To

Geoff, Heath

PROFESSOR CUSTARD

A little gift for you

Peter
April
2022

PROFESSOR CUSTARD

One boy's quest to fulfil his dreams

PETER GREGORY

Matador
Unit E2 Airfield Business Park,
Harrison Road, Market Harborough,
Leicestershire. LE16 7UL
Tel: 0116 2792299
Email: books@troubador.co.uk
Web: www.troubador.co.uk/matador
Twitter: @matadorbooks

ISBN 978 1803130 231

British Library Cataloguing in Publication Data.
A catalogue record for this book is available from the British Library.

Printed and bound by CPI Group (UK) Ltd, Croydon, CR0 4YY
Typeset in 10.5pt Adobe Garamond Pro by Troubador Publishing Ltd, Leicester, UK

Matador is an imprint of Troubador Publishing Ltd

For Joshua, my family and my friends

PROLOGUE

It is said that an autobiography is an act of revenge. A chance to 'put the record straight'. I beg to differ. As Stephen Fry says in his autobiography *Moab is my Washpot* it can also be a form of 'Thank-You' note. I concur wholeheartedly. An autobiography is a once in a lifetime chance to thank all the people who have contributed to your life. Who have made you happy (and sad). Who have made you laugh (and cry). Who have shared your triumphs (and disasters). In short, people who have made your life worth living.

To capture a whole lifetime in a single book is an impossible task. The enormous number of people and events are just too numerous. However, to those mentioned in the book, and to the many more that aren't, who have in any way enriched my life, I offer a heartfelt THANK-YOU. I just hope that my memory hasn't let me down.

PREFACE

My name is Peter Gregory and this is my story. It is the story of a boy born illegitimately on the 23 March 1946 into a poor working class family. Being immediately after the Second World War, it was a time of deprivation and rationing. Like most people's life stories, it consists of a mixture of many things. Of happiness and sadness. Of ambitions and triumphs. Of failures and disasters. Of love and hate. But, most of all, it is a story of the strength of the human spirit to overcome everything to achieve an ambition and a dream. And to never give up.

As you can see from my birthday, I was conceived at the end of the Second World War in June 1945, around VE (Victory in Europe) Day. In all probability, it was, in part, a celebration of the end of that war: the end of all the hardships, rationing, deprivation and death.

I was born out of wedlock. Apparently, my father wished to marry my mother but the rest of my family, particularly my grandma, were vigorously opposed to this course of action (I never found out why) and so the marriage never happened. Unlike nowadays, having a child out of wedlock in that era brought great shame on the family. Because of that fact (and probably others that I never knew about), the topic was considered taboo by my family and hardly ever discussed. The only thing I ever knew about my father was his name. What he looked like, what he did, where he lived, his family, his interests and hobbies, of these I knew absolutely nothing. Neither did I know if I had any half brothers or sisters. As I grew up I did ponder all these things very carefully but, in the end, decided not to pursue the matter. Why? For two reasons. First, because I didn't want to intrude upon his life, particularly if he had married and raised a family. And second, I didn't want to cause problems in my own family. The way the topic had been avoided for very many years meant that they didn't want it discussed. So I let sleeping dogs lie.

As mentioned earlier, I was born into a poor working class family in Aspull,* a small village about 3 miles from Wigan. My mother, Annie, was the youngest of the three sisters and two brothers of my grandma and grandad. Auntie Ellen (Nellie) was the oldest sister and Auntie Lily the middle one. The two brothers were Uncle Bill, the eldest, and Uncle Jack. Auntie Nellie married Evan and had my cousin, William, whilst Auntie Lily married John. Our whole family lived in a relatively new three-bedroom council house in Crawford Avenue. (Images 1a and 1b show maps of Aspull** in which the locations mentioned in the text can be found.[1])

How did nine adults and two small children squeeze into a fairly small three-bedroom semi-detached council house? They didn't! Our immediate neighbours were an old couple, whom we knew fondly as 'Owd Bill' and his wife. (I never knew his wife's name but I presume the adults did.) Since they didn't require three bedrooms, walls were knocked down and we 'acquired' their biggest bedroom. Even with four bedrooms, it was still a squash to accommodate all of us. Subsequently, Uncle Evan, Auntie Nellie and William moved to a new council house about quarter-of-a-mile away in St John's Road, Uncle Bill got married and moved to a council house in Westhoughton several miles away, and Auntie Lily and Uncle Jack (although his name was John everyone called him Jack) bought a terraced house in Ratcliffe Road, about half-a-mile away.

Later, my other Uncle Jack married Jean Copson, a local girl from nearby Horwich. Once their only child, Brian, my other cousin, was born when I was seven (Chapter 2), they also moved to a nearby council house in St Mary's Road, leaving just my mother, me and my two grandparents at 30 Crawford Avenue. No longer needing the extra bedroom, it was re-assigned to our new neighbours, Mr Whittle, the new postman, and his family.

And so to my story. The story of a small boy's journey on the path of life. Although he didn't know it, this small boy harboured not one but two burning desires within his chest. Two desires that became his dreams. But he didn't realise what they were until he was older. Would he fulfil his dreams? Well, that is for you to decide.

---

*   Aspull was first mentioned in 1212. Its name is derived from the old English 'aesp-leah' meaning 'aspen wood.'[1] The locals have a more amusing derivation of the name. On the outskirts of Aspull is a steep hill, Ivy Brow. Folklore has it that a city merchant, whose animal was struggling to pull his cart up the hill, kept urging it on by shouting, "Come on, Ass pull."

** After its first mention in 1212 Aspull was owned by the Ince and Gerard families until it was bought by the Earl of Crawford and Balcarres.[2] This history accounts for the many occurrences of their names in the district. Streets, such as Crawford Avenue and Balcarres Road, and several pubs, The Crawford Arms, Balcarres Arms and Gerard Arms, bear their names.

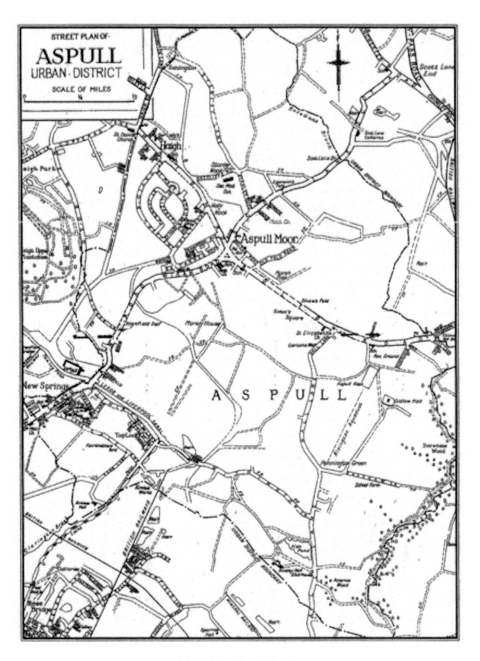

Map of Aspull and Haigh.

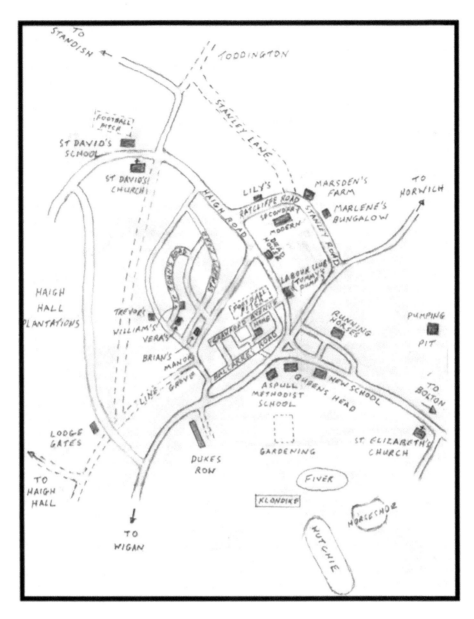

Map of central Aspull showing locations mentioned in text.

REFERENCES

1.   Smith, M. D., About Haigh and Aspull, Wyre Publishing, 2000, p. 73.
2.   A Guide To Wigan: Past and Present, Hallgate Press, Wigan, 1984, p.13.

CONTENTS

1

EARLY BEGINNINGS

Ooooh, what's this? A big patch of blue with a shiny yellow blob (which hurts your eyes if you look at it), framed by a black rectangle. Although there is no way that I could have written such a description, this is my earliest recollection of anything since my birth on the 23 March 1946. It is, in fact, the view from inside my black pram on a sunny summer's day.

Although I don't remember the next phase of my life I was, apparently, a chubby, happy-go-lucky toddler. A toddler with a distinctive shock of silvery blonde curly hair who loved to play on the beach (Image 2). A time when I was, by all accounts, very happy.

Me, age 16 months, on Southport beach.

Sadly, this idyllic state of affairs didn't last. By the tender young age of three my curly blonde hair had become manageable, my puppy fat had disappeared and, in contrast to my 'perky' younger cousin William, I had become somewhat reserved (Image 3).

The next thing that I remember clearly was my first day at school.

Me, age 3, on left, with my younger cousin
William in the Sitting Room of 30 Crawford Avenue.

1.1 PRIMARY SCHOOL

I had just turned five (Image 4) and both my cousin William (who is 9 months younger than me) and I were taken to Aspull Methodist School (the nearest local school) by my Auntie Lily and Auntie Nellie (William's mother). Being very timid and shy, we lagged some way behind our aunties as they talked to Mrs Dickson, the nice old lady who taught the first class. We leaned against the radiator, as far away as possible from the teacher, but gradually, as we gained a little confidence, inched further towards her. Having survived this daunting (to us) first visit to school, and seen what a lovely lady Mrs Dickson was, removed a lot of the fear from attending school for the very first time and ensured that it was not an unpleasant experience.

At that time it was not uncommon for church schools to be physically attached to the church (or chapel) itself. This was the case for Aspull Methodist School: the school was attached directly to the Methodist Chapel[1], the bulk of it being situated behind the chapel[2] (Image 5). Our first classroom, Mrs Dickson's, was the one on the far right. At the front of the school was a small tarmac playground, adjacent to the garden at the front of the Methodist Chapel (Image 5). At the other side of the playground was, rather surprisingly for a Methodist Chapel, a public house, the Queens Head[3] (Image 6). The Queens Head building still remains (it became an Indian restaurant, Aspull Spice, in 2012) but the school and chapel were demolished in 1990 to make way for apartments and a new chapel built, this time, at a more appropriate distance from the pub[4] (Image 7).

2

William (on left) and Me aged about 4 and 5
in the front garden of 30 Crawford Avenue.
We had been eating liquorice

The time spent in Mrs Dickson's class was wonderful. Although it's impossible to recall everything, I do remember how patient, tolerant and understanding she was towards a group of five and six year old boys and girls. One thing I do know is that I attribute much of my love of the countryside and wildlife to Mrs Dickson. On lovely summer's days this kindly old teacher would take the entire class out on a walk through the local fields and meadows, patiently pointing out and explaining the beauty of the plant and animal life. Without doubt, this planted the seeds of my passion for nature and wildlife, which, to this day, I still have.

Aspull Methodist Chapel 1990 with the school
(on the left and behind) attached, just before their demolition.

Aspull Methodist School – side view.

Aspull Methodist Chapel and school (1990)
showing their proximity to the Queens Head.

New Aspull Methodist Chapel on completion in 1992.
It is situated about 400 yards from the Queens Head pub.

Mrs Dickson also introduced me to the three R's, reading, writing and arithmetic, as well as to singing and school plays. Indeed, my very first feelings for a girl happened during rehearsals for a school play. I was seven years old. In the play, I was an Admiral in the Navy and had to stand on a platform on top of some ladders and pretend to scour the sea with a telescope. Below me several girls danced on the floor. At the end of the dance, they would glide to the floor with their dresses forming a neat circle. One girl did this really gracefully. Her name was Doris Corfield. I think I became instantly infatuated with her (or whatever passes for infatuation at that age) because I rushed home all excited and blurted out to my grandma that I 'wanted' Doris Corfield. Somewhat surprised, she looked at me for a moment and then said, quite calmly, "I'll tell you what. How about we go to the shop instead and I'll buy you a bag of toffees." What an offer! A bag of toffees in place of Doris Corfield. What seven-year-old boy could refuse. It was no contest. Thus ended my first encounter with girls.

Everyone became excited as the day to perform the play arrived. Dressed in a smart naval uniform with a telescope in my hand I must have looked quite dapper. A bad cold and runny nose shattered the illusion. During my time stood on the platform, I wiped the snot from my nose on to my sleeve several times, much to the amusement of the audience. It baffled me when everyone kept laughing. It was only at the end of the play when my mother and aunties explained it to me that I understood. They were a little bit annoyed at first but soon saw the funny side and forgave me.

During my time in Mrs Dickson's class another embarrassing incident occurred. "Peter, why aren't you playing with the other children in the playground?"

"Please Miss, because I've done a poo in my pants and now its dried my pants are glued to my bottom, so I can't run around. Also, I smell!" I did not utter this response to the question from the teacher on playground duty, but it was the truth. In the classroom, the urge to go to the toilet happened extremely quickly and by the time Mrs Dickson had noticed my upraised arm, it was too late. It was very embarrassing and it took a lot of effort to refrain from crying. But refrain I did, even though it was uncomfortable and would have been humiliating if other people had found out.

A similar incident almost happened many years later when I was a fully grown man. For several years a group of colleagues from work organised a walking weekend in the Lake District (Chapter 11). Normally, we stayed at Nether Wasdale near Wastwater, which is where the highest mountains, such as Scafell, Scafell Pike and Great Gable, are located. Springtime was the favourite time of year for this activity because the days were relatively long and the weather fine, being neither too hot nor too cold for strenuous walking. For this particular walking holiday we had chosen the Easter weekend. Being a public holiday, the Lake District was very busy. After a porcupine (pork-in-wine) dinner on the Friday evening, our landlady had packed pork sandwiches for lunch on the Saturday,

5

the day of our walk up Great Gable. Not only was it the Easter holidays, it was also a beautiful, scorching, sunny day. The area was filled with walkers, climbers and day-trippers. There were even a number of school outings comprising hordes of noisy excited children and their teachers. Undeterred, we first climbed Green Gable followed by the more daunting Great Gable and enjoyed our lunch of pork sandwiches at the summit. On the descent, I experienced terrible stomach pains and 'needed to go' urgently. I had severe diarrhoea.* The constant jarring action on the body caused by walking down the mountain exacerbated the situation. However, the mountain was full of other walkers and climbers, including, as I mentioned, parties of young school children. It was also quite open terrain with no hidden nooks or crannies to 'do the business'. Eventually, the strain became so unbearable that remedial action was needed. Immediately! The only option was to squat down away from prying eyes and relieve myself. The end result was pure bliss. But there was a major problem. Diarrhoea leaves a mess and walkers don't pack loo rolls! What a dilemma! In this barren landscape devoid of any grass or other soft vegetation, all that was available were pieces of rock and slate. Wiping your bottom with a piece of slate after disposing of a dollop of diarrhoea on a mountainside is not recommended! Painful it may have been but it was a better option than not wiping it. On arriving back at the hotel later that day (having kept silent in the car when people wondered what that funny smell was), I discovered that my underpants had become glued to my rear. The only option available was to soak myself in a bath until the offending garment relieved itself from my person. Since that eventful day I have avoided pork like the plague.

Tommy, a classmate at the Aspull Methodist School, continues the lavatorial theme. Tommy had a daily ritual. A bizarre daily ritual. Every day at lunchtime, come rain or shine, he would walk about 400 yards to a disused railway bridge and defecate under it. Every day. Without fail. At the same time and in the same place. Why he did it no one knows. But do it he did. Tommy and his lunchtime walk to the bridge to have a shit became well known throughout the village. Indeed, the bridge, which became the site first of the Labour Club, then the Aspull Village Club, (Images 1b, page xii, and 16, page 19), and now (2020) a Cooperative, became known as 'Tommy's dump'.

Living in the 1950s was different to today. It was a more gentle age with a much slower pace of life. People may not have had the material benefits and wealth that we enjoy, but they were certainly more relaxed, less stressed and more caring towards each other. Because people genuinely had little money and few material possessions, they gladly helped each other out as best they could. For example, if people fell on hard times, help would be provided in the form of food, clothes and even what little money people could afford to give. Indeed, it was not unknown for the children of

---

*   I later discovered that I have a reaction to pork – it gives me diarrhoea

unfortunate families to be taken in and cared for by their friends and neighbours until their circumstances improved. My family took in my cousin Alan from Westhoughton and cared for him for several months until his sick mother, Rose, recovered from her illness.

This caring, dedicated attitude extended to the professions. Generally, the professions were staffed by people who were passionate about their work and did it primarily because they enjoyed doing it. It was not done for money or status. Mrs Dickson was a shining example of these virtues. She carried on teaching well past her retirement age and, indeed, well into her late seventies. I'm sure she would have done it for free because she enjoyed it so much. Mrs Dickson never retired. She died while still teaching.

Her funeral took place on a warm summer's day. The whole school was given the day off and, rather appropriately, the cortege began from the school where she had devoted most of her life. The turnout was fantastic with hundreds of people, adults and children alike, giving her a fond farewell. It was a sad but touching occasion, one I have never forgotten.

From Mrs Dickson's class you progressed to Miss Moss's class. There were only three classes at Aspull Methodist School. Mrs Dickson took the beginner's class, Miss Moss taught the intermediate class, with the top class being taken by the headmaster, Mr Thomas. Like other schools in the area, Aspull Methodist School was an 'all-age' school. The few children who passed the 11-plus exam went on to the local grammar school (Rivington) but the remaining majority stayed at these schools until the school leaving age of fifteen. Thus, ten years were spent at these 'all-age' schools. There was no set time in any class. When an individual was deemed to have reached the required standard, they moved to the next class. Accordingly, an individual could spend anything from two to four years in one class.

The Miss Moss experience was totally different to that of Mrs Dickson. Miss Moss was a good teacher. However, she was a stern individual who was a strict disciplinarian. It was in her class that we really started to learn the three R's. As well as Enid Blyton's classic books, such as *Noddy and Big Ears* and the *Famous Five*, we also read the Emile series of books. To this day the bit on the train in *Emile and the Detective* where Emile is sat opposite a stranger who is following him is still fresh in my mind. In the book Emile is so tired that he can hardly keep awake but he knows that he has to so that he can keep his eye on the stranger following him. I often experienced the same feeling when staying up well past my bedtime and, as will become apparent later (Chapter 7), also on a train.

In Miss Moss's class I sat next to Roy Wood. Roy was a big strong lad who was keen on wrestling. (As far as I am aware, he still runs the Aspull Warriors Wrestling Club.) Roy was not one to be trifled with. However, he was a placid and modest boy who was well liked. Sometimes, I would play little jokes with him. One such joke was pretending to make a spelling mistake in a writing class. For example, when we had to write down the name of the person sitting next to us, I would write 'Roy Wooo' (for Wood). I would show him my mistake and ask to borrow his rubber. (We wrote in pencil then.) When he had rummaged through his desk and found the rubber, I started smiling and said I didn't need it. Putting a vertical stroke on the last 'o' converted it into a 'd'. Luckily, he enjoyed jokes.

Although she was a good teacher, Miss Moss didn't have the warmth of Mrs Dickson. One day, she kept me behind after school because I couldn't spell 'cat'. In those days healthy eating was unheard of. You ate what you could afford. As a child, my breakfast consisted of a glass of vimto and a kitkat. Because I was so used to seeing the word 'kitkat' every day, I naturally assumed that 'kat' was the correct spelling for a cat. Obviously not! When I didn't return home at the normal time, my grandma was worried and came to the school to see if I was still there. On learning that Miss Moss had kept her grandson behind (I don't think it was called detention then), all hell broke loose! She was furious and really tore into a frightened Miss Moss. Never again did Miss Moss detain me.

Whilst in Miss Moss's class I had two pleasant surprises, one at home and one at school.

"Peter, wake up. We've got a lovely surprise for you." My mother and grandma were gently shaking my shoulder as I awoke from my slumber. Bleary eyed, I followed them into the adjacent bedroom. Sitting up in bed was Auntie Jean. But she wasn't alone. Cradled in her arms was a tiny baby wrapped in white clothes. It looked so small, almost like a doll.

"Isn't he beautiful," my grandma said. "He's your new little cousin. They're going to call him Brian." Aged seven, I had a new cousin and a future playmate (Images 8 and 9).

Me, age 7, sat on back doorstep holding baby Brian and
Me, age 9, my mother and Brian, age 2, at rear of 30 Crawford Avenue

Me, age 7 (left), baby Brian and William, age 6. Brian, age 7 (1960).

The second surprise concerned mountaineers. A British led expedition had conquered the world's highest mountain, Mount Everest. Every attempt to conquer this inhospitable and hostile mountain had failed. Until 29 May 1953. On that momentous day, two climbers from the British expedition became the first in the world to reach the summit of Mount Everest. When Mr Thomas announced their feat at morning assembly, every child in the school felt immensely proud to be British. The fact that neither of the two climbers who reached the summit, Sir Edmund Hilary, a New Zealander, nor his faithful Nepalese Sherpa guide Tenzing Norgay, were British, was irrelevant. It had been a British expedition and the Union Flag sat proudly on the summit of the world's highest mountain.

This day, like all the others, began with school assembly. The pupils (and teachers) from all three classes congregated in the top classroom. Nestled in one corner was a small raised wooden platform. From this platform the headmaster took the assembly, assisted by a teacher (Mrs Dickson when she was alive) on the piano. Assembly was a brief affair, consisting, literally, of a song and a prayer. Along a side wall in the top classroom was a display cabinet. This was home to a variety of bits and bobs but one item in particular caught most people's attention. It was a green grass snake coiled up in a glass jar and preserved for eternity in formalin. A farmer had found the snake in the field directly adjacent to the school playground. Not knowing whether it was a harmless grass snake or a poisonous adder, the farmer had taken no chances and killed it. Now, I don't like snakes, never have done, and I used to dread having to stand right next to this jar during assembly, even though the snake was obviously dead.

My fear of snakes stems, I think, from two events. The first event happened when I was about four or five. I was in our garden and one of the adults put a large, slimy worm down my back. I could feel its wet, cold body writhing around next to my warm skin and it took me a while to get my shirt off and remove the worm. It's an experience I have never forgotten. The second influence was Rudyard Kipling. One of my favourite books when

9

I was young was Rikki Tikki Tavi. Rikki Tikki Tavi was a mongoose that was rescued from drowning in a flood by a young boy and adopted by his family as a pet. Rikki Tikki Tavi saved everyone from certain death from a family of king cobras that were living in the house and garden. At that age, you have a vivid imagination and I used to look with trepidation at all the nooks and crannies in our house and garden to check that no evil snakes were lurking around.

It was at Aspull Methodist School that I got my first taste of school dinners. The 'dining room' was a small room adjacent to the top classroom. Two 'dinner ladies' dished out the food to the hungry mob. School dinners arrived about 11-00 a.m. in metal containers reminiscent of milk churns. The food was already hot and no matter which class you were in, its arrival was unmistakable. The aroma would waft into every nook and cranny of the school. Sometimes the smell from the main course revealed its identity. It always consisted of mashed potatoes with meat of some kind and some vegetables. There was also a pudding. Things with custard, such as fruit sponge, were typical. However, the pudding that sticks forever in my memory was semolina. To me, semolina was frogspawn warmed up. It was like chewing slippery rubber and the feeling as the coagulated lumps slid down my throat made me gag. I never liked semolina but surprisingly I loved its cousin, rice pudding. Smooth and creamy, rice pudding was delicious. Sometimes, as a treat, there would be a blob of jam on the top. We also had the obligatory glass of milk.

Playtime was an important part of school life. At playtime you could run around and let off steam playing games. For the boys, football was the main game. During games of football, the ball occasionally went over the wall and into the adjacent chapel garden (Image 5, page 3). This created a dilemma. On the one hand we desperately wanted to continue playing football. On the other hand, Mr Thomas, the headmaster, was very strict and would severely punish anyone caught climbing over the wall into the chapel garden. A caning of six of the best on the buttocks was the summary punishment. A daring rescue operation was therefore required. A line of boys acted as lookouts for any sign of Mr Thomas whilst one boy would clamber quickly over the wall to retrieve the ball. Because of the real fear of being caught and our good system of keeping watch, punishments happened only occasionally.

The footballs, school football strip and gardening equipment (see later) were kept in the school storeroom. The quirky layout of the old school meant that the storeroom window directly overlooked the old-fashioned outdoor boys' toilets[5] (Images 5 and 10). Anyone looking through the window got a perfect view of the boys having a pee. Whenever the teacher asked for volunteers to collect some equipment from the storeroom, all the girls' hands shot up in unison. When we went to the toilet, you could see a load of girls' faces at the window eagerly peering down to get a good view.

Storeroom (upstairs window) directly
overlooking the boys' outside toilet.

Fights between boys to establish the hierarchy was also a common occurrence. One such fight occurred because of a football game. It was over a disputed goal. Jimmy, who was on the same team as me, said it was a goal. Norman, who was on the opposing side, said it wasn't. A trivial thing but neither would back down, so they agreed to settle it by having a fight after school near Tommy's dump. This presented me with a serious dilemma. Jimmy, who was also a neighbour of mine, was right. It was a goal. However, at the time Norman was my best friend with whom I went shooting. What was I to do! Trying to stop them going ahead with the fight failed. So, I offered to hold both their jackets whilst they got on with it. Fortunately, the fight didn't last long. It was stopped very quickly by a passing adult, Mr Fletcher.

Across the road from where the fight took place was a large tree. Located on spare land adjacent to the road, it was a favourite haunt for young boys and girls. As well as climbing the tree, ropes were tied around the branches and these makeshift swings provided hours of pleasure. It was whilst enjoying this activity that, for the first and only time in my life, I was admonished by a policeman.

Mr Chalmers, the local bobby, lived just down the road from our house. He was a stern, burly individual who was not averse to dispensing summary punishment in the form of a clip around the ears. We avoided this fate but got a real 'telling off' for playing dangerous games close to a busy main road. I was relieved he didn't tell my grandad or I would have got a clip around the ear.

By the time I reached the top class, aged nine, Mr Thomas had retired and our new headmaster was Mr Cadman. (For some reason the headmaster always took the top class.) Mr Cadman was less austere and more avuncular than Mr Thomas but he still maintained good discipline. He enjoyed telling anecdotes that had a real message. For example, he would emphasise how fortunate we were relative to the majority of children in the world. One tale he told made me feel extremely sad and humble. He said that in parts of India, people were so poor that they resorted to extreme measures just to survive. Parents placed a parasitic worm in the ears of their young children. This worm then burrowed into their brain causing blindness. The blind children were then sent on to the streets to beg and thereby earn a meagre amount of money to enable the family to survive. The reason for this awful act? Because blind children made better beggars. It really made us grateful for what we had.

In the top class our horizons were expanded. In addition to the usual lessons on the three R's, singing and football, we experienced three new activities; gardening, swimming and woodwork.

For the boys in the top class, Monday mornings meant woodwork. This entailed catching a bus to New Springs, approximately halfway to Wigan (Image 1a, page xi), where the woodworking facility was housed in an old building. Our woodwork teacher was Mr Chadwick. Here, we learned basic skills, such as how to saw, chisel, plane, sandpaper and French polish. Mr Chadwick also taught us the intricacies of mortice and tenon and dovetail joints, and how to use a lathe. We could also select which items of furniture to make: my selection was a seagrass stool and a card table. As was the case with gardening, I got an immense feeling of pride on taking my finished furniture home.

Wigan and the surrounding districts were hotbeds of mining and Aspull was littered with the remains of old mine-workings. It was on the site of a disused slag tip that the school had a small allotment. This was located about a quarter-of-a-mile from the school (Image 1b) and it was to here that the boys of the top class would trudge every Friday afternoon. (The girls went to a hut around the corner for cookery lessons.) We were shown the basics of gardening, particularly how to plant, tend and grow vegetables. I must admit to being fascinated with watching plants such as carrots, lettuce, onions, peas and potatoes grow from virtually nothing into quite large plants, and eagerly looked forward to seeing how much they had grown each week. The highlight, however, was taking the ripe vegetables home to be eaten. They tasted delicious. This produced a profound sense of achievement and, like Mrs Dickson and her walks, gave me another interest for life, gardening.

Swimming was different. I have never been a water baby. However, like most other children, I loved trips to the seaside. The thrills of the amusements parks, making sandcastles on the beach, paddling in the sea and even messing about in the swimming pool, were all great fun. However, I never hankered to actually swim. Therefore, I wasn't the most enthusiastic boy when it came to going to Wigan's Plunge Baths once a week to be taught how to swim. But there was no choice: it was deemed to be a good thing for people to be able to swim so I had to grin and bear it. Every Thursday morning the boys would catch the bus to Wigan for their weekly swimming lesson. After changing into our swimming trunks, the first ordeal was a cold shower. This was mandatory before entering the pool and it was so cold it took your breath away. Then, we were taken to the shallow (3 foot 6 inches) end of the pool. Our first task was to stand a few feet away from the edge of the pool, push off from the floor with our feet and glide to the side. I still remember the elation as my feet left the floor for the first time, my whole body being supported by the water. It was an exhilarating feeling, like a bird gliding through the air. Over the next few weeks we learned the breast-stroke and front crawl. Our spell at the baths culminated in gaining a certificate for swimming one length (25 yards). I failed to complete 25 yards doing the breast-stroke (the instructor had to haul me out of the pool using a large fishing net) but managed it doing the front crawl, so I got my certificate (Image 11).

As was the case for gardening, it was just the boys who went to the baths every Thursday morning. However, unlike gardening, the girls in the top class also went to the baths for swimming lessons, but not with the boys. In the 1950s, communal bathing was very rare. Therefore, the girls went on a different day to the boys. Because of this sexual segregation, Wednesday was the highlight of the week. Wednesday meant mixed bathing, the only day of the week when boys and girls and men and women were allowed to use the baths together. Not surprisingly, Wednesday was a very popular day at the baths.

After learning to swim, a group of us used to go to the baths twice a week: on a Wednesday evening after school and on a Saturday morning. The midweek excursion was, mainly, to sample the delights of mixed bathing. For example, we could see the rare sight of girls (and women) in their swimming costumes, getting a thrilling look at their bare legs and lovely cleavages. This was a real 'turn-on' for young adolescent boys in the 1950s. It would have been even more of a 'turn-on' if bikinis had been allowed. Unfortunately, they weren't. In contrast, the Saturday visit was to have fun and learn new skills, such as diving and underwater swimming. In Wigan's Plunge Baths a diving stage with three levels was situated at the deep (6 foot 6 inches) end. Although in reality the diving stages weren't very high, they seemed mountainous at the time and it became a personal quest to progress up the three stages to the very top one. Once again, it felt like a great achievement when I finally dived off the top stage (although I only did it once).

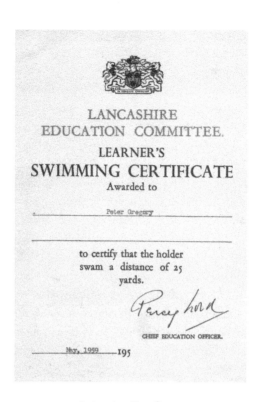

Swimming Certificate.

Going to the baths on a Saturday morning became a regular event for three of us, myself and two neighbours, Colin Heaton and Trevor Hough. We'd catch the bus to Wigan, have our session in the swimming baths and then hotfoot it to Woolworths to get some salted peanuts. On a fine day we walked home through Haigh Hall plantations. If it rained, the bus was employed. One distinctly amusing incident occurred in a changing cubicle I was sharing with Colin. We had showered and returned to the cubicle to get changed back into our clothes. Whilst towelling down after removing my trunks, my willy got a semi-erection from the rubbing with the towel. Colin was both fascinated and impressed telling me that I had a bigger willy than Jim Walsh, who was reputed to have the biggest willy in the school. Word quickly got around the school and I became somewhat embarrassed as the girls shot knowing glances in my direction.

The old Plunge Baths were demolished to make way for Wigan's International Pool. This impressive facility, built to Olympic standard, was opened in 1966. Having hosted many international tournaments, the baths remained an active part of Wigan life for many years. However, the years have taken their toll and the baths began to look old and tired. In 2010 they were demolished and a brand new swimming complex built. It opened in 2012.

Although we didn't have formal examinations at Aspull Methodist School, pupils in the top class would occasionally have a test. This consisted of the teacher asking 20 questions covering adding up (mental arithmetic), spelling and general knowledge. You would then exchange your answer sheet with your neighbour and mark the answers as the teacher read them out. Cheating was rife. However, one of the best lessons I ever learned came from Jackie Robinson. He refused point blank to cheat (by marking wrong answers right) saying that the only person you were cheating was yourself. It was far better, he said, to be honest, see how good (or bad) you really were, and try to improve. This was excellent advice. In the tests, Alan Seddon normally came top with Jackie Robinson and me vying for second place.

In no time at all I was fast approaching eleven and this required the first major decision of my life. At eleven, children could be entered for the 11-plus examination. Success meant a move to the local grammar school; in my case this was Rivington Grammar. Non-entry or failure meant staying at Aspull Methodist School until you left at 15. A small number of people from the top class were taking the 11-plus exam but I decided not to. My decision was influenced from a discussion I overheard between my mother, Auntie Lily and grandma. They were talking about Colin Seddon, our next-door neighbour, taking the 11-plus exam and wondered how his family could afford to send him to Rivington Grammar. (Colin attended St David's School at Haigh.) They said there was no way they could afford to send me to grammar school because of the expense involved – school uniforms, satchels, books, equipment, school trips, and bus fares to and from Rivington Grammar (about four miles away). Some time later I told them that I wasn't bothered about going to grammar school and quite happy to stay at Aspull Methodist School. This was actually true. However, I think they felt guilty about it, especially when one or two people from our school who were not in the top three passed the exam and went to grammar school. It wasn't too strange a decision since plans had just been announced to build a brand new secondary modern school in Aspull,[6] right in front of my Auntie Lily's house (Images 1b and 12). The secondary modern school was scheduled to open at the beginning of 1960 when I would be almost 14 years old. Furthermore, I would be able to stay with most of my friends.

1.2 FOOTBALL

At football we had fairly regular games against two other local all-age schools, the Church of England school, which was situated just around the corner from our school (and near to where the girls cookery lessons were held), and St David's School at Haigh, about a mile away (Image 1b). The Church of England school was known locally as the New School[7] (Image 13). This baffled me since it was at least as old as our school, which was built, along with the chapel,[5] in 1858.[*] Our school and the New School shared the same football pitch, about a quarter-of-a-mile away, but St David's School[7] (Image 14) had their own pitch behind the school[8] (Image 15).

SITE FOR ASPULL NEW SCHOOL.

The monthly meeting of the Division 13 Education Committee was held in the Wigan and District Mining and Technical College on Wednesday night when Mr. G. C. Bamforth presided.

NEW ASPULL SCHOOL.

It was reported that careful consideration had been given to a report of the County Architect regarding two sites suitable for the building of the new Aspull Secondary Modern School. The first site was an area of agricultural land situated on the south - west of Bolton Road, and the second site consisted of common land, bounded on the north by Ratcliffe Road, on the east by Stanley Road, and on the south and south-west by derelict land. The Development Plan Sub - Committee also reported that consideration had been given to the quesion of the time required for acquisition in view of the fact that the proposed school was included in the building programme for 1956-57.

Following reports that Aspull District Council favoured the adoption of the second site, the committee recommended that the land, approximately 13.25 acres, be acquired as the site for the school.

Commenting on the position, the Chairman said that he was very glad to see that Aspull were going to get a modern school, and he hoped that they would have it as quickly as possible.

Approval for Aspull Secondary Modern School.

---

[*] It was only whist doing the research for this book that I discovered why it was called the New School. Aspull once had a grammar school, the Aspull Endowed Grammar School, built in 1770. When the Church of England school was built adjacent to this grammar school in 1868, the two schools merged together. This was the 'New School'.[5]

16

Aspull C. of E. School (New School) 1978.

St David's School, Haigh 1995.

Aerial view of St David's School (top left) and football pitch.
The Balcarres Arms (centre left) and Culraven Garage (centre)
are also clearly visible, as is Haigh House (centre right).

It was considered an honour to be picked to play in the school football team and I was really excited the first time I was selected. However, it was with some trepidation that I entered the school dining room, which doubled up as the changing room, for the first time with the bigger, older boys, wondering what kind of things went on and getting undressed (and being naked) in public for the first time. As it turned out, there was nothing to be bothered about. Our colours were pale blue and dark blue halves with blue shorts, similar in a way to Blackburn Rovers who have blue and white halves. Wearing this strip for the first time, complimented with my new football boots, made me so proud.

In my first game for the team I was selected to play on the right wing. Wanting to do well and not let the side down made me very nervous. Since my home in Crawford Avenue was in-between the school and the football pitch (Image 1b) I decided to pop in to get a few last minute words of advice and encouragement from my grandad. I did, we won and I had a reasonable game.

Playing St David's away seemed a long trip. They were a better team than the New School and the games could go either way. Usually, we won at home and lost away. The games between us were more intense and physical than with the New School and sometimes erupted into violence, although this was rare. For an away game at St David's, we changed into our strip at our school and then caught the bus to Haigh. It must have been a strange sight for the passengers to see eleven boys with full football kit travelling on the bus.

It was after playing St David's at football that I heard the terrible news of the plane crash in Germany. On that fateful winter's day of 6 February 1958 on a snow covered runway in Munich, the plane carrying the entire Manchester United team crashed on take-off. Shock waves reverberated around the world. Twenty-three people lost their lives, including eight Manchester United players, and many more were injured. Duncan Edwards is the player who always comes to mind when I think of the tragedy. It is perhaps insensitive to remember the name of just one player, but the reason, I think, is that he survived the crash and appeared to be recovering when he died a few days later. The tragedy touched everyone, including me. Images of the wrecked plane in the snow are as poignant today as they were in 1958.

1.3 LABOUR CLUB

In the 1950s and 1960s the local Labour Club was a major feature of people's lives. So it was in Aspull. Labour clubs owed their existence to the mining communities who sought low cost entertainment in days of yesteryear. They were social meeting places supplying a cheap night out. In return, the workers provided a ready-made membership for the clubs.[10] The original Labour Club in Aspull was an old building in Harold

Street. It was the hub of social activity in the village. As its popularity grew, the building in Harold Street became too small and, in 1961, with help from a brewery, a brand new, bigger Labour Club was built. The site? Near to the disused bridge where Tommy did his business. (The new Labour Club is the large building seen in the distance on Image 55, page 73.) A fine building, the new club became even more popular with the locals. As social trends changed, it became the 'Aspull Village Club' (Image 16). In December 2015, this was converted into a Cooperative.

The Labour Club was also very popular with my family. My Uncle Jack was the club secretary, Evan and Jack (Brian's dad) were both on the committee, and later, when William and I were older, Lily and Nellie both worked behind the bar. In addition, my grandma used to clean the club and my mother and grandad were regular patrons. To be fair, people at the Labour Club tried to do their bit for the local community. For example, they organised various events, such as an old folks Christmas Party and an annual trip to the seaside for the children. The usual destinations were Blackpool and Southport. Now Southport is only 25 miles from Aspull and Blackpool 40 miles, but in those days they seemed to be on the other side of the world and the trips were a great adventure. On one of the trips to Southport it was a scorching day and Colin Heaton and me were desperate to cool down in the outdoor paddling pool. Unfortunately, we had forgotten to bring our swimming trunks. Being practical as ever, my mother said we should strip to our white underpants and paddle in these. Colin was reluctant at first but once he saw me splashing about and cooling down he quickly joined in. This improvisation created a problem. After our bathing was complete, our underpants were soaking wet. They had to be removed. For the rest of that day, Colin and I wandered around Southport without the comforting feel of this male undergarment.

Aspull Village Club 2008 (formerly the Labour Club)
now (2020) a Cooperative store.

One year, whilst paddling, I stepped on some shards of sharp glass from a broken bottle that some moron had thrown into the pool. Several shards penetrated the sole of my foot and the water was turning red from the bleeding. Luckily, our local newspaper man, Steve Whitfield, was nearby and he carried me on his shoulders to the local first aid room. The shards of glass were removed and my badly cut foot bandaged. For the remainder of that day I did as little walking as possible.

1.4 GRANDAD

My grandad, also called Peter Gregory (I presume I was named after him – Image 17), and me developed a strong bond.

My grandad at the front door of 30 Crawford Avenue
(circa 1957). His crushed right arm is clearly visible.

Until I was about seven, I always thought he was my dad. It was only when taunted by other boys did I realise he was my grandad. Nonetheless, we were very close. He used to work down the pit until his arm was crushed in an accident and he had to retire early, becoming the local postman. (A tradition carried on by my cousin Brian, who was also Aspull's postman until he retired, and currently by my youngest son, Michael.) At weekends and school holidays, he'd sit me on the front of his postman's bicycle and take me with him on his rounds. It often meant a very early start but I loved it since many of his rounds were through Haigh Hall plantations and the local fields and meadows.

It must have been an enjoyable experience because sometime later I did it again. Whilst studying for my 'A' levels, the long summer holidays could become boring. To relieve the boredom I volunteered to deliver the post to the far flung regions of the district, such as the outlying farms and distinguished houses dotted around the Haigh Hall estate. Joe Whittle and his wife, for many years the local 'postmen', agreed to let me help. They even paid me a small wage! At first the early starts were a problem but once I adjusted to them the job was really enjoyable. Cycling through the country lanes and meadows at the crack of dawn was idyllic. It was so peaceful. There was no one else around. It was as though I had the entire planet to myself. Everyone was still in bed and the only company were the birds and animals. I loved it so much that I volunteered to help over the busy Christmas period. Even today, I still walk the same lanes and meadows, though not at the crack of dawn.

Every evening before I went to bed my grandad would sit me on his knee near the open coal fire and talk with me. Sometimes it would be his reminiscences, sometimes his advice, sometimes his answers to my many questions, but always his patience and interest. Besides playing childhood games, we spent untold hours meandering aimlessly through daisy-filled meadows and haunted-looking woodlands. We even collected dant together (Chapter 2). However, his most endearing gift was that he would always be my champion, especially where guns were involved. These enriched moments still fill me with great pride.

1.5 GUNS

Guns have always been a passion of mine. When I was little, they were toy guns. My favourite game was Cowboys and Indians with me being a cowboy with a cap gun. As I got older, I yearned for a 'real' gun. My first real gun was a home-made 'peashooter' assembled from wood and elastic bands. This fired dried peas (or hawthorn berries, which were free) quite a distance (up to 50 yards). Our gang derived immense pleasure firing an array of weaponry – peashooters, catapults, guns, and bows and arrows.

My first proper gun was a potato gun. I was eleven years old. It was similar to a rifle but fired pieces of potato. The central part of the barrel was unscrewed, pushed into a potato, and then screwed back. After cocking the gun to load it with compressed air, the piece of potato was ejected. However, the range was only moderate (up to 25 yards) and the accuracy variable. A better weapon was required.

After school, I used to go shooting with my friend Norman Parkinson (the one who had a fight with Jimmy). He had a real air rifle, a Diana 16, which fired lead pellets (known by us as slugs), and made my potato gun seem rather silly. Therefore, I pestered and pestered for a real air gun like Norman's and eventually, with my grandad's help, got one. Shooting became our passion and we couldn't wait for four-o-clock to arrive so we could leave school and go shooting. The thrill of inserting the slug into the barrel of the rifle was irresistible.

We used to shoot in the local wastelands and fields. The most popular places were around the lanes of Toddington, the old pumping pit (Chapter 5) and Woodshaw, known locally as Wutchie (Image 18), a large ridge created from the waste slag of long lost coal mines. Reputedly, a house lies buried beneath this slag tip. Usually, tin cans and bottles were our targets. However, old light bulbs were the best. These were thrown into either a pond or the canal and we took great delight in trying to be the first one to hit and sink the floating bulb. There was something magical about shooting into water: the eruption of spray as the pellet hit the surface was something special.

Woodshaw (Wutchie) 2008. In the
1950s it was devoid of trees.

Not all things we fired at were inanimate. A water rat swimming across the surface was an even better target than a light bulb. However, these were rarely encountered and when they were they proved extremely difficult to hit. Birds sat in trees were a different proposition. These were the proverbial sitting ducks and were very easy to shoot. We must have killed many birds, especially starlings, which seemed great at the time, but in retrospect it was callous and cruel. It's amazing how cruel children can be without realising it.

Shooting became somewhat of an obsession. The Diana 16 was exchanged for a more powerful Original air rifle. This German gun was accurate to 60 yards. The gun was available in two calibre's. After much deliberation, I chose the smaller 0.177 calibre version rather than the 0.22 calibre because of its extra range and higher muzzle velocity (1,150 feet per second). Still only twelve, I was becoming something of an expert on air guns.

Aged thirteen, I began to go shooting with another friend, Brian Calland. Brian owned a shotgun. A 410 shotgun. A 410 shotgun with a bolt action to eject the spent cartridge, just like in the movies. Now this was a gun. Gunpowder replaced compressed air and the noise, and kickback, as you fired the shot was amazing. The acrid aroma of cordite was almost addictive. The damage a shotgun cartridge inflicted on cans and bottles and the like was awesome. I wanted one. Badly. I wanted a gun so much that I had vivid dreams about having been bought one. Indeed, the dreams were so vivid that I pictured the shotgun propped up at the bottom of the stairs. They were so real that when I woke up in the morning I would literally jump out of bed and dash excitedly down the stairs to get my gun. I just couldn't understand it when there was nothing there.

About this time my grandad finally received his redundancy pay from the pit after his accident some years earlier. It was £450. Now this may not seem a lot of money by today's standards but in the 1950s it was a substantial amount. To our family, it was a small fortune. My heart was set on getting a 410 shotgun. My mother, aunties and grandma all thought a boy of thirteen was too young to have a shotgun, which, on reflection, was probably true, but my grandad argued the case for me. A 410 shotgun was only £9 out of £450, but then everyone seemed to want something and it all mounted up. My grandma had always wanted leaded windows and she duly got them. Eventually, to my great delight, a 410 shotgun appeared. One of the last things my grandad did before he died was to take me shooting. We went to the old pumping pit (Image 74, page 103) where I managed to shoot a flying seagull from about 60 yards. He was quite impressed and told everyone that his grandson was a good shot. Although I didn't know it, this would be the last time that he would accompany me on a shooting trip.

Rats were a common sight, particularly around the marshes near the pumping pit. It's funny, but they always seemed more common when you didn't have a gun. One evening, whilst strolling through the fields looking for a suitable target, there was a commotion in the long grass about twenty yards in front of me. I stopped, and silently inserted a cartridge into the breech, taking care not to disturb my intended quarry. Directly ahead, in the failing dusk light, was a group of rats squabbling over some discarded food. One rat was huge, the size of a cat! Carefully, I took aim at this monster and squeezed the trigger. The crack of the shot was deafening in the still, evening air. The rats scurried away into the undergrowth but the monster that I had fired at turned around and headed in my direction. A series of emotions flashed through my brain. Disbelief. How could I have missed. And fear. Fear that the monster might reach and attack me before I had chance to reload. The fear was unfounded. After a few steps, the rat keeled over. If it wasn't dead then, it was an instant later when an Alsatian dog grabbed it by the neck and flung it over its shoulder. The owner of the dog had come to see what had been shot and the Alsatian was following its natural instinct. Closer inspection revealed the discarded delicacy was a lump of cheese. No wonder the rats had been excited.

1.6 DEATH

Approaching adolescence brought home to me just how old and frail-looking my grandma and grandad had become, and made me realise they were edging ever closer to their permanent retirement home in the sky. These unnerving thoughts sent a cold shiver down the spine of an adolescent boy, especially one who held his grandad in such high esteem. Thoughts like this crossed my mind most nights as my Auntie Nellie walked me home from my Auntie Lily's. We had to pass the 'dead-house', a place where the local dead people (the ones whose families preferred not to have the deceased in their front parlour) were taken. It was an eerie, foreboding building[11] (Image 19), especially at night, and I always increased my pace as we passed it.

Dead House 2000.

I first encountered death with our neighbours. As mentioned earlier, 'Owd Bill' and his wife lived in the other half of our semi-detached council house. They were pretty old. The thing I remember about 'Owd Bill' was the way he once despatched a rat. Plagued by these undesirable vermin, traps were set in the back garden ready to snare the ghastly pests. One night, a trap went off and caught this huge rat, which was squealing and making a terrible racket. On hearing the rumpus, 'Owd Bill' came around and promptly stamped his huge hobnailed boot on the poor creature's head. The squealing ceased instantly. I'm not squeamish but hearing the noise of the rat's skull being crushed sent a shiver up my spine. Despatching the rat in this manner seemed very cruel at the time but in retrospect it was the humane thing to do. A few months later 'Owd Bill' died. On the day of his funeral, I recall the coffin being carried in a dignified manner to the hearse in front of his house. As mentioned earlier, in those days it was the custom for the deceased's coffin to 'lie-in-state' in the parlour of the house until the day of the funeral. His wife died soon afterwards.

My grandad died suddenly, aged 63, in the November of 1959. I was thirteen years old. Suffering from emphysema from his time working down the pit, he had been coughing up blood for a while. As was normal at that time, his bed had been brought down to the front room to save him from climbing the stairs, and giving his carers easy access to cater for his everyday needs. On the day he died, I was playing with some friends around the disused pit remains at Wutchie. We had climbed (rather foolishly on reflection) on top of the wall that enclosed an old pit shaft. Rather foolishly because the previous year one boy, Don Fletcher, the son of Mr Fletcher who'd stopped the fight between Jimmy and Norman, had actually fallen down the pit shaft. He was saved from certain death only because his face had struck a metal hook projecting out near the top of the shaft. It left him disfigured for life. Staring down into the black abyss of the pit shaft produced a profound sense of foreboding. It proved prophetic because, on arriving home, my grandad was dead. Apparently, he had died around the time that I was looking down the pit shaft.

I don't remember much about the funeral, except standing at the grave in St Elizabeth's graveyard on a cold winter's day whilst the coffin was being lowered into the grave. It was my first funeral and it was rather daunting. Death was something that seemed to happen to other people, not to your own family. I felt sad and confused. About two weeks earlier, William and me had bought tickets to watch Wigan play Oldham away at the Watersheddings in the rugby league Challenge Cup later that afternoon. We must have seemed 'on edge' since people remarked that we were too young to understand. That wasn't so. We did understand: we were just two sad and upset young boys. It's a strange feeling when I visit the churchyard and see my grandad's grave. His name is the same as mine so it's like you are looking at your own grave (Image 20).

My Grandad's Grave.

25

The funeral heralded the end of my time at Aspull Methodist School. Shortly, I would have to leave. My final recollection of the school where I had spent the last eight years was a strange one. In the top class some of the older boys made it a quest to find a new rude or sexual word. By the time we were thirteen most of the coarser words, such as the 'F' word, were well known so the new words had to be something different. One morning Jim Walsh duly obliged. He came rushing to a group of us and blurted out a new word – rape. None of us had heard this one. Eagerly, we listened as Jim explained what it meant. Our vocabulary had increased by one. Not much, but every little helped as the school I would attend next, Aspull County Secondary Modern, was emerging from nothingness to near completion.

In a few weeks my life's journey would start a new chapter, leaving behind a host of cherished childhood memories.

REFERENCES

1.   www.wiganworld Aspull Methodist School and Chapel

2.   www.wiganworld Aspull Methodist School

3.   Smith, M. D., About Haigh and Aspull, Wyre Publishing, 2000, p. 82.

4.   Smith, M. D., About Haigh and Aspull, Wyre Publishing, 2000, p. 84.

5.   Smith, M. D., About Haigh and Aspull, Wyre Publishing, 2000, p. 93.

6.   The Wigan Observer and District Advertiser, Saturday March 24 1956.

7.   Smith, M. D., About Haigh and Aspull, Wyre Publishing, 2000, p. 96.

8.   Smith, M. D., About Haigh and Aspull, Wyre Publishing, 2000, p. 48.

9.   Smith, M. D., About Haigh and Aspull, Wyre Publishing, 2000, p. 57.

10. A Guide To Wigan: Past and Present, Hallgate Press, Wigan, 1984, p.151.

11. Smith, M. D., About Haigh and Aspull, Wyre Publishing, 2000, p. 142.

2

GROWING UP

Standing stark naked on the bathroom windowsill waving to some girls across the street. In addition to my first day at Aspull Methodist School (Chapter 1), this is one of my earliest recollections. My cousin William and me were having a bath when a group of giggling girls across the street dared us to stand in front of the window. Not wanting to disappoint, we duly obliged. Fortunately for us, but unfortunately for the girls, the glass in the window was frosted.

Until his family moved out of our house in Crawford Avenue, William and I used to have a bath together about once a week. This was all our families could afford. Hot water was expensive. The rest of the time we made do with a wash in the kitchen sink. Apart from the winter months we bathed in the bathroom. After our bath we would dash downstairs to the only warm place in the house: in front of the fire in the living room (there was no central heating then). As we stood in front of the coal fire, shivering, my mother and Auntie Lily would towel us down. Aged four and five, we had no shame being naked in front of a roomful of women, even when they talked about our 'bobbins', the word they used for our dangly bits. I have never heard it called that since and can only assume it had some connection with their working at the local cotton mill at Lostock, where the cotton was wound on a wooden bobbin. I hope it wasn't confused with 'Bobbitt', the name of the unfortunate man whose angry wife sliced off his manhood with a kitchen knife while he was asleep! Ours might have been small at the time but at least they were there.

In the depths of winter our house was so cold and uninviting that having a bath in the bathroom was out of the question. Another strategy was required. After moving the hearth rug aside, a tin bath was placed on the linoleum (lino) in front of the open coal fire. (Rooms had linoleum as floor cover, usually with just one rug near the hearth. Fitted carpets were unheard of, at least in our house.) The bath was filled with hot water from the tap, topped up if necessary with boiling water from the kettle on the coal fire. Being rather small the bath would only accommodate one person. This had repercussions. Whoever bathed first got clean water but subsequent bathers had to tolerate 'dirty' water. To be fair, William and I used to take turns at being first, although when we were small, both of us could, at a pinch, squeeze into the bath together. The adults too used the tin bath but, as expected, they did their bathing in private.

2.1 OUR HOUSE

The fireplace was the focal point of our home in Crawford Avenue. Located in the living room it had a black cast iron grate with an integrated black cast iron oven on its right hand side. On the left hand side of the fireplace a black cast iron kettle sat upon a trivet. This movable metal stand could be swivelled around so that it sat directly above the fire, thus allowing the kettle, or some other pan, to be heated. The fireplace housed an open coal fire which warmed both the oven and the living room but nowhere else. Encompassing the fireplace was a tiled hearth enclosed by a metal fender. On the hearth sat the usual suspects: a poker, a coal scuttle and shovel, a hearth brush, a toasting fork and a piece of felt. The functions of all these objects are obvious except, perhaps, for the felt. The felt was vital. It protected your hand when removing the hot kettle (or pan) from the trivet over the fire!

In our house the poker, apart from its traditional use of 'poking' the fire, had an additional, rather bizarre, use. Like other women of her generation, my grandma loved her daily glass of Guinness, but hers was a Guinness with a difference. Without exception, before consuming her beloved tipple she always plunged the red hot poker into her Guinness to give it some 'iron'. I doubt it did but it certainly warmed it up and probably reduced the alcohol content by evaporation. It also kept the poker clean.

A fireguard enclosed all the above objects. The fireguard's primary purpose was to protect the room from burning fragments of wood or coal that occasionally 'spat' from the fire. It had other purposes too, such as for drying and airing clothes. Thus, whilst bathing in the tin bath in front of a roaring fire, your clothes would be warming on the fireguard. Putting on warm clothes in winter after a cosy bath in front of a roaring fire was pure ecstasy.

The fire was a focal point not only for warmth but also for food. Bread would be toasted over the open fire using a toasting fork whilst food would be cooked in the oven or in a pan on the trivet. But what kind of food did we eat? Our staple diet was rabbit, eaten occasionally with boiled potatoes, but mostly consumed as rabbit stew. Coffee coloured, it tasted rather good, a sort of tender chicken with a hint of beef, but you had to be wary of the myriad of small bones. Rabbits were plentiful and cheap until the population was decimated by myxomatosis. Cockles and mussels prepared in a large brown dish was another common food. Each person would grab a handful from the dish, place them on their plate and gobble them down. Lobbies, potatoes boiled with corned beef and optionally carrots, were also part of our staple diet, as was the related potato pie. This was always made with a crust, which I found delicious. It is still made by my wife, Vera, especially in the cold winter months when it provides a warm, nourishing meal. Surprisingly, it is enjoyed by our younger generation, especially when served with mushy peas. Other 'delicacies' were tripe, the intestinal lining of cows and normally served cold with lashings of vinegar, pig's trotters (feet) and ox tongue. But the mainstay of our staple diet was chips. Chips are cheap. They were fried in fat in a cast iron 'chip pan' and served either alone or with baked beans and, occasionally, a fried egg. However, the best of all was a chip butty. These were delicious. Real meat, such as steak or lamb or chicken, cost an arm and a leg and was rarely served in our house.

The food was stored in the pantry, a small room off the kitchen. The pantry terrified me. In our house all the floors were wooden with a space beneath them. Normally, this space was about two feet. However, the pantry, I was told, was built over a mineshaft with a drop of thousands of feet. Whether this was a clever ruse to keep me away from the food, or whether it was actually true, I don't know. But it certainly worked. I was scared stiff of the floorboards collapsing and plunging down the deep, dark, void of a disused mineshaft. Only if it was absolutely necessary would I venture into the pantry and even then I would be in and out in a flash.

In winter, the oven had a dual purpose. Not only was it used for cooking, it was also used to heat 'bricks'. These were large, oval-shaped cobbles that, when hot, would be wrapped in a woollen cloth and taken upstairs to warm your bed. In bed you'd warm your feet on them and, as they cooled, remove the cloth and put your feet directly on to the brick itself to extract the last vestiges of warmth. They were a godsend on cold winter nights.

The fire was so important that the first priority every morning was to 'make the fire'. The first job involved removing yesterday's ashes from beneath the grate using the hearth brush and shovel. Next, old newspaper was scrunched up and placed on the grate. Then, firewood was placed on top of the paper. Finally, a few pieces of coal were placed on top of the firewood. After igniting the paper with a match came the tricky part. For the fire to really get going a vigorous supply of oxygen was required. This was achieved by creating a draft. A 'blower' (a square piece of metal sheeting with a handle in the centre), was placed in front of the fire. Covering the front of the fire except the grate, the blower allowed air to be sucked into the fire and up the chimney, ensuring that the fire burned with great gusto. For households without a blower, an alternative but more dangerous method was employed. Propping a shovel in front of the fire and placing a sheet of newspaper over it achieved the same purpose. However, there was always the danger that the newspaper would catch fire and burn.

Being a poor family we couldn't afford to burn pure coal. It was too expensive. Therefore, every Saturday morning my grandad would take me, together with his bicycle, spade and two coal sacks, to one of the old slag tips, relics from the abandoned coal mines scattered about the area. Our favourite was the slag tip around Wutchie (see Image 1b). On arrival, we filled the two coal sacks with the fine black dust we called 'dant', chatting and singing as we did so, before returning home with the booty slung over the bicycle. As well as helping my grandad fill the sacks I also indulged in a little exploration. It was great fun crawling up the disused mine tunnels or jumping across the small ravines on the slag tips. I remember seeing a beautiful yellow bird fly past nearby. My grandad said it was a yellowhammer. He seemed so knowledgeable, I thought he knew everything.

At home, the dant was stored alongside the coal in an outside building attached to the house. Before use, it would be moistened with a little water and then made into round balls, like black snowballs. They burned very well, especially when mixed with a little coal, and were an ideal source of free fuel. The only downside was that we always returned home covered in black dust, like two miners returning home after hewing coal at the coalface!

It wasn't only the coal store that was outside. The only toilet was also outside. This presented few problems in summer when the days were long and the weather was warm, but in winter, it was a different story. It was no fun having to venture outside on a freezing cold night to visit the toilet, especially when snuggled up in a warm bed. The absence of any lighting ensured that the toilet was dark as well as cold. For these reasons, a common, indeed almost universal, accessory of every bedroom was a poe. This 'basin with a handle' was kept under the bed and was your private toilet for the night. Used poes would be emptied in the morning. Although an unpleasant task, it was preferable to visiting the outside toilet in the cold and dark. The used poes were rinsed and then disinfected, usually with 'Dettol' or something similar. Just as the Queen thinks everywhere she visits smells of fresh paint, in winter every bedroom smelled of disinfectant.

Before the advent of television, games like cards, dominoes, ludo and snakes and ladders provided the entertainment. These were played on the kitchen table or, in winter, on the rug in front of the coal fire. Our kitchen table was a large, sturdy, wooden table with carved chunky legs, a table that wouldn't be out of place in an old National Trust house. Drawers beneath the tabletop housed the cutlery. Draped over the table was a thick yet flexible 'oilcloth', the tablecloth of the day. These came in various colours and patterns. Ours was yellow, patterned with blue squares. Red and green were other popular colours. The oilcloth would always be wiped clean before any meal was eaten or game played.

The hub of the kitchen was a rather bare, square, white, porcelain sink. Other essential items were a dolly, a dolly tub and a mangle. All three were needed to wash clothes. One day per week was set aside for washing. In our house washing day was Monday. Washing was a labour intensive task, completely different to the present age where washing machines and tumble driers do all the work. The dirty clothes would be placed in the dolly tub, water added and the dolly used to agitate the clothes. Dolly blue or a washing powder, such as 'Omo' or 'Acdo', would be added to aid the cleansing process. After washing, residual water was squeezed out using the hand operated mangle. Finally, the clothes were hung on the washing line to dry. In winter, they would be aired on the fireguard in front of the fire. For a week's washing, this entire operation had to be repeated several times. Washing day meant just that. A whole day devoted to washing.

Rag and bone merchants were a common sight in the 1950s. In exchange for a pile of old rags you received either a 'donkey stone' and/or some wooden clothing pegs. A donkey stone or rubbing stone was like a large tablet of soap. Except it was hard. Very hard. Its function was to clean the doorsteps. After moistening, the stone was rubbed vigorously on the step to produce a lovely white sheen. In some households, ours included, this activity was a daily occurrence.

Doorsteps had other functions too. They were used for sitting on, providing a cosy venue for chats with family and neighbours. Also, they were excellent for sharpening knives. Carving knives were particularly prone to this type of treatment. On the rare occasions when there was meat to be carved, the woman of the house would sharpen the knife on the front, not the back, doorstep. It was a way of showing off to the neighbours, of saying, "Hey, look at us. We can afford to eat meat." It was also a bluff. A way of keeping one step ahead of your neighbours. For example, even if you couldn't afford meat, by sharpening your knife in full view of them, your neighbours automatically assumed that you had indeed got some meat to eat.

2.2 ROUTINES

Like most children, my life followed a daily routine. Unlike other children, mine was a strange routine. I had two homes! Bed and breakfast was taken at 30 Crawford Avenue with my mother, grandma and grandad (and other family members initially), and tea (we never called it dinner) and supper at my Auntie Lily and Uncle Jack's house in Ratcliffe Road (Image 1b). On weekdays, I would have my breakfast of a glass of vimto and a kitkat, attend Aspull Methodist School and return home to Crawford Avenue. Then, after she had finished work as a home help (they are called carers now), my Auntie Lily would collect me and take me to their house. Here, I would have tea and stay until late evening. After supper, my Auntie Nellie escorted me back to Crawford Avenue (passing the 'dead house' on the way) and the routine would be repeated the following day.

This routine must have started very early in my life, too early for me to remember. Several factors probably caused it to happen. Being unmarried and having to work, my mother could not support me on her own. She needed help and the best source of help was from your extended family. Her older sister, my Auntie Lily, had recently married Jack and they had bought their own house, a rarity in those days, especially for anyone from our family. It was a two-up, two-down terraced house in Ratcliffe Road, about half-a-mile away. They were childless. So, the obvious solution for them was to share the upbringing of me with my mother (and grandma and grandad). I suppose I was the child that my auntie and uncle never had.

Was I growing up? On my many journeys to and from Auntie Lily's I would compare my height against the garden fences at the front of the houses on Crawford Avenue. At first the fences were taller than me but I remember the elation when, for the very first time, I could peer over the top of them. I was getting taller. The second part of the journey involved crossing common land, the same land upon which Aspull Secondary Modern would later be built. In summer the scene was sensational. Intricate swathes of yellow patterning a carpet of green was a joy to behold. It was amazing what beauty nature could achieve with grass and a few clumps of dandelions and buttercups. Even as a young boy, the wonder of nature fascinated me.

Every night before bedtime my grandad and I would sit and chat. He was fond of gadgets and would eagerly scour the newspaper for interesting items. If an interesting and, most importantly, inexpensive gadget was discovered, an order was placed. Normally, the gadgets were delivered on a Saturday morning. The pleasure and sense of achievement after constructing and then using radios and walkie-talkies in the back garden was immense. One morning, our task was interrupted when my mum and her sisters brought my grandma outside and sat her on the back doorstep. She was in agony and they looked concerned. Apparently, my grandma had heartburn. I felt really sorry for her. The pain must be excruciating when your heart's on fire. (As a small boy, this was my impression of heartburn.)

2.3 DESPERATE TIMES

Shortly after buying their house in Ratcliffe Road my uncle lost his job. It was a desperate time. They had a mortgage to pay with no way to pay it. Although my auntie worked as a home help her meagre wage didn't even cover the day-to-day bills, let alone pay the mortgage. Desperate times called for desperate measures and I remember my uncle trudging along to every local businessman with me in tow, virtually pleading for a job. I suppose I was there as a 'sympathy symbol', a little boy to tug at their heartstrings. It didn't work. My uncle didn't find regular work for several months and was reduced to doing whatever odd jobs he could find, sometimes alone, sometimes with other family members. He was quite adept at Do-It-Yourself (DIY) and I remember him, my other Uncle Jack and Uncle Evan building a wall at a house in Dark Lane, Little Scotland. Eventually, he got a job at Leyland Motors, the empire of Lord Stokes. This entailed travelling to Leyland but it was better than being jobless. My uncle remained at Leyland Motors until he retired in 1989.

The biggest DIY job my uncle undertook was converting his back bedroom into a bathroom and smaller bedroom. Although this was completed successfully, during its construction he had a nasty accident. He sliced the top off his thumb with a Stanley knife! After my uncle had positioned the severed part back in place and secured it with a handkerchief, I accompanied him the short distance to Dr Cooke's surgery in Haigh Road. This was located in a lovely old house* where Dr Cooke, obliging as ever, duly stitched the top of his thumb back on.

2.4 DREAMS AND NIGHTMARES

When I was young I had a very vivid imagination and nightmares, as well as dreams, were a common occurrence. For the most part I coped with the nightmares. A recurring one involved crossing the main road on my way to school. On reaching the middle of the road, I couldn't seem to move. No matter how hard I tried, my movements were in slow motion. The traffic was hurtling towards me and I couldn't move an inch! At the very last second, before the car hit me, I always awoke with a start, all sweaty and scared. It was frightening.

Falling was another recurring nightmare. Where I fell from would be different, sometimes from tall buildings, sometimes from cliffs or mountains, but it always involved falling. It was a scary sensation. Again, I always awoke before hitting the ground. These two nightmares, although frightening, were manageable. The third one wasn't. I didn't even seem to be asleep when an apparition of Colin Seddon, my next door neighbour, appeared in a corner of my bedroom. He seemed so real. At first, he was friendly and smiling but, without any warning, this friendly apparition suddenly changed into a snarling demonic monster that lunged towards me. It was so vivid. I was absolutely petrified and screamed the house down. Everyone came running upstairs to see what the commotion was but, of course, there was nothing. It was all in my imagination. The best way to describe it is like the scene in the library from the film

---

* This lovely old house with its beautiful back garden remained the doctor's surgery until old Dr Cooke died. His son Dr Peter and his daughter Dr Barbara built a new surgery adjacent to the Labour Club. Jean, my cousin Brian's mother, was the cleaner at this new surgery for many years. Sadly, the lovely old house has been demolished and replaced by apartments.

Ghostbusters when the ghost of a kind old lady suddenly transforms into an evil witch. Thankfully, this nightmare only happened once.

These experiences and my vivid imagination made me afraid of the dark. At bedtime, especially in the dark winter months, I would literally run up the stairs and dive into bed. When all the lights were turned off, the bedclothes would be pulled over my head. There was no way on Earth that I could ever have ventured on to the dark, still stairs in the dead of night. No way at all.

2.5 CHRISTMAS

Christmas. Ah, how I used to love Christmas. Of the many fond recollections of early Christmases, two events stand out since they were repeated nearly every year. The first event was a visit to Billy Croston's. Billy Croston's shop was located near the New School and every year, a few weeks before Christmas and always in the evening when it was dark, William and I would be taken to his shop. On arrival, Billy would usher us all upstairs to where the toys were kept. It was also where Billy had some toys, such as train sets, on display and actually working. We were two eager, excited little boys in wonderland: we had never seen so many toys. I think Billy enjoyed the experience too since he would willingly demonstrate all the toys in which we showed an interest. However, he took even greater pleasure in anticipating the money he would receive when they were sold.

At the time I couldn't understand why we always went to his shop in the dark but figured it out later. Billy Croston used to sell many of his goods 'on the slate' (on credit) and it was where many of the poorest families shopped. Billy Croston was a real character, a man who could tell a good tale, especially if you owed him money. And woe betide anyone who didn't keep up their repayments. He would ensure that everyone in Aspull knew you were indebted to him. Although a poor family, we had a modicum of pride and used to avoid using Billy Croston's unless it was absolutely necessary. Christmas was such a time. However, it was reasoned that, if we went to his shop in the dark, we had less chance of being spotted by prying eyes.

The second event involved writing a wish list for Father Christmas. (For some reason he was always called this and not Santa Claus.) As Christmas day drew near our mothers and aunties told us to write down on a piece of paper what we wanted from Father Christmas. Excitedly, William and I would scribble down our lists of presents for that Christmas. Then came the puzzling bit. We were instructed to 'post' the letters to Father Christmas up the chimney. This we did. But the chimney was over a blazing coal fire and the letters immediately caught fire and burned! So how did Father Christmas know what we wanted? Well, Father Christmas is magic and knows everything, was the answer. But there was always a caveat. Remember, they said, Father Christmas only delivers presents to children who have been good. Every year we had an anxious wait to see if we had been good.

I was born with an inquisitive nature and a fertile mind, attributes that would serve me well in later life. From an early age many things intrigued and puzzled me, including coal fires. At that time coal was being burned in fires all over the world. Now coal is heavy yet when it burns it disappears into nothing. Well, into heat and flames which, to a young boy, seemed to weigh either nothing or very little. So, with all the coal fires and all the coal power stations burning vast amounts of coal, the Earth must be getting a lot lighter. In that case, the Earth might be pulled into the sun and we'd all be burnt to a cinder, or it might fly off into space and we'd all be frozen to death. At eight years old, I couldn't work out which fate awaited me, being fried to death or being frozen to death. What a choice. Neither appealed. Despite reassurances from adults that everything would be fine, I was always a little scared.

Christmas is an exciting time for young children. After bonfire night, Christmas was the next big event* and I used to count down the days to December 25th. It's a strange fact that when you're young the days seem to last forever and time passes so slowly. (Oh for that feeling now. They speed by when you're older.) By Christmas Eve the excitement reached fever pitch. The big wait was almost over. I think Christmas Eve is the only day in the year that young children actually beg to go to bed early. They can't wait to sample the delights of all those wonderful presents the following day. One very cold and icy Christmas Eve, William and I made a slide on the road to help the time pass more quickly.

In those days the weather patterns were completely different to today. The winters were cold and often snowy and the summers hot and dry. The Bing Crosby song *White Christmas* was often literally true. Indeed, in severe winters the snowfalls could be really heavy and snowdrifts of ten feet or more were not uncommon[1] (Image 21). It was great fun making igloos and having snowball fights.

A typical winter snowdrift of the 1950s and 1960s.

---

* When I was a child Halloween was never celebrated in Britain. It was an American thing.

35

At Christmas we never had a real tree, just a small artificial tree with a few decorations and a small set of lights. It was always located in the living room on a table near the window. Other decorations consisted of a few paper chains and a couple of paper decorations, such as bells, hung from the ceiling with drawing pins. The decorations were completed with a few sprigs of holly collected from local holly trees, and, occasionally, a piece of mistletoe. Presents would be placed under the tree, unwrapped, on Christmas Eve after we had gone to bed.

I never got all the presents that were on my 'letter' to Father Christmas, just a few of them. But this hardly mattered. On Christmas morning, I would jump out of bed and dash down the stairs as fast I could, making straight for the presents under the Christmas tree. My main present would be found and opened. It was always from Billy Croston's. The first one that I remember was a wind-up train with just one carriage that ran on a small circular track. It was the very one that I had chosen in his shop! Father Christmas was so clever. I was so excited. Hurriedly, I assembled it in front of the fire and played with it for hours, still in my pyjamas. It was wonderful.

Like myself, many children only got one main present and a number of small presents. It was all that most families could afford. Some families couldn't afford even this and their children had to make do with second-hand toys and second-hand clothes donated by friends and neighbours. The small presents were usually books, chocolates and sweets. Annuals of comics, such as the *Beano* and *Dandy*, were typical books, but one book that I remember vividly was about the Wild West. On the front cover was a Red Indian sat astride his horse. He looked so strong, proud and dignified. It's an image that I have never forgotten.

Christmas presents for other years included cowboy outfits, complete with a gunbelt, holster and gun, a rifle, a Davy Crocket hat, and a cricket set, including a pair of whalebone cricket pads. One year, my main present was a football. A real leather football. I was so proud that I took it with me everywhere, even to 'jacksmudders' in Pemberton. I was puzzled when my Auntie Lily said we were going to 'jacksmudders'. (That's what it sounded like to me.) Where on Earth was 'jacksmudders'. She meant, of course, Jack's mother's.

New Year rapidly followed Christmas. This meant more merrymaking for the adults but no extra presents for the children. However, it did involve a strange ritual. Just before midnight on New Year's Eve either myself or William would be given a piece of coal and ushered outside. Then, after the clock had struck midnight, we had to knock on the front door. The door would open and we would step inside and offer our gift, a piece of coal. Apparently, this bestowed good luck and good fortune on the house and its occupants for the forthcoming year. It was known as 'letting the New Year in'.

2.6 BONFIRE NIGHT

A precursor to Christmas, bonfire night was another night to look forward to. There was the thrill of collecting your fireworks. Proper fireworks. Boys' fireworks, such as jackjumpers, bangers, roman candles and rockets, and girls' fireworks, such as mount vesuvius, snow fountain, catherine wheels and sparklers. Jackjumpers were great. They jumped around the floor in a haphazard way like a demented little dervish. Unfortunately, because of health and safety issues, jackjumpers have become extinct. Bangers were special too, particularly the large, loud ones. William and I used to keep our fireworks collections in cardboard boxes. Every night before November 5th we would diligently take them out, one by one, read the instructions and then replace them carefully. The anticipation of lighting the blue touch paper on the big day thrilled us to the core. They were treated with reverence were our fireworks.

The bonfire itself provided even greater excitement than the fireworks. When we were young, the wood for the bonfire was stored in the brick building in William's back garden. It was the size of a single garage and by bonfire night was over half full of wood and twigs. The bonfire was stored in the shed to keep it dry and to keep it safe. On bonfire night it would be assembled and set alight in their back garden. However, it was more fun in later years when the bonfire was built on open common land and required guarding against attack from rival bonfire gangs. Rivals would try and steal some of the wood from your bonfire or, even worse, set it alight before bonfire night. Vigilance was required to avoid these fates. Although guarding your bonfire against attack provided some excitement, the best thrill was planning and especially executing a raid on a rival bonfire. Hiding silently behind a garden wall, climbing over and stealthily stealing some of the wood, knowing that at any instant you might be observed and have to flee for your life. This was what got the adrenalin pumping and your heart racing. The meagre amount of wood actually stolen was irrelevant.

One year we made a respectable Guy Fawkes from old clothing and crumpled newspapers. Our intention was to just burn it on the bonfire. Anyhow, William's mother and Auntie Lily said it was good enough for us to show to the neighbours and try and earn a little more money for fireworks. Neither of us had done collecting of any kind before and, being quite shy boys, were very apprehensive. However, the thought of extra fireworks prevailed and our Guy was shown to a number of neighbours. To our surprise, they treated us kindly and a respectable sum was raised. We had a lot of fireworks that year.

At William's house in St John's Road various games were played. Playing with miniature soldiers and forts was a favourite and we took great delight in building our own forts from empty matchboxes and cigarette packets. Cowboys and Indians with cap guns and bows and arrows, and spacemen with ray guns, were other frequently played games. Firing ray guns with different coloured rays (beams of light) in the dark was brilliant. So were films about outer space. These were few and far between at the time but if one came out we would certainly go and see it. We also loved to listen to Dan Dare on the radio and make our own spacesuits from empty cardboard boxes.

Marbles and conkers were other popular games. 'Nooky' was the most common marbles game. A 'nook' or small hole about the size of an eggcup would be made in a patch of flat compacted dirt and a line drawn about three feet away. Starting from behind the line, the object of the game was to hit your opponent's marble and then to flick your marble into the hole before your opponent could return the compliment with his marble. The marbles were flicked using a thumb and forefinger and shots were taken alternately. The winner kept his opponent's marble. Conkers was played in the autumn when horse chestnuts were in season. It was amazing what treatments children bestowed on their conkers to make them successful in conker fights. Baking, lacquering and pickling in vinegar were but a few. It was a matter of pride to have a high-ranking conker, such as a niner or fifteener. Eventually, even the best conker met its match and was smashed to smithereens, but it was fun while it lasted.

Some days after school a group of us would make our way to our preferred playground, the area of common land between the school and Wutchie. It was littered with exciting places. As well as the old slag tips and disused mine tunnels, there were three ponds or lodges (Image 1b). The 'fiver' was the most popular (Image 22). This was an almost circular pond that at its deepest point was only five foot deep. Hence its name. A gently shelving sandy bottom made it popular for bathing, sailing boats and generally messing about. It was also a favoured fishing spot, reputedly containing a fierce pike!

The 'klondike' was a rectangular pond, probably a remnant from the mines, that had become filled with water. It was normally overgrown with weeds and 'ginny green teeth' and for these reasons wasn't popular. The 'horseshoe' completed the trio of ponds. Evidently, it got its name because of its shape: it was enclosed by a semi-circular slag tip. This made the water dirty so it wasn't good for bathing. However, when frozen in winter the 'horseshoe' was excellent for ice-skating.

Uncle Jack, Brian's dad, with a young William, at the
'Fiver' 1950. The pond has long since been filled in,
along with the Klondike and Horseshoe.

The fiver was a popular spot because not only was it adjacent to the slag tips, it was also close to farmers' fields. At harvest time these contained haystacks. Haystacks are magical things for young boys with lots of imagination. There are many things you can do but one of the best is sliding down from the top of the haystack and shooting off the 'roof' into a waiting pile of hay. Awesome.

As a small boy one of my esteemed toys was a tricycle. Pedalling my tricycle around the garden and nearby footpaths was a delight (Image 23). Many happy hours were expended on this delightful activity. As so often happens, Father Time intervened. Eventually, the tricycle became too small for my growing frame.

However, all was not lost. My ninth birthday present would be a bicycle. Surprised and excited, I asked what colour it would be. Maroon! Maroon, what colour was that? It was new to me. But, in the event, it was a beautiful colour. Not only did I get an amazing bicycle, it also came with two accessories, a bell and a dynamo. A dynamo to power the lights as you pedalled. I was in seventh heaven. My bicycle became a fond companion. At weekends and on long summer evenings our gang of about five would cycle around Wutchie to Top Lock (Image 1a). Our destination was a large granite boulder. Why? Because it had been used for target practice in World War II and was full of embedded bullets. We took great delight in digging them out, polishing them and attaching them to the tips of our arrows.

Me on my tricycle age six at 30 Crawford Avenue.

2.8 PETS

Despite shooting starlings and rats, I've always been fond of birds and animals and wanted a pet very much. A dog. A little puppy to play with and take for walks. For some reason we had never been a pet-owning family and it wasn't about to change on account of me. William also felt the same way and one day we did something mischievous. Without our parents' knowledge we toddled off to one of William's neighbours whose dog had just produced a lovely litter of puppies. We were smitten. They were gorgeous. Cute, cuddly, fluffy balls of pure delight. We picked our favourite there and then and said we would return later with our parents to collect it. On telling our families what we had done they weren't amused and William's mother had to go and apologise to the neighbour. We didn't get a puppy.

Thwarted in our attempt to get a dog, William and I decided to catch a bird. To do this a cunning trap was devised. An upturned garden sieve was wedged open at one end by a piece of firewood. A string was attached to the firewood and fed into the kitchen. Finally, pieces of bread, the bait, were placed around and under the sieve (Fig. 1). The trap was set. All we had to do now was watch and wait from our hidden vantage point behind the back door. Starlings (known by us as Sheppeys) were the most prevalent birds in our garden and it was no surprise when a flock of them arrived, attracted by the bread. At first, they ate the bread at the fringes of the trap. However, once that was gone they reluctantly and cautiously went for the bread under the sieve. As soon as that happened the trap was sprung by pulling on the string. This removed the piece of wood and the sieve fell to the ground trapping the bird underneath. It was a simple but ingenious trap that never failed. Carefully, the captured bird was extricated from beneath the sieve. Not surprisingly, our parents never allowed us to keep any of the birds as a pet. We had to let them go.

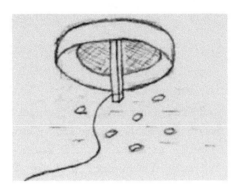

Trap to catch birds.

Eventually, I was allowed a pet, a blue budgerigar. I named him Joey. He lived in a cage at my Auntie Lily's house but was allowed out once a day to fly around the front room. This he did with gusto and sometimes it was a job to entice him back in his cage. Cuttlefish bones were bought to keep his beak in trim and I wondered what a funny shape a cuttlefish must be to have a bone like that.

2.9 ENTERTAINMENT

My first taste of formal entertainment happened when I was eight. Our entire family were having a rare night out at Wigan's Hippodrome theatre[2] to watch some live entertainment (Image 24). To a young boy it appeared massive, just like its namesake, a hippopotamus. It was my first experience of entertainment of any kind and one that I thoroughly enjoyed. Wigan Hippodrome, famous for its naughty vaudeville shows, really pulled in the crowds, but it was living on borrowed time. The era of live entertainment was coming to an end. Motion pictures, full of Hollywood stars of the 'silver screen', were the new fashion. Vaudeville shows just couldn't compete. And so it was with Wigan Hippodrome. Its final production, the typically saucy *We Never Clothed* was staged in April 1956. Shortly afterwards the building was destroyed by fire.[3]

Wigan's Hippodrome Theatre (circa 1950).

In the 1940s and early 1950s television ownership was rare. Indeed, it wasn't until 1955, when I was nine, that my Auntie Lily acquired a television set (in black and white of course). It was too late for the coronation of Queen Elizabeth II in 1953 but this new entertainment medium provided many hours of viewing pleasure. *The Trollenberg Terror*, a mini series that was shown on a Saturday night, was enthralling. It was about aliens who had landed on top of the Trollenberg, a mountain that always appeared to be shrouded in mist in a remote region of the Alps. Any humans brave enough to venture into the mist and survive became possessed. The give-away sign was their demented smile and the only way to kill them was to shoot them with 'dum-dum' bullets. Tame by today's standards, it was gripping entertainment for two small boys.

The *Lone Ranger*, the *Cisco Kid*, and *Chingachgook, Last of the Mohicans*, penned by James Fenemore Cooper, were other programmes that I watched. Whilst having my tea, I would watch a youthful Desmond Morris present *Zootime* from London Zoo. One episode from that programme is etched on my memory. A tree snake was hunting for bird's eggs in a large tree beside a South American river. It slithered slowly along a branch to a nest, unhinged its jaws and devoured one of the eggs. At that point the parent birds returned and began harassing the snake by dive-bombing it and trying to dislodge it from the branch with their talons. They succeeded and the snake fell into the river. Unfortunately for the snake, the river was infested with piranha. There was a feeding frenzy as the piranha tore into the hapless snake and in less than thirty seconds all that remained was the snake's skeleton at the bottom of the river. *Lassie*, a clever and affectionate Collie dog, *William Tell*, and *Robin Hood*, with the hero played by Richard Green, were other children's programmes popular at the time.

In those days it was the norm for the men to go to the Labour Club and for the women to stay at home and look after the children. With their husbands at the Labour Club, Auntie Lily and Auntie Nellie would stay in and look after William and me, sometimes at Nellie's house but more usually at Lily's house. Games were played, such as cards and dominoes. Gin rummy, find the queen and snap are games that I remember. Saturday nights were special: we got a treat. William and I were given some money to pop down the road to the New Inn pub to bring back some dandelion and burdock and bags of crisps. We looked forward to Saturday nights.

At home in Crawford Avenue I would wait for the men to return from their night out before going to bed. Reading a book or playing games such as snakes and ladders helped to pass the time. Fixed on to the inside of our back door was a real dartboard with a light above it. Occasionally, I would attempt to play but wasn't very good. For anyone playing darts, it was imperative they locked the back door beforehand, just in case someone tried to open it as a dart was being thrown! A dart in the forehead isn't recommended.

The women also had occasional nights out, usually at the pictures with their female friends. Auntie Lily had two such friends and sometimes they would take me with them to the pictures. There was a good choice of cinemas in Wigan. The Ritz, the County, the Court and the Princess. The Ritz was the largest and, because of its proximity to the bus stop in Station Road, the most popular cinema. Audrey Hepburn was my favourite film star. I thought she was the most beautiful woman in the world. (And still do.) James Stewart was my favourite male film star, although I also liked John Wayne (because most of his films were Westerns or war films) and Charlton Heston (because he was muscular).

My mother and her friend Margaret Fletcher (the sister of Don Fletcher mentioned earlier, and the daughter of Mr Fletcher) also took William and me to the pictures. Normally, we went to Wigan but occasionally they would take us to the Odeon in Bolton. Although only six miles away, the bus journey to Bolton seemed to take forever. In fact, it took one hour. After watching the film, we always called at the West End chippy. Rather than use the direct route from the Odeon cinema to the chippy, William and I became intrepid explorers and used the labyrinth of dark, winding, dimly lit alleyways. More than once we came perilously close to getting completely lost. My mother and Margaret would have fish and chips whilst William and I would share a bag of chips and mushy peas. Delicious!

2.10 WALKS

During summer, Sunday mornings became a ritual. Uncle Evan, William's dad, who had seen active service in the army in World War II,* was the 'rent collector' for Aspull. He loved to walk. Every Sunday morning he took William and me through Haigh Hall

---

* On one patrol, the soldier immediately next to Evan was shot in the head and killed by a German sniper. It could so easily have been Uncle Evan who was shot.

plantations to Wigan. Often, we stopped on the bridge overlooking the canal basin where Wigan Rowing Club had their headquarters in the lovely Haigh Boat House[4] (Image 25). Watching them rowing at speed along the Leeds-Liverpool canal was exciting. Not quite the Oxbridge boat race but a great spectacle nonetheless. Ice creams and lemonade in Mesnes Park preceded our return journey. Travelling on the little train (Image 30, page 47) with the wind in our hair was exhilarating but if, for whatever reason, this wasn't possible, we caught the bus.

Haigh Hall was built in 1827-40 for the 24th Earl of Crawford and Balcarres. Reputedly, it was the Earl himself who designed the building. Built of ashiar, slabs of square hewn stone, Haigh Hall is a grand old building reminiscent of a small stately home[5] (Image 26). It was given to the old County Borough of Wigan for a token price in 1947 to be used for the benefit of local people.[6]

Other treasures lay to the rear of the Hall. Three large greenhouses packed full of exotic plants nestled on the fringe of the wood and it was a joy to meander slowly through this tropical paradise. It was Kew gardens in miniature![7] (Image 27). Directly in front of the greenhouses was a circular lily pond filled with carp[7] (Images 27 and 28). Watching the waters of the fountain splashing on the surface of the pond with the fish gliding gracefully among the water lilies was tranquillity itself. A walled garden bristling with beautiful scented roses provided another delight.

The plantations were huge, stretching from Haigh in the north to Wigan in the south, a distance of over three miles. Covered with native English trees, such as oak, ash, sycamore and horse chestnut, and with masses of rhododendrons, they were a magnificent sight, especially in spring with the rhododendrons in full bloom. Bisecting the upper and lower plantations, the Leeds-Liverpool canal further enhances their beauty[8] (Image 29). In summer, a train, pulled by a tractor[7] (Image 30), ran a regular service between the Hall and the Plantation Gates on Wigan Lane[9] (Image 31). All these features made Haigh Hall and its plantations a very popular place.

Haigh Boat House in winter (circa 1950).
Sadly, it has long since been demolished.

Haigh Hall. It was used as a hotel for a few years
but has now (2020) reverted to its former status.

Greenhouses to the rear of Haigh Hall (circa 1958.)

Pond at Haigh Hall (circa 1958).

When we were older, Evan took us for bicycle rides. One that I remember was to Crank, a small country village beyond St Helens. Evan's brother-in-law was the headmaster of the local school and we had been invited for afternoon tea. The journey was enchanting. We cycled at a leisurely pace along quiet, winding country lanes to his house on a hill. Tea was taken in the back room: it had French doors that overlooked open fields full of grazing cows. Quintessentially English, it was also idyllic.

At 1,200 feet Rivington Pike (Image 69, page 94), on the edge of the West Pennine Moors, provides one of the highest vantage points in the district. A popular destination throughout the year, on Good Friday's it became a magnet, attracting people from near and far. Everyone flocked to its summit, including myself and a small group of friends. Come rain or shine, we undertook this strenuous journey every single year. Setting off from home in the morning with a packed lunch and a drink, we walked the four miles to Horwich, passing the Crown pub, and on into Lever Park. After finding a secluded spot, lunch would be taken. The weather determined which route we took to climb the Pike. In fine weather, a scenic route would be chosen. In bad weather we took the shortest route. On a fine day, thousands of people milled about, picnicking, playing or just lazing around. The splendid views from the summit made the arduous ascent worthwhile. Our thirst and hunger from the climb were satisfied by one of the many ice cream and burger vans parked a few hundred feet below the summit, having arrived in this lofty location via Georges Lane. After a visit to the Pigeon Tower,* our descent took us through the enchanting Japanese Gardens[10] (Image 32) and back into Horwich. An ice cream from Ferretti's fortified us for the journey home. One year it was so hot that by the time Blackrod was reached we were parched and gasping for a drink. Re-hydration was essential. After knocking on people's doors begging for a drink of water, one kind soul obliged and we managed to make it home.

The Leeds-Liverpool canal which bisects the Haigh Hall
estate (circa 1910). Haigh Hall can be seen in the
background. Taken from Haigh Boat House.

---

* The 'Pigeon Tower' is a famous landmark built by Lord Lever on his Rivington Estate. He kept
pigeons in the loft whilst Lady Lever used the tower as a sewing room to take advantage of the
panoramic views.

Miniature train that ran through Haigh
Hall plantations (circa 1958).

Plantation Gates, Wigan Lane (1909). They
are the same today except for the gas lamp.

Japanese Gardens, Lever Park,
Rivington (circa 1920).

As a youngster my only holidays were the occasional day trips to the seaside. Blackpool and Southport were the usual destinations. One day, whilst waiting for the train, my bucket and spade slipped from my hand and fell on to the track. Luckily, the station guard retrieved them before the train arrived. After travelling by train, our time was divided between the beach and the fairground, with a meal sandwiched in-between. On the rare occasions when the tide was actually in at Southport, we bathed near the pier. If it was out, a trip on the amphibious craft was taken. This was a boat on wheels. On the sand it drove like a truck and in the water it sailed like a boat.

Motor-boats were my favourite attraction. It was delightful driving them around the winding waterways of the fairground and the open spaces of Southport Marina. The thrill of the roller coaster rides and the scariness of the ghost train, combined with the hidden surprises inside Noah's Ark, especially the unexpected blasts of air up your trousers or into your face, added to the exuberant feeling. Gentler pursuits, such as drifting through the River Caves on a slow boat, were also hugely enjoyable. The Hall of Mirrors provided further fun. Some of the shapes and faces were hilarious. Very occasionally, we had a day out in North Wales. Rhyl was our usual destination. In the days before motorways and fast roads, the journey of approximately seventy miles took about four hours. It was so long that a stop was deemed necessary. This allowed passengers to use the toilets and obtain refreshments. Being roughly half-way between Wigan and Rhyl, Frodsham was an ideal stopping place. On the coach, we would peer through the windows looking for the unmistakable landmark of the Stanlow oil refinery, characterised by its flame of burning gas. Once that was spotted, we knew that a delicious meal of fish and chips from a Frodsham chippy wasn't far away.

Like most young children I had my share of tantrums. One occurred in Rhyl. I had spotted a boat in the window of a toy shop. A lovely boat. A boat that I really wanted. When the adults refused to buy it, I plonked down on the steps and wouldn't budge until they bought it. Eventually, they had to club their money together to buy it. At times, I must have been a selfish little child!

Auntie Lily and Uncle Jack had been going to the Isle of Man for the past few years with their friends, Mr and Mrs Fedegan. One year, without any warning, they decided that it was time for a change. Instead of going with their friends, they chose to take William and me for a weeks holiday. A weeks holiday away from home. In a hotel. In the Isle of Man. Where was it? It's a place that I had never heard of but, since you had to sail over the sea in a boat for four hours to get there, it must be a long way away. In fact, it might even be abroad!

The holiday was duly booked for July, the same time as Glasgow's fortnightly holiday, the Glasgow wakes. We were staying at the 'Waters Edge' guest house in

Port St Mary. It was expensive. The cost was 7 shillings 6 pence (37.5p) per night for the adults and 3 shillings 9 pence (18p) for us. I was eleven-years-old and William ten. We were so excited we could hardly wait.

Up at the crack of dawn on the Saturday, William and I virtually ran from my home in Crawford Avenue to my Auntie Lily's house in Ratcliffe Road. Full of energy and expectation, we played on the road until the taxi arrived to whisk us all to Wigan Wallgate station where we caught the train to Liverpool. A short bus ride and there we were. Liverpool docks. Ready to board the 9-00 a.m. boat. The Isle of Man Steam Packet boat that we boarded seemed gigantic. To two excited, thrilled little boys it seemed every bit as big as the Titanic or Queen Elizabeth! The company had a fleet of about four boats with names connected to the island. Lady of Mann and King Orry were two of the older boats, whilst Tynwald (the name of the Manx parliament) and Snaefell (the island's highest mountain) were the newest. It was potluck which one you got.

In the 1950s and early 1960s the Isle of Man was a very popular destination for the working class of the North West and the boats would be packed full of holiday makers. Once on board my uncle would tip a crewman to secure a cabin for us so we could enjoy the sail in comfort. The cabins were small. Nonetheless, they provided a refuge from the crowds, gave you privacy and provided the means to relax (they had bunks for four people). Standing on deck with the wind in your hair and the smell of the sea in your nostrils was brilliant. As the boat left Liverpool and made its way along the Mersey estuary, the sight of Liverpool, with its unmistakable Liver Birds, receding into the distance, lived long in my memory.

As soon as we set sail from Liverpool, a ritual was performed. Each one of us would write down the time we thought the boat would dock at Douglas, its destination in the Isle of Man. Many factors influenced the journey time. On a calm day one of the newer, faster boats could accomplish the trip in just over three-and-a-half hours. In contrast, a slower, older boat sailing in rough conditions could take over four hours. Although there was no prize at stake, it always got tense as the boat neared Douglas harbour since on many occasions people won or lost by a matter of minutes. The first bump as the boat made contact with the quayside was deemed to be the time of docking. This simple guessing game added an extra dimension to the already enjoyable journey.

After disembarking we boarded a charabanc (coach) to take us from Douglas to Port St Mary, about 15 miles away. The driver asked each party where their final destination was. When my uncle said the 'Waters Edge' guest house a man in the coach shouted, "You lucky people!" No, it wasn't Tommy Trinder but someone who had stayed there the previous year. The omens were promising.

On the way from Douglas to Port St Mary the road crosses what is known as the Fairy Bridge. According to Manx legend (the people who live on the island are known as Manx people) the Fairy Bridge is a favourite haunt of the little people, the fairies who inhabit the island. On crossing the Fairy Bridge everyone is encouraged to acknowledge the fairies by greeting them with "Hello Fairies". Failure to do so always brings bad luck during your stay on the island. We always said "Hello Fairies" and enjoyed good luck and marvellous holidays.

The Waters Edge was a small guest house located, not unnaturally, on the shore of a quiet part of Port St Mary (Image 33). It could only accommodate a maximum of five families. The rooms were small but adequate and none were *en suite*. The one bathroom per floor was communal. On arrival the landlady, Mrs Schofield, and her husband greeted us enthusiastically and served tea and biscuits in the small but cosy lounge. She was a large woman with a booming voice who reminded me very much of the late actress Peggy Mount. Her husband Jack was a quiet but knowledgeable man. We liked them both. All the other families who stayed at the Waters Edge were from Lancashire, usually from other mill towns such as Blackburn, Burnley, Bolton and Rochdale, although one year there was a family from Preston. Our rooms were on the top (second) floor. This was fabulous. As you walked down the stairs on to the first floor landing the window looked right out to the lifeboat, moored about fifty feet away in the bay. During our stays at the Waters Edge we never saw it launched in anger but it was still a thrill. The captain of the lifeboat actually lived directly opposite the Waters Edge guest house in a bungalow and told us of the many exploits of the lifeboat and its crew.

Me (left), Auntie Lily and William outside
the Waters Edge Guest House 1958.

In those days it was the norm to stay 'full board'. All the food was freshly cooked by Mrs Schofield and her husband and served in a small dining room by Mrs Schofield. Full board comprised three meals a day, breakfast, lunch and tea (as mentioned earlier, we never called it dinner). The food was lovely and I heartily ate everything. Except on one occasion. As we went down for our evening meal a strange, somewhat unpleasant, aroma greeted our nostrils. I had never smelled anything remotely like it before and hoped it wasn't part of our meal. I was disappointed. Soup was always the first course of our evening meal and so it was on this evening. But not any soup that I was aware of. A bowl of this vile green slime was placed before me and everyone else. More adventurous souls than me ventured one spoonful, but no more. I couldn't even try a tiny amount. Even now, when I adore most soups, asparagus soup is not one of my favourites.

About three times a week Mr Miller, the owner of the local coach firm in Port St Mary and a dead ringer for a Tommy Cooper look-a-like, would arrive at breakfast time and explain the trips they were running for the next few days. These ranged from full day round the island tours to short trips to nearby towns such as Port Erin, Peel and Castletown. The trips we actually went on most were those to Douglas, the capital of the island, and mystery tours. Douglas was visited in the evening, usually to watch a show, but my favourite was live wrestling. All right, so it's all fixed but it was quite spectacular. The mystery tours could, obviously, be to anywhere on the island but the journey was always through beautiful scenery. Niarbyl Bay was a popular destination. The view was breathtaking but if there is a windier spot in the United Kingdom I have yet to find it.

Rushen Abbey was another popular destination. This lovely spot is located near Ballasalla and, like Wimbledon, is famous for its strawberries and cream. It was an exquisite place to enjoy a relaxing few hours. On a bus journey from Port St Mary to Rushen Abbey William was trying to talk in a more refined manner than our normal broad Wigan accent. Admiring the wildlife in the countryside, we spotted some large birds in a field. William said, "Look at those lovely black birds," which was fine, and then spoiled it by continuing "with their breawn yeds" (brown heads). Spontaneous laughter erupted from all those within earshot.

Most mornings, after breakfast, the four of us walked the few hundred yards to a putting green attached to the local nine-hole golf course. Here, we played a game of putting. Normally, I'd team up with my auntie and we'd play against William and my uncle. Afterwards, we enjoyed a drink and a biscuit in the little café run by two kindly old ladies. (The café is still there but is now modernised and extended.) After our round of putting, my auntie and uncle rested (Image 34) whilst me and William went off to the rocks to explore and play games (Image 35).

Lily and Jack in Port St Mary 1959.

Me (left) and William on the rocks at Port St Mary 1958.

It was here that William and I had our very first game of golf. We hired the clubs, bought some balls and off we went. We weren't very good. It took us ages to get round the nine-hole course and most of our balls ended up in the sea, pulled or sliced over the cliffs, but we thoroughly enjoyed the experience. Indeed, in 2010 we returned to the Isle of Man for a short holiday with our wives and played the course again, this time much more successfully. On one of the longer (ca 350 yard) holes up a steep hill, William thought he'd played a shot that Tiger Woods would be proud of: his tee shot landed on the green! However, as we trudged up the hill, we realised there was another green about 150 yards further on. Puzzled as to why there were two greens for the same hole, we decided to ask the lady at the café why this was so. The answer was that the lower green was for those (elderly) golfers who couldn't make it to the higher green. (It was steep.) Unfortunately, a Tiger Wood's special it wasn't but it was still a damn fine shot.

The coastline near the golf course consisted of large slabs of rock sloping down to the sea. Piles of pebbles littered the periphery (Image 35). One of our favourite games was building a pile of rocks (a cairn) and then sliding large pebbles from a distance to try and demolish it. It was great fun, like curling with pebbles. We also loved feeding the seagulls. Using a large pebble, we dislodged limpets from the rocks and threw them to the waiting gulls. They went wild. Surrounded by hordes of screeching seagulls, it was like a scene from Alfred Hitchcock's film *The Birds*.

One day Mr Schofield lent us a hook and line to see if we could catch a fish. Excitedly, we skewered a limpet on the hook and, holding the other end of the line, threw it into the sea. We 'fished' for about half-an-hour without catching anything. Then, rather than give up, the end of the line was tied to a rock and we trudged dejectedly back to the hotel. To our utmost surprise, when we returned the following morning a large fish was attached to the line. It was brightly coloured and beautiful. It was too lovely to be taken back and eaten, so we let it go. Having described the fish, Mr Schofield said that it was probably a Pollack.

Some mornings William and I explored the surrounding cliffs and bays. On one of our expeditions towards Perwick Bay we discovered a cave in a cliff. Not just any cave but one that contained a pool. A very deep pool. We threw large stones into the pool and watched them sink in the crystal clear water. They seemed to sink in slow motion. We never saw any stone hit the bottom because the bottom was invisible. It was eerie.

Provided the weather was fine the afternoons were spent bathing. Being somewhat shy, at first we bathed in the sea around the rocks. Sometimes, Uncle Jack (aka Tarzan), but not Auntie Lily, would join us (Image 36). Rock bathing was both uncomfortable and dangerous since a wave could easily dash you against the rocks. Therefore, we decided to bathe where everyone else did, on Chapel Bay beach (Image 37). This is a large sandy beach that's overlooked by the resort's biggest hotel, the Balqueen Hydro. Rocks, with concomitant rock pools, flanked both ends of the half-mile long beach, whilst refreshments were available on the promenade. A floating diving stage moored in the bay provided additional fun. We enjoyed many happy hours on Chapel Bay beach.

The evenings were spent in different ways. When my auntie and uncle went to the local pub with the other adults, William and I would nip around the corner to Wilf's snack bar. Here, we indulged ourselves with the 'goodies' on offer, such as pop, chocolate and ice cream. Wilf was an amicable old gentleman who had 'retired' to the Isle of Man. As we became better acquainted, it transpired that he was originally from Standish, a small village on the outskirts of Wigan! It's such a small world.

Other evenings we all went for a walk. A spectacular but dangerous walk was over Cregneash, the local mountain, to Port Erin, a picturesque resort on the far side of the island. Near the summit of Cregneash lurked the chasms, fissures in the cliffs that dropped down to the sea several hundred feet below. Extreme caution was needed when visiting the chasms, not least because some of them were partly hidden by overgrowing vegetation. One false step and you were a goner! Surprisingly, you had to pay for the privilege of taking your life in your hands and viewing the chasms! On the summit was a café. Here, refreshments were provided and fees paid for viewing the chasms. Unfortunately, the café has been closed for many years but the chasms are still there, waiting for the unwary.

Bathing on the rocks at Port St Mary 1957. Me (left) and
William, Uncle Jack (middle) and Lily and Jack (right).

William (left) and me bathing
on Chapel Bay beach 1960

54

From the café at the summit of Cregneash the walk continued down past Harry Kelly's cottage and Cregneash village into the lovely resort of Port Erin. Overlooked by Bradda Head, Port Erin boasts one of the finest beaches on the island. Sheltered by mountains, this curved beach has lovely fine sand fronted by a nice promenade. Port Erin was also home to the late Norman Wisdom, one of Britain's best comic actors. Our return to Port St Mary was a gentle stroll along the road connecting the two resorts.

Midway between the two resorts was a park and a cinema. Many a game of tennis was enjoyed on the grass courts and it was here that my uncle introduced us to crown green bowling, including the intricacies of bias and spin. One year, we watched the film *Greyfriars Bobby,* the charming story of a Scottish terrier in Edinburgh.

The southern tip of the Isle of Man has some of the best scenery in Britain. It is reminiscent of Cornwall with its rugged cliffs and raging seas. The Calf of Man, a tiny island that is a nature reserve and home to both the grey seal and common seal, lies off the southernmost tip, separated from the main island by a strip of sea called 'The Sound'. These delightful creatures can be seen frolicking in this treacherous strip of sea or simply basking in the sun. Boat trips from Port St Mary to the Calf were run on a daily basis and I had been on several such trips, stopping at the Calf to admire the wildlife. On one trip, the sea became extremely choppy and a few of us became really sea sick. Rather than face a return boat trip back to Port St Mary, the skipper agreed to drop us off at The Sound, and we walked the four miles back.

It's strange but once Wednesday was over the rest of the holiday flew by. On our last night, we always went down to the rocks, made a cairn and watched the sea come in and demolish it. We also paid our final visit to Wilf's snack bar.

Returning home on the Saturday was a sad occasion. It could be awful if the sea was rough. One year it was very rough. Watching the boat bobbing up and down like a cork in Douglas harbour really excited me. It would be awesome sailing on a ship in such rough conditions. How wrong I was. Within half-an-hour I was physically sick and the feeling of extreme nausea was indescribable. But worst of all was the knowledge that there was no escape for the next four hours. We were all captives on the ship. On deck, suitcases floated in a sea of vomit. The journey was so bad that several passengers suffered broken arms and legs and many were violently ill. At Liverpool, a fleet of ambulances ferried the injured and sick to hospital. Getting off the ship didn't end the torment. Many hours later my bed seemed to be on the same rough sea. It took several days for me to recover fully.

William and I enjoyed five consecutive holidays in the Isle of Man with my auntie and uncle. Not only was our first holiday the most memorable, it produced some unexpected ramifications. Now my Auntie Lily and Uncle Jack had taken William and me for a week's holiday, both my mother and William's mother felt obliged to reciprocate. And reciprocate they did.

In the summer of 1959 my mother and her friend Margaret Fletcher took us for a week's holiday to Conway in a caravan (Image 38). We travelled by coach from Bolton and then by bus from Conway to the Bryn Morpha caravan site, which was situated on its outskirts. On the bus journey two Welsh men tried chatting up my mother and Margaret, without success. A lot of time was spent on the nearby beach (Image 39), where Margaret asked me to teach her how to swim. Most of the time we ate in the caravan but occasionally, the lure of the local chip shop proved irresistible. Their fish and chips were delicious. My most vivid memory was the sight of two men dressed in formal dinner suites, complete with top hats and tails, dancing and drinking on top of the small mountain opposite the caravan site. It was evening and they drank and danced around a roaring fire until well into the night. A pagan wedding ceremony it wasn't, so I presumed they were students from a local college who had passed some exams. Next morning, it was a relief to discover they hadn't got too drunk and fallen off the mountain.

Me outside our caravan in Conway 1959. It was
hardly big and luxurious but we enjoyed it.

Me (left) and William posing on the beach at Conway (1959).

Two years later William's mother and dad took us to Blackpool for a week's holiday with Brian and his mother and dad (Image 40). It was a different sort of holiday to those in the Isle of Man and Conway. Although we spent time on the beach (Image 41) and in Stanley Park (Image 42) a lot of time was spent on the amusements and Pleasure Beach rides. *The Grand National* roller coaster ride and the *Little Mouse* were breathtaking. We also went swimming in the renowned Derby Baths. This I remember well because my arm got stuck in the hand grip that ran around the baths and I had to be extricated by an attendant. It was a painful and embarrassing experience.

The following year my mother and Margaret took William and me to the Isle of Man. On arrival, everywhere was shut and we couldn't find anywhere to eat. All of us were starving. After wandering around for what seemed like hours in the forlorn search for food, we eventually stumbled upon a tiny café hidden away in the back streets. The menu was limited but beans on toast have never tasted as good as they did that day.

Brian, his Dad, his Mother, William, Me and William's mother (left)
and Uncle Evan, Uncle Jack and Brian outside the 'Cranville'(right).

We stayed in a small guest house in Port St Mary overlooking Chapel Bay beach. The landlady, Mrs Cayley, had a strange way of running it. "I don't do meals," she said, "but if you buy your own food I'll cook it for you." Although strange, this arrangement normally worked quite well, except she didn't always cook the food to my mother and Margaret's liking. For instance, the tea was always too weak and the gravy always too thin. But it wasn't them who complained. Instead, they sent William down to tell a displeased Mrs Cayley of these shortcomings!

Brian, Me and William on Blackpool beach 1961.

Me, posing in Stanley Park 1961.

Mrs Cayley had another trait. She was a stickler for cleanliness. Every time we returned from the beach she would literally follow us up the stairs with a brush and dustpan feverishly brushing up any specks of sand our feet had deposited on her precious carpet.

Despite our strange accommodation, we had a great holiday, not only spending time on the beach but also on the rocks (Images 43 and 44). It was a holiday that all four of us really enjoyed.

On the rocks at Port St Mary 1962. Margaret, Me
and my mother (left), Me and my mother (right).

My mother (left) and Margaret.

Aged fifteen and sixteen William and I realised that we were getting too old to holiday with our relatives. As adolescents, our hormones were playing havoc with our bodies. Our thoughts were turning towards members of the fairer sex. It was time for girlfriends. I was no longer a child. I was a teenager. I was growing up.

Although they hadn't yet appeared, this teenager's two burning desires simmered away nicely, awaiting their chance to burst to the surface.

REFERENCES

1. Wigan Evening Post, Images of Wigan, Breedon Books, Derby, 1995, p. 92.
2. Wigan Evening Post, Images of Wigan, Breedon Books, Derby, 1995, p. 109.
3. A Guide To Wigan: Past and Present, Hallgate Press, Wigan, 1984, p. 147.
4. Smith, M. D., About Haigh and Aspull, Wyre Publishing, 2000, p. 129.

5. Smith, M. D., About Haigh and Aspull, Wyre Publishing, 2000, p. 16.

6. Hannavay, J., History and Guide – Wigan, Tempus Publishing, Stroud, 2003, p. 30.

7. Smith, M. D., About Haigh and Aspull, Wyre Publishing, 2000, p. 34.

8. Smith, M. D., About Haigh and Aspull, Wyre Publishing, 2000, p. 17.

9. Smith, M. D., About Haigh and Aspull, Wyre Publishing, 2000, p. 24.

10. Smith, M. D., Old Rivington and District, Wyre Publishing, St Michaels' on Wyre, 1995, p. 78.

3

FEMININE FANCIES

3.1 THE INNOCENCE OF CHILDHOOD

As mentioned earlier, life in the 1950s was markedly different to life today. Nowhere was this difference more profound than in childhood. Children were not pressurised into growing up too quickly as is so often the case nowadays. In contrast, children were actively encouraged to be just that. Children. To enjoy the things that children enjoy. To play as children. To laugh like children. To cry like children. Responsibilities and pressures would come all too soon. This difference extended to matters of a sexual nature. In the 1950s sexual maturity (awareness) was attained at a later age. So, for most children, the period from when you were born to age about ten or eleven was an age of innocence.

Although we recognised that boys and girls were different, they weren't perceived as different in a 'sexual' sense, at least not in the early years. They were just different in the way they looked, the way they dressed, in their likes and dislikes, and what games they played. Just like boys, girls were treated as your friends and playmates, although in a different way. For instance, some activities, such as football, rugby, cricket and Cowboys and Indians, were generally regarded as boys' games. Netball, rounders, hopscotch, skipping and gossiping were activities primarily associated with girls. Listening to music, dancing, going for walks and playing games such as hide and seek were things that both boys and girls could enjoy together. Thoughts of romance or sexual attraction rarely entered your head. A girl was chosen because of her prowess in whatever activity or game you were engaged in.

It was a good time, this time of innocence. Of course, there were the odd exceptions. One such exception has been mentioned already. Doris Corfield. This was the first time I had 'feelings' towards a girl. I was seven years old. True love it most certainly wasn't since, as described earlier, I preferred a bag of toffees to Doris!

3.2 EARLY DELIGHTS

Aged about nine, I had another experience. At Auntie Lily's house the toilet was in a separate, small building outside the back of the house. A few yards away and directly opposite, was our next-door neighbour's toilet. The toilet doors faced each other. On opening the door to leave the toilet, I couldn't believe my eyes (or my luck). The neighbour's girl (I won't reveal her name to spare her blushes), who was a similar age to me, was sat on their toilet with the door fully open! She must have thought there was no one else around. With her skirt up and her knickers down, nothing was left to the imagination. I was transfixed. I couldn't take my eyes off her. It was the first time I had seen a girl's intimate region. The experience seemed to last for ages but, in reality, it probably lasted only a few seconds. The moment she realised that she was being watched, she hurriedly closed the door. Nonetheless, it aroused feelings in me that I didn't know I possessed.

One of our favourite haunts for playing games was Toddington and the old railway line leading to it[1] (Image 45). We loved to make small dens, usually by covering holes in the ground with a roof, made either from uprooted plants or from sticks and old tarpaulin. About six of us were playing around this den when, without warning, we were offered another glimpse of heaven. One of the two girls in the group (I can't remember her name) told us that her friend Dorothy was in the den and would show us her private parts if we wanted. If we wanted! We were dumbfounded. Nothing like this had ever been offered before. After the initial shock had worn off (after about one second) we excitedly agreed. However, there were three conditions. First, we could only enter the den one at a time. This was for practical reasons as much as anything else since the den wouldn't have held more than three people. Second, she would be present with Dorothy. And finally, the boys had to return the favour later.

Members of the Marsden family
ploughing fields at Toddington.

Which order the boys entered the den eludes me but I wasn't the first one. When my turn came, I entered, full of excitement and anticipation. Dorothy was at the rear of the den facing the entrance. She was in a squatting position and seemed fully clothed. Her friend was sat beside her. The den was well lit since the entrance was open so there was no problem with the view. After a few seconds, her friend lifted Dorothy's skirt to reveal her private parts. Dorothy had obviously removed her knickers beforehand. I stared at this sight and mumbled something like, "It's lovely," before her friend ended the 'consultation' by lowering Dorothy's skirt. It was a short yet sweet moment for an eleven-year-old boy.

We honoured our part of the bargain too. The girls had to 'tag' a boy before taking him into the den. In reality, none of us tried very hard to avoid being 'tagged'. As was the case with the girls, we went in one by one. I went in and knelt on the floor in front of Dorothy and her friend. Then, I lowered my pants. After they'd had a good look, I pulled up my pants and left the den. It was an unusual day. The age of innocence was coming to an end.

Before becoming a teenager I used to play with boys and girls who were neighbours or who lived close by. This was common practice. In addition to Dorothy and her friend, the other girls we played with were Kathryn Hurst, Josephine Ashton and Sylvia Rushton. Kathryn was a petite redhead who lived next door but one to my Auntie Lily. Her mother was a lovely woman with flowing red hair who died suddenly at a young age. Partly on account of this, I was always somewhat protective of Kathryn. Josephine was newer to the area. Her family had bought the local shop at the top of the road and her younger brother David was a member of our little gang. Both Josephine and Kathryn were of a similar age to me. Sylvia was different. Not only was she older, she seemed more 'posh'. Her family were the only family in the area that owned a car, a black Austin A40. Sylvia was very attractive. Actually, all three were lovely in their own way but only Sylvia appealed to me in a romantic sense. However, I felt her age and background meant she was out of reach.

3.3 UNREQUITED ROMANCE

With Barbara Lomax it was different. Like Josephine, Barbara and her family were relative newcomers to the district. Her father, Billy, had somewhat of a hero status. He was the centre forward of Wigan Athletic, a well-known and respected non-league side. Indeed, several years earlier in 1954, Wigan had almost pulled off one of the biggest shocks in FA (Football Association) Cup history. They had been drawn away to Newcastle United, one of the best First Division sides of the day and one of the favourites to win the FA Cup. To everyone's amazement, Wigan gained a 2-2 draw at St James Park and were unfortunate not to have won.

The replay at Springfield Park was scheduled for 2-00 p.m. on the afternoon of Wednesday 13 January. The whole town was buzzing with excitement and anticipation. Could little Wigan slay the mighty Newcastle? I can't remember if the match was an all-ticket affair but the terraces were packed to the rafters with a crowd of over 26,000 cramming into the tiny ground[2] (Image 46). Everyone in Wigan seemed to have taken the afternoon off. (I think many firms allowed their workers time off to see the game.) The tension was electric. It was the game everyone wanted to see and, aged eight, I was there with my Uncle Jack.

The match was not without incident. On arrival, the Toon stars refused to change in the visitors' dressing room, labelling it as crude, and hot-footed it across town to use the facilities at the local swimming baths! Suitably attired, the Newcastle captain Jimmy Scoular led his team out on to the pitch in their famous black-and-white stripes to polite applause. He looked very confident. The entire team looked very confident! Then the 'Latics', as Wigan were known, emerged in their traditional blue shirts and white shorts to rapturous applause. I think this was the first time that Wigan had played a team from the top flight of English football in a competitive match at Springfield Park. It was David against Goliath. The referee blew his whistle and, with a mighty roar from the crowd, the match kicked off.

Action from Wigan Athletic v Newcastle United at Springfield
Park 1954. The Wigan Athletic player (in the blue
top and white shorts) is Billy Lomax.

I can't remember the exact sequence of scoring but it was an exciting end-to-end game which Newcastle eventually won 3–2 with a late goal. Billy Lomax scored both of Wigan's goals. He died, aged 85, in 2008.

I found Barbara attractive. She was of medium height and build and had very dark, almost black, hair (Image 47). Her round face, full lips and slightly turned-up nose made her very appealing. These features, which are similar to those of the film star, Audrey Hepburn, are those that I have always liked.

Barbara's best friend was Jean Culshaw. Jean lived about half-a-mile away from my auntie's house, near the Running Horses pub (recently demolished in favour of apartments). It was where John Bolton, another friend, used to live. Myself, John and a few other boys would often play tag rugby on the road near his house. Occasionally, we would see Barbara and Jean since they used to baby-sit at a house nearby. Although I made it clear that I would like to date Barbara, it never happened. However, I did get an offer, via John, from Jean. He said that Jean wanted to meet me behind the Running Horses pub[3] (Image 48) and that she would let me do anything. Anything I wanted. I declined. Although Jean was a lovely girl with a voluptuous figure, it was Barbara that I fancied. At that stage of my life, I wouldn't have known what to do anyway.

Billy Lomax with his daughter Barbara (Torquay 1958).

The opening of the new Aspull Secondary Modern school on the 7 January 1960 (Chapter 4) had some unexpected side effects. Throwing together a lot of young adolescent boys and girls inevitably had some romantic repercussions. Boys saw girls they had never seen before and vice-versa. In my class were two girls, Gloria Lindsay and Helen Ainscough, from Dicconson Lane, about one mile away. Gloria was a swarthy, good-looking girl of half Italian descent. (She is the third girl from the left in Image 49.)[4] Her friend, Helen, was more of an English rose. Apparently, Gloria developed a crush on me but, at thirteen, I wasn't yet into dates and courting. It was normal for boys to call for me at home to come out and play. However, my mother was most surprised when, one evening, Gloria and her friend Helen turned up at our house to see if I would go out with her. She was a determined girl our Gloria! Unfortunately, I was out and the romance never happened.

Running Horses public house, Bolton Road, Aspull 2000.
It was demolished in 2005 to make way for apartments.

St Elizabeth's Choir assembled at the Cenotaph (circa 1960).

3.4 FIRST LOVE

My first true love happened at the age of sixteen. For some time I had secretly admired a classmate called Kathleen Moore. Being rather shy, particularly with girls, my request for a date with Kathleen was handled by my friend, Ronnie Bolton. To my complete surprise, she agreed. As the day of our first date approached, I became more and more nervous. I had never been on a real date before! What do you do? I reassured myself that lots of people went on dates and that there was nothing to worry about. Things would come naturally as they say. It was with these mixed emotions that I set off towards my first date.

We had agreed to meet at the top of the old railway line that led down to Haigh Hall plantations (Image 50). It was in the autumn of 1962 so it was going dark as I approached the meeting point. To my amazement, there was not one but two girls present! Kathleen had brought her best friend along. I was taken aback. This was something totally unexpected. I was already nervous and this just compounded the situation. Somewhat hesitantly, I approached the two girls and said hello. Kathleen said she hoped I didn't mind that she had brought her friend along and that she would wait there for us while we went for a walk down the line. Uttering a white lie I said it was fine. With that Kathleen and I set off down the dark line leaving her friend behind, sat on the garden wall of the end council house in Manor Grove.

Tentatively, I reached out and held Kathleen's hand. She didn't object and we made small talk as we walked slowly down the line, hand-in-hand. On reaching the Lodge Gates[5] (Image 51) at the bottom of the line Kathleen said we should start walking back. She was an attractive girl with a good figure and I wanted desperately to hold her tight and kiss her. But should I? I didn't know. I didn't and we started our walk back.

By now it was a moonlit starry night, a night for romance. So far, all we had done was talk and hold hands. It couldn't be left like that. Suddenly, I stopped walking, held her in a tight embrace and kissed her passionately on the mouth. Kathleen responded with equal passion and we spent the last ten minutes of our date hugging and kissing.

Top of the Line at Manor Grove 2008.

Over the following weeks the pattern was repeated. She would come along to the dates with her trusted friend, and Kathleen and I would go for a walk whilst her friend remained behind. The reason was simple. We didn't have any money so going to the pictures or for meals were non-starters. Walks cost nothing. Different venues would be used but the format remained the same. To my dismay, we were actually spied on. The people in the end house at Manor Grove told my family that I was courting a girl. This caused some consternation. They considered sixteen too young to be courting a girl. After a while the dates began to get a little boring and it came as no surprise when, on a date up Stanley Lane, Kathleen said she wanted to finish the relationship. Her friend was shocked. I wasn't. The romance had run its course and it was time to move on.

Lodge Gates, Aspull (circa 1905).

3.5 REBOUND ROMANCES

It was approaching Christmas and, as was the tradition, the school held a Christmas dance for staff and pupils. Christmas 1962 would be my last one at Aspull Secondary Modern and I wanted to make it a special one. Dressed in my new outfit, a sartorially elegant young man jauntily made his way to the school dance. My first dance was with Miss Eastwood, the deputy head. It went fine. Except at the end of the dance. Unaware of the etiquette required, I was about to leave her stranded in the middle of the dance floor and return to my seat. "Peter, do your duty." What did she mean? Sensing the bemused look on my face, Miss Eastwood explained that it was the man's duty to escort the lady from the dance floor at the end of the dance. Embarrassed, I performed my duty. The evening hadn't started well. It would get worse.

As happens so often on the rebound from romance, you do funny things. I was no exception. During my time going out with Kathleen, I developed an admiration and fondness for her loyal friend. She was called Vera. Vera Santus. She was an attractive girl.

She had black hair, a cute turned up nose, full lips and a lovely figure. A bold strategy was required. I bought some Christmas presents and would surprise Vera with them at the dance. Everything was going fine. We got talking and enjoyed several dances together. At the end of the last waltz, the time seemed right to offer the presents and ask her to go out with me. The presents were lovely; fine perfume and delicate toiletries. To my surprise and dismay, she refused to accept them and stormed off home. I was devastated. What sentient being wouldn't be? She must have thought I was being 'too forward'. Disconsolately, I trudged home. That year, my mother got some unexpected Christmas presents.

The following year I agreed to a date with Margaret Walkden, a quiet, studious classmate. (Margaret is the girl on the extreme right in Image 49, page 66 and is on Image 52.) We had known each other for some time. In fact, we were similar in many respects. Our first date, rather strangely, occurred underneath the school stairs. We met and kissed. I was pleasantly surprised. It was a hot kiss from a quiet, demure girl. We had just one further date, hot lips and I. In retrospect, we were probably too alike.

It was similar with Dorothy Beresford. Dorothy was a year older than me and both of us were prefects at school (Image 52). Being a prefect meant having responsibilities but it also had its privileges. One of these was being able to stay indoors at lunchtimes, a very useful privilege in the depths of winter. During winter lunchtimes Dorothy would stand near a radiator ostensibly knitting. In reality, she was flirting, throwing wistful glances to catch a boy's attention. It worked. She would often entice me to her side to have a chat. After a while, she would lead me to a secluded spot in the library and kiss me. But not any old kiss. Dorothy would gently gyrate her body against my groin to elicit the expected result. It never failed. She was an experienced girl was Dorothy.

School Prefects 1962. Left to right:
Back Row: William Fillingham, James Seddon, Ken Fielding, Graham Snape, Me, Trevor Pye.
Front Row: Pat Bynoth, Barbara Roby, Margaret Walkden, Mr Firth (Headmaster), Pauline Weeks, Christine Stott, Joan Fishwick. Dorothy Beresford had left school the previous year.

A strange liaison occurred at the Youth Club at Aspull Methodist School. Although not a regular participant, I attended occasionally. On one such visit, Julie, a big girl, sidled up to me and whispered in my ear that she wanted to kiss me. Not here in front of other people, but in private round the back of the building. This Amazonian woman grasped my hand and led me behind the building. Once we were out of sight she kissed me passionately. We kissed for a short while and then returned to the youth club, our brief encounter over.

Another brief liaison occurred with Marjorie. By the time we dated Marjorie had left school. There was no way on Earth that anyone would have paired Marjorie and me together. She was a self-confident, extrovert type of girl with different interests to me. Not surprisingly, Marjorie and I had just the single date before amicably calling it a day. As will become apparent later, this wasn't the end of Marjorie's involvement.

3.6 MARLENE

Two of my best friends in my early teenage years were Eric Marsden and Trevor Crane. (Trevor is third from the right in Image 56, page 75.) Eric's dad owned a farm at the junction of Ratcliffe Road, the road where my Auntie Lily lived, and Stanley Road (Image 53). It was a place where I spent many happy hours. We used the fields to play football, to go shooting and to build camps. Not only did we shoot with air rifles, we also had bows and arrows. Proper bows. Bows that would shoot an arrow a distance of over 100 yards. And proper arrows. Arrows with steel tips and feathers. One game we played was to see who could shoot an arrow around a roughly triangular course in the minimum number of shots. The course consisted of two telegraph poles and the burial mound of a horse, each about 250 yards apart. Starting from the burial mound, the arrow would be unleashed towards the first telegraph pole. A good shot would go about 150 yards, so the absolute minimum number required to hit the telegraph pole was two. However, even Robin Hood would have struggled to hit a telegraph pole from 100 yards so our usual scores were either three (very good) or four (average). Very occasionally, one of us would complete the course in nine shots, which was excellent, but usually it was more than nine.

Games of football were played in a depression at the edge of a grassy field near Stanley Lane (Image 54). Normally, they proceeded without incident. Except on the day Mr Smith's guard dog escaped from his property adjacent to Stanley Lane. It was a huge, fierce Alsatian. It posed no threat when enclosed in his garden but free of that constraint, it was a different matter. We were in the middle of a game of football when a deep, guttural snarl stopped us in our tracks. The Alsatian was crouched and ready to attack. Everyone scrambled to relative safety by crossing the brook and climbing over the fence into the next field. Everyone, that is, except me. Full of bravado, I stood my ground and confronted the attacker. It wouldn't attack. Nonetheless, I picked up a large stone, just in case. My bravado was misplaced. Suddenly, without warning, it charged straight at me! Unflinchingly, I took aim and threw the stone. It missed. But the Alsatian didn't. As the snarling creature got really close, I turned around and began to flee. It was too late. The dog bit my buttocks once and then ran off.

Marsden's Farm 2008.

The whole incident happened so quickly that I felt no fear. Surprise and shock but not fear. After a visit to Dr Cooke for an anti-tetanus jab and a few plasters to cover the bite marks, I was fine. A distraught Mr Smith came to see how I was, worried that his dog may have to be destroyed. The dog was doing its duty and my foolhardiness hadn't helped. I had no desire to have his beloved dog destroyed and with that message, a relieved Mr Smith returned home.

Great as it was to play in the fields, it didn't compare to frolicking in the barn. Without a doubt, playing in the barn gave us the greatest amount of pleasure, especially after harvest time when it was full of fresh hay. The smell was delicious. The feel and warmth were so comforting. What could be done in a barn was limited only by your imagination. Bales of hay were excellent for the construction of castles, steps and dens. Daring leaps could be performed without the fear of injury, and the barn was absolutely ideal for games of hide and seek and Cowboys and Indians. And it was always warm and dry, a huge bonus in the cold and wet winter months.

Depression in field where we played football and
where I was bitten by an Alsatian. Taken from Stanley Lane
from where the Alsatian launched its attack

During the dark, cold nights of winter, Eric would invite Trevor and me inside
his farmhouse to play with his favourite toy, a medium sized snooker table. We had to
wait until his family had finished their tea and cleared the kitchen table, since it was
upon this table that the snooker table was placed. It was normal for the three of us to
spend the whole evening playing snooker and related games, such as *Mystery*. All of
us watched Pot Black on the telly and fancied ourselves as budding snooker players.
Joe Davis's we weren't but we had a great time in the warm and cosy surroundings of
Eric's kitchen.

Next door but one to the farm was a large bungalow. It was obviously the
residence of a wealthy family. It was, in fact, the property of Mr Pilkington and his
family. Mr Pilkington was a successful businessman who owned a haulage company
called, I think, White Star. He had a son, David, and an elder daughter, Marlene.
Both children were schooled privately and neither I nor my friends knew them
very well. Rightly or wrongly we felt there was a class divide. We belonged to the
poor working class whereas Mr Pilkington and his family were members of the
wealthier middle class. Despite this, when making my way to the farm I had, on odd
occasions, spoken to Marlene when she was outside the front of their bungalow, so
we weren't complete strangers.

One winter's evening whilst waiting outside Roy and Eric Makinson's house,
which was located a little further down Stanley Road from Mr Pilkington's bungalow,
Marlene came walking past. She said hello and I returned the greeting. I asked her
where she was headed. Choir practice at St Elizabeth's church about a mile away
was her destination. She was making her way to the bus stop at the Fingerpost but

in order to do so had to cross some waste ground. The waste ground was uneven and could present problems in the dark[6] (Image 55). Being somewhat gallant (and having time on my hands), I offered to escort her across the waste ground to the bus stop. We made awkward small talk as we made our way tentatively over the uneven ground. As we crossed the ground, I slipped my arm around her, partly to make sure that she didn't stumble. I think Marlene interpreted this act as a sign of my romantic intentions (which in a way it was) and responded by putting her arm around me. A little further on we stopped and looked into each other's eyes. Then, I held her tight and kissed her. Gently at first and then, when she didn't resist, more passionately. We both liked it. That night, Marlene never made it to choir practice and I never got to play tag rugby. A chance encounter had sowed the seeds of a romance as we agreed to meet for a second date.

Marlene was a tall girl, almost as tall as I was (ca 6 foot) with a well-developed figure. (She is the fourth girl from the left in Image 49.) Knowledgeable and well educated with a good sense of humour, she also had a smattering of the tomboy in her too, a combination of traits that I found pleasing. We got on extremely well together and begun to have regular dates, about two or three times per week.

Being a little older, wiser and richer (I now received a small amount of pocket money) since my romance with Kathleen, Marlene and I had more options for our dates. We still went for walks since the cost was nothing yet the pleasure immense (from all the kissing and cuddling) but, in addition, we also went to the pictures, usually the Ritz in Wigan, and for meals (usually the local fish and chip shop).

Waste ground near Stanley Road. The large building in the
background is the new Aspull Labour Club (circa 1960).

73

Stanley Lane was our favourite walk. Not only was it close to both the farm and Marlene's bungalow, it also had a wooden stand designed for milk churns. It was a sort of outside wooden table on which we could sit under the stars and kiss and cuddle to our hearts content. We spent many happy hours in Stanley Lane.

Marlene and I went to the pictures a couple of times, usually on a Saturday night. Meeting at the bus stop in Haigh Road, we caught the bus to Wigan, hoping fervently that no one would be on the bus who recognised us. Which film was showing was largely irrelevant since we had other things in mind. Like every other courting couple, our preferred location in the cinema was the back row. Here, you could be romantic without being observed. To sit on the back row, you had to arrive early. We rarely sat on the back row. If I had enough money, sweets or ice creams were purchased. Because the boy paid for both himself and his girlfriend, a night out at the pictures was expensive. Accordingly, sweets and ice creams were savoured only occasionally.

One of my strangest dates occurred with Marlene. It was a foursome in a barn. Not the barn that I played in with Eric and Trevor, but a barn near Dukes Row at a farm owned by Eric's uncle. The date was arranged by Marlene's friend Joan and her boyfriend Freddie. The plan was to meet at the barn one evening whereby Freddie would unlock the barn door. (He had a key since he worked at the farm.) Freddie and Joan would go to one end of the barn whist Marlene and I went to the other end. This we duly did, eventually. It was hilarious. Not only was the inside of the barn packed tight with hay, leaving little room for manoeuvre, it was also pitch black. Two people trying to clamber to the top of the bales in total darkness in a confined space on a dark winter's night was something else. Nonetheless, after much huffing and puffing, the top was reached. It was so dark that we could hardly see each other. We literally had to use our sense of touch in order to do anything, such as embrace or kiss. The idea may have seemed romantic but in practice it wasn't.

At one point Marlene scared me witless. As we lay side-by-side in the hay she suddenly stopped moving and talking. I asked her what was wrong. There was no reply. Gently, I started to shake her. Again, there was no response. I was becoming very worried. What if she had fainted or, worse still, gone into a coma. What if she was dead! What should I do? I shook her again, more vigorously this time, and was on the point of trying CPR (Cardio Pulmonary Resuscitation) when she burst out laughing. She liked to play jokes, did Marlene.

Everything was wonderful. But it would soon come to an abrupt end.

Marlene and I went out together for a number of months. Both of us were happy. Then, without warning, came a bolt out of the blue. As I sat on the wall of Marlene's bungalow waiting for her to meet me, Eric's elder brother, George, who was significantly older, joined me. Later, Marlene came and joined us. At first the conversation was normal then George started making lewd allegations against Marlene. Protesting strongly, Marlene and I left to go for a walk. She denied vehemently what George had said and

I believed her, but it affected our relationship. We continued dating for several more weeks but it wasn't the same. Eventually, we split up. The end happened one night when I was playing snooker in Eric's kitchen. Marlene came to the door for me but I told her I couldn't go on seeing her. It wasn't the same. It was a shame. We were both upset. It had been a promising romance. Unfortunately, it wasn't the right one.

3.7 OLIVE

Once again I did strange things whilst on the rebound from my longest romance. A date was arranged with another classmate, Olive Brown. Olive would be the first to admit that she wasn't the most beautiful girl in the class but she was a fun-loving, dizzy sort of girl who was somewhat of an extrovert. She loved to talk, had a hearty laugh and was fun to be around. She also wore glasses that, to me, made her rather cute.[7] (Olive is third from the left in Image 56.) Being a quiet, shy boy, I was completely opposite to Olive so the date seemed strange to a lot of people. But, as the saying goes, opposites attract.

The rendezvous was near Olive's home in New Springs. Before the date, I was with my two friends Eric and Trevor at Eric's dad's farm. (Trevor is third from the right in Image 56.) As the time for the date approached, I departed and caught the bus to New Springs, arriving at the meeting point several minutes before Olive. The sound of high heel shoes on the pavement signalled her approach. Gradually she emerged from the shadows into the light. I was taken aback. This wasn't the schoolgirl I knew in class. This was a woman! Make-up, high heel shoes, nylon stockings and 'adult' clothes had transformed a schoolgirl into a woman. I began to feel out of my depth. What if she was experienced in other things as well? Still, it was too late to worry about such matters now so off we went on the dark path towards the canal.

Aspull County Secondary Modern Brass Band, June 1960.

75

We put our arms around each other and chatted happily all the way to the canal. Once there, we stopped and spent some time kissing. After a while, we started our return journey but before we reached the lighted street, stopped again for more kissing and cuddling. After escorting her home, we said our goodbyes. We both enjoyed the evening but there were no further dates. One of my shortest romances had just ended. However, my friendship with Olive would soon prove useful.

3.8 VERA

By now I was seventeen. Having left Aspull Secondary Modern that summer (1963), I was studying at Wigan Technical College. My academic career was going fine but I was beginning to feel that I needed some stability in my love life. The attraction I felt for the girl I had known and met many times still burned brightly. That girl was the friend of Kathleen Moore. The girl who had accompanied Kathleen on her dates with me and who was shocked when the relationship ended. Her name was Vera. Vera Santus. As mentioned previously, she was an attractive girl with all the features that I admired. She had very dark, almost black hair and a face with a cute turned up nose, and full lips. Vera's figure was gorgeous and her legs and ankles were sensational. Why hadn't I seen all this before? The answer was, of course, that I had. Indeed, it was the reason I had asked her to go out with me at the Christmas dance. She had refused me then but I needed to try again. This time, I didn't want to fail.*

I'd realised earlier that there was something different about Vera. At Friday lunchtimes at Aspull Secondary Modern a disco was held and at these discos the boys danced with the girls. Like the other boys I used to dance with a number of girls, not just one, and during these dances you sometimes held hands. One of my favourite records was *Poetry in Motion* and dancing to it with Vera was no different to dancing to it with the other girls. Until our hands touched! I had never experienced anything like it before. It was as though an electric current passed between us. It was exhilarating. I think I realised then that there was something special between us. I'm sure it was this that spurred me on to buy her those Christmas presents at the school dance, the ones she rejected. Should I try again? I wanted to. Desperately. But it wouldn't be easy. Vera had left school at sixteen and was now working at Harry Mayalls, a local decorator's shop in Wigan, whilst I was studying full-time at Wigan Technical College. This meant that occasionally Vera and I waited at the same bus stop at Dukes Row and caught the same bus into Wigan. However, we rarely spoke to each other.

---

* In retrospect, I needn't have worried. After we'd been married a few years, Vera informed me that when her classmate at school, Christine Smith, said, "Oh, that Peter Gregory's come top again," she replied, "I'm going to marry him."

At the time it was rare for a boy to ask a girl for a date face-to-face. Instead, it was done indirectly. A friend would either ask the girl for you or, more often, they would hand the girl a note from you asking for a date. This was the path I chose with Vera. I asked Olive Brown to be the go-between. Olive caught the same bus in New Springs and when she did we often sat together and had a chat. Apprehensively, I asked her if she would pass a note from me to Vera, a note in which I was asking Vera for a date. Olive agreed. All I had to do now was await the reply. I didn't have to wait long. It was just a few days later that Olive told me Vera's response. To my great relief, the answer was yes. There was more. The date, time and place had also been arranged. Somewhat ironically, Vera and I were to meet at exactly the same place that Kathleen and I had met on our first date, at the top of the line near Manor Grove (Image 50, page 67).

A few days before my first date with Vera, a strange thing happened. Normally, I caught the bus at the Fingerpost but on that morning I decided to catch the bus at Dukes Row, a row of 17th century cottages built by the lords of the manor (Image 57). There, waiting at the same bus stop, was Vera. We both knew about the imminent date but neither of us spoke to each other. Indeed, we hardly looked at each other. However, I do remember risking a furtive glance at her lovely legs and ankles and thinking that soon, they could be mine.

Bus Stop at Dukes Row.

The day of the date duly arrived. It was a special day. Not only was it the day of our first date, it was 14 February. We couldn't have chosen a more romantic day for our first date than St Valentine's Day. Expectantly, I made my way to the familiar meeting place at the top of the line. I don't know why but I seemed less nervous about this date than any of the others. Vera was already there, sitting on the garden wall. (I learned later that punctuality was one of her many virtues.) To my relief, there was no friend with her. I said hello and we set off down the line towards Haigh Hall plantations.

I longed to hold her hand but was reluctant to do so. What if she felt that I was rushing things again? What if the electric feeling wasn't there any more? After a short while I could wait no longer. I had to know. Cautiously, I reached out for her hand. The tingling sensation and flow of energy between us was as strong as it had been the first time. We continued walking hand-in-hand into the plantations. Eventually, we stopped, put our arms around each other and kissed. It was wonderful. We kissed and hugged for some time before returning back to our starting point. It had been a very good first date and, unsurprisingly, a second date was agreed. Everything was wonderful. Or was it? I would soon find out.

At the time, I was something of a flirt. It was in my nature. One evening in the school playground I was chatting to Marjorie, the girl I had dated briefly, who was waiting for her friend to arrive. After a while, her friend arrived. She was lovely. The three of us chatted and, almost without realising it, I had arranged a date with her friend. It was for the forthcoming Saturday evening, an evening when I also had a date with Vera. I was mortified. I couldn't believe what I had done. Although Marjorie's friend was a lovely girl, it was Vera that I wanted. What a mess! I didn't know where the girl lived so how could I contact her? I couldn't be completely callous and stand her up. So I did what seemed right at the time. I asked Trevor to go along to the date and explain what I had done. Cowardly, yes, but it was the best that I could think of. It was not one of my finest moments but it did confirm that Vera was something special to me. Not only that, but for the very first time I began to have an inkling of what one of my two burning desires was. It wasn't completely clear but I sensed that I was moving in the right direction. As yet, I had no idea what my second burning desire was. But I would find out, and soon!

REFERENCES

1. Smith, M. D., About Haigh and Aspull, Wyre Publishing, 2000, p. 107.
2. Wigan v Newcastle replay action.
3. Smith, M. D., About Haigh and Aspull, Wyre Publishing, 2000, p. 149.
4. Smith, M. D., About Haigh and Aspull, Wyre Publishing, 2000, p. 159.
5. Smith, M. D., About Haigh and Aspull, Wyre Publishing, 2000, p. 25.
6. Smith, M. D., About Haigh and Aspull, Wyre Publishing, 2000, p. 78.
7. The Wigan Observer and District Advertiser, June 3 1960.

4

SECONDARY EDUCATION

As explained in Chapter 1, until I was nearly fourteen all my education was provided by the all-age Aspull Methodist School. I was very happy with my life and had no worries or regrets. Although reasonably clever, I had no real ambitions or idea what I wanted to do. Like many other children, I just presumed that things would continue on in the same way.

It was with some curiosity therefore that I watched the building of the new Secondary Modern School as it emerged from nothingness into a fine building. The idea of a new school wasn't popular with everyone. Mr Joe Pimblett, a resident of Ratcliffe Road, from whom my Auntie Lily and Uncle Jack had bought a terraced house in 1950 for the princely sum of £250, put up a vigorous campaign against the school, saying it would blight village life by taking away a large area of common land enjoyed by adults and children alike. It was in vain. The objections were overruled and the school built.[1] It opened on the 7 January 1960 (Image 58).

The thought of attending Aspull Secondary Modern was both exciting yet nerve-wracking. Exciting because it was a brand new school with new facilities, new teachers and new subjects, not to mention new pupils, and nerve-wracking because most of the teachers for this new school were from St John's School in New Springs. There were no teachers from our school, the New School or St David's School. St John's School had a reputation for being very good, with clever pupils and good teachers. We were terrified that our simple education of gardening, football and singing, together with a smattering of the 3Rs, would expose us as dunces compared to the pupils of St John's.

Aspull County Secondary Modern 1962.

Aspull Secondary Modern meant to start off on the right foot. Mr Firth, the headmaster, sent out letters to the parents of all the children who were to attend the new school, extending a warm welcome and explaining the rules and procedures. One of the rules was that school uniform must be worn and that a satchel and certain books were deemed necessary. It was ironic. This was the main reason that I hadn't taken the 11-plus exam! For boys, the school uniform consisted of a navy blue blazer, a white shirt and grey trousers. The blazer was emblazoned with the school crest which was, for some reason, a yellow kiwi. The girls also wore blue blazers with white blouses and navy blue skirts. Ties for both boys and girls were mandatory (Images 52, page 69, and 56.) Mr Firth intended his pupils to be smartly dressed.

Once the start date for the new school became known, everyone began making plans. The pupils of Aspull Methodist School were no exception. Foremost in our plans was whom you were going to sit with. We didn't want to sit with strangers from other schools, especially the clever clogs from St John's School. Eventually, a plan was hatched. Colin Heaton and I were going to sit together. Not only were we good friends, we were also neighbours and could walk to school together. Most importantly, we were the same age and reasoned that age would be the key factor in deciding which class you would be in.

The start day arrived quicker than ever. Dressed in my smart new uniform with a satchel slung over my shoulder, I called for Colin and it was with some trepidation that we set off to the new school on our first day.

All our careful planning had been in vain. Although age was an important factor in deciding which class you were in, it wasn't the only consideration. The large number of pupils meant that each year was streamed into three separate classes. I was put into Form 3A whilst Colin was placed in Form 3B. Even our Plan B was foiled. We had decided beforehand that should Colin and I end up in different classes, we would still endeavour to sit with someone from our own school. No such luck. The first words from Mr Wardle, my form teacher, were that each person had to sit next to someone from a different school. This created a mild sense of panic. Everyone started scanning the room for the friendly face of a likely partner. Eventually, partners were found. Mine was a boy from the dreaded St John's school, called Trevor Pye (Image 52).

As time unfolded it became clear that our fears were unfounded. In general, the pupils from St John's were no brighter or better educated than we were and I became firm friends with Trevor. The teachers were nothing to be afraid of either. Indeed, most were good and cared about their pupils. One was inspirational.

4.1 CURRICULUM

The secondary school was a revelation. New subjects were on the curriculum which fired the imagination. Algebra, geometry and technical drawing were completely new, whilst history, geography, art and music were taught in a totally different way. However, the subject which blew my mind was science. Science was something that I had heard of only vaguely before and had little or no idea what it was. I was fortunate. The science teacher, Mr Wilkinson, was an inspiration. He undoubtedly had one of, if not the biggest, influences on my whole life.

He was an excellent teacher who got the points across in an entertaining way. For instance, I remember his lesson on the boiling points of liquids. He arranged the class into groups of four and equipped them with Bunsen burners, tripods, a glass beaker with water and a thermometer. He then placed a £5 note on his desk (£5 was a lot of money in 1960, especially to children) and said the first team to heat their water to 110°C would win the £5 note. There was a mad scramble as people frantically placed more Bunsen burners under their tripods to heat the water more quickly and be the first to reach 110°C. The excitement and tension increased in line with the temperature: 30°, 40°C, and upwards. Each team was watching their own temperature and comparing it to that of the other teams. Upwards it climbed, to 90°, 95°, 99° and finally 100°C. The tension was getting unbearable. Then a funny thing happened. No matter how many Bunsen burners were employed, the temperature would not budge from 100°C, the boiling point of water. Of course, no one won the £5 note but none of us would ever forget that the boiling point of water at atmospheric pressure was 100°C. This was my first introduction to physics.

A foreign language was also taught. A foreign language! Until I was eleven, the furthest I had ever ventured was Rhyl, about 70 miles away. Even the Isle of Man, where I was taken when I was eleven (Chapter 2), seemed like a foreign country to me. (Well, you did sail over the sea to it.) To my disappointment, I missed out on being taught

French. Those who were aged thirteen or over were deemed to be too old to learn a foreign language. Sometimes, when moving from one classroom to another between lessons, I would hear *Frere Jacque* and other strange sounds emanating from the French classroom. It intrigued me. I think being classed as too old had a profound effect since I have never since learned a foreign language (apart from some rudimentary German needed for science and later some basic Japanese for my trips to Japan – Chapters 14 and 21).

One of the first things the teachers asked the older pupils was what they wanted to do after leaving school. At age 14, having spent most of my time at primary school doing gardening, football, woodwork and the three Rs, I had no idea. It was something I had never thought about. However, people had remarked that a draughtsman was a good job, so I said that I would like to be a draughtsman. I had a vague idea what this involved, but no more than that. For instance, I knew it involved technical drawing, a subject that we had started to do for the very first time at the secondary school.

Mr Sutton taught technical drawing. However, Mr Sutton was primarily a maths teacher. He was an enthusiastic and committed maths teacher who knew his subject extremely well. He also had a very nervous disposition. He physically trembled all the time. Furthermore, he enjoyed playing jokes on unsuspecting pupils. One of his favourites, and the one that I remember, was his reply to anyone who raised their hand in class and asked, "Please sir. Can I go to the toilet?"

His response invariably was, "I don't know. Can you?" On seeing the bemused look on the questioner's face, he would add, "I don't know if you *can* or cannot go to the toilet. Of course, you *may* go to the toilet, but only you know if you can go to the toilet." It goes without saying that everyone quickly learned to phrase the request correctly.

It transpired that I wasn't very good at technical drawing. It's not that I was bad (Image 59), just that I wasn't very good. We had only been doing the subject for about eighteen months when our first taste of public examinations were upon us. Public exams were a new phenomenon to us. However, some of those who were aged sixteen were entered for the Union of Lancashire and Cheshire Institute (ULCI) exams. These were a step below the renowned General Certificate of Education Ordinary Level (GCE 'O' level) examinations. In the summer of 1962, aged sixteen, I took five ULCI subjects, gaining distinctions in three and a credit in one (Image 60). For one of the very few times in my life I failed an exam. That exam was ULCI technical drawing. Needless to say, I did not pursue a career as a draughtsman.

SUBJECT	Achievement	Endeavour	Exam. Mark	REMARKS	Teacher's Initials
English	A	A		A splendid year's work.	R.W.
French					
Mathematics	A	A.		Excellent work and progress	
Technical Drawing	A.	A.	84.	Always keen and conscientious	
History					
Geography	A	B		Has worked remarkably well.	
Science	A	A		An excellent effort	
Art					
Craft					
Arithmetic Needlework	A	A		Very good indeed.	R.W.
Domestic Science					
Woodwork	B	A	86	Good. Has worked hard	
P.E.	A	A		Excellent.	
Games				Senior champion - athletics.	

A = Excellent. B = Good. C = Average. D = Fair. E = Weak.

General Report: Another splendid report. I hope Peter will take full advantage of his academic ability. Excellent report.

Form Teacher R.N. Wardle.   Head Master J.A.Toth.

Parent Annie Gregory

School report for summer 1962 prior to taking the ULCI
examinations. I got an 'A' in Technical Drawing.

Aspull School successes

In the Secondary School certificate
examination of the Union of Lancashire
and Cheshire Institutes the following
pupils of Aspull County Secondary
school were successful:
   P Gregory (3 Dist. and 1 Credit).
W. Fillingham (1 Dist. and 3 Credits).
J. Mason (1 Credit and 2 Passes).

ULCI Results 1962.

Only two people took the technical drawing exam. After calling for William Fillingham on the morning of the exam at his house, which was halfway to the venue, the two of us made our way to the church hall in Harold Street (Image 1b). Mr Firth, the headmaster, was the invigilator. He handed out the exam papers and, precisely at 9.00 a.m., told us that we may open them and begin. There were several questions but the main one was an exploded view of some mechanical contraption. I was baffled. Whichever way I turned it around, looking at it from this direction and that, I just couldn't fathom out what it was. The drawing may as well have been in Martian, I just couldn't make head or tail of it. Two of the three hours were spent twiddling my thumbs. It was the worst exam experience of my life.

Basic biology was taught as part of general science, the only science we did at the secondary modern. As well as learning the theoretical aspects of biology, Mr Wilkinson also ensured that we learned the practical side too. He demonstrated a dramatic yet humane way of destroying unwanted fish from the aquarium; for example, when the fish had reproduced and there were too many babies. He would scoop them up in a fish net and then drop them into a beaker of concentrated sulphuric acid. There was an instant sizzling noise and a cloud of steam. When this ceased, after a few seconds, all that remained were the skeletons of the dead fish at the bottom of the beaker. It was fascinating, the equivalent of a chemical piranha.

Although biology and physics were interesting, the topic that really captured my imagination was chemistry. Chemistry was all flashes and bangs, the stuff of fireworks and explosives. It seemed colourful and exciting. It involved mysterious (to me) substances like acids and bases, and poisons such as cyanide. On a deeper level, it was about atoms and molecules, the building blocks of everything there is, and how these reacted together. Chemistry was the window to understanding everything I had ever wondered about. The second burning desire of that small boy was beginning to emerge.

I was hooked. I wanted to know everything. What are things made of? Why are they different? Why are some things solid or liquid, or soft or hard? Why are some things invisible, like air? What is a rock made of? What are grass and flowers made of? What makes them coloured? What are living things made of? What are we made of? I wanted the answers to these and many more questions, but I knew I wouldn't find the answers by just doing general science at a secondary school. So, aged sixteen, I plucked up courage and enrolled at the brand new Wigan and District Mining and Technical College to do chemistry and physics at GCE 'O' level for two evenings per week, whilst staying on at school for a further year to do other subjects to GCE 'O' level standard. One of these was biology. Biology wasn't taught at the technical college so I did my studying both at home and at school, aided by Mr Wilkinson. William Fillingham did the same. There were perhaps half-a-dozen of us who stayed at school an extra year to take some subjects to GCE 'O' level, but I was the only one to supplement this with an extra two nights per week at Wigan Technical College.

That single year from age sixteen to seventeen was one of the most demanding yet rewarding of my entire life. As well as attending school five days a week, studying mathematics, English language, geography, and general science (I gave up on technical drawing), I was also going to Wigan Technical College two nights per week to study chemistry and physics. GCE 'O' level subjects were normally studied over five years, from age 11 to 16. I had only one year to study seven subjects, three of which were completely new! It was a daunting task. Could a teenager of sixteen remain dedicated to such an arduous schedule whilst foregoing the pleasures of normal teenagers? The answer was most definitely YES! I was on the way to discovering my second burning desire. I was born for science, especially chemistry. It was my destiny. It was one of my dreams.

During my time at Wigan Technical College I quickly realised that chemistry was the subject for me. It was what I wanted to do. It was my reason for being alive. I was fascinated with the subject. I loved both the theoretical side and the practical or experimental side. To learn something in class and then to carry out the actual experiment in the laboratory was magic. I remember one lesson on acids and alkalis. These are very corrosive and destructive chemicals. However, when they react together, they produce an innocuous salt and water. For instance, when hydrochloric acid reacts with caustic soda (sodium hydroxide), harmless common table salt (sodium chloride) and water are produced. Not only can this reaction be expressed in words:

hydrochloric acid + sodium hydroxide = sodium chlo
ride + water

it can also be expressed in chemical symbols or molecules:

$$HCl + NaOH = NaCl + H_2O$$

I learned that there were just 92 kinds of naturally occurring atoms and that everything there is in the entire universe is made from these 92 types of atoms. Everything. From stars to planets, from mountains to molehills, from telescopes to televisions, from tulips to tigers, to you and me, we are all made from these atoms. This was absolutely amazing. How could just 92 types of atoms make all these things? I had to know.

I got so involved with chemistry that I ordered my own apparatus and set up a small 'laboratory' in my Auntie Lily's back bedroom. Here, experiments were conducted, sometimes with amusing effects. For example, I made nitrogen triiodide from ammonia and iodine. As long as it is kept moist, nitrogen triiodide is stable.

However, once it is allowed to dry, any contact with it causes a mild explosion accompanied with a flash of light. Feeling mischievous, one night I sprinkled some moist nitrogen triiodide around my Auntie Lily's house. I put a little on a light switch, a little on a door handle and a little on the handrail up the stairs. By the time my auntie and uncle had returned, I was already at home and only learned of the events the following day. On touching the internal door handle, they were startled by a mild explosion and flash of light. Although perplexed, they assumed it to be due to static electricity. However, when the same thing happened with a light switch, they suspected an electrical fault and turned off the electricity. Worse was to follow. After crawling up the stairs on their hands and knees in the dark, there was a bang and a flash from the top of the handrail. After spending a sleepless night, an electrician was called out the following morning to check the electrics. Needless to say, I wasn't the most popular person the following day.

It wasn't all work for the seven of us* who stayed on the extra year to do GCE 'O' levels. (Vera wasn't one of those who stayed on for the extra year, although she was certainly bright enough to have done so.) We had separate lessons to the rest of the school, lessons that were in a way akin to private tuition. Sometimes, these took place in the most unusual locations. Thus, we had lessons in the teachers' common room (on how a telephone worked), the headmaster's study, and the girls' domestic science (cookery) room. In other words, we used rooms that weren't being used for normal lessons. Also, we had ample time off for private study and to play sports, such as rugby and cricket. It was a year in which we all worked hard. But, as mentioned before, it was a year that was enjoyable and rewarding.

4.2 RUGBY LEAGUE

Before attending Aspull Secondary Modern the only sports that I had played were football and cricket. However, at Aspull Secondary Modern the major sport wasn't soccer, it was rugby. Rugby League. There were several reasons for this. First, Wigan has a world famous rugby league team and virtually all the secondary schools in Wigan had rugby league as their major sport. Second, our form teacher, Mr Wardle, was an avid rugby league fan and formed a school rugby league team from day one. Another reason was that our PE (Physical Education) teacher actually played for the Wigan 'A' team, Wigan's reserve team. Wigan regularly signed players with potential to make the first team and the valleys of South Wales, the hotbed of Welsh Rugby Union, was a favourite recruiting area. Mr Lindley was a rising Welsh rugby union

---

* The seven people who stayed on the extra year were Ronnie Bolton, William Fillingham, Brian Gormley, Sidney Jones, Valerie Naylor, my cousin William Jackson, and myself

player and had been lured to Wigan for trials. A guaranteed job was part of the lure. That job was PE instructor at Aspull Secondary Modern. Mr Lindley was a strapping 6 foot 5 inches of a man who, for whatever reason, never made the transition to Wigan's first team, but he was an excellent PE teacher. The final reason was that after playing rugby league, most of the boys preferred it to soccer. Actually, I had been a regular supporter of the Wigan rugby league team for some time, as had a number of boys. Sometimes, my uncle would take me. Other times, I would either go alone or with friends. In this case, I would watch the game from the 'Hen Pen', the section allocated to young supporters, at Wigan's famous Central Park stadium[2] (Image 61).

Another new concept was 'houses'. All the pupils were placed in one of four houses: Lancaster, York, Tudor and Stuart. Each house formed its own rugby team and played games against the other houses. This was not only to accumulate 'house points' but also to get accustomed to the new sport. The best twenty or so boys were selected and had further training sessions, usually after school, under the watchful eyes of Mr Lindley and Mr Wardle. When they deemed us ready, friendly games against other schools in the Wigan district were arranged.

The first year we lost more than we won but we were an improving team. The most accomplished thirteen rugby players had been found, including their best positions. I was the fastest boy at the school but didn't play on the wing where the fastest players normally play. Being a good tackler and passer of the ball, centre was my position. Since my inclination was to run towards the left, I played left centre. This was number 4 in a rugby league team and my wing partner was William Fillingham.

Hen Pen at Central Park, home of Wigan RLFC.

During our second year (1961) we entered the annual knock out competition for all the schools in the Wigan area. Approximately sixteen schools entered the competition. We won in the first round but were comprehensively beaten by St Judes in the second round. At the time our own playing fields weren't quite ready so we had to travel to Cale Lane at New Springs to play our home games. It wasn't ideal. In that game we played very poorly and were thirty points behind at half-time. Mr Wardle was furious and accused some of us, including me, of not trying. It wasn't entirely true. But his words had some effect since we won the second half but still lost the game quite heavily.

The following year was a different story. Our own playing fields were ready and this allowed us to have much more training and practice. In the knock out competition we won our first two games comfortably and were drawn against Pemberton in the semi-final. Even though it was the semi-final, being drawn first out of the hat meant a home tie. The stakes were very high. The final was to be played on Wigan Rugby League's famous Central Park pitch. Everyone was fired up. Pemberton were a decent side but so were we. The match drew a sizeable crowd. Not surprisingly, it was a tense low scoring affair but we prevailed and won through to the final. We were delighted. Many teams had been trying for years and never reached the final yet we had done it in only our second attempt.

Our opponents in the final were Rose Bridge. They were a formidable team, probably the best school team in the area. Indeed, Ince Rose Bridge were, and still are, a recognised force in amateur rugby league. They had several teams, ranging from juniors to open age, and all were successful. Several of their players were in both the Wigan Town team and the Lancashire team, including their captain, a lad called Gaskell. They also had a monster of a boy called Magnall who was actually training with and playing for the Wigan 'A' team! Fate decreed that we played Rose Bridge away from home in our last friendly game of the season, just two weeks before the final. The weather was atrocious but we won the game 5-0. I scored the only try, a length-of-the-field effort. However, we weren't fooled. Rose Bridge had rested many of their best players whilst we had fielded our strongest side. We knew it would be different in the final.

The day of the final duly arrived. It was a lovely warm summer's day, ideal for rugby. It was both a thrill and an honour to get changed in the same dressing room as my heroes, the Wigan rugby league players, and an even greater honour to run out on to the hallowed turf. The match kicked off. It seemed to fly by. All that I recall from the first half was chasing down my opposing centre, Gaskell, and tackling him into the corner flag to save a certain try. It was a close game. Rose Bridge led 5-3 at half-time, our try having been scored by our captain Jim Marsh.

In the second half their experience, size and skill began to take its toll and they took control of the game, eventually winning by 19 points to 3. Near the end I had to defend a two-on-one situation. I expected the centre to pass to his winger so I tackled the winger into touch. He didn't pass and scored. I had taken the proverbial dummy. It didn't really matter since it was the last try of the game but it was embarrassing nonetheless. More embarrassing were the comments from a group of girls stood near the touchline. "Hey," they shouted, "you with the red socks. Come and give us a kiss. You're gorgeous." These are not the sort of comments a rugby league player likes to hear! We were disappointed but not downhearted[3] (Image 62). Actually, I was paid a handsome compliment after the game. Gaskell, normally their best player, had been ineffective. He told his manager that the lad he played against (me) was too fast for him. At least it made me feel a little better.

Aspull Secondary Modern Rugby League Team 1962.
I am on the extreme left of the back row. On the front row,
William Fillingham is on the extreme left, Ronnie Bolton on the
extreme right and Jim Marsh is third from the right.

During my playing days in Aspull Secondary Modern rugby league team I broke three collar bones and two ribs. Not my own but those of my opponents. I was a hard but fair tackler.

As mentioned above I could run quite fast and was therefore entered into the inter-schools competition for the 100 yards. In the first year I made the final but finished last. I was only fourteen but competing against boys two years older than me. Defeat hurt and spurred me on. I bought some real running shoes and did lots of training, both at school and after school. After school, training took place on the disused railway lines leading to Toddington. I gave other boys starts ranging from twenty to forty yards and usually beat them over 100 yards. Never again did I lose a race over 100 or 220 yards. I was the senior school champion for two years (Images 59, page 83, and 63), winning the 100 yards race against a very strong wind in 10.5 seconds. In training, I had regularly clocked 10.2 seconds[4] (Image 63). I would have considered continuing my athletics (or indeed rugby) career except that I suffered a serious hamstring pull whilst playing rugby. I went down as though shot with an elephant gun and it took me fully four weeks to recover. In fact, I never recovered fully. The twinge is still there to this day.

SPORTS DAY

OVER 30 new athletic records were set up at Aspull County Secondary School last night — but that's not surprising because it was the two-year-old school's first-ever sports! The playing field, formerly a stretch of moorland near the school, has been in use for only six months and because there is no sand pit yet the long and high jump events had to be held earlier in the gymnasium.

More than 800 tickets were sold for the sports to help towards the provision of a house shield and individual shields and medals. So despite the cold, blustery weather, a large crowd saw some fine performances—among them that of 16-year-old Senior "A" champion Peter Gregory, who returned 10.8sec. in the 100 yards. Apparently he has done one-fifth of a second faster in practice.

Newspaper Cutting of Sports Day.

In the thirty-odd years before Aspull Secondary Modern was demolished to make way for a housing estate, my 100 yards record was only bettered on one occasion. It was beaten by a boy called Keith Maggs who went on to play professional rugby league as a winger for Leigh.

Our headmaster, Mr Firth, was educated at Keighley Grammar school. Keighley Grammar played rugby union and Mr Firth arranged for our school rugby league team to go to Keighley and play them at rugby union on their ground. The game would be played in the morning before we went to watch the Wigan rugby league team take on Keighley in the Challenge Cup in the afternoon. Although we all wanted to watch Wigan, none of us were really keen to play rugby union. It was a game none of us had ever played and it seemed so different and so technical compared to rugby league. Furthermore, their team was composed of boys who were all 18 years old. In contrast, ours consisted of boys aged 15 and 16. Compared to them we would be physically small. Despite these misgivings, the trip and the game went ahead.

Before the trip our parents had given us some pocket money to buy a little food and to pay for admission to the Keighley-Wigan game in the afternoon. Mine was 7s 6d (37.5p), a reasonable amount at the time. After getting changed in their dressing room I, like many others, left the money in my clothes. After all, it was a grammar school, a school attended by respectable, honest children, so it would be safe. Not surprisingly, we lost the game but were far from disgraced. In one of the mauls one of their players began throwing some punches. He thought being bigger made him safe. He was wrong. Completely wrong. They might have been bigger but they weren't tougher. Jim Marsh responded with a single punch and flattened him. They didn't try that tactic again.

Not only were they bullies, some of them were thieves. Those of us who had left money in their clothes returned to find it had all been stolen. We had to beg and borrow from our non-playing colleagues in order to buy some food and gain admission to the match. Evidently, honesty and veracity aren't virtues of all grammar school pupils. At least we gained some measure of revenge. Wigan trounced Keighley by 25 points to 3 in the Challenge Cup[5] (Image 64).

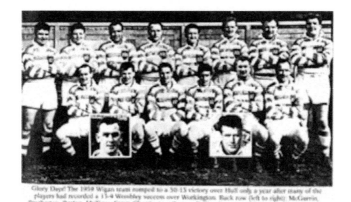

Glory Days! The 1959 Wigan team romped to a 50-15 victory over Hull only a year after many of the players had recorded a 13-9 Wembley success over Workington. Back row (left to right): McGurrin, Broughton, Boston, McTigue, Sayer, Cherrington, Barton, Collier. Front row: Thomas, Sullivan, Ashton, Bolton, Evans, Cunliffe. Inset: Griffiths, Holden.

Wigan Rugby League Football Team 1959.

4.3 EXAMINATIONS

As so often happens, the day of the first exam in May 1963 arrived with astonishing speed. Although I had worked hard and revised hard, I remember feeling nervous. GCE 'O' level qualifications were held in high esteem and weren't easy. Not only was I sitting seven 'O' level subjects, I was also taking four ULCI subjects. This was a precaution in case I failed the GCE 'O' level examinations. At least I would have some qualifications to fall back on. An exhausting few weeks lay ahead.

The first exam was always the worst. A mixture of emotions contributed to this feeling, such as the fear of the unknown, worrying that you had revised all the wrong topics, that the questions might be too difficult and that you would run out of time before answering all the questions. However, once that first exam was safely out of the way, the rest seemed less daunting.

The exams were spread over several weeks and, for me, several venues. The main venue was the assembly hall of Aspull Secondary Modern. It was weird to have just seven people and an invigilator in a deathly quiet hall that was normally filled with several hundred noisy people. The chemistry, physics and biology exams were taken at Wigan Technical College. Although the venue was less familiar, the presence of around one hundred students made it more reassuring. Because it was a different examining board, NUJMB (Northern Universities Joint Matriculation Board), I sat one of the general science exams at Upholland Grammar School.

It wasn't just the run up to the exams which was nerve-wracking, the waiting for the results was equally fraught. I thought I had done well enough to pass all the exams, indeed to have done really well in some of them, but there was always the nagging doubt that you hadn't. As the dreaded day drew nearer, all the questions you knew you had answered wrongly seemed to magnify, whilst all those that you thought you had answered well shrunk Therefore, it was with a mixture of apprehension and expectation that the seven of us entered school on the day of the results to ascertain our fate. We needn't have worried. The results were generally good with most of us passing the subjects we had taken[6] (Image 65).

I was slightly disappointed only to have got a grade five in English Language (the top grade was one and the bottom pass grade was six), but a grade one in general science and a two in mathematics restored the balance. So far so good but the key results for me were yet to come. For these, I had to travel to Wigan.

The technical college was teeming with people looking for their exam results. Excitedly, I made my way to the desk where the letters containing the results were located. Nervously, I opened the envelope. The results were in alphabetical order. Biology – grade two. That was pretty good. Chemistry, my favourite subject, was a grade one. Wow! That was excellent. Physics was also good, a grade two (Image 66). I was delighted. Given my results in the GCE 'O' level examinations, it wasn't surprising that I did well in the ULCI examinations, gaining three distinctions and a credit (Image 67).

Now came the key question. What should I do next?

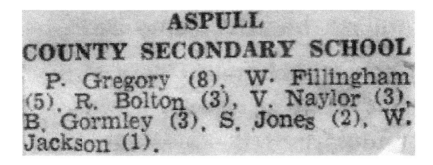

ASPULL COUNTY SECONDARY SCHOOL

P. Gregory (8), W. Fillingham (5), R. Bolton (3), V. Naylor (3), B. Gormley (3), S. Jones (2), W. Jackson (1).

GCE 'O' Level Results Newspaper cutting (Top)
Speech Day programme (Bottom).

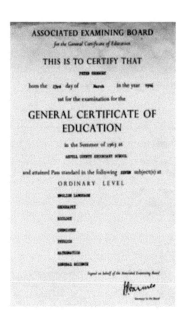

GCE 'O' Level Results 1963.

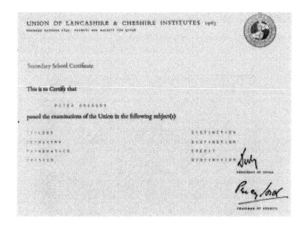

ULCI Results 1963.

4.4 'A' LEVEL STUDIES

As a family we had decided beforehand that if my results were good enough then I should carry on and study for the General Certificate of Education 'Advanced' Level (GCE 'A' level). The results were certainly good enough. I had attained grade one in chemistry and grade two in maths and biology, the three subjects I wished to continue studying. The question was, where should I do my GCE 'A' level studies?

Mr Firth, the headmaster at Aspull Secondary Modern, was adamant that my studies should be continued at the local grammar school, Rivington Grammar. This is the school that I would have attended if I had taken and passed the 11-plus exam. Indeed, Mr Firth had already contacted the headmaster of Rivington Grammar before the exam results came out, confident that his star pupil would do well, and had actually arranged for me to have an interview with him. The interview was held at the headmaster's house, located near to Rivington Grammar, one lovely summer's evening in the school holidays. It was at the same time that Wimbledon was reaching its climax, the time when a rank outsider, Chuck McKinley, was on his way to becoming the surprise winner of the men's singles title. We had a friendly and informative discussion in which the headmaster described the features of the school, explaining both its strengths and, to his credit, its weaknesses (although there weren't many of those). I left the interview feeling that Rivington Grammar could indeed be the place for me to do my 'A' levels, although deep down a nagging doubt still remained.

Rivington Grammar (Image 68) is a lovely old school located in a beautiful spot at the edge of the West Pennine Moors.[7] It is situated on the fringe of Lever Park, the former home and grounds of Lord Lever, the wealthy founder of what is now Unilever. The school has the well known landmarks of Rivington Pike and Winter Hill for its backdrop (Image 69), with its open playing fields, Lower Rivington Reservoir and Liverpool Castle for its front vista. The whole area is a beauty spot.

Rivington Grammar School (circa 1906).
It remains essentially unchanged today.

Rivington Pike and Winter Hill. Taken
from Ephraims Fold, Aspull 2010.

Rivington Hall Barn, the Great Hall Barn, with its café and information centre, and Rivington village are all nearby. It is a magnificent area for walking which is very popular with both locals and non-locals alike.

It was to this lovely scene that I arrived for my first day at Rivington Grammar School one August morning in 1963, full of enthusiasm and excitement. As was the norm, we had assembly in the school hall and then returned to our form room. My form teacher was also the chemistry teacher. Later that day I was shown the facilities for doing chemistry and physics. As mentioned previously, Rivington Grammar is a lovely old school, but so were the science laboratories. Although they were adequate, modern they were not. I felt disappointed. The science facilities at the brand new Wigan Technical College[8] (officially the Wigan and District Mining and Technical College) (Image 70), which I had attended in the evenings for my GCE 'O' levels, were infinitely superior. A further factor, which had occurred to me before but only now hit home hard, was isolation. All the people doing 'A' levels had been at this school since they were eleven. They all knew each other and were good friends. I felt alone and isolated. My early elation had turned to huge disappointment. It was with sadness and disappointment that I left Rivington Grammar after my first, and last, day.

Wigan and District Mining and Technical College.

Before agreeing to go to Rivington Grammar, I had enquired of the headmaster if I could study chemistry, mathematics and biology at 'A' level. Unfortunately, this wasn't possible. The subjects that were offered with chemistry were mathematics and physics. Although I preferred biology, physics was also an interesting topic so I agreed to this trio of subjects. Not being able to study biology was one of the nagging doubts referred to earlier. However, it was by no means the reason I left Rivington Grammar after just one day. Neither was the fact that I was the only new kid on the block, although this was more important than which subjects were available. The reason that I left Rivington Grammar was that the facilities for science were old and dated compared to what I had experienced at Wigan Technical College. The science laboratories at Wigan were brand new with completely modern equipment. This was the key factor in my decision to do my studies for GCE 'A' levels at Wigan Technical College.

The following days were difficult and embarrassing. I had to inform both the headmaster of Rivington Grammar and Mr Firth, my old headmaster, of my decision. Both urged me to give it another go but I knew in my heart that it wouldn't work. As I mentioned, not only did Wigan Technical College have excellent science facilities, I had also become familiar with the place and its lecturers. Eventually, both Mr Firth and the headmaster of Rivington Grammar reluctantly accepted my decision.

The two years at Wigan Technical College seemed to fly by. New friends were made and I thoroughly enjoyed my time there. One of my new friends was John Simmons, the son of a doctor (General Practitioner) for Aspull and New Springs. The Simmons' family lived in a lovely house on the fringes of Haigh Hall plantations. It is a house that I admired then and one that I still admire. Vera and I were courting steadily by this time and every Wednesday afternoon, after she had finished work at Harry Mayalls, a local decorator's shop, she would meet me at the college and we would walk home to Aspull together, either through Haigh Hall plantations or along the canal. Wednesday afternoons became special for John. He confessed that he loved to look at Vera's legs!

As expected, I found chemistry to be the 'easiest' and most enjoyable 'A' level subject, with physics the most difficult. Maths was somewhere in-between. A fourth subject, general studies, also had to be taken, although not the examination.

At 'A' level, the subjects were divided into separate disciplines. Maths was split into pure maths and applied maths. Pure maths entailed topics similar to those studied at GCE 'O' level but taken to a higher level, plus new topics such as calculus. Accordingly, it seemed more familiar than applied maths, which included a lot of new material such as mechanics and engineering. As the 'A' level examinations approached, I spent most of my maths revision on my weaker topic, applied maths, and devoted very little time to pure maths. As a result and, to my surprise, I did very well in the applied maths paper and less well on the pure maths paper, my supposedly stronger topic. Overall, I got a grade B. (GCE 'A' level results were graded A to F, with A being the top grade and F being a fail.)

Like maths, physics was also split into different disciplines. Light, heat, electricity, magnetism, gravity and mechanics are some that I remember. The physics exam consisted of two theoretical papers and a practical exam. As most students will testify, it is impossible to revise all the topics thoroughly, so you try and anticipate which topics will appear on the exam paper for that year. How is this achieved? Normally, by looking at the questions on previous papers (typically the last five years), and trying to spot a pattern. It's a risky tactic but it can work. This tactic was tried for the physics practical exam but it backfired. I assumed that 'light' wouldn't be one of the experiments since it was on the previous years practical exam. Wrong! It was on again and I struggled. Failing to do that 'light' experiment properly cost me a top grade. In physics, I also got a grade B.

As I've already mentioned, chemistry was my favourite subject and, like maths and physics, it was also divided into separate topics. Inorganic chemistry is the chemistry of metals and salts, ions and crystals. It is the chemistry of inanimate (non-living) things. It was primarily inorganic chemistry that had been studied at GCE 'O' level. Physical chemistry was new. It included topics like thermodynamics and was quite mathematical. This was my least favourite chemistry topic. Organic chemistry was the third and final topic. Organic chemistry is the chemistry of carbon, the chemistry of living things. Again, it was new but I loved it. This was the chemistry I wanted to do for a career. My second burning desire was becoming clearer by the day.

As was the case for physics, there was also a practical exam in chemistry. I finished early and got chatting with the lecturer, Mr Brindle. He asked me why sulphuric acid was used in one of the experiments (I think it was a titration of potassium permanganate with sodium thiosulphate), and not one of the other common mineral acids, hydrochloric acid and nitric acid. I replied that hydrochloric acid would have been oxidised to chlorine, a toxic gas, and that nitric acid would have behaved as an oxidant and ruined the experiment. He said I should go to university to study chemistry for an honours degree. I got a grade 'A' in chemistry[9] (Image 71).

I was selected to sit the GCE 'S' level papers in chemistry and physics. These 'Special' level papers are more difficult and demanding than 'A' levels and are intended to stretch even the brightest students. I was the lone candidate for chemistry but was joined by Stefan Baugh, a fellow student, for the 'S' level physics paper. We failed. Obviously, we weren't bright enough for Oxford or Cambridge!

GCE RESULTS—'A' LEVEL

WIGAN MINING and TECHNICAL COLLEGE

H. Anderson (2), P. Baldwin (2) S. Baugh (1), G. Birch (2), M. Bolland (2), A. Briers (1), B. Brown (1), E. Charlson (1), W. Daniels (2), R. Eyres (1), J. Forshaw (1), R. Gordon (2), S. Greer (1), P. Gregory (1), L. Jackson (2), P. Johnson (1), M. Knott (2), T. Liptrot (2), R. Lucas (2), J. Lyon (1), J. Medlock (1), J. Minto

London University Advanced Level:—

F. Ablett (3), P. Baldwin (1), S. Baugh (2), D. Bentwistle (1), G. Birch (1), M. Bolland (1), A. Briers (2), H. Charles (2), F. Cunliffe (1), C. Dawson (3), R. Eyres (2), R. Fishwick (1), J. Forshaw (1), P. Gregory (2), P. Hibbert (1), C. Hilton (3), P.

GCE 'A' Level Results Newspaper cutting.

What now? Having reached a crossroad, decisions had to be taken that would affect the rest of my life. Momentous decisions. Basically, three options were available. One option was to quit studying and apply for a full-time job. Another option was to get a full-time job and continue my studies on a part-time basis. The final option was to go to university. Decisions such as these couldn't be taken lightly. But they had to be made. It was decision time. But there was more to life than studying. I also had to negotiate those tricky teenage years.

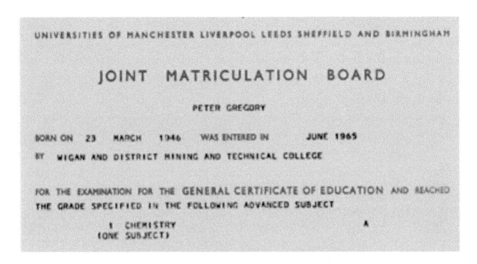

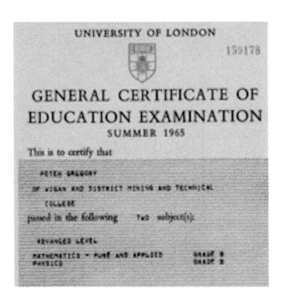

GCE 'A' Level Results Certificates.

REFERENCES

1. Lancashire Evening Post and Chronicle, April 12 1962.

2. Wigan Evening Post, Images of Wigan, Breedon Books, Derby, 1995 p. 145.

3. Lancashire Evening Post and Chronicle. Aspull Rugby Team 1962.

4. Lancashire Evening Post and Chronicle. 1962.

5. Wigan Evening Post, Images of Wigan, Breedon Books, Derby, 1995, p. 147.

6. Wigan Observer, Friday 30th August 1963, p. 15.

7. Smith, M. D., Old Rivington and District, Wyre Publishing, St Michael's on Wyre, 1995, p. 31.

8. Guide To Wigan: Past and Present, Hallgate Press, Wigan, 1984, p. 8.

9. Wigan Observer, Friday 30 August 1965.

5

TEENAGE YEARS

Becoming a teenager heralded the end of my age of innocence. Up to that time I and most other boys had only a vague notion of what sex was and what it entailed. The little we knew was gleaned from hearsay and innuendo, usually from other boys. Sex education was not on the school curriculum and my family certainly never discussed the topic with me. Never. However, my puberty was beginning and I was starting to experience wet dreams for the very first time. I had to find out more and the only source was from the older boys in school.

I had overheard the older boys speaking about masturbation (although they didn't call it that) and the immense thrill of orgasm and ejaculation (and they didn't call it that either), so I had an inkling of what was happening. Although you can fumble along, there is nothing quite like a real live demonstration and, to my complete amazement, that is precisely what I got. On one of our gardening sessions a strange thing happened. A small group of the bigger, older boys held down one boy (I won't mention names for obvious reasons), pulled down his pants and began to masturbate him. Right there, in front of everyone. At first he struggled but then relaxed and enjoyed it. I was totally shocked. I had witnessed a first hand demonstration of the act. It was a mystery no more.

There were lots of rumours and false truths about sex. The most prevalent rumour was that too much masturbation would cause blindness. This was spoken with such authority that everyone believed it to be true. What a shame that such a pleasurable act had to be rationed. The other rumour involved the quantity of sperm available. There was a fixed amount, about a bucketful per person, and once this had been used up that was it. There was no more. It seemed so unfair.

After experiencing the thrill of masturbation and orgasm I remember feeling extremely sorry for Katherine, Josephine and all the other girls. It seemed wrong that they couldn't experience such a feeling. They were missing out on one of life's most pleasurable sensations. I was so sad for them. (Of course, I have known differently for a long time.)

My neighbour, Jimmy Heaton, the one who had the fight with Norman, and I used to go for walks in Haigh Hall plantations. We would explore, build secret camps and, in the autumn, collect conkers. One day, Jimmy told me of a place near to Haigh Hall called the 'bonk'. It was a series of small grass clearings on a gentle hillside of rhododendron bushes. Apparently, it was the place where courting couples went to make love. Jimmy thought it would be exciting to conceal ourselves in the bushes and then wait to see if any couples came to make love. If they did, we could spy on them. It was risky. If discovered, we would have to flee for our lives. In the event, we gave it a go. We got lucky. A couple duly arrived and after a little kissing began to make love. Being a voyeur was exciting. However, our luck ran out when Jimmy coughed: we had to run like the wind. I had now witnessed two sexual acts firsthand. My sexual prowess was on the increase.

5.1 ADVENTURES

Being a teenager didn't stop me playing games. It's just that the games were different, more daring, more grown up. For instance, we still played Cowboys and Indians, but with a difference. Real guns were used. Air rifles. I remember the thrill as you hid behind a rock at Toddington and heard the 'bullets' whizzing overhead and ricocheting off the rocks behind. I accidentally hit someone who was running along the top of a hill, causing him to fall. Although it was exciting at the time, in hindsight it was dangerous and stupid. Being shot in the head with a lead pellet would have had serious consequences.

As mentioned earlier, I was the proud owner of a real bow and arrow purchased from Oliver Sumner's sports shop in Wigan. It was a powerful bow that fired real arrows equipped with feathers and a steel tip. One game involved firing the arrow vertically. The aim was to have it land as close as possible to the person who fired the arrow. Stupid really because a perfect shot would result in an arrow in your skull! Another game was for one person to stand with their legs apart at increasing distances from each other. The person with the bow had to shoot the arrow between the other person's outstretched feet. As William moved further away, I miscalculated and shot him in the leg. An arrow in the leg isn't pleasant. It made a hole that left a scar for eternity.

The slag tips around Wutchie were ideal for war games. One game involved the 'Germans' dispersing and hiding in the long ferns whilst the 'Allies' had to 'kill' them. This was achieved by lobbing dant 'snowballs' into the ferns in the places you thought they were hiding. A direct hit would cover the recipient in black dust. Great fun, provided people didn't cheat and place stones in the middle of their dant balls!

Rock climbing in the disused quarry at Toddington was another popular pastime. At about twenty feet the 'cliffs' weren't very high, but they were if you suffered a fall! A rope would be secured at the top of the cliff by tying it to a large boulder. Then, one at a time, we clambered down it. Normally, there were no accidents. On one occasion however, halfway down the descent Freddie Fielding lost his grip and fell to the floor. He was severely dazed so we carried him to a nearby horse trough and dunked his head in the water to revive him. Thankfully, he recovered and suffered no serious injuries.

A similar incident happened sometime later in Borsdane Wood. Borsdane Wood is located in a valley which runs from Aspull to Hindley. A stream meanders along the valley bottom flanked by wooded slopes[1] (Image 72). At one point, a pipeline traverses the valley horizontally, spanning its entire width (Image 73). A challenge was thrown down. Starting from one side, was it quicker to reach the other side by crossing the pipeline or by the conventional route of running down one side of the valley and up the other? I thought the former was quicker whilst another boy thought the latter was quicker. We decided to have a race. All was going well until I was about twenty feet from the finishing line. Then disaster struck. My right foot slipped down the pipe, my body followed suit and I plunged headlong to the forest floor. Dazed but not badly hurt, apart from a massive six-inch gash on my right leg sustained during the fall, I was fortunate not to have broken it. The rest of the boys carried me to a nearby pond where they splashed water on to my face to revive me and bathed my leg. With a handkerchief tied round the gash to stem the bleeding I managed to hobble home. After a visit to the doctors, some antibiotics and a properly bandaged leg, I was ready to meet Marlene, my girlfriend at that time, in the evening (Chapter 3). The scar on my leg today is testament to my misplaced bravado.

The old pumping pit was another frequent haunt. The ruins of the pumping pit building (Image 74) provided the opportunity to devise a series of daring leaps. There were about six leaps, ranging from easy to difficult. However, it was a dangerous game. The base of the pit consisted of concrete covered with piles of bricks and rubble so any slip would have resulted in serious injury if not death. Only a few of us were brave (or daft) enough to do all of the leaps.

Borsdane Wood (circa 1930).

102

Pipeline traversing Borsdane Wood 2008.

Pumping Pit ruins 2008.

5.2 ENTERTAINMENT

It was also a time for music. My grandad owned a phonograph, a strange contraption with a huge horn, that played records. It had the letters HMV (His Masters Voice) and a picture of a little dog. His collection of 78 rpm (revolutions per minute) vinyl records were mainly of classical singers such as Mario Lanza, Caruso and Joseph Locke. Once, my Uncle Jack asked me to go to Wigan to buy a record called *The Maharajah of Magador*. Asking for this record in the shop embarrassed me because it was the time of Elvis and The Beatles, not obscure records such as this. The shop attendant looked at me quizzically and, to my relief, replied, politely, that, "No, they didn't have that particular record."

The first record that I owned was, I think, Lonnie Donegan's *Hang Down Your Head Tom Dooley*. At the time, Lonnie Donegan was a well-known artist whose skiffle group appeared regularly in the charts. Two other early records of mine were *Chantilly Lace* and *When the Swallows fly back to Capistrano*, sung by Pat Boone. However, once Tommy Steele heralded the beginning of the rock and roll era with his *Singing the Blues*, it wasn't long before my tastes followed suit.

The sixties heralded an explosion of 'pop' music sung by some of the greatest singers and groups of all time. Cliff Richard and The Shadows, epitomised by Hank Marvin with his thick rimmed glasses, had many hits, such as *Living Doll* and *The Young Ones*, which was made into a film. Other famous artists included Buddy Holly, with classics such as *Heartbeat* that have stood the test of time. Tragically, his young life was cut short in a plane crash, the event being commemorated with the songs, The *Day the Music Died* and *American Pie*, the name of his plane. The Searchers were also popular and their *Sweets for my Sweet* was No.1 in the August of 1963. Cilla Black *(Anyone who has a Heart)* and Dusty Springfield *(I Only Want to be with You)* were female pop icons of the era. Neil Sedaka's *Only Sixteen* was one of my favourite songs but I hoped the words weren't prophetic of my romance with Vera, and that we weren't too young to fall in love.

Vera's pop idols were Gene Pitney, with his *Twenty-four hours from Tulsa*, and the Dave Clark Five, with *Glad all Over*.* But the kings of the decade and two of the most famous acts of all time were undoubtedly The Beatles and the king himself, Elvis Presley. Elvis was both Vera's favourite and mine. One of his songs, *Can't Help Falling in Love*, was our song.

For me, the sixties was the golden age of pop music. Before television became prevalent, listening to the radio was another common pastime. My grandad owned an old radio that had very poor reception. The interference produced a crackling noise and backgound buzzing that often drowned out the programme completely. I still remember the thrill when a new portable radio was purchased. It was great. Not only was the reception better, a portable radio also alleviated the boredom of bedtime. You could take it to bed with some chocolates and listen to Radio Luxembourg, the station that played more pop music than any other. DJs (Disc Jockeys) such as Pete Murray and Alan Freeman would introduce the records of Elvis and The Beatles as you lay cuddled up in bed. As well as established pop stars, new artists would also be aired. Helen Shapiro booming out *Walking Back to Happiness* sticks in my mind. She had a great voice and knew how to use it. I never understood why she didn't become a major star.

Boxing was also in the spotlight, particularly heavyweight boxing. The classy Floyd Patterson was the heavyweight champion of the world. His modesty and

---

* This record is always played at the DW stadium after a Wigan Warriors victory

respect for his opponents endeared him to the public. Suddenly, a black cloud appeared on the horizon. Sonny Liston. This monster of a man was everything that Floyd Patterson wasn't. An ex-convict, he was a brute of a boxer. In fact, Liston wasn't a boxer, he was a rugged, hard, street fighter. He quickly established himself as the number one contender and a championship fight with Floyd Patterson was arranged.

It was no contest. Normally classy and elegant in the boxing ring, Patterson just froze. He seemed in awe of the man-mountain facing him and was knocked out after just two minutes and five seconds, the third fastest knock-out in a world heavyweight fight and the first time the reigning champion had been knocked out in the first round. Exactly the same thing happened in the re-match. Psychologically, he was beaten before he entered the ring.

Liston was a frightening sight. Very few people fancied taking on this intimidating twenty-stone giant of raw power and thuggery. But one man did. A young man who had won the Olympic heavyweight title. A young man full of confidence in his own ability. A young man who, like Liston before him, quickly established himself as the number one contender. A young man that Liston couldn't ignore.

Cassius Clay was the best boxer I have ever seen. His physique was superb. Tall, lithe and muscular, the speed of his punches and footwork were unbelievable. Not only were his punches fast, they were also powerful. His self proclaimed slogan was 'to float like a butterfly and sting like a bee'. However, there is always a downside. With Cassius Clay, it was his arrogance. He never stopped boasting about his own prowess and what he would do to his opponents, predicting which round he would knock them out. He was a motor-mouth but, to be fair, most of his predictions were fulfilled.

Liston was unimpressed. He would soon despatch this young upstart and shut him up for good. This was the view that virtually everyone else shared too, except perhaps, for the friends of Cassius Clay. I had many discussions and arguments with my friends before the fight and the overwhelming view was that Liston would knock him out in the first round. It would be no contest. I begged to differ. Having watched both boxers there was no doubt in my mind that Cassius Clay was a far superior boxer than Liston. Provided he didn't freeze like Floyd Patterson, I thought he would win.

The world was enthralled. What would happen? The bell went and the fight began. It soon became apparent to everyone that Liston was being outclassed. He couldn't land a single blow on the lightning quick Clay and it was only a matter of time before the fight would either be stopped or Liston would retire. In the event, Liston retired after six rounds. Cassius Clay was jubilant. The inevitable re-match was arranged. This time, Cassius Clay knocked out Liston in the first round[2] by the legendary 'phantom punch' (Image 75). Liston was a broken man. Five years later, in 1970, he committed suicide.

Cassius Clay/Muhammad Ali
knocking out Sonny Liston.

Cassius Clay changed his name to Muhammad Ali. He dominated the realm of heavyweight boxing for many years, having a number of memorable fights along the way, especially with Joe Frazier and our own Henry Cooper. Indeed, I think 'our Henry' was the only person to knock him on his backside. It was a great punch but it only served to inspire Clay. He pummelled Cooper so much in the next round that the fight was stopped. Muhammad Ali was a joy to watch and I missed him when he retired.

5.3 FOOTBALL

Although I had played football at school, professional football never really interested me. Until, that is, my Auntie Lily acquired a television set. Then, Saturday afternoons became a ritual. Watching the final scores of the football matches became irresistible. I was fascinated by the names of the football teams. It was pretty obvious where teams like Manchester United, Bolton Wanderers and Blackpool were from. But Hibernian, St Johnston and Arsenal? These could be from anywhere. One day, my uncle asked which team was my favourite. I'd always had a soft spot for Blackburn Rovers. Why, I don't know. Maybe it was the name or because they usually seemed to win many of their games. Whatever the reason, he said that he would take me to watch one of their games. I was thrilled. (What would have happened had I chosen a team like Chelsea or Newcastle I don't know.) I never expected to be able to watch one of the teams mentioned on television, especially my favourite team Blackburn Rovers. I only had a rough idea where Blackburn was but we caught the bus to Wigan followed by a bus to Chorley. A coach from Chorley to Blackburn completed the journey.

5.4 BLACKBURN ROVERS

At that time Blackburn Rovers were in Division 2 of the Football League and were playing Liverpool. An excellent team, Liverpool were sweeping everyone aside in their promotion surge and no one expected Blackburn to beat them. By half-time, it appeared the pundits would be right. Liverpool had completely outplayed Blackburn and deservedly led 2-0. The second half was unbelievable. Blackburn played like men possessed, scored three unanswered goals, and won the game 3-2. My uncle said the teams must have swapped shirts at half-time. The match was a glorious introduction to football. I went to watch Blackburn on several more occasions, sometimes with my uncle, sometimes alone, but the extensive travelling, usually in the dark, meant that I didn't go as often as I would have liked. All that changed when Jack's brother, Bill, became involved.

Uncle Jack had two brothers, Bill and George. Bill had a car. He also liked football. On Saturday afternoons when Blackburn were playing at home Bill would pick up Jack and me and drive to Blackburn. It was far better than using public transport. Parking on a side street away from the ground, we invariably called at the Brown Cow to down a refreshing pint of beer (or two) before making our way to Ewood Park. It was around the time that I was seventeen to eighteen years old because Bill recommended a new film that had just come out, *Dr No*. The title didn't seem inspiring but he insisted that it was an excellent film. How right he was! It was the very first James Bond movie with the hero played by Sean Connery, one of the best Bond actors.

My visits to watch Blackburn Rovers with Bill and Jack continued for several years. We witnessed some good games. One memorable game was a 7-2 demolition of Tottenham Hotspur, one of the best teams of the day. Some good players wore the Blackburn shirt, such as the captain Ronnie Clayton and inside forward Brian Douglas. Matt Woods was the ageing centre-half who was being pushed for the first team place by a talented and ambitious Mike England. The strike force of Pickering and McEvoy was lethal and the right back Keith Newton played for England. They were a decent team and reached the FA Cup Final in 1960. Unfortunately, they had an off day and were soundly beaten 3-0 by Wolverhampton Wanderers. In that game, the Blackburn full back, Dave Whelan, the former owner of Wigan Athletic, broke his leg.

107

Travelling by car was so much better than public transport that I dreamed of having a car of my very own. But a dream it would remain. I had so little money that a car was out of the question. Or so I thought.

5.5 'UFFY'

Baby-sitting my young cousin Brian was a Sunday evening pursuit. In our early teens William and I would stay with our younger cousin Brian at his house in St Mary's Road whilst his parents, and ours, went to the Labour Club. Later, the custom was continued with Vera. She and I did the 'baby-sitting'. One of the rewards was that Brian's dad let me drive home in his works van. He'd taught me the rudiments of driving and this was just further driving practice in his eyes. To me, it was a thrilling end to the day. From a young age I had always wanted to drive.

When I was nineteen and completely out of the blue, my Uncle Jack bought me a car, a pale blue Ford Anglia from the Langtree Garage in Standish (Image 79, page 170). It was an old car but a car nonetheless, the first car that anyone in my family had ever owned. It's funny but you always remember the registration number of your first car. Mine was UFY 972 and we always referred to our car rather fondly as 'Uffy'. Having already learned the basics of driving from Brian's dad, my auntie and uncle insisted I take professional driving lessons too. The reasons were twofold. First, a professional instructor would teach me the correct things to pass the driving test. And second, it was the belief that taking your test in a driving school car enhanced your chance of passing.

Further tuition in Brian dad's van complemented the driving lessons and this additional driving was invaluable in preparing me for the driving test. Early in my tuition I had a fright. We were driving through Brian's estate when, without any warning, a young child ran out in front of the van. For what seemed an eternity but in reality was probably only a split second, I froze. Time was suspended. I didn't seem able to move. Shock has a strange effect. Just in time, my training kicked in and I slammed on the brakes. I had completed my first emergency stop. My second one would occur all too soon.

The driving instructor entered me for the driving test after just eight lessons. Presumably, all the extra tuition and practice received from Brian's dad had paid dividends. As was the norm I had a final lesson immediately before the actual test. It was the worst I had ever driven! Everything went wrong. "Don't worry," said the instructor, "this happens all the time. It means that you'll do everything right in the test." He was spot on. The test went wonderfully well, including an incident at the very beginning. I had just set off when a car pulled out directly in front of me and

I had to slam on the brakes. "Well," said the Examiner, "that's the emergency stop done." It was a good start to the test and I passed.

Passing the driving test meant that travelling to Blackburn became so much easier. My companions varied but usually were my Auntie Lily and my cousin Brian. Sometimes, Vera would also come along. It was on such an occasion that the radiator began to leak and we had to stop on Anglezarke Moor and nip down to a stream to get emergency supplies of water. As will become apparent later, a leaking radiator wasn't the only mishap to befall our beloved 'Uffy'.

Football and 'Uffy' provided us with other escapades. On the return journey home after playing Middlesborough away in an evening match, the fan belt broke, causing the radiator to overheat. We were in Preston. Not being members of any breakdown organisation we had to improvise. The solution? Vera took off her nylon stockings (stockings were the fashion then, not tights), and I tied them around the cooling fan in place of the broken fan belt. Heath-Robinson it may have been but they held and got us home safely.

Blackburn had drawn with Stoke City in the FA Cup and we decided to travel down to Stoke for the replay. This was scheduled for 7-30 p.m. on a Wednesday evening. The four of us travelling to the match assembled at my Auntie Lily's. Then disaster struck. As Brian closed the front passenger door, the handle fell off! The door would neither close nor remain closed. What should we do? Everyone was keen to see the match so we decided to press ahead as planned. This necessitated the front passenger continually holding the front door to keep it closed. Travelling down the M6 at 60 mph knowing that the front door might suddenly be ripped off if Brian's grip faltered was scary. Fortunately, we arrived safely, with the door intact. Suddenly, another problem reared its head. The car couldn't be locked. Normally considered a nuisance a group of young boys approached with their familiar question, "Shall we look after your car mister?" It was a blessing. We readily paid them the obligatory pound. Was it all worth the effort? Actually, it was. Blackburn won the game after having a purple patch in the second half.

Many people, including my family, dreamed of becoming rich by scooping a jackpot on the football pools. The top prize for correctly forecasting eight draws was a phenomenal £75,000! This was offered both by Littlewoods and Vernons, the two main players. A pools collector (the 'Coupon Mon') would deliver next weeks football coupon whilst, at the same time, taking the completed coupon (and your stake) in readiness for the weekend. Thursday was the most popular collection day. It was whilst helping my uncle fill in the pools that I had my first taste of combinations and permutations. He taught me how to 'perm any 8 from 11' draws.

5.6 CUBAN MISSILE CRISIS

The early 1960s was also the time when the Cold War between the two superpowers, the Soviet Union and the United States of America, reached fever pitch. The Soviet Union was annoyed that America had numerous nuclear missile bases ranged along its Western frontier on the soil of its NATO (North Atlantic Treaty Organisation) allies in Europe, so Kruschev, the Soviet leader, decided to retaliate. He did a deal with Fidel Castro, the pro-Soviet, anti-American leader of Cuba, to install a Soviet nuclear missile base in Cuba, right on the doorstep of America. President Kennedy was furious. He told the Soviets that under no circumstances would America allow the base to be built. Kruschev ignored the warning and the Soviet fleet sailed for Cuba with its cargo of nuclear missiles. Kennedy ordered the American navy to intercept the Soviet fleet and, by any means necessary, to stop the Soviets. The world held its breath. These were two very determined leaders flexing the muscles of the world's only two superpowers. A nuclear war appeared inevitable. Every time I went to bed I would stare out of the window expecting at any time to see a brilliant flash followed by the dreaded mushroom cloud of a nuclear explosion. It was so frightening, the nearest the world has come to a nuclear war. In the end, sanity prevailed and the Soviet fleet turned around. But it was a close shave.

5.7 TREVOR

I met Trevor Crane (Image 56) at Aspull Secondary Modern. We gelled immediately and quickly became good friends. One of the first things I learned from Trevor was how to play chess. It seemed so complicated compared to draughts but with his patience and understanding the game was learned quickly. During the many interesting games that we played, a curious fact emerged: I always played better after a few drinks! My moves became bolder and less inhibited.

Trevor was my companion on my first trip to the seaside without parents or relatives. I was fourteen. We travelled to Blackpool by train and enjoyed ourselves, first on the beach and then later in the Pleasure Beach. It's odd, but at tea-time we went to the same café that I had been taken to many times before by my relatives, the Brown Derby. We also had the same meal. It seemed strange ordering 'fish, chips and peas with tea, bread and butter for two' since this had always been done for us before. Nonetheless, it tasted as good as ever and, suitably refreshed, we returned home, tired but happy.

Everyone remembers what they were doing on the night that John F Kennedy, President of the United States of America, was shot. So do I. Trevor had called for me at my Auntie Lily's and we made our way to Eric's farm. On arrival, Eric blurted out the news that Kennedy had been shot. Where had he been shot? In the arm? In the leg? Was he badly wounded? Eric said these details hadn't been announced yet. We were shocked. However, we played snooker as normal, expecting further news later that evening. The announcement that he had been shot dead was met with utter disbelief! How could the most powerful man in the world have been shot dead in his own country? It was a reminder that the world was a dangerous place.

Trevor, Eric and myself became very close friends. We discussed many things, including death. One question asked, but never answered was, which one of us would die first? Although morbid, I suspect it's a question that other people think about too. But it's a question that came back to haunt me.

After my holidays in the Isle of Man with William and my Auntie Lily and Uncle Jack ended, I had my first holiday abroad. Lily and Jack were treating William and me to a week's holiday in Ostend. Even though I had just turned eighteen and William was seventeen, both of us were excited. We had never been abroad before. However, the week before we were due to depart, Trevor became ill. He suffered a mild cerebral haemorrhage and was taken to Wigan Infirmary.

On the Friday evening prior to our departure the following day, Eric, William and me walked through Haigh Hall plantations on our way to visit Trevor. It was a gorgeous summer's evening that July of 1964. Although our spirits were high, it was three anxious boys that entered the Red Cross ward where Trevor was located. Trevor quickly allayed our anxiety. He was sitting up in his bed as bright as a button and we talked and laughed throughout the whole visit. He said he was fine but that he had had a 'hard days night', the title of a Beatles' song popular at the time. Saying we'd see him in a weeks time, we bade him farewell and made our way home through the plantations. We had our holiday abroad to look forward to.

In Ostend, our hotel was the Trocadero. The weather was hot and sunny and we spent a lot of time on the fine sandy beach. A dip in the sea or a cooling glass of lager soothed our hot bodies. In the evenings, the lager was accompanied by a bag of frittes.

One evening was spent at the 'White Horse', a famous night club sporting a spectacular cabaret. Here, we downed steiners of lager (Image 76). The technical effect of the alcohol wove its magic. Back at the hotel, we fell asleep fully clothed, still wearing our silly hats!

During our stay we had two excursions. One was to Blankenberge, a nearby resort with a fabulous beach. At the time, I was a lean, mean running machine (Image 77). The other excursion was to Dunkirk to visit the war graves. It was a humbling experience to see how many young men had their lives so cruelly cut short. I was glad that I hadn't been in the war. Would I have been a hero, a coward or a normal soldier? I didn't know and I was relieved that I would never have to find out.

William (on left) and me at the
White Horse night club 1964.

William (on left) and me on the
beach at Blankenberge 1964.

Whilst in Ostend taxi rides were initially a source of puzzlement and amazement. William and I would watch in awe as the speedometer routinely reached speeds of 70 and 80 as the taxi travelled around the busy streets. What idiot would drive at this speed in a busy city centre? Only when we realised that it was kilometres per hour and not miles per hour were we relieved.

The journey home was long and tiring. Sailing from Ostend to Southend, we then travelled overnight by coach to Wigan. From Wigan, we caught the bus to Aspull, arriving at the Fingerpost bus stop early on the Sunday morning. As we alighted from the bus, a group of people beckoned my auntie and uncle to them. The expressions on their faces heralded the bombshell to come. Trevor had died! He'd suffered a massive cerebral haemorrhage. I felt weak with shock and disbelief. Worse was to follow. His parents wanted me to see him. Immediately. After a long tiring journey it was the last thing that I wanted. But I agreed. It seemed proper that his best friend should see him so we made our way to his house.

I had never seen a dead person before and didn't know what to expect. His distraught parents ushered me into the front room where his open coffin lay beside the window. Cautiously, I approached and peered inside. He looked like he was asleep. Tentatively, I touched his forehead. It was so white and cold! Suddenly, I felt dizzy and the room started to spin. For the only time in my life, I fainted.

I remember very little about Trevor's funeral but he was my best friend and he was gone. Gone forever. The loss of someone close is hard for anyone to bear, but for an eighteen-year-old teenager it was devastating. When old people die, the pain and grief are still there, of course they are, but it isn't really a shock. But when an apparently healthy child at the tender age of sixteen dies suddenly and without any warning it is one almighty shock. It took many years for me to come to terms with the tragic and unexpected death of my best friend on the 25 July 1964.

REFERENCES

1. Smith, M. D., About Haigh and Aspull, Wyre Publishing, 2000, p. 17.
2. Evans, G., Kings of the Ring, Weidenfeld and Nicolson, 2005, Front Cover.

6

A LONG ROMANCE

As mentioned previously, Vera and I started courting when I was seventeen and she was sixteen. It was 1963. I had started the first year of my GCE 'A' level studies at Wigan Technical College and Vera had left school and was working in Wigan at Harry Mayalls.

In the early stages of our courtship going for walks was our main activity. Occasionally, we treated ourselves to a night out at the cinema. There were a number of cinemas in Wigan but the Princess, the smallest and most obscure of them all, was the one that we frequented the most. Why? Because the Princess always showed the best horror films. Films such as *Dracula*, starring Peter Cushing as Dr Van Helsing and Christopher Lee as Count Dracula, and *Frankenstein*. These were my favourite films and I thought they were Vera's favourite too but, on reflection, I think she just went along with my wishes. We also went to the other cinemas as well, the Ritz, the County and the Court. Adjacent to the Court cinema in King Street was a confectionery shop where we bought sweets prior to watching the film. On special occasions, we indulged ourselves with a meal. Our favourite restaurant was the Turnkey, also in King Street. Here, we enjoyed T-bone steak and chips, our preferred meal at that time.

Many of our walks together were through Haigh Hall plantations. In the balmy summer months this was fine as the days were long and the weather warm. In winter, it was a different matter. Not only was it very cold, it was also very dark. Nonetheless, we still persisted in strolling through the dark lonely woods, partly out of routine and partly for the privacy, but that was about to change. One night as we were walking through the depths of the wood flanked on each side by rhododendron bushes, a faint rustling noise stopped us in our tracks. Slowly, we turned our heads to the direction of the noise. What we saw chilled us to the bone. A pair of red, evil eyes peered out from the bushes! Looking at us. Assessing us. Not from the ground, like a small animal, but from eye level. I grabbed Vera's hand and we ran as fast as we could towards the open spaces and relative safety of Haigh Hall. Only then did we pause to catch our breath and look behind us. There was nothing. Who or what those eyes belonged to we never found out.[*] However, after this major fright, in winter we confined our walks to the periphery of Haigh Hall plantations and avoided the dark depths of the interior. On reflection, the woods were a potentially dangerous place at night and we were foolish to have ventured alone in such a place, but such rational thoughts never entered the heads of two young lovers.

In addition to the walk through Haigh Hall plantations, another lovely walk was along the bank of the Leeds-Liverpool canal. There's something special about walking beside a stretch of water, especially at night. The fresh smell, the moonlit surface and the soft lapping of water against the riverbank, punctuated with the occasional splash of a fish leaping out of the water, is so romantic. However, our favourite walk was along Stanley Lane to Toddington. Not only was it a beautiful walk, it was also the one we undertook the most in our early courtship. Once, whilst on this walk, Vera twisted her ankle and I had to carry her for several hundred yards across a field to Haigh Road, passing beside a tall brick chimney, a poignant reminder of the area's coal mining history. Fortunately, she was very slim (see Image 79).

As pointed out earlier, walks cost nothing yet provided a great amount of pleasure. Although the walking itself was enjoyable the greatest pleasure was the romancing. Holding hands, embracing and kissing in complete privacy, lost to the world. I remember with dismay the frustration when Vera developed a contagious illness that prevented us from kissing. It only lasted for a couple of weeks or so but I had withdrawal symptoms. It was torture not being able to kiss her.

Once our relationship became more established, we decided to take a risk and stay in my Auntie Lily's house, especially on bleak winter nights. Discretion was required. At this early stage in our relationship we didn't want them to know we were staying in their house while they were out, so it had to be a night when my auntie and uncle could be guaranteed to be out. Friday was the best night since, without fail, Friday was their Labour Club night. To avoid detection by nosy neighbours I arranged with Vera that she should enter via the back door. As agreed, she carefully went through the alleyway and threaded her way cautiously down the backyards of the row of terraced houses. Everything was going to plan. Then, at the very last hurdle, disaster. In the deep, unlit gloom, she fell over next-door's dustbin! What a racket. Quickly, she scampered inside, hoping against hope that she hadn't been seen.

As time progressed a routine emerged. On Friday evenings we met at my Auntie Lily's, stayed there for an hour or so and then drove to a fish and chip shop in Chorley. After enjoying fish and chips in the car, we drove back to my aunties to watch Elliot Ness in *The Untouchables*. About one Friday per month, instead of staying at my aunties, we visited Trevor's parents, Mr and Mrs Crane. It was good to keep in touch.

---

[*]   On subsequent reflection I suspect the eyes may have belonged to an owl

The evenings always ended with me escorting Vera back to her home in St John's Road.

Early in our relationship two of our best friends were Irene and Tony Peet. (Tony is the second boy from the right on Image 49.) Vera had met Irene through work at the Hawker-Siddeley corporation in Lostock (to where she had moved from Harry Mayalls) and they got along really well. They thought Tony and I would also get along fine, partly because we shared similar interests, such as following Wigan rugby. They were spot on and the four of us enjoyed many good times together. We went to the pictures, to restaurants, to pubs and to dances. One film we saw together at the Ritz was *Guess Who's Coming to Dinner* starring Sidney Poitier, Katherine Hepburn and Spencer Tracey. It was a moving occasion since Spencer Tracey was dying from throat cancer and Katherine Hepburn's tears in the film were real. Our 'adopted' restaurant was the Turnkey and we ate there as often as our finances allowed. We didn't get fat. Christmas Eve meant a visit to the Berni Inn at the top of Library Street. The atmosphere was good, the food reasonably priced and they did an excellent steak and chips.

Saturday evenings were spent in different ways. Sometimes we went to a dinner-dance at the Pear Tree in Bamber Bridge. It was always a good evening. After enjoying a delicious meal of home cooked fare, we'd dance the night away. A packet of cockles from the 'cockle man' ended the evening. Other Saturdays meant a trip to the British Legion at Orrell, a place famed for its good entertainment. Once, we went to Haydock Park racecourse on Ladies Evening. We actually won a small amount of money and, feeling flush, decided to gamble it on a long shot in the last race. The horse was called *Freda's Legacy* and was something like 25-1 to win in a race of just four horses! It was a mistake. She was a grey mare that looked ready for the knackers yard. After leading for about five seconds, she was almost lapped by every other horse in a one-lap race! Still, it was an excellent night out.

One Saturday night we drove to Blackpool. First, we played a game of putting at Gynn Square. Later, as we strolled along the street, serendipity struck. On passing a wedding shop Vera spotted a dress that she liked. She and Irene were captivated and spent some time looking at the lovely dresses. Although we had no intention whatsoever of looking for wedding dresses, it had been a fortuitous break. Vera liked the dresses so much that it was from this very shop that her beautiful wedding dress was purchased (Images 88 and 90, pages 147 and 148.)

The destination for my first away day with Vera was Southport. Full of excitement, we boarded the steam train at Wigan Wallgate and settled down for the journey. Snuggled together near the window, we really enjoyed both the sound and the smell of the steam engine as it made its way noisily along the tracks. 'I think I can, I think I can' it sang as it merrily pulled us and all the other passengers along to Southport station. After spending a lovely day walking along the promenade, window shopping in Lord Street and smooching on the beach, the sunshine day ended in the sand hills.

We lay in each others arms as the golden sunbeams from the setting sun danced on the silver sea. It was so romantic. I still remember the dainty brown coat that Vera wore. We were getting along just fine.

However, it wasn't all sweetness and light. Like couples all over the world we had our fair share of rows and disagreements. Often, they were about the most trivial things. For instance, in 1965 Vera was recovering in hospital after having her appendix removed. It was a few weeks before the Challenge Cup Final at Wembley where Wigan were due to play Hunslet. It was a game we had planned to watch. Neither of us had been to Wembley and this would be our first visit to the famous 'twin towers'. Sat on her hospital bed, we chatted happily until this topic was broached. Then Vera, obviously feeling weak and sore from her recent operation, said she wouldn't be well enough to come to Wembley. Her stitches weren't due to be removed until after the cup final. One thing led to another and a row ensued. On my way home I felt terrible. The feeling in the pit of my stomach was indescribable. I wanted desperately to make things right again and I did. In the end Vera did come to Wembley and Wigan won, defeating Hunslet by 20 points to 16.

Every time we had a row I experienced the same awful feelings and the yearning to 'put things right'. Thankfully, we always did. The saying, 'You always hurt the one you love' is very true.

6.1 HAPPY FAMILIES

In due course Vera introduced me to her family and I introduced her to mine. Her family lived in a council house in St John's Road, just a stone's throw away from where my cousin William and his family lived (Image 1b). Anxiously, I entered Vera's house for the first time. I needn't have worried. Her dad, George, and her mum, Doris, were both down-to-earth friendly people who made me very welcome. She also had two sisters. June, the middle sister, was seven years younger than Vera whilst Elaine,* the youngest sister, was fourteen years younger. Laddie, an affectionate mongrel dog, completed their family. At last I had access to a dog.

Over the years I formed a very strong bond with George. In fact, he became one of my best friends. I have never met a more modest, unassuming, uncomplaining person in my whole life. He would do anything asked of him, immediately, and without complaint. He had simple interests: walking his dog, photography and Wigan Athletic. Although I preferred watching Wigan rugby, I would take him to watch Wigan Athletic at Springfield Park on Saturday afternoons.

---

* I always tease Elaine that she should have been named July, since July follows May, Vera's middle name, and June

117

Unfortunately, the friendliness and warmth I received from Vera's family was not reciprocated by my family towards Vera. My grandma was a matriarch (Image 78). She hadn't been in favour of any of her own sons courting or getting married and this feeling extended to her grandsons. As I proudly took Vera home to meet my family for the first time my grandma's 'greeting' astounded me. "Our Peter's not getting married until he's twenty-eight." I was furious. This was no way to greet the girl I loved and wished to spend the rest of my life with. Even my mother was lukewarm. My Auntie Lily and Uncle Jack weren't much better. I think they wanted me to marry a girl from a family who 'were someone', such as the Pilkingtons. In retrospect, whoever I'd chosen wouldn't have been good enough. It was an upsetting and distressing time for both myself and especially Vera. However, it made me even more determined to marry the girl I loved. Over time, I just hoped they would come to appreciate the qualities of my future wife.

My grandma (right) with her friend Mrs Bessie Taylor 1961.

They did, eventually. Two things changed their behaviour. As they got to know Vera they realised what a lovely girl she was. Not only was she attractive, of far more importance was her inner beauty. Caring, kind, thoughtful and loyal were but a few of her many attributes. She always thought of other people and put them before herself. I had been aware of her virtues for some time and now, rather belatedly, so were my family. The second factor was intent. Once they realised how serious we were about getting married they had little choice but to accept the situation.

Vera and I had our first holiday together in the summer of 1966. This was the year that England won the Jules Rimet World Cup for the first and only time. We had been courting for three years and decided that it was time to have a holiday together. It was a holiday we shared with my cousin William and his girlfriend, Jean. Our destination? Douglas in the Isle of Man. Partly because of the bad experience of my last boat trip but mainly because the seamen of the Steam Packet Company were likely to be on strike, we travelled by air. Flying from Blackpool airport to Ronaldsway takes less than 30 minutes and, after a short taxi ride, we arrived at our guest house in Douglas.

This was Vera's first visit to the island. Would she like it? To my immense relief she loved it. After we had checked in the four of us walked along the moonlit beach. It was so romantic. On one side the moonlight and coloured promenade lights danced and shimmered on the calm sea, whilst on the other side the tastefully lit promenade and hotels provided a kaleidoscope of colour. I think we realised there and then that one day we would return to the island to get engaged. The Isle of Man was to play a major part in our early life together.

It was a good holiday. Some things we did together, like visiting the Ocean Club in Ramsey with its famous, but very tiny, illuminated dance floor. Other things we did as couples. One of the highlights of the holiday was pony trekking. It was not an activity that either of us had contemplated and it had arisen purely by chance. In the summer of 1966 Douglas was teeming with holidaymakers from the North West of England and Glasgow. It was the time before cheap package holidays abroad had become established. Whilst walking down the promenade, we bumped into an old school friend, John Settle. He enthused about the pony trekking they'd done the previous day and insisted that we should give it a go. His persuasion succeeded. Next day we made our way to the pony trekking centre he'd recommended.

I was a little concerned that there mightn't be a horse big enough to carry me. How silly. The one they brought was a monster! It felt like I was sitting astride a two-storey building with legs on, the ground seemed so far away. With the guide leading the way we set off across the beautiful Manx countryside. My horse was a gentle giant. It walked at a leisurely pace along the winding country lanes, allowing me to enjoy the magnificent views. The only scary moments occurred when it broke into a slow trot and when it stopped to eat some grass. It felt like I would slide down its neck! To avoid this fate, I gripped the saddle very tightly. It was our first time on a horse and both Vera and I enjoyed the experience very much.

The Isle of Man lured us back the following summer when I was twenty-one. On this occasion our companions were my Auntie Lily and Uncle Jack. We stayed at the Stoneleigh Hotel on the Loch promenade. It was one my auntie and uncle had stayed in many times and they raved about the food and friendly service. I was disappointed. The hotel had overbooked and I had to share a room with three complete strangers. It wasn't a good start. However, this was no ordinary holiday. Vera and I had an ulterior motive.

On the north side of Douglas was a hidden gem. Summerhill Glen. We had discovered this gorgeous glen the previous year. Located on a hillside, it overlooks the magnificent expanse of Douglas bay. Although lovely in the daytime, it was at night when it really came alive. A brook babbled its noisy way to the sea far below but, without a shadow of doubt, the centrepiece was the array of fairies and other animals that were dotted along its meandering paths. These beautiful statues were illuminated in the most delightful way. Sat in one of the many little grottos, we drank in this wondrous scene. It was a perfect place for lovers. It was a perfect place to get engaged and it was in Summerhill Glen that I proposed to Vera. She said yes and I slipped the engagement ring on to her finger. Our only witnesses were the fairies and I think they approved.

The wedding date was set for July 1969, two years ahead, so our holiday the following year would be the final one before our wedding. For a change, Vera and I had decided to tour Scotland in our 'new' car. We planned to tour for about ten days, since we deemed a week was too short and two weeks too long. Deciding not to pre-book we went 'on spec'. The day of departure duly arrived and two expectant young people set off for Scotland.

Before the advent of motorways, travelling to Scotland took a long time. You travelled along the A6 over Shap and then on the equivalent roads in Scotland. Our plan was to make Oban our base but there was no way we could travel to Oban in one day. An overnight stop was required. On route to Glasgow we entered a quaint little village called Innerleithen. It was evening and both Vera and I were tired. We enquired at the local post office if accommodation was available. It was. We were directed to an old lady's house whose husband had just died. To help financially, but also to keep her occupied, she had decided to do bed and breakfast. She was so sweet. She made us very welcome and gave us some supper. The rooms were lovely and clean with really comfortable beds and we slept like logs. The breakfast was delicious. First cornflakes or porridge, followed by bacon, egg, sausage, tomato, mushrooms and fried bread, and finally toast. All washed down with lashings of tea. She really wanted us to stay for more nights and we were sorely tempted but decided that we should stick to our original plan and bade her farewell. It was a decision we came to regret.

On the drive to Oban the weather was atrocious. Strong winds and heavy rain made driving difficult but, undeterred, we proceeded on our journey. We drove through Glasgow, crossing the river Clyde, then on to Loch Lomond, where we stopped for a bite to eat. Suitably refreshed we set off on the long final leg to Oban.

Arriving at Oban in the early evening was a huge relief. The journey had been long and arduous and both Vera and I were exhausted and ready for some hot food and a warm, comfortable bed. With these thoughts in mind, we headed straight for the Tourist Information Centre to acquire accommodation for the night. "I'm sorry sir, there isn't a bed to be had in Oban. It's the peak season and its extremely busy." Our spirits sank. We were devastated. What an absolute bloody mess. If only we'd stayed at Innerleithen… Still, if there were no rooms available there were no rooms available and that was that. Instead of flying into a blind panic, we considered our options over a cup of coffee. To continue our holiday in Scotland meant driving to another location to try and find accommodation. There was no guarantee that we would. Also, Oban is pretty isolated and it was a fair distance to the next town. With no accommodation booked in advance it was deemed too risky to continue with our holiday in Scotland and a decision was made to return home. But where could we spend the night? It was getting late, too late to reach Glasgow. After an *al fresco* meal of fish and chips, we decided to start our journey south and, if the worst came to the worst, we would sleep in the car.

Two people sleeping in a Ford Anglia in a remote lay-by in the middle of the Scottish highlands is not recommended (Image 79). As we parked up and made ourselves as comfortable as possible for the night ahead, a violent thunderstorm broke out. It was frightening. Lightning bounced off the road in front of the car. However, I remembered my physics and as long as you remained inside the car you were perfectly safe. (The car acts like a Faraday Cage.) We survived but neither of us slept very much. At daybreak our bathroom was the stream at the bottom of the valley. We duly took our toothpaste and toothbrushes to the stream, cleaned our teeth, washed our faces and did anything else we needed to. Then, we started the long journey home.

Vera and 'Uffy' in the Scottish Highlands 1968.

It was late when we got home. Everyone had gone to bed and I had to throw some pebbles at my mother's bedroom window to awaken her. Both Vera and I were shattered after all the travelling and felt that we still needed a holiday. After all we hadn't spent much of the money we had allocated for our Scottish holiday. So, where did we go? We went back to our tried and trusted friend, Port St Mary in the Isle of Man. This was the third consecutive year that we had holidayed on the island. It wouldn't be our last. There was still the small matter of a honeymoon.

7

WORK AND STUDY

After the elation of an 'A' and two 'B's' at GCE 'A' level a difficult decision was required. Should I go to university full-time to study for an honours degree in chemistry, as Mr Brindle had suggested, or should I get a job and continue my studies part-time? I was nineteen-years-old and had been courting steadily with Vera for over two years. Although neither of us had actually mentioned it at the time, I think we both knew that we would get married. I had a strong preference for what course of action should be taken. To my relief, my family supported my decision and Vera didn't object either. I would apply for a job in chemistry and continue my studies part-time.

Several factors influenced my decision. To understand these factors, it is necessary to have an appreciation of the prevailing culture. In the 1960s only a few people went to university. Most of these were (bright) people from wealthy parents plus a few very bright children from poor parents. I fell into neither category. However, the majority of pupils left school at sixteen to start work. Some served apprenticeships in the trades, such as engineering, carpentry or bricklaying. Some entered into a vocation, such as typing, secretarial work or nursing. Indeed, this is what Vera did. She became a typist. Others just got a job, any job. The key factor was that all of them were earning money. Indeed, everyone I had known at Aspull Secondary Modern School was now in a job and earning money. In contrast, I hadn't contributed a penny to the family coffers. Because of this, I felt obliged to earn some money. This would help to repay my family for allowing me to study and to enable Vera and I to start saving towards our future together.

7.1 JOB HUNTING

Companies were recruiting. Our lecturers at Wigan Technical College informed us that the big chemical companies like ICI (Imperial Chemical Industries) and Shell were seeking a variety of new recruits, including people with GCE 'A' levels, so the time was right. Furthermore, in the 1960s part-time study was an established way of obtaining qualifications. It was possible, therefore, to gain full-time employment whilst simultaneously studying for the equivalent of an honours degree in chemistry. Another plus was that, initially, the studying would continue at Wigan Technical College. Finally, and perhaps most importantly, I didn't want to be apart from Vera for long periods.

After considering various options regarding my scientific career a shortlist of companies was compiled. It consisted of just three, ICI, Shell and the Atomic Energy Authority. Letters were written to all three. Each one sent me literature about their company and each one offered me an interview. Shell paid the highest salaries but required high quality staff whilst the Atomic Energy Authority paid the lowest salary. More important to me was the type of work, the working environment and the job itself. I wanted something that was interesting, challenging and had worthwhile benefits to society. In this respect, ICI seemed the most attractive. Their range of activities was enormous, spanning dyes, drugs, paints, plastics, polymers, fertilisers and much more. They employed a variety of people with different skills and abilities and, of paramount importance, appeared a caring company. Consequently, I decided that my first interview would be with ICI. For this I had to travel to Blackley, (pronounced Blakeley), North Manchester, headquarters of ICI Dyestuffs Division. Although Blackley was less than twenty miles from my home in Aspull, the journey by public transport was tortuous and time consuming. A bus journey to Wigan was followed by a train ride to Manchester. Another bus journey to Blackley completed the odyssey. The whole journey took almost two hours. On the bus to Blackley I asked the driver which stop was needed for ICI. "Oh, 'The ICI'. Yes, I'll tell you where to get off." Stepping from the bus I realised instantly why everyone in the area knew of 'The ICI'. It was enormous! A cluster of fine buildings nestled amongst the houses and shops of the village whilst the manufacturing facility, Blackley Works, followed the river Irk, stretching into the distance for almost a mile. It was an awesome sight. Taking a deep breath, I made my way to the main gate.

Dressed in a smart new suit, tie and shoes, I arrived at the gates of ICI Dyestuffs Division looking more confident than I felt. After the usual formalities, the security officer directed me to a fine old building called Hexagon* House New. (Hexagon House Old was an even older building.) Whilst sitting nervously in the lobby alongside several other candidates, something happened that reinforced my impression that ICI was a good company. An employee sitting in the same room offered his apologies to the receptionist saying that he had to return to his distillation. He wanted to make

---

*   The basic building block of dyes and pigments is benzene. The benzene molecule is hexagonal in shape. Hence the name 'hexagon'.

sure that everything was fine. It was obvious that he loved his work. The signs were looking good.

A smart silver-haired gentleman came dashing down the lovely spiral marble staircase. Dr Statham greeted me warmly and escorted me back to his office at the top of the stairs. His kind and relaxed manner soon put a nervous interviewee at ease. Briefly, he described his career. Most of it had been spent in the research laboratories and later, when he felt like a change, he'd moved to Personnel Department (now Human Resources), and that's where he was now. He lived in Chew Moor, a small village approximately half-way between Aspull and Bolton, a village that I'd passed through many times on the bus to Bolton. Then came the main part of the interview. Dr Statham asked me why I wanted to do chemistry and why I had chosen ICI. After answering these to his satisfaction, he then asked me some technical questions. "In the preparation of acetaldehyde from ethanol, why is it distilled continuously from the reaction mixture?"

On hearing the word 'distillation' my thoughts immediately flashed back to the employee in the lobby, although it had no connection to the question. But this was a question to which I knew the correct answer. "Because if it isn't, the oxidation proceeds further, converting the acetaldehyde into acetic acid (vinegar)." He seemed impressed. After answering a few more questions, Dr Statham asked if there was anything I wished to ask him. I did. I asked about the types of work, such as research, development and production, about the job prospects and, most importantly, if ICI supported employees wishing to continue their studies part-time.

"Yes, most definitely," he replied to my final question. "In fact, we positively encourage employees to continue further study and operate a day release scheme." With that, the interview concluded. I left feeling elated. ICI was the company for me.

A few days later a letter arrived. It was from Dr Statham. Subject to a satisfactory medical examination, ICI were offering me a job as a Laboratory Assistant. The starting salary was £495.00 per year. Eureka! It was what I wanted. After informing Vera and my family I wrote a letter of acceptance. Two more letters were written informing both Shell and the Atomic Energy Authority that I wouldn't be attending their interviews.

On the day of my medical I repeated the same journey as for my interview. From the same lobby as before a young lady from Personnel Department accompanied me to the Medical Centre. After a thorough examination I was pronounced healthy. At the conclusion of the medical came something completely new, a colour blindness test. On reflection this was to be expected. It was, after all, ICI Dyestuffs Division, where thousands of different dyes in a myriad of colours were produced. The test is called the 'Ishihara Colour Blindness Test'. It is a book containing a number of coloured patterns or mosaics, one per page. Hidden in each pattern is a number. For people who are not colour blind, the number is readily discernible and people with totally normal colour vision complete the whole test without problem. People with acute colour blindness can't even complete the first page.

I started quite well, completing the first five or six pages with ease. Then the numbers became more fuzzy and difficult to find. Struggling on, I managed to reach page ten. Progressing through the book, each successive page of the thirty or so pages becomes more difficult to 'read'. Try as I might there was no way I could see any numbers beyond page ten, despite the exasperation of the doctor. I was colour blind! Not totally colour blind, just a mild form of red-green colour blindness. Although this came as a shock, it was a blessing in disguise. Being colour blind ruled out any job in ARTS (Application Research and Technical Service) Department. This department tested and evaluated the novel dyes invented and synthesised by chemists in the Research Department, as well as providing technical service to ICI's customers. By necessity, anyone working in ARTS Department must have excellent colour acuity to be able to assess the colours of dyed fabrics. As a result of this finding I was assigned to work in the Research Department.

On completion of the medical examination, I was taken to the spacious canteen in Hexagon House New for lunch. I was impressed. The menu was comprehensive, the prices low and, most important of all, the food delicious. After lunch it was time for a tour of the site. I was shown several facilities, including the research laboratories, the library and the 'stores'. Here, I was fitted with my future working clothes, a white laboratory (lab) coat and safety glasses being the key items. Finally, we returned to the lobby in Hexagon House New.

The research building was extremely impressive. In the 1960s the Research Laboratories at ICI Blackley were the largest in Europe. Many memorable inventions originated from these laboratories, especially the famous PROCION reactive dyes for cotton. Also, it was here that ICI Pharmaceutical Division, now AstraZeneca, was spawned. It was a thriving site teeming with highly qualified people and I was amazed how any company could afford what must have been a massive wage bill.

7.2 MY FIRST DAY

Punctuality was paramount. The working hours were from 8-45 a.m. to 5-00 p.m. with 45 minutes for lunch, equating to a 37.5 hour working week and, on my first day, I was determined not to be late. On arrival, I was directed to a laboratory in the Research Department and introduced to my boss, Frank Robinson. My instant and overriding impression was his similarity to Kenneth Wolstenholme, the well-known football commentator. Frank was friendly and helpful. He gave me a guided tour of the laboratory, showed me how things worked, and explained the culture, including how Laboratory Assistants such as myself made tea and coffee for the chemists twice a day!

We chatted for a while. General chit-chat mainly but then Frank asked how much I knew about dyes. My knowledge surprised him. Dyes and colour chemistry were not taught at 'A' level. However, the hiatus between the job offer and starting work was put to good use. I learned as much as possible about dyes and colour chemistry, mainly out of interest but also to make a good first impression. It worked. My very first day at work was over.

Frank's boss was the Research Chemist Dr Gerald (Gerry) Booth. A Research Chemist was a highly qualified individual. Holding both a doctorate (PhD) and an honours degree (BSc) in chemistry, they led a 'chemist team'. The Research Chemist's main function was to provide the ideas and new dye molecules to meet agreed targets. An Experimental Chemist, such as Frank, worked for the Research Chemist. His job was to synthesise the molecules suggested by the Research Chemist. The minimum qualification for an Experimental Chemist was the Higher National Certificate (HNC) in chemistry but many Experimental Chemists also held a degree. A Laboratory Assistant helped the Experimental Chemist carry out his task. GCE 'A' levels in chemistry (obviously) and two other technical subjects, such as physics and mathematics, were required for a Laboratory Assistant.

Ours was one of four chemist teams in the spacious four-bench laboratory. We worked on the 'V-Dye Project', polymerisable vinyl dyes for nylon. The aim was to have three prototype dyes, a yellow, a red and a blue, at the end of two years. These V-Dyes would have excellent wash fastness. In other words, the dyes would be so tightly bound to the nylon that it would be impossible for them to wash off and stain adjacent garments, no matter how severe the washing conditions. It was a noble aim but a difficult one to achieve. My job was to assist Frank in making the dyes.

7.3 TRAVEL

At the end of the working day the roads around the site resembled a bus station. Dozens of red double-decker buses lined the streets waiting to ferry the workers to their various destinations. Hordes of workers piling on to the buses was reminiscent of a football crowd leaving the stadium after a match. Every evening I boarded the bus bound for Manchester's Victoria train station where I caught the train to Wigan. A bus journey from Wigan to Aspull completed my journey home.

The time taken to travel to and from work varied. Connections, delays and the weather were the main culprits. An average time was one-and-a-half hours. To arrive at work by 8-45 a.m. meant catching the 7-15 a.m. bus at the Fingerpost. For the return journey, if all went smoothly, I would get home by 6-30 p.m. Sometimes, things went wrong. One very cold and dark winter's evening the train from Manchester to Wigan was delayed by the severe weather. Standing on the freezing, wind swept, icy platform, I was chilled to the bone by the time the train eventually arrived. Boarding the train was heavenly. It was so warm and cosy, in stark contrast to the arctic conditions outside. Settled snugly in my seat, it wasn't long before the gentle swaying motion of the train produced a feeling of drowsiness. Soon, I succumbed and dozed off. It was like Emile in *Emile and the Detective* (Chapter 1). Suddenly, I awoke with a start. The train would be approaching Wigan shortly. I peered through the window looking for familiar landmarks. To my horror, there were none. Not a single one. All at once it dawned on me: I must have been asleep at Wigan and the next stop was... Liverpool! Panic set in. How could I let my family know that I would be very late arriving home. Not only were mobile phones not yet invented, no one in my family had a telephone of any description. There was nothing I could do except sit back and continue the journey.

It was 10-00 p.m. when I got home and my family were frantic with worry. All kinds of awful events had gone through their minds. Had I been in an accident? Worse still, had I been killed! They had been concerned for a while at the time (and expense) that it took me to travel to and from work and this latest incident was the last straw for my Auntie Lily and Uncle Jack. Soon afterwards they started saving up to buy me a car (Chapter 5).

7.4 PART TIME STUDY

My studies for the Higher National Certificate (HNC) in chemistry at Wigan Technical College began about the same time as I started work at ICI. The company allowed employees one full day per week to complete this two-year part-time course. The classes began at nine in the morning and continued through until nine at night. Except for myself and one girl (I can't recall her name), who had also arrived via the GCE 'A' level route, the remainder of the twenty or so students were from the Ordinary National Certificate (ONC) course from the previous year.

They were a friendly bunch and both myself and the girl were made most welcome. Mick Hoole in particular ensured that both newcomers integrated smoothly into their social group. Later, the girl became his girlfriend. Often, we enjoyed lunch together. Indeed, my very first introduction to Chinese food occurred one lunchtime when Mick and his girl took me to a Chinese restaurant near the Technical College. Chicken Chow Mein was certainly different but I still preferred my fish and chips from the local chippy.

On my first day of the HNC course I experienced 'tea' in the refectory. Used to a hot meal, such as steak and chips at Auntie Lily's, a cheese and tomato barm cake was something of a rarity for me. Apart from being healthier, which wasn't a consideration in those days, it actually tasted rather good and, to my utmost surprise, I really enjoyed it.

Unlike school, attendance at courses of further education is not mandatory. People attend because they want to. They want to learn the subject and, in doing so, enhance their career prospects. This environment fostered a feeling of camaraderie, and strong friendships were forged. Jim McCann and James Gainer became two close and dear friends. Both were married and had their own houses. James even had children. The three of us remained good friends throughout the duration of our studies (three years).

Twelve hours of lectures and practical work was a long day. Having joined the HNC course from 'A' level backgrounds, the practical skills of the two newcomers were below the standard required. Therefore, we had to attend an extra class on a different evening to remedy the situation. As a result, the working week became intensive and exhausting. Fortunately for both of us, after about two months our practical skills had attained the desired level and the extra evening class was no longer necessary.

7.5 MY FIRST JOB

I took to my job at ICI like a duck to water. Making dyes gave me an immense sense of satisfaction. It was most definitely the career for me. An added bonus was the social life. My colleagues in the laboratory were both friendly and gregarious and arranged several social events. One event remains prominent in my mind. It was a pitch and putt competition for the people in the laboratory, to be held one summer's evening after work. The prime organiser was Dave McKenzie, an enthusiastic, ebullient lad who loved to talk. For weeks before the actual event all the talk was about who was going to win. To me, it was pretty obvious. Dr Alex Blackhall, a polymer chemist, was the firm favourite. He was the only person in the laboratory who was a golfer!

The day duly arrived and, after work, twelve people made the short journey to the pitch and putt course at Heaton Park. We formed into six pairs. My partner was Dr Gerry Booth, the most senior person in our laboratory and my ultimate boss. During the banter before the event, Dave had asked Dr Booth what his handicap was. "Peter," he replied, but added quickly that he was just joking.

Dr Booth and I were the penultimate pair to tee off. Nervously, I placed the ball on the tee, took a deep breath, and played my shot. It was an air shot. I missed the ball completely! "Just a practice shot," I said.

"Oh no," said Gerry, "that counts as your first shot."

I took six shots on the first hole of the 18-hole course. Heaton Park's pitch and putt course resembles a miniature golf course with an average distance of approximately 100 yards for each hole. It is a tricky and undulating course with many obstacles. Embarrassed by my performance on the first hole, I quickly relaxed and soon got into a rhythm. Most of the remaining holes were accomplished with scores of threes and fours due, in the main, to a good putting performance. As we prepared to tee off for the eighteenth hole, Dave asked what our scores were. Mine was 67. "Bloody Hell," he shouted. "If you do this in a par four you'll have won!" Pressure like that I didn't need. The final hole was relatively straightforward. It was ca 120 yards long but, unless the ball was hooked or sliced, was obstacle free. All that was required was a good first shot. Having decided how the shot would be played, I took my stance, raised the club and then swung at the ball. To my relief, it sailed straight and true, landing on the edge of the green. Two putts later, it plopped into the hole. I had won with a score of 70. My putting and the odd game of golf in Port St Mary had served me well.

Later, over a few beers and some food in the White Hart pub, a few miles away, tales of the various rounds were recounted. The favourite, Alex Blackhall, had a decent round of 72 but hit the bunkers too many times. Dr Booth, my partner and ultimate boss, finished in the eighties. He paid me the compliment of saying that in any future competition he would back me to win. Most of the scores were in the high seventies and eighties, although one unfortunate person managed to break the one hundred barrier. However, the event had achieved its main purpose. It had been a good night out enjoyed by everyone.

Heaton Park was revisited a few months later with William. After our introduction to golf in the Isle of Man we managed to save enough money to purchase a half set of old golf clubs and decided to try the golf course at Heaton Park. When we started the weather was fine and sunny. Suddenly, it changed. It clouded over and thick fog descended like a blanket. With the course shrouded in fog it became extremely difficult to play golf. Rather than admit defeat, we tried to continue. As one person prepared to tee off, the other person would run down the fairway to a point where the ball would most likely land. After shouting that he was ready, the shot would be played. By listening and looking, the person on the fairway tried to ascertain where the ball had landed. Not surprisingly, it didn't work very well: one of William's tee shots nearly knocked me out! A dozen or so lost balls later we abandoned the idea and admitted defeat. The fog had beaten us.

In the laboratory a common topic of conversation was the latest film releases. Dave enthused over the first of Sergio Leonie's Spaghetti westerns, *A Fistful of Dollars*. He said this film, which launched Clint Eastwood's career, was great and that we should endeavour to see it. His favourite bit was at the beginning when the lone gunslinger, played by Clint Eastwood, asked the undertaker to prepare three coffins. On his way back from his gunfight with the bad guys, he remarked, casually, "Sorry, my mistake. Make it four." Another recommended film was *The Trap*, starring Oliver Reed and Rita Tushingham. They were alone and isolated in the wilderness, being pursued and attacked by a pack of ravenous wolves. I watched both films with Vera and really enjoyed them.

Part way through the V-Dye project Dr Booth was promoted and moved to his new position as Head of the Process Technology Department (PTD) at Huddersfield Works. His replacement was Dr Cyril Morris. Cyril had risen to the lofty position of Section Manager, a senior job in charge of about thirty or so highly qualified people. He was an intelligent, competent and thoroughly hard-working individual who was extremely good at his job. Unfortunately, he became so engrossed in the work that he suffered a nervous breakdown and had to leave ICI. He set up a thriving pie business in his village of Morris Green near Bolton but always hankered for his true vocation, chemistry. Therefore, it came as no surprise when, after recovering from his illness, he returned to ICI as leader of the V-Dye project and my ultimate boss.

Cyril was a thoughtful and studious chemist who evaluated every option before commencing work. Continuing the work that Dr Booth had originated, Cyril and his team developed a range of yellow, red and blue dyes that functioned really well. His work was impressive, so much so that he was asked to present it to one of Britain's foremost chemists, Professor Lord Todd! To stand in front of such an eminent person and present your work would have made me a nervous wreck. Not so Cyril. He was calmness personified. I was fascinated. Why wasn't he nervous? His advice was invaluable. "I am nervous," he said. "Anyone who says they aren't are either a liar or they don't care. The trick is in not showing you're nervous. Listen," he continued, "it doesn't matter what titles people have or where they're from, basically, they're no different to you or me." And, of course, he was right.

At that time Dr RR Davies, the Associate Research Manager, held his infamous Monday Morning Meetings. Each Monday morning one of the Research Chemists would have to present his latest work to the rest of the chemists from Research Department. The meetings were always chaired by Dr Davies himself and it was well known that he could ask some very awkward questions and be quite aggressive. This caused great consternation amongst the younger, more inexperienced chemists, including myself. Indeed, Dr Ramsay, my Section Manager, had said to me that when it became my turn to give a talk, he would 'protect' me! One poor soul got so worked up that, when he stood up to give his talk, he fainted! Before it was his turn, another chemist took a whiff of amyl nitrite, a powerful stimulant, to 'fortify' himself. Rather than give him courage it caused him to run around the Research Department corridors like a man possessed!

From a research point of view, the V-Dye project was completed successfully. A range of yellow, red and blue dyes had been invented that possessed excellent wash fastness properties. They were not, however, developed into a commercial product. This is one of the harsh realities of research. Several years can be spent developing a product that is technically excellent but which can fail for a number of other reasons. Research can be so rewarding but it could also be soul destroying.

For his excellent work on the V-Dye project plus his past record, Cyril became the first incumbent of the elevated new position of Company Research Associate, the highest position that a technical person could reach in ICI. It was a deserved honour for a thoroughly nice man and a brilliant chemist. That Christmas of 1967 I also gained a surprise but welcome promotion from Laboratory Assistant on Haslam Grade 4 to Experimental Chemist on Haslam Grade 5 (Section 7.10). It came with a total pay rise of 10 per cent paid in two instalments of 5 per cent, one immediately and the other 12 months later. Having your contribution recognised produced a profound sense of satisfaction. I was thrilled to bits. I rang Vera and said we'd celebrate by going out for a meal. Thus began another ritual: every pay rise would always be celebrated with a meal at one of our favourite restaurants.

Ken Dunkerley was another Experimental Chemist working for Dr Booth. An accomplished tennis player, Ken was a kind, helpful man who took an interest in everyone's welfare. Concerned about the length of my travelling time to and from work, he made enquiries and arranged for me to join a car club with people travelling from Wigan. A vacancy had arisen and Ken ensured that it was offered to me first. I grasped the offer with both hands. My pick-up point was the Fingerpost at 7-45 a.m. The car was a Morris Minor and I was the fourth passenger. It was a revelation. Instead of taking up to two hours, the journey now took less than one hour.

Everything in the garden was rosy. Settled at both ICI and at Wigan Technical College, the two years seemed to fly by. Vera and I were courting steadily and our engagement was in the offing (Chapter 6). Without warning, the examinations sprung into view. But I wasn't concerned. In fact, I couldn't wait to do them. Chemistry was in my blood. Organic chemistry, the kind that was done at work, was fabulous. I loved it. Inorganic chemistry and physical chemistry were also enjoyable but less so than organic chemistry. I passed the HNC examination with flying colours (Image 80). Indeed, the marks were high enough to warrant exemption from Part I of the Graduate of the Royal Institute of Chemistry (GRIC) examination (Image 81), although I still had to do the one-year course.

Full-time work and part-time studying curtailed my social life. Nonetheless, Vera and I went out when we could, often with our friends, Tony and Irene Peet. During the winter of 1966, my first winter as a car owner, I was driving along an icy Plodder Lane in Farnworth when the car encountered black ice. It seemed to acquire a mind of its own and started skidding uncontrollably towards a parked car at the side of the road. Time seemed to slow down. Everything was happening in slow motion. The parked car was coming inexorably closer and there was nothing I could do. With an almighty crash, the impact occurred. This jolted me out of the trance and back to reality. Although neither car was badly damaged, it was a frightening experience, one that I am in no hurry to repeat.

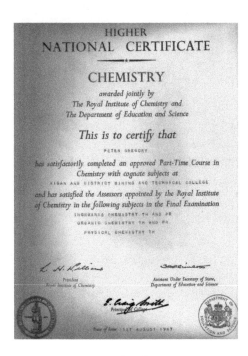

HNC Certificate.

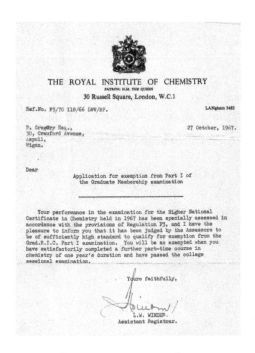

Letter stating exemption from
Part I of GRIC examination.

It was in this damaged car that the four of us went to the Research Dinner Dance. Held in the canteen area in Hexagon House New, they were fabulous events. The evening commenced with conversation and drinks, followed by a delicious four-course meal.

Dancing to a live band, games, raffles and prizes completed a memorable evening. It had been agreed that I could drink and Tony would drive. It was a wise decision. Being near Christmas, the police were having a blitz on drunken drivers. On the return journey, ironically at the end of Plodder Lane, a police car stopped us, no doubt attracted by the damaged wing. After a brief interrogation, with me sat in the back seat quite drunk and a sober Tony in the driving seat, he allowed us to proceed. Regrettably, as the site dwindled in size over the years, the Research Dances became a thing of the past.

As everyone knows, it is customary to celebrate your 21st birthday. When you are working, two celebrations are required, one for your work colleagues and one for your family. I had never hosted a celebration at work and was somewhat apprehensive as to what it entailed. What was expected? Ken said there was nothing to worry about. Just take a few friends and colleagues to a local pub at lunchtime and buy them some drinks. Would they expect some kind of speech? This bothered me since I had never done any public speaking. My fears were unfounded. About twenty of us toddled off to the White Lion pub and I bought the first round of drinks. People just came and chatted and everyone and his dog wanted to buy me a drink. Many were refused politely otherwise I'd have been completely legless, a state not recommended when in a chemical laboratory! In the event, it was a convivial session enjoyed by all.

The celebration of my 21st birthday by my family was a more formal affair. A meal had been arranged in the function room of the Labour Club for about twenty people. Sitting at the head of the table made me uncomfortable and I didn't enjoy the meal as much as I should have because of the speech I was expected to make at the end of it. Remembering Cyril's advice, I said a few words, thanking people for attending and for their presents, including a lovely silk dressing gown from Vera, and concluded by urging them to enjoy the rest of the evening. Short and sweet and, I hoped, delivered without them realising how nervous I actually was.

By this time Vera and I were saving up for our wedding and our future life together. It was customary to hand over all your wage to your family and in return receive a weekly allowance. From my starting wage of ca £10 per week, I kept £2.50 and my family kept the rest. After my promotion, my allowance was doubled to £5 per week. This arrangement wasn't too unfair since my family had played a major part in my upbringing and had, after all, just bought me a car. Nonetheless, we found it difficult to save for our future and enjoy any sort of social life. We compromised. Vera and I decided that all we could allow ourselves was one meal out per month. This we did, rotating the venues between the Turnkey, Berni Inn and the Atherton Steak House.

My final year of studies at Wigan Technical College commenced in the summer of 1967. A handful of students, including myself, Jim McCann and James Gainer, were determined to carry on towards a GRIC qualification. Many of the HNC class had decided to call it a day. In order to obtain the GRIC qualification, four GCE 'A' level subjects were required. And not just any four. The three technical subjects of chemistry, mathematics and physics were already in the bag. No problem there. But the fourth subject had to be chosen from a relatively short list. One of these was economics, a course being run that year at Wigan. It was the subject we all fancied. There were two potential problems. First, GCE 'A' level economics is normally a two-year course. And second, GCE 'O' level economics is normally required before 'A' level economics is attempted. Despite these problems we were allowed to study 'A' level economics. For my final year at Wigan therefore, I would be working full-time at ICI, doing the GRIC Part I course for a full day, including the evening, as well as an additional evening for 'A' level economics. It wouldn't be easy.

For students with a trained scientific mind, economics was relatively straightforward to understand. Many of the basic concepts, such as the 'Law of Diminishing Returns' and the 'Law of Diminishing Marginal Utility' only required a simple grasp of mathematics and common sense. And being exempt from the GRIC examination also helped. More time could be devoted to studying economics. Even so, it was a demanding year.

To improve the chance of success, all the economics students were entered for two 'A' level examinations. Thankfully, I passed both. Not surprisingly, I did better in the examination whose curriculum I'd studied. I achieved a grade B in the University of London paper (Image 82) and a grade D in the Joint Matriculation Board paper.

7.6 SALFORD UNIVERSITY

Excellent. Everything had gone to plan. But now, another crossroad had been reached, a major crossroad. Should I continue in full-time employment at ICI and study part-time for a further two years for the GRIC Part II qualification, or was it better to achieve this important qualification in one year's full-time study? The latter option meant resigning from my job at ICI, something I was reluctant to do. Whether it was full-time or part-time, the studying had to be done at Salford University.

It was a difficult decision. On the one hand I loved my job at ICI but on the other hand it was becoming increasingly hard to combine full-time employment with intensive studying. Also, Vera and I were now engaged and the wedding was planned for the following July. The decision was delicately balanced. What finally tipped it towards full-time study was the fact that both of my close friends, Jim McCann and James Gainer, had opted to go full-time. With some regret and a large measure of misgivings, I reluctantly handed in my resignation to ICI. Had I done the right thing? Time would tell.

GCE 'A' level certificate in economics.

Travel wasn't a problem. Salford University lies on the A6, a road that passes close to Aspull, making it a relatively straightforward journey. To cut costs, the travelling was shared with Jim McCann. He would drive from his home in Wigan to my Auntie Lily's house, leave his car, and travel with me in 'Uffy' to Salford. His car was a thirsty beast so we reasoned it was better to travel in my car with Jim paying me petrol money.

It was an intensive but enjoyable year. Prof. Ramage was head of the chemistry department and delivered lectures on terpenes. Often, the question of salaries would arise. The Royal Society of Chemistry (RSC) published the annual salaries of chemists from all walks of life, normally in the form of 'quartiles'. These never bore any relation to the salaries of the younger chemists. They were always much higher. Prof. Ramage acknowledged this and said that when he was young and poorly paid he shouted it from the rooftops, but now that he was well paid, he kept quiet. James asked the same question of a visiting lecturer from industry but received a less satisfactory answer.

The lecturers were good. I can't remember them all but Dr Ron Grigg delivered most of the organic chemistry lectures and made them very interesting whilst Dr LS

Bark took some of the inorganic lectures. He did an excellent job on 'Crystal Field Theory'. Dr Bark was an extrovert with a big personality. He loved to make an impact and usually succeeded, like the day we had our first lecture on lasers. As the class was settling down, Dr Bark strode into the room and, without warning, fired a powerful laser at the back wall. The red streak of laser light, followed immediately by a loud crack as it hit the wall, startled everyone. It certainly grabbed our attention.

In chemistry, it is often difficult to visualise three-dimensional images, particularly in group symmetry theory. The best way to overcome such problems was simple. Buy some plasticine and matches and construct the three-dimensional molecules from these simple materials! It was strange to watch a 22-year-old man playing with plasticine, but it worked. Rudimentary it may have been but it meant that the question on group symmetry on the final exam paper was a doddle.

Like those at Wigan Technical College, the chemistry laboratories at Salford University were relatively new, but not so the method of transport to the higher floors. The chemistry building had a unique elevator system. It was a conveyor belt with buckets that never stopped moving. Patrons had to wait for an empty bucket, time their leap to perfection and literally jump in! To exit the bucket, the same procedure was required in reverse. Scary at first, eventually it became second nature. It even became good fun.

It wasn't all study. Occasionally, the three of us went for a game of pitch and putt at Heaton Park. James was very good and usually won. Indeed, he was also a good footballer, playing for a respected amateur side. Because of this, we sometimes joined him for one of the many football games that took place on the university's playing fields. At other times we patronised the local pub. Here, Jim always put money into the jukebox to hear Jerry Lee Lewis blast out his favourite record, *Come on Baby Light my Fire*. He deafened us with the racket!

In the summer of 1969 we sat the final examinations. The GRIC Part II qualification was on a par with an honours degree from the best universities so the standards were high. There were three gruelling theoretical papers, each of three hours duration, and two full days of practical examinations. I had done my best. All that remained was the agonising wait for the results.

As mentioned before organic chemistry was my favourite subject. It was the chemistry I did at ICI and it really fired my imagination. One of the lecturers on organic chemistry was Hans Suchitski. He was an expert on halogenated heterocycles and supervised several post-graduates working towards their doctorates. His work was interesting and highly respected. Since my forte was organic chemistry we had agreed, in principle, that, subject to a satisfactory result in the final exams, I would undertake a research project on fluorinated heterocycles for my PhD. From the beginning of my studies at Aspull Secondary Modern School, one of my dreams was to achieve the ultimate academic qualification, a 'Doctor of Philosophy' (PhD). A PhD was the pinnacle of education, something I wanted very badly. Dr Peter Gregory sounded just fine.

7.7 WEDDING PLANS

Not only was the studying intensive, Vera and I were busily planning our wedding. The date had been set. On 12 July 1969 Peter Gregory and Vera Santus would become husband and wife. Many aspects about the wedding had been discussed but the key aspect had eluded me. Completely. In fact, it had never entered my mind. It was Vera who had the foresight and common sense to recognise it. Whilst escorting her back home after an evening baby-sitting Brian, she asked, "Where are we going to live?" It suddenly hit me that we needed a house. As mentioned earlier, Vera worked with Irene Peet at Hawker-Siddeley in Lostock and Irene's husband Tony worked as a bricklayer for a local builder, Jack Fishwick, father of Joan Fishwick, a fellow prefect at Aspull Secondary Modern (Image 52). Mr Fishwick was building a small estate of new houses off Bolton Road, near to Borsdane Wood. Indeed, Irene and Tony had bought a bungalow on the very same estate. With less than nine months to go before the wedding, this information was timely indeed.

7.8 DECISION TIME

After the hectic schedule of the exams I had some free time before the results were announced. Time in which to think and make one of the most important decisions in not just mine, but also Vera's life. A PhD was one of my dreams. But so was having a house, a lovely wife and, in the fullness of time, a beautiful family. Could I have both? I was certainly going to try.

The dream was shattered very quickly. There was no way that any bank or building society would offer a mortgage to a student doing a three-year PhD course. The meagre grant was totally insufficient to remotely cover the mortgage, let alone the other living costs. So the choice was simple. It was either a PhD or a new house. In reality, it was more complex. To buy a house, I first needed a good job.

Many people have unfilled dreams and I knew in my heart which dream was more important. I wanted to be part of a loving, caring family living in our own house. So, with some regret, I informed Hans Suchitski that I wouldn't be doing a PhD and set about finding a job. Not unnaturally, my first port of call was ICI. I penned a letter applying for another job with them. My results were through and I had passed with high marks (Image 83). Having resigned just twelve short months ago, I wasn't optimistic. To my surprise, they offered me two interviews, one at Blackley and one at their manufacturing site at Trafford Park.

Both interviews went well and a few days later a job offer arrived in the post. It was for a Senior Experimental Chemist on Haslam Grade 9. Grade 9! It was unbelievable. In just twelve short months, by resigning and rejoining I had jumped four grades! (Fig 2). It proved to be the biggest single promotion of my entire career. Vera and I were over the moon. My salary had doubled to £996 per annum. Armed with this information, we chose our new semi-detached house from Jack Fishwick and went in search of a mortgage.

7.9 OUR FIRST HOUSE

It was a short search. Our first destination was a small estate agency in Westhoughton run by Mr Cartwright. He took all the details and seemed fairly confident that we would be offered a mortgage. At £2,950 the house was priced at the higher end for a semi-detached property but then Mr Fishwick's houses were built to a bigger and better standard than comparable houses. We had managed to save a few hundred pounds so the deposit of 5 per cent wasn't a problem. Borrowing the remaining £2,800 shouldn't cause any worries either since it was less than three times my salary. Furthermore, Vera was also earning a reasonable salary. Following our meeting with Mr Cartwright we were directed to the Woolwich Building Society. After filling in our application forms, assisted by courteous and professional staff, we made our way home. The mortgage should be a formality but you never knew. All we could do now was wait.

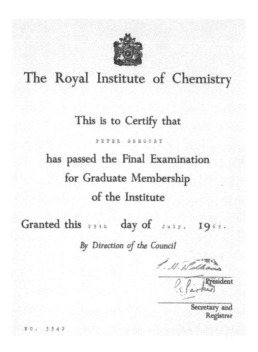

The Royal Institute of Chemistry

This is to Certify that

PETER GREGORY

has passed the Final Examination
for Graduate Membership
of the Institute

Granted this 29th day of July, 1969.

By Direction of the Council

President

Secretary and
Registrar

NO. 3342

GRIC Part II Certificate 1969.

In those days obtaining a mortgage was a 'big thing'. It represented a major stepping stone along the pathway of life. Securing a mortgage generated an immense feeling of pride, a feeling that you had achieved something really worthwhile. Virtually all the mortgages were standard repayment mortgages taken out over twenty-five years. There was none of the bewildering array of products available today. Also, once a mortgage had been granted people generally stayed with that mortgage provider for the entire term of the mortgage. There was no swapping and changing every few years. People accepted they had a mortgage for twenty-five years and that was it. There was no rush to pay it off early. It was just another part of life.

After several weeks, a formal offer of a mortgage for 95 per cent of the house price was received from the Woolwich Building Society. It was accepted with alacrity. Although not yet fully built, we owned our own house. Excited and proud, we couldn't wait to get married and move in. Before doing so, we had one or two final things to arrange.

First was the decision regarding the type of staircase. The house came with a standard staircase but for an additional amount of money you could have a lovely mahogany open tread staircase. Even though it stretched our small budget, having seen the latter in another house we were hooked. A mahogany open tread staircase it was. More important was the question of heating. Central heating wasn't included in the price of the house and cost an additional £300. There was no way we could afford that amount as well as the mahogany staircase. However, a stroke of luck came our way. The central heating contractor was Ken Livesey. A former rugby league player for Rochdale Hornets, Ken was a regular patron of Aspull Labour Club and a very good friend of my Auntie Lily and Uncle Jack. As a favour to them, he agreed to install a full gas central heating system for £150. This we could manage, just.

To my relief, in choosing to buy a house rather than study for a PhD the right decision had been made. In 1972, three years after making the decision, Britain was in the grip of a major recession. Not only weren't companies recruiting, they were making people redundant, including companies like ICI. If I had done a PhD, finding a job would have been nigh on impossible. My earlier impressions of how even ICI could afford to employ such large numbers of chemists flashed into my mind. Even the best companies couldn't escape the effects of a full-blown recession. I was grateful for the decision I had made. Serendipity had been kind.

7.10 THE IMPORTANCE OF QUALIFICATIONS

You may be wondering why a Doctor of Philosophy (PhD) was so important to me. The sense of achieving the highest pinnacle of education has already been mentioned but another equally important point is that a PhD opened the door to a better, more rewarding career. To understand why, it is necessary to take a brief look at the salary structure in a big company such as ICI.

At the time, ICI employed the Haslam scale for their salary structure (Fig 2). The Haslam scale is represented by a series of coloured books, namely Green Book, Blue Book, Black Book, White Book and Pink Book. Each book is sub-divided into grades. The starting position was the boxes D to A in Green Book. Clerical and administrative staff such as mail girls (and boys), typists, and telephonists, occupied these scales. In Research Department, grades 3 and 4 were Laboratory Assistants, grades 5 to 8 were Experimental Chemists and grades 9 and 10 were Senior Experimental Chemists.

The jump from Green Book to Blue Book was massive. The gap between the grades was ca 10 per cent but most people in Blue Book were eventually awarded an 'Agreement' with ICI (Chapter 9). These 'Agreements' were coveted. They were worth an extra 15 per cent, making the difference in salary between grades 10 and 11 a gigantic 25 per cent. This created an enormous differential between Green Book salaries and Blue Book salaries. To achieve a Blue Book position a PhD was almost invariably required. It was these Blue Book chemists, the Research Chemists on grades 11 and 12 and the Senior Research Chemists on grades 13 to 15, who produced the ideas for the new dye molecules and who led the 'chemist teams'.

In the 1960s industrial chemists were paid very well. For example, a Senior Research Chemist on grade 13 earned ca £3,500 per annum. To put that in context, our brand new semi-detached house cost £2,950. Therefore, in today's (2020) money, that would translate into a salary of over £150,000. Unbelievable!

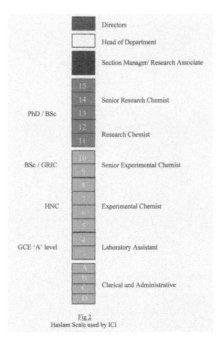

Fig 2
Haslam Scale used by ICI

The incumbents of the Black Book grades were the senior managers and the top scientists, such as the Research Associates. There were four Black Book grades ranging from 6 (the lowest) to 3, and two White Book grades, 2 and 1. Heads of Departments were the incumbents of White Book. Pink Book was the domain of the directors and chairman.

The pay freezes introduced by the Labour governments of the seventies prompted ICI and other companies to introduce 'benefit-in-kind' payments. As far as ICI was concerned, the biggest 'benefit-in-kind' payment was the award of company cars to Black Book staff and above. This created another large pay differential between Blue Book and Black Book staff.

It is evident why a PhD was such a prized qualification.

8

WEDDING BELLS

Planning a wedding is one of life's most stressful experiences. Not only do many things have to be chosen, they also have to be co-ordinated. Where do you start? It was daunting, there was so much to consider.

The first consideration was the date. We wanted a summer wedding, primarily for the prospect of good weather but also because my studies at Salford University would be complete. The next task was to secure the three most important aspects of the wedding, namely the church, the venue for the reception and the photographer. We were in luck. St David's church at Haigh, the one Vera attended, the Ridgeway Arms in Blackrod, our choice for the wedding reception, and Harold Ashton, the local photographer, were all available for the 12 July 1969. With these key things booked, we could relax and decide the remainder of the wedding at our leisure. I say we but in fact my involvement in the rest of the planning was minimal. The wedding dress, bridesmaids outfits, flowers, cake, entertainment and transport were the domain of the ladies and I was more than happy to leave them in their capable hands. My next major involvement was the stag night.

8.1 STAG NIGHT

Where should I go? Amsterdam, Prague, Dublin or some other overseas city? Unlike current stag nights these thoughts never entered my head. In those days it wasn't the 'done thing' and there was no way at all that I could afford such an extravagance anyway. The prevailing custom was to hold your stag night in a local pub or club and that is precisely what I did. Therefore, because of my family's involvement with Aspull Labour Club, my stag night would be held in the function room of that establishment.

Apart from inviting an assortment of friends and relatives, my main role in planning the stag night was deciding the date. Traditionally, the stag night was held on the evening prior to the wedding day. This wasn't a good idea. Many a groom imbibed so much alcohol that he was in a drunken stupor on his wedding day! Determined to avoid this fate, I chose the evening of Thursday 3 July for my final fling. That way I would have over a week to recover. It proved to be a wise decision.

I walked to the Labour Club with Les (Image 84), one of my friends and a neighbour of my Auntie Lily. Suspiciously, he was carrying a large cardboard box. I was both intrigued and apprehensive. What did it contain? When asked, Les was coy and evasive and I feared the worst. It was obviously part of the stag night but what was it? I would soon find out.

The evening was a blur. I drank far too much and got very drunk. Everyone really enjoyed themselves and, in what seemed a flash, it was time to go home. But a final surprise lay in store. Les unveiled the contents of his cardboard box. It was a brown poe, the receptacle that was your personal toilet (see Chapter 2), and some broken brown biscuits. Drunk as I was, I knew what was coming. The poe was filled to the brim with Double Diamond and the broken biscuits placed on top. It resembled a used poe full of urine with turds floating on the surface. "Drink it or wear it," came the command. Having already drunk more beer than at anytime in my entire life, there was no way that I could consume another three or four pints. However, since everyone was urging me on, I gave it a go. I managed no more than half of the contents before the inevitable happened. The remainder was poured over my head! Drunk and drenched in Double Diamond, William and Brian helped me stagger home. I was thankful the wedding wasn't until the following week.

From left to right: Me, Les, Brian and William.

144

It's considered bad luck for the bride and groom to see each other on the day before the wedding. Despite this 'tradition', Vera and I met briefly on the Friday evening, partly, I think, to confirm our commitment. Before we parted at her front gate there was one last thing to do. I held her close and whispered in her ear that I would always look after her. Gently, I let her go, watched as she walked down the steps to the front door and then, under a starlit sky, made my way home.

8.2 WEDDING DAY

The days leading up to the wedding were extremely fraught. Everything had been planned, booked, checked and double-checked to the last detail. No matter how much you worried, there was nothing else you could do. The success of the wedding day depended entirely on other people. It was out of your hands and it was scary.

As mentioned earlier, we had chosen a summer wedding primarily to ensure good weather but the weather thought otherwise. On the morning of our big day it was dull and cloudy with scattered showers. It was the last thing we expected or wanted. No matter how meticulous the planning, the weather is the one variable over which you have no control. It was just pot luck. There was nothing we could do except to make sure that everything else went really well.

Dressed in a complete set of new clothes[*] I made my way to the church with William, my best man. We were early. It was two-o-clock so we had an hour to kill before the actual wedding ceremony at three (Image 85). Thankfully, the weather had improved. The showers had been replaced by brief spells of sunshine and blue skies, although the rain clouds still scurried across the sky, waiting. A decision was made. We nipped across the road into the Balcarres Arms for a quick half to pass the time and soothe the nerves. Then, we made our way to the front of the church, sat down and waited.

A charming church, St David's is situated in a lovely location at the top of Copperas Lane, the gateway to Haigh Hall[1] (Image 86). Building of the church commenced in 1831 and it was opened on the 2 June 1833. It cost £3,433.[1] The inside of the church is as beautiful as the outside[1] (Image 87). Sitting nervously on the front pew as the guests arrived, I thought it a fitting location for the forthcoming ceremony.

---

[*]   The modern trend is to hire suits for the groom, best man, father-of-the-bride and ushers. This wasn't the case in the sixties. The groom bought a new suit and that was it.

St. David's Church
Haigh

Marriage
of
VERA MAY SANTUS
and
PETER GREGORY

July 12th, 1969
Ceremony 3.0 p.m.

Front cover of Wedding Ceremony.

St David's church Haigh.

Interior of St David's church Haigh.

Suddenly, the chattering ceased. A stillness and silence descended on the church that I found unnerving. Then, without warning, it was shattered as the sounds of the Bridal March bellowed from the organ. Everyone stood up. By now, the butterflies in my stomach were fluttering around frantically. I heard the footsteps on the flagged floor as Vera, escorted by her dad, approached. As they grew louder, I plucked up courage and slowly turned around. I couldn't believe my eyes. Never in my life had I witnessed a more lovely sight. My future wife looked absolutely stunning! Attractive, radiant, ravishing. Words could not adequately describe how beautiful she looked (Image 88). I felt like the luckiest man in the whole wide world.

The ceremony went without a hitch and the two hymns were lovely (Image 89). The only slight disappointment was that the regular vicar, Mr Southern, was unable to marry us. He was on holiday so a 'stand-in' vicar performed the ceremony. Outside the church the obligatory photographs were taken (Images 90, 91 and 92). Unfortunately, the sun had receded and the sky was leaden and overcast. It didn't reflect the mood of the wedding party. People were joyful and happy and there was a buzz of expectant conversation. I don't know about Vera but I was ecstatic.

After all the photographs had been taken, Vera and I walked through a hail of confetti to the wedding car whilst the guests boarded a bus.* Our destination was the Ridgeway Arms.** In the sixties, receptions were held at a local venue. Having weddings in remote locations and especially abroad was the province of the rich and famous. We were neither rich nor famous. A number of possible venues in and around Aspull had been considered. Good food, a suitable function room, a warm ambience and of course, an acceptable cost, were the reasons we chose the Ridgeway Arms. It was a large pub with a good sized function room and a private bowling green at the rear where photographs could be taken. And it was less than two miles away.

---

*   We'd hired a double-decker bus to transport all our guests from the church to the Ridgeway Arms

**   It is now called The Rivington

Me and Vera on our wedding day.

BRIDAL MARCH ("Lohengrin")   Wagner

ORDER OF SERVICE

HYMN   "O Father all creating."

O Father, all creating,
Whose wisdom, love and power
First bound two lives together
In Eden's primal hour.
To-day to these Thy children
Thine earliest gifts renew,—
A home by Thee made happy,
A love by Thee kept true.

O Saviour, Guest most bounteous
Of old in Galilee.
Vouchsafe to-day Thy presence
With these who call on Thee:
Their store of earthly gladness
Transform to heavenly wine,
And teach them in the tasting,
To know the gift is Thine.

O Spirit of the Father.
Breathe on them from above.
So mighty in Thy pureness,
So tender in Thy love;
That, guarded by Thy presence,
From sin and strife kept free,
Their lives may own Thy guidance.
Their hearts be ruled by Thee.

Except Thou build it, Father,
The house is built in vain;
Except Thou, Saviour, bless it,
The joy will turn to pain.
But nought can break the marriage
Of hearts in Thee made one;
And love Thy Spirit hallows
Is endless love begun.

MARRIAGE CEREMONY

PSALM 67

GOD be merciful unto us, and bless us: and shew us the
light of his countenance, and be merciful unto us:
That thy way may be known upon earth: thy saving health
among all nations

Let the people praise thee, O God, yea let all the people
praise thee.
O let the nations rejoice and be glad: for thou shalt judge
the folk righteously, and govern the nations upon earth.
Let the people praise thee, O God: let all the people praise
thee.
Then shall the earth bring forth her increase: and God,
even our own God, shall give us his blessing.
God shall bless us: and all the ends of the world shall
fear him.
Glory be to the Father, and to the Son: and to the Holy
Ghost:
As it was in the beginning, is now, and ever shall be:
world without end. Amen.

PRAYERS

HYMN   "Love divine, all loves excelling."

LOVE Divine, all loves excelling,
Joy of Heav'n to earth come down
Fix in us Thy humble dwelling,
All Thy faithful mercies crown

Jesu, Thou art all compassion.
Pure unbounded love Thou art:
Visit us with Thy salvation.
Enter every trembling heart.

Come, Almighty to deliver.
Let us all Thy grace receive:
Suddenly return, and never.
Never more Thy temples leave.

Thee we would be always blessing,
Serve Thee as Thy Hosts above:
Pray, and praise Thee, without ceasing.
Glory in Thy perfect love.

Finish then Thy new creation.
Pure and spotless let us be:
Let us see Thy great salvation
Perfectly restored in Thee.

Changed from glory into glory,
Till in Heav'n we take our place.
Till we cast our crowns before Thee.
Lost in wonder, love and praise

BLESSING

TRUMPET VOLUNTARY   Jeremiah Clarke

Order of Service of Wedding Ceremony.

Wedding photograph. Left to right: George (Vera's dad), June
(Vera's middle sister and bridesmaid), William, Lily, Louise Balfour (bridesmaid),
Me, Vera, Irene Peet (bridesmaid), Elaine (Vera's youngest sister and bridesmaid),
Doris (Vera's mother), and Jack.

Wedding photograph. Left to right: Jack, Mr Crane, Lily, Evan
(William's dad), Jack (Brian's dad), Brian, Alan (behind Brian), Bill,
Peter (Bill's youngest son), Sylvia (Alan's wife), Mrs Crane, David
(Bill's middle son), Margaret Lynch (Mr and Mrs Crane's daughter
and elder sister of Trevor), Joe Lynch (holding their son Trevor),
Mrs Meadows, my grandma and Auntie Nellie

Wedding photograph. Left to right: Jean (Brian's mother),
my mother, Jack (Brian's dad) and Margaret Fletcher,
my mother's friend.

The Wedding Breakfast was delicious. Although it's impossible to please everyone, we'd decided beforehand to choose traditional fare that should satisfy the majority of our guests. Accordingly, we had soup as a starter, a roast beef dinner as the main course, and a hot pudding for dessert. Coffee and mints concluded the meal. Judging by all the empty plates, we had chosen well. I don't remember much about the formal speeches and toasts, or cutting the cake, but the entertainer ensured that the evening was lively and huge fun with his selection of games and tricks. Everybody joined in. It was a good night. The only hiccup was the arrival of some guests that Vera and I hadn't invited. They were friends of my auntie and uncle from the Labour Club and it was they who had invited them. We were a little annoyed at their subterfuge. If they'd have informed us of their intentions, we would have gladly agreed that their friends could attend, since it was my auntie and uncle, together with Vera's parents, who'd paid for most of the wedding.

We partied with the rest of the guests until about ten-o-clock and then departed by taxi to Liverpool to catch the midnight boat to the Isle of Man. Our honeymoon in Port Erin awaited.

8.3 HONEYMOON

One large suitcase, that's all we had. One large suitcase and treasured memories of the happiest day of our lives. During the taxi ride to Liverpool we had, for the only time on our wedding day, a chance to relax and re-live the wondrous moments of a precious day. No longer were we Peter Gregory and Vera Santus, we were Mr and Mrs Gregory and a whole new life lay ahead of us. With these thoughts, we bade farewell to our taxi driver and climbed the ramp on to the midnight boat that would take us on the start of our new journey together.

Tired but happy, we should have grabbed the chance of a few hours sleep. But we didn't. Our minds were racing with the anticipation of what lay ahead. Under the starry sky, we embraced and watched in silence as the boat glided effortlessly over the silver sea.

We arrived at Douglas at about five in the morning, physically worn out but bubbling with excitement and expectation. After boarding the waiting bus, we arrived in Port Erin at six-o-clock on the Sunday morning. Our hotel was in an elevated position and I remember hauling the suitcase along a deserted promenade. As we gazed over Port Erin from the steps of the hotel, I hoped that our married life would be as calm and tranquil as Port Erin was on that Sunday morning. I knocked on the door and within a few moments it opened. We were expected.

The landlady directed us to the honeymoon suite, a grand name for a superior hotel room and, after wishing us well, closed the door. Mr and Mrs Gregory were alone for the very first time. Our exertions of the past twenty-four hours took their toll. We succumbed to tiredness and fell asleep.

The honeymoon was relaxing and enjoyable. We spent much of our time on the beach and going for walks, partly because of our depleted finances. Breakfast time was interesting. Every morning as Vera and I entered the breakfast room all the guests threw knowing glances in our direction. Embarrassing to begin with, we soon became accustomed to it. Our new life together had begun.

REFERENCES

1.   Smith, M. D., About Haigh and Aspull, Wyre Publishing, 2000, p. 38.

9

A DOUBLE DELIGHT

Disappointment! On arriving home from the honeymoon our new house wasn't quite ready. This created a problem. Where could we live? We had planned on moving straight into our new house but sadly this wasn't an option. The most sensible solution was for us to live with my mother and grandma until our own house was ready. There was ample room. It was a three-bedroom house and Vera could sleep with me in my 'old' bedroom. And she did, although it seemed strange sleeping together in the same house as my mother and grandma, even though we were married.

Not only was it the dawn of a new life together for Vera and me, on Monday I would start my new job at ICI. However, in order to squeeze the last vestige of pleasure from our 'honeymoon', we decided to take advantage of the fine spell of weekend weather and spend the Sunday at Southport. To our surprise, it was one of those rare occasions when the tide was actually in, allowing us to enjoy a refreshing paddle in the sea. Before returning home, we sat on the promenade steps and I pondered what lay ahead as the sun sank slowly below the horizon of the Irish Sea.

9.1 A NEW BEGINNING

Apprehensive, nervous, yet excited. These were the emotions coursing through my body as I drove to my new job on the Monday morning. I would be working with new colleagues on a new topic in a new laboratory. Also, having the equivalent of a good honours degree, the expectations of me would be higher.

My new job involved working on reactive dyes for cotton in Dr Ramsay's section. I was assigned two topics. One, to invent a reddish-brown dye having excellent bleach fastness for dyeing overalls and swimwear. And two, to find an economical, dull, green dye. It was ironic. These were hardly appropriate choices for someone with red-green colour blindness!

The shared office for the two laboratories of 235 and 237 accommodated eight Research Chemists. It comprised a mixture of characters and was referred to, rather unkindly in my opinion, as 'the snake pit'.

I was placed under the wing of Mr HF Andrew, one of the Senior Research Chemists. Herbert Francis, or Bert as he was known, was a Scotsman who had obtained his degree at St Andrews University and moved south for employment. He met and married a Cheshire girl and they lived in a lovely house in Hale Barns. Bert was renowned for investing in the stock market and, to be fair, was somewhat of an expert. He often gave tips and I remember buying some 'Northern Securities' shares on his recommendation. I made a modest profit. Bert would also buy stocks. When a coffee shortage seemed imminent he bought tonnes of the stuff and stored it in his loft! A few years later, he did the same with cornflakes. Neville Jackson, an experienced Experimental Chemist, worked for Bert. He was helpful and likeable and we became good friends.

Bert never tired of recounting one of his tales from his time in the army. His commanding officer, he said, was a prick. Apparently, he took great delight in humiliating men under his command, especially on the parade ground. As he strode along the line, each man had to give him their name, rank and number.

"And what's your name," he barked to Bert.

"Andrewsir," came the reply.

"Is that Andrew or Andrews?"

"Andrewsir," said Bert, deliberately slurring the two words together. Defeated, the officer moved on.

Dr CV Stead was another Senior Research Chemist. His forenames were Cecil Vivian but he preferred Viv and everyone knew him by that name. A Mancunian and avid Manchester City supporter, he was a gentle giant. At 6 foot 5 inches tall, he could literally stand with one foot resting in the four foot tall fume cupboard. He was an affable, easy going person who was liked by all who knew him. Viv was the archetypal inventor of big ideas, such as the PROCION H-E (High Exhaust) dyes. These dyes possessed excellent fixation for cotton, thereby minimising both cost and pollution. Whilst chemists like Viv produced the big ideas, it was chemists like Bert who invented the individual dyes. This was teamwork.

Dr G Griffiths was a portly and rather serious individual who nonetheless had an infectious chuckle. Geoff was a principled character who displayed tremendous loyalty to his friends and colleagues. Indeed, he once threatened to throw Bert through the window for speaking badly of Cyril Morris! He was a meticulous worker who was good at developing an idea. One of his major contributions was refining the synthesis of twice-coupled H-acid dyes, a development that was to prove useful in my work on dull greens.

Denis Harvey and his friend Denis Eckersley were other senior members of the office. Edwin Denis Harvey worked his way up from a junior Laboratory Assistant to a Senior Research Chemist and was used as a shining example by management that such a feat was possible. When he retired, he formed a cleaning company named, rather cleverly, DRV, after his name, D Harvey. A Boltonian, Denis Eckersley was an expert on anthraquinone dyes. Both were articulate men.

Richard Budziarek, Denis Ridyard and me made up the office complement. Richard was a Pole who escaped from the iron curtain by swimming across the River Danube to freedom. His neck was injured in the daring escape and he could never really turn his head properly. Richard was a smoothie, a bit of a ladies man but likeable nonetheless. He was the academic chemist of the section and published the mechanism of a chemical reaction that was affectionately known as the 'Budziarek Shuffle'.

Apart from myself, Denis Ridyard was the youngest chemist in the office. Like me, he had progressed by obtaining the GRIC qualification. About ten years older than me, Denis was a strong-willed individual who was quite ambitious. He was also an excellent fast bowler, as many batsmen found to their cost during the inter-departmental cricket competition (Chapter 11). His prowess was such that Northamptonshire offered him terms to turn professional. He declined, preferring a career in chemistry. As a newcomer, I remember asking Denis what was expected of us. "Not bloody miracles," he growled.

These then were my new colleagues and on Monday, 21 July 1969, my first day back at work after our honeymoon, the sole topic of conversation was the historic moon landing by the Apollo 11 astronauts the previous day. Who can ever forget the momentous pictures as Neil Armstrong took his final step from the spacecraft on to the moon with his now immortal phrase, "It's a small step for a man but a giant leap for mankind." I was so proud. As mentioned in Chapter 2, I have always been fascinated with space and I just wished it could have been me stepping on to the moon. If I could be granted one wish it would be to travel in space and see the magnificent sight of the stars and especially the Earth from such a vantage point. It would be truly amazing.

Over all of us was our Section Leader, Dr DW Ramsay. He was chosen to replace Cyril Morris after his nervous breakdown. Ron Davis, the Associate Research Manager, decided he didn't want another Section Leader to suffer a nervous breakdown so he appointed someone who was the exact opposite of Cyril. He did this to perfection. There was no way this calm, composed, imperturbable individual would ever suffer a nervous breakdown. His appointment personified the mantra of 'being in the right place at the right time'. To some, Dr Ramsay's placid, laid back nature labelled him as lazy. This was unfair. Yes, he was laid back in the extreme, but he was also clever and shrewd. Indeed, he had done some pioneering work on radar during World War II.

Weekly section meetings were a feature of life in Dr Ramsay's section. The twelve or so research chemists would assemble in his office and one of them would give a presentation of their work. This enabled the other chemists to contribute ideas and for Dr Ramsay to keep abreast of the ongoing work in his section. Without fail and at every meeting Dr Ramsay would be fast asleep within ten minutes. (I think he suffered from a form of narcolepsy.) Occasionally, rather than proceeding with the chemistry, topics such as football, films and TV were discussed. After about one hour, the presentation would revert back to chemistry and someone would bang loudly on the table. Dr Ramsay always awoke with a start but had the exceptional knack of being able to ask a meaningful question or make a useful suggestion. It was weird.

Another topic of conversation was the origin of the large bulge in his trousers. And I mean large. Very few men believed (or wanted to believe) that it was natural. (I don't know what the women thought.) The general consensus, although it was never proved, was that he suffered from a hernia and that a truss was the culprit.

Within six months Denis Harvey and Denis Eckersley moved out of the office and were replaced by Ray Windle and a new recruit, Dr Dave Waring. A Yorkshireman, Dave was a similar age to me and we immediately became good friends. We worked together on the reddish-brown target and within a year had invented one. It was developed and added to the commercial range as PROCION* Brown H-5R.

It was during this work that a valuable lesson was learned. We had invented a dye that wasn't destroyed by bleach, yet most dyes were completely decolourised by it. Why? I had an inquisitive mind and wanted to know. If the reason was known, this would facilitate the design of other bleach resistant dyes such as yellows, reds and blues. Accordingly, Dave, and especially Viv and I, did some fundamental research on the mechanism of the destruction of azo dyes by bleach, eventually publishing our findings in the academic literature.[1] My enquiring mind of wanting to know why certain events happened would prove useful in advancing my career.

A Research Chemist's main role was to invent novel dyes that overcame the deficiencies of existing commercial dyes. This entailed devising a completely new arrangement of atoms to form a completely new molecule which may or may not achieve the desired objective. It was amazing how an abstract idea in your brain could eventually be converted into concrete reality in the laboratory. Every time such a dye was made, you were, for the very first time, creating something totally new in the universe. Something that, until that instant, had never existed before! A brand new molecule. A brand new chemical. Something that nature, in the 13.7

---

* PROCION was ICI's tradename for the revolutionary reactive dyes invented by Rattee and Stephen at Blackley in 1954. Until then, cotton was dyed with direct dyes and vat dyes in order to impart a reasonable level of wash fastness. Unfortunately, these dyes were dull. A 'reactive group' could be attached to any class of dyes, including very bright ones, and they all exhibited excellent wash fastness. So, for the very first time, cotton garments were available in bright colours that wouldn't run or stain. Procyon is one of the brightest stars in the sky and ICI named their new range of reactive dyes after this star.

billion year history of the universe, had been unable to accomplish. It always left me with a feeling of wonder and awe. The icing on the cake was when one of your dyes satisfied a real target. Such a dye would be manufactured in quantities of tens, hundreds or occasionally thousands of tonnes per annum and used to colour garments around the world. Being the inventor of such a dye gave me an enormous buzz.

As well as the brown target described earlier, the dull green target was also met. Building on the splendid work of Geoff Griffiths on twice-coupled H-acid dyes, I managed to discover PROCION Green H-E4BD, a very economical bottle-green dye for cotton. This dye sold well but nothing like as well as its isomeric 'brother', PROCION Navy H-ER. This dye became one of the top selling dyes in the world. Partly because of these successes, and partly because I had been made an Associate Member of the Royal Institute of Chemistry (Image 93), I gained the magical promotion to Haslam Grade 11, crossing the great divide from green book to blue book without a PhD (Chapter 7).

After the successful research on browns, greens and navies I was assigned to work with Bert Andrew on a controversial topic, Darian Dyes. These were low cost reactive dyes that were aimed at replacing Direct Dyes. The idea was to confer the excellent wash fastness and brightness of the newly invented reactive dyes to the old and dated Direct Dyes, which had very poor wash fastness. The project had its critics, particularly Dr Booth. He argued, correctly as it turned out, that (i) Darian Dyes couldn't be as cheap as Direct Dyes because of the extra cost of adding the reactive group and (ii) that for most of their applications, such as colouring paper, Direct Dyes didn't need to have high wash fastness. For example, gift wrapping paper and toilet paper are used once and discarded. Unlike textile garments, they do not have to withstand the rigours of the washing machine. (However, dyes for toilet paper need to have good rub fastness!) At the start of the project Bert said that if we succeeded they would sing our praises from the rooftops but if we failed our names would be mud. After eighteen months, our names were mud. The project was abandoned and, in 1974, I was transferred to the Miscellaneous Dyes Section. Sadly, by this time, my friend Dave had left ICI to take up an appointment at Kodak in Liverpool.

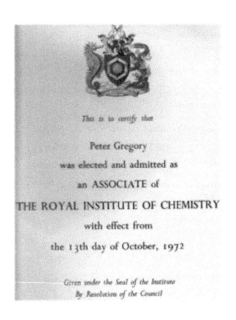

Associate Membership of the Royal Institute of Chemistry.

Dr Neville Corby, an Oxbridge man, was the Section Leader of the Miscellaneous Dyes Section. My role was to invent novel brown and yellow cationic dyes for polyacrylonitrile, probably more familiar under its tradenames of Dralon, Orlon and Courtelle. These SYNACRIL dyes could be difficult to make and one of my colleagues, Dr Dave Fawkes, said that the reactions were either 'pigs' or 'bastards'. In due course I invented SYNACRIL Yellow 2R whilst another colleague, Dr Brian Parton, invented SYNACRIL Yellow 8G.

Dr Corby was an 'old school' type manager who wanted things done by the book. Articulate and a good communicator, he was a stickler for protocols. Sometimes, he went too far. One morning he was pontificating to a group of chemists having their coffee break when Cyril Morris, as placid a man as I have known, could contain his frustration no longer. He stood up, shouted, "BALLS" and stormed off.

Visibly shaken by this outburst, Dr Corby went after him and said, curtly, "Cyril. My office. NOW!" He wasn't used to having his authority undermined.

9.2 A CALL TO SERVICE

It was at this time that I was summoned to do jury service. It wasn't something that I particularly fancied but, since I had to do it, I might as well enjoy it.

It was both an interesting yet strange experience participating in the wheels of justice. Interesting in watching the deliberate and painstakingly thorough machinations of the courtroom yet strange in some of the rituals. For instance, before a case commences the potential jurors are summoned to the courtroom to face the accused and his barrister. After looking each juror up and down they have the right to dismiss any they don't, for whatever reason, want on their jury. It felt like we were the ones on trial, not the accused.

Over my two week period I was a juror on two cases. The first case involved robbery from a school. The evidence against the accused was overwhelming. His fingerprints were everywhere, he had left his wallet behind with his name in it and, most incriminating of all, he had been caught red-handed leaving the scene by the police. I was astounded when it was announced that this man would be representing himself. My first thoughts were how clever and articulate he must be but I quickly realised the truth. He could hardly string two words together, let alone a simple sentence. Obviously his counsel had told him, in light of all the evidence against him, to plead guilty and, since he had declined, had refused to represent him.

What amazed me was that such a clear cut case took a full three days to reach a verdict! To its credit our justice system assumes nothing and conducts each case with extreme thoroughness. Not surprisingly, he was found guilty and it was only after the verdict had been pronounced that a string of previous offences was made public.

I can't recall the details of the second case but it involved someone getting drunk on Southern Comfort and committing an offence. This case wasn't as clear cut as the first one but a guilty verdict was delivered. On leaving the courtroom the guilty man's partner was waiting at the door and if looks could kill, all the jurors would have dropped dead on the spot.

9.3 AGREEMENT TIME

All the time that I was conducting my main targeted research, I also continued to use the allowed 10 per cent of my time to continue the fundamental studies. After the bleach fastness work discussed earlier, my focus was on the relationship between the colour and strength of dye molecules and their chemical constitution.

Azo dyes are the most important class of dye, comprising approximately 60 per cent of the world's annual dye consumption of approximately one million tonnes. Many azo dyes can exist in two forms, the azo form and the hydrazone form. These exhibit completely different properties. They have different colours, show different resistance to fading in light and to being decolourised by bleach, and have different colour strengths. All these are important features, particularly the last one. Since the azo and hydrazone forms are made in exactly the same way from the same intermediates, it is extremely cost effective to utilise the significantly higher colour strength (up to 40 per cent more) of the hydrazone form wherever possible. My studies addressed all these basic properties.

As well as presenting my work to leading academics, such as Professor Hazeldine, I was also asked to give a lecture to all the managers and chemists in the Research Department. This I duly did. It must have been fairly impressive because the Research Manager, Dr Frank Hall, who missed the lecture, was told that he had to hear it. Accordingly, I had to repeat the lecture at our Grangemouth Works site in Scotland at one of our Liaison Meetings. He must have been impressed too because a few months later I was promoted to Haslam Grade 12 and awarded the coveted ICI 'Agreement' which meant a whopping 15 per cent cash bonus paid every year (Image 94).

My studies on colour and constitution were largely empirical and qualitative.[*] Nonetheless, they were successful. Derek Thorp and I discovered several important and hitherto unexplained facts pertaining to azo dyes, particularly disperse type azo dyes, and our findings were published in the respected Journal of the Chemical Society.[2]

When Mike Hutchings joined the group in the early 1980s he brought a new dimension to the work. Mike was skilled in computational chemistry and was able to apply this technique to azo (and other) dyes. Thus, for the very first time, we were able to calculate, with a fair degree of accuracy, both the colour and tinctorial strength of a dye simply by knowing its molecular structure. This had important ramifications.

For instance, it was possible to write down dozens of hypothetical dye structures and, rather than having to devote weeks or even months of valuable time and effort synthesising the dyes in the laboratory, their colour and strength could be calculated in seconds on the computer. The work was widely acclaimed and Mike and me were invited to give a number of presentations around ICI, including one to a Main Road Director, Dr Charles Reece.

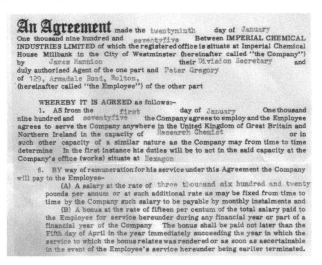

Part of the ICI 'Agreement'.

---

[*]   They were explained in terms of the Valence Bond theory

159

I remained in the Miscellaneous Dyes section until 1979, during which time some of my work on cationic dyes was published in the academic literature.[3]

9.4 A NEW HOME

In the August of 1969, just a few weeks after our honeymoon, our new house was completed and we were able to move in. Being handed the keys and opening the door of our very own house gave both me and Vera an immense thrill and sense of pride. A lovely lounge was separated from the dining room by wooden sliding doors and another door connected the dining room to the kitchen. Classy wooden panelling adorned the chimney breast. All the doors were made from 'sapele' wood. A beautiful open tread mahogany staircase graced the hall. Upstairs comprised three bedrooms, two decent sized ones and a small boxroom, plus a bathroom. It was a fine house for first-time buyers.

It was sparsely furnished. We had managed to buy carpets for the hall, stairs and landing, and for the lounge and dining room, from a local mill, negotiating a discount in the process. The rest remained as bare floorboards. The only furniture we could afford was a three-piece suite for the lounge, and a dining table and chairs. On our bus journeys from Wigan to Aspull we had seen a kingfisher coloured suite in Waring and Gillow and duly purchased it. The dining table and chairs, made by Beautility, were bought from Penningtons. A TV and bed made up the rest of our furniture.

With two wages and no children to support we gradually furnished our house. The first time we could afford a washing machine we spent the entire evening watching the clothes as they swished to and fro. It was better than watching telly. Bit by bit, items were bought until the house was fully furnished.

As well as furnishing the house we also decorated it. This was our first attempt at decorating and there were some hilarious moments. We began with the dining room. On the main wall we hung *Lincrusta*. *Lincrusta* was an expensive, thick, wall covering that was applied using special glue. Once in place, it was the devil's own job to remove. We painted it turquoise to match the carpet. The remaining three walls were papered with *Anaglypta*. The paper was duly pasted and hung. Pleased with our achievement of papering a room for the first time, we stood and admired our handiwork. But something wasn't quite right. It was difficult to pinpoint but something was wrong. It wasn't the pattern. That had been matched correctly. And it wasn't the *Lincrusta*. That was fine. Suddenly, it dawned on me. We had put the *Anaglypta* on back to front! It had to be stripped off, new wallpaper purchased and the room redecorated. It's a lesson I have never forgotten. I was glad it wasn't the Lincrusta that we put on the wrong way around.

As mentioned earlier we had bought a kingfisher coloured suite for the lounge and it was complemented by a patterned turquoise carpet and kingfisher curtains. We papered the lounge walls with Vymura. Off-white with vertical silvery stripes and a silken sheen, it was exquisite wallpaper. Not quite white or beige, as the 'House Doctor' would stipulate, but close enough to have gained her approval.

Our plan was for Vera to continue working for two years until we got the house fully furnished, but it took four years. It was a struggle. Just before we moved into the house the car needed replacing. Our beloved 'Uffy' was clapped out and we bought a red, second-hand Ford Escort from Fred Grimes in Wigan. To house the car, a concrete Banbury garage was purchased. That winter, we were literally penniless. We had over-stretched ourselves. It was so bad that when the fan belt broke we couldn't even afford the £1.50 to buy a new one. The money had to be borrowed. What made matters worse was the length of time to the next pay day. The December salary was paid a week early, on the eighteenth, so it meant a full six weeks until the next salary on the 25 January. It was a long wait over the most expensive period of the year. That year, the wait seemed forever.

9.5 A CHANGE FOR VERA

After we were married Vera changed her job. She moved from the Hawker-Siddeley corporation in Lostock to ICI in Blackley. Not only was the pay better, it meant we could travel to work together, reducing travelling costs. To reduce the costs even further, we formed a car club with Roy Glover and Derek Watkinson who both lived in Westhoughton. Our meeting point was the Mercury Motel. Here, we left two cars and travelled in the third. It was a good arrangement. In addition to the cost benefits, there was far less driving for each individual. It worked well except on one occasion when Roy and Derek were extremely late and we had to go without them.

Vera excelled at work. She started on the lowest grade (D) for clerical staff but, within two years, rocketed to the top grade (A), gaining three promotions in the process (Fig 2, Chapter 7). She was highly regarded by her supervisor, Mrs Byrne, and her ultimate boss, Mrs Margaret Smith. She was flexible and multi-tasked, working on the teleprinters as well as typing (Image 95). On Friday lunchtimes we bought fish and chips from the village chippy and, if it was sunny, ate them in the local churchyard.

Vera (centre left) at work in the
teleprinter room at ICI (circa 1973).

During her time at ICI Vera became friends with Christine, a local girl from Blackley, and Vivian. In Vivian, Vera had a friend she both trusted and confided in. They were like two peas in a pod. Most lunchtimes they went to the Black Cat café in the village. Sometimes, Vera went with Christine to her mother's house in nearby Chapel Road. Vera and I enjoyed some good times with Vivian and her husband Jan Fielden, who also worked at ICI, usually at each others houses.

The staff at ICI enjoyed a good social life. Out of work events were arranged on a regular basis. Two of the best ones were the Research Dances referred to in Chapter 7 and the Christmas Party. Each laboratory organised their own party and held it at a convenient venue. Wives and girlfriends were always invited. One year it was held at Smithills Coaching House in Bolton.

"Hey Steve, there's a tie in your soup!" Already the worse for wear, Steve Nebesniak, Dave Waring's Experimental Chemist, ate his soup completely oblivious to the fact that his tie hung in it all the time. After the meal, they all came to our new house in West Bolton (see later) for more drinks and chit-chat.

The following year the Christmas Party was held in a lovely restaurant in Cheshire. Having a small dance floor and an accomplished band, it was more refined than Smithills. After enjoying a sumptuous meal and some relaxed dancing, we retired to Bert's house in Hale Barns to have a nightcap. Everyone got on really well together. For me, these were the halcyon days at ICI.

9.6 A TRIO OF CHANGES

After we'd had our Ford Escort for a few years things started to go wrong. It needed to be changed. At the time Neville was selling his car. It was a lovely white Wolseley 1800 that was in very good condition. Both Vera and I liked it and we informed Neville that we would buy it. First, however, we had to sell our own car. It was advertised in the local newspaper but didn't sell. Indeed, on the Saturday that we were due to buy Neville's car, we still hadn't sold our own! In desperation, we got up very early and started taking it to a list of garages that bought cars for cash. Disaster struck. It broke down in Hindley and we had to call out Norman Johnson, a neighbour who serviced our car. Eventually, we managed to sell it to the Russ Rigby garage on the outskirts of Leigh, but for less than we expected. Relieved, we went for lunch to the UCP (United Cattle Products) restaurant in Wigan to celebrate.

In addition to servicing cars, Norman Johnson had another hobby. He bred Heelers. These black-and-tan dogs, similar in size and shape to a Corgi, were lovely. Boisterous and energetic, they were a bundle of fun. I had always wanted a dog but never been allowed to have one, whilst Vera's family had always had a dog. Norman's Heelers had just produced a litter of the most beautiful puppies and they were for sale at £5 each. We were sorely tempted. However, both Vera and I worked full-time and we felt it would be unfair on the dog to be left alone for long periods in the week. But help was at hand. Both our families, seeing how much we wanted a dog, said they would come to the house every weekday and take it for a walk. With this promise, we chose our little puppy. He was absolutely gorgeous. We named him Shandy to reflect his black-and-tan colouring (Image 96).

Both Vera and me liked our house at 18 Willowcroft Avenue very much but not the location. It felt like we were impostors, intruding on the locals who had lived their entire lives in the area. Also, we had bad neighbours. Therefore, we made the decision to look for a house nearer to our work in North Manchester, a bigger, detached house since we deemed it time to start a family.

On our trips to Bolton we had always admired the scenery of West Bolton, particularly the Lostock area. My mother used to work at the cotton mill in Lostock and during the summer holidays I would visit her at lunchtime. We went for walks along the stream beside the railway line and watched the water cascading down the steps from Rumworth Lake, and it was directly opposite this lake that a new estate of houses was being built.

Shandy, our black-and-tan heeler, digging a
hole on the beach at Birkdale (circa 1973).

Phase 2 was nearing completion and the plans for Phase 3 had been drawn up and submitted to the council for approval. In Phase 2, four houses occupied prime locations. Situated at the edge of the estate they overlooked Rumworth Lake. Surrounded by open pastures populated by grazing sheep and cows, and with Rivington Pike and Winter Hill as the backdrop, it was a view reminiscent of the Lake District. Furthermore, each house was built on a double-sized plot. Because of these attributes, the houses cost an extra 10 per cent more than comparable houses elsewhere on the estate. Despite the extra cost, potential buyers actually camped out overnight in order to secure the purchase of these four houses! In Phase 3, just one house occupied a double-sized plot and enjoyed the panoramic views over Rumworth Lake. Plot 1 on Armadale Road. This was the house we wanted. We made this perfectly plain to Alan Firth, the estate agent handling the sale of the houses. Every Saturday morning, without fail, Vera and I went to the estate agents office to check on the progress of Phase 3. We were determined not to miss the opportunity to acquire such a unique house, but so were hundreds of other people.

After about twelve months, the release date was announced. It was Sod's Law! I would be away on company business on the Monday morning that the houses were being released for sale. There was no way that I could be there to camp out overnight. Another strategy was required. Thankfully, because we had gone to the estate agents diligently for the past twelve months, and because they had known from the very outset that we wanted the house on Plot 1, Alan Firth kindly agreed to let us have it.

Both Vera and I breathed a huge sigh of relief. What he told the person at the head of the queue on the Monday morning I don't know.

Thus far, the price hadn't been fixed but Alan Firth informed us that it would be in the region of £10,500. This was at the top end of our budget but manageable. I had gone with Neville to his house in Shaw on the Monday lunchtime that the prices were being released. Excitedly, I rang them to discover the news. Neville remarked that I went white as a sheet and almost dropped the phone as I was told the price. It was £12,350! This was almost £2,000 more than we had bargained for. And that wasn't all. Because it was a premium house in a prime location with a double plot, there would be an additional 10 per cent surcharge. There was no way we could afford a house costing £13,500. I was devastated. I rang Vera with the news and returned dejectedly to work.

Our own house had been valued at £7,950, representing a handsome profit on our investment of £3,100 (including the central heating) in just four years. It was sold in the first week to a local couple for £7,750. After the outstanding mortgage of £2,758 had been deducted, plus the estate agents fees, solicitors fees and other expenses, we were left with ca £4,250. Even if we put all this amount as deposit, the balance of approximately £9,250 was still just over three times my salary. It seemed mission impossible. Out of the blue we received some good news. Alan Firth had negotiated with the builders and somehow got them to waive the extra 10 per cent surcharge. He argued that we had been committed to the house for eighteen months and that it was near a small substation. Surprisingly, the builders agreed. Everything was back on track.

A lovely lady called Miss White of Ackerley, Heaton and Pigot solicitors of Bank Chambers, Wigan, handled the transaction. The Woolwich Building Society agreed to loan us £8,250, meaning that we had to put down a deposit of £4,100. We responded in the affirmative and in July 1973, we moved into our new home (Images 97 and 98).*

Our home at 129 Armadale Road 1995. The double garage
was an original feature but the porch, conservatory, utility room
(not visible) and decorative walls were added later.

---

*   In 2015 we had an extension to make the kitchen much bigger, added a new utility room and converted the old utility room into a downstairs shower room (Chapter 28)

View from our home over Rumworth Lake (circa 1975).

9.7 THE STORK COMETH

The saying of new house, new baby, proved very prophetic. Within two months of moving into 129 Armadale Road, Vera became pregnant. We were thrilled to bits. Everyone was. However, the pregnancy did not go smoothly. In the latter stages Vera developed high blood pressure. Four weeks before the birth was due, it became so bad that Dr Frank Ratcliffe, our GP, insisted that she go into hospital. She did. It was a difficult time for both of us. Vera didn't like being away from home and inactive, confined to a hospital bed, whilst I found it a strain to continue working full-time and visit Vera every evening and weekends, in addition to fending for myself. Fortunately, we had good neighbours. Sheila and Don insisted that I went to their house for tea and our relatives were also very supportive. In the end, it didn't work out too bad.

Vera was on medication for her blood pressure and the baby had to be induced with a drip of oxy-tocin. For these reasons I wasn't encouraged to be present at the birth so I paced nervously around the hospital grounds. Eventually, I was summoned by the nurse. Vera had given birth to a beautiful baby boy. He looked so tiny and fragile. Andrew Ian, as we named him, was born at 4-50 p.m. on Thursday 11 April 1974. He weighed 7 pound 6 ounces and was 21 inches long (Chapter 10). It was one of the proudest moments of my life.

After ensuring that both mother and baby were fine, I dashed home to tell everyone the good news. On learning that it was a healthy baby boy, my grandma did a little jig of joy and Vera's parents had tears in their eyes. All and sundry were pleased. I was over the moon. To Vera and me it was irrelevant whether we had a boy or a girl. All we wanted was for the baby to be fine and healthy. And it was.

It wasn't all plain sailing. Our beautiful baby cried a lot, was reluctant to feed and was 'twitchy'. A blood test revealed that he suffered from 'hypocalcaemia', i.e. a calcium deficiency. This necessitated a further stay in hospital of one week whilst the problem was resolved. Eventually, mother and baby were allowed home. I already had a wonderful wife. Now, she was complemented by a lovely new house and a bouncing baby boy. Who could ask for more. It was a double delight.

REFERENCES

1. P Gregory and CV Stead, 'The Degradation of Water-Soluble Azo Compounds by Dilute Sodium Hypochlorite Solution', Journal of the Society of Dyers and Colourists, September 1978, pp 402 – 407.
2. P Gregory and D Thorp, 'The Electronic Absorption Spectra of 2-Substituted-4-NN-diethylamino-4'-nitroazobenzene Dyes and Their Monoacid Cations: The Applicability of Dewar's Rules to These and Related Dyestuffs', Journal of the Chemical Society, Perkin Transactions I, 1990, 1979.
3. D Brierley, P Gregory and B Parton, 'Cationic Azo Triazolium Dyes: Elucidation of the Structure of the Two Isomeric Components of C. I. Basic Red 22', Journal of Chemical Research (S), 174, 1980.

10

A BUNDLE OF JOY

A baby changes your life. Dramatically! This tiny addition to your family requires constant attention, morning, noon and night. Your whole life revolves around them. No matter how much planning is done beforehand, when a baby arrives the change in lifestyle comes as an almighty shock. In addition to all the time and effort devoted to the new baby, your finances take a massive hit. From the comfort of having two salaries to maintain two people, suddenly, you have just one salary to maintain three people! It's a double whammy.

Vera made the decision, which I fully endorsed, of becoming a full-time mum. From now on she wished to devote her life to looking after her family, a most noble and, in my opinion, a correct course of action. Babies and children, and not just young children, grow up better in a stable family where the mother remains at home. It was a courageous decision because she undoubtedly had a promising career ahead of her if she so wished. But she forfeited all that for the good of her family. I have no doubt whatsoever that her unselfish decision benefited not only our children, but me also. I could not have progressed in my career without her help and support.

It's unfortunate but your first baby is a 'guinea pig'. You learn with it. And you make mistakes. Bombarded with well-meaning advice from doctors, nurses and midwives it is difficult to follow your own instincts when the baby is so tiny and fragile. But follow them you should. If they cry, pick them up and comfort them. If they're hungry, feed them. Don't wait for the prescribed feeding times. And, most importantly of all, give them lots of love and attention. As a baby Andrew wanted feeding little but often. He was unable to or didn't want a large feed in one go but preferred smaller feeds more often. Despite advice to the contrary from the health visitor, this is what we did. And he flourished (Image 99). But, like most babies, he had his share of mishaps and illnesses.

Colic is a scourge of babies and Andrew didn't escape its clutches. He suffered from it terribly and it made him cry a lot. We spent countless hours, both day and night, pacing up and down the lounge with Andrew draped over our shoulder to relieve the symptoms. Many times I arrived at work tired and bleary eyed. However, it was worth all the effort. It is impossible to put into words the untold joy that a baby brings. I remember the first word he uttered. Dada. It brought tears to my eyes. And the time he took his first, faltering steps. They were beautiful moments that I will cherish forever.

Andrew aged about six months.

But there were mishaps too. Serious mishaps. One, which has left a deep scar on my memory and which I still have nightmares about, happened when he was about twelve months old. A few months earlier, I had replaced the solid balustrade around the landing with some ranch-style pine wood. One Saturday morning I was knelt on the landing doing some work on a bedroom door when Andrew toddled out from the bathroom. Having been bathed and dressed by Vera, he was radiant in his sky blue babygrow. "Dada," he shouted, and toddled towards me as fast as his little legs could carry him. As toddlers do, he plonked down beside me and leant back. But there was nothing to lean on! He fell through the bottom gap of the ranch-style fencing, landing on the stairs some eight feet below with a sickening thud. Then, he tumbled down the few remaining stairs making a terrifying 'thud-thud-thud' noise, finishing up on the hall floor. I was horrified. Vera heard the commotion and beat me to the bottom of the stairs. Gently, she picked him up. He was crying his eyes out. There didn't appear to be any blood and he didn't seem to be hurt but we couldn't take any chances. We dashed to the Accident and Emergency unit of the Royal Bolton Hospital to have him checked thoroughly, including a brain scan. To our immense relief he was fine. Everything was in order. Two things helped. First, babies of that age are a bit like rubber. They 'bounce'. Second, the carpet on the stairs was thick and almost certainly cushioned the impact of his fall. But the incident signalled the end of our ranch-style decor. Almost immediately, we had it replaced with a mahogany banister and spindles so that such an event could never happen again.

Although we didn't realise it initially, Andrew was born with a congenital hernia. As time progressed it got worse. When he was about fifteen months old our doctor advised that he should have an operation. Our first thoughts were that he was too young and tiny to have an operation and be confined to hospital but the hernia was quite bad and would only get worse so, somewhat reluctantly, we agreed. Although the operation proceeded smoothly, it was a distressing time. The smile on his face as he greeted us in his cot at visiting time was a joy to behold. It warmed our hearts. In contrast, the end of visiting time was heart-wrenching. He wailed and wailed and beseeched us not to leave him, his little outstretched arms begging us to return. I think we cried as much as he did. Thankfully, he was only in hospital for about a week.

Gradually, a routine developed. His feeding habits improved and he responded well to 'potty training'. Vera took him to playschool in Junction Road West, Lostock, where he formed a strong bond with one of the teachers, Mrs Curley. He was so fond of her that he couldn't wait to go to playschool. It reminded me very much of myself and Mrs Dickson many years earlier (Chapter 1). At home, both Vera and I lavished lots of love and attention on Andrew, not only playing with him but also encouraging him to read. Indeed, we made a scrapbook entitled *My Family* with pictures of family members and their names.

10.1 A BAD NIGHT IN BLACKPOOL

It was a busy time. Not only had Andrew been born my cousin Brian's wedding to Valerie was just a few months away. Brian had decided to hold his stag night in Blackpool, somewhat adventurous in those days. It was on a Friday evening, eight days before his wedding. The plan was to meet at Aspull Labour Club where a coach would transport us to Blackpool. I remember chatting to William, whose wife Jean had just had their first baby, saying that all they seemed to do was eat, sleep, poo and cry. A tad unfair perhaps, but not too far from the truth, especially to two new dads.

Once in Blackpool, it was the usual stuff of pub crawling and drinking. Lots of beer puts a tremendous strain on the bladder and whilst walking to the next pub I could wait no longer. My bladder was at bursting point, aching to release the pressure exerted by untold pints of beer. I had to relieve myself. After dashing down the steps to the beach, the pressure was released. The never-ending stream seemed to go on forever and the sense of relief was overwhelming. Free of my unwanted burden, I ascended the steps to rejoin my friends. There was no one there! They had gone. I felt betrayed. We were barely halfway through the long evening and Brian, William and Arthur Groves had left me all alone in Blackpool. Disappointed and angry, I spent the next three hours wandering the pubs of Blackpool. The saying that you can be completely alone in a crowded bar is most definitely true. I spent a miserable four hours all alone in an unfamiliar town until it was time to board the coach for the return journey home. I was so angry and upset I told Brian that I wouldn't be attending his wedding the following Saturday.

Various people tried to change my view. Although what had happened was unforgivable, a wedding was a once-in-a-lifetime occasion that shouldn't be missed. However, I dug my heels in and wouldn't change my mind.* Vera, loyal as ever, stood by my decision although I think she thought I should have relented and that we should have attended his wedding. We didn't and it is one of the biggest regrets of my life. With hindsight I realise how many people I upset and let down, most notably Brian, Valerie and their families. It was a selfish act for which I am truly sorry.

10.2 A SUMMER SIZZLER

The summer of 1976, when Andrew was two-years-old, was a scorcher, one of the hottest and driest since records began. Initially, it was great. Waking every day to a clear blue sky without the slightest wisp of cloud was paradise itself. However, after several weeks it became unbearable and people were praying for rain. A hosepipe ban was quickly imposed and, after more than six weeks without a single drop of rain, Denis Howell, the environment minister, made his famous proclamation to 'let the plants die'. The drought became so severe that watering the garden by any means was strictly forbidden. Indeed, many activities involving the use of water were either banned or restricted. Cars couldn't be cleaned, windows weren't allowed to be washed and people were urged to be conservative in their use of baths and toilet flushes. *If it's yellow let it mellow. If it's brown flush it down* was the mantra of the day. Anyone found breaking the ban was promptly informed on by neighbours. The whole episode had an eerie feel to it. Like most other people we lost many of our plants.

I took advantage of the good weather to build a porch on the front of the house and to get the garden in order. Digging the foundations in the scorched, dry earth wasn't easy but at least they didn't fill up with water. Vera and I designed the porch ourselves. Built in stone, it wasn't a straightforward building job. However, by taking my time and with help from Neville with the roof, it was completed successfully (Image 97, page 165). It must have been impressive because a neighbour asked me to build one for them! In the event, it didn't materialise. I think the cost put them off. I also landscaped the garden, including building walls and laying flags (Image 100).

---

* Stubbornness is one of my faults

As well as helping to build the porch, Neville also introduced us to the delights of caravanning. He and his wife Phyllis had bought a Cavalier touring caravan and they had kindly agreed to let us use it. It was a kind and timely gesture since money was tight, and we took up their offer when Vera was pregnant with Andrew. One balmy autumn evening Neville placed it on a quiet, secluded site at Great Eccleston, near Blackpool, where Vera and I enjoyed a really relaxing week's holiday. On our travels we crossed a beautiful stone bridge over a river, a bridge that, despite our best efforts, we have been unable to find since that holiday.

Me landscaping the back garden 1976.

When Andrew was just a few months old Neville offered us the use of his caravan in the Lake District, one of our favourite places. The plan was simple. Neville and Phyllis would call at our house on the Friday evening and we would follow them to the caravan site in our car. But it didn't work out like that. That same Friday my white Wolseley was being repaired by Jim Routledge in Blackley. It was having the power steering converted to normal steering. Unfortunately, the work took longer than anticipated and the car wasn't ready for me to collect at the agreed time after work. Jim said the best he could do was to deliver the car to my home later that evening.

After arranging a lift home, I phoned Neville and told him to proceed without us and that we would meet up with them at the Limefitt Park caravan site later that evening.

It was 10-30 p.m. when Jim delivered the car and it was already going dark. We set off immediately, arriving at Limefitt Park at around midnight. Located on the side of a mountain in the middle of nowhere, the park was pitch black. Being summer, there were hundreds of caravans. Finding Neville's was like finding a needle in a haystack! (There were no mobile phones in those days.) After riding around for about half-an-hour, we eventually found his caravan. It was a huge relief. Andrew was hungry and needed feeding and we were tired. It had been a long day.

More drama followed. Neville was unimpressed with the facilities at the park, especially for a family with a young baby. He wouldn't allow us to stay and so, on the Saturday morning, we upped sticks and relocated to the nearby White Cross Bay caravan park on the shores of Lake Windermere. Before they returned home, we treated Neville and Phyllis to a meal in Windermere, a meal we all enjoyed. Then, we had time to relax and savour our first holiday as a young family.

Later that same year Eddie Slater, a neighbour, loaned us his caravan at Arnside. We were hooked. Caravanning was great, especially for families like ourselves with young children. Indeed, holidaying in caravans had made such an impression on us that sometime later we would buy our own caravan (Chapter 18). Before then, however, we had other holidays to look forward to.

10.4 HOLIDAY TIME

Our next holiday with Andrew was spent in Tenby in 1976. David Fawkes, a colleague at work, had recommended Tenby after spending a week's holiday there the previous year. Accompanied by Auntie Lily and Uncle Jack, we stayed in the same hotel and, helped by the beautiful weather, had a marvellous time.

However, as always, there was the odd hiccup. One evening at dinner Andrew cried his heart out and, despite our best efforts, we couldn't console him. To be fair to the other guests, I took him to our bedroom leaving Vera, Lily and Jack to enjoy the three course dinner. I didn't miss out completely. They brought my hot dessert to the bedroom.

The following year we returned to our old friend the Isle of Man. In the late summer of 1977 Vera and I decided that we should treat my mother to a week's holiday with us in Port Erin. The boat set sail from Liverpool at 4-00 p.m. in atrocious weather. Gale force winds whipped the sea into a frenzy and torrential rain reduced visibility to a few yards. To compound the situation even further, darkness had fallen by the time the boat docked in Douglas harbour. The rain was still lashing down and the sea was so rough that the boat was bobbing up and down like a cork. This created a major problem unloading the cars. A car could only be driven off the boat at the very instant it was at the top of a wave, since this was the only point the ramp was level with the jetty. Just one car per time could disembark and the timing had to be perfect. Too early or too late would have resulted in a damaged car or, worse still, a car in the sea. It was hair-raising stuff but we managed it.

On arrival at our flat (they weren't called apartments then) in Port Erin the rain was still sweeping down. Making the short dash from the car to the front door drenched me to the skin. "Sorry, sir. We don't appear to have a booking under your name. Are you sure it's the right place?" I was perplexed. This was the place that my mother and Vera had sent me to so it must be the right place. I dashed back to the car with the bad news.

"Sorry," they said, "we've sent you to the wrong flat. It's the one next door." After making my apologies to the landlady, we all scampered next door to the warmth and shelter of our flat. Although the holiday hadn't got off to a great start, the weather improved and we had a really good time. The only downside was that I developed a sore throat. My voice became so hoarse that I could hardly speak.

10.5 A THROATY PROBLEM

I've suffered from sore throats and loss of voice throughout my life. My throat is my Achilles heel. Usually, however, they clear up after a course of antibiotics. Not on this occasion. (And not on another occasion either – Chapter 29.) After the first dose of antibiotics failed to solve the problem, Dr Ratcliffe, my GP, prescribed another, more powerful, antibiotic. When this also failed, he referred me to a throat specialist at the hospital. The specialist prodded, probed and peered down my throat for what seemed an eternity. Then followed the disturbing pronouncement. "I think you need to come into hospital so we can take a better look. Can you come in on Sunday?" It was Thursday. Sunday was only three days away. He must have suspected something serious to want me in so quickly. As I trudged disconsolately back to the car all manner of horrible thoughts crossed my mind. It was a worrying time.

On that Sunday afternoon, I entered hospital for the first and, until I had a hernia operation in 2010 (followed later by two scares, one in 2016 and one in 2020 – Chapter 29), the only time in my life, relieved that the problem would be addressed but worried that it may not be curable. The surgeon came to have another look down my throat and, satisfied with what he saw, informed me they would operate the following day.

After having my pre-op injection, I was wheeled on a gurney to the operating theatre. I remember chatting happily to the nurse about Dr Ian Barben, a colleague from work. She knew him because his wife was a doctor at the hospital. Suddenly, she asked me to count backwards from twenty. My next recollection was waking up on a trolley in the recovery room! I was choking and a nurse came over to suck fluid from my mouth using some kind of vacuum instrument. Later, I was wheeled back to my ward.

My throat felt as dry and rough as sandpaper. I was parched. When the nurse asked if I would like anything to eat or drink, I said that I would love a glass of cold milk and an ice-cream. But no sound came from my mouth. I couldn't utter a word! "Don't worry," said the nurse. "This is perfectly normal after your operation." Apparently, I wouldn't be able to speak for about two weeks. At the post-op debrief, the surgeon explained, with the aid of a diagram, that he had removed a growth on my vocal chords. It was so large that it completely covered the gap between the two forks of the wishbone-shaped vocal chords, preventing them from vibrating. This was the reason why I had been unable to speak. The excision of the benign growth, or polyp as they called it, had left the vocal chords raw and inflamed and this was the cause of my temporary speech loss.

After several more days I was discharged and allowed to complete my convalescence at home. It is hard to describe the relief I felt knowing that the problem had been resolved. Although I had to have a number of six-monthly check-ups to ensure that the growth hadn't returned, in due course I was discharged completely. The upside of the operation is that sore throats have been much fewer, but the downside is that too much talking or shouting quickly results in hoarseness and loss of voice. My vocal chords were my new Achilles heel.

10.6 BABY BLUES

About a year before Andrew was born my cousin Alan (the one who stayed at our house in Crawford Avenue – Chapter 1) and his wife Sylvia (Image 91, page 149) had their first (and only) baby, a girl they named Wendy. Every Monday evening Vera and I took Andrew around to their house in Westhoughton to play with Wendy. In summer, it was ball games and hide-and-seek at Haigh Hall whilst in winter, we stayed indoors at Alan's house. The arrangement worked well with both Andrew and Wendy benefiting from each others company. Seeing them playing together, with laughter, giggling, (and the occasional tears), made us realise that we wanted another baby. A brother or sister for Andrew.

Our original plan had been to have a second baby about two years after Andrew was born so there wouldn't be a big age difference but, although we tried and tried, it didn't happen. Neville said that tomatoes and brown bread did it for him so I ate lots of tomatoes and brown bread. And Vera got pregnant. Our elation was short-lived. To our dismay, she had a miscarriage. Undeterred, we continued trying and within a few months Vera was pregnant again, this time without the tomatoes and brown bread. On account of the previous miscarriage, the doctors kept a watchful eye on her. She had to attend both the doctor's surgery and the hospital on a regular basis.

At approximately twelve weeks into the pregnancy an 'amniocentesis' test was performed. We got the result on a Friday afternoon. To our complete horror, it was positive! This meant there was a high probability that the 'baby' had 'spina bifida', a very debilitating and incurable disease. The doctor strongly recommended terminating the pregnancy. However, to be absolutely sure, a re-test would be done but the result wouldn't be known until the following Monday.

That weekend was one of the worst of our entire lives. We agonised over what would happen if the test result came back positive again. It was a dreadful position to be in. The whole weekend was spent considering our options but no firm decision was reached. I think we clung to the faint hope that the test result was wrong. If it wasn't, termination seemed the best thing to do but it was so final. It was a terrible time.

It never rains but it pours. On the very same Friday that we received the awful news about the foetus, I was on company business attending a Colour Chemistry course at the University of Manchester Institute of Science and Technology (UMIST). On returning to the multi-storey car park, another shock awaited. My car had gone. Vanished. The spot where I'd parked was empty. My white Wolseley had been stolen. After informing the police, I phoned my friend Derek Thorp to give me a lift home. It couldn't have happened at a worse time. Already upset and distressed about the test result, losing the car made matters even worse.

Of all the times we needed a car, this was it. A car was essential. Vera was visiting both her local doctor and the hospital on a regular basis and we had no transport. The bus service was infrequent so we had to use taxis and that was expensive. Colleagues at work sympathised with my plight and urged me to ask the Research Manager, Dr Frank Hall, to loan me a 'Pool' car until mine was recovered. He refused and this caused a big rumpus. It certainly didn't help my career prospects. Eventually, my car was found abandoned by 'joyriders' in Sale and yet again Derek helped me out by driving me to Sale. It was a stressful time.

After enduring the worst weekend of our lives, it was with a mixture of fear and foreboding that we made our way to the Royal Bolton Hospital on the Monday morning for the results of the re-test. No one had been told of the drama. We had borne the burden ourselves. Only if the positive result was confirmed would people be informed. We hoped with all our hearts that they wouldn't have to be.

NEGATIVE! The re-test was a definite negative. It is impossible to describe the way we felt at that instant, but the relief was huge. It's as though a massive weight had been lifted from our shoulders. We could resume our lives again.

Thereafter, for obvious reasons, Vera was monitored extremely carefully for the remainder of her pregnancy. Fortunately, there were no more scares.

176

Her contractions began in the middle of the night. The ambulance arrived at six in the morning to whisk Vera to hospital. I took Andrew to her parents' house in Aspull and then dashed back to the hospital to be present at the birth. I arrived just in time. Michael Jonathan was born at 7-50 a.m. (Image 101). As soon as the head popped out I just knew it was a boy. I didn't need to see the rest of him. He yelled heartily. It was a bloody but beautiful experience, one I wish I could have experienced with Andrew. This was one birthday that was easy to remember. Our second baby had been born on Tuesday, 4 July 1978, America's Independence Day.

Weighing in at 8 pounds 4 ounces and twenty inches long, Michael was a fine healthy baby boy. Except for one thing. He was slightly jaundiced. To rectify this condition he was placed under a special lamp for several hours a day. The treatment worked and, within a few days, both mother and baby were allowed home.

For the time that Vera was in hospital with Michael her little sister, Elaine, was an angel. She volunteered to come and stay with me to help with the meals and housework. Although only thirteen-years-old, she was a tremendous help to both me and Andrew. In hindsight, we couldn't have managed without her.

In contrast to Andrew, Michael wanted feeding a lot. Large feeds and often. Feeding times were normally every four hours. However, in addition to his evening feeds at six-o-clock and ten-o-clock, Michael also wanted one at eight-o-clock. Not surprisingly, he developed into a chubby, but extremely happy, toddler (Image 102).

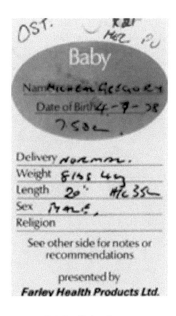

Michael's birth tag.

At three months of age, just before his inoculations were due, Michael contracted whooping cough. It was a worrying time. Dr Hall, another of our GPs, who lived in a bungalow near to our house, had no hesitation in whisking him off to the isolation hospital on Hulton Lane, where he was detained for several weeks until the infection had been cured. As was the case with Andrew, it was a most distressing time but for different reasons. Andrew could walk and speak during his stay in hospital and, as mentioned already, it was heart-breaking having to leave him after visiting time. At three-months-old Michael just lay in his cot, obviously very ill, and it was equally heart-breaking having to see him in such a condition. Yet again it was a difficult few weeks but we managed to cope, just.

Having learned important lessons from our first baby, bringing up our second baby was relatively easier. Michael was fed when he was hungry, comforted when he cried and, like Andrew, given lots of love and attention. Michael quickly settled into a routine. Every afternoon, as regular as clockwork, he would grab a cushion at one-o-clock and sleep on the settee for three hours, awakening at four-o-clock. Every day, without fail. Also, he had six dummies, one on each finger, and thumb, of his right hand, plus one in his mouth. And he took great delight in continually swapping them around, giving each of his dummies their time in his mouth (Image 103). This habit became so strong that Vera and I became concerned that it would be a difficult one to break. We needn't have worried. When we deemed it appropriate, we said, "Come on, Michael. You're old enough now to go to bed without dummies." Without any fuss, he handed them over. All of them. Just as a precaution, we didn't throw them away in case he asked for them back, but he never did.

Michael, aged about twelve months, with
his mum at Manchester airport.

Like his elder brother, Michael was also easy to potty train. During the day his nappies were replaced with a small pair of underpants, without mishap. Revelling in being 'nappy free', he actually asked not to wear nappies at bedtime. He had recovered well from whooping cough but, as will become apparent later, the antibiotics had a disastrous effect on his first set of teeth.

When he turned four, Michael followed in Andrew's footsteps by attending playschool, this time the Ladybridge playschool. Whilst at playschool Michael became a minor celebrity! He and his friend Gavin Beevers were chosen to appear in a photograph with police officers for the Bolton Evening News to highlight a road safety campaign (Image 104). They must have had photogenic faces.

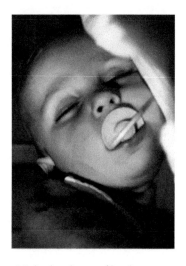

Michael with one of his dummies.

Michael (left) and Gavin Beevers with
the two road safety police officers.

179

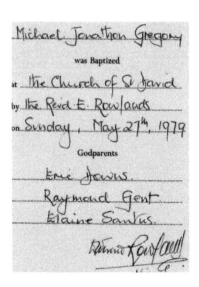

Andrew's baptism certificate.

Both Andrew and Michael were baptised at St David's church, Haigh, the church were Vera and I were married. Andrew was baptised on the 1 September 1974 (Image 105) and Michael on the 27 May 1979 (Image 106). Although he was unable to marry me and Vera because of holiday commitments (Chapter 8), Reverend Southern baptised Andrew. However, by the time Michael was baptised five years later, Reverend Southern had retired.

We had already experienced one delight with the birth of Andrew. The birth of Michael was our second bundle of joy.

Michael's baptism certificate.

11

PLAYTIME

Although building a career and starting a family were by far the most important things in my life, I also wanted to play sport and to indulge in some new activities. I'd really enjoyed playing rugby league at secondary school but the time was right to try something different. I began with football, a game I hadn't played much since primary school. I began at ICI.

11.1 FOOTBALL

The sporting facilities at ICI were excellent. The Recreation Club boasted two football pitches, a cricket pitch, tennis courts, five-a-side football pitches and a bowling green. Each year, inter-departmental competitions were held. In the football competitions, Research Department, with over two hundred employees, was able to enter several teams.

In preparation for the five-a-side football competition our team (Image 107) played friendly games against other research teams, usually about twice a week. On these days a quick lunch was required since the allotted 45 minutes for the lunch break had already been exceeded. This provided an opportunity to visit Marr's Sandwich Shop in the village for a cheese and tomato barm cake, a Mars bar and a carton of milk, a healthy snack to replenish all the lost calories from the strenuous exercise.

One of Research Departments early Five-a-Side Football teams 1971.
Left to right: Back Row: Me, Phil Gabriel, John Lawson.
Front row: Andy Logan, Steve Hallam.
We lost 6-1 to Distribution Centre in the quarter-final.

Initially, I started out as a central defender (Image 107) but, as my girth size increased and my fitness decreased, I switched to goalkeeper (Image 108). Some people jokingly compared me to 'The Refrigerator', the enormous American grid-iron footballer. He was so big he would have blocked the entire goal just by lying down! I was big but not that big.

In the early years of the competition Distribution Centre from Heywood were the team to beat, not only at five-a-side and eleven-a-side football, but also at cricket too. Although they had good players, they were successful because they put all their best players into one team. As the saying goes, the only way to beat them is to join them so we decided to follow suit and Research Colours, as we were known, became a formidable team. In fact, we were more than formidable, we were virtually unbeatable, winning the five-a-side football competition for an incredible five successive years. John Campbell was our key striker. Strong and fast with a lethal shot, he was an excellent goalscorer. Up front, he was ably assisted by Steve Hallam, a good all-round footballer who was also supremely fit. The two defenders were John Lawson and Mick Clarkson. John was a Manx man who had played football at a high level in the Isle of Man. (Yet another connection with the island!) Mick was a Boltonian who also played regular football at a good standard. Both John and Mick were cultured, unflappable footballers. Our substitute, Andy Logan, was a little livewire. He never let the team down (Image 108).

Research Colours All-Conquering Five-a-Side Football Team 1975.
Left to right: Back Row: John Lawson, Me, John Campbell.
Front Row: Andy Logan, Steve Hallam, Mick Clarkson

Aspull Moor Football Team, circa 1973, with a
Championship Trophy. Left to Right: Back Row: Me, Gerry Hughes, Kenny Crompton, Brian,
Jimmy Whitfield, Alan Birchall, Ian
Wilson. Front Row: Alan Harrison, Brian Beresford, William,
Freddie Fielding, Alan Ainscough, Alan Crompton.

The same six players formed the core of the Research Colours eleven-a-side football team and we won that competition three times.

As well as playing football at ICI, I also played for Aspull Moor. My cousin Brian and I still frequented Ewood Park to watch Blackburn Rovers, but we were becoming bored. Many of the games were dull and ended in drab 0-0 draws. The thrill and the excitement had disappeared and it wasn't enjoyable any more. So, in 1968, we decided to form our own football team and play the game rather than watch it.

Aspull Moor Football Club was formed the following year. We had secured a football pitch and a place in the Wigan Sunday League. Finding players hadn't been a problem either and, with a brand new kit of blue shirts, blue shorts and yellow socks, we began our first season. Surprisingly, we did rather well and won promotion to the next division. I revelled in my position as central defender and captain whilst Brian played really well in goal. William had also joined the team and made an excellent full-back. However, a few years later I hung up my boots and became the manager (Image 109).

Aspull Moor Football Club existed for over ten years and in that time was pretty successful. We gained successive promotions from Division 3 to Division 1, the top division, and, in 1973, had a good cup run, reaching the latter stages of the Lancashire Sunday Trophy. In the first round of the competition we defeated, away from home, a team from the Premier Division of the Middleton League called the Dyers and Polishers. It was such an achievement that we made the headlines in the local paper[1] (Image 110). Our opponents in the next round were the 'Wheatsheaf' from Westhoughton. They were a formidable team, unbeaten and runaway leaders of the third division. Boasting a sprinkling of ex-professional footballers, they had reached the final of the Wigan Challenge Cup, defeating the Division 1 leaders, the White Duck, along the way. The match drew a sizeable crowd and, in an exciting encounter, we prevailed by two goals to one. Once again we made the headlines[2] (Image 111). One more win would make us the first team from the Wigan Sunday League to have reached the quarter finals of the Lancashire Sunday Trophy. Unfortunately, we lost to the White Bull from Preston who, incidentally, were comprehensively beaten by the White Duck in the quarter-final by five goals to one.

Aspull Moor polish off the Dyers

ASPULL MOOR, of the Wigan Sunday Soccer League, pulled off one of the best performances in the first round of the Lancashire Sunday Trophy when they defeated Middleton Premier Division side Dyers and Polishers 3-1.

Down 1-0 at half-time, Aspull Moor came storming back to get a quick equaliser, and then clinch a second round ticket with two goals in the last 10 minutes.

Victoria also went through. A solitary first half goal by Bradburn gave them victory at Wildbores.

Wigan Sunday Soccer League

Division IV: Conquering Hero 2 (Ashcroft 2), Hindley Celtic 1 (Baines); Interhough 2 (Johnson 2), Free

Newspaper cutting of our win
over the Dyers and Polishers.

Aspull Moor, White Duck carry flag

ASPULL MOOR and White Duck "A" are day Soccer League teams which figured in Lancashire Sunday Trophy first round games — and both played teams in their own league.

A goal by Holmes gave White Duck "A" a victory at Bryn, while a goal 15 minutes into the second half gave Aspull Moor a 2-1 win over last season's Division IV champions, Wheatsheaf.

2 (Hodson, Shilton); Travellers Rest "B" 0, St William's 14 (Egan 5, Hill 3, Perry 3, McNamee 2, Hart); St Jude's "B" 0, Wagon and Horses 11.

Division IV: Wigan Observer 2 (Ferrish Hotel...

Newspaper cutting of our win over the Wheatsheaf.

185

I also played cricket. The players from our five-a-side soccer team also dominated the five-a-side cricket competition, winning a hat trick of trophies. As was the case for football, these five players formed the core of our eleven-a-side cricket team called, for some obscure reason, David Niven's Fridge.

The Fridge, as we were affectionately known, won the eleven-a-side cricket competition a number of times. In one memorable final we were rank underdogs, playing a team containing many of ICI's first eleven cricketers, including their captain, Duncan. The games were twenty over affairs in which no player could bowl more than four overs. Having won the toss we elected to bat first. Batting at number three I made a quickfire 34 runs. The highlight of the innings was hitting a huge six off Duncan's bowling. He was ICI's first choice fast bowler and a renowned cricketer. As he ran in to bowl I decided to go for a massive hit. Striking the ball sweetly in the middle of the bat, not only did it clear the boundary rope, it sailed right out of the ground, clearing the ten foot concrete fence with ease! The look on Duncan's face said it all. He wasn't accustomed to being treated in that manner. No doubt he would exact revenge when it was my turn to bowl at him.

We amassed over 120 runs from our allotted twenty overs, a respectable but not insurmountable total. Not surprisingly, Duncan opened their batting and John Campbell, our quickest bowler, opened our bowling. It was a cautious opening but Duncan ensured that he was on strike to face the second bowler. Me!

I could see that he intended to seek revenge for his earlier humiliation at my hands but I wasn't prepared to let him have it. Bowling fast right arm round the wicket, I was determined to put everything that I had into my first delivery. My intention was to bowl a 'yorker' between his bat and feet with all the venom that I could muster. After measuring my stride length, I took a few deep breaths to compose myself then began my run up. Completely focused on what I had to do, I delivered the ball as fast and accurate as I could. The rest was up to Duncan. As expected, he took an almighty swipe to hit the ball out of the ground. To my complete delight, he missed, and his stumps went flying. I was mobbed by ecstatic team mates. Their star player had been dismissed for a paltry score. Now, we had a chance to win. Inspired by that early success, I took a further three wickets in my allotted four overs and we went on to win the match comfortably. It was my finest hour of cricket.

The presentation of the awards were held in the Recreation Club on Delauney's Road. They were very enjoyable events. As well as the presentation of the trophies and medals (Image 112), entertainment was provided. One of the funniest 'acts' was a balloon dance, performed by one of the cricket teams (not ours). The sight of eleven naked men dancing to music with just a balloon to preserve their modesty was a hoot. The occasional mishap meant the girls got more than they bargained for.

David Niven's Fridge receiving their medals and 11-a-side cricket trophy in 1983. Left to right: John Lawson, Phil Gabriel, Mike Hutchings, John Moore, Derek Thorp, John Campbell, Me, Steve Hallam (with trophy), Brian Bothwell, Unknown, Ian Ferguson, Jim Campbell and Mick Clarkson. Stan Shaw and Denis McKay are the two people at the back.

11.3 BADMINTON

In addition to football and cricket I also played badminton. Mr Gaffiken, the PE (Physical Education) teacher who succeeded Mr Lindley, Mrs Parkinson, the English teacher and Miss Twist, the art teacher, introduced me to this new sport. Once a week, after lessons had ended, we enjoyed some entertaining games of chasing the shuttle in the gymnasium of Aspull Secondary Modern School. Like my games of golf in the Isle of Man, it would serve me well later.

As well as organising the walking weekends in the Lake District (see later), Brian Parton, a colleague from Research Department, also organised a badminton group. The core members of the group were those from the walking weekends and we played at the local Abraham Moss leisure centre every Thursday evening. To make the evening more enjoyable (and competitive), the seven regulars (Brian, Steve Hallam, John Yates, Phil Rowbotham, Joe Bereza, Jim Campbell and me) held a competition. We played games of doubles, playing with each of the other six players against all the other combinations. With two points for a win and zero for a loss, there was a league table and, once all the games had been played (after about three months), the champion was crowned. To my complete surprise, I won the first competition, with Steve and Brian winning subsequent ones.

We chased the shuttle from six-o-clock until eight-o-clock. Afterwards, a refreshing shower revived our tired, sweaty bodies. Normally, this proceeded without incident. Except on one occasion. On that evening I was the last person into the showers and, not surprisingly, I was the last person to leave. As I turned off the shower and prepared to depart, the sound of stilleto heels on the tiled floor grew louder and louder. Suddenly, two ladies emerged into view. I was taken aback. There I was, stark naked, with two fully clothed ladies standing right in front of me. They didn't bat an eyelid. It was as though talking to a naked man in a public place was an everyday occurrence! Completely unabashed, they started talking to me, eventually asking directions to the bar. Even more amazing was that I didn't feel embarrassed either. It was a weird encounter.

The badminton continued for about eight years. In addition to providing much needed exercise, it also provided immense enjoyment. Playing badminton was thirsty work and the highlight of the evening was downing that first ice cold pint of Stella Artois in the leisure centre bar. It was pure bliss.

As well as the refreshing after-match lagers, an annual night out was organised. Normally, this was in Manchester, usually at a strip club such as the 'Twenty-One Club'. We witnessed some incredible sights, not all of them pretty. One year, an old banger of a stripper took a fancy to Brian, gyrating her bruised and flabby flesh in his face. He thought it was great but the rest of us didn't know whether to laugh or cry.

11.4 WALKING WEEKENDS

Brian Parton was a fellow research chemist. I knew him well since we had worked together on both reactive dyes for cotton and dyes for acrylics* (Chapter 9). This modest, pipe-smoking person with a ruddy complexion and rapidly receding hairline (Image 115, page 191) was one of the cleverest chemists I ever encountered. Early in his career, he was asked, along with Denis Eckersley, to invent the holy grail of a cost effective, bright blue reactive dye having excellent fixation. Many had tried, and failed, to meet this challenging target. Initially, both Brian and Denis worked on the tried and tested anthraquinone dyes, but were continually treading on each others toes. Exasperated, Brian switched his attention to a new and relatively obscure class of dye, the triphendioxazines, and came up with a blockbuster. He invented PROCION Blue H-EGN, one of the best selling dyes of all time.

Brian was also an experienced fell walker and decided to organise a walking weekend in the Lake District for anyone in Research Department who wished to join him. A number of people expressed interest but in the end just five people went on that first walk, Brian, John Yates, Phil Rowbotham, Pete Mathias and me. It was almost only four. Brian had booked the Low Wood Hall hotel in Nether Wasdale for the weekend that was either on or near our baby's first birthday on 11 April 1975. I wanted to go, badly, but I also wanted to be with my family for Andrew's first birthday. Vera was kind and understanding and insisted that I go. I did, but had to borrow some walking boots from my brother-in-law, Ray, since fell walking was a completely new activity for me.

---

*   Scientifically, these are cationic dyes for polyacrylonitrile

That Friday morning the 'famous five' set off in Brian's brand new Morris Marina 1.8 litre car for our weekend in the Lake District. Rydal Mount, near Grasmere, was our first destination. Ever thoughtful, John had planned a 'warm-up' walk to get us in trim for the big one the next day, Scafell Pike. Some warm-up! It took us over 5 hours to complete the Fairfield Horseshoe. At over 3,000 feet, it was almost as high as Scafell Pike, the highest mountain in England. Not only that, the weather was bad too. As we sat huddled behind rocks on the snow-clad summit, the howling gale almost blew us away (Image 113).

With the Fairfield Horseshoe tucked safely under our belt, we staggered into the Badger Bar to sink a few pints of beer and warm ourselves up in front of the roaring log fire. Reluctant to leave these cosy surroundings, we set off, eventually, for Nether Wasdale.

It was dusk as we turned off the A595 at Duddon Bridge and drove along the Duddon valley towards the tiny village of Ulpha. After turning sharp left and climbing the very steep hill, Brian made a startling announcement. He'd forgotten to fill up with petrol and the car was running on empty! By now, it was pitch black and we were, literally, in the middle of nowhere. The moors between Ulpha and the next tiny hamlet of Eskdale Green, a good few miles away, were desolate and barren. At the top of the moors the car stuttered and spluttered and ran out of petrol. Fortunately, we had just begun to descend and had to free wheel for several miles to the only garage in Eskdale Green. Not surprisingly, at this time of night it was closed. Brian made his way to the small house adjacent to the garage. He knocked repeatedly on the door but there was no answer. As panic was rearing its ugly head, the door finally opened and a burly man, accompanied by two large, fierce, Alsatians, peered cautiously outside. I didn't fancy being bitten again (Chapter 3) so I stayed in the car. After Brian explained our predicament, he grudgingly filled up the car, muttering something like "bloody stupid townies."

Left to right: Me, Phil Rowbotham and John Yates
at the summit of the Fairfield Horseshoe.

189

Next morning, after devouring our breakfast, we drove to Wasdale Head, parked the car and donned our walking gear. Already sore and blistered from the previous day's walk, my feet would be in a far worse condition after the ascent of Scafell Pike. From Wasdale Head, we climbed to Sty Head and then took the Brown Tongue route up Scafell Pike, following diligently Alfred Wainwright's guide. The ascent seemed to take forever. Although not steep, it was a long, steady slog. After taking the obligatory photograph beside the cairn at the summit (Image 114), we ate our lunch before beginning the descent.

Left to right: Phil (you can just see his head behind the rocks), Me (in blue),
Peter Gale and Steve Hallam at the summit of Scafell Pike.
(This was from the walking weekend the following year).

For me, the descent was an ordeal. Ray's boots were at least one size too big and by now my feet were badly blistered and bleeding. The pain was excruciating. I was so relieved to get back to the car and take them off. Grateful for the loan of his boots, I vowed to buy a pair of my own at the earliest opportunity.

In the evening we relaxed in the hotel bar in front of a open log fire, playing games and drinking beer. It allowed our tired, aching bodies to recover in time for more gentler pursuits on Sunday.

Following a leisurely breakfast, we bade our hosts farewell and drove the short distance to a little gift shop at nearby Santon Bridge to buy some presents for our families. Next, it was on to Fell Foot park at the bottom of Lake Windermere, England's largest lake. After enjoying a light lunch in the café, we sauntered down to the rowing boats. A one hour row around the bottom of the lake, where we almost collided with the Windermere ferry at Lakeside, was our final activity of the weekend.

The walking weekend became a regular event. It was held every spring, and sometimes in the autumn too, for the next seven or eight years. The seven core members of Brian, John, Phil, Dave Devonald, Paul Gordon, Steve Hallam and myself were joined occasionally by Andy Logan, Tony Nelson and Peter Gale (Image 115). There were many memorable moments, one of which I recounted in Chapter 1. A few others deserve a brief mention.

My room mate on these weekends was Paul. We got along very well, but there was an issue. My snoring! As discussed later in Chapter 13, it was so bad that it forced Bryan Backhouse to vacate the bedroom in Antibe, and it forced Paul to take action too. Unlike Bryan, Paul couldn't relocate to the relative quiet of a hallway since there wasn't one. Instead, he threw Mars bars at me! I didn't mind. I just ate them and threw the wrappers back.

Undoubtedly the most amusing event occurred on Muncaster Fell. It was meant to be a gentle stroll on the Sunday morning before departing for home and four of the five walkers treated it that way. One didn't. Tony was determined to show how fit he was and pressed ahead at a searing pace. To the laggards he remarked, jokingly I presume, that we geriatrics should get a move on. One of these was Steve Hallam. Steve, who was by far the fittest person on the walk, was incensed and decided to teach Tony a lesson. As Tony strode off yet again, Steve outlined his plan. It was simple but effective. Eventually, after catching up with Tony we all stopped for lunch. Before resuming our 'stroll', Steve propped his camera on an appropriate rock, set the timer and asked us all to stand together for the obligatory group photograph. Then, as planned, he executed his plan. "Right lads," he said. "All turn round and drop your pants for a 'moonie'." The resulting photograph of four bare bottoms next to a startled and fully clothed Tony became an icon at ICI Blackley. Unfortunately, I forgot to keep my legs closed and revealed more than my bare bottom!

Members of the walking weekend. Left to right:
John Yates, Me, Paul Gordon, Steve Hallam, Brian Parton,
Andy Logan, Peter Gale and Phil Rowbotham.

191

As is evident from Image 115, Andy is not the biggest of guys yet he brought an enormous rucksack. And I mean enormous. What it contained I'm not sure but it certainly wasn't water. One blisteringly hot day on a strenuous climb with sweat pouring from his small body he literally begged every passing walker for a drink. It was so funny. It got even funnier on the descent. At one point, we had to walk in a stream that was gushing down the bottom of a ravine. Everyone negotiated it successfully except Andy. The size and weight of his rucksack caused him to topple backwards and he slid down the stream for a good hundred yards with his rucksack acting as a sled. It was so comical, we split our sides laughing.

All good things come to and end and regretfully, so did the walking weekends. As people dispersed to different sites or retired, the walking weekends petered out.

11.5 MASONIC WEEKENDS

During my research on reactive dyes, Steve Bostock was my Experimental Chemist. Steve was a strong character who called a spade a spade. He synthesised many of the twice-coupled H-acid dyes, including PROCION Green H-E4BD. One of his favourite TV programmes was the 1970s western series *Alias Smith and Jones* starring Pete Duel* and Ben Murphy, but he hated James Bond films. Later, Steve replaced the iconic Tony Woolham as head of our Fine Chemical Service and Derek Thorp became my new Experimental Chemist.

Like Steve before him, Derek was a diligent worker and skilled experimentalist. He successfully continued the work on twice-coupled H-acid dyes, synthesising PROCION Navy H-ER. He also did a lot of the fundamental work, particularly on the colour and constitution of azo dyes. Indeed, he was a co-author on one of my publications.[3] It also transpired that he was a freemason. In this respect, he was following in the footsteps of his father, who had been a freemason for many years. Every spring, their lodge held a 'Ladies Evening', usually at the Savoy Hotel in Blackpool. Vera and I were invited to attend and we did, leaving Andrew and Michael in the capable hands of our parents.

The 'Ladies Evenings' followed a regular routine. Vera and I always arrived at the Savoy Hotel, located just beyond Gynn Square, early on the Saturday afternoon, checked in to our room and then enjoyed a stimulating walk along the promenade towards Blackpool. A coffee and cake in one of the many cafes kept our hunger at bay. Suitably refreshed, we'd return to our room, bathe and don our evening attire. For these occasions, I wore a dark blue dinner jacket with a matching bow tie whilst Vera wore an evening gown (Images 116-118).

---

*   Pete Duel committed suicide at a young age by blowing his brains out with a gun

The evening began with a few drinks and some conversation. Then, it was time for the main event, the evening dinner. But before any food was served, we first had to perform the ritual of 'clapping in' the 'Grand Master' and his lady. Only then was it time to eat. The meals were always sumptuous affairs, consisting of at least three courses. The ladies got a double treat. Not only were they serenaded by a male singer, they also received a present from the Grand Master.

Vera and Me at the Savoy Hotel 23 April 1983.

Derek, Yvonne, Bill, Sue, Me and Vera.

Derek, Yvonne, Dave, Anne, Vera and Me.

The remainder of the evening was enjoyed in different ways. There were 'Whist Drives', games, dancing and raffles. And, of course, there was talking and drinking. Normally, the men did most of the drinking and the ladies most of the talking. Then, at 1-00 a.m. in the morning, a strange thing happened. A very strange thing. Supper was served in the dining room. Supper was actually a full English breakfast: bacon, egg, sausage, fried bread, and tomato, followed by tea and toast. At 1-00 a.m. in the morning and on top of a bellyful of beer! It was bizarre but, for me, the defining moment of a Masonic weekend.

On the Sunday morning breakfast was usually taken late. Then it was a long walk with friends to clear our heads. After lunch, we all said our goodbyes and departed for home.

On our first Masonic weekend Derek and Yvonne also invited their neighbours Bill and Sue. They were a lovely couple and we all got along extremely well (Image 117). On subsequent weekends, Dave Thompson and his wife Anne (Image 118), and Ron Kenyon and his wife Daisy (you'll hear more about Ron later), were also invited.

The Savoy hosted most of the Ladies Evenings but the Queens Hotel, near the South Pier, was another venue. The event was very popular. So popular that one year we ended up staying in the 'overspill' hotel, the Viking. For a change, one 'Ladies Evening' was held in Llandudno. The year that Derek's dad was the secretary, Vera typed the lodge accounts.

The sports, fell walking and Ladies Evenings were an enjoyable period of our lives but there was more fun to be had. Like most parents, Vera and I strived hard to give our children the best possible childhood and this included holidays.

REFERENCES

1. Lancashire Evening Post and Chronicle, Tuesday 25th September 1973, p. 24.

2. Lancashire Evening Post and Chronicle, Tuesday 16th October 1973, p. 7.

3. P Gregory and D Thorp, 'The Electronic Absorption Spectra of 2-Substituted-4-NN-diethylamino-4'-nitroazobenzene Dyes and their Monoacid Cations: The Applicability of Dewar's Rules to these and Related Dyestuffs', Journal of the Chemical Society, Perkin Transactions I, 1990, 1979.

12

HAPPY HOLIDAYS

We endeavoured to take as many holidays as was practicable, both in the UK and abroad and, in the spring of 1980, we experienced the delights of our first holiday away from home as a family of four. It was in the Lake District, a place that Vera and I have always loved. Andrew was six and Michael almost two. The stunning scenery, bustling villages and friendly people make the Lake District a magical place. On one of my walking weekends with colleagues from ICI (the one mentioned in Chapter 1), we stayed in the heart of the Lake District at Nether Wasdale near Wastwater where the highest mountains are located. It was an excellent, if eventful, weekend and it was to here that we decided to have our first family holiday.

The view from the road as Wasdale emerges into sight is simply breathtaking. It's scenic heaven! To the west the famous screes sweep down into the depths of England's deepest lake, Wastwater, whilst at the head of the lake three of England's highest mountains dominate the skyline. At over three thousand feet Great Gable, Scafell and Scafell Pike, England's highest mountain, are simply awesome. It is a magnificent vista, so beautiful that it won the 'Best View in Britain' competition in 2007.

As we pulled on to the gravel driveway of the Low Wood Hall Hotel on a sunny Good Friday afternoon we were greeted by the landlord, a local Cumbrian. "I know you," he said, as I exited from the car. Indeed he did. I had stayed at his hotel twice in the previous year, at Easter and again in October, with my colleagues from ICI. He introduced us to the rest of his family, his lovely Austrian wife and their two young children, Heidi and Tim. As children do, Andrew and Michael quickly became friends with Heidi and Tim and the four of them enjoyed many hours in each other's company. The weekend had started well.

The exceptionally fine weather allowed us to spend most of our time outdoors, particularly on the gentler East shore of Wastwater and the tranquil beck of Backbarrow (Image 119). Muncaster Castle, with its World Owl Sanctuary, was our destination on Saturday morning. We had a marvellous time exploring the castle grounds and watching an owl display before travelling to nearby Ravensglass. Here, we caught the quaint little steam train, known fondly as 'Ratty', to Boot in Eskdale. Running alongside the foot of Muncaster Fell, it was a splendid journey, providing panoramic views of the magnificent scenery.

Vera, Andrew (with his new hiking boots)
and Michael at Backbarrow 1980.

The food at the hotel was delicious, a mix of traditional English with a smattering of Austrian. To start the day there was a choice of either a full English or a continental breakfast. The evening meal consisted of a starter, a main course and a dessert. In addition to pork-in-wine (Chapter 1), we also enjoyed some delicious roast lamb and a scrumptious apple strudel dessert.

Without doubt the highlight of the holiday occurred on the morning of Easter Sunday. Entering the dining room for breakfast everything seemed perfectly normal. It wasn't! As Andrew and Michael pulled out their chairs from under the table, whoops of delight emanated from their surprised faces. On each chair sat a lovely Easter egg! Excitedly, they scooped them up and sat down. Further surprises lay in store. Under each upturned cereal bowl nestled a clutch of smaller eggs, with even more eggs under the upturned cups. Eggs were even hidden in the sugar bowl! Watching the surprised and delighted faces of the children as they unearthed these hidden treasures was the kindly face of the old lady who had placed them there. Peering around the door, her face was a picture. It was hard to tell who was happiest, the children or the lady who had hidden the Easter eggs. It was obvious that she derived enormous pleasure from her kind gesture.

This unexpected event began a tradition that has lasted over 40 years to the present day. Our children enjoyed it so much that every Easter Sunday we had to re-enact the 'Great Easter Egg Treasure Hunt' at home. At first, we hid them under items at the breakfast table, just like in the Lake District. However, as time progressed, the Treasure Hunt became more sophisticated (and expensive). Not only eggs but also fluffy toys were hidden in various places around the house, especially the garden, and clues provided as to their whereabouts. I used to rack my brains devising the clues, easy ones when they young but more difficult ones as they grew older.

Baa baa black sheep have you any eggs?
Yes sir, yes sir, between my legs
(Small eggs 'hidden' between the legs of a decorative garden sheep we'd bought to remind us of our children's encounter with the birth of a lamb – Chapter 18.)

I'm small and red
Behind the shed
Under my lid
An egg lies hid
(A large egg hidden in the red milk container behind the garden shed.)

were two of the easier rhymes, whilst two of the more difficult ones were:-

Under the table
If you're able
Lift up your eyes
To find the prize
(A fluffy toy in a plastic bag taped under the roof of our bird table.)

I'm not in the reeds
And I'm not in the weeds
I'm not in the phlox
But look in the Box

Over the years so many eggs were hidden in our large egg shaped box shrub *(buxus sempevirens)* that I'm sure many went uncollected and provided a feast for the local wildlife. This annual ritual became so popular that we carried it on with Michelle and Natalie, the children of Keith and Elaine, and it was only discontinued when they were well into their teenage years.

It began again in 2014 with Layla, Natalie's daughter, Jessica, Stuart's daughter, and Joshua, Michael and Kathryn's son (Chapter 29).

12.1 MAGIC AND MYSTERY

That summer we spent two weeks in another of our favourite holiday destinations, Cornwall. Vera had spotted some lovely old cottages in Tintagel advertised in a national newspaper and the largest one became our home for the duration of our holiday. The accommodation was spread out over two spacious floors. The kitchen, lounge, dining room and main bedroom were on the first floor, with the bathroom, toilet and two smaller bedrooms on the ground floor. After allowing Andrew and Michael to sleep in the downstairs bedrooms on the first night, we all slept upstairs for the rest of the holiday. (The main bedroom had two double beds.) Why? Partly for safety reasons since the downstairs bedrooms were situated near to the front door but also because the cottage had an aura of 'spookiness' about it. In the stillness of the dawn and dusk mists it was all to easy to imagine the ghosts of generations past lurking in the dark nooks and crannies of the old, creaky building, especially when by yourself. Even upstairs, we moved our bed from beneath the large head of a bull fixed to the wall. We didn't fancy being speared by it's enormous horns should it happen to fall down.

Two amusing incidents occurred at the cottage. A 'billy goat' was tethered on the front lawn, presumably to keep the grass tidy. A lover of animals, Michael quickly befriended the goat, offering it clumps of grass to eat. One day, as he was walking away after feeding it, the goat suddenly charged and butted him in the rear, sending him sprawling to the ground. Surprised but unhurt, it didn't deter him from feeding the goat for the remainder of the holiday. In the second incident, two older boys, who were staying in an adjacent cottage, began to bully Michael, pushing and shoving him around. As soon as Andrew saw this, he immediately ran to his rescue, placing himself between Michael and the two bullies, even though he was considerably younger and smaller than they were. After Andrew gave them a good telling off, they both ran back to their cottage. Andrew was very protective of his younger brother.

Steeped in mystery and magic, Tintagel was a wondrous spot for young children. The legend of King Arthur and his knights of the round table at Camelot, and especially Merlin the wizard, were enthralling for young inquisitive minds. A visit to Merlin's cave at the foot of the cliffs was a must, although it was a relief to catch the jeep for the arduous return journey. Tintagel's only drawback was that it lacked a beach. For this, we travelled either to Newquay or Bude.

Our frequent trips to Newquay were fine except for the traffic bottleneck at Wadebridge. It was a pain and increased the journey time considerably. In Newquay, Fistral beach, with its big Atlantic waves, was our children's favourite. They took great delight in holding their dad's hands as the raging surf tried to knock us off our feet. Although the traffic may have been problematic, finding a place to eat certainly wasn't. They enjoyed *The Rif* restaurant so much on our first visit that we ate there on virtually every subsequent visit to Newquay. One reason was the unusual view. A table near the window afforded the rare sight of baby seagulls in a roof nest across the street.

Although the Newquay beaches were fine, the beach at Bude was the one our children liked best. Here, Andrew and Michael spent whole days digging holes in the sand, filling them with sea water collected in their buckets, and then spending hours splashing about in them (Image 120). Their laughter and joy as they messed about in the improvised pool is etched on my memory.

Andrew and Michael
on Bude beach 1980.

Vera, Andrew and Michael
on Bodmin Moor 1980.

Vera, Michael and Andrew on a
boating lake at Newquay 1980.

Cornwall has more to offer than its craggy coastline and sandy beaches. Bodmin Moor, with its wide open spaces, rugged scenery and wild ponies, was another idyllic place (Image 121). The peace and quiet on the moors was stunning. It didn't take much travelling to escape the madding crowds. Happy days were also spent at the theme park and zoo at Newquay, particularly on the boats (Image 122). Watching the eels slithering around the boat in the clear, shallow water of the boating lake fascinated our children. All-in-all, it was a brilliant family holiday, the first of many that we would enjoy together.

12.2 TOMFOOLERY IN TORQUAY

Torquay, on the English Riviera, was our holiday destination the following summer. On this occasion we didn't holiday alone. Elaine and Keith, who were engaged to be married the following year, also came along. The hotel was lovely. Situated on a hillside in a quiet corner of Torquay, not only did it provided a magnificent view of the bay, it also provided some hilarity.

After we'd finished unpacking our belongings in our family room, Andrew and Michael dashed off to find Elaine and Keith's room(s). This they did. Partly. Elaine was in room 13. But so was Keith. And they weren't married! At that time this wasn't the done thing. You only stayed in the same room and slept together if you were married. Hurriedly, Keith remarked that room 13 was Elaine's room and that he was just visiting. Inquisitive as ever, Andrew asked Keith which room he was staying in. Put on the spot, Keith told a 'white lie' and said that his room was 13A. Intrigued, Andrew, with Michael in tow, spent the whole week searching the hotel for this fictitious room. Needless to say, they never found it.

We visited many places but the two that stick in my mind are Kent's Cavern and Buckfast Abbey. Deep inside the bowels of Kent's Cavern our offspring were awestruck, and a little scared, at the sensation of complete and utter 'blackness' when the tour guide switched off all the lights. In contrast, it was a gorgeous sunny day when we visited Buckfast Abbey and, before embarking on a guided tour of the Abbey, we refreshed ourselves with some cold drinks and ice cream. Then, after purchasing our tickets, we made our way to the starting point to meet our guide.

Michael bowled the monk off his feet. His cherubic face, charming smile and blond hair (Images 120-122) were just too much for the poor monk. He scooped Michael up into his arms and literally carried him all the way round the hour long tour. This could have been a ploy to ensure that we stayed with him for the full duration of the tour, but I think not because, even at the end of the tour, the monk was reluctant to release him. If he had a son, he would have wanted one like Michael.

Even at the tender ages of seven and three, Andrew and Michael aspired to be 'cool'. One of the most obvious ways to achieve the 'cool look' was to follow in the footsteps of film stars and celebrities and wear sunglasses. The result, as they posed beside a panda bear, was hilarious (Image 123).

It was a good holiday. What made it even better was that England beat the Australians in the third Test at Headingley. Needing just 130 runs from their second innings to win the match, it looked a formality for Australia. But Botham and Willis had other ideas. Botham hit a magnificent unbeaten 149 in England's second innings to give them an outside chance of victory and Willis duly obliged by taking eight Australian wickets for just 43 runs as they bowled the Australians out for 111. Against all the odds (at one stage the bookies were offering 500:1 against an England victory) England won.

Andrew and Michael's cool
look at Torquay 1981.

12.3 TWO SHORT BREAKS

That year, as well as the main summer holiday, we also had weekend breaks in spring and autumn. Our destination in spring was the Richmond Hill Hotel. Near to Windsor Great Park and the River Thames, it was an ideal location. On Saturday, the train took us into London, passing through Clapham Junction on the way. Excitedly, we clambered into one of London's famous black cabs. What a delight. Andrew and Michael were fascinated with the drop-down seats. Perched atop these seats, they smiled incessantly as the cab wound its way to our first stop, Buckingham Palace, just in time to watch the changing of the guard. As we searched for a good vantage point a middle-aged London man introduced himself and said he would take us to the best viewing point. Without warning, he picked up Michael, placed him on his shoulders and set off at a brisk pace through the gathering crowd. We followed, making sure that we kept right behind him. At the time we thought nothing of it but, with all the paedophiles in today's society, it was most unwise. In the event, he did find us a good vantage point and, somewhat reluctantly, returned Michael to us. It may have been a narrow escape.

London is a vibrant city with lots to do. We visited the Natural History Museum to see the dinosaurs, the Tower of London to see the crown jewels and traitor's gate, and HMS (Her Majesty's Ship) Belfast, wondering how on earth the sailors coped in such cramped conditions. However, our children were enthralled by the uniforms and armour of the Grenadier Guards and Coldstream Guards, including the horses, and never missed an opportunity to have their photograph taken with them (Image 124).

Andrew and Michael standing to attention with
a Grenadier Guard at Windsor Castle 1981.

The lure of the Lakes proved irresistible. That September we stayed in the Royal Hotel in Windermere. It was a memorable holiday because we bought Michael his first pair of hiking boots from a local shop. He was thrilled to bits. Andrew's boot's had been bought some years earlier (Image 119, page 196) and so, dressed in real hiking gear, we were able to enjoy many hours of walking.

Easedale Tarn was one of our first walks. After I'd parked the car in the charming hamlet of Grasmere, Andrew and Michael performed their usual ritual, dashing straight to the book shop on the corner of the main street. They couldn't wait to buy one of the *Three Investigators* books, endorsed by Alfred Hitchcock. With their book thirst sated, we set off on the wonderful walk to the tranquillity and beauty of

Easedale Tarn (Image 125). On the ascent, we stopped alongside Sourmilk Ghyll, marvelling at the cascading water, so churned up with air bubbles that it really did look like sour milk. After finding a secluded spot on the shore of the tarn, we ate our picnic lunch, throwing scraps to the countless small fish darting around the crystal clear water. After making our descent, a visit to the 'Copper Kettle' café for refreshments completed the walk.

Andrew and Michael in full hiking
gear at Easedale Tarn 1981.

In the February half-term break of 1982, the snow clad mountains of Lakeland beckoned us yet again. Parking at Rydal Mount, we ascended Nab Scar, the mountain which marks the beginning of the Fairfield Horseshoe (Chapter 11, Image 113). The top was covered in thick snow and it wasn't long before our offspring had made a snow slide in a deep depression on the summit. They had a smashing time sliding and frolicking around in the cold, crisp snow. Suddenly, out of nowhere, a couple of RAF (Royal Air Force) fighter jets screamed past, so close that you could almost touch their wingtips! It put the icing on a marvellous day.

We returned to the Lakes in the autumn, this time staying at a small hotel on a hill near Skelwith Bridge, a hotel I'd stayed at on one of our walking weekends. It was a strange experience. Although the hotel was clean and functional, the proprietors were quiet people who hardly spoke to their guests, even when serving the meals. Not only was the atmosphere cold, so was the food! The breakfasts were continental style and the evening meals were cold meat and salad. The only hot items were the drinks. Not quite the Munsters, but almost. However, it didn't spoil our break. One day we drove to Wasdale and climbed Yewbarrow, a lovely fell shaped like an upturned wheelbarrow. To add to the adventure, on part of the descent we slid down the screes on our bottoms. The boys thought it was cool, although I think Vera disagreed.

That summer, sandwiched between our two Lake District holidays, we took Andrew and Michael to the Isle of Man. To the island where Vera and I had many happy memories. To the island where we got engaged. To the island where we spent our honeymoon. We stayed in Douglas at a small family-run hotel where Ray and June had stayed earlier that year with their young son, Stuart. We chose Douglas because it is by far the largest and busiest town on the island, with loads of activities to amuse young children. It was a mistake. Our children preferred to visit every other place on the island. Days were spent at Ramsay, Peel, Laxey, Port St Mary and especially Port Erin. They loved Port Erin. The sheltered sandy beach was their idea of heaven. Not only that, we weren't allowed to drive to Port Erin, we had to take the little steam train! (Image 126). It cost us a fortune. But it was worth every penny to see the joy and delight on their faces as they frolicked in the sand and the sea (Image 127).

Boarding the Steam Train at Douglas 1982.

Peel, also boasting a fine beach and a lovely fishing harbour, was another favoured destination. Peel was also the hub of the Manx kipper trade. Here, smoked herrings were processed and you could send these kippers to friends and relatives back home. But of most interest were the Viking longboats moored in the harbour. If you were lucky (and we weren't) you could witness the re-enactment of a Viking 'invasion'.

Laxey and Mooragh Park at Ramsay were other places of interest. On returning from Ramsay along the famous TT (Tourist Trophy) route one wet and foggy afternoon, we stopped at the Motorbike Museum. Situated on the lower slopes of Snaefell, the island's highest mountain, it was just about visible in the mist and rain. Not surprisingly, we were the sole visitors. Because of this, the proprietor treated us like royalty, allowing Andrew and Michael the freedom of the museum. They had a brilliant time sitting astride many of the famous old motorbikes.

Andrew and Michael, with his cheeky
grin, on Port Erin beach 1982.

Climbing to the top of Lady Isabella, Laxey's famous waterwheel, with its connection to Wigan (parts of the wheel were made in Wigan), provided a further thrill, as did exploring the nearby mine. Laxey's little pebble beach provided further enjoyment. Our children spent hours throwing pebbles into the sea, trying to 'kill' the incoming waves. Yet again, we couldn't use the car. They took great delight in riding on the Manx Electric Railway, particularly where it meandered close to the cliffs and the sea.

One of the reasons we travelled a lot was the weather. It was awful. Many days it rained incessantly and on one occasion it blew a gale. On that very day we'd gone to Summerland,* a relatively new indoor amusement facility at the north end of Douglas promenade. On returning to the car in a howling gale, disaster awaited. It had a flat tyre. After changing the tyre I was literally soaked to the skin. Shivering, wet and cold, it was the last straw. We were so fed up with the atrocious weather that we vowed there and then to holiday abroad the following year. At the very least the weather would be better.

12.5 THE ALGARVE AWAITS

In the summer of 1983 we ventured abroad as a family for the very first time. From Manchester we flew to Faro on the Algarve. In complete contrast to the rain and gales experienced in the Isle of Man the previous year, clear blue skies and a hot sun welcomed

---

*   Tragically, later that same year Summerland burned down with the loss of many lives

us to Portugal. It was such a nice feeling not having to worry about the weather. Our final destination was a modern holiday complex near to the small picturesque fishing village of Alvor. This location had been chosen because of the many facilities provided, such as swimming pools, amusement arcades, a small water park and sandy beaches. We should have known better. As was the case in Tintagel and the Isle of Man, most of the time was spent either on the beach or visiting other places. To my surprise, our children shunned the other facilities.

The hotel was situated on a beautiful sandy beach. Caressed by the gentle waves of the surprisingly warm Mediterranean sea, it was an ideal setting for two energetic youngsters. Splashing about in the sea, riding on pedaloes, playing with frisbees and beach balls, the time flew by. Although it was June, the weather was exceptionally hot. "This is the August weather come early," remarked the beach attendant. He was right, as I found to my cost. I underestimated the strength of the sun and got badly blistered, suffering slight sunstroke at the same time. However, it was a small price to pay to see their happy, smiling faces.

The hotel accommodation was first class. Our apartment was spacious, modern and finished to a very high standard. A typical day began with a continental style breakfast on the balcony of our apartment, the food being purchased from the on-site supermarket. Evening meals were taken at restaurants. In Alvor, we patronised a small, family-run restaurant. It was recommended by an English family who had discovered its delights during their holiday. It proved an excellent recommendation. Located near the centre of the village, it also doubled up as a bar/café for the locals and you had to walk through the bar to reach the small restaurant. The food was delicious. Cooked over charcoal, the steak and chips were to die for. Every time we walked the short distance from the hotel to the restaurant the same ritual occurred. Standing in their doorways, the old Portugese women couldn't resist patting Michael's blonde head! All the Portugese children had jet black hair so Michael's crop of blonde hair was a novelty.

Most evenings, with the children safely tucked up in bed, Vera and I sipped a cool glass of *vino verde* on the balcony as we watched the setting sun sink slowly into the Mediterranean. One evening, she surprised me. She discarded her blouse and bra and sat topless, letting the cool evening breeze caress her warm skin. Emboldened by this act, she surprised me even more by repeating the feat on a crowded beach! It must have taken courage for a shy, reserved girl to go topless, but I wasn't complaining. She had a lovely figure so why not show it off.

We had brilliant days out at Albufeira, the capital of the Algarve, Lagos, Praia de Rocha (Beach of Rocks), and Portimao, the main fishing port, famous for its sardine dishes eaten *al fresco* in the many waterfront cafes. It was here that Vera bought a beautiful lace tablecloth, displaying excellent haggling skills in the process. However, two of the best excursions were to the Monchique Mountains, the highest point in the Algarve, and Cape St Vincent, the most westerly point of Europe.

Cape St Vincent is the point where, in 1497, Vasco da Gama set off on his epic voyage to discover the vital sea route to India. Andrew and Michael had a wow of a time exploring the rocky headland and looking through the powerful telescopes out to sea. The large old cannons (Image 128) that once protected the headland from potential invaders also proved compelling artefacts for inquisitive young minds. But, despite all the travelling, there was still plenty of time to relax and soak up the hot sunshine.

Andrew, Michael and Vera at Cape St
Vincent in Portugal 1983

The journey to the Monchique Mountains in a modern air-conditioned coach afforded stunning views of the beautiful scenery. The greenery of the cultivated olive groves contrasted sharply with the dry and arid natural flora. As we got off the coach, a small group of local children approached, babbling away in Portugese. It was obvious they were begging for money, so we gave them a little. At that point, our tour guide arrived on the scene and gave the children a good telling off in Portugese Somewhat embarrassed, I asked her what she had said. "If you are going to beg for money, then at least be clean," is what she told them. I felt even more sorry for the poor children and gave them a little more money.

The Monchique Mountains are famous for their sulphurous spring water. Drinking a glass of this foul smelling and equally foul tasting liquid is claimed to endow the drinker with an extra ten years of life. Like other tourists, I participated in this myth, mainly to be polite to our hosts. Not surprisingly, before leaving you had to drink some other alcoholic liquid which, surprise, surprise, negated the effect of the extra longevity. All part of the tourist trap, it was still good fun. Before leaving, we duly climbed to the 'summit' to be recorded on film for posterity (Image 129).

Vera, Andrew and Me at the summit of the Monchique
Mountains 1983. Taken by Michael.

12.6 A MEMORABLE DAY

How did a family of four, on a single salary and living in a large detached house, manage to afford all these holidays? ICI shares, that's how. The company ran a generous profit-sharing scheme and each year paid a bonus to employees in the form of ICI shares. Ranging from 10 per cent of salary for an excellent year to zero for an abysmal year, the bonus was typically around 5 – 7 per cent. Selling the shares provided the cash for our holidays. However, in the recession of the early eighties the company, like many others, performed very badly and no profit-sharing bonus was paid. Accordingly, that year (1984) we had to curtail our holiday spending. We still managed to enjoy our spring and autumn weekend breaks in the Lake District and Richmond respectively, but instead of a two week holiday we decided to have days out with our families. We had many such days out but one sticks in my memory. Leighton Hall.

Located on the southern fringes of the Lake District Leighton Hall is a small stately home. Although the house and gardens are beautiful in their own right, Leighton Hall is famous for its displays of falconry. Vera's dad, George, was an avid amateur photographer and keen walker who loved the outdoor life. So it was Vera's mother and dad that we took to Leighton Hall on a lovely summer's day. After enjoying a tour of the house and gardens, it was time for the main event, a falconry display. George was in his element. Armed with both his still camera and his beloved 'super eight' cine camera, he got some breathtaking pictures. But the highlight of the day was yet to come.

For the finale of the falconry display, the instructor asked all the keen photographers to stand in a line with their cameras at the ready. Standing about a hundred yards away the instructor, with a magnificent golden eagle perched on his arm, told the photographers to get ready for some wonderful shots as the eagle flew towards them and over their heads. However, unbeknown to the photographers, his accomplice had secretly placed some food on the ground just behind them. A sweep of the instructor's arm and the eagle was released. With its eight foot wing span it was an awesome sight as it flew at great speed towards the line of photographers. But its flight path wasn't over their heads but directly at their midriffs! It was going straight for the food on the ground. I have never seen so many grown men scatter so swiftly. It was hilarious to the onlookers but not, I suspect, for the frightened photographers. They needn't have worried. At the very last instant, the eagle soared up and over their heads, dropping swiftly to the ground to reap its reward. No doubt it had performed this feat many times before. Realising they had been 'conned', the photographers joined in the fun and got their close up pictures of the eagle enjoying its food. I think that was one of George's best ever days out.

The exposure of our children to the sea and swimming pools on our holidays triggered a safety alert and prompted us to arrange swimming lessons for Andrew who, by the time of these holidays, was attending primary school (Chapter 19). When he was about seven we enrolled him into Rick's Swim School. Many other parents followed suit and a large proportion of Rick's learners were pupils of Beaumont Primary School. Rick was a good instructor who quickly gained the confidence of the children. He made sure the lessons were fun and gradually transformed the children from non-swimmers afraid of the water to swimmers who were confident in the water. He accomplished this in stages. At the beginning, each learner wore fully inflated lifebelts and armbands. As they gained confidence, the lifebelt was discarded first then, surreptitiously, he gradually deflated the armbands until they too could be discarded. Each swimmer learned the breaststroke, front crawl and backstroke and chose which one to specialise in. The finale entailed each swimmer doing 50 metres in their stroke of choice to earn their certificate. Andrew chose the backstroke and duly gained his certificate. Like myself and Vera, he never became a water baby but at least he could swim.

However, it wasn't all holidays and play. These pastimes required money and that came from my work at ICI.

13

A TIME FOR CHANGE

It wasn't all play. At work, times they were a changing. In 1979, after ten consecutive years of research into novel dyes for textiles, I was offered a totally different role. A role away from the coloured world of dyestuffs to the colourless world of biocides. It was a challenge I couldn't refuse. Biocides was an emerging business with huge potential. These industrial 'bug killers' were in demand and ICI had two of the best products on the market.

13.1 BIOCIDES

VANTOCIL,* a colourless, odourless, tasteless, safe biocide, was a leading alternative to chlorine and had the potential to command a massive market share of the lucrative swimming pool sanitisation business, especially in the private pools of the USA. Even bigger was our prime product, PROXEL. The active ingredient was BIT (benzisothiazolone), a very effective anti-bacterial which had many uses, especially paint preservation. It controlled and eradicated all the insidious bacteria such as Escherichia Coli, Aspergillus Niger and Staphylococcus Aureus. (MRSA – Methycillin Resistant Staphylococcus Aureus – wasn't a problem then but it would have killed that too.) BIT's only downside was that, in a concentrated form, it occasionally caused dermatitis to people who handled it. A similar product without this adverse effect would be ideal. My main task was to help discover such a product.

The Section that included the Biocides Group was run by Dr Jim Wilde. Small in stature, he was a shrewd manager who knew the strengths and weaknesses of his staff very well. The Biocides Group was led by Dr Denis Pemberton. Denis supervised three chemist teams, Dr Alan Buckley and his assistant Jeff Wilton, Bernard Tury and Janet Blake, and myself and Ray White. Bernard had made a mini-breakthrough

---

* It is based on the oligomeric PHMB (poly-hexamethylene biguanide)

with his discovery of 1-thiocyanato-8-nitronaphthalene. This novel molecule exhibited almost the same anti-bacterial activity as BIT but without the adverse side effect. Could this lead to something better than BIT? I worked closely with Bernard pursuing his lead and although we made steady progress, all the products failed to match the outstanding stability of BIT. It was a dead end. Reluctantly, I turned my attention to different types of molecules, molecules more similar in structure to BIT.

A vital source of information to any research chemist was the academic and patent literature. It was tedious, but essential, work trawling through the hundreds of published papers and patents on a weekly basis. The majority were irrelevant but occasionally, a gem would appear. And so it proved in biocides. My technical marketing colleague, Dr Bryan Backhouse, deserves the credit for he was first to spot an obscure publication from Dr Brahram Shroot at CIRD in the South of France. This International Centre for Research on Dermatology had just published a patent on MIT (methylene isothiazolone), a closely related chemical to BIT, for use in hand creams. Eureka! If it was for use in human hand creams then it must be perfectly safe on human skin. And, being a very similar structure to BIT, it should exhibit similar stability and anti-bacterial activity. Brimming with expectation, Bryan and I arranged a meeting with Braham Shroot at CIRD to pursue the matter further.

The journey to the French Riviera represented my first overseas business trip for the company. After flying to Nice, we collected the pre-booked hire car and drove to our hotel on the lovely Riviera resort of Antibe. Quaint and quintessentially French, Antibe abounded with street cafes and restaurants. After a delicious evening meal washed down with equally delicious wine, we retired to our hotel to prepare for the meeting the following day.

To minimise the cost Bryan and I shared a twin room. Tired after my long day of travelling, I soon fell asleep. The next morning I was awoken by a loud banging on the bedroom door. It was the maid. She wanted to make up the room. But where was Bryan? His bed was empty. As I went into the hallway to greet the maid, I stumbled over Bryan. He was huddled on the hall floor wrapped in blankets. Apparently, my snoring was so bad that he had shut himself in the hallway to grab a few hours sleep!

The meeting with CIRD had a positive outcome. Permission was given for us to explore the efficacy of MIT as a biocide and, if it proved promising, a licence would be granted. In the event, it was effective, a licence was granted and MIT was added to our product range.

My passion for understanding why things happen followed me into biocides. I continued my fundamental studies on structure-activity, this time on anti-bacterials, a study that would later lead me into the relationship between the chemical structure of a dye and its toxicity, especially its mutagenicity and carcinogenicity (cancer causing ability).[1] These structure-toxicity relationships would prove useful in my next assignment as I returned from the colourless world of biocides back to the world of colour. But not to the traditional world of colour for textiles, but to an exciting new world of colour. Before I do so, allow me to recount two strange incidents.

Once a week, on Friday lunchtimes, Ray, myself and two of his friends, Pat Harrell and Alan Morrissey, went to the local baths at Harpurhey for a swim. It was a refreshing end to the working week. Alan was a keen student of karate and, to display his skill, he invited a number of colleagues to a demonstration in his laboratory. I was intrigued. What was he going to do? On a laboratory bench a plank of wood was supported between two blocks. He was going to break it with his hand! He rolled up his sleeve, composed himself and, with a loud Japanese war cry, slammed his clenched hand into the wood. There was a sickening crack. Unfortunately, it wasn't the sound of breaking wood, but of breaking bone. He had broken his wrist. The management were not amused and soon afterwards Alan changed career to become a policeman in Bermuda.

The second strange event concerned the disappearing act of Les Mather, a chemist in Bill Black's Formulation Section. Bill was an amiable Scotsman who, at lunchtime, would wander round the laboratories of his staff looking for someone to chat to. Without fail, his opening remark was, "Hey laddie. How you're doing?" Once started, Bill could chat for ages and some staff, particularly Les, devised an ingenious way of avoiding such lunchtime banter. He removed the side panels of two storage cupboards beneath a laboratory bench to provide a space big enough for him to lie down and, just before Bill approached, he would secrete himself within this space and have a snooze in his sleeping bag. Every lunchtime. The absence of Les puzzled Bill and he would ask the other staff where he was. "I don't know," was the usual answer but one day, one of the less bright people replied, "He's asleep under the bench."

"Don't be daft," said Bill with a chuckle as he walked jauntily out of the laboratory.

13.2 DIFFERENT COLOURS

William Henry Perkin invented the first synthetic dye *Mauveine* in 1856 so the textile dyes industry can be described, quite rightly, as mature. By the 1970s dyes were available in all colours for all substrates. Essentially, it was just a matter of who could manufacture them at the lowest cost. Historically, the bulk of the world's dye production was located in just three countries; Germany (Bayer, BASF (Badische Anilin Soda Fabriken) and Hoechst), Switzerland (Ciba-Geigy and Sandoz) and Britain (ICI). However, by the late 1970s, this situation began to change.

Several Third World and Far Eastern countries were starting to manufacture dyes in significant quantities and, because of their lower labour costs, the dyes were manufactured more cheaply than in the European countries. The fact that many of the dyes were no longer protected by patents, plus the fourfold increase in the early 1970s in the price of oil, the basic feedstock of the dyestuffs industry, exacerbated the already difficult situation for the large European dye producers. Accordingly, as commodity dye production began to switch to the lower cost producers, most dye companies in the Western world began to diversify, seeking high technology (hi-tech) applications offering both patent protection and higher profit margins for their dyes. ICI led the way. In 1980, an embryonic group was created, ICI Electronics Group. Based at Runcorn, this group, led by John Mellersh, evaluated a number of hi-tech areas that required sophisticated organic chemicals, including dyes. Several emerging applications were identified and prioritised, including telecommunications (non-linear optics and infrared absorbers), flat screen displays (liquid crystal dyes), and printing and imaging (e.g. thermal printing). The dye research for these new hi-tech applications would be done by the chemists at Blackley. A team led by Mike Hutchings worked on dyes for non-linear optics, one led by Paul Gordon on infrared absorbers and one led by Dave Thompson on liquid crystal dyes. In 1983, after four enjoyable years on biocides research, I was recalled back into the colours fold to lead a small team on dyes for thermal printing, as well as dyes for charge control agents (CCAs) used in photocopiers and laser printers. I was back where I belonged.

13.3 IN PRINT

Because of the new emphasis on dyes for hi-tech applications, a recruitment drive resulted in an influx of bright, young, highly qualified individuals, some of whom I have mentioned above. Even though at the time I was working on biocides and not dyes, several of these new recruits asked me for advice. One went further. Dismayed at the lack of a suitable book on dye chemistry for graduates new to the field, Paul Gordon suggested that we write such a book. It was an excellent suggestion but a daunting task. Full of youthful enthusiasm, we decided to go for it.

Our decision was helped by the fact that we had recently written a chapter for a book edited by Dr John Griffiths of Leeds University.[2] Being one of the few industrial dyestuff chemists who published articles in the academic literature, John asked me to write a chapter on the non-textile uses of dyes. Because I was working on biocides, not dyes, and because of Paul's desire to learn about the hi-tech uses of dyes, we wrote the chapter together.

Paul's supervisor for his PhD, Professor Charles W Rees of Imperial College, London, was a leading UK academic. Well respected by government and industry alike, he had influential contacts with several publishers. He recommended that we send a synopsis of the proposed book to Springer-Verlag, a well known German publisher of scientific books. We did and it was accepted. A contract was signed whereby we would produce the finished manuscript for the book within two years. It was 1980 so we had until 1982 to complete the task.

The format of the book was quickly agreed and we shared the writing. In some cases we each wrote 50 per cent of a chapter but, more usually, we wrote whole chapters. Paul tended to write the synthetic organic chemistry chapters whilst I focused on the colour and constitution aspects. It worked well. We spent lots of time together, checking and cross-checking our work. These sessions normally took place at our house with Vera making our tea. Indeed, it was Vera who converted our scribbled longhand into readable text on her trusty old typewriter, although Paul's mother did a little of the typing too. Paul was also a very keen amateur photographer and took some charming photographs of Andrew and Michael (Image 130).

Michael and Andrew taken by Paul (circa 1980).

The manuscript for the book was completed on schedule. Having joint authors helped since each of us encouraged and motivated the other. Damaging my back playing five-a-side football, although excruciating at the time, was also beneficial since I needed two weeks off work. (And no, I didn't do it deliberately.) It was a timely injury, providing more time at the proofing stage.

All that remained was to decide a suitable title for the book. Thus far, we had used the uninspiring but working title of *Dye Chemistry*. We needed something more catchy. More sexy. Something with a bit more panache. After wracking our brains for several weeks it was Paul who came up with the ingenious title of *Organic Chemistry in Colour*.

The book was published in hardback in 1983.[3] It received excellent reviews and quickly sold out. The publisher brought out a cheaper paperback edition, which also sold extremely well. Its popularity was such that a Russian edition was issued in 1987. I could now see my name in Russian! (Image 131).

Publication of our book was recognised by our employers. A photograph and short article appeared in the in-house magazine, Hexagon News (Image 132).

П.Гордон П.Грегори

ОРГАНИЧЕСКАЯ ХИМИЯ КРАСИТЕЛЕЙ

Перевод с английского
Ю. М. Славина-Мирского

под редакцией
д-ра хим. наук Г. Н. Ворожцова

Title of our book in Russian. My name is on the top right.

A gap in the scientific book market has been filled by the publication of 'Organic Chemistry in Colour' written by Peter Gregory and Paul Gordon of Research Department.
The book which deals with theoretical calculations in the dyestuffs field is published by Springer-Verlag and costs 71 US dollars, though copies are available in the Division Library.
Mr Gregory of Special Chemicals Section said he and Dr Gordon of Application Intermediates and Design Section had noticed that books on dyestuffs tended to concentrate on the technological aspect of the subject.
They decided that as there was little or nothing on theoretical calculations they would produce one themselves. In their own time they spent two and a half years researching and writing and a further eighteen months checking proofs and awaiting publication before their book was available. The authors are pictured above with Mr Gregory, left, and Dr Gordon, right.

Article in Hexagon News about the publication of our book.

13.4 FOILED AGAIN

At the time we were writing the book (and I was still working on biocides), a plethora of posters suddenly appeared around the research building advertising a new MSc (Master of Science) course at Manchester Metropolitan University. The course, entitled *Strategies on Organic Synthesis*, was devised by Dr Vic Garner, a former chemist from ICI Pharmaceutical Division at Alderley Park. He had decided to change career and become a lecturer. Having missed out on the opportunity to obtain a PhD (Chapter 7), I was sorely tempted to enrol for this two year part-time evening course and obtain a

Masters degree. However, fate decreed that, rather than being a student on the course, I would be a lecturer!

The course consisted of several modules, one of which was dye chemistry. Peter Bamfield, my Section Leader and boss, had been approached by Vic Garner to do this module and he had, somewhat reluctantly, agreed. (Giving lectures was not one of his favourite activities.) Aware that Paul and I were in the process of writing such a book, he deemed it highly appropriate for us to take over the role. We agreed and began preparing a course of about twelve lectures.

I remember feeling very nervous before delivering the first lecture, partly because it was breaking new ground by lecturing at a university but also because a good number of people on the course were from ICI, both the Research Department at Blackley where I worked, and from ICI Pharmaceutical Division. One such person was Roy Bradbury, whom we'll meet again later. I needn't have worried. The lecture was extremely well received. As for the book, Paul did the organic synthesis lectures and I did the colour and constitution ones. Later that night, I drove home 'on a high'* listening to Barbara Dickson blasting out 'Caravan' from the tape in my car.

The course was a resounding success and ran for a number of years. The dye chemistry lectures were refined into a 'Colour Chemistry Course' which I gave for over two decades, both in-house and externally. (Paul had been promoted and moved to our Huddersfield Works site.) Within ICI, I must have given the Colour Chemistry Course over a dozen times, usually at Blackley to new recruits, but also at other sites such as Grangemouth and Runcorn. I also gave the course at universities, conferences and other companies (see Chapter 21). I never got an MSc but, sometime later, I would receive something even better.

13.5 NEW GROUP

As pointed out previously, I returned to dyestuffs research in 1983 to lead a small team on novel dyes for thermal printing. ICI Imagedata, as that part of Electronics Group had become, had chosen Dye Diffusion Thermal Transfer (D2T2) – reminiscent of the cute little robot R2D2 of Star Wars fame – as one of their key technologies. Three solvent soluble dyes were required; a yellow, a magenta and a cyan, the famous YMC trichromat used in all colour printing systems. The dyes needed to have demanding properties. For example, the colours had to be matched precisely. These three dyes had to produce millions of colours just by mixing them in the correct proportions! Their colours had to be vivid and vibrant. (It's impossible to make a dull dye bright but you can make a bright dye duller.)

---

* Giving a good lecture always left me with a feeling of euphoria

And, they had to display excellent light fastness. In other words, any prints or photographs made from these dyes had to survive for many years without fading. These were just a few of the exacting properties that D2T2 dyes needed to possess. Not surprisingly, none of the existing dyes fulfilled all these criteria. It was up to our team to invent three new dyes.

Although we had the 'chemistry set' we needed to collaborate with a partner who possessed the 'electronics set'. It is common practice in industry for companies with complementary skills to collaborate. In this case, our partner with the 'electronic set' was Nikon.

As everyone is aware, Nikon is a Japanese camera company. For this envisaged new technology of electronic photography (now known as digital photography), an electronic (digital) camera was required. The idea of digital photography was both simple and appealing.[4] (An established technology nowadays, it was revolutionary in the early 1980s.) In a digital camera, a memory card replaced the silver halide film. Hundreds of photographs could be stored on the memory card and viewed on your computer. (Nowadays of course they appear instantly on the screen of your camera.) Bad photographs could be deleted immediately and new ones taken. Indeed, once a digital camera and memory card had been purchased, it didn't cost a single penny to take, and subsequently view, literally hundreds of pictures, since the memory card can be used over and over again. The only cost incurred, apart from batteries, was when a photograph was printed. D2T2 was the technology aiming for this lucrative multi-billion dollar photographic market. But, as we shall see later, it had competition from ink jet printing.

As was the norm in collaborations, people from each company met face-to-face on a regular basis to discuss progress (plus any problems). Although other forms of communication were also employed, such as the telephone, emails, faxes and even video conferences, nothing came close to matching face-to-face meetings. In the July of 1985, such a meeting with Nikon was arranged in Tokyo. The original plan was for Derek Toms, the project leader, and Richard Hann (Image 204, page 349), the key scientist, both of whom were based at Runcorn, to fly out to Japan for the meeting. However, for some reason, Richard was unable to go and a replacement was needed.

We had already booked our summer holiday in Newquay and it clashed with the Nikon meeting in Japan. Therefore, I was reluctant to go. Because the meeting was deemed extremely important, I was put under enormous pressure to attend. Eventually, I relented. We re-booked our holiday for August, with ICI Imagedata bearing the extra cost. Richard Marboro, a polymer chemist from ICI Wilton, was also going on the trip. Apparently, it took two of us to replace Richard Hann!

My trip to Tokyo was my first long haul trip for the company. After catching the shuttle from Manchester to London, we flew business class in the upstairs cabin of a jumbo jet. I had never experienced such opulence. It was lovely. The only slight downsides were that Derek became a little unwell and that, because of poor relations with Russia, we had to fly to Japan the long way round via Anchorage in Alaska. Never having been to Japan, I didn't know what to expect.

I was impressed. Everything worked. The trains and buses were clean and punctual. Streets were tidy and safe. Taxis had white linen cloths draped over their seats, the drivers wore white gloves and the doors opened automatically. The Japanese people were so polite and friendly I couldn't believe how they had committed such unspeakable atrocities in World War II.* Finally, to cap it all, tipping was not allowed. Anywhere.

The meetings with Nikon proceeded well. On the first day, our Japanese hostesses were amazed at the amount of coffee we drank as we perused the reams and reams of data generated by Nikon on our products. However, we faced a strong competitor in Dai Nippon Printing (DNP). One of the largest Japanese printing companies (Dai Nippon Printing translates, literally, as Big Japanese Printing), they always seemed to be one step ahead of us.

Towards the end of the week Derek's boss, Dr Bill Barlow, joined us in Japan for the final day of meetings with Nikon and, on the Thursday evening, our hosts took us to a Japanese restaurant. As is the custom, we took off our shoes before entering the restaurant. After a typical Japanese meal, eaten whilst sitting cross-legged on the floor,** we exchanged presents. Bottles of single malt whisky, purchased at Heathrow airport, were gratefully received by our Japanese hosts. They reciprocated with beautiful fans and fine silk scarves. After the meal, we put our shoes back on, bade farewell to our hosts and departed back to the Palace Hotel for a nightcap.

On Friday, after several days of technical meetings had ended, we were ushered into the lofty echelon of Nikon's main boardroom. The final act of the visit was to have a discussion with their chairman and senior directors over a cup of Japanese green tea. Our hosts were so obliging we felt like royalty.

Saturday was a free day prior to our return home on the Sunday afternoon. Derek had kindly arranged a visit to Expo 85 which, in 1985, was held in Tokyo.

---

* An employee at Blackley, who'd spent time in a Japanese prisoner-of-war camp, witnessed these atrocities first hand. Each morning the camp commandant lined up all the prisoners, walked along the line and selected one prisoner at random. The unfortunate soul was forced to kneel, whereupon the commandant cut off his head with his sword. Each night you never knew if you'd be the one selected the following morning. It was so horrific the prisoners were scarred for life. Indeed, it left the employee with such a fierce hatred of the Japanese that he was always given the day off when any Japanese visited the site. Otherwise, he would have gone beserk.

** One tip. When visiting Japan, always wear loose fitting trousers. Sitting cross-legged on a floor in tight-fitting trousers for several hours is not recommended.

It was a mixture of business and pleasure. One of the digital photography stands was using materials from DNP, our competitor, for their photographs. To obtain a photograph a member of the audience had to re-enact a scene to a video clip. There were several clips to choose from, including a wild west gunslinger and an orchestral conductor. Derek opted to conduct the orchestra, much to the amusement of the Japanese onlookers. Unfortunately, when it came to getting his photograph, the thermal printer had broken down and all he got was a laser print. We never did get to analyse DNP's dyes. Such was Sod's Law.

We also got some pleasure from the many rides available. One, the Python, made me feel dizzy and sickly. Strapped upright in a standing position, the ride twisted and turned at high speed around a tortuous track, doing several loop-the-loops in the process. I recovered by having a coffee and a cake at one of the many outdoor cafes, watching the Japanese girls go by. "They're quite pretty, aren't they," I remarked. And they were. Many Japanese girls, with their jet black hair and dusky complexions, were indeed attractive.

"Yes," replied Derek, "except they've got no tits."* Sadly, it was a crude, but true, remark. They were flat-chested. But, as I was to discover some years later, the advent of McDonalds would change all that.

On the Sunday morning I was up early, arriving outside the breakfast room at 6-55 a.m. On the menu, it stated that breakfast was served from 7-00 a.m. to 10-30 a.m. I watched the clock on the wall as the time crept ever nearer to 7-00 a.m. To my utter amazement, and, it must be said, admiration, at the very instant that the second finger signalled that it was 7-00 a.m., the doors to the breakfast room opened. In Japan, punctuality was the norm.

After consuming a hearty (English) breakfast, I crossed the busy main road and walked to the entrance of the Emperor's East Garden. What a treat. Surrounded by a moat of green water, it was an oasis of peace and tranquillity in the heart of bustling Tokyo. Watching the koi carp gliding gracefully amongst the lily beds was so relaxing. The intricate red and black wooden bridges across the ponds completed the very Japanese scene. Transported to another world, I lingered as long as possible before heading for downtown Tokyo to buy some presents.

The attendants in a shop selling Japanese clothes were most helpful. For Vera, I bought a beautiful silk kimono. "Would you like to buy one for your secretary too?" they asked.

"No thank-you," I replied politely, but secretly intrigued by their culture of present-giving. Red, typified by the rising sun, is the national colour of Japan and a row of red T-shirts with black kanji characters caught my eye. "What do they say?" I asked.

---

* On a separate occasion, Ian Wasson also remarked that they were bow-legged

"Ichi ban, meaning Number 1," came the reply. Both Andrew and Michael were so delighted with their 'Number 1' Japanese T-shirts they literally wore them out.

Something wasn't quite right. I'd been aware of this since the evening meal at the Japanese restaurant. I couldn't quite put my finger on what it was but I knew there was something wrong. Settling into my seat for the long 12 hour flight home, I pondered what it might be, but still it eluded me. No matter, I thought, it will come to me eventually. And it did. As I removed my shoes, it hit me like a thunderbolt! These weren't mine. Yes, they were the same make. Yes, they were the same style and colour. And yes, they were the same size. But they weren't mine. I had purchased a brand new pair of shoes for the trip to Japan and these were old and worn. Someone in our party had identical shoes to me and we had put on the wrong pairs after the meal. For Bill Barlow, Christmas had come early.

The D2T2 project was proceeding well but strong competition from Japanese companies such as DNP meant that we had to work really hard to stay one step ahead. It quickly became apparent that the small team of two, myself and Ray White, wasn't enough to achieve this objective. More effort was required. Richard recognised this and one of his young chemists, Roy Bradbury, was seconded to Blackley for six months. Roy was a revelation. He had never worked on dyes before but, like me before him, he took to dye chemistry like the proverbial duck to water. Roy loved it so much that his six month secondment turned into a lifetime career! He never returned to Runcorn.

Our team played a major role in the success of the D2T2 project. We invented three novel dyes, a yellow, a magenta and a cyan, having the demanding properties described earlier.[4] Deservedly, the D2T2 team were rewarded with a special bonus for a job well done. That Christmas, I also showed my appreciation. I took my small group of three (Roy, Ray, and Kevin) for a meal at the White Hart. Next time you get your passport photographs from a booth or when you buy a picture of yourself on a ride at Disney World or Alton Towers or any other attraction, you may be viewing our D2T2 dyes.

13.6 TONER TALKS

In addition to Roy and Ray working on dyes for D2T2, I also had Kevin Birkett working on charge control agents (CCAs) for toners. A toner is the 'powder' in photocopiers and laser printers that produces the image (copies or prints) on the paper. In black-and-white photocopiers and laser printers, the toner is black, but in colour copiers and printers yellow, magenta and cyan toners are also required.[5]

A toner containing a charge control agent produces better quality copies and prints. Like many other discoveries, this one was also accidental. A researcher in the

Orient Chemical Company laboratories in Japan added a small amount of a black dye to a toner to improve its 'blackness'. To his amazement, not only did it improve its 'blackness', it dramatically enhanced the quality of the image! The company developed these chromium complex azo dyes into a commercial range of products and sold them under the tradename BONTRON.

Our task was to develop charge control agents superior to the BONTRONS. ICI manufactured and marketed a number of chromium complex azo dyes and these were our starting point. Gestetner, a medium size German photocopier company with a base in Tottenham, was our first partner in this venture. Kevin and I visited Gestetner many times, catching the early morning train from Manchester Piccadilly to London Euston followed by the tube to Tottenham. Our contact was Derek McGee, a likeable, pipe-smoking avuncular person and his young female assistant whom Kevin christened 'thunderthighs'. (Although, of course, she was never aware of this nickname.) In due course, two products were developed, CCA7 and CCA9.[*] The following year, Kevin and I published our work in the academic literature.[6]

At the time Dr Frank Hauxwell, formerly of Research Department, was the Business Manager. Enthusiastic, committed and articulate, Frank played a key role in ensuring the success of the hi-tech colours venture in its early days. Most of all, he was optimistic and championed the project at every opportunity. I felt that he never got the credit he deserved. It was Frank who introduced us to the founder of a company called *Advanced Technology Resources (ATR)*, a man called Ian Mallender. Ian was steeped in the new technologies, particularly electrophotography, and told an amusing after dinner tale about Chester Carlson, the founder of electrophotography. I can't remember the details but it involved Carlson attempting to get funding for his discovery from a large number of companies. In 1938, on a kitchen table at the Waldorf Astoria in New York, Carlson successfully demonstrated the principle of photocopying for the very first time (Image 133). He used basic materials such as wax paper, a sulphur plate, lycopodium powder and a handkerchief and, in his own words, received "an enthusiastic lack of response from over twenty major companies." It was a classic "don't call us, we'll call you" scenario. More setbacks followed. First, his wife left him and then, a little later, his only assistant left him. Despite all these disappointments, Carlson persevered and, in 1944, a small independent company, the Battelle Institute, took up the idea. Three years later Haloid, later to become Xerox, acquired a licence and funded him to the tune of $25,000 per year. The rest, as they say, is history.

ATR were holding a symposium in Vienna and I was invited to attend as ICI's representative. The venue was the Hilton Hotel. It was classy but expensive. Even in 1984 a bottle of lager cost £3.00! It was an informative and productive course.

---

[*]   CCA7 was a chromium complex azo dye and CCA9 a cobalt complex azo dye

Not only did I learn about these new technologies, I also made a number of useful contacts with people from other companies. After the first day of the course we were treated to a demonstration of 'apple strudel making' at our evening meal. To break the ice, each participant had to stand up and introduce himself and his company. I have never forgotten what the man from one company said, although I can't remember his name. "When you think what Dr Johnson, the famous explorer, achieved, just think what Johnson and Johnson can achieve!' I thought it was very witty.

The first ever photocopy made by Chester Carlson.

Ian's assistant was an attractive lady called Grace Moyles. A former British Airways air stewardess, she was graceful, elegant and sophisticated. Both Ian and Grace were excellent hosts as we explored the beautiful city of Vienna. I bought Vera a fine porcelain vase which still takes pride of place in our dining room.

In the September of 1985 the city of Manchester was hosting a large international conference on dye chemistry. Since the headquarters of ICI Dyestuffs Division was in Manchester, both myself and Nigel Hughes, a Senior Research Chemist, were asked by our management to give lectures at this conference. I was to lecture on charge control agents whilst Nigel would speak about the new red benzodifuranone dyes for polyester. The venue for the lectures, rather surprisingly, was the Royal Northern College of Music. We were ICI's ambassadors at this prestigious event and many of the senior managers, including Dr Booth, the Research Manager and our ultimate boss, would be present. Accordingly, we prepared thoroughly for the lectures, including having a 'dress rehearsal' in our own lecture theatre. Neither Nigel nor I wanted to let ourselves, or the company, down.

As the time for my lecture approached (mine was the second one after lunch), I remember visiting the toilets to splash my face with water, brush my hair and straighten my tie. A colleague, Trevor Smith, remarked that I acted like someone preparing to give a lecture! In the event, both mine and Nigel's lectures were good, two of the best of the day. Later, as we were walking along a street in the centre of Manchester, Nigel said that Dr Booth 'looked like a dog with two dicks'. Obviously, he thought we had done well too. This was my first lecture at a major international conference. It wouldn't be my last.

After the rigours of the trip to Japan and lecturing at the conference, I was ready for a break. It was time for me and my family to enjoy some rest and relaxation.

13.7 NEWQUAY

Michael (left) and Andrew enjoying
the Surf on Fistral Beach 1985.

First up was our rearranged holiday in Newquay. The Trebaron Hotel occupied an elevated position overlooking Fistral Beach. It was an ideal location because Andrew and Michael spent a great deal of time frolicking in the sea and surfing (Image 134). They also loved exploring the rocky headland (Image 135). The holiday was a welcome break for the whole family. But it wasn't the only one. Denmark awaited.

Andrew (left) and Michael on the rocks at Newquay 1985.

13.8 LEGOLAND

Our children loved playing with Lego so Vera decided that a holiday in Legoland would be a nice treat. Driving down to Harwich in the October of 1985 the weather was remarkably spring-like. Once our car was safely parked, we boarded the DFDS ship the *Tor Brittania*. It was a magnificent ship (Image 136). During the sea crossing to Esbjerg, we took advantage of the on-board cinema and watched the first of the Police Academy movies. It was a very funny film which we enjoyed immensely.

Despite the cold and inclement weather, our children really enjoyed Legoland. They experienced all the delights that Legoland had to offer, including dressing up as Red Indians (Image 137). In Andrew's case, the highlight was undoubtedly taking and passing his driving test (Image 138). Sadly, Michael missed out on this treat. He wasn't the obligatory 11-years-old. However, he still got to ride in a car (Image 139).

The Tor Brittania cruise ship.

Michael and Andrew at the Indian Village, Legoland 1985.

Andrew taking his driving test.

Michael in his car.

Our accommodation at Legoland was strange. The hotel room was fine. It was clean and modern with an *en suite* bathroom and panoramic views over the Legoland park. However, we could only see two beds. We searched and searched for the missing two beds but to no avail. What should we do? Unpack, that's what we did. As we looked for storage space to put our clothes, Vera pulled out two large drawers under each of the two beds. But they weren't drawers at all, they were the two missing beds! It was an unusual arrangement, but it sufficed.

As we boarded the *Tor Brittania* for our journey home, a nurse greeted us at the top of the gangplank. "Would you like an anti-sea sickness pill, sir?" I was bemused. It was a fine calm day. "The weather in the North Sea is so bad that the sailing has been delayed by four hours. Even so, the crossing will still be very rough. I strongly recommend that you take the pills." We took the nurse's advice and took our pills.

The delay was used to our advantage. After settling in our cabin, we strolled down to the restaurant and graciously accepted the offer of a free meal from the *Smorgabord*. The quantity and choice of food was unbelievable. There was meat of every description, cheeses from around the world, a variety of vegetables and a vast array of fruit, the choice was endless. It was a help yourself meal but it was delicious. We over indulged ourselves and later would be extremely thankful for the efficacy of the anti-sea sickness pills.

Sat in our cabin, we listened apprehensively as the *Tor Brittania*, by no means a small ship, was tossed about like a cork. It creaked and groaned under the onslaught of the raging sea. Our children's faces were ashen but, fortunately, they had fallen asleep. Eventually, Vera and I followed suit, but not without thinking the ship might break up and sink.

The weather relented. The following morning we awoke to clear blue skies and a calm sea. This made the final part of our sail most agreeable. Then, after disembarking at Harwich, it was a car ride home and back to the routine of work.

13.9 CARLSON CONTINUED

Later that year Tony Nelson joined our little group to work on organic photoconductors (OPCs). These ingenious chemicals are the magic ingredient in the working of photocopiers and laser printers,[5] replacing the sulphur used by Carlson. Light years behind established companies such as Xerox, IBM and Canon, we still wanted a slice of the action.

Tony did a good job. He set up testing equipment, devised suitable test protocols and evaluated some of our pigments. A red pigment, dibromoanthanthrone (DBA), when present in the correct crystalline form, proved a useful organic photoconductor for photocopiers and was added to the selling range. Metal-free phthalocyanine was a good organic photoconductor for laser printers.[*] However, there was a problem. How to make it reliably. Derek Dobson from the Formulation Section found a way. Taking crude metal free phthalocyanine (H_2Pc) made by Bert McKay at Grangemouth, he milled the dry product with steel balls in a steel container for 48 hours. The crude x-form metal free phthalocyanine was treated with nitric acid, filtered and washed acid free with water. After careful drying, the product was suitable for use as an organic photoconductor.

Out of the blue Fuji-Xerox of Japan required 10kg of our x-form metal free phthalocyanine. Urgently. It may not seem very much, but 10kg was an awful lot of chemical to make in the Research Department. A few grams up to a few hundred grams was the norm. However, since a little organic photoconductor went a long way and commanded a high price, we pressed ahead. Six more steel cylinders were hastily made by our engineering department, the crude metal free phthalocyanine synthesis was cranked up at Grangemouth and the milling operation at Blackley was carried out seven days per week. This meant that I had to go to work on Saturdays

---

[*]   As the x-form polymorph (x-H_2Pc)

and Sundays to empty the cylinders and treat the crude product as described above. Wearing a boiler suit, gloves and face mask was no protection against the superfine blue powder. It got everywhere. On getting into the bath at home, the water always turned deep blue.

13.10 FRIENDLY COMPETITION

Our limited range of products for hi-tech applications was selling reasonably well but they weren't the blockbusters we had been hoping for. Our Section Manager, Peter Bamfield, held weekly Monday morning meetings with his six or so Group Leaders. Once per month, the sales figures for each of the businesses were discussed. This created a friendly rivalry between myself, who led the hi-tech colours group, and Dr John Schofield, who led the SOLSPERSE hyperdispersants group. Both were embryonic businesses with the potential for rapid growth. Although growing steadily, the sales figures were relatively low (ca £5 million). A big breakthrough was needed.

REFERENCES

1. P Gregory, 'Azo Dyes: Structure-Carcinogenicity Relationships' in: Dyes and Pigments, Vol. 7, pp. 45-56, 1986.
2. PF Gordon and P Gregory, 'Non-Textile Uses of Dyes' in: Developments in the Chemistry and Technology of Dyes, J Griffiths (ed.), Blackwell 1984.
3. PF Gordon and P Gregory, 'Organic Chemistry in Colour', Springer-Verlag, Berlin, Heidelberg, New York, London, Paris, Tokyo 1983.
4. P Gregory, 'Electronic Photography – The Future' in: Chemistry in Britain, January 1989, pp. 47-50.
5. P Gregory, 'Modern Reprographics' in: Review of Progress in Colouration, Vol. 24, 1994, p. 1.
6. KL Birkett and P Gregory, 'Metal Complex Dyes as Charge Control Agents' in: Dyes and Pigments, Vol. 7, pp. 341-350, 1986.

14

LEADING THE
JET SET

In the seventies and early eighties home and office printing was the domain of conventional 'impact' printing technologies such as typewriters, daisywheel and especially dot matrix printers. Although functional, they had a number of serious deficiencies. For example, they were noisy, slow, and could print only in black-and-white. Furthermore, typewriters and daisywheel printers produced only text, not graphics. Therefore, the time was ripe for better printing technologies.

From a number of contenders, just three so-called 'non-impact printing' technologies vied for the expanding home and office printing market.[1] All three overcame the deficiencies of the impact printers. Thus, laser, thermal transfer and ink jet printers were quiet, fast, could print (or copy) in colour as well as black-and-white, and produce graphics (pictures) as easily as text.

At that time, electrophotography, perhaps more familiar as photocopying and laser printing (Chapter 13), was the most prevalent non-impact printing technology. Direct thermal printing had been around for some time and was in decline, due in part to technical deficiencies. (Till receipts are a common example of direct thermal printing and, as most of us are no doubt aware, they fade quickly and become unreadable.) However, thermal transfer printing, particularly Dye Diffusion Thermal Transfer (D2T2), was new. Dye Diffusion Thermal Transfer was aimed, primarily, at the embryonic digital photography market (Chapter 13). Ink jet printing, the third technology, was the new kid on the block. Thermal 'drop-on-demand' (DOD) ink jet printing, the system used in most ink jet printers for the home and office, was discovered independently in 1979 by both Canon in Japan and Hewlett-Packard (HP) in the USA. Yet again it was an accidental discovery, as Canon's account[2] testifies:-

A Canon discovery, Bubble Jet Technology is based on the simple natural phenomenon that when fluids are heated, bubbles are produced. Who would have imagined, even a

228

mere thirty years ago, that this phenomenon, which we have always taken for granted, was bound to have a revolutionary impact on modern printing technology.

An unsuspecting Canon researcher had no idea that he was on the brink of translating this wonder of nature into a technological application. By sheer accident, he brought a soldering iron in contact with an ink-filled syringe. A bubble formed in the syringe, forcing a spurt of ink out of the needle. He was so intrigued he decided this 'accident' was worth reporting: and did so, back in the seventies.

Today, in the nineties, Canon is still grateful to their researcher for having reported this 'accident' because his discovery launched further research into the application of bubbles. The result: Canon's exclusive Bubble Jet Technology, which works wonders in printers and copiers, naturally, as it were. In its current advanced form, the Bubble Jet principle does not differ at all from the accidental discovery: a pulsed signal (electric current) in the heater produces several thousand sudden temperature rises (up to 300 to 4000C) per second: each of these in turn forms a tiny bubble: this bubble exerts pressure and forces a single, ultra-fine droplet to be ejected: the pressure drops, a vacuum is created, attracting new ink and the process begins all over again.

These then were the three technologies that would dominate the lucrative home and office printing market. And we were involved in all three. The photocopying, laser printing and ink jet businesses were based at Blackley, whilst, as mentioned in the previous chapter, we also did the dye research for ICI Imagedata's D2T2 business.

Within a few years, laser printers and especially ink jet printers had replaced virtually all the impact printers. Dot matrix printers suffered the most. These ubiquitous printers of the sixties, seventies and early eighties were wiped out completely. It was a disaster for the company who made them, the Seiko Epson Corporation (SEC) in Japan. Having lost a major part of their business, they had to respond quickly. And they did. Seiko Epson became the third main player in the ink jet business. Unable to use the thermal (bubble jet) technology because of HP and Canon patents, they used a different technology, piezoelectric ink jet. Between them, these three companies dominated the ink jet printer market, holding about 90 per cent of the total market in the early to mid-nineties. Ink jet printing was big business and we wanted to be the major supplier of ink jet dyes.

The ink jet research done by Tony Baxter and his team for Canon in the mid-eighties was unsuccessful in that it didn't result in any commercial products. However, it gave us a sound knowledge of ink jet dyes and ink jet printing that proved invaluable in later collaborations. One of the reasons for the failure of the Canon collaboration was that, unbeknown to us, Canon were also collaborating with a Japanese dye company, Mitsubishi. Apparently, Mitsubishi were given 'achievable' dye targets whilst those assigned to ICI were almost impossible. We needed a big breakthrough.

Of all the printing technologies ink jet was the simplest. It involved squirting coloured water (the ink) on to paper. The squirting was done either thermally[3] (Canon and HP) or by a piezoelectric crystal[4] (SEC). The simplicity of the technology is what made it so appealing. To some dye companies, ink jet printing was just an interesting curiosity that would be here today and gone tomorrow. Not so ICI. We believed fervently that ink jet would become THE dominant printing technology for the home/office market. Simplicity is excellence and you can't get much simpler than squirting coloured water on to paper. Therefore, when HP came looking for a dye partner, we were determined to be the company chosen.

The simplicity of ink jet printers meant they were much cheaper than laser printers. This was the main reason that HP's first ink jet printer, the THINK JET (THINK is an acronym of THermal INK), and also Canon's 'Bubble Jet' printers, were selling extremely well. But they had a weakness, an Achilles heel. Unlike laser printers, which utilise a water insoluble pigment (carbon black) and a resin to bind the image to the paper, ink jet prints were not water fast. They smudged. Badly. Very badly. Any contact with water caused them to smudge. For example, if tea or coffee was accidentally spilt on them, the prints became illegible. Even handling ink jet prints with moist fingers caused them to smudge. This deficiency was exploited fully by laser printer salesmen. Armed with water pistols, they took great delight in demonstrating the superior water fastness of their product compared to that of ink jet. It was becoming a major problem for the manufacturers of ink jet printers, a problem they needed to address.

HP were basically a computer company. They had no dye expertise whatsoever. Furthermore, as mentioned in Chapter 13, the bulk of the world's dyestuffs industry was located in Europe, not the USA. Accordingly, in 1988 representatives from HP visited all the major dye companies in Germany (Bayer, BASF and Hoechst), Switzerland (Ciba-Geigy and Sandoz) and the UK (ICI) to find a partner with the right 'dye chemistry set' to complement their 'ink jet printer' set.

By this time the ink jet research had been transferred to Nigel Hughes, one of our most experienced and capable dye chemists. Nigel prepared an impressive presentation for the HP delegation, including a number of stunning practical demonstrations. One of these involved overprinting a dyed sheet of paper with one of our colourless biocides, VANTOCIL (Chapter 13). The biocide bound the dye to the paper 100 per cent so that when the paper was placed in a beaker of water, all the dye which wasn't treated washed away leaving the message from the dye overprinted with VANTOCIL.*

---

* It is a demonstration I have used many times in talks to schoolchildren. Watching their faces as a red piece of paper in a beaker of water gradually transforms into 'Man Utd' (or some other message) 'by magic' is a delight.

The HP delegates, who included Ron Prevost, their project leader, and Norm Palowski, an ink scientist, were most impressed and it was ICI who they chose as their partner for a 12 month collaboration for a water fast black dye for HP's ink jet printers. And so, in the autumn of 1988, Nigel and his small team of Dave Greenwood (Image 140, page 232) and Christine Millard (Image 196, page 322) embarked on the quest for a water fast black dye.

It wasn't an easy task. Dyes having 100 per cent water fastness on paper had proved extremely difficult to obtain (Chapter 9). Achieving this result for a dye in an ink jet printer ink was even harder. On one hand the dye had to be very soluble in water to give a robust and reliable ink. Even a tiny amount of dye that crystallised or precipitated from the ink would clog the printer nozzles, causing failure. Yet, on the other hand, once this highly water soluble dye hit the paper, it had to become water insoluble. Instantly! How could this apparently impossible situation be resolved? By a chemist's ingenuity, that's how.

After exploring several avenues without success, Nigel and his team struck gold. The principles of differential solubility and smelling salts solved the problem. The ink jet ink was slightly alkaline (pH 8-10) whilst most papers were acidic (pH 4-6). Therefore, a dye was required that was soluble in the alkaline ink but insoluble on the acidic paper. Such dyes were already known. They contained carboxylic acid groups, the group present in acetic acid (vinegar). Taking the black dye used in HP's printers, namely CI (Colour Index) Food Black 2,[*] Nigel's team replaced three of the four sulphonic acid groups, the groups that conferred high water solubility to the dye, with carboxylic acid groups to produce a dye having 80 per cent water fastness. This was substantially better than the 30 per cent water fastness of CI Food Black 2 but still not good enough. Changing the dye cation from sodium to ammonium did the rest.[3] The volatile ammonium cation is the active ingredient in smelling salt. It breaks down into the pungent gas ammonia and a proton. This simple change increased the water fastness to 98 per cent and the resulting dye, PROJET Fast Black 2, was launched in 1990. It became our best selling ink jet dye and provided the big breakthrough that we needed. Within a few years, our ink jet dye business alone grew from one or two million pounds per annum to over £50 million.

The collaboration with HP on the water fast black was a WIN-WIN situation. For HP, it gave their ink jet printers a technical advantage over their competitors

---

[*]   Safety was one of the reasons why a food dye was used. Many homes had an ink jet printer and there was always the possibility that ink from the print cartridge would be accidentally spilled on to a person's skin or, even worse, that a child might swallow some ink. Food dyes were eaten so they were deemed to be safe.

(water fast black prints) whilst we at ICI had a leading position supplying novel, patented and highly profitable dyes in a rapidly expanding hi-tech market.

At the Imaging Science and Technology (IS and T) conference in Orlando in October 1991, a joint ICI/HP paper[5] on the water fast black was presented by Suraj Hindagolla from HP. The water fast black was a landmark discovery in the evolution of ink jet printing and, not surprisingly, the paper aroused extreme excitement amongst the audience. This was great kudos for both ICI and HP but it presented a serious dilemma for me. I was the next speaker! The one who had to follow such an explosive lecture. As the applause for Suraj died down and my name was announced by the chairman, I remember saying to Dave Greenwood (Image 140), the joint inventor of the water fast black dye, who was sat next to me, "How do you follow that!"

My lecture on a novel, safe, alcohol soluble black dye for industrial ink jet printers was also well received.[6] Such a dye had been a prime requirement for a number of years and Prahalad Mistry and I executed one of, if not the quickest, dye research projects ever. In just three months, we invented the ideal dye. Taking the water soluble CI Direct Black 168, we made the dye increasingly less water soluble and more alcohol soluble by making fatty amine salts. The best product was the salt with tertiary octylamine. PROJET Black ETOH was launched eleven months after the research was begun and was the fastest ever dye project conducted at Blackley.

As well as participating in the conference Dave and I also had some time exploring the delights of Disney World. Even in October the weather was surprisingly warm and conducive to both shorts and ice cream (Image 140).

Me (left) and Dave at Disney World 1991. The tub
of ice cream wasn't the only tub I was carrying.

Dr Ohta (Images 141 and 142, pages 238 and 239), the leader of the ink jet work at Canon, and several of his colleagues were at the conference. After hearing the water fast black lecture, they invited Peter Bamfield, my boss, and me to a meeting with them in a private room. Intrigued, we accepted their invitation. What would it be about? Our collaboration with Canon had come to nought yet they had just learned of our successful work with their main competitor, HP. After exchanging pleasantries, Ohtasan* complemented us on achieving a water fast black, something they and their collaborators had been unable to achieve. Furthermore, within days of HP launching their Desk Jet printer, Canon had analysed the ink and Ohtasan drew the structure of the black dye on the board.

"Have we got the structure correct?" he asked. Not knowing how to respond, I looked at Peter for assistance.

"Ten out of ten," beamed Peter. "You've got it spot on." I was a little surprised at first by his answer but on reflection it's what every company did: analyse their competitor's products. Ohtasan asked if we would collaborate with them although I think he knew the answer. It wasn't possible at that time due to our commitment to HP, but things would change.

HP were impressed with our work on the water fast black. From starting the research to launching the product had taken less than two years. Normally, this process took between four to seven years. After the research phase, in which a novel dye having the desired properties may or may not be invented, came the toxicological testing. This took a minimum of twelve months and was costly. Next came process development to find the best (most economical and safest) way to make the dye on a large scale. Finally, the dye had to be manufactured. These processes were usually done sequentially but, in the case of the water fast black, they were done in parallel. This was risky in the extreme but, unlike the traditional dyes industry, the hi-tech market moved very quickly. Speed was of the essence.

In 1990, all the ink jet dye research was transferred into my group. It was near the end of the water fast black project. Buoyed by the success of this project, HP wanted more. One of the advantages of ink jet printers is their ability to produce coloured, as well as black, prints at low cost and HP required water fast colour dyes to complement their new water fast black. I remember discussing the possibility of water fast colour dyes with Skip Rung, the boss of Ron Prevost. Instead of just one dye, like the black, three colour dyes were needed; a yellow, a magenta and a cyan. The black dye research took one year. However, the principles required to achieve high water fastness had been discovered so a two year project was agreed to invent a trichromat of yellow, magenta and cyan (YMC) water fast dyes. The agreement was signed and work duly commenced.

Ron Kenyon and Christine Millard, with a little input from me, were the team for this new adventure. Our counterparts in HP were John Coyer, their project leader, and

---

*   In Japan, it is respectful to address someone by adding 'san' to their surname. Ohtasan means, literally, Mr Ohta.

John Skeene. It was a good collaboration. Face-to-face meetings were held every three months to discuss progress, alternating between Manchester and Corvallis, Oregon. In addition, John Skeene spent several weeks at our research laboratories to set up suitable test equipment and test protocols. He loved English pubs, especially those which served a 'Ploughman's Lunch'. Near the end of the project, a large meeting was held at our manufacturing site at Grangemouth. No expense was spared. Everyone stayed at the magnificent Stirling Castle. In the evening a sumptuous Scottish meal was preceded by the ceremony of 'piping in the haggis'. A Scotsman in full Scottish attire played the bagpipes as the haggis was ceremonially paraded into the room. After a convivial evening in which too much food and alcohol was imbibed, it was time for bed. My room was in the dungeons. It was deathly quiet and pitch black when the lights were extinguished. Although I'm not superstitious, the small bedside light remained on throughout the night, partly as a precaution in case I needed the bathroom (or so I convinced myself).

Towards the end of the project we discovered that HP had been simultaneously collaborating with duPont. One of duPont's major projects on pigment-based inks had collapsed leaving dozens of highly specialised ink formulation chemists with nothing to do. DuPont decided to switch them to ink jet ink formulation. And it worked. Led by Ray Work, they successfully developed a water fast black pigment ink and were developing yellow, magenta and cyan pigment-based inks. It boiled down to a straight fight between our dye-based inks and duPont's pigment-based inks. HP asked us to produce large quantities (ca 2 kg) of each of the yellow, magenta and cyan dyes for extensive testing. This we did, with the help of extra effort from Tony Watson and Prahalad Mistry (see Image 196). It proved futile. HP decided not to go with our dyes but to continue with duPont's pigments.* Our whole team was devastated. The dyes were good but HP didn't want them. However, someone else did.

14.2 CANON

After clearing the legalities with HP, our water fast trichromat of dyes was offered to Canon. They seized the opportunity with both hands. The yellow and cyan dyes were fine but we had to develop a different magenta. HP had wanted a really bright dye based on a xanthene, but the penalty was moderate light fastness. Canon were prepared to sacrifice a little brightness in order to obtain better light fastness and this is what we did. And so, in 1993, Canon included our water fast colour dyes PROJET Fast Yellow 2, PROJET Fast Magenta 2 and PROJET Fast Cyan 2 in their latest printers. Ohtasan was pleased and so were we.

---

*   * HP didn't go with duPont's pigments either. They didn't get their water fast colour inks.

This was the beginning of a long and fruitful collaboration with Canon on inkjet dyes. Initially, I was the technical contact and Ian Wasson the technical marketing contact.

Dr Francis Ian Wasson got his degree and PhD at St Andrews University. He was the archetypal English gentleman; slim, balding head and articulate (Image 141). Ian was also good at his job. Not only did we make a good team, crucially, we also got on well together, a key requisite on long business trips. Later, one of our ink jet formulation chemists, Aidan Lavery, an Irishman, also accompanied us. Ohmichisan, from ICI Japan, was our host, guide and interpreter (Images 142 and 143).

A typical visit to Japan began with a taxi to Manchester airport to meet up with Ian and Aidan, followed by the shuttle to Heathrow. Here, single malt whiskys were bought for our Canon hosts before making the twelve hour flight to Japan. Departing Saturday afternoon, the plane touched down at Narita airport in the early hours of Sunday morning. A one hour coach ride conveyed us from the airport on the outskirts of Tokyo to the central bus station. A short taxi ride to the Fairmont Hotel completed the journey, some twenty hours after starting out from home. After a quick wash and brush-up it was time to explore the local park and get some much needed exercise and fresh air. Then, it was time to eat.

On the first evening we always ate at Tony Roma's. There were a number of reasons for this. First, it was within walking distance of the hotel. Second, they did Western type food. And third, it had become a tradition. A fourth reason, certainly for me, was that the Japanese waitresses were young and pretty and wore very short mini skirts. I am not very adventurous with food and played safe. Soup, barbecued spare ribs with French fries followed by apple pie and custard was my usual fare. Ohmichisan used to joke that we all looked like Siberian huskies as we devoured the spare ribs using our fingers. By nightfall, after a 'thirty hour day', we were shattered and tumbled into bed. Unfortunately, the jet lag meant that we got at best a few hours sleep.

Most of the flights proceeded without incident but there was always the odd exception. Following a decent three course meal and oodles of wine, the stewardess came round with a box of chocolates. "Oh, yes please," I said and removed one from the box. It was a chocolate caramel, one of my favourites. Slowly, I let the chocolate coating melt from the caramel centre and, when the caramel had softened, began to chew. It was a huge mistake. The caramel acted like a lump of glue and removed a large filling from my back tooth! Completely. I could feel this large hole in my tooth and it was so sensitive. Even breathing air through my mouth activated the nerve endings. It was so painful, eating or drinking was out of the question. I needed a dentist. And fast.

Whatever else British Airways have on their planes it wasn't a dentist so I had to wait until we arrived at the Fairmont Hotel in Tokyo. Even though it was Sunday, the hotel staff arranged for me to see a local dentist. Escorted by my two 'minders', Roy and Aidan, I made my way to the Japanese dentist. It was a strange situation. I spoke very little Japanese and the dentist and his assistant spoke very little English so communication was mainly by improvised sign language. He quickly realised the problem and rectified it. I was so grateful, even though it took most of the money I had brought. Although they felt a little sorry for me, I think both Roy and Aidan found the episode quite amusing.

The second incident occurred when Roy and I were travelling alone. Sleeping on planes is difficult for me but I must have dozed off as we approached Tokyo. I awoke next to an empty seat. Where was Roy? The toilet. He must have gone to the toilet. I settled back into my seat to await his return and prepare for landing. But he didn't return. Five minutes, ten minutes, twenty minutes elapsed and still no Roy. I was getting worried. The announcement to return to your seats and fasten your seat belts in preparation for landing came over the tannoy. He must return now, surely. But he didn't. There was nothing I could do except sit back and await the landing. As the plane taxied to a halt, Roy suddenly appeared, grinning from ear to ear. Apparently, while I dozed he'd been chatting to a stewardess and told her that his boyhood dream had been to sit in the cockpit of a jumbo jet as it landed. The stewardess had relayed this to the captain and, surprisingly, Roy was allowed into the cockpit to live his dream. (This certainly wouldn't be allowed nowadays.)

The meetings with Canon took place at their Tomaegawa plant on the outskirts of Tokyo. Normally, they lasted about three days. Ohtasan led the Canon delegation with Muraisan his second-in-command. Yamamotosan and Haradasan, their two ink chemists, completed their complement. Our delegation was Ohmichisan, who acted as interpreter, Ian, Aidan and myself. (Later, I would relinquish my role as 'Mr Canon' to Roy.) Mutual respect was established quickly and over the years a strong bond developed between ourselves and our Japanese hosts.

Technically, we came up with some very good concepts. Dye-resin, polymeric dyes and CPI dyes displayed excellent properties but there was always a defect. For dye-resin and polymeric dyes it was robustness of the ink and the complexity of manufacture. For CPI dyes,* well, they almost made it, especially the cyan. The Japanese are fond of mysterious acronyms so we duly obliged with the Close Proximity Interaction (CPI) dyes. It was amusing hearing our hosts saying, "Ah so. Cee Pee Aye dyes." Yet again, it reminded me of the other robot in the Star Wars films, C3PO.

Canon were wonderful hosts. At the meetings we had a 'boxed' lunch. Canon quickly learned my culinary traits and were extremely obliging. Whilst all the other

---

* The principles of CPI dyes were zwitterion formation and anchoring.[3] This produced dyes having instant, 100 per cent water fastness, a highly desirable feature that matched laser prints.

boxes contained a selection of Japanese delicacies complete with chopsticks, mine contained a burger and fries with a knife and fork! On the middle day of meetings Canon always arranged an evening dinner in a private room at the Elcy Hotel. Once again, whilst everyone else had typical Japanese fare, I was served steak and chips. However, I did eat Japanese food too: it would have been offensive to our hosts not to have done so. But I always kept a cold beer handy to wash away any unpalatable tastes.

During the meal the array of drinks was bewildering. There was, of course, sake, the traditional Japanese rice wine. Not just warm sake, but also the higher quality and more expensive cold sake. In addition, there was cold beer, wine and whisky. Then there was the quaint Japanese etiquette of drinking. The guest does not pour or replenish his own drink. That is the duty of your host and so, as soon as you took a sip of any drink, your host would immediately top it up. And it was the custom for you to reciprocate with their drinks. Unlike the Europeans, the Japanese do not have genetic resistance to alcohol so they cannot drink very much before becoming inebriated.* Therefore, at these dinners, it was us who did most of the drinking with our hosts continually replenishing our glasses.

The evening always ended with the exchanging of presents. Silk scarves, ties and fans from our hosts were reciprocated with fine, single malt whiskies. One evening there was an almost full bottle of Bushmills finest whisky left on the table. Ohtasan insisted that we took it back to our hotel, so we did. The Fairmont Hotel had a cosy bar with a lovely wooden sculpture of a naked lady and Aidan and I spent a relaxing time enjoying the delights of the Bushmills well into the early hours of the morning.

It was a mistake. The next thing I remember was being awoken by the ringing of the telephone. "Gregorysan, we are in the lobby waiting for you." It was Ohmichisan. I had overslept. My head was pounding and my throat felt like sandpaper. Worse still, I was due to give a talk to Canon in less than an hour. On the plus side, I was already dressed (I must have fallen asleep fully dressed) so, after a quick wash and brush-up, I dashed downstairs to my waiting colleagues and we set off for our meeting with Canon. There was no time for breakfast but I managed to grab a carton of orange juice and gulped it all down in the taxi on the way to the train station. Even so, my throat still felt extremely rough as I gave my talk. But I managed, just.

Our short train journeys to Canon coincided with the morning rush hour when the station was crowded with business commuters and noisy schoolchildren. Without fail, the sight of three foreigners always aroused the curiosity of the

---

*   Over the preceding millennia Europeans drank alcohol based drinks such as Mead because water alone was unfit to drink. Consequently, they developed a genetic tolerance to alcohol. In Japan, they drank water and didn't.

Japanese schoolchildren, with Ian's balding head the main attraction. As we sat on the train waiting for it to depart, dozens of excited faces peered through the window, pointing and gabbling away in Japanese. It made their day when we smiled and waved to them. Jumping up and down with joy, they smiled, waved back and ran away, giggling, to tell their friends about the three strange foreigners.

The embodiment of Canon's ability as hosts came with the retirement of Ian Wasson. A few months before his retirement in 1998 Ian made his last visit to Canon. On learning this fact, Canon pushed the boat out, literally. They arranged an evening dinner cruise on a luxury boat around Tokyo harbour for Ian and his friends. The secretarial staff of Canon were also invited so that each of us would have a female companion for the evening. It was a great gesture and a most enjoyable evening (Image 141) which ended with a group photograph (Image 142).

The tradition of entertaining your guests extended to Geisha girls. On someone's first visit to Japan Yamamotosan, the head of ICI Japan (Image 142), arranged an evening at an establishment for gentlemen. Run by a 'Madam', they employed sophisticated, pretty Japanese girls, usually university educated, who could speak reasonable English. Each guest had their own girl to look after them for the entire evening. It was an interesting and enjoyable experience. The girls would chat to you about anything (they were always keen to talk about Princess Diana), place food into your mouth and constantly replenish your drinks. They even washed and dried your hands with a warm flannel after a visit to the toilet! It made you feel special.

Ohtasan presenting Ian with a retirement gift on
the boat. My head is just visible behind the lady.

238

Group photograph taken after the cruise around Tokyo bay
with the boat in the background. L to R: Unknown,
Yamamotosan, Muraisan, Ohtasan, Ian, Me, Charles Shields
and Ohmichisan. The three ladies are the secretarial staff.
My companion was the lady in red.

14.3 SEC

Our success with HP and Canon meant that other ink jet companies were also keen
to collaborate with us. Although this was good, it also presented problems. When
companies collaborate they learn, at least in part, the business plans and strategies of
each company.

This is sensitive information confidential to that company. Legally binding
'Confidentiality Agreements' were signed and strenuous efforts were made to ensure
that each company's confidentiality was respected. Consequently, each company had
their own dedicated technical contact and technical marketing contact. In the case
of Seiko Epson, these were Paul Wight and John Presgrave respectively. Our contact
at Seiko Epson was Ohwatarisan, the dynamic leader of their ink jet business (Image
143). Accordingly, I had less involvement with Seiko Epson than with Canon and HP
but I still had some. For example, as well as providing input into their dye research
programmes, I also made the occasional visit to Seiko Epson in Japan.

An ink jet meeting with Seiko Epson at Blackley. Left
to right: Ian Wasson, John McCarthy, Paul Wight,
Aidan Lavery, Ohwatarisan, John Presgrave and Me.

On one such visit I was asked to give a lecture on ink jet dyes to the entire ink jet
business community of Seiko Epson. Those staff who visited Japanese companies were
invited to learn rudimentary Japanese on Friday lunchtimes and I began my lecture
by speaking in Japanese. It only lasted for thirty seconds or so before I switched to
my native tongue but it impressed the audience. However, there was a problem. The
microphone didn't work. It was a one hour lecture to a large audience in a large room
and this meant that I had to project my voice throughout the entire lecture. A couple
of hours later, I lost my voice. Completely. This was embarrassing since at the evening
dinner I was literally speechless. Although there were many things I wished to say, I
couldn't utter a sound.

It was at this same meal that I encountered the most vile tasting starter of my life.
The only reason that stopped me gagging was by gulping down a copious amount
of cold beer to remove the taste. And it wasn't just me. Everyone else thought it was
horrible too. The rest of the meal was fine, then it was coffee and what we thought
were funny shaped chocolate mints. I was wary and let some of my more adventurous
colleagues try them first. John Meyers, an American, duly obliged. "Mm," he said,
"crunchy and different."

"Yes," said Ohwatarisan proudly, "chocolate coated beetles are a Japanese delicacy."

Russell Bond (Image 201, page 347) taught me to be wary of Far Eastern food.
Russell succeeded Frank Hauxwell as Business Manager of Specialist Colours and
recounted a tale from one of his visits to Korea. As is the norm, he was taken out to
dinner by his hosts. Russell is not squeamish when it comes to food but even he was
taken aback when the waiter arrived with his dinner. The plate contained a solitary
item. A large sea slug! Not wanting to offend his host, Russell bit the bullet and
decided the best option was to eat the slimy slug as quickly as possible. And he did.
"Ah, you like," said his host and promptly ordered two more!

240

Ohwatarisan and his colleagues were concerned by my loss of voice and arranged for me to see their company doctor. After a thorough examination, he said that I was very tired, exhausted even, and that I should rest. It wasn't surprising. The long haul trips were taxing. The shortest trips involved visiting at least Canon and Seiko Epson but some trips involved consecutive visits to both Japanese and American companies. These trips lasted almost two weeks (Chapter 21). The doctor prescribed some antibiotics for the sore throat. Even so, it took a further four days for my voice to return.

14.4 LEXMARK

Lexmark, a spin-off company from IBM, were also becoming a serious player in the ink jet printer market and we collaborated with them too, but in a less formal manner than with Canon, HP and Seiko Epson. I had several visits to their headquarters at Lexington in the blue grass state of Kentucky. Famous for its horse racing, such as the Kentucky Derby, it is a lovely place. Most visits were uneventful. Except one. At this visit I was giving a presentation to a group of about twelve Lexmark people. Anne Piekonka, a lovely young lady, was the host. I duly gave the presentation and was intrigued by the intense interest shown, especially by Anne and some other ladies sat near the front in the cosy room. At the end, a male colleague of Anne's sidled up to me and said, "Great presentation, Peter. By the way, do you know your flies are undone."

"Why didn't you tell me sooner?" I enquired.

"Because I didn't want to spoil it for the ladies," he grinned. Now I know why they were so captivated!

REFERENCES

1. P Gregory, 'Modern Reprographics' in: Review of Progress in Colouration, Vol. 24, 1994, p. 1.
2. Canon Press Release, 1991.
3. P Gregory, 'Colouring the Jet Set' in: Chemistry in Britain, August 2000, p. 39.
4. P Gregory, 'Colorants: Use in High Technology' in: Chemistry and Industry, October 1989, p. 179.
5. S Hindogalla, N Hughes and D Greenwood, 'A Novel Waterfast Black Dye for Ink Jet Printing'. SPSE's 6th International Congress on Advances in Non-Impact Printing Technologies, Orlando, October 21-26th 1990.
6. P Gregory, RW Kenyon and PM Mistry, 'The Discovery of a Novel Alcohol Soluble Black Dye for Industrial Ink Jet Printing'. SPSE's 6th International Congress on Advances in Non-Impact Printing Technologies, Orlando, October 21-26th 1990.

15

THREE-IN-ONE

Things happen in threes. That's how the saying goes and in 1988 three things certainly happened to me. Two were good but one was awful.

15.1 A LAST GOODBYE

Like most other couples with young children, at the weekend we visited our families. Geographically, this presented no problems since my mother, Vera's parents and my Auntie Lily and Uncle Jack lived within a quarter-of-a-mile of each other in Aspull (Chapter 1 and Image 1b). However, it meant that we had to visit three households in one day.

Our first port of call was my mother's house. Normally, we arrived late Saturday morning and stayed for about an hour. Seeing Andrew and Michael, and to a lesser extent Vera and me, was the highlight of her week. She was always thrilled to bits and went out of her way to please them. Being poor, she couldn't shower them with gifts but she always had some little treats, such as their favourite chocolate bars. One year, when conkers were scarce, she arranged for Jimmy Heaton, her neighbour, to collect some from the woods at Haigh Hall. The delight on our children's faces as she handed them a huge bag full of conkers was matched only by the pleasure on her own face.

In the early days my mother would make us some 'lobbies'. This traditional Lancashire dish, to which beetroot or red cabbage could be added, was simple but tasty. We loved it. She also had a cast iron chip pan which made the most delicious chips, some of the best I have ever tasted (Chapter 2). Usually, however, we ate at my Auntie Lily's, whom we visited next.

As was the case with my mother, our visit was the highlight of their week. Here, I played football with our children on the spacious playing fields of my old school, Aspull Secondary Modern, sometimes for hours. A few years later, it also became a playground for Sam, our beloved yellow Labrador (Chapter 17). When the school was demolished to make way for a housing estate in the mid-nineties, instead of football, it was a walk around Toddington.

Lily insisted on making our dinner, partly, I think, to extend our time at her house. A roast beef dinner, including boiled potatoes, roast potatoes, mushy peas, carrots and gravy, became the norm. It was a kind gesture and we enjoyed it but, as she got older, it was obvious to us that it was getting too hard for her. Also, by this time our 'children' were grown up. Andrew had started university and Michael was well into his teens. It was an extremely delicate situation. On the one hand she desperately wanted the weekly visits and the roast beef dinners to continue but, on the other hand, it was becoming virtually impossible for us to comply with this request. In the end we had to tell her, as gently and tactfully as possible, that we could no longer guarantee to visit every Saturday, but that we would endeavour to visit as many times as possible. And we kept our promise. Our children, loyal as ever, continued to visit until she died in 1999 (Chapter 24).

George and Doris, Vera's mother and dad, were our final destination. By now, they had moved from their house in St John's Road to a nicer, more spacious house in Manor Grove, close to where Vera and I had our first date (Image 50). In contrast to my family, George and Doris were much more flexible regarding visiting times. They were always extremely pleased to see us and made us very welcome, but I think they realised that it wasn't always possible for us to visit on the same day and at the same time week after week. In a sense, they were more understanding. Weather permitting, we walked down the line to Haigh Hall plantations, the very same line where Vera and I did our courting. In the evening, after a drink and a biscuit, it was time to return home, tired but happy in the knowledge that we'd done our duty.

The ritual of weekend visits began when Andrew was a toddler and, because we adhered to the routine religiously, it became the done thing. It was set in stone. It was expected of us, especially by my family. When the children were young, we didn't mind since none of our families owned a car. If, for whatever reason, we couldn't go, they became extremely upset and this was one of the reasons the ritual persisted for so long. Vera and I decided that when our children left home, visiting would be flexible and not to a set schedule.

Our families desire for us to visit them with our children could sometimes be used to our advantage. For example, if there was a dispute, which thankfully was very rare, rather than have an argument we simply excused ourselves from visiting them the following weekend. It always produced the intended effect. Our point had been made without resorting to arguments or rows.

The routine of Saturday visits became such a part of our lives that we thought it would go on forever. But we were wrong. Very wrong. In the early hours of Thursday 9 June 1988, Vera and I were awoken by the shrill sound of the telephone. "Who on earth is ringing at this unearthly hour," I mumbled. Bleary eyed, I stumbled out of

243

bed and made my way downstairs to the phone. Whoever it was wasn't going to give up. I picked up the receiver and said, somewhat grumpily, "hello."

"I'm sorry to disturb you so early in the morning," said Mrs Whittle, my mother's next door neighbour, "but your mother has been taken to hospital. Can you come now?"

"Yes, I'll come right away," I replied, becoming instantly wide awake, and dashed upstairs to get dressed. All kinds of thoughts flashed through my mind. How ill was she? Would she be in intensive care with lots of tubes attached? I was in a whirl. Suddenly, the phone rang again. What was it now. It was Mrs Whittle again.

"Peter, I'm very sorry but your mother is dead. I wanted to break it to you gently. That's why I didn't tell you the first time." I heard the words but I couldn't comprehend what they meant. Dead. How could she be dead. We had only seen her a few days ago and she seemed fine. It must be a mistake, surely. Everything would be alright. I was in shock.

On arriving at my mother's house in Crawford Avenue I was greeted by Mrs Whittle and my Auntie Nellie. Both were distraught. I was bewildered and felt like a zombie. It just didn't seem real. Apparently, my mother had suffered a massive heart attack in the very early hours of the morning and Auntie Nellie's 'kiss of life' attempts were in vain. My mother died. She had been taken to Wigan Infirmary and I needed to go there to identify the body. It was the last thing I wanted but, accompanied by Vera, we set off for Wigan.

In the event, I didn't have to identify the body. They just needed her next of kin to fill in some forms. For this small mercy I was so grateful.

The next few days were hectic. There was the funeral to arrange, work had to be informed and we had to decide the best course of action for our children. They had grown fond of my mother, as indeed they had of all our close family, and this was their first encounter with a sudden death. Should they attend the funeral or not? My mind went back to William and me attending my grandad's funeral at a similar age (Chapter 1). It wasn't right then so Vera and I decided that our children should stay with her mother and dad on the day of the funeral.

At the request of my family we used Bolton's, the local undertakers, for the funeral. I remember discussing the arrangements with Mrs Bolton at her bungalow in St David's Crescent on a beautiful June day. Their Chapel of Rest was situated opposite the Balcarres Arms in Haigh, not far from the church where Vera and I were married. Looking at my mother as she lay in the open coffin didn't reassure me at all. I had the distinct feeling that at any moment her eyes would spring open and she would sit up. It was an unsettling sensation.

Most of the funeral was a blur, except for part of the vicar's address. As he surveyed the congregation, he remarked, rather chillingly, "Take a good look at the coffin and reflect because one day, it will be you lying in a coffin." I didn't think it appropriate then and I still think it was an inappropriate thing to say at a funeral. My mother was laid to rest beside my grandma and grandad in St Elizabeth's graveyard (Image 20, page 35).

Although Vera and I were both deeply upset, my mother's two sisters were badly affected by her untimely death. It was a beautiful summer's day so, after the funeral, we took my Auntie Lily and Auntie Nellie to the Marton Mere Wildfowl Trust to help take their mind off the past few days. My mother had always been fond of birds and walking around the sanctuary watching the antics of the ducks and their ducklings did provide a small measure of relief.

Towards the end, my mother's life was hard. Following my marriage to Vera in 1969, she was left by herself to care for my grandma. It wasn't easy. As she got older, my grandma required constant attention. This included, amongst other things, lifting her from her bed into her rocking chair and vice-versa on a daily basis. My grandma had never learned to read or write and it was heart-breaking watching her staring into space as she rocked in her chair. "God is good," she kept mumbling as she whiled away her days. The stress and sheer physical exertion of coping with an ageing person certainly took its toll on my mother, as did her heavy smoking and poor diet. To alleviate the situation, Auntie Nellie moved in to help her cope. Her husband, Evan, was obviously a very understanding man.

My grandma died on Saturday, 20 September 1980. The nurse had prepared my family for the worst and visited every few hours in her final days. On the Saturday afternoon, she told my two aunties that the end was very near and asked them to go to the bedroom and hold my grandma's hand. For whatever reason, my aunties were reluctant to do this and, when I arrived home from the football match, it was just Vera and I who saw my grandma draw her last breath. "She hung on until she saw you one last time," they said to me as we returned downstairs with the sad news. It is the first time that either I or Vera had been present at a person's moment of death and it's not an experience that we are in a hurry to repeat.

With hindsight the warning signs were there. They always are. You just don't see them until it's too late. My mother had always been an active woman but in the months prior to her death she had slowed down dramatically. As we picked her up on the Saturday before her death, she shuffled, rather than walked, to the car. Dressed in her trademark green bobcap, she looked a forlorn figure. During the roast beef dinner at Auntie Lily's she smiled at me in a way that was reminiscent of someone saying farewell. Sadly, it was.

15.2 DISNEY WORLD

Ironically, the year had started really well. Our children were growing up fast so Vera and I decided to splash out on a special holiday before they became too old. A special two week, two centre holiday in Florida. We had seen such holidays advertised by St Andrews Travel, a local travel agent in Bolton. They claimed to be the specialists in this type of holiday and, after discussing the arrangements with them, the holiday was booked for the last week in June and the first week in July. Not only were our children excited, we were excited too. All of us eagerly counted down the days to our departure on the jumbo jet to Orlando. Then came the bombshell of my mother's death.

My mother's sudden and untimely death occurred just two weeks before our holiday. It was a difficult time. What should we do? Andrew and Michael were really looking forward to this special holiday yet it was so soon after my mother's death. Everyone said that we should go ahead and have our holiday. This was also the view shared by our next door neighbour, Mildred. She sat on the wall in our back garden, put her arms around Vera and me and said, "Go. It's what your mother would have wanted." There was another reason too. One of Michael's classmates at school, Paul Rooney, had also booked the same holiday with his mum, and Michael and Paul had been chatting for ages about what they were going to do. It seemed only fair not to disappoint the children and so, with a tinge of sadness, we went ahead with the holiday.

It was a DC10, not a jumbo, that flew us first to Bangor, Maine, the home of Stephen King, the horror writer, and then to Orlando, the home of Mickey Mouse. This was a good ploy. Clearing customs at Bangor was done in a jiffy and, since the flight from Bangor to Orlando was internal, there was no hold up at Orlando either. Although a car had been booked for the entire holiday, it wouldn't be collected until the following morning. I didn't feel like driving after a long flight and, furthermore, this strategy allowed me to drink whilst on the plane. A coach transferred us to our hotel, the Quality Inn on International Drive. There were two Quality Inns, the Low Q, meaning a two storey hotel, and the High Q, a multi-storey hotel. Ours was the former. It was evening and International Drive was packed with local youngsters driving their vehicles up and down the Drive honking their horns. Apparently, this was a local tradition.

The following morning we attended a presentation from the tour representative. Our week in Orlando was already pretty full but we managed to squeeze in two further activities, a trip to a water ski school and a Wild West night.

Nothing prepares you for your first visit to Disney World. On entering the grounds of the Magic Kingdom we were amazed by the sheer scale and size of the park and the car parks. They were enormous. I was grateful for the advice given by the attendant to write down where we parked our car. Some didn't and regretted it when they couldn't find their vehicles in the vastness of the car parks. A little road train then transported us from the car park to the entrance of the Magic Kingdom.

Just like the entrance to the car parks, the many entry points meant that queuing was minimal. Everything was so organised. Once inside, a further surprise awaited. There was a choice of transport to complete your journey to the Magic Kingdom. You could cross the lake by boat or by monorail. We chose the latter. On its short journey the monorail stopped at a Disney hotel beside the lake. It was so lovely with its pools, gardens and man-made beach. At the entrance to the Magic Kingdom we chose to walk down Main Street USA rather than board the quaint little train that ran around the periphery (Image 144). That delight would come later.

As its name implies, the Magic Kingdom was enthralling and enchanting. The centre piece was Cinderella's Castle. Whilst eating lunch in a charming café beside the castle (Image 145), we met an elderly lady from Bolton. She was on the same tour as ourselves and was treating her grandchildren to the holiday of a lifetime. The food was both plentiful and delicious, as it would be for the entire holiday. I had frozen yoghurt for the very first time and loved it. Also, the food was reasonably priced. There was no ripping off a captive audience at Disney! And everywhere was so clean. It was a welcome change from England.

Mickey's Train (left) and Main Street, with
Cinderella's Castle in the background (right).

Me, Michael and Vera outside the café.
Taken by Andrew.

We spent a whole day sampling the delights of the Magic Kingdom. Vera doesn't like white-knuckle rides so didn't accompany my two sons and me on the *Thunder Mountain Railway* or the *White Water Rapids*, where we got soaked to the skin but dried out in no time at all. She preferred gentler pursuits such as *Mickey's Birthday Party*. A ride on Mickey's train (Image 144) transported us to this attraction. His birthday party was brilliant but without doubt Vera's favourite ride was *It's a Small World*. She loved the animation and especially the music. *Captain Nemo's underwater voyage in the Nautilus*, *Pirates of the Caribbean* and the *Haunted House* were also great fun, particularly the witty tombstones in the graveyard.

Our children also had their pictures taken with some of the Disney characters. These included *Pluto* (Image 146) and the *White Rabbit* (Image 147). It's hard to discern the difference between the *White Rabbit's* buck teeth and Michaels! As mentioned earlier, the extensive use of antibiotics to cure Michael's whooping cough affected his first teeth very badly. As is evident from the picture, they didn't affect his two front teeth.

Andrew and Michael, in full Disney gear, with Pluto.

One morning, whilst approaching the Magic Kingdom on the monorail, Andrew's camera broke. He fiddled with it and tweaked it but to no avail. It wouldn't work. He was really distraught. He loved taking photographs and in this respect took after his grandad, George. I took him to the camera shop more in hope than expectation. To our complete amazement, the pleasant young lady stripped down his camera, reassembled it and Hey Presto, it worked! It had taken her literally just two minutes. "How much do we owe?" I asked.

Michael with the White Rabbit from
Disney's Alice in Wonderland.

"Nothing," she replied. "It's all part of the Disney service. Have a nice day."
Thanks to her kindness, we did.

EPCOT, with its famous golf ball landmark (Image 148), was more spacious,
less crowded and less hectic than the Magic Kingdom. Its rides, such as *Spaceship
Earth* and *Living with the Land* were more educational than those at the Magic
Kingdom. It also had 3D cinema shows. *Honey I Shrunk the Audience*, with all the
special effects, captivated adults and children alike, particularly near the end when
everyone could feel dozens of mice running up their legs. The screaming from
the ladies was deafening. However, the main attraction of EPCOT was the twelve
showcase countries set around the shore of a large lake. All of them were good but
our favourites were Germany and China.

Andrew, Vera and Michael at EPCOT.

The shops and markets in Germany sold a host of gorgeous articles, the best of which were the beautiful bears and dolls. They were simply exquisite. China had a 360 degree cinema. Standing in the middle, surrounded by a wrap-around screen, the effect was awesome. Several short films were shown but the flight in the hot air balloon, especially when it sailed over the edge of a gigantic cliff without any warning, took your breath away.

EPCOT was also famous for its evening fireworks display. Synchronised to music, water fountains and laser lights, it was a most magnificent spectacle and therefore extremely popular. The trick was to secure a good vantage point. Normally, this entailed selecting your position over an hour in advance and then staying put. To circumvent this problem, we booked an evening dinner at the Rose and Crown pub in 'England'. Our reserved table was on the outside patio overlooking the lake. It was an excellent viewing spot but it came at a price. The roast beef dinner was really expensive. But we didn't mind; we just wanted to have a good view.

Catastrophe Canyon, King Kong, Jaws and *Star Wars* were all spectacular but the attraction we enjoyed the most at the MGM (Metro-Goldwyn-Mayer) theme park was *Indiana Jones*. The stunts and special effects were first class.

Another full day was spent at Sea World. The shows were spectacular, particularly *The Legend of Shamu*, a killer whale. We laughed at the antics of the sea lions and marvelled at the power and tricks of *Shamu*. Indeed, *Shamu* ended the show swimming round the edge of the pool slapping his tail fin into the water so hard that the resulting splashes reached the front rows of the audience, drenching everyone sat there.

Half a day was spent at Wet and Wild but one of the highlights of the holiday was the visit to the Kennedy Space Centre. On our drive to the Space Centre we were lucky enough to spot an American Bald Eagle, as well as some strange looking logs beside the river. I'm glad we didn't get out of the car to investigate. The 'logs' were sunbathing alligators! There were more of these fearsome beasts in the man-made pool at the Space Centre and it was fascinating watching them devour the food thrown by the tourists. I certainly didn't want to fall in!

If Disney was big, the things at the Space Centre were colossal. Not only did it boast the largest building in the world, it also had a Saturn V rocket on display (Image 149). I couldn't believe how big it was. How such a monster ever got into space I just don't know.

The caterpillar tracks needed to transport rockets such as the Saturn V to the launch pad were mind boggling. You had to see them to believe their size. During the guided tour, I was amazed at how low tech the moon buggy was. It seemed like a 'Meccano' contraption that a teenager had assembled. However, the astronaut looked authentic (Image 150).

Saturn V rocket at the Kennedy Space Centre.

Andrew and Michael with an Astronaut.

Every morning we hopped across the road to Dennys. Breakfast at Dennys became a ritual. We loved it. Not only was it exceptional value at $1.99 for the adults and $1.0 for the children, the food was excellent too. Crispy bacon, sausage, eggs sunny side up and hash browns, followed by toast and coffee. Delicious. And the orange juice was out of this world. We became friendly with a waiter who said that he enjoyed serving us. The sentiment was reciprocated: we enjoyed being served by him.

In the middle of the week we had our date with the ski school. This was the opportunity to try something different as well as breaking up the visits to the theme parks. Michael was too young to participate but Andrew and I gave it our best shot. Located on a shallow inland lake, it was great fun being dragged around at high speed in a rubber tyre in preparation for the water skiing to come. I found the water skiing extremely hard on the legs and wasn't very good but Andrew was better, gaining his certificate (Image 151).

Andrew's certificate from Dave and Vince's ski school.

Our second pre-booked date was the Wild West show. Paul and his mum had also booked for this show and the six of us boarded the coach with high expectations for the evening ahead. We weren't disappointed. It was an excellent show with Indians, the Cavalry and Country and Western music and dancers. The food was cowboy style and I was appointed the head of our table and had to dish it out. (The food, that is.) It was bacon and baked beans! Not fine dining but tasty nonetheless. Our hosts were very liberal with the beer and I had far too much to drink (Image 152). Testament to this fact was that I left our hotel room door unlocked all night. Even worse, I'd left the key in the lock on the outside of the door. On his patrols the security guard had discovered it and pushed it under the door with an explanatory note. I'm grateful it wasn't a criminal who found it.

At the conclusion of the evening, our children had their picture taken with several of the show's cast, including the Indian Chief (Image 153). He looked a proud and fearsome warrior and reminded me of the Indian on the front cover of a book I received as a Christmas present when I was a child (Chapter 2).

A drunken me, with Mrs Rooney and Paul at the
Wild West night. Note the large flagon of beer on the
left with the enormous blue coffee pot on the right.

252

It wasn't bacon and baked beans at Sizzlers where we dined most evenings. Here, we enjoyed a hearty three course meal, including steak and chips for the main course, for less than ten dollars, and only half that for the children. There was the usual free fruit and salad bar but the highlight as far as our children were concerned was the dessert. It was help yourself to as much ice cream as you wanted from the ice cream machine. For them, it was heaven on earth. Sizzlers was very popular, and no wonder.

Andrew, Michael and the Indian chief.

After we had dined it was off to the Pirates Cove mini golf. These floodlit mini golf courses were a common feature in America but the course itself was anything but common. Pirates Cove was built in the form of a small mountain. The first nine holes were up the mountain and the last nine holes down it. There were caves, waterfalls, rivers, bridges and lagoons. And the playing surface was top class. It was a very popular venue. On completing our round, we joined Vera and Mrs Rooney at the cafe for refreshments.

Other evenings were spent at the nearby Mercado shopping centre and the Florida Shopping Mall. At the time, these seemed wonderful but nowadays the Trafford Centre is far superior.

Our hectic week in Orlando was coming to an end. As Winston Churchill would have said, "Never has so much been crammed into so little by so few." We were ready for a more relaxing week on the Gulf Coast to recover and recuperate.

The drive from Orlando to Treasure Island took over two hours. Passing through Tampa we were alarmed as cars whizzed by on both sides on the seven lane highway. The final approach was along a road flanked on both sides by the ocean and, perched along the railings, were thousands of pelicans. It was reminiscent of a scene from Alfred Hitchcock's famous film *The Birds*. I think they scared Vera. Eventually, however, we arrived at our destination.

Treasure Island is a small resort located between Clearwater and St Petersburg on Florida's Gulf Coast. Directly opposite our hotel was a small store and, as soon as I had parked the car, Andrew and Michael dashed across the road to buy their fix of Hershey chocolate bars. It was a taste they had grown fond of during their short time in America.

Our week at Treasure Island was, as expected, a stark contrast to that in Orlando. It was relaxing, tranquil and peaceful, a time to recharge our batteries. The stretch of beach was like something from a South Sea island (Images 154 and 155). It was pure paradise. The fine silver sand, the azure sea and the blue sky were idyllic. The temperature of the water was amazing. Bathing in the sea was like having a warm bath. It made the Mediterranean seem positively cold. We spent most afternoons on the beach (Images 154-156), sometimes with Paul and his mum.*

Pot roast. We ate this strangely named dish in a cosy waterfront café on the way to Clearwater. It had been recommended by some guests at the hotel as an excellent place to dine, with pot roast the speciality. And they were right. Essentially, pot roast was a large piece of succulent, tender roast beef served with potatoes and vegetables, very similar in fact to an English roast beef dinner. Our waitress, a buxom middle-aged American lady, was both friendly and informative, telling us about the local customs and attractions. The whole atmosphere was geniality itself. It was so nice to eat good food in a friendly environment whilst watching the world go by.

Our family on Treasure Island beach 1988.

---

* Tragically, Paul's dad died at a young age from complications associated with haemophilia

Michael on Treasure Island beach. St Petersburg
can be seen in the background.

The restaurant, like all the other shops, cafes and stores on the waterfront, was built of wood. It was a bustling, thriving area with people frequenting the original little shops hunting for unique souvenirs to take home. It was fascinating exploring the shops, many with a nautical flavour, as the sun set over the horizon and nightfall approached. There's something magical about being close to the sea at night, with the lights twinkling on the ocean and the soft sound of waves lapping gently on the shore.

Michael, Paul and Andrew having a dip in the sea.

We also ate on a boat. The early diner specials were excellent value, better even than Sizzlers. In fact, it was reminiscent of a Sizzlers-on-Sea.

One evening we decided to drive to downtown St Petersburg, a few miles away. Accompanied by Paul and his mum we parked the car and began to walk along the seafront. It was dusk. With the sea to one side and the city to the other, it was a beautiful sight. Suddenly, out of nowhere, a large gang of youths appeared ahead. It was an intimidating situation. Realising our vulnerability, we hurriedly turned around and retraced our steps back to the car as quickly as possible.

The following day we learned that a murder had taken place close to where we had ventured. On the very same night that we had been there! Apparently, certain areas of downtown St Petersburg were places to avoid at night. We had had a lucky escape.

All good things come to an end and, rather reluctantly, on the Saturday morning it was time to make our way back to Orlando airport for the return flight home.

15.3 A PLEASANT SURPRISE

In the spring of 1988 Dr Gerry Booth, the Research Manager, retired. His replacement was Dr Alan Calder, a Scotsman, who had been head of the Process Technology Department at Huddersfield. One of the first things that he did was to review the roles, achievements and performance of the senior staff in his new department. Effectively, he was selecting his technical leaders for the future, his 'Calder Men'.

Three chemists were selected for promotion to the relatively new position of Senior Scientist. Brian Parton was chosen primarily for his work on inventing the blockbusting dye PROCION Blue H-EGN (Chapter 9), Mike Hutchings for his work on Non-Linear Optics and computational chemistry, and myself for the work on hi-tech colours. It was a pleasant surprise.

All three of us were promoted to Hay 37, crossing the great divide from blue book to black book (Chapter 7). A few years earlier ICI's salary structure had changed from the in-house Haslam system (Chapter 7) to the universally used Hay system. The four Haslam black book grades of 6 (the lowest) to 3 (the highest) were replaced by three Hay grades, Hay 37 (the lowest) to Hay 39 (the highest). It was a massive promotion because people on black book grades got a company car as part of their remuneration package.

Any car up to a certain value could be chosen. After much deliberation, I chose, with the help of my family, a Rover 820i in white from Lookers in Manchester, one of the designated garages. Not only was I excited, the whole family was excited. We were getting an expensive luxury car for free. Well, almost free. The company paid for everything. The car, road tax, insurance, repairs, accident damage, servicing and even membership of the AA. The only cost incurred was a benefit-in-kind tax which, at the time, was about £900 per year. It was incredible. I had got a substantial pay rise and an £18,000 car for peanuts. This time, I was like a dog with two dicks.

It was agreed that Lookers would deliver the car to me at work. I was so excited when the receptionist phoned to say that the man from Lookers had brought the car and would I come down to inspect it and sign the paperwork. Full of expectation, I dashed into the lift to descend to the ground floor. He greeted me warmly and escorted me to the car. It was lovely. I couldn't wait to sit inside and drive it. As I inspected the outside, my heart sank. The badge said 820e, the model below the one that I had ordered. They had delivered the wrong car! It was so disappointing. However, it was only temporary. After a few days the right car was delivered. The wait was worth it. The white Rover 820i was a lovely car.

It was a good end to a mixed year but I was so sad that my mother had missed our holiday in Florida, my promotion and the company car.

16

RUGBY

I got my first taste of rugby when, as a little boy, my Uncle Jack took me to watch Wigan on a Saturday afternoon. We entered the ground through separate turnstiles, me through the children's turnstile and Jack through the adult turnstile. We met up inside the ground and then walked to our usual spot on the corner of the Spion Kop. For me, it was a day out. I didn't really understand the rules but I wanted Wigan to win. Usually they did. Once, against Widnes, they lost. In contrast to most games, this one was as dull and boring as the black-and-white strip of Widnes.* The game was ruined, my uncle said, by Widnes adopting 'spotting' tactics.

We were also at the traditional Good Friday fixture against St Helens on the day that Central Park posted its biggest ever attendance. Anticipating a big crowd, we'd arrived early to claim our usual spot on the Spion Kop. Even so, the 46,674 spectators crammed into the ground exerted such a crush that we had to move from standing behind the crash barrier to standing in front of it. It was frightening.

My passion for Wigan rugby reached its peak in my early teens. I had begun playing the game at Aspull Secondary Modern and actually played on the famous Central Park pitch (Chapter 4). In the seventies and early eighties I stopped watching Wigan, partly because of other commitments, such as a young family and work. However, on one of our Saturday afternoon walks through Haigh Hall plantations whilst visiting Vera's parents (Chapter 15), our young children were intrigued by the roar from the crowd at Central Park. "What's that noise, Dad?" they asked. It rekindled my interest and I decided to take Andrew and Michael to watch a game to see if they liked it. In 1984, they witnessed their first ever game of rugby league. I can't remember who Wigan played but there was a good crowd, a great atmosphere

---

* There's an amusing, but true, tale about a Widnes player, Jim Mills. Big Jim, as he was known, was a really hard man. During the warm up before a cup tie at Barrow, a spectator noticed that Jim had his shin pads on 'back-to-front'. On pointing this out to him Jim growled that no one kicks Big Jim from the front.

and they thoroughly enjoyed the experience. That year, we went to several more games, not just at home but also away. It was the beginning of a long association with Wigan Rugby League Football Club.

16.1 WEMBLEY

Without a shadow of doubt the pinnacle of the Rugby League season was the Challenge Cup Final. Played at the famous Wembley stadium in May, it was every fans dream to cheer their team to victory in this prestigious showpiece event. The road to Wembley was long and hard but, after a decade in the doldrums, Wigan finally made it to the final. Their opponents were Widnes, the 'cup kings' of the era. Not having been to Wembley since my visit with Vera in 1965 (Chapter 6), a few of us decided to go. After all, it was Wigan's first visit to the famous twin towers for many years. Since the only tickets available were for the terraces, our young children wouldn't have been tall enough to see the game. Therefore, George, Keith, Alan, my cousin, and myself attended the game whilst Vera, Elaine and Sylvia, Alan's wife, spent the day in London with the children.

Wigan lost. What made the defeat harder to take was that two of the star players for Widnes were Wigan lads. Both Andy Gregory, their scrum half, and Joe Lydon, their speedy winger, were products of the Wigan St Patrick's Amateur Rugby League Football Club and both had cracking games. Indeed, Lydon scored a length-of-the-field match-winning try. Wigan were losers that year but things would change.

The following year Wigan reached Wembley again. This time, against Hull, they were determined to make amends for their defeat the previous year. But it wouldn't be easy. Although Wigan had some world class players, such as Graeme West, Brett Kenny and John Ferguson, so did Hull with Peter Sterling, James Leuluai and Fred Ah Kuoi.

View of the Wigan players in their pre-match
walkabout against Halifax in1988.

This time, we managed to purchase seating tickets but they were on the front row. On the plus side, our children got to shake hands with the players during their pre-match walkabout (Image 157) but the downside was that the seats were too low to offer a good view of the game. That final of 1985, in which Wigan won a thrilling encounter 28-24, was considered by many to be the best ever. Who can forget the beaming smile on Henderson Gill's face as he touched down for a try after a scintillating dash down the wing. It lit up Wembley. Or Brett Kenny's majestic arcing run to the try line. No team deserved to lose and this was reflected in the camaraderie of the Hull and Wigan fans as they made their way back to the coaches and trains for the journey home.

By now our children were keen Wigan fans and watching them became a regular event. The three of us, plus George, attended virtually every game, both home and away. Every Sunday (the games had switched to Sunday rather than Saturday afternoons to avoid conflict with soccer), we donned our gear in readiness for the match. Standing on the terraces or sitting in the stands in the depths of winter chilled you to the bone and so, for the first time in my life, I bought a pair of 'Long Johns' and a thermal vest. Neither George nor I wore Wigan shirts, preferring instead to wear a Wigan bob cap and a Wigan scarf (Image 159). Not so our children. They wore the full monty. A Wigan shirt, a Wigan track suit, a Wigan scarf and a Wigan hat (Image 158). They even had Wigan bags (Image 159).

Michael (left) and Andrew in full Wigan gear
in front of Wembley's twin towers 1988.

Vera made a flask of hot coffee for me and George and packed Ribena for our children. Bars of Cadburys chocolate and kitkats completed the refreshments. These were most welcome at half-time. Away games in deepest Yorkshire required an additional strategy. As well as taking some refreshments for later, we always set off early and stopped for lunch on the way, usually at a Little Chef. The 'Chef's Grill' of bacon, hamburger, sausage, egg, chips and beans was delicious, especially on freezing winter days. Hull and Hull KR were the furthest outposts but we also ate out when playing Bradford, Castleford and Wakefield. On some away games Joe Lynch, my late friend Trevor's uncle, also came along (Image 159).

Left to right: Joe, Margaret, George, Vera, Me and
Michael. Wembley 1988. Taken by Andrew.

We all enjoyed our Sunday rugby. Vera never hankered to come. Instead, she took her mother for a ride in the car with our yellow Labrador, Sam (Chapter 17). After a walk in the park (Beacon Country Park at Dalton was one of their favourites), they listened to the rugby on the radio whilst enjoying a cup of tea and a burger and fries from the mobile 'sausage man'. And yes, they bought one for Sam too. He slavered uncontrollably in anticipation of his treat.

Watching Wigan was great but there was a problem. The big games against the top teams drew large crowds and, because of their small stature, our young children had difficulty seeing the game. In the biggest game of the season against St Helens, they couldn't see a thing! This was the last straw so, for the 1987 season, we bought season tickets in the Douglas Stand. It was a smart move. Not only did we get excellent views for every game, including all the big games, we also got preferential treatment when it came to purchasing tickets for the really big games, such as the Wembley Cup Finals and the World Club Challenge games. Furthermore, during our twelve years in the Douglas Stand, we became firm friends with our companions sat around us. It was a golden era for us and for Wigan rugby.

After the lean times of the seventies, Wigan's outdated and unwieldy committee of approximately 16 members was replaced with the 'gang of four'. Maurice Lindsay, the leader, Jack Robinson, a local antiques dealer, Tom Rathbone of Rathbones bread and Jack Hilton, a former Wigan winger, transformed Wigan from the flops of the seventies to the best team in the world. How was this amazing feat achieved? It was achieved by having a backbone of proud, local Wigan lads complemented by a sprinkling of top quality Australian, New Zealand and later, British players.

Graeme West, the 6 foot 5 inch New Zealand second row forward began the transformation. Graeme was an inspirational captain who gave his all to Wigan, playing for them until he retired. In the early years he was assisted in no small part by his fellow countryman Dean Bell and the two Australians Brett Kenny and John Ferguson. Wigan's improving fortunes also ensured that the best Wigan youngsters, such as Shaun Edwards, didn't slip the net as had happened in the past. Now, they were proud to play for Wigan. Indeed, those who had slipped the net, such as Joe Lydon and Andy Gregory, returned to the fold to become part of a great Wigan side. Top British stars such as Ellery Hanley, one of the finest players I have seen, and Martin Offiah, certainly the fastest player I have ever seen, made Wigan almost invincible in the late eighties and early nineties. Indeed, the Wigan team of 1992, boasting most of these players plus Gene Miles, a giant Australian centre, was, in my opinion, one of the finest club sides of all time (Fig. 3).

It takes more than good players to be successful. A top class management team is also required. When they defeated Hull in the 1985 Challenge Cup Final Wigan were in the unusual position of having two coaches, Colin Clarke and Alan McInnes. Strengthened by an influx of top talent, Wigan were expected to do even better in 1986. But they didn't. One wag said we had a million dollar team and a ten bob coach. A tad unfair perhaps but it was a view obviously shared by the 'gang of four'. After their surprise home defeat to Castleford by 10 points to 2 in the third round of the Challenge Cup, the joint coaches were sacked and Graeme Lowe, a no-nonsense New Zealander, took over the reins for the 1987 season.

Joe Lydon

Frano Botica   Dean Bell   Gene Miles   Martin Offiah

Shaun Edwards   Andy Gregory

Kelvin Skerret   Martin Dermott   Andy Platt

Denis Betts   Billy McGinty

Phil Clarke

Wigan RLFC Team of 1992.
Ellery Hanley had moved to Leeds the previous season.

Graeme Lowe cracked the whip. He was a strong character who wanted things done his way. He improved their fitness levels, work ethic and defence. As a player, you either did as he wanted or you were dropped. It was harsh but it worked. In the league Wigan were sweeping all before them. They were unstoppable. Not surprisingly, they were red hot favourites to lift the Challenge Cup. Following the disappointment of 1986, Andrew and Michael were desperate to return to Wembley with Wigan. I was confident they would and promised them that Wigan would get to Wembley and win the cup.

We had drawn Oldham away. Anchored close to the bottom of the league, they shouldn't prove much of a threat. But the weather was a different matter. Because of the severe wintry conditions, the Sunday afternoon game was postponed and rescheduled for a Tuesday evening. Oldham's Watersheddings ground was cold even in summer. In the depths of winter, it would be perishing, especially at night. Suitably wrapped up, we set off for Oldham.

Wigan totally dominated the first half and came within inches of scoring several tries but somehow Oldham, enjoying a measure of good fortune, kept them out. Astonishingly, at half-time we were losing by four points to nil courtesy of two penalty goals kicked by Mick Burke, the Oldham full back. No matter. Wigan's superior skill and fitness would tell in the second half and so it seemed when Dean Bell rounded the Oldham full back to score a try and put Wigan 8-4 ahead. With Wigan totally in control, it was just a case of waiting for the final hooter. Then disaster struck. Joe Lydon fumbled a nothing kick close to the Wigan line and from the resulting scrum Oldham's Paddy Kirwan dived over for a try to level the scores. With just a minute of the game remaining, it all hinged on the goal kick. To the delight of the home fans and the abject dismay of the travelling Wigan fans, it sailed between the uprights giving Oldham a shock 10-8 victory.

We couldn't believe it. Wigan had been unceremoniously dumped out of the cup at the first hurdle by an unfancied team near the foot of the table. I was in shock and our children were heartbroken. We trudged back to the car in a daze, not believing what had just happened. I had promised them that Wigan would get to Wembley and win the cup and now that promise was in tatters. They believed what their dad had told them and I had let them down. It was this that hurt more than Wigan losing. It took us weeks to recover.

If 1987 was our nemesis, then the golden years from 1988 to 1995 would be our zenith. During this period Wigan won the Challenge Cup an amazing eight consecutive times! Eight consecutive years without a single defeat in Rugby League's most prestigious competition. Almost forty games without losing. It is a feat unrivalled in any sport and one that will, in all probability, never be equalled.

In this fantastic run Wigan beat Halifax, St Helens (twice), Warrington, Castleford, Widnes and Leeds (twice) at Wembley (Fig. 4). In the 1987 final Halifax had defeated St Helens by 19 points to 18 and Wembley was a sell out for their clash against Wigan the following year. Indeed, the crowd was so big that many were allowed to sit around the perimeter of the pitch to alleviate the crush. On a lovely May day, Wigan were simply too good and crushed Halifax by 32 points to 12. The following year they kept their arch rivals St Helens scoreless[*] and were the first team to defeat Castleford at Wembley. Although all the games were memorable, the one that sticks in my mind was the first of their two games against Leeds. In this game, Martin Offiah scored an absolutely superb try. Collecting the ball near his own try line he beat three defenders and then sped down the field towards the Leeds tryline. Only Alan Tait, the speedy Leeds full back, stood in his way. Tait had boasted that no one passed him on the outside. Wrong. Offiah rounded the Leeds last line of defence with ease to complete a magnificent length-of-the-field try. It was a try that Ray French, the BBC commentator, described as the best he had ever seen in 41 years of watching Wembley finals.

1988	Wigan	32 – 12	Halifax
1989	Wigan	27 – 0	St Helens
1990	Wigan	36 – 14	Warrington
1991	Wigan	13 – 8	St Helens
1992	Wigan	28 – 12	Castleford
1993	Wigan	20 – 14	Widnes
1994	Wigan	26 – 16	Leeds
1995	Wigan	30 – 10	Leeds

Wigan's Wembley Finals 1988 – 1995

For the majority of finals we travelled down just for the day. Against Widnes and Hull we took one of the chartered trains from Wigan to London, then the tube to Wembley. This arrangement worked well, allowing the ladies to do some shopping and sight-seeing in London whilst we went to the game. After boarding the train at Euston for the journey home, still excited at Wigan's win in a wonderful game, Michael suddenly decided that he wanted a Mars bar. And he wanted it now! We didn't have one and he sulked and sulked until one was eventually purchased from the trolley lady.

The one exception to our day returns was 1988. That year, we booked a package weekend at the Spiders Web hotel in Watford. The deal included bed and breakfast for the Friday and Saturday evenings, coach travel and tickets for the game. It was one of the rare occasions that not only did Vera make the trip, she also went to the match (Image 159).

---

[*]   Andy Gregory uses this game in his after dinner speeches, citing the 29-0 drubbing of arch rivals St Helens in the Challenge Cup Final at Wembley as one of the most satisfying victories of his entire career. When corrected by St Helens' fans that it was 27-0 not 29-0, he responds by saying that he got their score right.

On the Friday evening we caught the coach into London to do some sight-seeing and have our evening meal. Saturday evening, we did something different. On returning to the hotel from Wembley we took a taxi into Watford town centre to find a relaxing restaurant in which to enjoy our evening dinner. It was relatively quiet but we found a nice family run restaurant with a menu that included steak (for Andrew) and roast lamb (for Michael). (You'll hear more about Michael and his roast lamb later – Chapter 18.) The waitress, who I think was also the owner, accompanied by a young boy, obviously her little helper, came to take the order. She said they had been run off their feet earlier in the day because of the rugby union final at Twickenham, and that they had run out of some dishes on the menu. Thankfully, they still had some steak and roast lamb. She seemed a little surprised when asked if Michael could have some mint sauce with his roast lamb. "Er, yes. That's alright," she said rather hesitantly, before making her way to the kitchen.

Well, we waited and waited for the food to arrive. Fifteen minutes, half-an-hour, forty-five minutes. Just as we were about to complain, in they breezed with our meals. She was very apologetic for the delay and the meals were delicious. During the meal there was much discussion as to the cause of the delay with the general consensus being that she had sent her little helper to the local supermarket to buy a bottle of mint sauce. Indeed, Joe said he saw the little boy running down the street shortly after we had placed our order. Whether this was true or not is open to debate but Vera, myself, Joe, Margaret (his wife) and George were highly amused and recounted this tale for many years. Obviously, the mint sauce had run out earlier in the day.

For all the other Wembley finals, including Wigan's shock 17-8 loss to Sheffield Eagles in 1998, we travelled by car. It became a ritual. Vera would dress our mascot, a teddy bear, in Wigan colours, including a little cherry and white hat, and sit him proudly on the shelf at the rear of the car. Then, cherry and white scarves were draped from the car windows and our refreshments loaded into the boot. Finally, Andrew and Michael, in full Wigan paraphernalia (Image 158, page 260), and myself would pick up George and drive down the M6, stopping at the Corley Services for a break. Upon leaving the M1, the car was parked at Stanmore, the final stop on the Jubilee Line. After eating lunch in our favourite café, we boarded the tube to Wembley. It was a good arrangement. Being north of Wembley, the trains avoided the crowds in both directions, unlike those heading to and from London.

In addition to winning the Challenge Cup a record eight consecutive times, Wigan also won, at the same time, a record seven consecutive Championships, from 1989/90 to 1995/96. They were an incredible team.

16.2 SPEED TO BURN

How fast was he? Wigan's unprecedented run in the Challenge Cup, televised by the BBC, meant that many people witnessed Offiah's extraordinary pace and harboured the same thought. It was a question asked not only by the general public but also by other sportsmen and sports commentators, especially after his spectacular length-of-the-field try at Wembley. Could anyone beat him? Was there a footballer, another rugby league player, a player from rugby union or even a sprinter who was faster? Even Ade Mafe, the Great Britain 200 and 400 metre Olympic sprinter, wondered just how fast Offiah really was. In sprint training with the Great Britain Rugby League team, Offiah, after a terrible start, still managed to clock 10.5 seconds for the 100 metres. Although respectable, it was slower than that of the top sprinters who regularly clocked around 10.0 seconds.

Because of all the speculation, a challenge was thrown down. Offiah issued an open invitation to all sportsmen to race against him in a 100 yard sprint at one of Wigan's end of season 'Fun Days' at Central Park. It would be run on grass on Wigan's Central Park pitch. Around twelve sportsmen took up the challenge. These included speedsters from both codes of rugby, local sprinters and, of course, Ade Mafe.

The Fun Day drew a sizeable crowd. Although there were other events, such as five-a-side football, the sprint challenge was the main attraction. On a beautiful summer's day, the dozen or so athletes took up their positions on the starting line alongside the Douglas Stand.

Ade Mafe was the favourite. Being a top Olympic sprinter he was expected to win. But how close would Offiah be? "Take your marks. Get set." At the crack of the starter's gun, they were off. It was over in a flash. As anticipated, it was a two horse race. But it wasn't Ade Mafe who won, it was Martin Offiah! He beat the Olympic sprinter by 2-3 yards. Anthony Sullivan, the St Helens flyer, came third, some eight yards behind. Offiah had answered the question. He really was exceptionally fast.

16.3 WORLD SEVENS

Offiah's speed was most apparent in 'seven-a-side' competitions. Wigan normally hosted a pre-season 'Sevens' competition at Central Park. These were rather parochial affairs consisting of Rugby League teams from Lancashire plus the odd one or two from Yorkshire. However, in 1992 the Australians decided to hold a World Sevens competition. The majority of the twelve teams were from the Australian Rugby League, the best league in the world, but two other teams were also invited – Wigan, because of their dominance of the English game, and Fiji, the recently crowned champions of the World Rugby Union Sevens.

Wigan scraped through from the group stage by the skin of their teeth but Fiji, the best sevens team in the world of Rugby Union, were eliminated. As the tournament progressed Wigan were simply unstoppable, primarily because of the lightning pace of Offiah. Not for nothing was he nicknamed 'Chariots Offiah' after the film Chariots of Fire about the great British sprinter, Harold Abrahams. Every time he touched the ball, he scored. Wigan beat Manly in the semi-final and the Brisbane Broncos in the final, with Offiah scoring a hat trick. Not surprisingly, Offiah was easily the top try scorer of the tournament with a haul of ten tries. The Australians were miffed: they didn't take kindly to a bunch of 'Pommies' beating them at their national sport in their own backyard. And it wouldn't be the last time either.

As the 100 year rift between the two codes of League and Union began to heal, Wigan were invited to take part in the Twickenham Sevens. Here, they would lock horns with the best rugby union sides in England at their national stadium and at their own game. Despite these drawbacks, Wigan were favourites to win the tournament. And they did, defeating most of their opponents convincingly, including Wasps in the final. The superior skill and fitness of rugby league players compared to their union counterparts was plain for all to see.

In the following years competition, another rugby league team, the Bradford Bulls, emulated Wigan by also winning the Twickenham Sevens.

16.4 CROSS-CODE CHALLENGE

In addition to seven-a-side matches, a full blown cross-code challenge was arranged between the two dominant sides of English rugby, Wigan from Rugby League and Bath from Rugby Union. The first of these two matches, staged at Manchester City's Maine Road stadium in 1996, was played under League rules. Wigan were far, far too good for Bath, racing into a 56-0 lead by half-time! In the second half, they took their foot off the gas and were leading by 82-0 when, to the biggest cheer of the night, Mike Catt dived over for Bath's only try of the game. The Bath fans just couldn't believe how fit, fast and skilful the Wigan players were.

The return game at Twickenham, played under Union rules, was a different matter. Bath deservedly won an entertaining encounter by 44 points to 19. I think the intricacies of the rules of the rucks and mauls, plus the lineouts, were too much for the League players.

16.5 WORLD CLUB CHALLENGE

Who was the best Rugby League club side in the world? England and Australia were the two top Rugby League playing nations but who was the top team, the English champions or the Australian champions. A challenge match between the two had been mooted often in the past but, for a variety of reasons, the game never materialised. However, in 1987, due mainly to the sterling efforts of Maurice Lindsay, the Wigan chairman, the first World Club Challenge match was arranged. On 7 October, Wigan would face Manly at Central Park.

The match created enormous interest, not just with Wigan fans but with Rugby League fans everywhere. Even the leading Rugby Union dignitaries were invited! A capacity crowd of 36,895 packed into a cold Central Park and, sat in the Douglas Stand, we couldn't wait for the match to start.

The general consensus in the press was that Manly would win comfortably. After all, the Australian game was superior to ours. And it seemed they would be right. In their very first attack, Manly sliced through the Wigan defence and nearly scored. For the remainder of the game Wigan's defence held firm and prevented Manly from crossing the Wigan line. However, so did the Manly defence. In a tryless yet absorbing game, Wigan won by 8 points to 2, thanks to the boot of their goal-kicker, David Stephenson. In a very physical encounter, the turning point was the sending off of Manly's 'hard man' Ron Gibbs in the 45th minute for elbowing Joe Lydon. Brian Case (Wigan – Image 162, page 270) and Cliff Lyons (Manly) were sin binned. What made the victory even sweeter was that Wigan's starting thirteen players that evening were British. Even three of the four substitutes were British, the one exception being Graeme West, a New Zealander. Shaun Wane, the former Wigan head coach (Image 161), was named 'man of the match'.

Wigan went on to win three more World Club Challenges, one against Penrith at Anfield in 1991, a famous one against the Brisbane Broncos in Australia in 1994, and the Cronulla Sharks at the DW Stadium in 2017. Brisbane had beaten Wigan at Central Park in the 1992 World Club Challenge by 22 points to 8 and were expected to win handsomely in Australia. The Broncos were the best team in Australia and, to the Australian press, that meant they were the best team in the world. Wigan had no chance. According to the Australian media, Wigan had wasted their time simply by boarding the plane. However, in a thrilling match, Wigan triumphed by 20 points to 14 in front of a capacity 54,000 crowd. A new young winger by the name of Jason Robinson, who was destined to become a dual international,* scored one of Wigan's tries that momentous evening in 1994. Yet again, Wigan had beaten the Aussies in their own backyard.

---

*   He also scored England's only try in their 20 points to 17 defeat of Australia in the 2003 rugby union world cup final

16.6 OKELLS CHARITY SHIELD

The Charity Shield was a pre-season pot-warmer where the Champions entertained the Challenge Cup winners with the proceeds going to charity. In the late eighties the match was sponsored by Okells Brewery in the Isle of Man. Having missed the previous years game against Hull KR, we decided it was time to revisit our favourite island for the match against Halifax and so, in the September of 1987, Joe, George, myself and our two children boarded the plane at Blackpool airport for the short hop to Ronaldsway airport in the Isle of Man. After collecting our hire car, we drove to the Palace Hotel in Douglas.

We had chosen the Palace Hotel because it was where both the Halifax and Wigan teams were staying. To our dismay, the Wigan team decided, at the last minute, to stay at a hotel in Castletown on the evening before the match. Apparently, Graeme Lowe didn't want his players fraternising with the 'enemy' prior to the game. Later that day as the Halifax team coach pulled up in front of the Palace Hotel, they were met with a chorus of 'Here come the losers' from the Wigan fans.

They were right. Wigan thrashed Halifax in front of a full house at the small but picturesque stadium (Image 160). At the evening disco in the Palace Lido, Chris Anderson, the Halifax coach, was gracious in defeat saying it took a great side to beat his team by such a margin. That evening, the Wigan players did stay at the Palace Hotel and Andrew and Michael got their pictures taken with their heroes (Images 161 and 162).

On Sunday morning we paid a visit to Nobles Park. Because of its lofty location half-way up the hillside, Nobles Park provided a magnificent view of the Douglas seafront. Even though it rained, we played bowls and laughed as streams of spray flew from the bowls as they rolled along, leaving a tell-tale track on the rain covered grass. After a drink and a cake in the little café, it was time to make our way to the airport for our flight home. On crossing the Fairy Bridge, we said goodbye to the fairies to ensure a safe return.

It was such an enjoyable weekend that we went the following year too. Although Wigan lost to Widnes, we still had a brilliant time. It seemed surreal sitting in the same bar as the Wigan and Widnes players (Image 162) and their coaches, Graeme Lowe and Doug Laughton. Unfortunately, that was the last time the event was held in the Isle of Man.

The Wigan and Halifax teams line up at
the stadium before the game.

Left to right: Michael, Andy Gregory, our
Andy Gregory and Shaun Wane.

Andrew and Michael with some of the Wigan
players in the Palace Hotel bar. Left to right: Ian Potter,
Richard Russell, Andrew, Dean Bell, Michael and Brian Case.

The launch of the European Super League in 1996 meant that, for the first time, a French club was included. This provided an ideal opportunity to visit Paris in the summer to watch Wigan play Paris St Germaine. Even Vera couldn't resist the lure of Paris and she accompanied Michael and myself for a weekend in Gay Paree.

We stayed in a small hotel at the Place de Italie. It was a good location, close to the *Stade Charlety* where the game would be played, yet not too far away from the bustling city centre. Furthermore, it was close to a host of cafes and restaurants, including MacDonalds! Even though Paris is not Michael's favourite city, we had a great time despite Wigan suffering an unexpected defeat at the charming stadium (Image 163).

The following year we went back again, this time accompanied by Michelle and Keith. Michelle was also an avid Wigan supporter and the opportunity to see Wigan play rugby in Paris was too good to miss. This time, things didn't go smoothly. At Charles de Gaulle airport we waited for an eternity at the carousel for our baggage. It never arrived and we had to fill in a lost luggage form before departing the airport for our hotel.

Michael outside the Paris St Germaine ground 1998.

The weather was scorching. However, we were dressed for the cool Wigan weather with thick jeans and woolly sweaters. We sweltered in the heat but there was nothing we could do. Our shorts and lightweight clothes were in our suitcases. In complete compliance with Sod's Law, our suitcases arrived on the morning of our departure home. In spite of this mishap, Wigan won and we had an enjoyable weekend.

16.8 AN EVENING TO FORGET

Tuesday, 12 February 1991. It was a cold, dark, wintry day. The heavy snow of the past week had turned to a dismal grey slush, as wet and depressing as the brooding grey sky. The severe weather had caused the postponement of Wigan's Challenge Cup tie at Castleford and the new date was tonight. I had taken the day off work and, in the morning, gone with Vera to Wigan to do some shopping. However, my mind was elsewhere. The dark clouds looked laden with snow and I wondered if we should bother with our trip to Castleford. A further snowfall would result in another postponement and a wasted trip. These thoughts whirled around my head as we trudged wearily through the deep, grey slush. There was something foreboding about the place in these conditions, something quite eerie. Maybe it reflected my melancholy mood since I secretly hoped it would snow and that we wouldn't have to make the long trip over the Pennines in the cold and dark in such atrocious conditions.

It didn't happen. The snow held off and so, in the late afternoon, Andrew, Michael and myself went to collect George for our trip to Castleford. He was sat in his favourite armchair near a roaring coal fire sipping the last contents of his cup of tea. He looked so settled, it seemed a shame to disturb him. "You don't have to come if you don't want to. It's a bad night. If you'd rather stay here, it's fine," I said.

"No," said George, "I want to come." After he'd donned his coat, hat, scarf and gloves, we set off.

After crossing the Pennines, the plan was to take a short detour from the M62 along the M606 to a Little Chef on the outskirts of Bradford, one that we had used before and really liked. As we turned off the M62, my early fears came home to roost. Thick, heavy snow fell from the sky. What should we do? We decided to continue on to the Little Chef, have our meal and then reassess the situation.

By the time we reached the Little Chef the snow had abated but the heavy snow flurry had left its mark. The car park had a two inch covering of the white stuff. It was lovely sitting in a cosy warm cafe looking through the window at the winter wonderland. The food was delicious too. George had fish, chips and peas with tea, bread and butter. The fish was as white as the freshly fallen snow and George remarked that it was the best fish and chips he had had in his entire life.

On returning to the car we listened to the radio to see if the match was still on. It was, so we resumed our journey to Castleford.

The light covering of fresh snow ensured that we made our way from the car to the ground cautiously. Near the ground, people were offering collectable cards of famous rugby league players to the passing children. George knew that Michael collected them and, despite the cold, insisted that he went and got some.

After taking our seats in the small stand I took out the flask of coffee that Vera had packed and began to unscrew the top. A cup of hot coffee before the game would warm us up nicely. As the Wigan team emerged on to the field for their pre-match warm up, someone tapped my shoulder from behind. And again, this time more urgently. Bemused, I turned around. Was it someone I knew? No, it was a complete stranger. He looked concerned. "I think your friend is unwell," he said. "He needs help."

He was right. Sat two seats away from me (Andrew and Michael always sat between us), George's head was jerking backwards and forwards as if he were having a fit. I dashed the few feet to the nearest steward and said that someone had taken ill and needed medical assistance. Immediately! By a stroke of good fortune, the person he was talking to was the Castleford team doctor. He was at George's side in a flash. "I think he's having a heart attack," he said, and immediately called for an ambulance and a stretcher.

It was so unreal that it didn't seem to be happening. We had just had a lovely meal, sat down to watch a game of rugby and now all this commotion. I ushered Andrew and Michael to the safety of the aisle as the medical team arrived with the stretcher. Carefully, they lifted George on to the stretcher and began to carry him down to the pitch. Holding my children's hands, we followed behind as they took him down the touchline to the waiting ambulance. I asked if we could come with him in the ambulance and they agreed.

It was a harrowing journey as the ambulance sped along snow covered roads, its siren blaring, to the nearest large hospital at Pontefract. The paramedics were doing all they could, supplying oxygen and giving artificial respiration. I was so proud of our children. Although they were extremely upset and distressed and their faces were ashen, they held my hands tightly and never uttered a word.

We waited for what seemed like an eternity in the small reception area of the hospital. "Will he be alright Dad?" they asked. I didn't know what to say. I hoped with all my heart that he would. George wasn't just my father-in-law, he was my best friend. But the omens didn't look good. I couldn't bring myself to tell them the truth, nor could I tell them a lie, so I said that I didn't know. By then, I think we all knew what the outcome would be.

Eventually, a doctor in a white coat came and took us into a small private room. Gently, he broke the news that none of us wanted to hear. "I'm very sorry," he said. "We did all we could but I'm afraid your father-in-law is dead." I was speechless, numb with shock. But for Andrew and Michael it was too much. They could hold back no longer and burst into floods of tears. It was a terrible situation for two young boys. I felt so helpless. The doctor kindly arranged for a police car to take us back to our parked car and then we faced the long drive home.

273

That car journey home was the worst of my whole life. None of us spoke a word. Four of us had set out to watch a game of rugby yet only three were returning. It just couldn't be true. But it was. My thoughts were as bleak and desolate as the dark, snow covered hills. As for my children, I couldn't begin to comprehend what they were feeling. They had set out with their grandad a few hours ago and now he was dead. Gone forever. I wanted desperately to comfort them but I didn't know what to say. So I said nothing.

How was I going to break the news to Vera and especially to his wife? These thoughts troubled me all the way home. Who should I tell first? Normally, I would take George home first before returning to our own home, but I didn't think that was the best course of action tonight. It would be better to take our children home and break the sad news to Vera first. It was something I was dreading.

After parking the car on the drive we made our sombre way to the back door. Andrew and Michael were doing their best to compose themselves but I knew that tears weren't far away. Slowly, we made our way into the lounge. I was struggling to find the words to say but Vera spoke first. "What's up. Have they lost?" With that, our children broke into tears and sobbed uncontrollably. I'll never forget the look on Vera's face as she turned to me for an explanation, although I think she realised at that instant what had happened. I just shook my head and said that her dad had had a heart attack at the ground and died in hospital. It was already the worst night of our lives, but it wasn't over yet. We had to tell Doris, his wife.

I drove Vera to George's house in Manor Grove and we knocked on the door. Doris greeted us warmly, looking a little bemused as to why Vera was with me and not George and our children. Lovingly, Vera embraced her mother and told her what had happened. Looking on, I saw Doris visibly slump: I thought she was going to fall. Her response haunts me to this day. "But he can't be," she said. "I've got his supper ready."

Vera then had the harrowing task of informing her two sisters of the tragedy. We couldn't leave Doris alone but we only had one car at her house. What should we do? To compound the situation, Keith worked nights meaning that Elaine was home alone. It was unfair to ring her with such dreadful news so late at night so it was decided that Vera would drive to Elaine's to break the news in person whilst I remained with Doris. Whilst she was gone, I had the unenviable task of phoning June.

It was an awful thing to have to do but it was equally awful for June on the other end of the phone but at least Ray, her husband, would be with her. Receiving an unexpected call after midnight to tell her that her dad had died suddenly at a rugby match must have been terrible. On hearing the tragic news, June's response was, "You're joking!" Sadly, I wasn't.

That night everyone was supportive. Elaine returned with Vera to her mother's house and we deemed it best if Doris stayed with us, at least for that night. Elaine had telephoned Keith at work and he also insisted on driving to our house to offer his support, whilst June and Ray came the following morning. Numb with shock and disbelief, it was a long night for all of us.

George's death was reported in the Wigan Evening Post (Image 164).

Again, with hindsight, all the little warning signs were there. For instance, for the home games at Central Park I parked our car at the top of a small hill. In the past, climbing the hill after the match had presented no problems but in the previous few months George had become a little breathless. Furthermore, on returning home from away trips his legs ached more than usual. Little things maybe, but they were the harbinger of what was to come. What made his death more surprising was that he seemed so fit. Always an active man, George took his dog 'Miffy' for at least one long walk every day. He looked a picture of health. It was so perplexing. However, he did smoke in the early part of his life and this must have been the main cause. We couldn't think of anything else.

Devastated by the loss of a dear friend and fellow Wigan supporter, I said to Michael that I wouldn't have anyone to watch Wigan with.[*] "Don't worry, Dad," he said. "I'll come with you." And, true to his word, we still go to watch Wigan together to this day. Nowadays, however, we watch the games in comfort.

Shortly after Wigan moved from Central Park to the brand new JJB stadium (now renamed the DW stadium) in 1999, Michael and I became members of the Cherry and Whites Club. Membership has many advantages. As well as getting the best seats in the ground, members also have the exclusive use of a large lounge, with your own dedicated table, both before and after the game. It is also where the players come after the match. A compere, hostesses, quiz, plus food and drink, complete the package. But, most important of all, it is where you meet and make friends with other like-minded supporters.

Over the last ten years we have become firm friends with Ian Taylor and his family (Image 165), sharing the same table with Ian, his wife Sharon, their two daughters Vicky and Laura and, until recently, Sharon's mother, Janet, and Pat, her sister. Steve, his wife Carol and her brother Robert, also shared our table.

In 2014 Sharon couldn't attend the AGM so Ian invited me to take her place. It was the year Wigan defeated Hull in the Challenge Cup final and I duly had my picture taken alongside the famous trophy (Image 165).

---

[*]   Andrew would be starting university the following year – see Chapter 19

Devoted rugby fan dies at game

A DEVOTED rugby league fan collapsed and died as he watched his team in a cup match.

Lifelong Wigan supporter George Santus of Manor Grove, Aspull, keeled over during Wigan's first round cup tie in Castleford on Tuesday.

Ambulancemen struggled in vain to revive the 71-year-old fan after he collapsed in the stands alongside his son-in-law and two grand-children.

He died almost instantly of a massive heart attack.

His daughter June said today: "He loved rugby, he rarely missed a match, he followed Wigan everywhere.

"I think he would have thought it was the ideal place to die — watching a match."

Born and brought up in Wigan, Mr Santus worked at British Loco in Horwich. He moved to Aspull when he married his wife, Doris, 45 years ago.

Mr Santus, whose funeral is on February 20, leaves a wife, three daughters and five grandchildren.

Report of George's death in the Wigan Evening Post.

Ian, Laura, Sharon and Vicky.

Me with the Challenge Cup.

We have also made friends with people who don't sit at our table, particularly John and Helen Evans. If there are two more passionate and devoted fans of Wigan Warriors, I have yet to meet them. Not only do John and Helen travel from Chester for every game, they also sponsor one of the Wigan players, Jake Shorrocks, and organise an annual meal at Rigolettos for about 20 or so fans from the Cherry and Whites lounge at the end of every season. A larger than life character, John makes everyone laugh with his witty humour. Being with these people is something we look forward to every year.

16.9 RUGBY HOLIDAYS

Not only have we become firm friends with Ian and his family, we also have 'rugby holidays' together. In 2015 Michael and I had a weekend break with Sharon and Ian for the 'Magic Weekend' in Newcastle. The event is so popular that there wasn't a single hotel room to be had in Newcastle so we ended up staying at the Sunderland Marriott in Seaburn. It was a good choice. The hotel is situated in a prime position on the charming seafront, the interior was modern yet homely and the bedrooms spacious. Furthermore, all the staff were locals. We had a wonderful time and, to put the icing on the cake, Wigan beat Leeds. Indeed, we booked the same hotel for the 2016 and 2017 'Magic Weekends' but had to book a different one for 2018 and 2019 because the Sunderland Marriott was fully booked.

Also, in 2016 we thoroughly enjoyed a five day break at Lloret de Mar to watch Wigan play the Catalan Dragons in Perpignan. Sharon's pre-trip research unearthed a real gem of a watering hole, El Pub. Run by an enthusiastic English couple, the pub really caters for the rugby fans like ourselves staying at the nearby Fenals Garden Hotel. They even recorded the match on TV so we could enjoy watching it on our return over a few glasses of cold beer. The only downsides were that my old sandals disintegrated on the first day causing my feet to become sore and blistered, and the return Easy Jet flight home was cancelled at short notice, necessitating an unscheduled extra nights stay. Nonetheless, we all enjoyed the holiday so much that we went their again in 2017, this time accompanied by my brother-in-law, Keith. This time, however, we flew with a different airline, Jet 2, and there were no problems.

The games in both 2016 and 2017 were played in the middle of summer when the weather was hot and sunny. In 2018, the match was in early April when the weather is not so hot and sunny, so we gave it a miss. However, in 2019 the fixture returned to its original slot in summer. Not only that, the match was played at the famous Nou Camp stadium in Barcelona. Therefore, instead of staying at Lloret de Mar, which is ideal for matches at Perpignan, we stayed at Santa Susannah, which is closer to Barcelona. It was a good choice.

Boasting a fine sandy beach with mountains as its backdrop, Santa Susannah is a most picturesque resort. As well as enjoying the beach, we also enjoyed a lovely ride on a road train along the foothills of the mountains. Situated right on the beach, our hotel too was lovely. And, as she did in Lloret de Mar, Sharon also found a gem of a drinking hole, the Drunken Duck pub, which we frequented regularly.

Not only was the resort, and the hotel, lovely, so was the train journey along the beautiful coastline to Barcelona. The track hugs the coast all the way to Barcelona, affording splendid views along the way. The only downside to a most enjoyable holiday was that Wigan lost.

This year (2020) the Covid 19 pandemic has caused the cancellation of both the Magic Weekend in Newcastle and our trip to Perpignan. We're all hoping for better luck next year.

17

SAM

What on earth was that? This thought flashed simultaneously through the minds of Vera, Andrew and Michael. It sounded like a deafening bark but it couldn't be. Our old Heeler, Shandy, who was frail and going blind, hadn't barked for over a year so it couldn't be him. Perplexed, they all dashed towards the source of the sound in the back garden; Vera from the kitchen where she had been preparing tea, Andrew from the garage where he had been playing with his chemistry set and Michael from his bedroom. What they found both astounded and saddened them. It had been Shandy who had barked. He lay dead on the flags beside the back door, his mouth still open from the bark. From somewhere, he had summoned the strength to produce one final bark. It was his last act before he died, his way, I suppose, of saying farewell.

That summer afternoon in 1987 I received a phone call from Vera informing me that our dog had died and promptly made my way home. It was distressing seeing his lifeless form lying so still on the flagged patio when normally he would be dashing around and yapping away. What made it worse was that the flies had already started to settle on his prone, defenceless, little body. None of us wanted that so, as gently as I could, I placed him in a black bin bag and sealed the end with string. At least it would keep the flies out and preserve some degree of dignity. But what do you do with a dead dog? We considered burying him in our back garden but quickly dismissed it on health grounds. In the past we had given small animals, such as hedgehogs, a decent burial plot in our garden but a dog was a different matter. In the end I telephoned the council and they agreed to send someone round to collect him. Thankfully, they took him away that same afternoon to be cremated. We didn't want our dead pet to start decomposing in our garden in the summer heat.

Shandy had a good, long life. As mentioned in Chapter 9, we bought him as a puppy in 1970, the year after we were married, and he lived to the ripe old age of 17. Coming from a farm he wasn't the cleanest of dogs and, being terrier like, he yapped a lot too but despite these shortcomings we were very fond of him. One of his best party tricks was his 'singing'. He would imitate people who 'sang' in a high pitched voice and it was so funny. Everyone who saw it was in fits of laughter. Every night before going to bed Vera and I took him for a walk around the estate. One night, he had been so badly behaved that we told him off and went on the walk without him. On our return, his greeting was so friendly, enthusiastic and affectionate that we had no option but to relent and do the walk again, this time accompanied by our canine friend.

I had fulfilled my childhood dream of owning a dog and therefore, after Shandy's death, Vera and I weren't really bothered about having another one. Granted, they were lovely, affectionate and loyal companions but they were also quite demanding and restrictive. Dogs need a lot of time and attention. With two children to bring up, we felt like having a breather. However, our children, especially Michael, kept on and on at us to get another dog. He said, jokingly, that it was child cruelty not to let him have one! They promised that they would look after it; feed it, take it for walks and clean it. But they would say that, wouldn't they? In our hearts we knew that most of those tasks would fall upon us.

The joint onslaught from Andrew and Michael was resisted staunchly, until the day that a stray dog found its way into our garden. Our children had a whale of a time playing with it both in the garden and later in our house. The following day the dog was re-united with its owner but the damage had been done. The joy and delight on our children's faces melted our resolve and we granted them their wish.

We bought books on dogs and several breeds were considered but the one that we all kept coming back to was a Yellow Labrador. Not only were they absolutely beautiful, they also had an excellent temperament, a crucial consideration when children are around. You couldn't better a Labrador for that. We were hooked and, in the late summer of 1988 after our holiday in Florida (Chapter 15), we set out to the Mayfield Kennels at Agecroft to choose our little Labrador puppy.

17.1 PUPPY LOVE

The Mayfield kennels were quite big and it took us a while to look at all the cuddly little fluffs of yellow as they played boisterously with, I presume, their siblings. However, two stood out. We asked the attendant if we could hold them. "Yes, no problem," she said. "Which one do you want to hold first?" This was problematical. I think we all favoured one puppy over the other, but only slightly. Which one should we handle first? It is cruel, I know, to handle and caress a puppy and then not to take it home. But we had no choice. Rightly or wrongly, I decided that we should look first at the 'second favourite' since, if we chose the other one, they would both have been handled only once. We all handled him and he was lovely. But we instructed the attendant to put him back and hand us the other one. It was unanimous. This one was special. He melted our hearts. He was so cute, a fluffy, cuddly yellow ball with a hint of mischievousness (Image 166). He was most definitely the one and, with joy in our hearts and a spring in our step, we toddled off to the spacious pet shop to buy some goodies for our new little friend.

We perused the pet shop hunting for things to buy our new addition, who was held in turn by all of us. Food, yes, we'd need some food, and a nice cosy basket for him to sleep in, together with a woollen blanket to keep him warm. And a small collar and lead were also essential. These were some of the things we purchased although I'm sure there were more. Amidst all the excitement the attendant almost forgot to let us pay for our fluffy yellow bundle. Unfortunately, she didn't and we duly paid the £375 price tag for our puppy and his Kennel Club certificate. It had been a happy if expensive day. But it wasn't over yet. We had to show off our new addition to our families.

A cute, yellow puppy.

Our first stop was my Auntie Lily's. They had never been a pet-owning family and were somewhat surprised when we walked in with our yellow bundle. However, he was so cute and adorable that he quickly enrolled them into his band of followers until, that is, he decided to stage a demonstration. Look at me, his face said, as he proudly stood on the rug in front of the fire and unleashed a liquid torrent from beneath his gangly legs. It seemed to go on forever, like someone with diabetes. We were so embarrassed. Lily quickly fetched a cloth and wiped it up but my uncle was, as the Queen would say, not amused. Hurriedly, we made our excuses and departed to our second destination, Vera's parents.

Having been dog owners for most of their lives they were delighted to see our new little puppy. And he was delighted to see them. He ran around their lounge and loved the attention they bestowed upon him, although I think George's own dog Miffy was, how can I put it, a little miffed. Fortunately, there were no more accidents and we whisked our little bundle of joy off to his new home.

What should we call him? It's something that we hadn't really considered but it didn't matter. He seemed to name himself. On the way home in the car it was obvious what he should be called. He was, most definitely and unequivocally, a SAM!

Sam loved our house. He bounded around, full of the joys of life, exploring every nook and cranny. He settled into his new surroundings instantly. Or so we thought. In the evening we placed his basket next to the radiator in the kitchen, complete with his cosy new blanket, and then lifted him in gently. He looked so cute and cuddly curled up in his new basket. A bowl of fresh water and some food were placed nearby and, pleased with our efforts, we slowly edged our way out of the kitchen and closed the door. Then, all hell broke loose. He started yelping frantically and clawing away at the door. We tried to talk soothingly to him but to no avail. Eventually, we had to open the door, go back into the kitchen and stay with him until he dozed off. It was quiet for a while but as soon as he awoke the same thing happened again. In the end we had to leave him. None of us got much sleep that night.

We were determined not to let him sleep in any of the bedrooms and to get him used to sleeping in the kitchen, at least until he was house trained. The kitchen had a tiled floor so any 'accidents' could be cleaned up swiftly and efficiently. However, his scratching was making such a mess of the door that I had to fix a piece of hardboard to the bottom half to protect it from further damage. Eventually, the whining and scratching abated and, after a few weeks, ended completely. Sam had become accustomed to his sleeping place.

Like most owners of pedigree puppies we took him to the vets to have his inoculations. The vet said there was a lot of the Parvo virus about and that Sam would have to be confined to the house and garden for two weeks, when his booster jab was due. This wasn't too bad: it gave us, or rather Vera, time to begin his training. And not just house training, which he learned pretty quickly, but also obedience and 'trick' training, which he also learned quickly.

The two weeks passed fairly rapidly and it was with great expectations that we took him to the vets for the second time to get his booster jabs. To our dismay, the vet said that he needed to be kept housebound for a further two weeks. The same thing happened on the next two visits, so it was nine weeks before Sam could be released from the confines of his house and garden for his first taste of the outside world. It placed a huge burden on Vera since it was she who had to spend time at home looking after him during those nine weeks. However, she used the time well.

17.2 PUPPY TRAINING

Sam learned to associate the command 'Here' with a food treat and positively raced to anyone who shouted this word, waiting eagerly for his biscuit or Bonio. Eventually, it was possible to dispense with the treat. 'Sit' was learned very easily by pushing down gently on his rear end as the command was spoken. The commands 'Lie (down)', 'Roll over', 'Say hello' (wave his front paw in the air) and 'Shake a paw' (offering his front paw from a sitting position for someone to shake) weren't much more difficult either. 'Fetch' was another command learned easily but 'Leave' and especially 'Stay' were another matter.

Like most dogs, but particularly Labradors, Sam was eager in the extreme to please his master. But, just like most other dogs, he was equally keen to consume any food or treats on offer. To learn these last two commands we made him sit and held his collar to restrain him. Then, a treat, such as a Bonio, would be placed a few feet away followed by the command 'Leave' in a very stern voice. It was hilarious watching him stare intently at the food, his eyes pleading, his mouth slavering, until he was released from his torment by the command 'Get it'. 'Stay' was more difficult since he never wanted to be away from his 'master' and it was the one command that he never really mastered.

Accidents were rare during his house training but they did happen occasionally. One I remember well. Vera and I had returned home early from a shopping trip and, on opening the back door, we were met with the view of Michael on his hands and knees in the kitchen cleaning up an 'accident'. The culprit, Sam, huddled sheepishly in a corner. The look on Michael's surprised face was a picture. It was one of, "Oh no, they might not want a dog if it does this," mixed with a pleading look that, "He won't do it again." He needn't have worried. We had all become very attached to our new member of the family.

When Sam was finally cleared to leave the house and garden, one of the first places we took him was the Beaumont Primary School playing fields. Located close to our house they were an ideal spot for an energetic Labrador puppy to let off steam. One game he adored was 'chase the children'. I held Sam's collar whilst Andrew and Michael ran away across the football field. Sam was like a coiled spring waiting to explode. When he was released, I'm sure he'd have given a cheetah a run for its money as he sped after his two companions. Although he liked Vera and myself, it was obvious who his two best friends were.

17.3 VETS

When Sam was a puppy we carried him into the vets. He had grown a little but was still small and lightweight compared to a fully grown Labrador. "You won't be doing that in six months time," a man in the waiting room said with a smile. And he was right. Sam changed from a gangly puppy with legs far too big for his small body (Image 167) into a proud, powerful Labrador weighing over two stones (Image 168).

Sam as a Puppy.

Sam, fully grown.

Sam hated going to the vets. In his mind, a trip to the vets meant being lifted on to a table by a stranger in a white coat and then being prodded and probed and, even worse, having sharp little spears stuck into you! It wasn't a pleasant experience, completely different to chasing sticks on a walk and swimming in a lake. No, a trip to the vets was one thing he could do without, thank-you very much. But, although he didn't know it, it was for his own good. He dreaded a visit to the vets so much that he quickly became familiar with the word and would run a mile once anyone uttered it. Not only that, he learned to lip read because, even when we mimed the word, he still recognised it!

17.4 MISCHIEF MAKER

Sam grew into a lovely dog. He was gentle, affectionate, loyal and handsome with a mouth like the TARDIS and a tongue like a car wash. In the morning he would stride proudly into the lounge, open his mouth and all manner of things would fall out (Image 169). Dirty knickers, handkerchiefs, underpants (dirty preferable to clean), socks and yet more dirty knickers. It was like a magician pulling a never-ending stream of paraphernalia from his hat. And you certainly didn't need to wash your face or especially your hair if Sam was around. Just sit in front of him, lower your head and, Hey Presto, he would give you the best face wash and hair cleaning ever. He would lick you until the cows came home, and then some more. He would even perform this task lying down. If you fancied lying on the floor, Sam would come and lie next to you, place his face next to your head and lick you clean for England. And he wasn't fussy. Baldies were just as good to lick as the hirsute, as George found to his cost.

Sam with his mouth full.

Once he was fully house trained, Andrew and Michael would sometimes let Sam sleep on their beds. (Vera expressed surprise when this was mentioned recently although I can't believe she wasn't aware of it at the time.) He was a big, heavy dog and on the occasions that he actually lied across their bodies, they'd push him off. Reluctantly, he would drop to the floor, give them a baleful look and release a sigh so big that the flaps of his mouth reverberated for several seconds. He wasn't used to being treated in such a manner.

Sam had another foible. He pinched pillows. People stayed at our house quite often, particularly at weekends and school holidays; Elaine and her friends when they were young (but before we had Sam), and then her two children, Michelle and Natalie. Every morning we awoke to find Sam lying on a pile of pillows on the

285

landing whilst Michelle and Natalie lay on beds devoid of pillows. He would sneak into their bedrooms at night, pull the pillows from under their sleeping heads and stockpile them on the landing. On the occasions that he woke them, they had to win a tug-of-war to retrieve their pillows. But it was only a temporary victory. As soon as they were asleep, he would pinch them again.

Food. Sam loved food and eagerly awaited the evening meal that Vera, myself and our two children invariably ate at the dining table. To his credit, he was exceptionally well behaved. At meal times he would sit quietly and patiently near the table between two of the diners, waiting. Waiting for one of us to throw him a titbit. As he waited, saliva dripped incessantly from his mouth in anticipation of the treat to come. Indeed, after several years, there was an unmistakable pattern around the oval table caused by his constant saliva drops impregnating the carpet. Although I can't be absolutely certain, I'm sure that the amount of drooling increased in proportion to the type of food being eaten, culminating in a steady drip for his favourites of fish, steak and his absolute favourite, chicken. He loved chicken so much that he sat near the oven as it was being roasted and would voraciously gobble up any bits that fell to the floor as it was being carved. After he'd received a morsel from one person, he would move round the table to the next one for his next treat. And so on. And he always mopped up any leftovers. There were no dirty plates in our house.

Although chicken was probably Sam's favourite food, kippers ran it a close second. As a family we rarely ate kippers but Vera would occasionally buy some just for Sam. He devoured them as though he was at starvation's door. Tripe was another food that we didn't eat but Sam adored. Roast beef was a different matter. We all loved a roast beef dinner: this is what we had on our Saturday visits to my Auntie Lily's (Chapter 15). But she didn't stop at four roast dinners. Sam had one too, his own personal spread of roast beef, mashed potatoes and gravy. No wonder he dashed from our car and through my auntie's door like a bat out of hell.

He didn't always behave impeccably. If an opportunity arose, Sam would take it. For instance, like the time that Michael left his lunchtime sandwich unattended for a moment on the lounge coffee table while he nipped into the kitchen for a drink. On his return, the plate was empty. The sandwich was safely tucked away in Sam's belly.

17.5 WALKIES

Once Sam had been released from the confines of his house and garden a routine was established. Part of this routine was that he got five walks a day. His first walk was at 7-30 in the morning. Before setting off for work, I took him across the busy Beaumont Road and into the fields opposite our house (Image 98, page 165). Just before 9-00 a.m. and again at lunchtime, either Andrew or Michael walked him along the grass verge between Armadale Road and Beaumont Road (Image 98). His penultimate walk took place after school had finished. However, before taking him, our children always watched *Home and Away* on television. The music that signalled the end of the programme was the cue for his walk. Sam realised this connection very quickly and as soon as the music started, dashed off to get his lead and drop it at their feet. He performed the same trick to a bemused June. George had kindly agreed to look after Sam while we were away on holiday and was used to his trick of bringing the lead at the end of *Home and Away*. June wasn't and was most surprised when he dropped the lead at her feet, wagging his tail vigorously in anticipation of his walk. He was a clever dog.

His final walk of the day was after tea. Sometimes, it would be round the estate but more usually Vera and I took him into the fields opposite our house. Although he had a healthy appetite, he certainly got enough exercise to burn off any excess calories.

As mentioned in Chapter 15, on Saturdays we visited our parents' homes and Sam got not one but two walks. At my Auntie Lily's he was taken on to the playing fields of Aspull Secondary Modern School, where he was sometimes joined by her neighbour's Doberman Pincher, Dan. Dan was a soft dog and they chased each other around the field for ages. Just before the school was demolished to make way for a housing estate, the grass had grown extremely long and we had great fun by running off and hiding in it. It was to no avail. Sam always found us in no time at all. After the houses were built, we took him round Toddington.

Later, when visiting Vera's parents, Sam got his second walk. It was down the same line and into the same plantations where Vera and I did much of our courting. (It was also where we heard the roar from Central Park – Chapter 16.) He revelled in the woods and could seek out water better than any water diviner. Haigh Hall plantations are home to a number of ponds. Some have clear, fresh water whilst others are a swamp of black, stinking, muddy water. And yes, you've guessed the ones he preferred. In less time than it takes to utter 'Jack Robinson', he transformed himself from a Yellow Labrador into a black one.

After the sudden and unexpected death of her dad Chapter 16), Vera and her two sisters shared the visits to her mother's house on a daily basis. On her visiting days Vera was invariably accompanied by Sam. Without fail, come rain or shine, they always took him for a walk in the same plantations (usually with the same result).

Taking Sam for a walk gave them immense pleasure. However, this came to an abrupt end when Doris's house was burgled (Chapter 24). Living alone, the burglary made her insecure and shortly afterwards she moved into sheltered accommodation at nearby Hollydene. Unfortunately, dogs weren't allowed and, much to Sam's disgust and Vera's regret, this spelled the end of his midweek forays into Haigh Hall plantations.

On Sundays and in the summer evenings Sam was taken farther afield. Lever Park at Rivington, with its wide open spaces and numerous reservoirs, was Labrador heaven. As a puppy, he did his first swim in the pond at the Japanese Gardens (Image 32, page 47). Gently, we placed him in a shallow spot. Would he clamber out or would he venture in and have a swim? We should have known the answer. Labradors simply adore water, even as puppies, and he duly had his first taste of swimming. It was by no means his last. Lever Park remained one of his favourite spots for walks, influenced no doubt by the numerous reservoirs available for swimming. He must have swum miles retrieving the countless sticks thrown in the reservoirs for him.

Sam's *creme de la creme* of walks wasn't to be found in Lever Park or Haigh Hall plantations. No, it was much further afield than that. His favourite walk resided in our favourite place, the Lake District. It was the walk around Rydal Water, near Grasmere. Starting from the car park at White Moss common, we followed the path beside the river to a wooden bridge. The humans cross the river using the bridge. Not Sam. He splashed about in the crystal clear water like a toddler in the sea. After traversing a small wood (plenty of sticks to fetch), it was a climb up the hillside to a cave. About half-way up was a large rock. Here, we took a breather whilst, at the same time, throwing sticks down the hill to tire Sam out. It didn't. He was always fresher than we were even after half-an-hour's continuous running. After he'd had a quick dip in the cold waters of the cave, we began the descent down the rocky path to the southern tip of Rydal Water. The instant he saw the lake, Sam was off like a shot. He literally hurtled at full throttle into the water creating an enormous splash (Image 170), much to the astonishment of the people sat on the lake shore. Then, he swam all the way back to the starting point of the walk, whence he emerged an exhausted, wet, but very happy Labrador.

Sam making a splash.

In his later years we took an ageing Sam to Coniston. Our companions were Elaine and Keith, together with Charlie, their young, energetic and boisterous Beagle. Along the lake shore it was Charlie who was the star of the show. With his boundless energy he dashed hither and thither, whilst Sam simply plodded along like the old dog he was. However, as we reached a secluded pool, the situation changed. Without hesitation, Sam waded straight in and, just before it was deep enough to swim, turned around to Charlie as if beckoning him to follow. To his credit, he tried. Placing one paw tentatively after another, Charlie slowly inched his way towards the waiting Sam. He was doing fine. Until the moment the cold water touched his underbelly. "Whoa," he must have thought, this is not for me and made a quick U-turn, leaving Sam to swim alone.

Occasionally, we took Sam to the seaside, usually to Freshfields. Near to Formby, Freshfields is ideal for dogs. Flanked by the sea on one side and giant sandhills on the other, the vast expanse of sandy beach, frequented by so few humans, was doggy paradise. Sam really enjoyed chasing balls on the beach and splashing through the pools, but he was less certain about the sea. I think the waves confused him. Despite this, he still retrieved sticks thrown into the sea, his head constantly disappearing from view in the wave troughs. But sea water and Sam didn't mix. That evening, he was ill. Very ill. He couldn't stand and Vera had to massage him for hours to make him well. The treatment even included holding a hot water bottle next to his rear legs! Rightly or wrongly, we attributed the cause to sea water that he had swallowed. Accordingly, this spelt the end of his trips to Freshfields, but not to the seaside.

17.6 HOLIDAYS

Labradors are designed for holidays. Unlike most other breeds, they adore travelling in cars. Short hops or long hauls, it made no difference. Sam was no exception. Whether it was a short trip to Rivington or an eight hour marathon to Cornwall, he sat in the back seat like royalty, surveying the scene. Sometimes, I half expected him to wave his paw at the passers-by! Not only that, he also had the uncanny knack of being able to sense the presence of water, even from miles away. He would sit bolt upright, his nostrils sniffing the air, and make a low keening sound. And, without fail, within a few miles either a lake or the sea would suddenly spring into view. He was a water-diviner *par excellence*.

Sam also had his own car! In the mid-nineties I bought a Peugeot 106 for Vera and Michael. A few years later, when Vera acquired a Peugeot 206, the 106 became Sam's car. It was used for all the local destinations and sometimes for trips as far afield as the Lakes. But for really long journeys, we needed something bigger.

Taking a dog on holiday isn't easy. Most hotels don't welcome pets. But that didn't matter. We had our own holiday home. A home away from home. A caravan. Bought in 1986 (Chapter 18), our first touring caravan proved a sound investment. For any dog-owning family, a caravan is a godsend. It is your own private place with your own set of rules. It is a home for both you and your canine companion. You can go where you want, when you want. You get up when you want, eat when you want and go to bed when you want. For dogs, it is perfect.

Although the Lake District was our preferred holiday destination, Cornwall ran it a close second, and it was to Cornwall that we took Sam on his first holiday. The car was always packed on the Friday evening, allowing an early morning departure the following day. Sam was always the first one into the car, partly because he relished the journey ahead and partly because he didn't want to be left behind. On long journeys such as this, he sat in the middle of the rear seat, flanked by Andrew and Michael. However, it didn't take long before he was sprawled out across both their laps. After two comfort stops at Birmingham and Bristol, it would be evening by the time we arrived at our destination, usually the Hendra Caravan Park in Newquay.

Sam loved caravanning. He quickly found a place to lie (in front of the fire) and a place to sleep (under our bed). In the morning, he would crawl from his sleeping place and peek around to see if anyone was up and about. If not, he gave a big sigh and retreated, bleary eyed, back under the bed.

Everywhere we went, Sam went. Well, almost everywhere. On the odd occasions that we ate out, Sam was left in the car. With his face against the partially open window, he would watch us depart and then plonk down to have a snooze.

Without a doubt one of his favourite spots was Holywell Bay. This lovely sandy beach, with its warm pools and rocky outcrops, was doggy heaven. He splashed about in the pools (Image 171), frolicked in the sea and dashed along the beach. In other words, he mimicked Andrew and Michael. When he needed a rest, which wasn't very often, he lay down beside me and Vera.

Sam splashing about in a pool at Holywell Bay.

One year, we took our caravan to Crocketford, a small village beyond Dumfries. It was a perfect location. There was a beautiful, sparsely populated, beach at Sandyhills, walks through unspoilt countryside, and Auchencairn. Auchencairn was a delight. This secluded spot had everything. Tranquillity, clear blue sea, a rocky shore and a beach of shells. Our children and Sam adored it. They spent hours exploring the rock pools, throwing shells into the sea and generally messing about. Sam spent so much time on the rocks (Image 172) that his paws bled. But it didn't matter. He literally swam around the entire bay (Image 173), allowing the salt water sufficient time to weave its magic and heal his wounds.

Sam, Michael and Andrew on the
rocky beach at Auchencairn 1991.

Andrew and Michael encouraging Sam to swim around
Auchencairn Bayby throwing stones ahead of him 1991.

17.7 CHRISTMAS

Sam 'knew' when Christmas was approaching. How, I can hear you say, can a dog be aware of some future event. He 'knew' because of the tell tale signs that preceded Christmas, such as the cold weather; the frost and ice and, if we were lucky, the snow. He revelled in the snow, chasing and 'eating' snowballs, and demolishing the snowmen built by Andrew and Michael. He was intrigued by the patterns his warm yellow wee made in the pure white snow. It didn't make patterns in anything else! One very cold winter the lake opposite our house froze solid. Watching him chase a stick on the frozen ice was hilarious. Running from the land was fine but as soon as he reached the ice his legs splayed out and he slid along like a sled, way past his intended target. It was so funny.

Although the frost and the ice and the snow gave him clues that Christmas was coming, the clincher was the Christmas tree. As soon as he saw the tree, he knew that Christmas was near (Image 174). And, like any excited child, he wanted to participate in decorating it. I hesitate to say helped because that's not what he did. In fact, it was the opposite. As fast as we placed the decorations on the tree, Sam promptly removed them with his mouth, took them into 'his' corner of the lounge, and deposited them ever so gently on the carpet. In spite of the flimsiness and fragility of Christmas tree decorations, he never once broke a single one.

Michael with an excited Sam near the Christmas Tree.
And the coffee table where he pinched Michael's sandwich.

Sam was always the first one up on Christmas morning, his eyes glistening and his body quivering with the excitement to come. However, he knew that no presents would be opened until everyone was assembled in the lounge. Accordingly, he woke any sleepyheads by dashing into their bedrooms and licking their faces. "Come on, come on," he must have thought. "I want to open my presents."

The presents were opened in an orderly manner and Sam, like everyone else, waited patiently until it was his turn. Once the command 'Open it' had been given, he attacked the job with gusto. Placing one paw on top of the present to anchor it to the floor, he used his mouth to tear the wrapping paper to shreds. The presents containing food were 'attacked' first, presumably because he could sniff the food inside. Only when all his presents were safely opened would he relax and enjoy the fruits of his labour. Although his opening of presents was frantic and frenzied, it was extremely rare for him to damage any of them.

It wasn't only Sam who opened his presents. We did too. And one Christmas, a present for Michael caused no end of amusement. It wasn't the present itself but the purchase of it. Like most adolescent teenagers Michael wanted a pin-up calendar to hang in his bedroom and asked his mum to get it for him. As ever, Vera duly obliged.

The shop assistant seemed bemused. "Oliver Lance? A pin-up calendar of Oliver Lance?"

"Yes, that's right," replied Vera. "I'm sure that's what he told me." To her dismay, none of the shops seemed to have heard of Oliver Lance, let alone stock a calendar of him. Dejected by her lack of success, she returned home.

"Michael, I've been everywhere and no one has a calendar of Oliver Lance."

Michael looked quizzically at his mum, smiled and said, "Mum. It's Holly Valance, not Oliver Lance."

One year, during the quiet period between Christmas and New Year, I took Sam for a walk along the Leeds-Liverpool canal at Red Rock. Suddenly, there was a splash. He had decided to go for a swim. It wasn't a good idea. That stretch of the canal had been strengthened with concrete piles and the sides were too steep for him to clamber out. I knelt down and grabbed his front legs but I couldn't pull him out. His weight would have caused me to topple into the canal too! It was a dilemma. He needed to be pulled from the freezing water quickly or he would succumb to the cold. I gambled. The portion of the canal around the bend near Arley Hall golf club was popular, at least in the summer, with fishermen. But would any be foolish enough to fish in the depths of winter. I sincerely hoped so. Therefore, I released his legs and began to walk towards the bend, keeping pace with Sam's swimming. To my immense relief there was not one but two fishermen. On seeing my predicament, one of them held me whilst I pulled Sam from the canal. Needless to say, he didn't jump in again.

Christmas wasn't the only time that Sam and presents were linked together. Always eager to please, Sam just had to offer every visitor to our home a present. As soon as he heard someone approach (at which he excelled), he dashed around frantically until he found a 'present'. A cushion, a pillow, a toy or, if desperate, even a dirty pair of knickers would be scooped up into his mouth. Then, like an excited child, he stood, literally quivering with excitement at the door, ready to offer his esteemed gift. As the door opened, Sam proudly dropped his present at the feet of the surprised visitor. His look of smug satisfaction on his face spoke volumes. Aren't I a clever, friendly dog. I'm not sure all our visitors agreed, especially the ones who got dirty knickers.

17.8 A SHOULDER TO CRY ON

A dog has a calming influence. Not just on you but, as silly as it seems, on the house as well. The presence of another living, breathing animal inside the home makes it, well, more homely (Image 175).

Sam sensed when you were upset or sad or stressed and would come and place his head on your lap. It's amazing how simply stroking his head and running his floppy, silky ears through your fingers made you so relaxed. Any troubles simply melted away. Whenever there was a row or raised voices, he retreated under the stairs until it was over and then came out and lay at your feet.

In the garden he was my friend. If I pottered around the plants, he pottered around the plants. If I sat down, he sat down. If I mowed the lawn, he… sat in the way and had to be moved. He rested when I rested and he ate when I ate. He was a faithful companion. Sadly, all good things come to an end.

Sam and his two best friends on Andrew's 21st birthday.

17.9 A FINAL GOODBYE

It was the phone call that we had been dreading. We were in our caravan at the Lakelands Leisure Park in the southern Lake District (Chapter 18). Elaine and Keith were also present that Easter Sunday 2002, having come up for the day. Having just returned from a walk, we were enjoying a refreshing cup of tea when Vera's mobile phone rang. It was Michael. Sam had become very ill. He'd collapsed in the back garden and couldn't get up. And he was too heavy for Michael to move on his own. We had no choice but to return home immediately.

When we arrived home Sam was lying beside the radiator in the hall. A distressed Michael had telephoned his brother, who by then had moved to his own house in Westhoughton with his fiancee Helen (see Chapter 28), and together Andrew and Michael had managed to manoeuvre Sam on to a blanket and carry him into the house. We stroked and caressed him and massaged his legs, but to no avail. Even a hot water bottle had no effect. He still couldn't stand up. It was heartrending seeing our beloved pet in this condition. All of us were really upset.

Gathered together in the hall, we knew what had to be done. None of us wanted it but it had to be done. Sam had to be taken to the vets to be put to sleep. For Andrew, this was too much. With tears in his eyes, he bade Sam a final farewell and departed for home. By now, it was getting late so, clinging on to one final hope, we decided to stay with him for the night to see if there would be any improvement by the morning.

There wasn't. Sam was still in the same condition the following morning. It was time to say goodbye. After Michael had said his final goodbyes, Vera and I carried our beloved pet into the car in a blanket. Michael remarked that from the look in Sam's eyes, he knew that he wasn't coming back.

The weather was atrocious. Vera and I drove to the vets in Horwich in torrential rain. Even though we parked directly outside the front door, just carrying Sam the few steps from the car to the door drenched us to the skin. We laid him on a table inside a small room where the vet and his assistant were waiting. Carefully, the vet examined him.

"I'm afraid he's very ill," he said. "His heart is very weak and he has a cancer. There's nothing we can do except put him to sleep." At this point, Vera burst into tears and I felt my own eyes water. It's difficult to explain but although you know what is going to be said, when it actually is said it still comes as a shock. "I'll just give him an injection. He won't feel any pain," the vet said.

"Can we stroke him whilst you do that?"

"Yes. That's fine." And then the vet began preparing the injection.

Sam passed away peacefully. We stroked his head and talked soothingly to him as the lethal dose was delivered. He died almost immediately. It was an experience that both Vera and I had been dreading but, in reality, it wasn't horrible at all. I'm so glad that we were both there at the end so see him slip peacefully away.

We chose to have Sam cremated by himself and to have his ashes sent to us in a beautiful casket. Then, at the first available weekend, Andrew, Helen, Michael, Vera and myself drove to White Moss common in the Lake District, parked the car and, armed with some of his ashes, set out on his favourite walk around Rydal Water. At the point where he always charged into the lake, we paused. Then, each of us scattered a handful of his ashes into the clear waters he adored so much. "Swim forever, Sam," I thought as I scattered my handful of ashes. My companions no doubt had their own fond memories as they performed the same ritual. After a lovely meal at the Rose and Crown pub in Cark, we made our way home.

At home, we buried some more of his ashes at his favourite spot in the back garden, and planted a Brilliantisimum Acer tree in his memory (Image 207, page 363), together with a stone bearing his name. Sam. Every Christmas, some of his treats, such as a Bonio and some chocolate drops, are buried beneath the tree. They are always eaten though not, I suspect, by Sam.

With that wonderful gift called hindsight we probably held on to our dog for too long. About nine months earlier Sam had become very ill. One night, he ventured into the garden, lied down on the grass and wouldn't come in. He stayed out all night. Later, he lay in the lounge looking listless and tired. I remember lying beside him and beseeching him to get better. He did seem to recover but, looking back, he was never really well. I had to make a ramp for him to get in and out of the back door (and the caravan) and his walks got shorter and shorter. On a small, circular walk at Rivington, I even had to park next to a small hump at the side of the road to enable him to get in and out of the car. In the Lakes, his appetite for swims dwindled. In the end, Vera said that he was doing the short walks not for himself, but for me. She was probably right. But when you have owned a lovely dog for a long time, you never want to let go.

18

CARAVANNING

We've been good friends with Neville and Phyllis (Image 176) for over 50 years. When we were young, we'd visit them in their house in Shaw, where they lived, and they'd visit us in Bolton. We continued our reciprocal visits when they moved to Arnside after Neville's retirement but, because of Covid 19, have been unable to do so this year (2020). As mentioned in Chapter 10, Neville built the roof on our porch and also installed a side door on our double garage. When money was tight, they let us use their caravan for holidays, even towing it to the holiday sites (see later). They have been, and still are, good friends.

Until Neville let us use his caravan (Chapter 10), owning one had never crossed my mind. As a child, the few holidays that I'd had the privilege to enjoy were in boarding houses or small hotels, typically in the Isle of Man. My one and only experience of a caravan was when my mother and her friend Margaret treated me and William to a week's holiday in Conway (Chapter 2). I was thirteen years old and, from what I recall, it didn't stand out as something special. Consequently, I never harboured any desire to holiday in a caravan let alone buy one.

Neville and Phyllis celebrating their
Golden Wedding in 2009.

All that changed when Neville agreed to let us use his Cavalier touring caravan. Having just bought a large detached house (Chapter 9), money was tight, especially for holidays, and we were so grateful for his kind gesture. In the autumn of 1973, when Vera was pregnant with Andrew, Neville placed his caravan on a small, family run site at Great Eccleston near Blackpool so that Vera and I could enjoy a week's holiday. We had a wonderful time and really appreciated the freedom that a caravan holiday allowed.

These sentiments were reinforced the following year when Neville towed his caravan to the Lake District so that we could enjoy another low cost holiday, this time with our first baby (Chapter 10). This, I think, was the clincher. A caravan was ideal for holidays involving children and we knew there and then that, sometime in the future, we would buy one of our own. But first, I had a landmark birthday to celebrate.

18.1 SPRINGTIME IN PARIS

Father Time creeps up on you so quickly that, before I knew it, it was almost the day of my big 'Four O'. My fortieth birthday. Vera and I had decided beforehand that my fortieth birthday would be celebrated in that most romantic of cities, Paris. Paris in springtime, how romantic. It would be a special treat for the two of us. Although we loved our children to bits, some adult 'me' time was also essential and this special treat provided the ideal opportunity.

After perusing several brochures, we opted for an 'Independent Traveller' holiday with Paris Travel and, on the weekend of my birthday on 23 March 1986, we boarded the Pullman train at Wigan and travelled first class to Dover (via London). At Dover, for the first and only time in our lives, we boarded a hovercraft. I watched in awe as the huge amphibious brainchild of Sir John Cockcroft skimmed over the waves and then, just as effortlessly, continued on its way over the sandy beach, coming to a standstill a mere few yards from the waiting passengers (Image 177). It was so weird. You boarded a plane at an airport, a train at a train station and a boat at a port, but you boarded a hovercraft on a beach!

Boarding the hovercraft on the sandy beach at Dover.

That day, the bad weather meant the sea was choppy but the hovercraft handled the conditions well. It wasn't exactly a smooth crossing but smoother than it would have been on a boat. However, we still felt queasy. Not from the motion of the hovercraft, but from the noise. It was extremely noisy. The bad weather also caused a switch of destination from Calais to Boulogne. It wasn't a problem. Just as it did at Dover, the hovercraft swept from the sea on to the sandy beach. A short walk took us to a waiting train. Not only was it warm and comfortable, everyone had a reserved seat. Hot food was also available, which was most welcome on that cold spring day. In what seemed like no time at all, we arrived at the Gare de Nord station in Paris.

Ben Gunn, a colleague at ICI (see Image 201), had informed me that the Metro, the underground railway system, was the best way to get around Paris, and that the cheapest way to use the Metro was to purchase a *carnet* of tickets. We did and, in the early evening dusk, alighted from the Metro at a station outside our hotel.

Feeling hungry, we sauntered down the Boulevard to a small local café. As mentioned in Chapter 4, I didn't learn a foreign language at school but was determined to order our meals in French. The waiter stood by patiently whilst I struggled to order a cheese omelette and fries for myself, steak and chips for Vera (well done of course) and two glasses of red wine. After I had finished, the waiter said, in perfect English, "So you want a cheese omelette and fries for yourself, a well done steak and chips for your lady, and two glasses of red wine." I was so embarrassed at my stuttering French compared to his perfect English. Nonetheless, I think he appreciated my attempt to address him in his native tongue. My meal was fine but Vera's steak was more than a little underdone. The French 'well done' must be different to ours.

We saw the usual sights. *The Louvre*, with its smiling Mona Lisa, the *Champs-Elysees*, where a cup of coffee cost a fortune, and the *Arc de Triomphe*, where a kind stranger took our picture (Image 178). The volume of traffic whizzing around that famous monument was unbelievable and to reach it we used the underpass. Not so Ray and June. When they visited Paris a few years later they took their lives in their hands by actually crossing the busy roads! June said it was one of the most scary experiences of her life. *At Notre-Dame, we climbed the spiral staircase to reach the ramparts, whereupon Vera had an attack of vertigo. Needless to say, the even loftier heights of the Eiffel Tower remained unexplored.*

Vera and me at the Arc de Triomphe 1986.

On the Saturday evening we savoured a delicious meal in one of the 'brown cafés' on the Left Bank of the River Seine. From the outside the café looked distinctly unappealing, and the interior wasn't much better either. But the food was superb. Once again, Ben's recommendation proved first class.

The weather on the Sunday was appalling. Gale force winds and squally showers whipped across the city. Hardly the weather for a sail on the river. But a sail on the romantic River Seine was one of our 'must do' activities and so, against our better judgement, we hopped aboard a *Bateaux Mouche* for a one hour sail. It was a mistake. The wind was so fierce that, within minutes of setting off, several of the plastic windows were ripped from their supports and blown into the river. Not surprisingly, the sail was curtailed there and then. (And no, we didn't get a refund.)

Before departing for home we did some shopping at two of Paris's most famous stores, *Printemps* and *Galleries Lafayette*. Neither disappointed. A fellow guest at our hotel had recommended a visit to a small market and, since we had a little time left, we made our way down a busy Boulevard to seek it out. Suddenly, from out of nowhere, a group of street urchins surrounded us, babbling away in French. At first, I presumed they were begging for money but, in fact, they were after stealing my wallet. They didn't succeed. Having read about such dangers, my wallet remained in the firm grip of my hand inside my trouser pocket.

On the train journey home, Vera and I treated ourselves to a sumptuous meal in the first class Pullman carriage. It put the icing on a memorable weekend. Although sad that the weekend was over, we had something else to look forward to.

18.2 OUR FIRST TOURER

In the summer of 1986 we took the plunge and bought our first touring caravan. Vera and I had been browsing around local caravan dealers such as Stewart Longton and Dave Barron for a while, looking at various models and trying to decide which one suited our needs (and budget). We even visited a small dealership in Blackpool on one of our masonic weekends! (Chapter 11). The owner was friendly and knowledgeable and offered us a good deal, a 20 per cent discount, on the caravan we wanted, an ABI Ambassador (Image 179). It was a tempting deal but, rather than accept this first offer, we decided to see what Dave Barron would offer. "I'll tell you what Dave Barron's will say to you," he said. "They'll ask what discount you want? And you'll have to haggle very hard to match the discount I'm offering."

Michael outside our ABI Ambassador caravan at
Warmwell Bay, Dorset 1987. Andrew can be seen peering through
the side window, with Vera behind the front window.

In the end we did buy our caravan from Dave Barron. Several factors influenced our decision. Based in Coppull, it was local; it had a large repair and service facility; and it had both a large accessories shop and awning store. Unfortunately, the man from Blackpool was spot on. They behaved exactly as he predicted and we had to haggle extremely hard to approach his 20 per cent discount. With hindsight, it may have been better to have bought it in Blackpool after all. After taking our children and families to see our intended purchase, a cheque for £4,500 was handed over and the caravan was ours.

Towing a caravan, particularly for the first time, is a strange experience. I must admit to being more than a little apprehensive as our new purchase was hooked to the back of our Nissan Bluebird estate on the forecourt of Dave Barron's. The roads to and from Dave Barron's dealership were narrow and winding, hardly ideal for a nervous first time caravanner. But it had to be done and so I put the car into gear, pressed the accelerator, and inched forward. The car is the same, obviously, but with this big 'thing' attached, it behaves differently. It's like a chunk of its power has disappeared, gobbled up by the 'thing'.

At road junctions and traffic lights, more time, and care, was needed and towing the thing up steep hills was like driving in treacle. It was a slog. However, on normal roads towing wasn't too bad. But the worst was yet to come. On arriving home, it had to be reversed on to the new drive.

Work had started on preparing a new drive for the caravan several months earlier. The council had been informed and they duly lowered the kerbstones (for a fee of course) whilst myself and our two sons laid a countless number of flags for the caravan's hard standing area and driveway.

Reversing a caravan is an art. It takes time and practice to master, but I had neither. On arriving home, I, a complete novice, had to reverse the thing on to the new caravan drive. And quickly, because the car and the caravan were blocking a busy road. The prying eyes of the neighbours and those waiting impatiently in their cars while I completed the manoeuvre added to the pressure. Somehow, I managed to reverse it on to the drive sufficiently for it to be unhooked and pushed the rest of the way by hand. It was a daunting experience, not one that I enjoyed.

To get accustomed to towing the caravan, our first destination was a local one, a quiet site at the southern end of Blackpool, not too far, in fact, from the dealership mentioned previously. I remember that first night vividly. The weather had turned windy and it had begun to rain, yet we were so cosy and warm cocooned in our little aluminium shell. There is something magical about being inside a caravan in the rain, listening to the sound of the raindrops as they patter on the roof.

On Saturday it was off to the Pleasure Beach, the Sand Castle and the amusement arcades where, by sheer coincidence, we ran into Viv Stead (Chapter 9). At the Winter Gardens cafe, Vera and I enjoyed a relaxing drink whilst our two children amused themselves in the adjacent arcade, occasionally coming for more funds to replenish their depleted resources. Whilst there, we booked for the Freddie Starr show later that evening. He was a scream. His antics had the whole audience in stitches. To add to the pleasure, the magician, much to Andrew's delight, mingled with the audience before the show on a one-to-one basis and amazed Andrew with some of his tricks. Our first caravanning weekend had been a great success. We were eager for more.

18.3 CARAVAN HOLIDAYS

For our first big holiday we selected the Warmwell Bay caravan site in Dorset (Image 179). It was a wise choice. The site was central to many of the tourist spots. At

Weymouth, we spent untold hours on the sandy beach and even bought a dinghy (Image 180).

Two boys in a boat, Weymouth 1987.

Lawrence of Arabia's house and Corfe Castle, where Esther Rantzen was performing, were also visited. In Bournemouth, a charity stall on the promenade caught our attention. It had the most adorable Teddy Bears imaginable. "Can we try and win one, daddy?" they pleaded. It was Michael who took the money to the lady to buy a ticket and, to our complete and utter amazement, won a cuddly Teddy Bear (Image 185, page 307).

For our children, the highlight of the holiday was undoubtedly the Bovington Tank Museum (Image 181). But it wasn't just the museum that excited them. Equally exciting was driving through the army's firing ranges and seeing the 'Unexploded Shell' signs, where they insisted on having their picture taken (Image 182).

Andrew at the Bovington Tank Museum.

Andrew and Michael being brave. I think
Michael is pretending to pray.

The following year we joined the 'Caravan Club'. It had been recommended by Arnold Winder, a member of our car club and a veteran caravanner. The Caravan Club has some prime locations in the Lake District, such as Park Coppice at Coniston, Braithwaite Fold in Bowness and Low Manesty at Derwent Water. It was having access to prime locations such as these that persuaded us to join.

All of these sites were frequented but our favourite was Low Manesty, near to the tiny hamlet of Grange. Located in a wood at the southern end of Derwent Water, it was a most magnificent setting. The southern part of the lake is so shallow (two feet deep at most) that it is not uncommon to see herds of cows 'paddling' in the centre of the lake! It was ideal for bathing and for sailing our dinghy. To my surprise, George declined a sail in the dinghy but the quiet and demure Doris accepted and looked most serene as we paddled our way around the lake.

But the real treasure of Low Manesty wasn't the wood or the lake. It was something else. Something far better. Something that was extremely rare in England. Low Manesty was one of last refuges of the red squirrel, England's native squirrel species. One of the few remaining places that remained untouched by that ubiquitous invader, the grey squirrel. To our children's delight, the friendly warden had shown them how to construct a feeding table for the squirrels and, within minutes of his departure, they had constructed one near to the rear window of the caravan. Placing bits of chocolate and some nuts on their virgin table, they settled back and waited. Waited for the first little visitor to arrive.

They didn't have to wait long. Within a few minutes a beautiful red squirrel appeared out of nowhere and sat down to eat the treats on offer (Image 183). Michael and Andrew were entranced. As the squirrels got used to the feeder, our children moved it closer and closer to the caravan. After a day or so, the feeder was so close to the window they could almost touch the squirrel. Sat on his haunches nibbling a nut clasped between his front feet, he was so cute. And unafraid. Obviously, it was a routine he was accustomed to. By the end of the holiday, the red squirrels were eating out of our children's hands.

A red squirrel on the feeder.

During our stay we rambled along the foothills of Cat Bells, sampled the delights of Keswick, one of the most beautiful Lake District towns, and visited Ashness Bridge, imagining the trolls emerging at night and searching for naughty children to eat. All too soon however, it was time to go home.

We left Low Manesty early on the Sunday morning to get home in time for Wigan's match at neighbours Leigh in the afternoon, when Wigan's new signing Dean Bell (Chapter 16) would make his debut. He did and Wigan won 35-0. It was a fitting end to a fabulous weekend.

Lying on the southern fringe of the Lake District, Meathop Fell is yet another of the Caravan Club's charming locations. The site occupies a flat plateau that provides a panoramic view of Morecambe Bay to the west (Image 184). To the east lies gentle rolling farmland populated by the occasional cow or sheep. Early one spring morning we set off on a leisurely stroll down the lane, uplifted by the crispness of a new day. With the dewdrops sparkling like diamonds and the sweet song of the birds drifting on the breeze, it was like a picture postcard. Suddenly, we stopped. In a field less than ten feet away a sheep lay on the grass. Initially, we thought it was asleep or simply resting. But it wasn't. On closer inspection, it was in the throes of giving birth. Of bringing a new life into the world. A baby lamb. All of us were fascinated, captivated by this wonder of nature.

View over Morecambe Bay from
Meathop Fell caravan site.

Within a few minutes, the lamb was born. Gently, its mother licked it clean and, to our astonishment, the new born lamb struggled to its feet. It was one of the most moving scenes we had witnessed, a chance encounter which had a lifetime effect on Michael. Up until then his favourite meal was roast lamb and mint sauce (Chapter 16). Not any more. After that momentous day, he never ate roast lamb again. He switched to steak! Obviously, he didn't have the same affection for cows.

After the Lake District our most frequented destination was Cornwall. For our first holiday there in the tourer we stuck to tradition and used the Caravan Club site at Newquay. With the car and the van all packed up and ready to go, we were up at the crack of dawn ready for the long and exhausting journey ahead. Then disaster struck. On coupling the caravan to the car, none of the caravan lights worked! The wet weather of the previous few weeks must have been the culprit. There was no way the caravan could be towed in such a condition so there was no other option than to wait until the accessories shop opened at Dave Barron's.

It was 11-00 a.m. before the electrics were fixed and we were ready to go, four hours behind schedule. According to the brochure, the site closed at 8-00 p.m. so we had just nine hours to reach our destination, a tall order when towing a caravan on a 350 mile journey.

As we entered the county of Cornwall it was getting late and we still had a fair distance to cover. Michael was the map reader. "How much farther is it?" I asked.

"It's just past Indian Queens," he replied. Indian Queens, where the hell was that? We seemed to be going on and on and getting nowhere.

"Are you sure?" I enquired.

"I'm positive," came the response. "It's just past Indian Queens." And he was right. It was just past Indian Queens, but it wasn't in Newquay. It was a considerable distance further on. We arrived just before 8-00 p.m. and, with the help of some fellow caravanners, managed to manoeuvre the van into position on yet another hilly site. On future holidays in Newquay, we patronised the more central commercial site of Hendra.

The caravan was used by our relatives too. One year, we towed the van to Torquay for Elaine and Keith to use. They too had chosen a commercial site which was, to put it mildly, rather hilly. And, in keeping with Sod's Law, our spot was at the top of a steep hill. Trying to tow the van up the hill on the wet grass almost burned out the clutch of my new BMW (Image 186, page 308). In the end, the van had to be positioned by the Park's four wheel drive tractor.

18.4 A DIFFERENT TYPE OF HOLIDAY

Life in a caravan is totally different to life in a house or a hotel. The drastically reduced living space sees to that. A space of just sixteen feet by eight feet has to accommodate the lounge, kitchen, dining room, bathroom and bedroom(s). Amazingly, the ingenuity of caravan designers ensures that not only is this achieved, it is achieved with distinction. However, there is a caveat. The reduced living space imposes the twin virtues of economy and tidiness on the caravan's occupants.

In a house, a constant supply of fresh water is taken for granted. Water for drinking, water for cooking, water for washing up, water for bathing and water for flushing the toilet is available at the turn of a tap. Not so in a touring caravan. There is no water on tap. The only water available is that which you bring to the caravan. Initially, we used a plastic Jerry Can to transport several gallons of water from a 'water point' to the caravan. But water is heavy and it was no fun lugging a full Jerry Can from the water tap to the caravan, so we invested in a 'AquaRoll', a plastic cylindrical container which could be rolled along the ground. Not only did it hold more water than a Jerry Can, it was also very easy to transport it. Nonetheless, you still had to ration the amount of water used.

All that clean water gets converted into dirty water and it is obvious that the amount of dirty water leaving the caravan is equal to the amount of clean water that entered it. The water from washing your face or cleaning your teeth in the bathroom, and from washing up in the kitchen sink, was collected in Jerry Cans placed at the outlet pipe outside the caravan and taken to the water disposal unit. It could have been collected in a second AquaRoll but, to avoid any confusion, we preferred to use Jerry Cans, emptying them when they were half-full. Toilet waste, however, was a different matter.

Although all the caravan sites had toilet and shower blocks, all of us preferred to use our own private toilet in the caravan, a 'Porta Potty'. This plastic commode, housed in the small bathroom, was very popular with our family but other families preferred to use the public toilets. And I can see why. Emptying the 'Porta Potty' on a daily basis was not a pleasant task. The used container had to be carried to a disposal unit, emptied into an open 'sewer', and then rinsed with water. It was then refilled with a blue liquid containing chemicals that were designed to both disinfect and mask the odour of human excrement, thus making it ready for the next day.

Despite this unpleasant chore, life in a caravan was special. It provided a complete change of environment from living in a house. The cramped space ensured that you were in intimate contact with your companions. It was cosy (Image 185). Armed with bars of Cadbury's chocolate and Ribena, our children loved to curl up in a corner munching their chocolate and sipping their drinks as they read the Alfred Hitchcock endorsed *Three Investigators* books. This scenario was particularly satisfying in bad weather, like the year we had a severe storm in the middle of July. Snuggled up in our warm caravan with food, drink and a good book was heavenly.

Michael, with the Teddy Bear he won, and Andrew
in the lounge section of our ABI Ambassador caravan.

We had many memorable holidays in our ABI Ambassador caravan, particularly in the Lakes and Newquay, but also in Henley-on-Thames. But it was time for a change. Our children were growing up and getting bigger and we had acquired Sam, our Yellow Labrador (Chapter 17). The space in our caravan was becoming too cramped and so, in 1990 when Andrew was sixteen and Michael twelve, we upgraded to a Van Royce.

18.5 VAN ROYCE

A Van Royce was the Rolls Royce of touring caravans. Frustrated by the lack of a caravan having all the features they deemed necessary, two experienced caravanners started their own company in Standish, near Wigan. The caravans were superb and, in 1990, Vera and I bought one from Stewart Longton. It cost £10,500, a considerable sum in those days, but we had negotiated a good deal. We got £4,500 trade-in for our old caravan, exactly the amount it had cost us new four years ago.

Our new Van Royce caravan was not only considerably bigger than our ABI Ambassador, it was also much heavier. And weight is an important consideration when towing a caravan. For example, our 1.6 litre Nissan Bluebird was adequate for towing the much lighter Ambassador caravan but you couldn't half tell the difference when we had the more powerful Rover 820i. You didn't even notice you had a caravan in tow! Not so with the Van Royce. Even the Rover found it difficult to tow, as did the BMW 518i that I got in 1990. However, the extra space and comforts of the Van Royce made it worthwhile.

The Van Royce had a spacious lounge, a separate kitchen and dining room and a separate bedroom for the children. It also had a reasonable sized bathroom with its own toilet and shower. The fittings were to a very high standard, including flyscreens on all the windows. It also had a kind of central heating, a boon since caravans can get pretty cold at night.

To increase the space even further, we bought an Isabella Ambassador awning to go with the Van Royce caravan (Image 186). An awning served a number of purposes. It provided much needed extra storage space: it provided space for visitors to sleep: and it acted as a 'games room'. We had great fun playing table tennis in the sheltered confines of the awning (Image 186).

Our Van Royce caravan provided years of holiday pleasure. The Lakes and Newquay were the main destinations but we also had a brilliant holiday in Scotland (Chapter 17). However, as both we and our children grew older, it was used less and less and so, in 1995, we sold it, although not without one or two amusing moments.

We had decided to sell in the spring of 1995. That summer, a conservatory and utility room would be added to the rear of the house (Chapter 22). This involved removing a large part of the caravan hard standing area and completely rearranging that section of the back garden, a major undertaking. Adverts in local papers and Loot elicited few responses. One caller left a message that he was interested and to ring him back. I did. But it wasn't the caravan he wished to buy, it was the wheel-lock!

Eventually, we sold it to Callenders Caravans at Carnforth. But there was a problem. I had just changed my company car from a BMW which had a towbar to a Rover 600 that didn't. Normally, the used company car was returned to the company for sale at auction. However, the employee had the option of buying the car at an attractive price, a price that an auction house would pay. This was way below the retail price so my car club colleague, Ian Macnab, bought all my company cars. Fortunately, he was kind enough to let me borrow the BMW to tow the Van Royce to Callenders Caravans. It saved a lot of hassle (and expense).

Our Van Royce caravan with its awning, and
our white BMW 518i, at Hendra, Newquay.

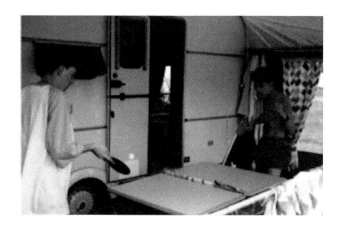

Andrew (left) and Michael enjoying a
game of Table Tennis in the Awning.

18.6 A HOLIDAY HOME

For the next few years Vera and I took advantage of a five day springtime special offer break at the Hendra caravan park in Newquay. It was a good way of banishing the winter blues. During these mini breaks we became increasingly fond of the static caravans or holiday homes as they are now known. The space inside was huge compared to a touring caravan. Instead of a 16 foot by 8 foot living space, a static caravan boasted the gargantuan proportions of a 40 foot by 12 foot living area, accommodating a lounge, dining room, kitchen, hallway, bathroom and two (or three) bedrooms, one with an *en suite*. Just like a house, they were plumbed into a mains water supply and sewage system. There was no need to lug water and sewage to and from the caravan. What's more, the better models also had full central heating and double glazing. They were a home-from-home.

And so, in 1999, we bought a Willerby Bermuda holiday home at the Lakeland Leisure Park in Flookburgh in the Southern Lake District. We'd spent months scouring Lake District caravan sites, visiting numerous caravan manufacturers and attending caravan shows at Manchester's G-Mex arena, and were beginning to despair that we couldn't find a caravan with the desired layout. Then we saw the Bermuda. It was perfect. It had all the mod cons referred to above, plus a large master bedroom with an *en suite*. However, there was a snag. Willerby made the Bermuda exclusively for Bourne Leisure, the owners of Lakeland Leisure Park, so if we wanted this van, we had to buy it from them. It was difficult to negotiate a discount in such a situation but, since Lakelands was our preferred site anyway, we decided to go ahead and buy, but not before we had found a pitch to our liking.

Eventually we did. It was in Dearham, a horseshoe of about a dozen caravans set around a landscaped area. Dearham was in the premier section of the park and as such had better pitches than the standard ones. But at a price. They cost more. Number 16 Dearham was the fourth pitch around the horseshoe. It was one of the largest and had open views both to the front and rear (Image 187). It was a fine pitch. So, after handing over the cheque for about £30,000, the holiday home was ours.

It proved a mixed blessing. A few months after we bought the caravan, my Auntie Lily died suddenly of a heart attack, leaving my disabled Uncle Jack alone (Chapter 24). The strain of looking after two lonely, elderly people (Vera's mother had been widowed in 1991 – Chapter 16), particularly on Vera, meant that finding time to use the caravan wasn't easy. Also, it was whilst at the caravan that we received the dreaded phone call from Michael informing us that Sam was very ill (Chapter 17). Although we enjoyed some happy times in our Bermuda caravan, events such as these left some unhappy memories too. In 2009, after ten years of ownership, we sold our Bermuda. Our caravanning days were over.

Our Willerby Bermuda caravan on 16
Dearham at Lakelands Leisure Park 2009.

Our children enjoyed a happy childhood. But it wasn't all holidays, Labradors and rugby, they had their schooling to attend to.

19

EDUCATION, EDUCATION, EDUCATION

The big day had arrived. It was the morning of Andrew's first day at school. His first day at Beaumont Primary School. His very first steps on the long road of education. The day that we had been looking forward to yet, at the same time, secretly dreading. From now on, instead of spending all his time in the safe and secure surroundings of his home, he would spend the best part of five days a week with total strangers. And it was with these mixed emotions whirling around our heads that we got him ready for school that first morning.

19.1 PRIMARY SCHOOL

He looked so small and vulnerable stood against the lounge wall (Image 188). Dressed in his school uniform, he seemed too young to go to school. Every year on his birthday we'd charted the progress of his growth by marking his height on the lounge wall. This fifth mark represented something special: it recorded his height on his first day at school.

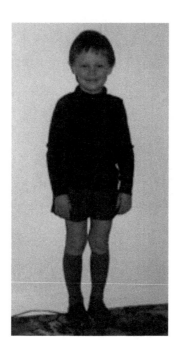

Andrew, age 5, on the morning
of his first day at school.

After some last minute adjustments to his uniform, Andrew, with his little satchel slung over his shoulder, set off with his mum on the short walk to Beaumont Primary School. I was a little concerned there may have been some tears or, even worse, a tantrum, and that he may have refused point blank to enter the school. After all, such things did happen. But there were no such problems. Reassured by his mum and met by a friendly teacher, Andrew walked into the school playground to join his new playmates. His first day at school had begun.

Like most of the other pupils, Andrew settled in quickly. Under the guidance of its headmistress, Mrs Wilde, the school employed traditional teaching methods to instil the 3R's into its pupils. Indeed, in the short time that it had been open, Beaumont Primary School had established a good reputation and was one of the reasons why families moved into its catchment area. It certainly worked for our children. They really enjoyed their time at Beaumont Primary School, receiving a sound primary education in the process.

In summer, the school held an annual sports day and, like his dad before him (Chapter 4), Andrew excelled at sprinting, though not at fun races (Image 189).

Andrew sprinting to victory in the 60 yard dash
(left) and struggling in a fun race (right).

Christmas was synonymous with the nativity play. To her credit, Vera attended every single one, sometimes accompanied by my Auntie Lily and sometimes by her mother. Andrew always participated but, judging from his expression (Image 190), not always enthusiastically!

Four years later Michael followed in Andrew's footsteps. However, Michael preferred soccer to sprinting and was an accomplished footballer, both as an outfield player and as a goalkeeper. He was a regular fixture in the Beaumont Primary School football team (Image 191). He also participated in the school nativity plays, ostensibly showing a little more enthusiasm than his elder brother (Image 192).

A less than enthusiastic Andrew (extreme left)
in a school nativity play.

Beaumont Primary School football
team with Michael as the goalie.

Both Andrew and later Michael did well at primary school, not only academically but also socially too. They were liked by their teachers and by their fellow pupils. As is evident from Image 193, one of my favourite school photographs, they were two happy boys.

Michael, second from the right,
in a school nativity play.

Andrew and Michael at Beaumont
Primary School 1984.

Parents' evenings were a pleasure. From an early age we had taught our children to behave properly, to respect other people and to know right from wrong. And we had encouraged them to learn. Therefore, we weren't surprised when the teachers said that our children were well behaved, studious and generally performed well. This was the case every Parents' Evening. Except one. Towards the end of his time at Beaumont Primary School, Andrew's class was taken by Miss Ryan, a temporary supply teacher. "Andrew is a solid performer, not a bright spark and not a dimwit." Fair enough. However, when she said, "Really, he's too quiet and reserved. He needs to be more forceful and outgoing so that in the future he can look top executives in the eye and not be intimidated. And the best way for him to develop these traits is to send him to Bolton School."

I wasn't pleased that some temporary supply teacher, whose report was completely at odds with all the others, should tell us what we should do with our son. I stood up, looked her straight in the eye and said, "Miss Ryan, thank you for your report but we'll decide our son's future, not you," and, with that, Vera and I walked away. I could have said more but decided not to. But, Miss Ryan, I wish you could see him now.

19.2 SECONDARY SCHOOL

As Andrew approached eleven, we had a decision to make. Where should he do his secondary education, at the independent, fee paying Bolton School favoured by Miss Ryan, or at Deane School,* the local comprehensive? My mind flashed back to the dilemma that I faced when I was eleven and the course of action that I took (Chapter 1). However, in Andrew's case money wasn't an issue. It boiled down to which school he wanted to go to, Bolton School or Deane School.

Several of our friends and neighbours, including my car club colleague, Ian Macnab, had elected to send their progeny to Bolton School. This was fine providing that the child itself wanted to go to Bolton School. Unfortunately, in some cases it was just an ego trip for the parents. It made them feel good to say that their child attended Bolton School. In such cases it usually backfired. The child either rebelled or dropped out (or both) and did far worse than it would have done by going to Deane School. In our case, we left the decision entirely up to our children. Both elected to go to Deane School.**

Deane School was literally 400 yards up the road from our house, in the opposite direction to Beaumont Primary School, allowing our siblings to yet again walk the short distance to school. The headmaster was Warren Bradley, the former Manchester

---

*   Now Ladybridge High School

**   Our seven-year-old grandson, Joshua (see Chapter 29), doesn't want to go to Bolton School either. Every time we pass it on our way to Bolton he always says I don't want to go there.

United and England footballer. As was the case with primary school, both our sons received good reports, and both did extremely well in their GCSE exams, achieving mainly A and A* grades in nine subjects.

Again, they declined the opportunity to do their sixth form studying at Bolton School, preferring instead to go to Bolton North College to study for their GCE 'A' levels. Which subjects did they choose? I hope I didn't put any pressure on them or influence them in any way, but both Andrew and Michael elected to study mathematics, physics and chemistry. Their dad was a chemist and they could see that I enjoyed my work and that it had provided a comfortable living, so maybe these factors did have some effect on their decision. I don't know, but those are the subjects they chose.

Bolton North College is situated in a lovely location on the fringes of the West Pennine Moors, not far in fact from Smithills Coaching House (see Section 9.5). For the first time in their school career, they had to catch a bus to school. Both our sons did very well at sixth form college, gaining grade A's in mathematics and physics and B's in chemistry.

Now came the big decisions. Should they go to university and, if so, which one. And what subject should they study? I couldn't help but remember the decisions I faced and the choices I made at a similar stage in my life (Chapters 4 and 7) but again, I tried not to influence their decisions. It was their life and they had to make the choices that were right for them.

19.3 TERTIARY EDUCATION

At sixth form college Andrew had excelled at physics. He loved the subject and dreamed of becoming a famous nuclear physicist earning loads of money in America. Also, he was fond of his physics teacher. She had been educated at York University and thoroughly enjoyed her time there and I think it was a combination of all these factors that culminated in Andrew choosing to study physics at York University. Secretly, Vera and I had our reservations. Not over the choice of subject, but the choice of university. York was a two hour drive over the Pennines, a difficult trip in winter. We'd have preferred him to go to Manchester University, a mere sixteen miles away, but it was his choice and we respected it. And so, one September morning in 1992 with the car packed to the rafters with Andrew's belongings, Vera, myself and Andrew set off for York.

Located in Heslington, parts of the university were indeed attractive with lakes and landscaped gardens adding a feel of the countryside to the campus buildings. Other parts, however, were less attractive. Nonetheless, we queued up with Andrew whilst his papers were processed and he was allocated a room. The building we were in had some fine rooms and I hoped that Andrew would be allocated one of these. But it wasn't to be. These were the superior rooms for the post-graduate students.

As the girl escorted us to Andrew's room, my heart sank. It was the end, ground floor room of a dated two storey 1960s type building. Not only that, a murder had been committed in one of the rooms of that very building a few months earlier! To disguise the actual room, several had been redecorated. Fortunately, Andrew's wasn't one of them. To make matters worse, Vera and I weren't enamoured with some of his flatmates. They were loud and brash southerners, completely opposite to Andrew. Reluctantly, we said our goodbyes and made our way back to the car.

On reaching the car, Vera started to cry. It was a mixture of things. The fact that she didn't believe York was the right place, the fact that she didn't like his room or his flatmates but, most importantly, the fact that she was losing her son for the first time in her life. I reacted badly and told her not to be so soft. I was trying to be 'manly' when in fact I was being the exact opposite. I shared the same feelings myself and should have comforted her. Once again, another apology is needed.

Most weekends Vera and I would drive to York to pick up our son and bring him home for the weekend. I was always relieved when I saw him walking towards the car. Vera worried he might not be eating well and that whilst he was home at least he would be fed properly. I worried that he had chosen the wrong university (or subject) and might be regretting it. Either way, we enjoyed our weekends together but never relished the return drive back from York on a Sunday night in the dark. When I was away on company business, Vera had the dual task of both picking him up from York and taking him back on her own.

One Sunday night our worst fears came true. It was winter and we had duly dropped Andrew off at York and were making our way home. It was a horrible night. Not only was it freezing cold, a gale force wind whipped across the moors. Everything seemed fine until we reached the top of the M62 just past the Huddersfield exit. The traffic had come to a complete standstill. It was stationary for miles ahead. Nothing was moving. Minutes passed, then hours. Vera was becoming desperate. Michael, who was only fourteen, was at home by himself and there was no way we could let him know we were stuck in a traffic jam. It was getting really late and after two hours without moving Vera ran along the stationary vehicles searching for someone with a mobile phone. Eventually, she found one and phoned both Michael and her sister Elaine who, with her husband Keith, were kind enough to go to our house and stay with Michael until we arrived home. We did, about five hours later. A journey that normally took no more than two hours had, on this fateful night, taken seven. This incident prompted us, for the very first time, to buy a mobile phone.

Later, we learned the cause of the delay. The wind was so fierce it had blown one of the motorway lights down on to the carriageway and, fearful that more might be blown down with horrendous consequences, the police had taken no chances and closed the motorway. In the end, everyone had to exit the motorway via a dirt track used by farmers.

318

After his first year at York, Andrew decided to switch to UMIST (University of Manchester Institute of Science and Technology) to complete his degree. Moving from the Halls of Residence to a rented house in the quiet suburbs of Heslington left him feeling isolated. It's doing my head in, were, I think, his exact words. So, for the final two years of his undergraduate studies, he commuted from home to Manchester. I think he was glad he made the switch. We were.

In 1995 Andrew graduated from UMIST with a BSc Honours degree in physics, a 2:1 in one of the most difficult subjects. It was a tremendous achievement. He was pleased and we were pleased for him. We were so proud as he received his certificate at the graduation ceremony (Image 194), a ceremony that was videoed for posterity.

Andrew on his graduation from UMIST 1995.

The following year Andrew undertook a Master of Science (MSc) degree in Computational Physics at Salford University, the university where, many years ago, I studied for my GRIC qualification* (Chapter 7). He really loved it. He had a natural aptitude for computation and felt right at home at Salford. I think it was the best year of his educational life.

After obtaining his Masters degree, Andrew opted to go the whole hog and study for his doctorate. Several interviews later he chose to study for his PhD at Lancaster University. Under the tutelage of Dr Fisher he explored the properties of superfluids, where some of the ultra-low temperature physics involved was analogous to the cosmological physics of the Big Bang. The creation of the universe with the Big Bang is a topic that I have been interested in for a long time and, obviously, it interested Andrew too.

---

* I didn't attend the graduation ceremony for my own degree in 1969. Why? I don't really know except that I didn't fancy all the 'pomp' and because I thought my family weren't all that interested either.

His accommodation at Lancaster was superb. Situated in a new building his room was worthy of a four star hotel, a complete contrast to that at York. It was modern, well furnished and had an *en suite* bathroom. Although the accommodation was excellent, the research project wasn't. Despite the grand aims of researching the Big Bang, the reality was disappointing. I don't know the full story but, after the first year, Andrew became disillusioned and decided to terminate his PhD project. Now, all he had to do was find a job (see Chapter 23).

Michael learned from Andrew's experiences. He chose a university closer to home in which to study for his degree. Salford. Furthermore, rather than live in the Halls of Residence, he commuted daily from home. Less clear cut was which subject to study. Andrew chose the right subject but the wrong university. Michael chose the right university but the wrong subject. Having achieved good grades in mathematics, physics and chemistry, Michael elected to study chemistry. However, after the first term at university, he stunned us by announcing that there was no way he could do chemistry for a living. It wasn't for him. He wanted to switch to physics. And so, from the December of 1996 to the following September, he enjoyed a nine month 'sabbatical'. In other words, he lounged about for nine months.

Michael commenced his physics degree at Manchester University in 1997. This time, for the first year, rather than commute from home, he stayed in the Owens Park Halls of Residence. He settled in well, joining in sports activities such as football. And, in the millennium year of 2000, we had a second physics graduate in the family. As was the case with Andrew, we were so proud as he received his BSc Honours degree certificate at the graduation ceremony (Image 195), again recorded on video. And, like his brother before him, he also had to find a job (see Chapter 23).

In the meantime, however, their dad still had to 'earn a crust' to sustain the family.

Michael on his graduation from
Manchester University 2000.

20

EXPANSIONS AND EXPLOSIONS

The success of our ink jet business with Hewlett-Packard (HP) and Canon in the early nineties (Chapter 14) fuelled a big expansion of the entire hi-tech colours area, which meant a big increase in the size of my research group. In less than twelve months it grew from an average size group of approximately six people to a group of around twenty people. In fact, it was almost a section in its own right. As well as funding more ink jet research (obviously), the revenue from our ink jet business was also used to fund other hi-tech areas, such as electrophotography and infrared absorbers. It was an exciting time, a time of rapid change.

20.1 MANAGEMENT

The expansion of the group meant that I had to devote much more of my time to management and administrative duties. It wasn't something I particularly enjoyed. My passion was chemistry and I got my thrills from inventing new molecules, solving problems and understanding why things happened (Chapter 13). I just had to know. The biggest thrill of all was when a new molecule met a target and resulted in a commercial product (Chapter 9). It was so satisfying to walk into a shop, see a Canon, HP or Seiko Epson ink jet printer, and know that your dye was in the print cartridge. Nonetheless, I took the management role seriously. I had to. It was only fair. A person's effectiveness, happiness at work, salary and career prospects depended upon good management.

Was I a good manager? I don't know. In my time at ICI I had worked under managers good and not so good and tried to practice the best features of what I had experienced and avoid the worst. I tried to be a good listener, to treat my staff fairly, to respect them and to motivate them. Most of the time it seemed to work okay, but there were some surprises. For instance, I was shocked when Steve Leary handed me his resignation. Steve (Image 196) was a hard working, productive Experimental Chemist who became frustrated by his perceived lack of progress. It was something I hadn't seen coming. However, to paraphrase Abraham Lincoln, "You can please all of the people some of the time and some of the people all of the time, but you can't please all of the people all of the time." How right he was.

Paul Gordon must have thought that I was doing a good job because he arranged for me and my team to meet John Whatmore, a psychologist, who was writing a book called 'Releasing Creativity'[1] about how leaders develop creativity in their teams. John said that creativity had never been so highly valued and nor have those leaders who are able to stimulate and optimise their teams' creative talents. It was his quest to try and discover what special skills such leaders possessed. For example, was it possible to let creativity flourish yet at the same time manage it? Along with Professor JP, I was invited to John's inaugural lecture in London to launch his book.

In the late nineties the management burden was relieved by the arrival of Charles Shields (Image 142, page 239). He took over the management of the bulk of the group leaving me free to concentrate on the chemistry.

Ron and his friends and colleagues on the occasion of his retirement in 1996. Left to right: Unknown, Steve Leary, Prahalad Mistry, Kath Carr, Tony Watson, Jim Campbell, Ron Kenyon, Me, Zoonia Hussein, Unknown, Ian Ferguson, Mick Clarkson, Neil Tallant, Paul Wight and Christine Millard.

20.2 INK JET

In ink jet the main focus was still on the lucrative small office and home office (SOHO) printing area. Dedicated teams were assigned to work on the requirements for our three major customers, HP, Canon and Seiko Epson. The influx of people needed to fill these new jobs were recruited both from within the company and from university (see later). They included experienced experimental chemists, graduates and doctorates.

The HP research team was headed by Dr Kath Carr (Image 196). Kath was a relatively new recruit to the company and worked on disperse dyes for polyester prior to her move to ink jet. A deep thinker, careful planner and studious worker, Kath had given a presentation of her work on disperse dyes at one of the 'Chemists Meetings' a few months earlier. She was one of our best presenters and was talking about azo dyes with a *meta* acetylamino group, but couldn't really explain the unexpected brightness of these dyes. Derek and I had discovered and theoretically explained this very fact some years earlier[2] (Chapter 9) and I remember going to the whiteboard to explain it both to Kath and her audience. Little did I know that within a few months she would be in my group. Mark Kenworthy, a young ambitious chemist who had dropped out of medical school to pursue a career in dye chemistry, Rachel Vaudrey, who had relinquished a better paid but boring job as a radiographer, and Steve Leary, an experienced Experimental Chemist, completed the team.

At that time the Canon team was still headed by myself, working with Ron Kenyon and Christine Millard (Image 196). Later, after the conclusion of the D2T2 dye project (Chapter 14), Roy Bradbury would become Mr Canon. Prahalad Mistry, who along with Christine had the most experience of synthesising ink jet dyes, worked on the important black dyes. His work provided black dyes for all the companies.

One of our brightest young chemists, Dr Paul Wight, ran the Seiko Epson team, assisted by Dr Phil Double, a new recruit, and Mick Clarkson (Plate 196). Later, when he moved to lead the fundamental studies work, he was replaced by Dr Maria Hadjisteriou, a young Greek recruit from Leeds University. Like Kath, she thought deeply about her work, was well organised and very focused.

Initially, a chemist makes just a few grams of a new molecule, just enough to see if it is any good. Most don't satisfy the demanding criteria. However, for the few that look promising, more material is needed for further testing. In our group, Ian Ferguson (Image 196) performed this scale-up role, producing up to several hundred grams of the most promising dyes.

The other areas, such as wide format ink jet printing and industrial ink jet printing, were addressed by Janette Watkinson, later to become Janette Cordwell. Wide format ink jet printing is used to produce large size prints for applications such as posters, banners and signage, whilst industrial ink jet printers have a wide ranging role from printing sell-by-dates on food products as diverse as eggs, cornflakes and coca cola cans, to printing your electricity and gas bills.

We were also active in the ink jet printing of textiles, a subject that I had written about in the academic literature,[3] but this work was run by Dr John Provost (Image 199, page 340) from our Technical Marketing Department.

20.3 ELECTROPHOTOGRAPHY

Electrophotography (photocopying and laser printing) still formed a major plank of our hi-tech strategy but Tony Nelson had moved on and the team was now led by Dr Ray Gairns. Tony Watson, Zoonia Hussein (Image 196) and Ray White worked alongside Ray Gairns on organic photoconductors whilst Kevin Birkett continued his work on charge control agents (Chapter 13).

An organic photoconductor consists of two parts, a charge generation material and a charge transport material.[4,5] Inventing products better than those already on the market was a tall order. To put this in context, in the fifty-odd years since Chester Carlson discovered electrophotography (Chapter 13), only a handful of charge generation materials and charge transport materials had been developed into commercial products. There were many valid reasons for this. For example, charge transport materials had to satisfy conflicting requirements. On the one hand they had to release an electron readily in order to form a positive hole. In other words, they had to be easily oxidised. Yet, if they were easily oxidised, they would be oxidised by the oxygen in the atmosphere and rendered useless as a viable product.[4,5] Also, both charge transport materials and charge generation materials had to have exceptional levels of purity. Just a few parts per million of an impurity would cause them to fail.

Not surprisingly, we found it extremely difficult to invent products superior to those already developed by major companies devoted to photocopying and laser printing. Giants such as IBM, Xerox and Canon had, as I said earlier, only managed to discover a handful of such products over many years of research. Our chances of beating them were very slim. Indeed, the lack of superior products caused some consternation amongst our Technical Marketing colleagues, particularly Arthur Quayle. Arthur had championed electrophotography as a major technology for us to exploit, but it was misplaced optimism. Yes, it was a major imaging technology. And yes, it was a multi-billion dollar industry. However, we were late entrants into a technology that wasn't really our field of expertise. We were experts in dye chemistry, not electronic chemicals. That's why we did so well with ink jet dyes.

At one stage the situation became so bad that our Technical Marketing colleagues blamed the research chemists for the failure to invent new products and wanted Ray and his team replaced with different chemists. This was unfair. For the reasons mentioned above, it would have made no difference who worked on charge transport materials and charge generation materials, the targets were just so difficult. I had to attend an evening dinner with Paul Gordon, who had succeeded Peter Bamfield as my Section Manager, to explain and defend our position to Ian Wasson, Arthur's boss, and Mark Carrier, the Business Manager. Fortunately, sanity prevailed and the status quo was maintained, but it did nothing for Research/Technical Marketing relationships.

As mentioned in Chapter 13, we had developed two charge generation materials, the red pigment dibromoanthanthrone for white light photocopiers, and x-form metal free phthalocyanine for laser printers. Although adequate, neither was state-of-the-art. Something superior was required.

Charge generation materials are pigments and as a company we had manufactured pigments for many years. Indeed, in 1928 chemists at the Grangemouth plant of ICI had discovered, again by serendipity, arguably the world's most important class of pigments, the copper phthalocyanines (Image 197). The account of this momentous discovery, recorded in a letter written by Ron Grieg, an analytical chemist at the time of their discovery, is worth recounting.[6] To set the scene, batches of phthalimide, a white chemical manufactured from the equally white phthalic anhydride, had become contaminated with a dark blue substance, resulting in complaints from customers. The letter attempts to clarify the 'inventor' of the phthalocyanine pigments. (The blue impurity turned out to be iron phthalocyanine.)

It was A G Dandridge, a plant chemist, who noticed the blue colour around the charge hole of the phthalimide one morning and, as it was customary each morning to raise merry hell in the interests of good discipline, he proceeded to give the foreman a roasting for allowing careless work which had culminated in the contamination of the phthalimide. On the face of it there was enough circumstantial evidence to obtain a conviction because, sited about five yards away, was the plant for the production of dibromo-indanthrone (CALEDON Blue GCD).

The foreman was vehement in his denials and an incensed AGD brought a sample to the Analytical Department, handed it over to me personally, told me the blue colour was dibromo-indanthrone and almost ordered me to confirm his statement! Fortunately for the foreman, and incidentally ICI, I was able to demonstrate that the blue colour was not dibromo-indanthrone. Dandridge, although disappointed at his failure to substantiate his charge against the foreman (I think he told him he would let him off this time but it must not occur again), asked me to collect more of the blue stuff, which I did by scraping material from around the charge hole. The colour was a kind of 'efflorescing sublimation' and Dandridge gave specific instructions that this material should be left until I returned the samples.

Dunworth (the analytical chemist who was Grieg's boss) and Dandridge had many discussions. I can recollect Dunworth doing a few tests by himself but I have no idea what they were although there was an attempt to put the colour on cotton using a vat dyeing technique. Dr Thomas was in on the discussions by this time and it was on his instructions that I was given the job of working out the empirical formula. During the 'combustions' I noted the presence of iron, which could not be removed by extraction with HCl.

Drescher took over at this stage and the idea that iron was an integral part of the molecule was proved by him but I think that his conjecture was that the substance was a pigment of the 'lake' type. He used different metals in his preparations, including copper, and it fell to me to carry out the estimations of the metal content.

Drescher was killed when he collided with a steam roller while riding to work on his Sunbeam motorcycle. The steam roller was working on the wrong side of the road and Drescher came round the bend at speed.

Finally, Arthur G Dandridge was, without doubt, the originator of the work on the phthalocyanines and, although I was only carrying out the instructions, I was probably the first person to know that the original compound contained iron.

Ron Grieg   25 March 1971

Consequently, phthalocyanines had been an area of expertise at ICI for many years and phthalocyanine pigments were the pigments of choice as laser printer charge generation materials. Titanyl oxy phthalocyanine had been shown to be a very good charge generation material,[*] and this was the molecule we worked on to develop further as a commercial product. Some innovative molecular modelling on the computer[4] aided our understanding why this molecule performed so well and facilitated its development (Image 197).

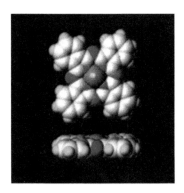

Copper phthalocyanine.

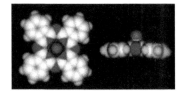

Titanyl oxy phthalocyanine.

---

[*]   Particularly the Type IV polymorph of titanyl oxy phthalocyanine (TiOPc)

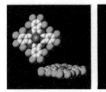

Molecular models of some phthalocyanine
pigments and an infrared absorber. CuPc-Cl$_{16}$ VYNAMON
Green (left) and CuPc-(SPh)$_{16}$ (right).

20.4 A FORTUNATE ESCAPE

It was early evening. Most of the staff had gone home and I was sat in my office perusing a problem when I heard a dull thud from down the corridor. I thought nothing of it and continued with my deliberations. Suddenly, Mick Clarkson burst into the office. "Peter, you'd better come quick. There's been an explosion in the laboratory." I dashed down the corridor to Lab 237 and couldn't believe my eyes. It was as though a bomb had gone off! Apparently, a chemical that was being dried in the large drying oven had exploded, propelling the oven across the lab where it smashed through the windows on the opposite side, destroying everything in its path. Anyone in its way would have been killed instantly. Fortunately, all the occupants had gone home, except one, and he had been standing at the other end of the lab from where the explosion occurred. Dean Thetford had had a lucky escape.

Having ascertained that everyone was okay, we evacuated the building, called our own security staff and then the Fire Brigade. They arrived within minutes and, with full breathing apparatus, entered the building. A large batch of a leuco-triphenylmethane compound had been placed in the oven to dry overnight. It had been washed in methanol. As the methanol evaporated in the heat, its vapours had built to a high level and a spark from the oven caused them to explode. Although rigorous safety procedures were followed, the odd incident always seemed unavoidable. This time we had been lucky. As mentioned in Chapter 2, flashes and bangs were one of the reasons that attracted me to chemistry, but flashes and bangs of this kind I could do without.

20.5 INFRARED ABSORBERS

The infrared absorber work was started by Paul Gordon and Peter Duggan[7] (Chapter 13). It was targeted at the new technology of optical data storage.[8] Optical data storage uses near infrared lasers to both write and then read compact discs (CDs) and later digital versatile discs (DVDs), including rewritable DVDs.[4] In the early nineties this infrared absorber work was transferred to our group, led initially by Dean Thetford and later by Jim Campbell.

Paul and Peter's work[7] had produced some excellent infrared absorbers by replacing the sixteen chlorine atoms on the copper phthalocyanine pigment VYNAMON Green with sulphur nucleophiles (Image 197). In our group, these products were tweaked to meet the requirements of our customers (see later). The thiols (or mercaptans as they are also called), used in these experiments stank to high heaven. Indeed, thiols are amongst the most pungent and foul smelling of all chemicals. For example, it is butyl thiol that is emitted by the skunk and it can be detected at one part in ten billion! Because their smell is detectable at such low concentrations thiols* are added to natural gas to give it its characteristic odour. (Without this, any gas leak would be undetectable because natural gas is odourless.) Despite taking the most stringent scrubbing and deodorising precautions during the experiments, it was impossible to contain the smell completely. Consequently, Dean and Ray White, his Laboratory Assistant, used to wait until most people had gone home before carrying out experiments involving thiols. Even so, residents living near to the site were forever reporting gas leaks.

Not only did thiols stink, the smell became ingrained in a person's clothing and, worse still, their skin, and it lingered for weeks. For this reason no one rushed to work with thiols. Anyone who did found it almost impossible to attract a partner. Although I wasn't in close contact with the thiols, Vera and our children used to remark that I smelled funny. God knows what Ray and Dean's partners said!

However, it was worth the smell. Our infrared absorbing phthalocyanines (which, by the way, were completely odourless) were almost invisible yet absorbed strongly in the near infrared region of the electromagnetic spectrum. Not only that, we learned how to 'fingerprint' the entire infrared region from 700 nm to 2000 nm by chemically modifying their structure.[4,9] We were confident these unique molecules would have important applications in security and camouflage. Furthermore, they furnished a positive charging organic photoconductor, which became the subject of my first lecture at the Society of Photographic Scientists and Engineers (SPSE) conference in New Orleans in 1988 (Chapter 21).

In addition to the sulphur-based nucleophiles, we also evaluated the effect of oxygen- and amino-based nucleophiles on VYNAMON Green. And boy, did they produce some unusual molecules! We couldn't believe our luck. Simply by switching from sulphur to oxygen produced novel molecules having a range of unusual yet potentially useful effects.[4,6] These included 'Singlet Oxygen Generators', molecules which could be used both as environmentally friendly washing powders and as anti-

---

*   Tertiary butyl thiol is the thiol normally added to natural gas

cancer drugs, and 'Reverse Saturable Absorbers', a class of compounds extremely useful in modern warfare (Section 20.6).

It was fine having all these wonderful molecules, but they were no use without having customers to exploit them. And it was part of our job to help find such customers.

20.6 FINDING CUSTOMERS

In the textile dyes industry the research chemists were confined to the laboratory. They never met the customer. This task was the province of the Technical Marketing personnel. It was they who met the customers on a regular basis, finding out their needs and wants and relaying these back to the Research Department. This wasn't the case in the hi-tech colours industry. The topics were so technical and so science-based that it was essential that those doing the research met with their technical counterparts from the customer. It was a paradigm shift in inter-company relations but it worked. There was no alternative.

The search for customers fell into two categories. For established technologies such as ink jet and electrophotography, we simply had to demonstrate that our products were superior to those of our competitors and that they met the customer's needs. However, for the molecules that exhibited an unusual effect, we had to think of an application for that effect and, if possible, devise a working example to demonstrate the effect to potential customers. Then, we needed to visit the relevant companies who might exploit such an effect. Finally, presentations of our work at key international conferences was another way of advertising our expertise (Chapter 21). All these scenarios involved extensive travelling.

Trips to America could last up to two weeks. And they weren't always plain sailing. On one of my first trips to America I arrived with Russell Bond* at Boston's Logan airport in the late evening. Waiting for us should have been our American host and guide, Mark Carrier (Image 198), but he wasn't there. We waited for several hours and still there was no Mark. By ten in the evening we decided he wasn't coming so we had no alternative but to book a hire car. The following morning, at 8-00 a.m. sharp, we had an important meeting with Nashua, one of America's leading toner manufacturers.

After being bussed to the compound to collect our hire car, we set off towards Nashua with Russell driving and me navigating. Finding the town wasn't a problem but finding

---

* The last three digits of Russell Bond's passport were ...007. He took great delight in showing people his passport, exposing only the last three digits and the name Bond. "The name's Bond. Russell Bond."

the hotel was a different matter. We seemed to go round in circles, even after following the directions provided by a garage attendant. Actually, we ended up on a private housing estate. It was 2 a.m. Suddenly, out of nowhere, a police car drew alongside, suspecting we were burglars. After hearing our English accents and our predicament, they pointed us in the right direction and, at 2-30 a.m., we finally found our hotel.

I got a few hours fitful sleep but awoke too late to get any breakfast. Mark and Russell were already waiting in the lobby. Apparently, Mark's flight had been severely delayed. His plane had been stuck on the runway for over four hours and he had been unable to contact us. This meant he arrived at the hotel later than we did. It wasn't a good start to a gruelling trip and I felt terrible during the meeting with Nashua.

In the US, all the big companies involved in the hi-tech area were visited, including HP, Xerox, IBM, Lexmark, Pitney Bowes, du Pont, 3M and Nashua, as well as a number of smaller companies. Some of the companies welcomed us whilst some gave us a grilling. Pitney Bowes fell into the latter category. However, despite this hostile reception, I made a good friend. Until I retired, Judith Auslander and I had many meetings, both at Blackley and at conferences around the world (Chapter 21), and shared many insights and ideas.

For the trips to the USA it was Mark who arranged the itinerary. He also did the driving (Image 198). Like everyone else, he had his idiosyncrasies. Whilst driving, he always drank a cup of coffee through a straw, constantly switching between radio channels until he found one he liked, and then drumming his fingers on the dashboard. It's a wonder we didn't crash.

On a subsequent trip with Ben Gunn, our luggage was lost. Instead of following us to Philadelphia it went to Phoenix. (Well, they did both begin with Ph.) My suitcase was unmistakable. It was a large, rigid, beige Delsey, fondly referred to as 'Big Bertha' by Ben and Mark. We managed in the same clothes for a day or two but then had to go to K Mart to buy some fresh ones. We were beginning to smell.

Mark preparing to drive us on one of our trips.

In Japan, Ohmichisan was our host and guide (Image 142). Occasionally, his boss, Yamamotosan, tagged along too. Yamamotosan was a character, a bit of an extrovert. He was a trained opera singer and, after a few drinks, would often burst into song. He also had an eye for the ladies and would patronise prostitutes on his travels. One, he said, was so sweaty and smelly that he placed a newspaper between them during the act. Unfortunately, during the sex act the print transferred from the paper to his body. He had become the Sunday Times.[*]

In the UK and Europe potential customers were found in a number of ways. One way was a direct visit to a company we thought might be interested in our offering. Our exploitation of infrared absorbers was such a case.

It was our belief that the infrared absorbers would be excellent in security applications.[4,6] Governments and companies were increasingly seeking new, hi-tech ways to keep one step ahead of the counterfeiter and forger whose illegal activities had been made easier by the availability of low cost colour photocopiers and printers. A novel, unique chemical that was impossible to replicate was the ultimate security feature. Therefore, Arthur and Jim arranged for a company called Welch Allyn to develop a hand-held infrared detector whilst we developed inks containing the infrared absorbers. Using the infrared ink and an ink jet printer, invisible messages (bar codes) were printed on various coloured articles, including bank notes. Scanning with the detector revealed the message (Image 220, page 378). We had our demonstration kit to show potential customers.

In the UK, the Bank of England and De la Rue were very interested whilst in Switzerland Sicpa were also keen to pursue the concept. Jim and I had many visits to De la Rue at Maidenhead, meeting with David Ezra and Derek Wallace, and with Robin Bratchley at the Bank of England. We also travelled to Switzerland to meet with Sicpa. Eventually, both De la Rue and Sicpa adopted our infrared absorbers, incorporating them as the highest level security feature in both UK bank notes and the Euro.

The security aspects of bank notes proved a big hit in my talks to secondary school children. (And to Princess Anne – Chapter 23.) I would ask them (the schoolchildren, not Princess Anne) who wanted to be millionaires. Almost immediately, all their hands would shoot up in the air. Tongue-in-cheek, I said I would tell them how to become one. Getting out their notepads and pens, their attention levels went into overdrive as I began my explanation.

Bank note paper, I said, is the only paper that doesn't contain a 'Fluorescent Brightening Agent'. These are the chemicals that produce the characteristic blue fluorescence seen on clothing (and some drinks) under the ultraviolet (uv) lights encountered in nightclubs and discos. (Clothes fluoresce blue because fluorescent

---

[*]   That's what he always said but I thought the *Sunday Times* a highbrow paper for a prostitute to buy. It's more likely he became The News of the World.

brightening agents are also added to washing powders to produce the blue whitening effect.) It is the effect a shop assistant is looking for when she shines a uv lamp on your banknote. If it displays a blue fluorescence, then it is a forgery.* Therefore, the first step in producing a counterfeit banknote is to eliminate the blue fluorescence. How is this done? It is done by using a chemical that quenches the fluorescence, a uv absorber. Unless you work in a chemical laboratory or know a friendly chemistry teacher, you will have to make do with something else, something that is readily available from any chemist shop. Sun tan lotion. High factor sun tan lotion.

Ultraviolet absorbers are the key ingredient of suntan lotions. They absorb the harmful ultraviolet rays of the sun, preventing them from causing damage to your skin.

They also absorb (quench) the blue fluorescence from the fluorescent brightening agents in the paper. Smearing diluted suntan lotion over ordinary paper 'converts' it into bank note paper. The rest is easy. By using a good quality colour photocopier (either laser-based or ink jet-based) to copy banknotes on to this paper, you have produced passable forgeries.

However, a word of caution. The average life of a banknote is only six months. After six months, the used notes are returned to the central banks where they are scanned automatically for the infrared absorber. If it isn't found (and it wouldn't be in this case), then the Fraud Squad is activated to find the source of the forgeries and punish those responsible. It is at this point that the faces of the children took on a look of despondency. Still, it was good fun while it lasted.

Infrared absorbers are also useful for camouflage.[4,6] They absorb the infrared radiation emitted by the human body, therefore negating the infrared sights on an enemy's weapon. Accordingly, a company in Devon successfully employed one of our broad band infrared absorbers in the manufacture of military uniforms and webbing.

In the eighties and early nineties any patent or publication containing the words 'infrared absorber' immediately alerted the military establishment, particularly the boffins at the Royal Signals and Radar Establishment (RSRE) at Malvern. (It later became the Defence Research Agency and is now known as the QinetiQ Group.) And that is precisely how we came to be in contact with Ken Harrison and his colleagues. Ken was a real boffin and a true gentleman. He was interested in our infrared absorbers but of more interest were some of our oxygenated phthalocyanines. Ken and his team had found these to be excellent 'Reverse Saturable Absorbers'. The theory was too complicated for me to understand but I could certainly understand why they were so interested.

---

* Be careful that you never leave any banknotes in the pockets of garments destined for the washing machine. They would be authentic before the wash but after washing they would exhibit blue fluorescence (from the washing powder) and be classed as forgeries!

Military commanders were worried that in any war the enemy might use high powered lasers against our forces, especially pilots and tank commanders. Such a laser would blast a person's eyeballs, causing immediate blindness. This would be catastrophic. For protection, goggles could be worn to intercept the laser radiation, but they would have to be intensely coloured, so coloured in fact that the wearer would be unable to see! A reverse saturable absorber, however, is a completely colourless material that only becomes coloured when activated by laser light. Remove the laser light and the colour disappears, instantly. Eureka. Problem solved. Of all the reverse saturable absorbers tested, ours were the best. It was a timely discovery since the Gulf War was about to start. Not surprisingly, they requested more material.

Another type of molecule we made, namely oxygenated zinc phthalocyanine, proved an extremely effective 'Singlet Oxygen Generator'. Singlet oxygen generators have a number of applications, such as hard surface disinfectants, soaps and insecticides, but two of the more important are their use in washing powders and as anti-cancer drugs.[5,7]

Singlet oxygen generators were already being used to treat certain types of cancer. In this treatment, known as 'Photo Dynamic Therapy', a singlet oxygen generator is injected into the patient. The patient is then kept away from any light sources for twenty-four hours, during which time the drug accumulates preferentially in the cancer tissue. Irradiation of the cancer tissue with a laser stimulates the singlet oxygen generator to produce singlet oxygen, which kills the cancer cells.

Although photodynamic therapy is a useful treatment, it has its drawbacks. Thus, it can only treat cancers that are accessible by a light source. Also, the distribution of the drug throughout the body renders the patient susceptible to light for several days because their skin becomes photosensitive. Finally, because the available singlet oxygen generators were blue, this meant that the patient also turned blue, at least for several days. In the worst case scenario, if a patient died during the treatment, their body would be blue. This was extremely distressing for their relatives.

Our singlet oxygen generators had distinct advantages. For a start, they weren't blue. They absorbed in the infrared and were almost colourless. Not only did this obviate the patient turning blue, it also meant that more inaccessible tumours could be treated because human tissue is transparent to infrared radiation.[*] So, by using an infrared laser, the infrared singlet oxygen generator could, in theory, be activated anywhere in the body. Despite these advantages, and the fact that Leeds University, one of the foremost centres for photodynamic therapy in Europe thought they were

---

[*] This is easily demonstrated by holding a torch to the tips of your fingers. The reverse side of your fingers look red because the red light passes through them. The invisible infrared radiation passes through your fingers even more readily than the red light.

a breakthrough, we found it difficult to get any drug company, including our own Zeneca Pharmaceuticals, to develop our infrared singlet oxygen generators. Photo Dynamic Therapy wasn't part of their anti-cancer strategy.

Singlet oxygen generators are also environmentally friendly photobleaches. In the presence of light they convert normal triplet oxygen ($^3O_2$) into the highly reactive singlet oxygen ($^1O_2$). Just a few milligrams of a singlet oxygen generator could replace all the hypochlorite or perborate bleaches which make up the bulk of a conventional washing powder. With a singlet oxygen generator, the stains aren't removed in the washing machine (because there isn't any light), but when the clothes are hung on the washing line. The process is relatively fast. It's fascinating watching the stains as they disappear in a matter of minutes.

Our singlet oxygen generators were also evaluated by ICI's Plastics and Polymers Division on Teeside, and by Procter and Gamble. I remember a joke one of our colleagues made about two workers at a sewage works. As one of them ended his shift, he said to the other, do you realise we're like two ships that pass in the shite.

We also did some work on 'Dark Oxidation Catalysts'.* These work by catalysing the action of traditional bleaches. Unilever had developed a so-called 'manganese accelerator' and marketed it as Persil Power. It was a disaster. Not only did it remove all the dirt and stains, it also attacked the textile fabric, causing the articles to disintegrate. It made headline news in the newspapers and on television. Regrettably, the 'manganese accelerator' was blamed, but it was a false accusation. The real culprit was human error. Unilever had inadvertently added twenty times too much of the catalyst to the product. Nonetheless, the damage was done and Procter and Gamble decided to shelve their manganese accelerator.

To me, it was amazing how one class of molecule, the phthalocyanines, could lead you in so many different directions. It also amazed the Research Manager, Dr Alan Calder, too (Chapter 22), and my ex-boss, Dr Peter Bamfield, a prominent figure in the Royal Society of Chemistry (Chapter 23).

20.7 EUROPEAN COLLABORATIONS

In the late eighties, as well as collaborating with Gestetner on charge control agents we also collaborated with Coates Electrographics. As a company, Gestetner were in decline whereas Coates Electrographics were the largest toner producer in the UK. Derek Wilson, the head of their Technical Department, was a strong advocate of the SPSE conferences and urged us to present our work at these events (Chapter 21). Derek was a straight talking no-nonsense type of guy who didn't mince his words.

---

*   The one we developed was manganese phthalocyanine tetra-sulphonic acid[4]

At one conference a German man was aghast when Derek didn't wash his hands after urinating in the toilet. Derek was incensed by the German's effrontery and said, "In England, we don't piss on our fingers." Based in Midsomer Norton, Coates Electrographics became one of our biggest users of CCA7 and CCA9 (Chapter 14).

The European Union (EU) positively encouraged collaboration between European institutions, particularly in hi-tech industries. The aims were to foster synergies between companies in different countries with complementary skills, and to involve small companies and universities, especially from the less industrialised nations. As a company ICI, and later Zeneca, participated in quite a number of European collaborations. Our group participated in two.

The aim of the MASCOT project (the EU loved acronyms)* was to produce an ink jet printer and ink system to compete with the Americans and Japanese. Olivetti, based near Milan, was the ink jet printer company and ICI the dye/ink company. Complementing these two large companies was a small Greek company based in Athens with an input on paper, and a university in Belgium that helped with the software. In these collaborations, the EU funded 50 per cent of the cost, including travel expenses. Not surprisingly, Blackley was a less popular venue for holding meetings than Ghent, Milan and Athens.

At the start of the project Dave Thompson (Image 118, page 193), my Section Manager, accompanied me to Milan. Whilst waiting for a taxi outside Milan railway station a group of women appeared from nowhere and began begging for money. Two of them knelt at my feet 'pawing' my legs whilst others were touching my upper torso. They were wailing and I was becoming extremely uncomfortable and embarrassed. The local Italians in the queue beside me were so ashamed and annoyed that a visitor to their country should be subjected to such treatment that they gave the beggars some money so they would leave me alone, and apologised profusely for the beggars' behaviour. I don't know why I was singled out. Perhaps I had a kind and compassionate face.

Prahalad and I attended the Athens meetings, enjoying some good evenings in one of the many hillside bars, whilst Jim came with me to some of the Milan meetings. This two year project proved relatively successful, helping to discover some new dyes, such as a yellow and a black.

The other project was COTEL. This was aimed at devising colour filters for flat screen displays such as computers and LCD (Liquid Crystal Display) televisions. These have now become the mainstream TVs, replacing the older cathode ray tube televisions. Again, we were the dye/ink partner and this time GEC (General Electric

---

*   So did ICI, but some could be unfortunate. For example, the 'Analytical Research Section' (ARS) quickly changed its name (to the 'Analytical Sciences Group'), as did the 'Applications, Intermediates and Design Section' (AIDS).

Company) was the electronics partner. The French company SAGEM, based in Paris, together with another small European company and a university, completed the partners. Neil Tallant (Image 196) led our COTEL team and although reasonable progress was made, the project didn't lead directly to a commercial product.

20.8 STAFF RECRUITMENT

Staff recruitment was an ongoing process but, unlike some other people, I was only involved in a few of these recruitment events. At least once a year promising candidates from our list of preferred 'red brick' universities were invited for an interview at one of our sites. The one that sticks in my memory was held at our Grangemouth site near Edinburgh. It followed the usual pattern. The 12 to 15 candidates would assemble in the late afternoon and be given a welcome and a short introductory speech by the Research Manager. After Paul Gordon (Image 132, page 301) had finished, each of the interviewers would introduce themselves and give a brief account of their role in the company. Jokingly, I said that Paul was a lapsed research chemist who had moved on to management. Somewhat taken aback by my pronouncement, he replied that, "Peter, once a research chemist, always a research chemist!" I had been politely reprimanded for my 'joke'.

Next, the candidates (and interviewers) were split into two groups. Each candidate gave a 15 minute presentation to the interviewers, followed by a question and answer session. Then, it was time to eat. At the evening dinner, the candidates moved two places round the table after each course, so that the interviewers could speak to all of them. It was like musical chairs with food. However, it was a good way of seeing each of the potential candidates with their guard down. You learned a lot about a person when they were inebriated! (And, I suppose, they learned a lot about the interviewers too.) During the first course, one girl literally fell asleep with her hair dangling in her soup. Thankfully, she wasn't sat next to me. Another girl threw a tantrum when it was announced that the technical interviews would take place the following morning. "I've already proved my technical ability by obtaining my BSc and there's no way I'm doing a f…ing technical interview," she barked. And, with that outburst, she stormed off. Needless to say, neither of these two were offered a job.

At the technical interviews two people from ICI would each present the candidate with a real chemical problem to see how they handled it. As expected, some were very good, others poor and some average. Each candidate was awarded a mark out of five for each problem. The 'wash up' session took place in the afternoon when all the interviewers gathered to discuss the results and draw up a short list of candidates to be offered jobs. There was generally good agreement for the bulk of the candidates but some arguments over the fringe candidates. One person was labelled 'boring'. I disagreed. Okay, he wasn't as extrovert as some of the others but he was technically excellent and that was the prime consideration. And, in my opinion, he wasn't boring at all. In the end, he was offered a job and not only did well at it but he also turned out to be one of the 'characters' of Research Department. Finally, all the candidates were thanked for attending (all their expenses were paid by ICI) and we wished them well for the future. The following day, the successful candidates were contacted by telephone to be told the good news and letters sent to all the candidates, irrespective of whether they had been offered a job or not, thanking them for their time and their interest in ICI. It was only courtesy to do so.

20.9 CORPORATE CHANGES

The hi-tech colours business had come a long way since its embryonic beginning as one man and his dog (Chapter 13). It had a name, Specialist Colours, and a formalised structure. Specialist Colours was headed by David Greensmith, a sensible, clear thinker who listened to every point of view and rarely made a rash decision. A leader I held in high esteem. Answering to David were the three wise men. Mark Carrier, an American, was head of the Technical Marketing Department, having replaced Russell Bond, John Meyers, another American, was head of the Process Technology Department, whilst Steve Jennings, a Yorkshireman, was head of manufacturing (Image 199).

In the Technical Marketing Department Ian Wasson was the Canon contact whilst John Presgrave looked after SEC and HP. Ian also looked after electrophotography and infrared absorbers, assisted by Arthur Quayle.

These changes were minuscule compared to what happened to ICI in 1993. In the late eighties, Lord Hanson had launched an audacious bid to buy ICI. By breaking up the cumbersome giant into small pieces and selling them off, he reckoned he could make a financial killing. This hostile bid shook ICI to the core. ICI had been a revered bastion of British Industry since its formation in 1928. Indeed, it was regarded as the bell-weather of British Industry. If ICI was doing well, then so was the rest of British industry. That someone should seek to dismantle such a renowned company sent shock waves throughout Britain.

However, Lord Hanson was proved right. Within a few years, ICI, under its new chairman Denys Henderson, who had succeeded the flamboyant Sir John Harvey-Jones, split ICI into two separate companies. Those parts of ICI that relied heavily on intensive Research and Development to continually invent new molecules to sustain and grow their business were spun off to form a new company, Zeneca.

The Pharmaceutical Division of the 'old' ICI, with its ongoing search for ever better drugs, was the flagship business of Zeneca. Agrochemicals, the business devoted to plant protection products such as fertilisers, insecticides and herbicides (e.g. weedkillers like Paraquat, marketed as Weedol), was the second Zeneca business. The third and final business was Zeneca Specialties. Specialties comprised a handful of smaller businesses that relied on research and development for their survival. Our Specialist Colours business was one of the five that comprised Zeneca Specialties.*

The remaining businesses formed the 'New ICI'. Generally, these were businesses that produced commodity chemicals on a large scale, where economies of scale were more important than Research and Development. Thus, paints (e.g. the famous Dulux brand popularised on TV with the Old English Sheepdog), polymers, plastics and petrochemicals comprised the 'New ICI'.

Did I learn of these momentous changes to ICI from an announcement at work? I did not. The first I knew that my employers were no longer ICI, that trusted and respected company, but a completely new company, Zeneca, was in our caravan at Newquay (Chapter 18). We were taking our two week summer holiday when I read about this bombshell in the daily newspaper. In fairness to ICI, they had sent a letter to my home address and there was no way they could have contacted me in a touring caravan. Nevertheless, it was a shock to learn that I was now an employee of Zeneca Specialties and not ICI.

20.10 AWAY DAYS

To celebrate the rapid growth and success of the Specialist Colours business, 'Away Days' were held. Virtually everyone involved in the business was invited to participate. It was a way of team building, fostering camaraderie and networking. Instead of a voice at the end of a phone, people could chat face-to-face with colleagues from Grangemouth, America or even Japan.

The first 'Away Day' was held at the Cottons Club, an hotel near to Tatton Park in Cheshire, in 1994. People arrived in the afternoon and, after a few drinks and a bit of a chit-chat, got changed in readiness for the main event, the evening dinner. Typically, the tables were set for about eight people, selected from various functions and geographical locations to promote networking. At the Cottons Club, our table included Roger Pugsley, the head of our Intellectual Property Group (formerly the Patents Group), Christine Millard and Ron Kenyon from my own

---

* The traditional textile colours business, along with the staff (including Mike Hutchings), was sold to BASF in 1993

group, Bob Bowker from Technical Marketing, John Stewart and another person from Grangemouth, and one from the USA. After a delicious meal, where the wine and beer flowed freely, it was quiz time. Hosted by an ex-ICI employee, it was an enjoyable yet keenly contested affair. At the end of the questions (about forty in all) our team, named rather inappropriately as it transpired, 'Norfolk and Chance',* finished in joint first place with the even more stupidly named 'Hoof Hearted' team. This meant a sudden death tie-breaker. I think the tie-breaker involved writing down as many countries as possible beginning with the letter 'S' in just two minutes. It was a close shave but we won by managing to name just one more country than our rivals.

Later, there were more competitions and games (one involved identifying the owners of the four bare bottoms – Chapter 11) but most people preferred to relax, having conversations with friends old and new, and enjoying the free drink. However, some people had to limit their intake because, on the following day, they had to give a presentation. Unfortunately, I was one of those.

The next 'Away Day' was held nearer to our Scottish colleagues at Drymen, Loch Lomond, in 1996. It followed a similar format to before, beginning with an evening meal. This time, however, there was no quiz or games, just some serious drinking. Geoff Rothwell (Image 199), a colleague from the Formulations Group, unleashed his wicked sense of humour on the unsuspecting Scottish ladies. He had one entranced with his athletic prowess, proclaiming that before the evening meal he had swam the entire length of Loch Lomond to 'work up an appetite'. (I don't think he could even swim!) Later in the evening, after he had drunk far too much beer, he engaged in some friendly banter with another young Scottish lady. After a while he asked, "Are you married?"

Rather coyly, she said, no, she wasn't married. I don't know if she expected Geoff to follow up this enquiry with an offer of marriage. If so, she would be bitterly disappointed.

"I'm not surprised," he said. "You're bloody ugly." He could be so hurtful.

David Greensmith (Image 199) did what a good boss does. He drank with his colleagues, talked with his colleagues and made jokes with his colleagues, making sure that he mingled with everyone. But he went further. Not only did he stay up into the early hours of the morning, he also chatted with the hotel staff, including an ageing barmaid! To his credit, he was up the following morning to give his presentation, which was more than some of us could manage. Before departing for home, most of us posed for a photograph (Image 199).

---

*   For those who haven't twigged, it sounds like 'No F...ing Chance'

Group photograph of some attendees at the Loch Lomond
'Away Day' 1996. People mentioned in text. Standing, left to right: 7th from left David Greensmith
(wearing the grey and white hooped top), 8th John Presgrave, 9th Mark James, 10th John Schofield
(stood behind Mark James), 11th Bill Fern, 13th Paul Wight, 14th Geoff Rothwell (Geoff is the second
person to the right of the lamp), 15th John Meyers. Aidan Lavery is stood on the far right, next to
Steve Jennings and then Mark Carrier in the check shirt. Front row, kneeling, left to right: Exreme
left: Ian Wasson, 3rd from left, Me, 5th John Provost, 7th Dr Roy, 8th Roy Bradbury (Roy is the one with
the white top knelt behind Dr Roy), and Ilesh Bidd is the one knelt on the extreme right.

Although I travelled the world visiting companies to extol the virtues of our products, I spent an even greater amount of time giving lectures at prestigious international conferences, promoting our work and, indirectly, our products, to an even wider audience. But it wasn't all jet setting. I also gave lectures at such far flung and exotic locations as Warwick and Whitehaven!

REFERENCES

1. J Whatmore, 'Dr PG: Determination, curiosity and 'doings' as drivers of learning'. In: Releasing Creativity, Kogan Page, London 1999, pp. 222-227.

2. P Gregory and D Thorp, 'The Electronic Absorption Spectra of 2-Substituted-4-NN-diethylamino-4'-nitroazobenzene Dyes and Their Monoacid Cations: The Applicability of Dewar's Rules to These and Related Dyestuffs', Journal of the Chemical Society, Perkin Transactions I, 1990, 1979.

3. P Gregory, 'Ink Jet Printing on Textiles' in: Textile Ink Jet Printing: A Review of Ink Jet Printing of Textiles, including ITMA 2003, TL Dawson and B Glover(eds), The Society of Dyers and Colourists Technical Monograph, 2004, pp. 69-97.

4. P Gregory, 'Metal Complexes as Speciality Dyes and Pigments'. In: Comprehensive Coordination Chemistry II: From Biology to Nanotechnology. JA McCleverty and T J Meyer (editors-in-chief), Elsevier, London 2004. pp. 549-579.

5. P Gregory, 'Colorants: Use in High Technology' in Chemistry and Industry, October 1989, pp. 75-87.

6. P Gregory, 'Industrial Applications of Phthalocyanines', Journal of Porphyrins and Phthalocyanines, 4 432-437, 2000.

7. PJ Duggan and PF Gordon (ICI), Infrared Absorber. European Patent 55,780. March 28th 1990.

8. P Gregory, 'Colorants: Use in High Technology' in: Chemistry and Industry, October 1989, p. 247.

9. P Gregory, 'Steamrollers, Sports Cars and Security: Phthalocyanine Progress Through the Ages', Journal of Porphyrins and Phthalocyanines, 3 468-476, 1999.

341

21

CONFERENCES, COURSES AND PRESENTATIONS

I have always been inquisitive (Chapter 1). It's in my nature. I needed to know about things, to understand them, to know why they happened. Therefore, if any opportunity came along to increase my knowledge, it was grasped with both hands. And that's why I was on the Colour Chemistry course at UMIST in 1974 when my car was stolen from the car park (Chapter 10). It was the spark that ignited my passion for an even deeper understanding of the relationship between a molecule and its colour. The spark that ensured Paul and I wrote the book[1] and gave the Colour Chemistry course at Manchester Metropolitan University (Chapter 13). The spark that was the launch pad for our own Colour Chemistry course. A course that would run for the next two decades.

21.1 COLOUR CHEMISTRY COURSES

When Dr Gerald Booth, who had succeeded Frank Hall as the Research Manager, learned from Peter Bamfield that Paul and I were to give a Colour Chemistry course, he invited me to his office to discuss a colour chemistry course he once gave. Slouched in his chair with his shirt undone, his belly exposed and his feet on the desk, he was not your typical Head of Department. However, he was a very knowledgeable 'hands on' chemist and I listened politely as he showed me some of his slides. His course centred around the concept of a 'Balance Factor'. Essentially, this meant that a particular molecule 'wanted' to be a particular colour. Altering the molecule to change that colour 'strained' it, worsening its properties. Although there was some truth to this conjecture, the pivotal slide contained a key structure that was plainly wrong. The molecule, which had a pentavalent nitrogen atom, just couldn't exist! When I pointed this out, he was dumbfounded. In all the courses he had given no one had ever noticed this serious error (or did and were too scared to mention it) and he himself had never spotted it. Although disappointed that a major tenet of his theory was flawed, I think his estimation of me increased after that discussion.

The Colour Chemistry course at Manchester Metropolitan University was our first. It ran for six years, from 1982 to 1988, and comprised twelve lectures written in longhand on overhead transparencies, the technology of the day. As time and technology evolved, so did the lectures. Not only was the material updated and refined, so was the method of presentation. Hand written overhead transparencies were replaced by Power Point transparencies which in turn were replaced by 35mm slides. Eventually, the lectures were delivered directly from a laptop computer.

A typical Colour Chemistry course comprised between eight to twelve individual lectures, each lasting about 45 minutes. Wherever possible, the lectures were embellished with exhibits and live, practical demonstrations, including wet chemistry. For example, yellow, red and blue dyes were synthesised in large glass beakers in front of a captivated audience. However, the most spectacular and 'magical' demonstration was the 'Flag' experiment (Appendix II).

In the Flag experiment a piece of white cloth was placed in a beaker of hot water. Then, a yellow dye was added, turning the water a bright yellow colour. Next, a red dye was added, changing the colour from yellow to orange-scarlet. Finally, a blue dye was added, turning the water a horrible brown-black colour. (Mixing dyes is like mixing paints. Mixing yellow, red and blue dyes produces a murky brown-black.) After adding a spot of salt and vinegar, the murky brown-black mixture was left to stew for a couple of minutes. Then, it was time for the magic. As the piece of cloth was pulled out of the mixture, it wasn't the expected dirty brown-black colour, it was a vibrant yellow, red and blue tricolour flag! I have lost count the number of times that moment received a standing ovation. To the audience, it was pure magic. To the chemist, it was clever chemistry.*

I also gave the Colour Chemistry course at the University of East Anglia (UEA) at Norwich. Dr Ray Price, our Company Research Associate, had lectured there on dye chemistry but, like Peter Bamfield (Chapter 13), decided to pass the baton to the younger chemists. It turned out to be a long association: the course was popular and ran from 1984 to 1996. My initial contact at UEA was Alan Haines and, on my first stint at the university, he took me out for dinner to the Red Lion pub in Eaton. It was a cold January evening and, sat in front of a roaring log fire, we consumed a delicious

---

* The single piece of cloth that enters the beaker is, in fact, three separate types of cloth, acetate rayon, silk and viscose rayon, sewn together in the shape of a flag. By careful selection of the dyes, the yellow dye only dyes the acetate rayon, the red dye the silk and the blue dye the viscose rayon. Nonetheless, it is a stunning demonstration (see Appendix II).

meal. Later, after Alan retired, Mike Cooke, a phthalocyanine expert, became my contact. Accompanied by his Norwegian wife, Mike also took me out for dinner. I was fascinated by her strange yet charming accent.

During my visits to UEA, I became very fond of the Norfolk coastline, particularly the North Norfolk Heritage Coast. Starting at Cromer, a typical English seaside resort, I'd drive along the coast to Hunstanton, stopping at Cley-next-to sea, the secluded fishing village of Blakeney, and Wells-next-to-sea. Great Yarmouth, Norfolk's largest and best known seaside resort, was also visited. The inland scenery was less impressive. It was too flat. However, Sandringham was an exception. Royalty certainly selected the best locations for their homes.

Only a handful of British universities taught colour chemistry. Leeds, Bradford and the Herriot-Watt Borders Campus at Galashiels were the main ones, but Strathclyde University included a 'Dyes and Dye Analysis' module in their Forensic Science degree. And it was Peter White, an ex-forensic scientist with the London Metropolitan Police, who invited me to give a six-lecture Colour Chemistry course for this module in 1988. Later, after Peter moved on to pastures new, the reigns were taken over by Prof. Ewen Smith. Like it did at UEA, the course proved very popular and ran for over fifteen years.

As a course tutor I was invited to attend the graduation ceremonies of the students I had helped teach at Strathclyde. One year, I accepted. It was a strange yet uplifting experience to stand on the stage with all the other tutors and watch as the students received their certificates. I may have missed out on my own graduation (Chapter 19) but in a way this helped to make up for it.

I thoroughly enjoyed my time at Strathclyde. Initially, I stayed at the university's Graduate Business School and, when that closed, at the nearby Travel Inn. This was located at the foot of a very steep hill, known locally as 'Induction Hill'. Why? Because climbing it induced the babies of many pregnant women making their way to the maternity hospital at the top.

The courses were popular and well attended and I became good friends with both Ewen Smith and Debbie Willison, the course organiser. Indeed, it was Debbie who invited me to give a talk to several hundred Scottish schoolchildren when 'how to become a millionaire' (Chapter 20) and the 'Flag' experiment were once again the stars of the show. I enjoyed many good meals in Glasgow, some with Ewen and some alone, at both the Babbity Bowser and especially the City Merchant restaurant.

However, most of the Colour Chemistry courses were presented 'in-house'. The majority were held at Blackley but they were also given to our Scottish colleagues at Grangemouth and to our American colleagues at New Castle, Delaware. Paul had moved to our Huddersfield Works site and it was left to me to present the course by myself. Giving twelve 45 minute lectures over one-and-a-half days meant a lot of talking, a lot of strain on your vocal chords. Following the operation to remove a polyp (Chapter 10), my vocal chords were my new Achilles Heel and too much talking resulted in hoarseness or, even worse, a complete loss of voice. On several occasions my voice became so hoarse that I was hardly able to speak for the final few lectures. Help was required. I needed someone to share the lectures with to alleviate the strain on my voice. Fortunately, Kath Carr (Image 196) agreed to present half of the lectures. It was a wise move. Not only did it ease the strain on me, it also improved the course. Having two presenters with different voices and different styles added extra variety to an already good course.

The Colour Chemistry course was an excellent introduction to dyestuffs chemistry for graduates new from university, as well as for those moving into the colours area from other parts of ICI. Furthermore, it was a useful refresher course for people within the colours field itself. For these reasons, it was run on a regular basis, at least once per year, from the early 1980s until after I retired in 2002.

In addition to giving the Colour Chemistry course at universities and in-house, it was also given elsewhere. Surprising as it may seem, it was given at another company, Unilever. Being heavily involved in detergents and washing powders, they were keen to learn more about dyes and dyed fabrics to help them design better products. Provided any sensitive information was removed from the talks, it wasn't a problem. Kath and I also gave the course in New York for the Center for Professional Advancement. In order to get cheaper taxi fares, we had to pose as man and wife!

At the request of Mike Willis and Al Keene of IMI (Institute for Management Information) the Colour Chemistry course was given at two of their conferences, both after I had retired.

The first was at Clare College, Cambridge, in the July of 2002. Clare College is a beautiful college in a most wonderful setting beside the lovely River Cam and I felt privileged to be lecturing in such a historic place. Ten lectures comprised the one and a half day course (Image 200). These were similar to the in-house Colour Chemistry course, except that the lectures on Carbocyclic Synthesis and Heterocyclic Synthesis, which describe the chemistry of the basic building blocks of all dyes and pigments, were omitted. The high attendance and favourable comments resulted in Al asking me to repeat the course the following year at Sugarloaf mountain in the USA. Although retired, I was still in demand.

21.2 CONFERENCES

My first ever lecture[2] at a major international conference was in Manchester in 1985 (Chapter 13). Two years later, Al Keene, who ran the Institute for Graphics Communication (IGC – later to become IMI), asked if someone from ICI would present a paper at their upcoming European conference in Amsterdam (Appendix I).[*]

---

[*] Appendix I lists all the papers that I have presented at major international conferences

Dave Thompson (Image 118), our Section Manager, said it would have to be him, Nigel Hughes or me. In the event, the task fell to me. I was quickly becoming the person from ICI to speak at major international conferences.

Colour Chemistry course given at Clare College 2002.

However, the major conference for hi-tech imaging was that hosted by the Society for Photographic Scientists and Engineers (SPSE), which later became the Imaging Science and Technology (IS and T) organisation. This organisation held an annual 'International Congress on Advances in Non Impact Printing', usually in the USA, although occasionally it was also held in Japan and Europe. It is the conference that Derek Wilson from Coates Electrographics advised us to present our work (Chapter 20). His advice was heeded. Big time. I presented not one but two lectures at SPSE's Fourth International Congress on Advances in Non Impact Printing (NIP) in New Orleans. At that conference, I really earned my corn.

Wanting to make a good impression, the 35mm slides for both presentations were done professionally by an external company. It wasn't a wise choice. Not being *au fait* with chemistry, they made countless errors with the chemical structures, causing innumerable delays. It took them so long that the slides were only delivered to my home on the night prior to my departure for the USA! Furthermore, they charged an absolute fortune, about £4,500 for just twenty slides! It was a rip-off. In future, we produced our own.

Ben Gunn and Russell Bond accompanied me to New Orleans. Arriving on the Saturday, we had the whole Sunday to relax before the conference began on the Monday. Being keen golfers, Ben and Russell fancied a game at the local golf club and asked me to join them (Image 201). I'm not a golfer but I enjoyed the game and was by no means disgraced, although I did hit a few balls into the lake.

Left to right: Ben Gunn, Russell Bond and
Me on New Orleans Golf Course 1988.

My first presentation was on positive charging organic photoconductors.[3] Our work using thiols to replace the chlorine atoms on phthalocyanines (Chapter 20) led to these unusual molecules. I felt nervous both before and during the lecture. Electronic chemicals wasn't our *forte* and here I was lecturing to an audience of experts. It was a daunting experience. However, I felt much more confident and relaxed giving the second lecture.[4] When it came to D2T2 dyes, *we* were the experts.

New Orleans is a strange city. A city of contrasts. The French Quarter is charming, a reminder of a gentler age. Indeed, it wouldn't have surprised me if elegant ladies in costumes from the 1900s had alighted from a horse and carriage. Down by the mighty Mississippi, the paddle steamers (Image 202) evoked memories of Mark Twain and also Rhett Butler in *Gone with the Wind*. It was a bustling scene. Jazz artists belted out the blues on the wooden jetties (Image 203), hoping to elicit tips from the tourists in the countless cafes dotted along the busy waterfront. In the Riverwalk Center, throngs of tourists milled around the myriad of stalls searching for that special gift. Others simply relaxed, watching the world go by as they savoured authentic cajun cuisine in one of the many eating establishments.

Paddle steamer on the Mississippi.

In downtown New Orleans the bars and cafes abounded with entertainers, dancers and jazz bands. One evening, on the famous Bourbon Street, 'Skeet, the man with the dancing feet', entertained us by dancing on the bar. We even sampled the delights of naked female mud wrestlers! But there were seedy parts too, parts where murders were not uncommon. Overall though, it was a pleasant experience.

Jazz artist by the river.

The following year I gave a presentation on infrared absorbers[5] at the Fifth NIP conference in San Diego. On the flight from Chicago to San Diego the stewardess asked if a middle-aged lady could move seats and sit next to me. She had become increasingly upset by the antics of a young boy sat next to her and asked to be moved. She was very friendly and even invited me to her house for a drink. Politely, I declined.

San Diego is a beautiful city with a wonderful climate. With a temperature constantly in the mid-seventies, it is neither too hot nor too cool. Like Goldilock's porridge, it was just right. The whales must have thought the same about the sea temperature too because they abound in the coastal waters, making San Diego ideal for whale watching. It is also a major US naval base and some of the warships moored in the harbour, especially the gigantic aircraft carriers, took your breath away. They were an awesome sight.

The Embrocadero on the Bay was the conference hotel. Modern, with a smattering of old world charm, it overlooked a small harbour in which an old sailing ship was moored. In the evening, I met up with my boss, Peter Bamfield, for a meal. We had a 'steerburger', an enormous hamburger, with fries. They did things big in San Diego.

Derek Toms and Richard Hann, from the D2T2 dye project (Chapter 13), were also at the conference. I accepted the offer of a drive in their hire car, stopping above the bay to have our pictures taken (Image 204).

Left to right: Richard Hann and Derek Toms.

In 1991, IS and T's Seventh International Congress on Advances in Non Impact Printing was held in Portland, Oregon, not far from Corvallis, the Hewlett-Packard site where we held most of our meetings. (The 1990 conference in Orlando was covered in Chapter 14.) On the first night Ron Kenyon, Ian Wasson and myself wandered around for ages trying to find a restaurant. In desperation, we eventually asked some locals, who directed us to a small waterfront café. It wasn't very good. The following evening, Ron and I asked the hotel concierge to recommend a good restaurant. "Certainly sir. You are spoiled for choice in Portland, the City of Restaurants." I still don't know if he was being truthful or facetious, but his recommendation was excellent. We had a superb meal in a lovely city centre restaurant.

Me in San Diego 1989.

On the Sunday, I hired a car so we could go for a drive through the magnificent Oregon countryside and stop at a remote mountain location for brunch. In reciprocation of his gesture at San Diego, I invited Derek Toms to join us. Not only did he accept, he also offered to drive, allowing Ron and myself to relax and admire the beautiful scenery.

After I had given my talk on water fast black dyes for ink jet printers,[6] Wayne Jaeger and his team from Tektronix invited me to meet them in a private room. Tektronix were the leading supplier of hot melt ink jet printers, a niche market of ink jet printing, and wanted ICI to develop novel dyes for them. It wasn't in our business plan but Wayne and his five colleagues (I was outnumbered by six to one) gave me a real grilling. They were desperate to collaborate with us. They had used the chemistry I presented at the 1990 conference for the alcohol soluble black[7] (Chapter 14) to produce some good dyes and wanted us to develop them further. Being as diplomatic as possible, I said I would put their suggestion to my business colleagues. In the end, we did do a little work for them by esterifying the water soluble carboxy-based dyes but, as far as I am aware, I don't think they became commercial products.

In 1992, Japan hosted the prestigious 'Chemistry of Functional Dyes' conference in Kobe. I met up with my boss Peter Bamfield and, on the Sunday, enjoyed a sightseeing trip in the city of Kyoto. We did some contemplating in the rock garden, trying in vain to locate the thirteen rocks (I'm sure there were only twelve – Image 205), but the highlight was the visit to one of the many temples. With their typical Japanese roofs and red and black colouring, they were absolutely lovely (Image 206). The guided tour revealed some fascinating facts. For instance, the wooden floor of the temple creaked as loudly as any in the oldest stately homes of England, not because

350

it was old but because it had been designed that way. It acted as an early warning system, making it almost impossible for any would be assassin to sneak up on the Emperor undetected. A further precaution was that anyone visiting the Emperor had to wear a long flowing robe that trailed on the floor, in the way that a wedding dress does. Should the visitor try to lunge towards the Emperor, he would be stopped in his tracks by the guards standing on his robe.

One evening an ICI Japan colleague offered to take us out for dinner to sample the famous Kobe beef. Kobe beef is expensive, very expensive, but our colleague said he knew a restaurant that offered high quality Kobe beef at an affordable price. To his embarrassment, he couldn't find the restaurant. After wandering the streets for over an hour, we had no option but to dine in a different restaurant. It cost the earth, over £70 each! But the Kobe beef was to die for. It is the tenderest, tastiest beef I have ever had. It literally melted in your mouth.

Japanese Rock Garden.

Japanese Temple, Kyoto 1992.

351

The following year, I returned to Japan with Ron Kenyon, this time to Yokohama, the home of the Japanese naval fleet. But Japan wasn't our first port of call. Far from it. We'd spent the previous week visiting HP's research facility at Palo Alto in California. After an intensive week of important meetings, Ron and I were exhausted. To recuperate, we spent our final night in the USA in the cabaret bar of the hotel. It was a good decision. The entertainment was provided by a bubbly blonde singer, a veritable pocket dynamo. She entranced us. She was excellent, so good in fact that we stayed up until her act ended in the early hours of Saturday morning. But it cost us a good night's sleep. We had to be up at the crack of dawn to drive our hire car to San Jose. Our plane to Tokyo awaited.

After snatching a few hour's sleep and a hurried breakfast, Ron and I made our way to the parking lot to collect our hire car. It started fine but there was a problem. How to release the handbrake. It was a completely different set up to a European car. Flummoxed, we had to wait until a passing American solved our dilemma.

We boarded the plane at 10-00 a.m. on the Saturday morning for the eight hour flight, expecting to arrive in Tokyo at about 6-00 p.m. But we had reckoned without crossing the International Date Line. Crossing this line of longitude from West to East means that you lose a whole day! A full 24 hours. So, rather than arriving at 6-00 p.m. on Saturday evening, we arrived at our hotel at 6-00 p.m. on Sunday evening! The entire weekend had gone. Disappeared. We'd set off from America on Saturday morning on an eight hour flight and arrived in Japan on Sunday night! Talk about disorientating, it was weird in the extreme.

Two years later in 1995, the trip was done in reverse. Ian Wasson and I had been visiting Canon and Seiko Epson in Japan and our next appointment was IS and T's Eleventh NIP conference at Hilton Head in North Carolina. Setting off from Tokyo at about 6-00 p.m. on the Saturday evening for the 14 hour flight, we expected to arrive on the east coast of America at around 8-00 a.m. on the Sunday morning. But, by crossing the International Date Line from West to East, you gain a full day. So, having left Tokyo at 6-00 p.m. on Saturday evening, we arrived in North Carolina at 8-00 a.m. on the morning of the very same day!! We arrived ten hours before we'd set off!! It is so strange that it has to be experienced in order to understand just how weird it really is.

Hilton Head is a secluded spot on the North Carolina coast. It has two main attractions; a sandy beach that stretches for miles and miles, and a host of golf courses. At the evening reception we met up with two old friends from HP's facility at Corvallis, the husband and wife team of Dave and Barbara Halko. It was most pleasant sipping drinks, eating canapés and catching up on gossip as the sun sank slowly below the horizon of the Atlantic Ocean.

My role at the conference was to present a two hour tutorial on Advanced Colour Chemistry. Unfortunately, in my zest to promote dyes rather than pigments, I made a slight error, saying that Pigment Yellow 12, which is based on the carcinogen

3,3'-dichlorobenzidine, was carcinogenic. Although it has the potential to be carcinogenic, in everyday usage it isn't, and the company had to issue a retraction. This was the one blemish on my lecturing career.

IS and T's twelfth NIP conference was held in the Lone Star state of Texas at San Antonio, famous as the site of the Alamo. It was here that less than two hundred Texans held the invading Mexican army at bay long enough for General Sam Houston to assemble an army that would later defeat them. But the defenders paid a terrible price. Every one of them perished,[*] including famous names like Davy Crockett and Jim Bowie.

Although small, San Antonio is quaint. A river meanders lazily through its centre, flanked on both sides by an assortment of bars, cafes and restaurants. In the evening, dining with friends and colleagues in one of the restaurants overlooking the river provided a fitting end to a San Antonio day.

Nineteen ninety-eight presented a completely new travel experience. China. I had been invited to give a lecture on ink jet dyes but was uncertain whether or not to accept the invitation. China was a totally different kettle of fish to Japan or the USA. It was unknown territory. Also, there was no locally based Zeneca representative to assist me. However, urged by Judith Auslander, an inveterate traveller, and Ray Work, our competitor on pigment-based ink jet inks from du Pont, I agreed to go.

Beijing airport was a complete contrast to Tokyo's Narita airport. As soon as I emerged from passport control a horde of gabbling Chinese taxi drivers surrounded me, all vying for my custom. It was intimidating. Eventually, I agreed to let one of them help me put my luggage in storage since my connecting flight to Chongqing, my final destination, was eight hours away. He was quite aggressive in wanting to take me to the Great Wall of China, saying that we had ample time, but I wasn't so sure. The last thing I wanted was to miss my connecting flight. Furthermore, he was charging about ten times the going rate. Firmly, I declined and gave him a hundred Yuan, the Chinese currency, to leave me alone.

I sat in the bar having a few drinks and catching up on some reading whilst trying to gauge the time to board the flight. It wasn't easy. All the announcements and notices were in Chinese, so they were no use. But I almost got it completely wrong. I think the flight must have been brought forward by an hour because, although I arrived at the right departure gate at what I had estimated to be the right time, everyone had already boarded except me. The plane was sitting on the runway waiting for the single missing passenger. I felt so ashamed as I walked down the aisle to my seat with hundreds of Chinese eyes glaring at me.

---

[*]   Legend has it that before the decisive battle Colonel Jim Travers drew a line in the sand and said that any men who wished to leave were free to do so. Only one man crossed the line, a man with a wife and young children.

The situation was better organised at Chongqing airport, presumably because of all the foreign delegates, like me, making their way to ICISH 98 (International Conference of Imaging Science and Hardcopy 1998). At the taxi rank an official wrote each person's final destination on a slip of paper. It had both the destination and the fare, which was exceptionally cheap. On handing this to the taxi driver, I was driven to my hotel in the centre of Chongqing. As we approached the city centre I couldn't believe my eyes. The streets were literally teeming with bicycles. They were everywhere. Millions of them! Everyone seemed to have one. Never in my life have I seen so many bicycles. By comparison, the number in Cambridge seemed minuscule. I arrived at the five star hotel exhausted but relieved that the long journey was over, but I couldn't relax just yet.

The Chinese were completely different to the Japanese. Where the Japanese were polite, courteous and helpful, the Chinese were brash, in-your-face and very money orientated, traits that reared their ugly head as soon I checked-in. To my utter amazement, the hotel receptionist wanted payment in full, in advance, for the whole of my stay! I had been advised to take the bulk of the money in US dollars but they refused to accept that currency. They wanted payment in their own currency, the Yuan. They wanted it in cash. And they wanted it now. One of their staff even escorted me down the street to the local bank to make sure the dollars were exchanged for the Yuan to ensure they got their money. I was not impressed.

The culture shocks didn't end at reception. En route to breakfast on the first morning I was amazed to see a large glass case half-full of live, writhing snakes. What on earth were these for? I would soon find out. As I was munching my cornflakes, two Chinese men came and sat at a nearby table. They placed their order with the waiter, which was fine, but what happened next sickened me. The waiter relayed their order to a man in a butcher's apron who stood inside a tiled, circular counter at the entrance to the restaurant. He went to the glass case and grabbed two live snakes. Placing them on the counter, he chopped off their heads and 'tails', skinned them and then sliced them up. Pleased with his handiwork, he beckoned to waiter. Carefully, the waiter placed the raw slices of snake on to two plates and served them to the two diners. As mentioned in Chapter 1, I don't like snakes but I felt sorry for these poor creatures. The sea slug saga (Chapter 14) was bad enough, but this was worse. Far worse.

One excursion was to the Terracotta Army. (I don't think it was THE Terracotta Army.) It was a long journey and, before leaving the motorway, the coach made a comfort stop at a service station. It was unlike any service station in the UK. On entering the communal toilet block, I couldn't believe my eyes. Two large, circular, tiled trenches, one to the left for the ladies and one to right for the men, were the only features in an otherwise featureless room. They were the toilets, the place where you 'did your business', whether it be solid or liquid, in full view of everyone, including members of the opposite sex. Not only that, the open trenches were full of urine and excrement, which meant the stench was overwhelming. I was glad that I only wanted

354

a wee because there was nothing to wipe your bum with. (I don't know if anyone ever overbalanced while squatting down to do a poo. If so, they would have ended up at the bottom of the trench covered in urine and excrement.)

On the final part of the drive through rice fields and small villages, I was fascinated by the local children. They wore strange clothes. The boys didn't wear pants nor the girls skirts. They both wore something which left their bare bottoms exposed! The tour guide informed us the children wore split-crotch pants so they could just squat down anywhere, anytime, for a wee or a poo. It certainly did away with the need for nappies.

The excursion was fascinating but not so the evening dinner. It was, apparently, authentic Chinese cuisine. To my surprise, the first course was soup. Fine, I like soup, but not the soup they served up. It was a bowl of clear warm water with two or three young, fledgling, hairless birds floating in it, complete with heads, beaks and legs. I watched in horror as people picked them up with their fingers and tore chunks out of them with their teeth. It made me feel sick. If this was the first course, I shuddered to think what the other courses might be. Politely, I excused myself and caught a taxi back to the hotel where I had steak and chips (although where the steak came from didn't bear thinking about, but it tasted okay).

On my journey home, Beijing airport provided another scare, this time a potentially serious one. I clambered into a taxi from the official taxi rank and settled back for the journey into central Beijing for my final night in China. Within minutes, the taxi was halted in no uncertain terms by a police car with its sirens blazing. A gun-toting policeman ordered the taxi back to the airport and then escorted me to a genuinely official taxi. Apparently, the previous one was a rogue taxi that had somehow managed to evade the airport's security system. It could have taken me anywhere.

As I checked into the impressive Hilton Hotel an attractive young lady approached me asking if I required a taxi to the airport the following morning. Before accepting her offer, I asked the hotel receptionist if she represented a genuine taxi firm. "Yes," replied the receptionist, "she belongs to one of the most reputable taxi firms in Beijing. They are the company we recommend." Reassured, I said I did indeed need a taxi the following morning. Slowly, she started taking some details whilst I continued checking-in. Once my check-in was complete, she asked if she could finish taking the details in my room. As I sat on the edge of the bed, she knelt down provocatively on the floor in front of me, taking details and displaying her cleavage. "You are a nice man, a very nice man. I like you very much." She probably made more money selling her body than she did from her taxis. But not on this occasion. I have never been unfaithful to Vera and I wasn't going to start now.

Judith had booked an extra five day trip on a dhow on the Yangtse river and wanted me to join her. I declined. I'd had my fill of China, thank-you very much.

355

After presenting a paper on 'Enhanced Light Fastness from Photofading Studies' at the International Congress on Imaging Science in Antwerp in 1998, I participated in two Diamond Research Conferences, the first in 1999 and the second in 2001. Run by Art Diamond, they were prominent conferences in the hi-tech imaging area. A further lure was their location, normally Santa Barbara in California. It is a beautiful small resort boasting a superb sandy beach, a beach where countless courting couples sit and embrace as they watch the glorious sunsets.

At the conference I was befriended by three attendees from Mitsubishi, our major competitor in ink jet dyes. They even invited me to join them on an excursion to a vineyard. Driving through the beautiful Californian countryside in the failing dusk light was a delight. After a simple meal, it was time for the main event. The wine tasting. There were dozens of wines and all of them were delicious. As the evening drew to a close, Mitsubishi, they said, was finding it increasingly difficult to compete with us on ink jet dyes. With du Pont entering the fray with their pigment-based inks, they were feeling the squeeze. In a way, it was a complement.

My final overseas trip before I retired was to Las Vegas to attend my second Diamond Research Conference. Arriving at Chicago's O'Hare airport on 10 September, an early evening connecting flight to Las Vegas completed the journey. Seeing the famous Las Vegas 'Strip' from the air at night was awesome. It was a ribbon of colour.

Located about twenty minutes drive from downtown Las Vegas, the plush five star hotel had everything. Extensive landscaped gardens, numerous pools, waterfalls and its own shops. It was a delight. Spending a few days here would be no hardship at all.

On entering the breakfast room on the morning of 9/11, I was surprised to see a large crowd gathered in front of the television. They seemed to be watching a movie. A plane was crashing into a skyscraper. And, a little later, a second plane crashed into another skyscraper. As the waitress came to take my order, I asked her what they were watching. "It's awful, absolutely awful," she said. "Two planes have crashed into the World Trade Center in New York and one has crashed into the Pentagon." I was speechless. Who on earth would commit such atrocities? It not only spoiled everyone's breakfast, it also spoiled the conference. Although it went ahead, it was a very subdued and sombre affair.

In response to the atrocities, the US authorities grounded all flights for almost a week. I was stranded. Stranded in Las Vegas. I called Vera to let her know that I was okay but couldn't tell her when I would be home. To his credit, John Schofield was the only person from work to ring Vera to enquire how she was. The chaos caused by the atrocities and the cancellation of all flights meant that I was stuck in Las Vegas for over a week. However, it wasn't a bad place to be stranded as I divided my time between the pools and downtown Las Vegas. The flight home had to be arranged from the UK. It proved impossible to get through to any American airport or airline from the hotel.

On reflection, if I had flown just 24 hours later, it could so easily have been me on one of those fateful flights. 'There but for the grace of God go I'. It made me realise just how tenuous life is.

21.3 PRESENTATIONS

It wasn't all jet setting to exotic locations around the world to speak at prestigious international conferences. Giving presentations at such far flung places as Warwick and Whitehaven was also part and parcel of the job, as was participating and organising conferences in the UK.

John Pagett, a colleague from Runcorn, had organised a successful 'in-house' Polymer Symposium. Our Specialist Colours business was equally important and I thought that an 'in-house' conference on 'Colour Chemistry' would also be appropriate. The idea was readily supported by senior management and four colleagues from different parts of the Colours Business were appointed to organise the event.

I remember giving the opening lecture of the conference just a few hours after touching down from Japan. Jet lagged I may have been but I impressed the audience by speaking my opening remarks in Japanese, even though they only lasted for about a minute or so. The conference was huge success, gathering together people from disparate parts of the business and bringing them up to speed with the latest developments. I was pleased and so too was Peter Doyle, our main board Research Director, who said it was one of the best conferences he had attended.

It may sound strange but in many ways the UK trips were more enjoyable than the overseas ones. You were only away for one or two days rather than one or two weeks and there was none of the hassle associated with international travel.

My assistant or, more correctly, my 'right hand man' for most of these UK trips was Christine Millard (Image 196), although on some occasions it was Jim Campbell and later, Julie Stocks. The majority of lectures were given at universities, presumably, I think, to expose the students to the 'cutting edge' of industrial research in a fashionable high technology area. All the lectures resulted from invitations either from people I knew, such as Bert Mather at Herriot-Watt University at Galashiels, Ewen Smith at Strathclyde University, John Plater at Aberdeen University, John Griffiths at Leeds University and Ron Grigg from Queens University, Belfast, or from people aware of my published work. Invitations from Lancaster, York, Bangor and Canterbury fell into this latter category. The majority of lectures and trips proceeded without incident, but not all.

Professor Ron Grigg, who was my organic chemistry lecturer at Salford University in 1968 (Chapter 7), had requested help from ICI regarding one of their

PhD projects. They were attempting to fine-tune the colour of 'Rheumann's Purple' by modifying its chemical structure, but were struggling. Ron said it was like 'the blind leading the blind'. They were desperate for some expert help.

I arrived at Aldergrove airport in 1988 feeling a little apprehensive. Not about the visit to Queens University to discuss the problem. That was fine. But because of 'The Troubles' at that time. The drive through downtown Belfast, with its barbed wire barricades, IRA and Loyalist murals and the presence of army vehicles, did nothing to allay my fears. I asked Ron if there had been any trouble at the university. "Oh, just once," he replied. "There was one man who was a very vocal and outspoken critic of the IRA. One evening, two masked men walked calmly into the university and blew his brains out." It was said in such a matter-of-fact way that it seemed a normal, everyday event. In those troubled times, I suppose it was.

Christine, Jim and Julie assisted me in the lectures because we endeavoured to include as many visual, practical demonstrations as possible. Their role was to perform these practical demonstrations as I gave the lecture. If a picture is worth a thousand words, a demonstration is worth a million. They brought the lectures to life. However, it meant transporting a lot of equipment and chemicals, some of it very heavy, from our laboratories to the place of the lecture. I think my arms grew a few inches in length carrying laser printers from the car to the various lecture theatres!

Right in the middle of my lecture at Leeds University, the door to the lecture theatre burst open and an irate man stormed into the room. "Who's blocked my bloody car in!" he shouted. It was me. Parking space was non-existent and John had told me to park there, thinking the lecture would be finished before the man departed for home. Obviously not! John was very annoyed by the man's uncouth behaviour but I had no option but to temporarily suspend the lecture and move my car. It is the first and only time that one of my lectures has been so rudely interrupted.

Mike Hutchings, one of my colleagues (Chapter 9 and Image 112, page 260) and an organiser of a prestigious International Chemistry Conference being held at Warwick University, asked me if I would give a short talk on D2T2 dyes for electronic photography on one of the evenings. "There's no need to go to a lot of trouble," he said. "It'll be an informal affair to an audience of about thirty." Fine. I had already given the talk a few years ago in New Orleans (page 490) so I cobbled together a dozen or so slides and, together with Christine and the electronic camera, set off for Warwick.

Mike must have been joking! The lecture theatre was the size of the Albert Hall and it was filled to capacity. Instead of 30, there were over 300 people! I was taken aback. However, I went ahead and the talk created a lot of interest. So far, so good. In an hour's time after Christine had taken some of the participant's photos and printed them out as souvenirs, she and I could go back to the hotel and enjoy a well-earned evening meal with a bottle of wine. But it didn't work out like that. A multitude of people queued up for hours to have their photo taken by this revolutionary new and exciting technology, so many in fact that it was after 11-00 p.m. when we finally packed up. Instead of a sumptuous three-course dinner in the hotel, we ended the night eating fish and chips in a lay-by in the car!

The potentially most embarrassing situation occurred at Bangor University. I had been invited to give a public lecture on Colour Chemistry. In such cases I tended to keep the material simple and visual, including lots of photographs and amusing anecdotes. Near the beginning of the lecture were two full colour slides, one of a naked man and one of a naked woman. I used them in the Colour Chemistry course to show that images were better in full colour than in black-and-white. As was the norm, the carousel containing the 35mm slides was handed to the projectionist before the lecture, leaving Christine and me time for a leisurely coffee. Sipping my coffee, I watched as the attendees began to arrive. Usually, university students comprised the bulk of the audience, together with a smattering of interested people from the general public. Not here! To my complete surprise, it was a stream of elderly, well-to-do, genteel ladies that trooped into the lecture theatre! I was horrified! I could see the headlines already. 'Respectable chemist in the dock for displaying pornographic material in a public lecture to old ladies'. But it was too late. There was nothing I could do now except deliver the lecture and hope they weren't offended.

To my immense relief, they took it in the right spirit and had a good chuckle. Indeed, several elderly ladies came to me after the lecture to have a chat. A few weeks previously they had been to a lecture by Michael Fish, the TV weather presenter. He also had shown a naked lady, in this case standing in front of a roaring log fire. "This," he said, "is a warm front."

As mentioned earlier, I gave a Colour Chemistry course at The University of East Anglia and, during one visit, was asked to give a public lecture. The girl who introduced me to the audience obviously had a profound dislike for one of the lecturers. In her introduction, she said something like, "And now, Dr Wilkins (not his real name), this is how a lecture should be given." No pressure there, then.

21.4 EXTERNAL EXAMINER

The aftermath of one lecture resulted in a new appointment. Bert Mather had invited me to give a lecture on hi-tech colorants to students at Heriot-Watt University at Galashiels. I duly obliged and, some weeks later, was invited to become the university's External Examiner. It was a job I thoroughly enjoyed. Making suggestions to the courses and exam papers was fine but the really rewarding part was interacting with the staff and students. During my three year stint from 1997 to 2000 I became firm friends with Bert, Keith Morgan, Bob Christie, Margot Baird and Roger Wardman.

I was also the External Examiner for the oral exam (the viva) for two PhD students, Rachel Brown at Strathclyde University in 2002 and Syed Iqbal Ahmed at Heriot-Watt in 2005. Both, I am happy to say, received their doctorates.

21.5 PROFESSOR CUSTARD

My propensity for custard became a source of immense amusement at Blackley. I always ended my lunches in the canteen with a custard-based dessert. Jam roly poly was my favourite although spotted dick, chocolate sponge and Eve's pudding ran it a close second. Indeed, I enjoyed almost anything with custard. Out of curiosity, I calculated the amount of custard I must have consumed during my 37 year career at work. To my utter amazement, I had eaten 3.5 tonnes of the stuff! And that's without the jam roly polys, spotted dicks, chocolate sponges… Because of this, I was referred to, rather fondly, as Professor Custard,* and was often introduced as such during lectures to schoolchildren. I was like a character in Cluedo.

However, in addition to presenting lectures, Professor Custard had a number of other events to look forward to.

REFERENCES

1. PF Gordon and P Gregory, 'Organic Chemistry in Colour', Springer-Verlag, Berlin, Heidelberg, New York, London, Paris, Tokyo 1983.

2. KL Birkett and P Gregory, 'Metal Complex Dyes as Charge Control Agents' in: Dyes and Pigments, Vol. 7, pp. 341-350, 1986.

3. P Gregory, 'Novel Phthalocyanines for Positive Charging OPCs'. SPSE's 4th International Congress on Advances in Non-Impact Printing Technologies, New Orleans, March 20-25th 1988.

4. P Gregory, 'Dye Diffusion Thermal Transfer Dyes'. SPSE's 4th International Congress on Advances in Non-Impact Printing Technologies, New Orleans, March 20-25th 1988.

5. P Gregory, JS Campbell and A Quayle, 'Novel Infrared Absorbers for Non-Impact Printing Applications'. SPSE's 5th International Congress on Advances in Non- Impact Printing Technologies, San Diego, November 12-17th 1989.

---

* As you will have no doubt noticed, this is the title of the book you are reading, my autobiography

6. JS Campbell, P Gregory and PM Mistry, 'Novel Waterfast Black Dyes for Ink Jet Printing'. IS and T's 7ᵗʰ International Congress on Advances in Non-Impact Printing Technologies, Portland, Oregon, October 6-11ᵗʰ 1991.

7. P Gregory, RW Kenyon and PM Mistry, 'The Discovery of a Novel Alcohol Soluble Black Dye for Industrial Ink Jet Printing'. SPSE's 6ᵗʰ International Congress on Advances in Non-Impact Printing Technologies, Orlando, October 21-26th 1990.

22

FIVE OF THE BEST

Although I didn't know it, 1995 would be a good year. A year that would finally fulfil one of the two desires that had burned brightly within my chest for many years. A year in which five notable events would occur, beginning with improvements to our house.

22.1 TWO WELCOME ADDITIONS

No, it wasn't twins but a conservatory and utility room. Vera and I had fancied a conservatory for a number of years. We sat in them at garden centres and thought how lovely it would be to sit in our own and look out over the garden. They were so light and airy. It was like sitting in the garden without getting cold or wet. A utility room would serve a double purpose. Not only would it house the gas boiler and washing machine, it would also provide more cupboard space both in the kitchen and in the utility room itself. And so, in 1995, we took the plunge and decided to go ahead.*

There were lots of conservatory companies around and we looked at quite a few but we always kept coming back to Croston Conservatories. Based, not surprisingly, in Croston, they displayed their wares at the nearby Auldene Garden Centre. Several factors influenced our decision. First, Croston Conservatories were built and finished to a high standard. Second, they did everything 'in-house', including knocking a large hole in the lounge wall and fitting patio doors. And they would tile the floor and carry out all the electrical work, including buying and fitting the ceiling fan and radiator. Finally, they would also build the utility room, which was important since the conservatory and utility room shared a common wall. It was costly but the end result was worth it (Image 207).

---

*   In 2015 we added an extension to the side of the house to make the kitchen much bigger and add a new utility room, converting the old one into a downstairs shower room. We also had quoins (cornerstones) incorporated into both the extension and the front of the house (see Chapter 28).

Rear of house showing conservatory, utility room
and part of the patio 2008. The tall tree with the pale
foliage is the one planted in memory of Sam.

Before they could begin, Andrew, Michael and myself had some hard labouring to do. The hard standing area made for the touring caravan (Chapter 18) needed to be demolished. This necessitated digging out and removing about 20 tons of brick and rubble, enough in fact to fill two large skips. The demolition phase was followed by the construction phase, building the decorative walls and laying the patio flags. It was hard, back-breaking work that took several weeks to complete. One thing was for sure. That year, we were certainly ready for our holidays.

22.2 A FINAL FAMILY HOLIDAY

As a family, we had enjoyed some wonderful holidays (Chapters 12, 15 and 18) and, in 1995, we decided it was time to have not one but two final holidays with our boys. But we had left it too late for Andrew. Aged 21 and having been away at university (Chapter 19), he considered himself 'too old' to holiday with his parents. Not so Michael. Still only seventeen, he readily agreed to a week's holiday in Cala Dor* followed by two weeks in Florida and so, in the May sunshine, the three of us departed for Majorca.

---

*   We liked Cala Dor so much that a few years later Vera and I had a week's holiday at the Parque Mar holiday park. Situated just outside Cala Dor, it was in a lovely location and we enjoyed a most relaxing holiday. In the morning we'd relax on our loungers on the rocks watching the boats entering and leaving Cala Dor harbour, including Michael Schumacher's black yacht, whilst in the evening we enjoyed refreshing drinks in the poolside bar.

We stayed in an apartment at the Club Ferrara Playa in a room with a balcony that overlooked the swimming pool (Image 208). The accommodation was spacious and of a good standard, except the mattresses on the beds were too thin. Every morning we ate breakfast at one of the cafes on the main street, the Marivent Bar being one of our favourites. Our evening meals were taken at either the small café opposite the Hollywood Diner or at one of the many cafes overlooking the picturesque harbour.

Most afternoons we chilled out on one of the secluded little beaches, waiting for the familiar call of 'oranges, melons, pineapples' from the boy touting his fresh fruit (and ice creams) on the beach, without fail, every day. Enjoying a fresh orange or licking a cold ice cream whilst resting in the shade was pure paradise.

In the evenings we had fun playing crazy golf and then relaxing in one of the bars, sipping a cold beer as we listened to music and watched the world go by. It was a rejuvenating, refreshing break, an ideal way to recharge the batteries after a long winter. But it was only a taster. The main holiday was yet to come.

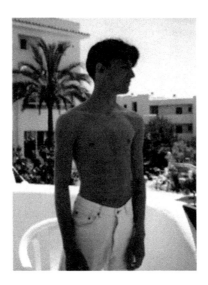

Michael on the balcony of our
apartment in Cala Dor, May 1995.

Three months later in late July we arrived in Florida. The timing couldn't have been worse. The day after we arrived, Orlando was hit by a hurricane. Our first full day at the Marriott Hotel was a complete and utter wash out. The hurricane had moderated to a tropical storm but it was still so bad that we had to vacate our room in case the windows shattered, and congregate in the restaurant. Just dashing the fifty yards or so soaked us to the skin.

Breakfast was a self-serve affair. Finding the bacon and eggs (sunnyside up) was no problem but locating the sausages was hilarious. We looked and looked but could we find the sausages. They were nowhere to be seen. In desperation, I asked one of the waiters, "Where are the sausages?"

In his heavy Hispanic accent he said, "Sausages, sausages, over there." Following his pointing hand, all we could find were thin slices of some round meat. There were no sausages. Eventually, the penny dropped. There weren't any real sausages, just very thin sausage slices. It was so funny.

The following day revealed the extent of the damage caused by the hurricane. Uprooted trees, street lights and signs were strewn around like confetti and a number of buildings were damaged. Fortunately, our part of the hotel and our hire car were still intact (Image 209).

Michael stood beside our hire car at the
Marriott Hotel, Orlando, July 1995.

In Orlando we spent alternate days at the theme parks, using the other days to relax, visit the shopping malls, play floodlit mini golf and patronise *Rosie O'Gradies*. The attractions Michael and I enjoyed the most were the *Tower of Terror* and *Alien*. In the *Tower of Terror* you are strapped into an elevator at the bottom of a very tall building. The ride begins gently, ascending slowly to the top of the building and then proceeds at a leisurely pace towards some double doors. Suddenly, the doors fling open, leaving nothing between you and a sheer drop of several hundred feet to the ground below! It returns slowly to the elevator, and stops. Then, without warning, the elevator drops. It's a false start. After falling a few feet, it shudders to a halt. After the uncertainty induced by a few false starts, it drops for real, plummeting in free-fall the entire height of the building, leaving yours and everyone else's stomach behind, before coming to an abrupt halt. The actual free-fall only lasts a few seconds, but it's a few seconds of pure exhilaration. We thought it was great but Vera sat outside on a wall waiting for us to return.

The alien encounter took place in a circular amphitheatre in the dark. An excellent life-size replica of the fearsome alien monster was housed in a cage in the centre of the theatre. Suddenly, there was a power failure. All the lights went out, plunging the room into total darkness. Amidst the resulting chaos and confusion, the alien monster escaped. It could be heard but not seen as it 'flew' around in the darkened room. Suddenly, with a bone jarring thud, the evil monster landed on the back of *your* seat, its claws gripping your shoulder, its hot steamy breath on the back of your neck sending shivers down your spine. It was great! Yet again, Vera sat this one out, waiting for the gentler pursuits of *ET (Extra Terrestrial)*. She even thought the ET ride was scary, especially the bit where you passed through the mist. It made her breathless!

On the Saturday morning we bade farewell to Orlando and set off on the two-and-a-half hour drive to St Petersburg. With the exception of the seven-lane highway in downtown Tampa, where cars whizzed by on both sides, it was a pleasant journey. However, for some reason, Vera didn't like the multitudes of pelicans perched on the railings beside the 'highway over the sea' as we approached our destination.

We had admired the Tradewinds Hotel on our previous visit to the Gulf Coast (Chapter 15). Located next to a beautiful expanse of white, sandy beach (Image 210), it was a most splendid hotel. As we pulled on to the forecourt, we were greeted by a friendly porter. To my surprise, he wasn't wearing a typical porter's uniform. He wore a traditional porter's jacket but, instead of wearing a porter's trousers, he was attired in shorts! He reminded me of a Bermudan policeman. (And no, it wasn't Alan Morrissey – Chapter 13). It wasn't the hotel's only connection to the Caribbean. A network of waterways criss-crossed the extensive landscaped gardens and it was lovely to hop aboard one of the little boats and enjoy a leisurely sail, stopping off at one of the Caribbean style huts for a morning breakfast or an afternoon drink.

The Tradewinds Hotel, St Petersburg 1995.

We spent many hours on the beach (Image 211), having an occasional dip in the warm Gulf Sea. Sometimes, we drove along the narrow promontory, enjoying a picnic at one of the many secluded spots. Treasure Island was visited too, but, to our dismay, the Pot Roast restaurant and the 'floating Sizzlers' were gone (Chapter 15). Things changed quickly in the USA.

Michael on St Petersburg beach.

One afternoon, Michael fancied a session in the well-equipped hotel gymnasium. Not a gym person myself, I didn't exert myself. In contrast, Michael really exerted himself, especially on the stepping machines, so much so that sweat literally poured from his body. He was fine in the air conditioned surroundings of the gym but, on venturing outside into the sweltering heat, he became faint and I had to help him back to our room. Once there, he had to lie down for several hours, sipping cold drinks and having wet towels placed on his head to help him cool down. It was a harsh lesson learned the hard way. Never over exert yourself in a hot country.

It's a small world. No, not the Disney ride, which was Vera's favourite, but a cosy restaurant near to the hotel that served traditional English breakfasts. The husband-and-wife owners were helped by a friend who, it transpired, used to work at, and part own, the Georgian House, a hotel situated a mere two miles from our home in West Bolton. We patronised that restaurant a lot. Full English breakfasts, delicious evening meals and a lovely roast beef Sunday lunch, all went down a treat.

All too soon it was time to drive back to Orlando and board the plane for Manchester. A Long Service Award beckoned.

22.3 THIRTY YEAR AWARD

Nineteen ninety-five was my thirtieth year with the company (they didn't seem to count the year that I left to do the GRIC Part II course at Salford University – Chapter 7) and my loyalty was about to be rewarded for the second time.* Ten years earlier, I was one of many recipients of the 20 year Long Service Award, but there would, I suspected, be fewer recipients of the 30 year award.

The Long Service Award Presentation Dinners were grand affairs. Taxis were despatched to pick up the recipient and their spouse and transport them to the venue, Hexagon House New. Here, you were met at reception by your host and escorted up the grand marble staircase to the spacious dining area on the first floor, where a number of tables were set for dinner. Drinks and canapés were served and then it was time for the main events, the dinner and the presentations.

Each table of approximately ten people was hosted by either a head of department or a senior manager. Our table was composed of people mainly from Research Department, such as Geoff Rothwell, Derek Thorp, Geoff Dent and their wives, with Alan Calder, the Research Manager, the host. The meals were very good but, for Vera and I, a little too pretentious (Image 212).

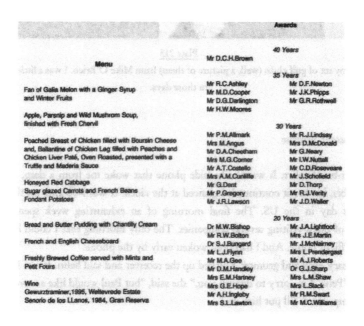

Menu

Fan of Galia Melon with a Ginger Syrup and Winter Fruits

Apple, Parsnip and Wild Mushroom Soup, finished with Fresh Chervil

Poached Breast of Chicken filled with Boursin Cheese and, Ballantine of Chicken Leg filled with Peaches and Chicken Liver Paté, Oven Roasted, presented with a Truffle and Madeira Sauce

Honeyed Red Cabbage
Sugar glazed Carrots and French Beans
Fondant Potatoes

Bread and Butter Pudding with Chantilly Cream

French and English Cheeseboard

Freshly Brewed Coffee served with Mints and Petit Fours

Wine
Gewurztraminer,1995, Weltevrede Estate
Senorio de los Llanos, 1984, Gran Reserva

Awards

40 Years
Mr D.C.H.Brown

35 Years

Mr R.C.Ashley	Mr D.F.Newton
Mr M.D.Cooper	Mr J.K.Phipps
Mr D.G.Darlington	Mr G.R.Rothwell
Mr H.W.Moores	

30 Years

Mr P.M.Allmark	Mr R.J.Lindsay
Mrs M.Angus	Mrs D.McDonald
Mr D.A.Cheetham	Mr G.Neary
Mrs M.G.Corner	Mr I.W.Nuttall
Mr A.T.Costello	Mr C.D.Roseveare
Mrs A.M.Cunliffe	Mr J.Schofield
Mr G.Dent	Mr D.Thorp
Mr P.Gregory	Mr R.J.Verity
Mr J.R.Lawson	Mr J.D.Waller

20 Years

Dr M.W.Bishop	Mr J.A.Lightfoot
Mr R.W.Bolton	Mrs J.E.Martin
Dr S.J.Bungard	Mr J.McNairney
Mr L.J.Flynn	Mrs L.Prendergast
Mr M.A.Gee	Mr A.J.Roberts
Mr D.M.Handley	Dr G.J.Sharp
Mrs E.M.Hartney	Mrs L.M.Shaw
Mrs G.E.Hope	Mrs L.Slack
Mr A.H.Ingleby	Mr R.M.Swart
Mrs S.L.Lawton	Mr M.C.Williams

Menu and recipients at the Long Service Awards 1995.

---

* At ICI and Zeneca, Long Service Awards were presented after 20, 30, 35 and 40 years, although there were very few recipients of the 40 year award (Image 212)

After a speech by the Chief Executive Officer (CEO), in this case Mr M J O'Brien, the individual awards were presented (Image 213). Thinking ahead to my retirement, I chose a set of golf clubs. The ceremony ended with the longest serving member giving a short speech, thanking the company for the evening and the gifts. Then, after more drinking and chatting, the taxis returned to whisk us all home.

Receiving my set of golf clubs (well, a picture of them) from
Mike O'Brien. I was a little overweight in those days.

22.4 A PLEASANT SURPRISE

Brr-brr, brr-brr, brr-brr. It was the bedside phone that woke me from a deep, comforting sleep. Brr-brr, brr-brr it continued. I glanced at the clock. It was 7-30 a.m. on the morning of my last day in the US. The final morning of an exhausting week spent travelling thousands of miles visiting several companies. The only morning that I could have a lie-in before my flight home. And I had been woken early by the phone.

Bleary eyed and grumpy, I picked up the receiver and said hello. It was Rose, Paul's secretary. "Peter, I'm sorry to disturb you," she said, "but Paul would like a word with you. It's quite important. I'll put him on."

"Hi Peter, it's Paul. I've got some great news! The International Scientific Panel at Zeneca have approved your promotion to the position of Company Research Associate. Congratulations." I was speechless. Still not fully awake, I thought I was dreaming. "I've rung you now because the news is being released within the company later today and I thought it only fair that you should know beforehand. Once again, well done!"

It wasn't a dream, it was real. I had been promoted to the highest possible technical position in Zeneca. Paul had mentioned at my appraisal a few months earlier that I was being considered for the position but I didn't think it would materialise. However, it is something to which I had secretly aspired, to reach the pinnacle of your chosen career. Ken Henderson, the head of Personnel Department, had likened it to winning a Nobel Prize! I don't think it was that rare, or prestigious, but it wasn't easy either.

When the news finally sank in, I said, "That's great. Thanks, Paul," and literally jumped out of bed. I was awake now! Unfortunately, at that very instant there was a knock on the door and the maid walked in to make up the room. Met with the sight of a naked 49-year-old man jumping out of bed as she entered the room was too much for the poor girl to bear. She departed far quicker than she'd entered!

Apparently, both Paul Gordon, my Section Manager, and Alan Calder, the Head of Research Department, had been very supportive regarding my promotion. Alan remarked that he was impressed and amazed by the bewildering array of molecules emanating from my lab (Chapter 20), whilst Paul had supplied one of the five references needed in support of my promotion (Image 214). Ohtasan of Canon and Ron Prevost of HP supplied the two industrial references, with John Griffiths of Leeds University and Mike Cooke of the University of East Anglia providing the two from academia.

What did the promotion mean financially? It meant a jump of two grades, from Hay 37 to Hay 39, the highest black book grade. I couldn't go any higher. With a 12.5 per cent differential between each grade, it also meant a 25 per cent increase in salary, although not all at once. I felt so proud. Not because of the extra money or status. Yes, these were important, of course they were. I felt proud because I had started my career in 1965 as a humble Laboratory Assistant on Haslam grade 4 (Chapter 7) and worked my way up to reach the highest possible grade for a technical person. One of my two childhood dreams had been realised. Well almost (Section 22.5).

On returning to work, I received the official letter confirming my promotion (Image 215). As Prof. Ramage said (Chapter 7), when you earn a lot, you keep quiet.

The letter wasn't all that awaited me on my return. My staff had immortalised the promotion by writing a poem. I was very touched.

PERSONNEL/CONFIDENTIAL

P.GREGORY - RESEARCH ASSOCIATE

Dear Nigel

In response to your note concerning a reference for Peter Gregory I have no hesitation in supporting his promotion to Research Associate. I have known Peter for some considerable time and recognise his qualities well. In my opinion he is now the foremost 'Colours' expert within Zeneca and this expertise extends not just to the design of coloured molecules for various applications (ink jet dyes, textile dyes etc.) but to a deeper understanding of the cause of the colour, i.e. their intrinsic electronic/molecular properties.

Peter is achievement orientated and over the last few years has lead teams which have developed so called Generation 2 and 3 ink jet dyes which are a step change in performance over anything else currently on the market. During this work he has used molecular modelling and computational methods to aid him in his molecular design work. In this respect Peter has been one of the leading lights in the application of such modern technology to his work and this goes back over ten years when computational methods and their application in the Specialties Business were in their infancy. This points to a desire for a deeper appreciation of the science and the willingness to tackle areas outside of his immediate comfort zone. This tendency is also shown in his work for new applications of coloured molecules leading to, for example, the design of singlet oxygen generators for a number of applications. Peters general approach always impresses me and marks him out from many of his BRA colleagues, especially when the success realised in hard Business results is accounted for.

It is also quite noticeable how Peters standing in the scientific community has risen in the last few years and he is now widely consulted by those within and outside of Zeneca. I am quite sure there are many in companies such as Hewlett-Packard and Canon who would testify to his expertise and I am aware that he is regularly invited to write articles and present his work (and his view of the industry) at major international conferences. Clearly he is well respected at the international level.

I hope the above comments and observations help to support Peters case but if you would like further examples I would be happy to supply them. I am quite convinced of his suitability for a Research Associate post and am in no doubt that he will fulfil the role in the future satisfactorily.

Regards

Reference written by Paul Gordon in support of
my promotion to Company Research Associate.

Dear Mr.Gregory,

I am pleased to confirm that at the recent meeting of the International Scientific Ladder Panel, you were recommended for promotion to the position of Company Research Associate and that this has been agreed.

The job grade associated with this position is Grade 39 and in consequence your salary will be increased to £   per annum with effect from 1st October, 1995. Your salary will be paid at the new rate from 1st October, 1995, onwards and your November salary will also include the backpayment due to you.

Please accept my congratulations on your new appointment.

Yours sincerely,

S.M.Shierson (Mrs)
Personnel Manager - Headquarters

Formal letter concerning my promotion.

ODE TO OUR BOSS

Our Boss is just one of them men
Tucked his shirt in his undies again!
But hang on a sec
We'd better just check
'Cos that 'lastic could go, who knows when

Far be it for us lot to fuss
For all we know it could be a truss
From reports that we've heard
From a Huddersfield 'bird'
It's a hernia that makes our man cuss

Could be a chance in a million
We were laughing at Ayyub's squarylium
But really we know
That his truss was on show
And stood there, he looked such a silly 'un!

Is it something to do with the pies
That puts too much strain on his flies?
Or sponge pudding and custard
That gets him so flustered
And brings all the tears to his eyes?

The effect of the wall building lingers
He's got no ends left on his fingers
He's got a bad back
But he's still got the knack
To join in with the falsetto singers

At the thirty year long-service ball
TVs and stuff weren't in his haul
But golf clubs he picked
And if they get nicked
Will this change his swing? Not at all!

He's just got to grade thirty-nine
But there's nothing for Hutchings, poor swine!
He gets dirty looks
But he's written more books
"And his remit is smaller than mine!!"

For the ladies he has quite an eye
Especially when hemlines are high
Better still in the buff
When they're strutting their stuff
"Mm, I'd like one of them in a pie!"

The third and fourth verses refer to the episode at Lexmark (Chapter 14) and, for the record, I have never worn a truss, it's just that…

22.5 A BOLT FROM THE BLUE

It couldn't get any better, could it? An ordinary year had just become something special. But it did get better. Following hot on the heels of my promotion, I got another pleasant surprise. I was appointed a Visiting Professor at the University of East Anglia, a university where I had been giving a Colour Chemistry course for about ten years (Chapter 21). One of my boyhood dreams was to obtain a PhD and become Dr Peter Gregory, but it didn't happen (Chapter 7). Becoming a professor was beyond my wildest dreams. It's something I had never, ever considered. And now, completely out of the blue, it had happened. Dr Peter Gregory sounded good but Professor Peter Gregory sounded even better. Furthermore, it was a timely appointment, coinciding nicely with the promotion to Company Research Associate. Not only had I reached the highest technical position in Zeneca, a major international chemical company, I was also a professor. Not just Professor Custard but a real Professor. Professor Peter Gregory. It put the icing on the cake. One of my two childhood dreams had more than been fulfilled.

The year of 1995 had been a good one, culminating in three special occasions. However, they weren't the only ones. During my career, there were several more.

23

SPECIAL OCCASIONS

During my life there have been a number of 'Special Occasions' or events. Some of the most important, such as my wedding and the births of our two sons, I have described already (Chapters 8, 9 and 10). Other events, which I consider as special occasions, are described in this chapter. Some occurred at work whilst other, perhaps more important, events took place at home.

23.1 WORK RELATED SPECIAL EVENTS

Built in the 1920s the Research Building, for many years the finest and largest collection of research laboratories in Europe, was starting to show its age and so, in 1990, it underwent extensive refurbishment. Many of the laboratories were updated and the reception area was completely revamped. To recognise these improvements an important dignitary was invited to officially open the rejuvenated Research Building. On Monday, 4 March 1991, the Princess Royal, Princess Anne, came to Blackley to perform the opening ceremony.

23.2 PRINCESS ANNE

It was a cold, blustery day, surely too cold and windy for the Princess Royal to go walkabout and meet the assembled throng. But no, on arrival, Princess Anne's first act was to walk through the village to greet the crowd of onlookers (Image 216), who had waited patiently to catch a glimpse of the Princess Royal, even finding time to stop and chat to several of them.

Princess Anne's (second from left) arrival at Blackley on a
cold and windy day. The building is Hexagon House New.

After entering the Research Building, the Princess Royal listened to four short presentations about the kind of work done at ICI Specialties. Peter Jessop, the managing director of Stahl, told her about the finishing of leather products, Dr Peter Tasker gave her an insight into the work of ICI Mining Chemicals, in particular the pioneering work in the field of solvent extraction of copper, whilst Dr Roger Lloyd spoke about the biodegradable plastic BIOPOL made from renewable resources. BIOPOL was an environmentally friendly, alternative plastic which, by degrading to harmless products, was aimed at reducing the burgeoning litter problem associated with conventional plastics. It was something that ICI was proud of. However, during Roger's presentation, Princess Anne stopped him in his tracks by remarking that such a biodegradable plastic might encourage litter, not reduce it!

The fourth and final presentation was by myself on the hi-tech applications of dyes. These included dyes for ink jet printers, infrared absorbers for security applications and dyes for electronic photography (Images 217 and 218). Indeed, by using the innovative D2T2 process (Chapter 13), we were able to show the Princess Royal photographic prints of her arrival some 30 minutes earlier.

Christine, myself and the Princess Royal as I explained about
ink jet printing and infrared absorbers. Dr Alan Calder, the Research Manager, and Rodney
Brown, the CEO, are in the background.

Not only was Princess Anne a good listener, she was also an astute and knowledgeable lady. She asked some relevant questions and even knew that bank note paper was the only paper that didn't fluoresce! (Chapter 20). Furthermore, at the end of the presentation, she took time to ask both Christine, who'd done some demonstrations, and myself about our careers and our families. She was a shrewd and likeable lady, most unlike the impression that many people have of the Princess Royal.

The day was a great success and we received a complimentary letter from Buckingham Palace thanking us for a fascinating visit (Image 219).

Letter from Buckingham Palace regarding Princess Anne's visit.

23.3 ESSENTIAL CHEMISTRY

"Peter, Alan Calder would like to see you in the Research Conference Room. Would you stop whatever you're doing and see him immediately." It was Pat Walton, Alan's secretary. What had I done now! This was my first thought as I made my way to the conference room. After knocking politely, I entered the room. To my surprise, the large conference room was occupied by just three people. There was Alan of course plus two middle-aged strangers, a man and a woman.

"Ah Peter, come in, come in. This is Jenny Lucas and (I can't remember the man's name). Please sit down and make yourself comfortable. We're just waiting for Nigel (Hughes) to arrive." A few minutes later, after Nigel had made his entrance, Alan asked the two strangers to explain why we had been summoned.

They were from a film production company and wanted to make a video promoting chemistry. It was intended for schoolchildren, especially secondary school children, to get them interested in pursuing chemistry as a career. They had made several award-winning videos in the past and wanted to produce another. Nigel and I had been selected for two reasons. One, because of the nature of our work. And two, because we were the two most senior research chemists. Nigel worked on the revolutionary benzodifuranone red dyes for polyester whilst I worked on dyes for hi-tech applications, particularly D2T2 dyes for electronic photography (Chapter 13). The topics were fine. What they wanted to know was, were we suitable people for a video!

We passed the first test. After talking to us for about an hour, they deemed us to be knowledgeable, likeable and interesting people who should come across well in a video. Next came the sound test. We had to answer some questions into a special tape recorder so they could assess the sound quality of our voices. The results would be known the following day.

Our sound bytes were fine too, so it was full steam ahead. Over the next two weeks we had many meetings with the production team regarding the locations for the shoot, the content, the demonstrations and the length. Although everything went well, there was one proviso. All the shots of Nigel and myself had to be front-on shots. Side shots were banned. Why? Because both Nigel and I were deemed to be too 'portly'.

After its release in 1989 the 'Essential Chemistry' video won its makers yet another award and was very popular with both schoolchildren and the general public. Whether it enticed lots of them into chemistry I don't know, but I hope it did.

23.4 LONDON CALLING

In the spring of 1994 Peter Tasker and myself were invited by the chairman of Zeneca, Sir Tom McKillop, to present our work at a Science Journalists reception at Stanhope Gate in London. It was an event designed to promote some of the most exciting and potentially valuable topics to an invited gathering of the country's top science writers from all the national newspapers. It was an honour to be one of the half-a-dozen or so scientists selected for this prestigious event. I was thrilled to bits.

On the afternoon before the event Peter and I loaded all our equipment into his car in readiness for the trip to London. As we made our way around Marble Arch in the failing dusk light I was so glad that it was Peter who was driving and not me. He said that you weren't a true Londoner (Peter was born in London) until you had driven around Marble Arch at rush hour.

Our hotel for the evening was the upmarket Dorchester on Park Lane, the haunt of the rich and famous. I could see why. It was opulent. After a short stroll down Park Lane, followed by a few drinks in the bar, we retired to bed in readiness for the day ahead.

The Dorchester breakfast was delicious. Served by attentive waiters, the full English breakfast was without doubt one of the best I have ever had. Suitably refreshed, we made our way to the car and drove the short distance to Stanhope Gate to set up our demonstrations.

My demonstrations included water fast dyes for ink jet printers, D2T2 dyes for electronic photography, infrared absorbers for security (Image 220) and the Flag experiment (see Appendix II). The latter was almost a disaster. I had been talking to Peter Doyle, our main board Research Director when, without warning, he tinkled his glass and announced that I would show them an impressive demonstration. Unfortunately, the girl who had been looking after the beaker of hot water had let it cool too much and I had to waffle on for several minutes before it got hot enough to perform the experiment. It was a touch-and-go situation.

Science Journalists' Reception

Christina McGourty of the Daily Telegraph talks to Peter Gregory about infra red dyes used to combat counterfeiting

After the press conference, it was time to pack up and make the long drive home. However, in the summer of that same year I would return to London for an even more daunting experience.

June 4 1994 was 'Parliamentary Links Day'. On this day just four topics from the whole of the UK chemical industry were selected to be presented to Members of Parliament at the Palace of Westminster. Our pioneering work on water fast dyes for ink jet printers was one of them. Not only that, because the title of my presentation was 'Leading the Jet Set', I was to be the first speaker at this prestigious event.

As the audience of eminent parliamentarians began to gather, including several ministers such as Tony Benn,[*] the butterflies in my stomach began to flutter frantically. Two things calmed my nerves. First, the chairman was Prof. Charles Rees, Paul's PhD supervisor who I had come to know during the writing of the book (Chapter 13). And second was the advice received from Cyril Morris many years earlier (Chapter 7). In the event, the presentation prompted a lot of interest and the MPs were reassured that Britain still led the world in some of the emerging hi-tech applications.

On completion of the presentations and the subsequent press interviews, it was time for a pleasant lunch on the Cholmondley Terrace overlooking the River Thames. It was a sweltering day and it was so lovely to down some refreshing cold beer. In his wisdom Paul, who had accompanied me to the event, decided we should walk back to our hotel through Hyde Park, a distance of over two miles. It was fine if you were dressed in shorts and a tee shirt but not in a suit and tie and carrying a heavy briefcase! On reaching the hotel we made straight for the bar. Hot and drenched in sweat, we were gasping for a drink. To my surprise, Paul ordered four bottles of ice cold lager, two each. One was to drink immediately but Paul had an innovative use for the second one. He rolled the ice cold bottle over his face, his hands and even his feet to cool down. I followed suit and it worked a treat.

23.5 AN UNEXPECTED AWARD

To highlight the importance of collaboration between scientists involved in different disciplines the 'Royal Society of Chemistry' presents an annual 'Interdisciplinary Award' to the chemist who has been, in their opinion, successfully involved in many different disciplines. To my utter amazement, in 1996 I became the first industrial chemist to win this award (Image 221).

---

[*] I was surprised that Margaret Thatcher, who was a chemist by training, wasn't in the audience. Perhaps she hadn't recovered from being ousted as Prime Minister.

RSC 'First' for Peter Gregory

Congratulations to Professor Peter Gregory, leader of the inkjet synthetic group of Specialist Colours Research, who has been awarded the "Interdisciplinary Award for 1996" by the Royal Society of Chemistry. This award aims to highlight the importance of collaboration between chemists and scientists working in other fields.

Previous winners of this prestgious award have been from academia, however Peter is the first industrialist to receive this accolade. His studies on the High Technology Applications of Organic Colourants, particularly the chemistry and applications of phthalocyanines, have led to strong collaborations in areas such as electronic printing, security devices, military applications, medicine, toxicology and environment. Peter has worked with scientists as diverse as engineers, laser specialists, biologists and theoretical physicists. A wide range of applications such as dyes for ink-jet printers, infrared absorbers, singlet oxygen generators for anti-cancer treatment and environmentally friendly washing powders have arisen from this work.

Peter Gregory

Professor Gregory (Peter was made a visiting professor of the University of East Anglia in 1995) is expected to present a lecture based on his work to the British Association for the Advancement of Science in 1998.

Article from Hexfiles in May 1997
about the Interdisciplinary Award.

To receive the engraved decanter and a cheque for £500, I had to present a lecture to the Association for the Advancement of British Science. Because most of the work that involved me in other disciplines was based on phthalocyanines, it was deemed appropriate to present the lecture in Edinburgh in 1998 to commemorate the 70th anniversary of the discovery of the phthalocyanines at Grangemouth (Chapter 20). My former boss, Peter Bamfield, who had retired in 1993, presented me with the award (Image 222).

Dr Peter Bamfield (right) presenting me with the engraved
decanter and cheque before my lecture at Edinburgh in 1998.

From time to time the company instigated programmes of staff improvement. For instance, in the 1970s ICI implemented a 'Staff Development Programme' and in the 1980s a 'Management Award' scheme was introduced. In the late nineties Zeneca Specialties introduced a programme aimed at promoting openness, trust, honesty and creative thinking amongst their staff. It was run by an external company using two people but, in order to disseminate the scheme throughout the company, 'Change Agents' were required.

A Change Agent was someone who was experienced in the ways of the company, who was known throughout their respective departments and, above all, who was trusted and respected by the staff. For my sins, I was one of those chosen to represent Research Department.

A Change Agent's role was to assist the two external staff to implement the programme of change. After a brief training session, groups of about twenty staff were gathered together and subjected to the 'change' programme. This involved a number of activities, including the 'Prisoners Dilemma' game, to foster co-operation.

During morning and afternoon 'tea breaks', it was the custom to serve tea (and coffee) and biscuits. Because one aim of the programme was to change the culture, I suggested that, instead of biscuits, hot bacon barmcakes and sausage barmcakes should be served. They were, they went down extremely well with the participants (pardon the pun) and they became the new norm for future tea breaks. At least I had left one useful legacy!

I think most staff derived some benefit from the programme but most benefit was derived by the Change Agents themselves. It taught us how to assess people's needs and desires, listen to and empathise with their concerns, and, last but by no means least, we met and interacted with a great variety of people from across the company. At the end of the year, in recognition of our efforts, a party was held for all the Change Agents at our Grangemouth site near Edinburgh. The location was the Inchyra Grange hotel.

After a three course evening dinner, people from each site were invited to do a 'turn'. Craig Johnston from Grangemouth did a really funny impersonation of Rolf Harris (he probably wouldn't do that now) whilst the two external people Mark Brechtl and his New Zealand colleague (I can't remember his name), a former rugby union player, taught us the 'Haka'. A few months earlier we had divested out textile colours business to BASF so myself and Graham McPherson performed our own version of the 'Haka':-

BASF, BASF

NO, NO

ZENECA, ZENECA

YES, YES

Also, for one of the few times in my life, I won a game of musical chairs.

During one of the early meetings at which Mark Brechtl and his colleague were explaining the change programme to the senior managers and Change Agents, he said he would pick someone at random to stand up and spend five minutes telling the whole group why they were a unique and special person. At this point, every single person in the room shuffled their feet, looked down at the floor to avoid eye contact, and prayed that it wouldn't be them! After a suitable pause he remarked that we could relax, he wasn't going to do it, but said it highlighted how a simple remark could cause such an uncomfortable feeling. He didn't do it but, a year later, someone else did.

23.7 TEAM BUILDING

The Change Agent initiative was followed up by an Away Weekend at Lake Vrnwy in Wales, chosen for its remoteness and isolation. The two day team building course was run several times for groups of about a dozen senior and middle management staff. Peter Walker, a man with a very varied past, was the course leader. After a brief and informal introductory session, it began in earnest with dinner on the Friday evening.

But it was no ordinary dinner. Each person had to team up with a partner and then decide which one of them would wear a blindfold for the entire evening, including eating dinner! It was, said Peter, an excellent way to build trust: the blindfolded person had to rely entirely on his (or her) non-blindfolded companion for everything. Now this may reveal something about my character for I opted immediately not to be blindfolded.* Instead, I preferred to guide and direct my companion, Graham McPherson, throughout the evening. This involved carefully steering him through the crowded bar to the restaurant, much to the bewilderment and amusement of the other hotel guests, who must have wondered what the hell was going on. What made it even more difficult was that no physical contact of any kind was allowed. All the communication had to be verbal. Left a little, right a bit, forward two paces, stop, was the language of the night.

The three course meal took ages. Detailed instructions were needed for everything. Which utensil to pick up, directions on how to pick up the food and then transfer it from the plate to the mouth. It's amazing how extraordinarily difficult it is to explain the simple task of eating to someone who is blindfolded. And, at the same time as delivering all these detailed instructions to your companion, you also had to eat your own food! Not surprisingly, much of our meals were cold by the time they were eaten.

The following morning, at the crack of dawn, it was yoga. I had never done yoga before but I must confess that I enjoyed it immensely. Then, after breakfast,

---

* One reason, I think, was that I didn't fancy going hungry by not getting enough food at dinner

there were a number of different games and activities, each with a powerful message. One activity involved playing musical instruments. It was an activity to take us far away from our comfort zone. I have never liked or found it easy to play a musical instrument. Even the simple recorder baffled me, but I really loved playing the Bongo drums, as did a number of other people. We had a whale of a time.

However, one game in particular had a profound effect on four of us. It was a game where the group was split into three teams of four and each team was given a large bag of individual letters. The aim was simple. Make as many words as possible in a short space of time on the table top, similar in a way to Scrabble. But there was a catch. Once this phase of the game was over, all the letters had to be placed back in the bag and, on a given command, emptied back on to the table. You then had just two minutes to rearrange them back into the words you had assembled before. Having explained the rules, the teams were then allowed a brief planning phase to devise their strategies.

On the first round no team did particularly well. In fact, Peter taunted us by saying that we were the worst of the groups, far worse than our Scottish colleagues from Grangemouth the previous week. Well, that did it. It lit the blue touch paper. We weren't going to be beaten by them!

For the second round ingenious new strategies came into play. The best was that of John Schofield's team who stuck their words together using sellotape before replacing them in the bag. Once the command to empty the bag was given, their words were already assembled.

Peter said we had done much better the second time but it still wasn't good enough. We needed a third attempt. This produced much more innovative solutions. I think we won by simply putting together: WE HAVE PRODUCED AN INFINITE NUMBER OF WORDS. This, Peter said, was what he wanted. To think 'out of the box' and not be constrained by pre-conceived ideas.

Prior to the course we had been instructed to bring with us an item, something special that meant a lot. Why, we didn't know. I took Michael's first pair of walking boots, boots that we had treated with copper to preserve them for eternity. They were the ones we bought in the Lakes when he was small and they held very special memories (Chapter 12).

On Saturday evening we found out why. "In half-an-hour," said Peter, "I want each one of you to stand in front of the group and spend five minutes telling them why you are a unique and special person. You may use the special item you brought along if you wish. Oh, and the session will be recorded on video." It was a bombshell. None of us had expected this. I went back to my room for a quick wash and brush-up and to think of what I was going to say.

Having composed myself, I volunteered to be first. This was partly to 'get it out of the way' and partly because what I intended to say would still be fresh in my mind.

In the event it wasn't too daunting since the audience was supportive knowing that later it would be their turn.

The course came to a close on Sunday with a strange activity. We were instructed to take off our watches and go for a walk for two hours. We could walk anywhere but had to return in precisely two hours time. Furthermore, we had to go alone and were forbidden from speaking to anyone, either fellow course participants or locals. But how, we protested, would we know when two hours had elapsed without a watch? "That's part of the challenge," Peter said. "Now off you go."

It was an interesting spectacle watching people set off on their short journey. People who were extremely confident in a work environment suddenly looked lost and frightened, whereas people who were reserved and unsure at work were confident and jaunty. It was weird.

I found a beautiful spot in a field overlooking the lake and lay down to admire the view. The colours of the flowers, the smell of nature, the song of the birds and the complete absence of any man-made sound was absolute bliss. This, I thought, was what life was all about. After a short stroll along the Lake, where I was spotted relieving myself by a passing Kath Carr, I returned to the hotel.

I was a little early, but not by much. A few others had returned before me and were sat around the conference room chatting quietly. After about two-and-a-quarter hours everyone had returned, everyone except one. John Schofield. Where was he? Two-and-a-half hours passed, then two-and-three-quarter hours and still no John. I think Peter was beginning to get worried when, just before three hours had elapsed, in breezed John eating an ice cream. "Sorry I'm late," he said, "but I fell asleep."

As mentioned earlier, four of us found the message behind the 'Scrabble' game extremely relevant to our work at AstraZeneca.* In ink jet printing a magenta dye having the dual properties of brightness and high light fastness had proved impossible to achieve. Myself, Kath and Maria all thought the same thought: had we been pursuing traditional chemistry too much and not trying outlandish approaches? Ron Swart, a colleague from Biocides, entertained the same thought about his work and the four of us spent many hours discussing what could be done. We approached David Greensmith, the head of the Specialist Colours business, with our idea and, supportive as ever, he agreed to fund a special one-off event, Creativity 2000. He even agreed to give a talk on creativity.

23.8 CREATIVITY 2000

It took many months to organise but the 'Creativity 2000' event, held on the atrium floor of Hexagon House New, proved a big hit.

---

*   In 1999, Zeneca merged with the Swedish pharmaceutical company Astra to form AstraZeneca

It was a full day event hosted by one of the gurus used by our management, namely Brian Weller. However, the main highlight of the day was the keynote guest speaker. Originally, we had tried, unsuccessfully, to lure first Sir Alex Ferguson, the Manchester United manager and then Frank Endacott, the Wigan Rugby League Coach, to speak about motivation. Both were unavailable. However, we found an excellent replacement.

Adam Hart-Davis, the well known TV presenter, agreed to speak about motivation, invention and creativity and gave an enthralling lecture with practical demonstrations. A second guest speaker, an architect, gave an intriguing talk about creative design in construction. There were many other attractions too, including Brian Weller's seminar on 'The Great Masters', and the talk by David Greensmith on creativity. Creativity 2000 proved a popular event.

Later, in 2002, a magenta dye having the desired properties was invented using a completely different type of chemistry. It was developed, manufactured and added to the selling range. Perhaps the two events did inspire us.

23.9 WHO'S WHO LISTING

Another pleasant surprise. In 2001 I was included in the prestigious 'Who's Who in the World' publication in recognition of my contribution to colour chemistry, particularly ink jet printing (Image 223). Such a listing is by invitation only. I was chuffed to bits.

Who's Who listing for Ink Jet research associate

Peter Gregory, a research associate with the Ink Jet Printing Materials business, is to be included in the 19th edition of the prestigious publication 'Who's Who in the World'.

Peter, who has been with the company for over 30 years, is a recognised authority on the subject of colour chemistry. He has given presentations at conferences around the world and published articles and books on the subject.

Inclusion in Who's Who is by invitation of the publishers and is in recognition of major achievements in an individual's particular field of endeavour.

Peter Gregory

Article in the Avecia News, October 2001.

385

23.10 A RELUCTANT EXPERT

Because of my involvement and interest in the toxicology of dyes, particularly the relationship between the chemical structure of a dye and its mutagenic and carcinogenic (cancer-causing) effects, I was asked by the company to be their 'Expert' on a number of litigation cases. These cases were brought against the company by the wives of former workers of ICI who had died, or were dying, from cancer. They believed, rightly or wrongly, that the disease was a direct result of their husband's exposure to certain chemicals during their time at ICI.

In the 1950s it was recognised for the first time that too much exposure to chemicals such as benzidine and β-naphthylamine, two of the building blocks of a number of important dyes, did indeed cause cancer of the bladder* and it was on this basis that the litigation cases were brought.

Of the four cases that I was involved in, three were dropped, mainly because of the evidence I provided. Despite convincing evidence against them, the fourth case was going to court. On the morning of the trial, myself and Sue Bostock, the wife of Steve Bostock, my Experimental Chemist in the 1970s, travelled to London to meet our legal team at the courtroom. (Sue had started her career in the Research Department but did a law degree and moved into our Legal Department.) Sat in a briefing room, our barrister was giving us our final instructions when, without any warning, we received a message from their counsel. At the very last minute, they had decided to drop the case.

At the time I thought it was brinkmanship in the extreme, but later I felt terrible. Although we had 'won' all four cases and saved the company a considerable amount of money, it left me with a bad taste. I had this mental picture of some kindly old ladies struggling along with little money and just wanting a small amount of compensation to ease their struggles in the twilight of their lives. And it was me who had helped to deny them this small comfort. I was only doing my duty for the company but this clash of conscience always troubled me.

Although I didn't have to testify in the courtroom on this occasion, I would have to do so at a later date.

23.11 DUTY CASE

This is what Avecia** called it. The 'Duty Case'.

---

* As soon as this was known, all responsible dye manufacturers banned the use of benzidine and β-naphthylamine and all the dyes based on them, but it was too late for some workers

** In 1999, shortly after the merger of Zeneca with Astra, the board of Zeneca Specialties decided to split from AstraZeneca and become a new, independent company, Avecia

As mentioned in Chapter 14, our company was the world leader in supplying dyes and inks to the ink jet printer market. Most of our products were shipped overseas, especially to the USA and Japan, where the leading ink jet printer companies, such as Hewlett Packard, Canon and Seiko Epson, were located.

We rarely supplied the finished ink, the final ink that went into the print cartridges. The printer manufacturers themselves wanted to 'customise' the final ink, adding whatever special ingredients they desired. However, another important reason was cost. The main component of any ink jet ink is water,* plain simple water, and it would be foolish in the extreme to spend a lot of money shipping water half-way round the world. Instead, we shipped a 'dye-based ink', a highly concentrated form of the ink containing mainly dye plus a little water and, optionally, other additives.

The US Customs classified these 'dye-based inks' as conventional, bog standard 'dyes' mainly, I think, because imported 'dyes' attracted a much higher import duty than a 'finished ink'. This practice was costing the company millions of dollars a year in import duty. It was a lot of money and we felt that not only was it unfair, it was just plain wrong. Accordingly, in the late nineties, Avecia launched a legal action against the US Customs Office to have their imported products classified as 'dye-based inks' rather than 'dyes'.

I was asked to write a short document explaining why our products were indeed 'dye-based inks' and not dyes, including tests we could perform to demonstrate this. I did and believed that it would signal the end of my involvement with the case since Harold Freeman, Ciba-Geigy Professor of Dyestuffs Chemistry, North Carolina State University, had been 'hired' by the company as an independent 'Expert Witness' to provide the necessary evidence.

I was wrong. Over the next few years our legal team from the USA made frequent visits to Blackley during which I was identified as a key witness. However, the wheels of justice turn very slowly and, a few years later, in 2002, I retired.

Suddenly, out of the blue, a date had been arranged for the trial. But Vera and I had already booked two long weekends away, the first in Bristol and the second in Glasgow, using her Tesco vouchers before they expired, and the date clashed with the Glasgow weekend. Fortunately, the judge was kind enough to reschedule my testimony from the Monday to the Wednesday, thereby allowing us to enjoy our two short breaks.

The man's fart reverberated like a thunderclap around the bowels of SS Great Britain, the world's first metal steamship. Designed by the legendary Isambard Kingdom Brunel, it lay moored in Bristol harbour. Vera and I were standing on the

---

*   Except Tektronix's hot melt ink jet inks

387

viewing platform overlooking the ship's engines when the solitary man at the other end unleashed this deafening sound. Then, nonchalant as ever, he simply turned around and continued on his way. On reaching the spot where he had farted, the stench from his bodily expulsion of foul smelling gas lingered in the still air. It was bad but it produced something so funny that Vera and I found it nigh impossible not to break out in fits of laughter. A few feet opposite the viewing platform was an authentic replication of a crewman's cabin, a small, cramped space. Inside, we heard an American family extol the virtues of the authentication. "Gee honey," the man said, "they've even recreated the smell." Once out of earshot, we broke out in fits of uncontrollable laughter. If only they knew.

After arriving back from our weekend in Glasgow, where we visited the stunning Culzeath Castle, an abode of General Eisenhower in the Second World War, I duly flew out to New York on that Tuesday in the middle of May 2006. The company had booked me, along with the rest of our team, into the expensive Hilton Hotel, located adjacent to Ground Zero in the financial sector of the city. When I saw the tariff of $375.00, I assumed it was for the entire three night stay. Silly me. It was per night and breakfast was extra! After a leisurely swim in the hotel pool, followed by a few (expensive) beers, I met my colleagues and in the evening we went for a lovely meal on Pier 17.* Ideally, a good nights sleep was needed in readiness for the ordeal the following day but, as usual, I didn't get one.

Jet lag was the main culprit but I never slept well on my first night away from home.

The following morning myself, Ilesh Bidd, my former manager, and our legal team set off on the short walk to the Supreme Courts of Justice. Not being allowed in the courtroom before my testimony gave me the chance to read the lengthy proceedings of the previous day, and to meet the US prosecutor. Eventually, it was my turn to testify. After the usual formalities of being sworn in I was questioned by our own attorney. No problem there. Then came the difficult part. I was cross-examined by their prosecutor. They tried usual tricks to unsettle me, but I more than held my own. After a gruelling three hours or so, it was time to stand down. "They didn't lay a finger on you," said one of our legal team. Our attorney was also very pleased. He remarked that we had all performed very well and 'were home and dry'. Time would tell…

The verdict was a long time coming. It took about nine months for the judge to deliver his verdict but when he did it was worth the wait. Our attorney had been right. The judgement went in our favour. We had won the case.

---

* My companion, Ilesh Bidd, said it was Pier 42, which had some unfortunate consequences later (Section 27.4)

23.12 HOME RELATED SPECIAL OCCASIONS

As mentioned earlier, some of these have been described already and others, such as our sons' weddings, are described in Chapter 26. The rest are covered here.

23.13 ANDREW AND MICHAEL'S 21ST BIRTHDAYS

Eleventh of April 1995. How time flies. The 21 years from Andrew's birth on the 11 April 1974 (Chapter 9) to his 'coming of age' had passed so quickly. Although we had made a fuss at his 18th birthday, it was his 21st that was really celebrated. In addition to some wonderful presents and a birthday cake in the shape of a Wigan rugby jersey (Image 224), his 21st birthday was celebrated with a meal at the Mawdesley Eating House.

It was an evening meal to which all the family were invited. The setting was superb (Image 225) and, after pre-dinner drinks (Image 226) and much conversation, everyone tucked in to a delicious three-course dinner. After further drinks and laughter, the evening ended with some tired but happy people (Image 227).

Because it fell slap bang in the middle of the holiday season, Michael was often away on holiday when it was his birthday. And so it was on his 21st birthday. On 4 July 1999 he was in Ibiza with his friends, two of whom would be his best men at his wedding (Chapter 26).

Andrew with his cards and
Wigan birthday cake 1995.

389

Andrew (3rd from left) enjoying dinner with his relatives.
Left to right: Michael, Me, Andrew, June, Stuart, Ray. On the
other side of the table Vera is obscuring Elaine and Keith.

Doris (Vera's mother) and Michael
enjoying a pre-dinner drink.

A tired Ray with two equally tired
little girls, Michelle and Natalie.

By terminating his PhD studies at Lancaster University after just 12 months (Chapter 19), Andrew was concerned that this action would adversely affect his job prospects. However, on the plus side, his career's advisor at the university said it could be seen as a positive decision, a difficult decision taken bravely to end an unsatisfactory course.

Andrew's first action in that winter of 1998 was to embark on a 'Computeach' computer course, at which he excelled, and then to begin the unenviable task of applying for a job. He wrote letters to dozens of companies, usually in IT (Information Technology), and every morning he would sit at the bottom of the stairs waiting for the postman. It was heart-breaking watching his face as he opened the letters from the few companies courteous enough to reply. Sorry, we have no vacancies at present, was the usual response.

After a while he became disillusioned, saying that, "Nobody wants me." Every time I took Sam for his walk in the morning (Chapter 17), I just wished that someone would give him a chance. To offer him that first step on the ladder of employment.

Then, one evening, the phone rang. Andrew picked up the receiver and said hello. Suddenly, his face lit up. DMR, a Canadian company with a base in Manchester, were inviting him to attend an interview. He was elated and so were we. The interview was to be held in a hotel in Derby at 9-00 a.m. in a few days time. To ensure that he was there on time, fresh-faced and bushy-tailed, we decided that the safest option was for him to stay at the hotel on the night prior to his interview. And so, on that evening, Vera and I drove him to Derby, hoping with all our hearts that he would do well.

For the next few days after the interview Andrew, uncharacteristically it might be said, was up early waiting for either the telephone to ring or the post to be delivered. He didn't have to wait long. One morning the phone rang. Trembling with excitement and anticipation, he dashed to answer it. Within seconds, an enormous smile spread across his face and he literally jumped into the air. "They've offered me a job," he yelled. "At last somebody wants me."

DMR, like many other IT companies, were recruiting in readiness for Year 2000. All the doom mongers were predicting horrific events at the turn of the millennium, a veritable apocalypse. The reason, they argued, was that all the computers would fail as the 20th century changed into the 21st century. They would be unable to cope with such a massive change. Planes would fall out of the sky, cars would cease to function, household appliances would fail and companies and governments would be paralysed because their communication networks wouldn't work. The list was endless. Anything that involved a computer would fail. If any or part of this happened, IT companies would be in great demand.

In the event, very little of the above actually happened. Nonetheless, it helped Andrew and many others to get their foot on that first rung of the employment ladder. Andrew spent eighteen happy months at DMR (Plate 228), including a six week stint in Canada, a country he became very fond of. He also became firm friends with a work colleague, Keith McKnight, a friendship that has lasted to the present day. Indeed, Keith was Andrew's best man at his wedding (Chapter 26).

Like many in the IT industry, Andrew changes jobs frequently. His longest spell at a job was at Alliance Publicity Services in Stockport, where he became the IT Development Manager. After a short stint at Top Cash Back at the Middlebrook Retail Park in Bolton, only two miles from where he lived in Westhoughton,* he now (2020) works in a start-up company in St Helens. He loves new challenges.

A smart looking Andrew at one of
DMR's Christmas parties.

23.15 MICHAEL'S FIRST JOB

After obtaining his physics degree from Manchester University in 1999 Michael decided to 'chill out' for a few months before looking for gainful employment. This reflected his character: he is an extremely laid back individual who is calmness personified. He never, ever gets angry or loses his temper.

As boredom began to rear its ugly head, he decided to accept an offer from Frank Hinks, the father of his two best friends, John and Phil, to accept a temporary job

---

*   In 2015, Andrew, Helen and their two cats moved from a modern detached house in Westhoughton first to a large 1930s semi-detached house in Standish and 18 months later to a large, new build home in the same area (Chapter 28). They later sold their house in Westhoughton.

at his business in Wigan. Frank owned and ran a successful tyre business, Best Way Tyres,* located on the Lamberhead Industrial Estate. Their main business was re-treading the tyres of industrial vehicles, such as vans, lorries and buses. Ostensibly, the job was for six to twelve months but Michael enjoyed it so much and did so well (he became the Factory Manager) that he worked there until the business closed in 2017. He then changed career and became a postman, carrying on the tradition started by my grandad (Chapter 1) and continued by my cousin Brian. A degree in physics may seem a strange qualification for a manager in a tyre business and a postman, but a degree in a science subject helps you to think clearly and logically and to solve problems, useful attributes for any job. Indeed, a degree in chemistry didn't do Margaret Thatcher any harm.

23.16 SILVER WEDDING ANNIVERSARY

On July 12 1994, the date of our 25th wedding anniversary, I was away on company business in Japan. It was something I couldn't get out of. It didn't seem fair that on one of the most important dates of our life Vera and I were unable to share it together. It wasn't the first time either. Company commitments meant that I had missed other important events, such as birthdays, not only of Vera and myself, but also our children.

Although the rewards of being a senior member of staff were very good, the pressures and sacrifices that you had to make were considerable. Mainly because of this, a fair proportion of the marriages of the senior staff ended in divorce. I certainly didn't want to add to this statistic and tried my best to avoid being away on special occasions but sometimes it was just unavoidable.

The previous year I had attended a conference in Antwerp. It is a lovely city with stunning architecture (Image 229), beautiful platz's (squares) and stylish shopping streets (Image 230). My hotel was the five star Hilton Hotel on the 'Grunplatz' (Grand Square), right in the centre of the city. It was a luxury hotel in a superb location and it was here that I booked a five day holiday for Vera and me to celebrate our silver wedding. I know it wasn't the same as being away on the exact day but it was still a beautiful place to go. In the event, we had a good time. The weather was kind, the food delicious and the people friendly. Indeed, the weather was so good that on most occasions we ate al fresco, including our breakfast at the hotel.

One evening there was a minor mishap when a waiter accidentally spilt some soup on Vera's dress. He was so apologetic. On another occasion, we were sauntering along the main shopping street when we decided to stop for a coffee. As we sipped

---

* The business changed hands in 2012 to Direct Tyre Sales. It closed in 2017.

our coffee in the in the warm summer sunshine, I heard the unmistakable sound of a familiar voice. "I'm sure I know that voice," I said to Vera, and turned around to locate its source. Sat a few tables away was Keith Denham, a colleague from my days working in Biocides. We recognised each other instantly. Keith, who had retired a few years earlier, and his wife were visiting their son at Ghent University. It's such a small world.

Antwerp's stunning Town Hall,
located on the Grunplatz.

One of the many beautiful squares in Antwerp (left).
And a stylish shopping street (right).

23.17 GOLDEN WEDDING ANNIVERSARY

No, it wasn't ours but that of my Auntie Lily and Uncle Jack. In 1995 they celebrated 50 years of marriage (Image 231), a considerable achievement in today's world. Normally, we would have held a lavish celebration at our house but, because of the work on the conservatory and utility room (Chapter 22), our house was in no fit state to host such an event. Therefore, at the behest of Lily and Jack, their fiftieth wedding anniversary was celebrated at the Balcarres Arms in Haigh.

It was a mixed occasion. The buffet wasn't that great but the amount of beer and wine imbibed by the assembled throng compensated for that shortcoming. Jack presented Lily with an eternity ring (Image 231), and everyone enjoyed themselves (Images 232 and 233). However, on looking at the photographs now, both Lily and Jack appeared old and frail.

Lily and Jack on the occasion of their Golden Wedding anniversary s
howing Jack placing an eternity ring on Lily's finger

23.18 RUBY WEDDING ANNIVERSARY

Two thousand and nine was a special year. It was our fortieth year of being married, our ruby wedding year. Vera and I began courting when I was 17 (Chapter 3) so it meant I had spent 46 years of my life with Vera, 46 years out of a total of 63.* It's a sobering thought to have shared the majority of my life with just one woman, yet I wouldn't swap those years for anything. Like most couples we have had our ups and downs, but we have had far more of the former than the latter. Also, we have raised two wonderful sons. Two sons of which we are very proud. And a lovely grandson (Chapter 29). My second dream was almost complete.

---

* Now (2020), aged 74, I have spent 57 years of my life with Vera

William offering an undecided Jean a sandwich.

Jack, Andrew and half of Valerie sharing a joke (left).
And Me and Michael (right).

As was the norm on these special occasions, Vera and I had intended to celebrate our Ruby Wedding Anniversary with a meal for our family and friends, but it wasn't easy. The close proximity of Andrew and Helen's wedding anniversary on 15 July, just three days after ours, the summer holiday season, and particularly Michael and Kathryn's imminent wedding on 8 August (Chapter 26), meant that it proved impossible to find a date that suited everyone. Then we had a brainwave. Everyone we intended to invite would be at Michael and Kathryn's wedding so it seemed natural to kill two birds with one stone and have the meal then. It was a great idea since all the guests were staying for the weekend and so, on Friday 7 August we celebrated our Ruby Wedding Anniversary with a delicious meal at the Aspinall Arms at Mitton, adjacent to the wedding venue of Mitton Hall. I even acted as a waiter, taking the dessert board round to each table in turn (Image 234).

A man with a menu.

The only minor blot on the weekend occurred that evening. Vera picked at her food, obviously not enjoying it. "Is there something wrong?" I asked.

"No," she replied. "I'm just not very hungry." But something was wrong. I had left for the Aspinall Arms to greet our guests arriving by minibus from the Swan Hotel and, whilst getting ready in our room, Vera had lost the diamond encrusted heart that I had bought her for our Ruby Wedding Anniversary. It was losing this special gift that caused her loss of appetite. She was utterly distraught. Only after Helen, with her keen young eyes, discovered the missing item on the bathroom floor later that evening, did Vera tell me what had been wrong. Later, John Schofield said that I was the only one who didn't know!

A few days after the wedding Vera and I had a short holiday, both to recuperate from the stresses of the wedding but, more importantly, to celebrate further our ruby wedding anniversary. We stayed at the Marriott hotel in Gosforth to explore a part of the country we had rarely visited before, the towns and coast of North Yorkshire and Northumbria.

We chose a Marriott hotel because earlier in the year we stayed at the Marriott in Huntingdon to explore Cambridge. It was a lovely hotel and the dining room served traditional 'English' food that we both liked and that was reasonably priced. For instance, on the first evening I enjoyed soup, an Aberdeen Angus cheeseburger with fries, and an ice cream, whilst Vera had fish, chips and mushy peas. We also enjoyed one of our best days ever, punting on a crowded River Cam in glorious sunshine.

After suffering a major delay on the way up to Gosforth because of a serious accident on the motorway, we arrived at the hotel about tea-time, tired and weary. Therefore, we decided to eat in the hotel restaurant and were advised by the receptionist to book a table since, he said, it got very busy on Saturday night. We did and, at 7-30 p.m. were escorted to our table. The attentive waiters (there were many) brought the menu and retired whilst we decided what to have. But there was no sign of a cheeseburger or fish and chips. It was a special menu for the Saturday evening 'Dinner Dance' to live music! And it wasn't cheap. At £32.50 per person, plus a bottle of wine, the evening cost a cool £87.00, a far cry from what we paid at Huntingdon. Still, it was a special occasion and we made the most of it.

On Sunday we drove to the small seaside hamlet of Craster and walked along the scenic coast to the atmospheric ruins of Dunstanburgh Castle. Then it was off to Alnwick Castle, better known as Hogwarts School of Magic and Wizardry in the Harry Potter films, where we enjoyed a coffee and cake. Before departing Alnwick, we took a (free to pensioners) tour on the open top bus, marvelling at the beautiful scenery and the fact that the lady of the castle spent a cool £3.8 million on a tree house, making it the most expensive tree house in the world. Apparently, so far she has spent an amazing £43 million on the Castle Gardens. Her husband has told her that any future spending must be financed from her round-the-world lecture tours.

Beamish museum took all of Monday and on Tuesday, on the way home, we spent half-a-day at Durham, where we visited Durham Cathedral. The senior tour guide, a knowledgeable elderly lady, took our tour and gave an enthralling account of its history. As we were leaving the cathedral a succession of vintage cars arrived, reminding us of 'Hughie', the car that would transport first Michael, and then Vera and myself, to the church for his wedding. We half expected David, the enthusiastic owner of 'Hughie', to appear, but he didn't. However, he most certainly did at Michael's wedding (Chapter 26).

23.19 FANCY DRESS PARTIES

In addition to the above 'Special Events' we also attended several fancy dress parties. These were invariably organised by Ray, usually in the function room of his local pub, The Squires. They were fun events helped in no small measure by everyone dressing up. I made a rather credible Sherlock Holmes whilst Vera looked lovely as the Queen of Hearts (Image 235). Michael went for the medieval look as a knight in shining armour and Kathryn made a stunning Cleopatra (Image 236). Andrew and Helen opted for something completely different and made a most realistic pair of pirates (Image 237).

Me as Sherlock Holmes (left) and Vera as
the Queen of Hearts (right).

Michael as a knight (left) and
Kathryn as Cleopatra (right).

Andrew and Helen as pirates.

However. in addition to the good things in life, there are also the bad. As described in the next chapter, the last decade of the twentieth century fitted that to a tee. It was a very bad ten years.

24

A DECADE OF DEATHS

The final chapters focus on the two extremes of human emotions. The deep sadness, despair and feeling of utter hopelessness at the loss of a loved one and the sheer exuberance, joy and happiness at the wedding of a son or close relative. And, of course, the birth of your first grandson. There is also a chapter on house moves and extensions. In this chapter we'll discuss the deaths of my family and relatives.

The untimely and premature death of my mother in 1988 (Chapter 15) followed by Vera's dad George in 1991 (Chapter 16) heralded a decade in which an entire generation of my family was wiped out. An entire generation obliterated whilst I was still a relatively young man. It was something that was difficult to come to terms with, especially since most other people of my age still had their parents.

24.1 BRIAN'S DAD

The first to go was Uncle Jack, Brian's dad. It was Friday 2 March in the winter of 1991 and we had been invited to William and Jean's bungalow in Blackrod to celebrate the Golden Wedding of his mother and dad, Uncle Evan and Auntie Nellie (Image 239, page 406). All the close family were present and the atmosphere was cosy and convivial. As is the norm on these occasions, there was a lot of catching up to do. How have you been? How are your children? What are they doing? Have you had your holidays? How's so and so? Conversation filled the room. The drink flowed freely too and the buffet went down a treat. After a short interlude, during which Evan gave a short, yet sweet, speech the drinking and talking resumed in earnest. Brian's dad had claimed a warm and comfortable spot beside the fire. He chatted merrily to everyone and, with a glass of whisky in his hand and the rest of the bottle beside his chair, was in extremely good spirits (Image 238). He even led the singing later in the evening! And he was still there in the early hours of the morning when Vera and I left to take Auntie Lily and her husband home.

The following morning Vera and I, together with Andrew and Michael, headed off to Auntie Lily's. As usual, Sam was the first out of the car, dashing like a demented dervish to their front gate, followed closely by our children. As Vera and I brought up the rear, Uncle Jack was waiting at the gate. "Jack's dead," he said. Both Vera and I stared at him blankly. "Brian's dad is dead. He died last night after the party."

We were speechless. "Are you sure?" I asked. "He seemed fine when we left."

"Yes, I'm sure," he replied, and went inside.

Brian's dad with his glass of whisky at Evan and Nellie's
Golden Wedding. A few hours later, he was dead.

Apparently, when it was time for Jack to leave, William and Brian had to carry him to the car because they thought he was drunk. "It was like carrying a dead weight," William remarked later. On reaching his house, they had to repeat the feat and carry him from the car to the sofa.

He was still there in the morning, cold and lifeless. The doctor pronounced him dead and said that he had died sometime earlier, probably in the early hours of the morning. William's words had been prophetic.

The funeral, at St David's church in Haigh, was barely two weeks after that of Vera's dad, George, and I remember the vicar putting a consoling hand on my shoulder as I had attended both. Indeed, Brian's dad is buried in the adjacent grave to George in the churchyard.

When I mentioned the shock of Jack's death to Auntie Lily, she said a strange yet, on reflection, a perfectly understandable thing for an elderly person. "Well, at least he's got it over with." The elderly may fear death but the actual process of dying terrifies them far more.

24.2 BILL

Jack's wake was held at Brian and Valerie's house in Aspull. As expected, it was a sombre occasion. Eventually, the conversation got round to the topic of death, particularly who would be the next one to go. "You needn't worry about that," said Bill. "I'll be the next to go. And it won't be long either." I thought it was a strange and morbid thing to say but, as it turned out, it was accurate. A little later, Uncle Bill died.

Alan, my cousin, said that whilst on his death bed at home, Bill had severe delusions and hallucinations. He would sit up in bed and ramble on and on, talking, he said, to his long dead son, Peter. "He's there, sat at the bottom of the bed as clear as daylight. Why can't you see him!" It's weird what visions people close to death conjure up.

Auntie Nellie didn't conjure up any weird hallucinations but, immediately before her death in the spring of 1994, she did exhibit some strange behaviour.

Auntie Nellie was a small, frail looking but wiry woman. A quiet, unassuming woman who wouldn't hurt a fly. A woman who I never once heard raise her voice. But a woman who, in her younger days, hadn't enjoyed the best of health.

As a young boy I remember visiting their house in St John's Road to play with William. For what seemed like an eternity (but was probably no more than several weeks), Auntie Nellie would be lying in her bed in the living room, sandwiched between the fire and the back window. The exact nature of her illness eludes me but she did have a course of electric shock treatment and I felt really sorry for her.

Auntie Nellie was very friendly with my Auntie Lily. In fact, Lily was her best friend. When their husbands went to the Labour Club, she would bring William to my Auntie Lily's for the evening so we could play together. In summer, they took us for walks around Toddington and Haigh Hall and in winter we stayed in and played games or watched television (Chapter 2).

A few days before she died Auntie Nellie developed a cough. A chesty type of cough that seemed to have settled on her lungs. On one of their regular visits, William and Jean found Nellie sat on the sofa accounting her money. "I owe Lily ten pounds three shillings and sixpence, and Annie three pounds two shillings and tuppence," she muttered, and was writing it down on a scrap of paper. William asked her what she was doing. She had never behaved in this way before and it puzzled him. Like most people would, he dismissed it as the quirk of an old person.

Before returning home, William called at the chemist to get some medication for his mother's cough. After dropping it off, he drove the short distance to his bungalow in Blackrod. As he stepped through the door, the phone rang. It was his dad. Would he come quickly. His mother had collapsed on the kitchen floor whilst making a brew and he needed help. But it was too late. Auntie Nellie had died within seconds from a pulmonary embolism, a blood clot on the lungs.

Obviously, Auntie Nellie's accounting heralded something more serious than the quirk of an old person. Somehow, it's as though she knew what was coming and was attempting to tidy up her affairs beforehand.

Although the death of his mother in the April of 1994 came as a shock to William, the death of his dad some six weeks later did not.

24.4 EVAN

Evan, in his younger days, was a fairly active man who loved to walk. Every Sunday morning he took a young William and me through Haigh Hall plantations to Wigan (Chapter 2) and, for a while, he was the rent collector for Aspull and Haigh. His love of walking provided plenty of exercise but, as he got older, long walks became a distant memory. Instead, he enjoyed a more sedate game of bowls at the Aspull Civic Centre.

Evan's outdoor activities were tempered by his drinking and smoking. In common with most people of his generation, Uncle Evan liked his pint of beer. Initially, he drank at Aspull Labour Club with Brian's dad and Uncle Jack and then, when the fortunes of Aspull Labour Club declined, it was at the Victoria, a local pub in Haigh. Over the years, the drinking took its toll.

Some five years before his death the doctor had informed William that his dad had cirrhosis of the liver. It was at an advanced stage and the prognosis wasn't good. Uncle Evan had, the doctors said, just 12 to 18 months to live. This placed William and Jean in a difficult position. Should they tell Evan or should they keep quiet and let nature take its course? After much deliberation, they chose not to tell him but warned him that if he didn't stop drinking he would die. To their utmost surprise, he stopped drinking alcohol and began drinking orange cordial, which was unbelievable considering what he used to drink. When William asked his dad if he regretted his lifestyle, he said, "No. I would do the same all over again."

About a year later, and just three weeks before the Golden Wedding (Image 239), the consultant informed William he didn't think his dad would survive that long and they should use the food and drink for his funeral, not his Golden Wedding! But the doctors were wrong. Very wrong. For whatever reason, Uncle Evan lived for another three-and-a-half years. Another three-and-a-half years to carry on enjoying his orange cordial, his pipe and his bowls. Indeed, he would probably have lived even longer but for Nellie's untimely death. The sudden and unexpected loss of his wife was the last straw. It sapped his will to live. His resolve crumbled. He literally gave up.

Nellie and Evan cutting the
cake at their Golden Wedding.

One day in June 1994, Jean arrived at his house to find it empty. Where was he? Where had he gone? Matches were scattered on the rug and on the kitchen floor. This was most unusual. It wasn't right. Frantic with worry, Jean rang the local hospitals, but no one of Evan's name had been admitted. Finally, she rang the police.

They took the fact that Evan was missing very seriously and said they would pursue their investigations with a matter of urgency. Then, just as the police were leaving, a man came to the door. "Are you looking for Evan?" he asked.

"Yes, we are. Do you know where he is?"

"Well, there was an ambulance here at 6-30 this morning. I presume it took him to hospital." Bewildered, Jean rang Wigan Infirmary again. This time, they confirmed that Evan had indeed been admitted. Admitted almost thirteen hours earlier. For fully thirteen hours they hadn't had the decency to contact his next of kin. It was appalling.

A few days later, Evan died. Losing both his parents in the space of six weeks had a profound effect on William. I'm not sure that he ever got over it fully.

24.5 LILY

I had always thought of my Auntie Lily as one of those people who was indestructible. Someone who would be around forever. Someone who would withstand the ravages of time. Sadly, I was wrong.

The first sign that something was amiss occurred when Vera and I took Lily and Jack to the Lakes to show them our new holiday home in the autumn of 1999 (Chapter 18). They were so excited. "It's a beautiful caravan in a lovely location," she said. Leaving Jack in the caravan (he found walking difficult by that time), we set off to take Lily on a short tour of the site. To my surprise, after walking only a few hundred yards, she asked if we could return to the caravan as she was out of breath. This was most unlike her. Unfortunately, it was a harbinger of things to come.

The years of looking after Jack, especially after he had become immobile, had taken their toll. It was hard work for Lily, particularly as they still lived in their two-up, two-down terraced house. Every night she literally had to push Jack up the stairs. Then, one night, the roles were reversed. Lily could hardly breathe and it was Jack who had to push her up the stairs.

The following day we received a call from Jack saying that Lily had been taken to Wigan Hospital and could we take him to visit her in the evening. We duly picked him up and, a little later, entered the ward where she was staying. I couldn't believe my eyes! This wasn't the Lily I knew. Her face was so grey and ashen and her skin so pallid and wrinkled that I hardly recognised her. However, she recognised us and made an attempt at conversation, but it was a struggle. "Thanks for coming, love," were her final words as we departed. What she didn't add was, "See you tomorrow."

As we were leaving the ward, the nurse beckoned me to one side and asked for my telephone number. "Just a precaution in case we need to get in touch with you," she said. It wasn't a good omen.

After we had dropped off Jack at his house and seen that he was alright, I remarked to Vera on the way home in the car that looking at Lily in the hospital was like looking at a dead person.

It was a prophetic pronouncement. The following morning the phone rang. It was the nurse at the hospital. Would we come quickly, my auntie was gravely ill. There wasn't much time.

We collected Jack on the way and sped to the hospital. It was in vain. On arrival, Lily was dead. She had died a few minutes earlier from a heart attack. Her still warm body lay where it had lain the previous night, in the same hospital bed. It wasn't a pretty sight. One of her naked breasts lay outside her nightgown, visible to all and sundry. It was so undignified. I was angry that the hospital staff had let us see her in such a state. The very least they could have done was to make her 'presentable' at such a difficult and emotional time.

Neither Lily nor Jack had talked about their funeral arrangements but we were surprised when Jack remarked that Lily had asked to be cremated. All of our family had been buried, not cremated. This was bucking the trend. But, if it was her wish, we had no alternative but to honour it. And honour it we did.

The funeral service was held at Overdale Crematorium in Bolton. The vicar had asked me to prepare something personal to say about Lily, which was fine, but also to present him with a list of people who had helped her in her final years, which was not. I resisted but, in the end, his persistence paid off and I reluctantly handed him what he wanted. It was a mistake. The worst fears of Vera came true. As he read out the list at the service, I realised that two of the most important people had been omitted. Two of the people sat near us in the congregation. Tom and Linda. I was mortified. There was nothing I could do except offer my profound apologies to the couple concerned. It was a salutary lesson. I won't do it again.

24.6 DORIS

After her husband George's sudden death at a rugby match (Chapter 16), Doris continued to live at the same house in Manor Grove. It was understandable. It was a large, spacious house in a fine location. It was something she had become used to. It was her home.

With one of her daughters visiting each day and with a friendly neighbour in Lynette, everything was fine, or at least as fine as it could be after the death of her lifelong partner. Suddenly, a single event changed everything.

One night, asleep in bed, a noise awoke her. A strange noise from downstairs. A noise like someone trying to force their way into the house through a door. It was the dead of night and pitch black. Trembling with fear and trepidation, she switched on as many lights as possible, hoping against hope that this would cause any intruder to leave. Fortunately, it did.

The following morning Vera and her sisters found that someone had indeed tried to force open the downstairs back door. They even found the implement used, a scewdriver, discarded at the bottom of the garden. The police were informed and, some time later, the offender apprehended. It was the son of a neighbour, a family to whom Doris had been kind and helped considerably, and this was the way they repaid her! It beggared belief that such kindness should be repaid with such a callous act. In due course the son was put on trial for attempted burglary and jailed. But it was too late. His cowardly act had unsettled Doris so much that she felt too vulnerable being all alone in that house and it was decided to move her into sheltered accommodation at nearby Hollydene.

We had mixed feelings about the move. Doris and her family had always lived in a house with a garden and were used to the freedom and independence this allowed. They had their own front (and back) doors, their own living room, their own kitchen, their own bedrooms and their own bathroom. The flat she moved in had few of these. It was a small bedsit with a tiny attached kitchen and no bathroom or toilet. These were communal. Worse still, it meant that while Doris was having a bath, anyone could walk in and use the toilets. It was a far cry from what she had been used to but it's where she had opted to go.

The flat was given a complete makeover. After gutting it, Keith, Ray and myself redecorated it completely, wallpapering and painting the entire flat. New carpets and curtains were fitted and all new furniture bought. We tried to make it as homely as possible. It was the least we could do. But, despite our best efforts, whenever Vera visited Hollydene, it filled her with a feeling of dread and foreboding. She hated the place.

Her three daughters took it in turns to visit their mother, sharing the duties so that one of them visited each day. As mentioned earlier, this proved hard on Vera. Not only had she her own family to care for, but she also had to visit Jack virtually every day and her own mother three times a week. It was a very demanding schedule and it took a special person to do it.

Doris became very frail. She had always been a slim woman (Image 240) but she seemed to wither away. On the occasions that Vera helped her mother to bathe, she remarked to me later she was so thin you could see all her bones. It was extremely distressing for both Vera and her sisters to see their mother in such a state. She seemed to lose her appetite and, to compound it all, suffered a fall and hurt her back. Gradually, she deteriorated and, in the February of 2002, was taken to Leigh Hospital.

Doris and George at Elaine
and Keith's Wedding.

One evening, when I visited with Vera, Doris was propped up in bed on a pillow. She was so gaunt and emaciated. Although we talked to her, she seemed far away, in a world of her own. The nurse brought her a light meal, saying that she had to eat to keep her strength up. Surreptitiously, Doris took the piece of chicken from the plate and, with what little strength she had left, slid it into the pocket of her nightgown. Obviously, her appetite had gone.

After about a week, the inevitable happened. Doris died. Elaine, June and Vera all went to see her shortly after her death and, on her return, Vera remarked that she looked so at peace, almost as if she was happy. Although this reassured her, she was most unhappy with the treatment provided to her mother by the staff at Leigh Hospital. She said they could have done more, such as ensuring that she ate her food and attending to her basic needs. Never, ever, she told me and her sons, let them take me into that place.

24.7 JACK

And so to the sole survivor, Jack.[*] If anyone had told me that Jack would be the last one of his generation alive, I would have thought they were mad. He had smoked and drunk a lot during his time as secretary of Aspull Labour Club. He was the most infirm, least active and, I presumed, least healthy of them all, but he couldn't have been. He outlived people I thought were much healthier and fitter.

Ever since Jack had found walking difficult, he and Lily had taken their summer holiday in a flat in Cleveleys with two close friends, Tom and Linda. Cleveleys is a Mecca for old people. It caters for their every need. It must have the highest number of cafes per square mile than any other place in the UK. It is flat. And it boasts an abundance of shops and markets aimed at the elderly. Later, as Jack's immobility worsened, they changed to a hotel that had a stair lift to transport the infirm to their bedrooms. This impressed Jack and prompted him to have one installed at home. And it was during the redecorating phase after the stair lift had been fitted that Lily died.

After Lily's death Jack required carers. He was adamant he wanted to remain in his own house and, because of his immobility, carers were essential. As mentioned earlier, as well as visiting her own mother three days per week, Vera, to her eternal credit, also managed to visit Jack almost every single day. Even though he could be cantankerous and awkward, she never once missed a single day, running his errands and attending to his various whims. I don't know how she did it, especially as she would sometimes come home in tears after one of his many rants.

I didn't escape either. Because of his frailty we occasionally received calls from his neighbours saying that Jack had fallen and hurt himself and could we come and see to him. It was invariably at night and, after a long day at work, it wasn't what I wanted. It may seem selfish but I must admit that I got annoyed at having to disrupt my evening and drive to Aspull to see to Jack. Sometimes it was nothing more than a few minor bumps and bruises but other times it meant calling for an ambulance and a visit to the hospital.

After one such mishap, a doctor took me to one side and said, "I'm very sorry but I think there's something very sinister down there (meaning his abdomen). We'll have to keep him in for a while."

That evening, driving home in the car, I had a strange experience. Just for one fleeting moment, a split second, a feeling of relief flashed through my mind. A feeling that soon it would be all over and that Vera and I would be relieved of a heavy burden. Then, almost simultaneously, I felt extreme guilt. And shame. How could I have thought such a thing. It was a weird experience.

Jack recovered on that occasion but, a few months later, he was taken in again. This time, he didn't recover.

---

[*]   Actually, Jean, Brian's mother, is the sole survivor. She is still alive today (2020).

Vera and I visited him every day for about a week. For the first few days he seemed fine. He was quite chatty but, invariably, the conversation always returned to the ailments of fellow patients in the ward. "See that man over there in the end bed. He's got cancer. He looks okay but he's only got a few weeks to live. And that man over there. He's got cancer too." It never seemed to occur to Jack that everyone in that particular ward seemed to have cancer, which meant that he probably had it too.

After a few days the consultant took Vera and me into a private room. "I'm afraid your uncle's very ill. We think he's got pancreatitis. In someone his age and in his condition, it's usually fatal."

Although we hadn't expected good news, when you hear words such as those it still comes as a shock. Shaken, we returned to his bedside and tried to act normally. But, however positive we tried to be, I think he knew. On more than one occasion, he said, "I'm not coming out of here."

"Should we tell your brother George* that you're in hospital?"

"No, don't bother," he replied. So we didn't. But, a few days later when he was taken into intensive care, we felt we had no option but to inform his only surviving brother that he was gravely ill.

George did come to visit, once, but Jack was oblivious to everyone, lying unconscious in intensive care. George was angry saying that he should have been informed earlier so he could have said goodbye. We reiterated what Jack had said but it didn't placate him and he left the hospital an angry man.

Just before he died, we offered both our children the chance to see Uncle Jack one last time, having forewarned them what state he was in. Andrew declined but, to our utmost surprise, Michael accepted. Somewhat reluctantly, I entered the Intensive Care Unit with Michael. Slowly, we made our sombre way to where he was lying.

It was a distressing sight. A bloated Jack was lying motionless on a raised bed with a plethora of tubes protruding from his still body. This sight, mixed with the overpowering smell of chemicals, proved a step too far for Michael. He didn't actually faint but would have done if the nurse hadn't sat him down and brought him a glass of cold water. Sadly, this was the last time we saw Jack alive. The following day he died.

Like Lily before him, Jack was cremated at Overdale Crematorium. The cortege was almost delayed because George and his wife arrived late, blaming us for giving them the wrong time (which we hadn't). Obviously, his anger still lingered.

A few years earlier, Lily and Jack did something which surprised me. They made a will. This was most unusual. No one in our family had ever made a will, mainly, I presume, because none of them had anything to pass on. But Lily and Jack had. They had bought their own house (Chapter 2).

---

*   His other brother, Bill, the one who used to take us in his car to watch Blackburn Rovers (Chapter 5), had died some years earlier

On one of our regular Saturday visits they told us about the will and asked if I would be the 'Executor'. "Yes, of course I will," I said, a little taken aback. "No problem at all."

"We've made a will," Lily said, "because we want to leave what we have to you. We don't want George to have a penny."

There were, I think, three main reasons for their decision. First, they had treated me as their only son. As the child they never had. Second, Vera, myself and our children had been very kind and considerate to them, visiting them every Saturday without fail for over twenty years. (George and his wife Linda hardly ever visited.) And third, they blamed George for the death of Jack's mother. Some years earlier his mother had an accident, a collision with a small motorised vehicle in Wigan's indoor market. Immediately, George saw the opportunity for a hefty compensation payment. For this to happen, his mother had to tell lies. This placed unbearable stress on his elderly mother and, in the eyes of Lily and Jack, hastened her death.

At the funeral, George took me to one side and said, "We'll have to decide how to split up the money. There'll be a tidy sum with the house. As his brother, I suppose it'll all go to me. But don't worry, I'll make sure you get a bit."

"He's made a will," I said, and turned away.

A few weeks later I was in Las Vegas on that fateful trip of 9/11 (Chapter 21). Whilst I was away, George rang Vera and ranted and raved about why Jack had left the money to me and not him. He really upset her and, when she told me following my return, I was furious. So furious that I wanted to drive to his house there and then and tell him in no uncertain terms what I thought. But Vera said, no, don't bother. He's not worth it. I heeded her advice but what he did still rankles to this day.

24.8 MOVING ON

Enough of deaths and funerals for a while. Let's move on to happier times beginning with my retirement, although, unfortunately, this also includes some sudden and unexpected deaths.

25

RETIREMENT

I retired at the beginning of April 2002, just a week after my 56th birthday.

You know when it's time to retire. I did. I thoroughly enjoyed my time at work and wouldn't have swapped it for anything. The chemistry, the colorants, my colleagues, the collaborations, the conferences, they were all brilliant. But there comes a time when things begin to change. Little things at first but then, all of a sudden, it hits you like a thunderbolt that your time has come. That things have changed so much that you don't, or don't want to, fit in anymore. You're like a dinosaur.

The majority of people that I had worked with had either retired, or left or, in some cases, died. The influx of new, young people with their different ideas of how the research should be conducted was alien both to me and many more of the older staff. Their rigid methodology was more suited to a factory churning out widgets than to a Research Department trying to invent new, hi-tech molecules. And, finally, at that time and that time only, the company was offering excellent terms for those wishing to take early retirement. It was a combination of all these factors that prompted me to leave the job I had loved for 37 years and take up pastures new (Image 241).

Reluctantly, the company accepted my decision to take early retirement. But there was a caveat. A condition. For the first two years I had to act as a 'Consultant', partly to pass on my knowledge to the younger people but mainly, I think, to stop me being a consultant to their competitors. I didn't object. It allowed me to visit the site about four or five times a month, enabling me to keep in touch with the people I had worked with for many years. It also provided a bridge between full time employment and full time retirement. In addition, lunchtime meals were arranged at the nearby *Three Arrows* pub for former colleagues and friends, such as Christine, Roy, Derek, Jim, Prahalad and Dave Devonald. It was shortly after one of these meals that I received a call from Roy saying that Christine had been taken into hospital. It was the spring of 2006.

Myself (left) with Christine and Prahalad at
my Retirement Dinner, April 2002.

25.1 CHRISTINE

Apparently, her friend had rung Christine to ask her to go shopping but realised that something was wrong with her speech. It was a little hesitant and slightly slurred. This was most unusual since Christine was a highly articulate person. Her friend immediately dashed round, saw that all was not well and persuaded Christine to call the doctor. She was taken into Hope Hospital and, a few days later, the cause was diagnosed. It was a brain tumour.

Later that week I visited Christine with Roy and Prahalad. She and I had worked together for many years and, as mentioned earlier, she had been my 'right hand man' for many of my lectures. I wanted to see her. It was my duty.

After experiencing some difficulty finding the ward (Hope is a big hospital), we recognised her right away. She was sat up in bed with her headphones on doing the puzzles in the paper, just as she did most lunchtimes at work. Her face lit up when she saw us and we spent an enjoyable hour reminiscing about past times. Only in a few instances did I detect the slightest hesitancy in her speech. For most of the time, she appeared completely normal. "I'm just looking forward to getting back to work," she said. And on that note we bade her farewell and departed.

A few days later Christine was allowed home. But it wasn't to recuperate. Oh no, it was something far worse than that. Roy informed me that she had been diagnosed with a Type IV brain tumour. A very malignant brain tumour, the most aggressive tumour of all. It was untreatable. She had been sent home to die.

On a beautiful Tuesday afternoon I went to visit Christine at her home in Brinnington, near Stockport. She had never married and both her parents had died some years ago, so she lived alone in the family home. She had changed profoundly. Greeting me warmly at the door, she ushered me into the living room on unsteady legs. "Would… you … like… a drink?" she asked with great difficulty.

"I'd love a cup of tea. You sit down and I'll make us one."

"No, no," she responded. "I'll… make… it." Somewhat reluctantly, I relented and she disappeared slowly into the kitchen.

As we sipped our cups of tea I was astonished how quickly her speech and her movements had deteriorated. She had only been home a couple of weeks yet, in that short time, she found it difficult to walk and even more difficult to speak. I felt so sorry for her and so angry that nothing could be done. I could see she was tired and, after a little while, decided it was time to leave and let her rest. She insisted on accompanying me to the door and, before I left, we hugged each other tightly. I don't know if Christine shared the same feeling but I knew this would be the last time I would see her alive. There was a tear in my eye as I said my final goodbye.

Three days later, on the Friday, Roy called me to say that Christine had died. Died at the tender age of 50. It was the news I had been dreading yet, at the same time, expecting. "The funeral is next week," he said, "and her only brother has asked if someone from work would give a eulogy. Seeing that you have known her for a long time, we'd like you to do it. Is that okay?"

"Yes," I replied. "It's fine. Of course I'll do it."

And I did. I was used to speaking in front of large audiences. I'd done it many times at conferences. But I had never, ever had to do it under such emotional circumstances. It was one of the most difficult things I have ever done. But it wouldn't be the most difficult. Those were yet to come.

25.2 CHRISTINE'S EULOGY

Most people at work are regarded as colleagues. Christine was different. She was more than a colleague. To those who knew her, she was a friend.

416

Christine started work in the Research Department of ICI in September 1973 as a Scientific Assistant, working with Ron Hyde on dyes for textiles and has remained with the company through its various rebirths as Zeneca, Avecia and now FujiFilm. Christine's qualities of hard work, self-motivation and reliability enabled her to reach the respected position of Research Chemist.

Without a doubt, one of Christine's career highlights was being a key member of the embryonic Specialist Colours research team of four people which laid the foundations of a business that was recently purchased for 150 million pounds. Indeed, for many years she was my "right hand man" (so to speak) on the various roadshows we did to promote the Specialist Colours area. We travelled to such exotic locations as Canterbury and Cornwall, Glasgow and Leeds, and Whitehaven and Warwick. After the lecture and demonstrations, we usually looked forward to a good meal with some wine. Except for Warwick! Mike Hutchings, a colleague, had asked us to give a short talk and a demonstration of electronic photography to a "couple of dozen" people at 7-00 p.m. at a conference at Warwick University. We agreed, expecting to be finished by 8-00 p.m. Instead of a couple of dozen people, there were over 300! By the time Chris had finished taking peoples' photos with the electronic camera, all the restaurants were shut and we finished up eating fish and chips in a lay-by at midnight. But, as usual, she never complained.

Everyone you speak to seems to describe Christine in pretty much the same way, as a well-liked, hard-working and respected colleague, as highly self-motivated now as she was when she began her career almost 33 years ago. Chris was a private, sincere and loyal person and was always more than willing to help others. At the same time Chris had a "mischievous" (in the nicest sense of the word) sense of humour, being a co-conspirator, if not instigator, of a few good natured wind-ups over the years. At lunch-time she could usually be found trying her hand at some quiz questions or puzzles. (I don't think she was fond of the canteen food.)

Chris was a very well organised person and, as a Chemist-in-Charge, served on an internal safety committee for many years. It was at one of these meetings not too long ago that Chris amply demonstrated her organising skills. The meetings held by this safety committee often lasted for anything up to two hours but in the absence of the regular chairman Chris took on the responsibility of driving the meeting and completed everything within about 30 minutes, leaving no agenda items untouched. Chris was so well organised that she had plans in place for the lab Christmas meal by mid-year.

There was a recent example of a situation where an important piece of equipment had failed, causing chemical contamination within the Fine Chemicals store. Chris was straight in there, volunteering to help one of her colleagues and getting things decontaminated and back on track. This was above and beyond the call of duty and was duly recognised by the award of a bonus to Chris. It speaks volumes about Chris when she turned up the next day armed with a selection of sweets and cakes for the people in the office so that everyone could share in her good fortune.

Although the company has evolved and many people have moved on to new companies or retired, Chris was always one for keeping in touch wherever possible, especially with those she had worked most closely with. A number of people here today are testament to this.

When we heard the very sad news on Monday there was an air of complete disbelief that this could happen to Chris. In some ways you never knew she was there but you certainly missed her when she wasn't. The place won't be the same without her and she will be sadly missed by all.

25.3 GOLF

After I retired me and William (who'd retired nine months earlier) began playing golf together. I'd started going for a walk on Tuesday, Vera's day out with her two sisters June and Elaine, so we chose Thursday for our round of golf. Every Thursday we played different local courses, usually just nine holes, although occasionally we'd play 18 holes. Sometimes we were joined by Keith and his dad Howarth. And it was whilst playing a round at the nine hole Haigh Hall course with William, Keith and Howarth that I had my golfing Eureka moment. It was on the eighth hole, a relatively short (91 yards – Image 242) but tricky hole. The hole was up a rather steep hill which meant the green was invisible from the tee. I think I was the last to play. William, Keith and Howarth had all played decent shots so the pressure was on, especially since this was a hole I didn't play well. I took one last look towards the (invisible) green and played my shot. It sailed up towards the green then disappeared from view over the top of the hill. I heard the ball land, hopefully on the green. Keith went one step further: he said he'd heard it plop into the hole. "Don't be daft," I said as we strolled up the hill to the green. When we got to the green, William's, Keith's and Howarth's balls were there, but where was mine?

Scorecard of my 'Hole-in-One' Round.
Whoever totted up the scores wasn't very good at arithmetic.

"It's in the hole," said Keith as he walked briskly towards the flag. And he was right, it was in the hole. I achieved what every golfer dreams of: I'd hit a hole in one! (Image 242).

25.4 WALKING WITH WILLIAM AND BRIAN

A few years later when Brian retired, William and I thought he should join us on our Thursday day out. However, Brian isn't a golfer so we swapped playing golf for walking. A routine was quickly established. When I drove, we did our walks either locally around Aspull and Blackrod, where Brian and William lived, or to the west of Aspull, such as Parbold, Eccleston, Croston and Southport. When they drove (we took it in turns to drive), we either walked around where I lived in Lostock, or further east such as Edgworth (no 'e'), Darwen, Holcombe Moor, Hollingworth Lake and Pendle. Sometimes, in the longer days of summer, we ventured further afield to Lancaster, the Lake District and the Yorkshire Dales. Before commencing our walks we always had a coffee (or hot chocolate) and cake in a cafe.* Then, after completing the walk, which could last from two to six hours, but was usually of two to three hours duration, we always ended the walk by downing a couple of pints, plus a bag of crisps, in a pub. Over the years we must have patronised scores of pubs.

In winter, when the days are short and the weather wet and cold, we did local walks, such as the moors around Rivington, the plantations of Haigh Hall or canal walks. Indeed, we've walked the complete stretch of the Leeds-Liverpool canal from Leigh to Tarleton, though not in one go. Two of the most beautiful stretches are those through Haigh Hall plantations (Image 29, page 46) and those either side of Parbold. *The Ring O Bells* pub (sadly now – 2020 – closed) at Lathom near Parbold was one of our watering holes.

Walks through Haigh Hall plantations to Wigan were done often, using a variety of routes. In Wigan, we stopped for refreshments at the *Orchid* (now the *Allotment*) cafe, formerly the site of one of the most awful public conveniences in the land. Local walks meant local pubs and those we frequented most were The *Poacher* at Blackrod, *Suzannahs* (now the *Goose and Gander*) at nearby Little Scotland, and the *White Crow* and the *Crown* at Worthington. The latter was a real ale pub, which is ideal for Brian but not so me and William. We prefer traditional beers such as Tetleys, Boddingtons, John Smiths and Thwaites. Real ale is too warm for us, especially in summer, so we drink lager. In pubs without real ales, which are few and far between, it's Brian who has to resort to lager.

Walks to the west include Eccleston to Croston along the River Yarrow, where we sampled the delights of the *Grapes* pub, Roby Mill to the Leeds-Liverpool canal,

---

* Sometimes, if there was no cafe, we'd have our coffees in a pub with a bowl of chips

where I did a double somersault and forward roll on a slippy hillside, and where we stopped at *Sam's Place*, a weird pub with a flagged floor and strange clientele. It was here we met a young girl who asked us to escort her to the top of a steep hill. As it was on our way back we duly obliged but found it extremely hard going to keep up with her, especially after a long walk and two pints. One day we followed one of Tim Barnaby's walks from the Lancashire Magazine[1] around Wrea Green, the home of the *Dizzy Ducks* tea room – the start and finish of the walk – run by Sharon Dooley, the wife of Wade Dooley, the former British Lions and England rugby union lock forward. It was on this walk that Brian informed me that Adam's girlfriend Kaylea was pregnant. Wheelton, where Andy Goodway ran the Post Office after retiring from playing rugby league with Wigan, to Botany Bay, was another short but pretty canal walk with a welcoming pub at the end. However, our favourite area for walks to the west was Parbold.

Bisected by both the canal and the railway Parbold is a lovely old village. Boasting two quaint cafes, it's the *Yours is the Earth* cafe directly beside the canal that we tend to visit before commencing our walk. There are several walks around Parbold. Harrock Hill,[2] Fairy Glen and the quarries are all lovely but our favourite is the one to Ashurst Beacon.[3] It is a relatively long (6.5 miles) and arduous walk which begins at the top of Parbold Hill itself. You descend to the valley below down a steep path at the edge of a wood, cross the valley and ascend the other side through rolling fields and enchanted little woods before passing the picturesque Dalton Cricket Club and on to the Beacon. At the summit there are magnificent views over the Lancashire Plain to the Lancashire Coast, where Blackpool, with its famous tower, and Southport, are clearly visible. From here, Tim's instructions state that 'after admiring the views to drop down along the obvious path' for the descent, which is hardly much help when there are four or five 'obvious' paths. However, we took the one in the general direction of Parbold Hill, which proved to be the right one. As we crossed the valley it suddenly dawned on us that the final part of the walk involved the ascent of the steep path that we'd descended at the start. This is most certainly not recommended at the end of an arduous six-and-a-half mile walk, especially in hot weather. However, the thought of a refreshing ice cream and a cold pint of lager from the *Miller and Carter* pub (formerly the *Wiggin Tree*) at the top of Parbold Hill spurred us on.

In inclement weather we'd visit Derby House in Wrightington, Heskin Hall and the nearby Bygone Times in Eccleston, and Botany Bay in Chorley (also now closed), all of which have excellent cafes, though not all on the same day. Brian in particular loves to rummage through the antiques and bric-a-brac of Bygone Times but both his wife and mine hate the place. However, like Brian, I like it. It is quaint and different.

When Brian or William drove, we walked either around Rivington and Winter Hill, or further to the east. Over the years we must have done all the walks around

Rivington (and there are many), some more than once. Rivington Pike, the Upper and Lower Rivington reservoirs, Anglezark reservoir, the Wellington Bomber Memorial (a Wellington bomber crashed on the moors during World War II), the river walk from White Coppice to Brinscall, and Winter Hill, are but a few. For most of these walks we'd fortify ourselves with a coffee and cake at the *Rivington Village Cafe* or the nearby *Bowling Green Cafe*, which does a brilliant hot chocolate. When we began our walks at Georges Lane we took our refreshments at *Curleys Tea Rooms* or the *Jolly Crofters* pub.

On one winter walk with William (Brian couldn't come) we set off from Botany Bay, walked over Chorley Nab and dropped down into the picturesque village of White Coppice. With a stream meandering beside the old cottages and the most beautiful setting for the village cricket pitch, it is the quintessential English village. After admiring the view (we never stopped for a rest, just a view), we set off beside the stream heading uphill to the reservoirs. Ahead, a huge patch of mud blocked our path. Completely. There was no way around it. At the edge of the mud and right beside the swollen stream lay a plank of wood. A slippery plank of wood. After some deliberation William decided that was the route he'd take. Tentatively he inched his way forward. As he neared the far end of the plank his foot slipped and he almost plunged headlong into the dark, icy water. Fortunately, he managed to grab a branch, regain his balance and haul himself to the other side.

Having witnessed this near disaster the plank route wasn't for me. (I don't have the best balance anyway.) Therefore, I had no option but to go through the mud. All was going well until, near the middle, instead of hitting *terra firma* my right foot kept going down and down, causing me to overbalance and fall face first into the cloying mud. I was covered in the stuff and had to crawl on my belly to the other side. It must have been a funny sight for William but, to his credit, he didn't laugh. When we reached the first reservoir, I spent ages trying to wash the mud off my hands, face and clothes with the icy water. However, as you will discover later, I wasn't the only one to befall this fate.

Walking to the TV mast on Winter Hill, the highest location in the area and a famous landmark for miles around, was another walk that we enjoyed. One winter's afternoon William and me (Brian was unavailable) parked our car at the bottom of the tarmac road leading up to the mast and walked the mile or so to the top. The remote building on top of the hill always reminded me of the Trollenberg Terror TV series (Chapter 2), especially in the mist. A group of sheep huddled together near the building's heat exchanger to keep warm fascinated us. They're obviously not as dim as people make out.

After reading the plaques commemorating the tragic plane crash in 1958 (Image 243) and an unsolved murder in 1838 (Image 244), we decided to take a new route for our descent. It was one that William had taken a few years earlier with his son

Neil. It ran along the edge of a steep escarpment and then through thick woods before coming out on to a tarmac road. To our dismay the route we'd intended to take had a large red sign proclaiming, 'PRIVATE. NO PUBLIC ACCESS'.

We decided to obey the law and set off on a five mile detour along Scout Road. After about two-and-a-half miles we faced a dilemma. The darkness was descending and we were still a long way from our car. We had two choices. Either continue along Scout Road to Bob's Smithy pub and catch a bus to Horwich, the safer option in the deepening gloom, or take a shorter, riskier route over the moors.

Walking on uneven paths on remote moors in pitch black darkness without a torch is not a sane thing to do. It was so dark we couldn't see where we were placing our feet, let alone where we were heading. Keeping to the path was difficult enough but when the path forked, which path should we take? Fortunately, we'd walked this route in the daylight and, by sheer instinct and good fortune, a relieved William and I managed to make it back to the car. A few minutes later the two pints of Tetley's Smooth in the warm and cosy surroundings of the *Jolly Crofters* were never more welcome.

Plaque on Winter Hill commemorating
the plane crash in 1958.

Further eastward Peel Tower on Holcombe Moor lured us on more than one occasion. William and Brian first did this walk in my absence and said it was one that I had to do. They enthused about the walk itself and the views from the top and so, one Thursday afternoon, the three of us parked our car on the outskirts of Ramsbottom and set off towards Beetle Hill at the far end of Holcombe Moor. The weather was fine as we climbed Beetle Hill and started our trek along the ridge of the moor. To our right the army's firing range sheltered us from the steadily increasing wind. However, as we emerged from our sheltered position, not only had the wind had increased to gale force, it was accompanied by torrential rain. Indeed, the wind was so strong the rain was literally horizontal! By the time we'd crossed that bleak expanse of Holcombe Moor and reached the shelter of Peel Tower we were absolutely drenched, but only on one side. As for the magnificent views, I saw nothing. Later, we warmed up and dried ourselves at the *Shoulder of Mutton* pub whilst downing a refreshing couple of pints, so it wasn't all bad. We've done the walk several times since then and yes, the views are great.

The Scotchsman's *(sic)* Stump commemorating the brutal murder
of twenty year old George Henderson on 9 November 1838.

I'd walked Pendle Hill both with Ray in the summer (see later) and with Andrew and Helen in the winter snow, so it was my turn to enthuse about the views when, for the first time, I did the walk with William and Brian. It was a beautiful sunny day as we parked near the ski slope and set off on the climb towards the top of the first hill. As we approached the top a dark cloud descended from nowhere, enveloping both ourselves and Pendle Hill. We were dumbfounded. There hadn't been the slightest sign of any dark clouds when we set off. The visibility was down to just a few yards. We could hardly see anything. Since I knew the route from previous walks we carried on along the top until we reached the stone slabs that led over the boggy ground to the cairn at the summit. We chatted for a while with a family of walkers who'd come well prepared with maps, compasses and emergency supplies. They were astounded when we said we hadn't any of these things. No map, no compass, no directions. You'll never get off the top in weather like this was their parting comment as we followed a stone wall for our return journey. Unfortunately, it turned out to be the wrong stone wall and we ended up in a deep ravine. We all became a little concerned as we followed this ravine for what seemed like ages with no idea where we were headed. As we were becoming really worried, a small stone building emerged from the mist. I recognised it instantly. At last we were on the right path and we made it safely back to the car. Like me on Holcombe Moor, William didn't get to see the magnificent views.

Other walks to the east included a circular walk around the Jumbles reservoir, where there is a cafe that is open all year round, over the moors to Affetside, where there is a lovely pub, Turton Tower, and the Wayoh and Entwistle reservoirs at Edgworth, where the *Strawbury Duck*, a real ale pub, is ideally located between the two reservoirs. William and me drank Starapramen lager which was surprisingly good.

Darwen Tower and the Roddlesworth reservoirs are two other walks we do fairly often. For both walks we park at *Vaughs Country Cafe* in Tockholes, the village we passed through when driving to Blackburn to watch the football (Chapter 5). The cafe has an unusual attraction: a large one way glass window which allows customers to get up close and personal with feeding wild birds whilst enjoying their refreshments. On completion of the walk we usually drank in the small but quaint *Royal* pub.

The walk from Clough Head Country Park near Haslingden, first around the quarries and then the Ogden and Calf Hey reservoirs, is another walk we enjoy Near the Ogden Reservoir Dam are the remains of an old haulage system known as 'Donkey Bill', and a tunnel. There is a cafe at the Clough Head Visitor Centre, the start and finish of the walk, and a pleasant pub, the *Duke of Wellington Inn*, about half way round the walk, where we down a pint or two.

Nearer to home Pennington Flash, near Leigh, with the *Robin Hood* pub at its entrance, and the Moses Gate Country Park in Farnworth, are two shorter circular walks for the winter months.

However, in summer when the days are long and the weather warm, we venture farther afield for walks around the Pennines, Lancaster and the Yorkshire Dales. Whilst walking around Piethorne reservoir in the foothills of the Pennines Brian and I fed a friendly horse with clumps of grass. William didn't. The horse must have known for, as we were about to leave the field, it sidled up to William and tupped him in the rear. It served him right for his lack of consideration for a hungry horse. (Good name for a restaurant chain!) At Wycoller Country Park we stood on the same stone bridge as Jenny Agutter did in *The Railway Children*, although it took us an age looking for the pub that was the starting point of the walk. It didn't seem to exist. Flummoxed, we asked a local where it was. No wonder we couldn't find it: it had changed its name!

Two of our favourite walks are Malham Tarn in the Yorkshire Dales and Sambo's Grave near Lancaster. Not only is the Dales village of Malham quaint, so is the car park. It is patronised by cheeky chickens which amble up to your car looking for food. At the start of the walk beside a babbling brook William found a digital camera which he handed in at the end of the walk. (The owner phoned him a few days later thanking him for his kind deed.) After passing through a delightful wood with a strong smell of garlic and a lovely waterfall, we emerged to the awesome sight of Gordale Scar, a vast fissure in the towering limestone cliff. At the edge of the nearby campsite we stopped for refreshments at a mobile van on a stone bridge over a stream, where a photographer took our picture. (Last of the Summer Wine and all that.) Suitably refreshed, we continued on to Malham Tarn, where we dangled our hot sweaty feet in the cool water. Then it was onwards and upwards to the grykes at the top of Malham Cove, another spectacular feature, before descending the 300 or so limestone steps, which are treacherous in wet weather, to the valley below, and then back to the car.

The walk to Sambo's Grave (Image 245) begins at *The Globe* pub in Overton.[4] Heading across open fields and country lanes towards the massive hulk of Heysham power station, we eventually arrived at the Shorefields caravan park. Here, we stopped for refreshments in the small but beautifully situated cafe right on the beach, with panoramic views over Morecambe Bay to the Lake District mountains. From here, the walk continues along the shoreline to Sambo's Grave, the final resting place of a negro slave who died after coming ashore. The locals were moved by the tragic death of a young slave boy and buried him in a beautiful spot beside the sea. His grave is still festooned with tributes and lovingly tended almost three centuries after his death. After admiring his grave, we cut inland to the lovely seaside hamlet of Sunderland Point, where we almost got cut off by the incoming tide. *The Globe* was shut so we downed our beers at the recently rejuvenated *Golden Ball* on the banks of the River Lune, just a few miles away.

Sambo's Grave, a memorial to a young black slave
who is thought to have arrived, and died, in 1736.

On our way to a walk at Cockersands Abbey,[5] on the opposite side of the River Lune to Sunderland Point, a man we'd asked for directions in Galgate was so impressed with my S-type Jaguar that he wanted to buy it! On these longer walks, and indeed on most of our walks now, we've learned from bitter experience to always pack a loo roll. It's much more preferable to having grass in your bum.

25.5 WALKING WITH RAY

After Ray retired from his role of Financial Adviser we used Tuesdays, our wives day out, to go walking. Ray shared similar hobbies to myself. He loved rugby league, being an avid St Helens supporter, gardening, visiting National Trust properties and especially walking. As was the case with William and Brian, we walked both locally (we did a lot around Billinge where Ray lived, and Rivington near to where I lived) as well as farther afield. One of his favourite walks began and ended at his house at 2 Upholland Road. We set off across the fields towards Winstanley College, then on to the picturesque Orrell Water Park. Carrying on through Orrell past Edge Hall Road, the training ground of Wigan Warriors, and the tiny hamlet of Tontine near the M58 motorway, we headed uphill over the rolling fields towards the lovely little reservoir. On reaching this farthest point of the walk, we returned over undulating meadows, pastures full of grazing cows and sheep, Houghwood Golf Club and finally the landmark Billinge Lump. From here, we descended along the road to the *Ice Cream Parlour* in Billinge, where we finished the walk with a refreshing hot drink and a cake.

The walk around Crank Caverns and Carr Mill Dam was another one we did from Ray's home. These rather eerie caves are located in the village of Crank, the same village that Uncle Evan took William and me on a bicycle ride when we were small (Chapter 2). On this walk we always refreshed ourselves at the *Waterside Inn* situated, as the name suggests, beside the waters of Carr Mill Dam.

Carr Mill Dam was one of Ray's childhood haunts and partly because of this, but also because it was a lovely place to walk, we frequented this area a lot. Indeed, we used it as the starting point to walk the entire length of the Sankey Valley Canal, right through to the River Mersey. Ray's love of canal and river walks meant we did many such walks. We walked long stretches of the Leeds-Liverpool canal, where he introduced me to the delicious Aberdeen Angus beef burgers at the *Fettlers Wharf Coffee Shop* in Rufford (and to the enormous cakes in the newer *Tastebuds* cafe), as well as the tearooms at Burscough Wharf where, on more than one occasion, his teapot lid fell into his cup as he poured his beloved cuppa. (Ray loved his pots of tea.)

We also walked from Rufford along the River Douglas to the quaint little marina at Tarleton. At one point the vegetation was so dense and overgrown – it was literally over six feet high – we couldn't see where we were headed. Not only that, it stripped my pedometer from my waist causing one of my prized possessions to be lost forever. (I always liked to record the length of each walk.) It was akin to walking in a jungle without a machete. On our return journey we followed the more sedate Leeds-Liverpool canal without any further mishaps. However, that wasn't the case on our walk from the White Bear Marina in Adlington along the Douglas Valley to Worthington Lakes.

The weather had been particularly wet and, rather foolishly, we continued to follow the River Douglas long after we should have headed uphill. Ray was leading the way when suddenly, and without any warning, he inadvertently entered a swamp. As he struggled to extricate himself first one, and then both, his feet parted company with his boots, causing him to plunge headlong into the muddy swamp. Like me earlier, he had to crawl on his belly to reach the side of the swamp. It was so funny but, like William, I didn't laugh, especially as I nearly suffered the same fate extricating his boots from the clinging mud. It was like pulling them out of concrete. Later, when we told the waitress in the *Marina Cafe*, where we'd gone to clean ourselves and get a welcoming warm brew, she couldn't help herself and burst out laughing.

Like William and Brian, Ray also liked walks around Parbold. One such walk ended up much longer than anticipated. As we crossed the field from the quarries down to the only stile, disaster struck. At the other side of the stile a huge bull blocked our path. Sniffing and snorting, it eyed up these two interlopers. We had two choices. Cross the stile and risk being gored to death by this fearsome brute, or find an alternative route. Discretion is the better part of valour and we followed our noses on a three mile detour rather than risk the wrath of a raging bull.

In summer, we walked further afield. Both Ray and I like the Ribble Valley and we did a number of walks in this beautiful part of the country which, incidentally, is also one of the Queen's favourite areas. On a walk from Chipping the guidebook instructed us to head diagonally upfield and then make towards a white post at the edge of a wood. Well, we searched and searched for this elusive white post but to no avail. It didn't seem to exist. As we were on the verge of giving up we found it lying on the ground hidden in long grass. It must have blown down. At the end of the walk in the *Corner Cafe* I had my first taste of Bungo soup, so called because the chef bungs everything into it! It was so thick and nutritious.

We also did some lovely walks around Whalley and Hurst Green, near to where Michael and Kathryn held their wedding (Chapter 26). The walk from Hurst Green began at Stoneyhurst College, one of Lancashire's top public schools, and the place where such famous people as Sir Arthur Conan Doyle (his name is carved into his desk), creator of *Sherlock Holmes*, and JRR Tolkien, author of *The Hobbit* and the *Lord of the Rings* trilogy, were educated. It is said that Tolkien found the inspiration for the fabled *Middle Earth* in his blockbusting books from the countryside surrounding

Stoneyhurst College. The college was also the setting for the film *Three Men and a Baby*. The eight mile walk, another one of Tim Barnaby's,[6] is delightful, with the stretch along the River Ribble providing a blissful finale.

Spike Island in Widnes was the starting point for several more of our walks. Situated near to the Catalyst Museum, where I had a latte and a cake and Ray his pot of tea, and on the banks of the River Mersey, it is an ideal hub for a number of lovely walks.

Following the Mersey westwards as it winds its way to the Irish Sea offers a plethora of pleasures. The changing views of the river at different tide levels, the quirky little inlets and bays, the quaint wooden bridges over numerous small tributaries, and the varied wildlife, are a delight on the eye. After approximately four miles, the village of Hale is reached, famous for John Middleton, the English giant known as the *Childe of Hale*, who grew to an incredible nine feet three inches tall. He is buried in the local churchyard and his statue adorns the village square. After refreshing ourselves at the pub bearing his name (we sometimes had a meal there too), we returned along the same route back to Spike Island.

The only blot on this otherwise delightful walk is the bone works. Located near the start of the walk, the stench emanating from the factory is overpowering. It is so nauseating it makes you want to puke. However, a few minutes stench is a price worth paying for such a memorable walk.

Once, and only once, we headed eastward from Spike Island towards the imposing bulk of Fiddlers Ferry power station, but turned back because it was boring. Instead, we crossed the iconic Runcorn Bridge, strolled through the town of Runcorn and crossed the bridge over the Manchester Ship Canal to Wigg Island, walking to its far end to survey the construction of the new bridge being built over the Mersey.

On another day, after crossing Runcorn Bridge we followed the Bridgewater canal for several miles, passing a small marina, a picturesque park and a lovely lake. It was a gorgeous summer's day and we'd walked further than planned so Ray had to phone our wives to tell them we'd be late back.

As well as canal and river walks both Ray and myself loved coastal walks. We walked through the National Trust's Formby Point nature reserve, one of the last strongholds of Britain's native red squirrel, to the impressive sand dunes on Freshfield beach, walking for several miles along this beautiful stretch of coastline. We also walked along the beach from Crosby, the home of Anthony Gormley's statues gazing out to sea, down past Blundellsands and on to the Marine Lake at Waterloo. One rainy day we walked the other way to the army's firing range at Hightown, where we had to take off our boots and socks and wade through two feet of water to escape the incoming tide.

We did a lovely circular walk at West Kirkby on the Wirral, where people walk on water (Image 246), and a long (12 mile) walk from New Brighton to Hoylake and back.

Because it was flat and good underfoot, and the weather hot, I decided not to change into my hiking boots and wear my Reiker shoes instead. (Wearing hiking boots in hot weather always make my feet hot and sweaty.) What a mistake! By the time we returned to the car I was in agony. Both my feet were blistered and bleeding. I didn't make that mistake again.

People apparently walking on
water at West Kirkby Marina.

The walks around the Lancashire and Wirral coasts were fine but without a doubt our favourite coastal walk was the Great Orme in Llandudno. As is Malham Cove in the Yorkshire Dales, the Great Orme is limestone country, which I like. On top of the Orme there is so much to admire. St Tudno's church, the ski lift, the funicular railway, the ski slope and the complex at the summit are all attractions, but it is the craggy cliffs and the magnificent views which are the real attraction. The feeling of space and solitude and the fresh sea air are a joy to behold. Indeed, Ray loved the place so much he wanted his ashes scattered here.

Ray's elder brother Harry lives at Degawny near Conway and he showed Ray a number of local walks, including one from the quiet West Shore of Llandudno along the coast to Conway, with its famous castle and pretty harbour. On these walks we sometimes treated ourselves to fish and chips from the Galleon chippy. As you will see later (Chapter 27), Llandudno is a place that Vera and I love too.

Like Brian, Ray liked his real ales. His favourite was Speckled Hen so, one long summer's day we drove to Masham in the Yorkshire Dales and did a tour of the small but quirky Black Sheep Brewery, where we sampled a number of his favourite tipples, including Speckled Hen, and enjoyed a delicious meal in a local pub. He also took me on a walk in Delamere Forest in Cheshire, stopping at the *Station Cafe* for refreshments. He'd enthused about this cafe for ages, citing the enormity of the dishes. (Ray loved big portions.) Soups, main meals and desserts, he said, were all giant sized. And he was right. The jam roly poly and custard that I had was huge.

429

If the weather was too bad for walking we'd go to either Liverpool or Manchester and visit the museums or libraries. In Manchester we visited The *John Rylands Library*, a beautiful example of Gothic architecture, and the *Imperial War Museum* at Salford Quays. In Liverpool, we sampled the delights of the *Central Library*, with its circular design, the *World Museum*, including the planetarium, and the *Williamson Tunnels* built, apparently, for no other reason than to provide employment for the people of Liverpool. He'd recently written a book on football so we visited the *National Football Museum* when it was in Preston.

Sadly, all good things come to an end and on 27 February 2015 I lost a walking companion and good friend (Chapter 26).

REFERENCES

1. Tim Barnaby, 'Scrum on Down', Lancashire Magazine p. 128
2. Tim Barnaby, 'Setting the Pace in Parbold', Lancashire Magazine, September 2008, p. 78
3. Tim Barnaby, 'Many Happy Returns', Lancashire Magazine, p.184
4. Tim Barnaby, 'A Salute to Sambo', Lancashire Magazine, p. 198
5. Tim Barnaby, 'Coasting Along', Lancashire Magazine, December 2007 p. 52
6. Tim Barnaby, 'Top of the Class', Lancashire Magazine, p.134

26

WEDDINGS

After the sadness of the deaths and funerals (Chapter 24), this chapter focuses on the sheer exuberance, joy and happiness at the marriage of a son, daughter or close relative although, tragically, there are two more sudden and unexpected deaths to report.

26.1 WILLIAM AND JEAN'S WEDDING

Saturday 27 September 1969 was a very special day for Jean. A day of double celebration. Not only was it the day of her wedding to William, it was also the day of her 21st birthday. On that single day, Miss Jean Berry became both Mrs Jean Jackson and got the 'key to the door'.

Jean's family lived in Chorley and, not surprisingly, she and William decided to get married at the Trinity Methodist Church in that town. Transport had been provided to take William's family and friends from his house in Aspull to the church in Chorley and, as the weather was fine that Saturday morning, Vera and I decided to walk the one mile or so from our new house in Willowcroft Avenue to William's house in St John's Road. It wasn't a wise choice. As we approached half-way, the heavens opened and we got absolutely drenched, arriving at his house bedraggled and soaked to the skin. In fact, I think my new suit got so wet that, by the time it dried out, it had actually shrunk!

As far as I recall, the wedding ceremony went without a hitch with William and Jean making a fine couple (Image 247). The reception was held at the De Trafford Arms in the picturesque village of Croston, just a few miles away from the church. After a most enjoyable Wedding Breakfast I vaguely remember, as his best man, giving a short speech and reading a few cards. After that, my memory fails me. I must have got drunk!

431

Jean and William on their Wedding Day.

William and Jean forewent the pleasures of a formal honeymoon. In preparation for married life they'd begun refurbishing a cottage they'd rented in Coppull Moor. The cost of the wedding plus the refurbishment left a huge hole in their finances. They were left with the princely sum of £1.50! Therefore, they had no option but to spend their 'honeymoon' in the cottage. But it didn't get off to a good start. As they opened the front door, a shock awaited. The cottage was flooded. Water was everywhere. Apparently, during a severe storm, rainwater had seeped under the door. It wasn't the best of starts to married life but they survived and remained together until their untimely deaths (Chapter 29), having raised a son, Neil, whose partner Liz has presented them with two grandaughters, Elsa and Theia, and a daughter, Helen, who has presented them with two further grandaughters, Bella and Stevie.

26.2 BRIAN AND VALERIE'S WEDDING

As mentioned in Chapter 10, this is a wedding I didn't attend and it is something that I regret to this day. However, by all accounts Brian and Valerie had a wonderful wedding and looked lovely on their special day (Image 248). Like William and Jean, they have raised both a son, Adam, and a daughter, Catherine. Adam's first partner Kayley presented them with a grandson, Dylan, and his current partner, Louise, has also presented them with a grandson, Reuben. In contrast, Catherine has given them the gift of two grandaughters, Elodie and Willow.

Valerie and Brian on their Wedding Day.

26.3 RAY AND JUNE'S WEDDING

Like her elder sister before her June got married at St David's church, Haigh. On a beautiful afternoon on Saturday 27 May 1978, Miss June Santus married Mr Ray Gent. They made a charming couple (Image 249).

The wedding almost never happened. Not because of any bust up but on account of a technicality. For some reason, the wedding banns hadn't been read out at Ray's church in St Helens and because of this oversight, Ray and June didn't know until the Thursday if they could get married on the Saturday. In the event, they did, but only because the vicar had applied for, and was granted, a special licence.

June and Ray on their Wedding Day.

Although he hailed from nearby St Helens, June and Ray did not meet locally. In one of life's bizarre twists, their paths crossed whilst on holiday in Spain. In a Spanish bar, a group of lads from St Helens met a couple of girls from Wigan and for one of the girls, romance blossomed.

June and Ray held their Wedding Breakfast at the Baronay restaurant near Haigh Hall. It was a fine meal in a room that generated an intimate atmosphere. After the formalities of the speeches and toasts, of which I remember very little, everyone took advantage of the beautiful weather to frolic outdoors, where Andrew amused himself by showering the happy couple with confetti (Image 250).

Andrew looked quite dapper as a pageboy but he had given a heavily pregnant Vera and me cause for concern. A few days before the wedding he trapped his finger in a 'Tonka' toy, causing it to swell up horrendously. The doctor gave him antibiotics to treat the infection and was on the verge of lancing the swelling when, to our utmost relief, it burst of its own accord on the morning of the wedding. Even so, his left forefinger was still heavily bandaged (Image 250).

Ray, June and Andrew (left) and Angela Whittaker,
Andrew, Vera and her mum (right).

In those days money was tight, especially in our families, and honeymoons, if they could be afforded at all, were a world away from those of today's generation. There was no jetting off to exotic locations for a one or two week stay. If you were lucky, it would be a few days at a local holiday destination. Ray and June were lucky. They managed to enjoy a four day honeymoon at one of their favourite places, Windermere in the Lake District.

26.4 RAY

As mentioned in Chapter 25, Ray shared similar hobbies to myself, particularly rugby league (he was an avid St Helen's supporter) and walking. Because of our weekly walks on Tuesdays, Ray and I became firm friends.

Tragically, Ray died suddenly on 27 February 2015, aged just 66. Not only had I lost a brother-in-law and walking companion, I'd also lost a true friend. June, his wife, and Stuart, their only son, asked if I'd give a 'Tribute' to Ray at his funeral. I did, but it was a very emotional occasion.

26.5 RAY'S TRIBUTE

Stunned. Shocked. Complete and utter disbelief. These are some of the emotions we all felt on hearing the terrible news about Ray.

Ray was unique. He was a jolly, gentle giant who loved being with people. He organised several fancy dress parties where, as usual, he was the life-and-soul of the party. With children, he was fantastic. He'd fool around and play silly games, and his cheeky grin was infectious. Except for the size difference, it was hard to tell who were the children and who was the adult he enjoyed himself that much.

Ray had many hobbies. One of his favourite was rugby league, particularly his beloved Saints. He'd followed St Helens since he was a boy and loved recounting how he and his mates would travel far and wide following their favourite team. More recently, whenever St Helens and Wigan met in the Challenge Cup Final, both our families made a weekend of it, but we supported different teams. We enjoyed two wonderful weekends, one in Cardiff, where Saints won, and one in Edinburgh, where Wigan won. The fact that I'm a Wigan fan could have caused problems, but it didn't, at least most of the time, just friendly banter. However, I never, ever thought I'd see the day when I'd be wearing a St Helens scarf!*

Ray wrote two books on rugby league and was an active contributor to the Fans Forum on the Total RL website.

Visiting old churches, cathedrals and National Trust properties was another of Ray's passions, one he shared with his wife June. Indeed, he'd just renewed their membership for the forthcoming year. Ray and June often took short breaks around Britain, visiting National Trust properties in their chosen area. One of Ray's favourites was Snowshill, a house packed full of old relics.

Gardening was another of Ray's hobbies. His large garden was always immaculate. Every tree and bush was tended with loving care, shaped and pruned to perfection. He

---

*   I wore a Saints scarf whilst delivering the tribute

even shaped one bush to look like Alien from the science fiction film of the same name! After retiring, he continued his love of gardening by doing gardening jobs for other people.

Perhaps Ray's favourite activity was walking. From a young age he'd always loved to walk, having walked the Pennine Way in his twenties. For the past few years, Tuesdays became our walking day. Tuesdays was June's, Vera's and Elaine's day out, so me and Ray went walking. In our younger days we'd think nothing of climbing the lofty heights of Pendle Hill and Rivington Pike, even in 2 feet of snow but, as Father Time caught up with us, we reverted to the gentler pursuits of the Leeds/Liverpool and Sankey valley canals. But Ray had two strict provisos – we had to take a packed lunch and there had to be a cafe. He loved his food and his pot of tea.

Beautiful as they were, my overriding impression of the walks was the packed lunches. As I tucked into a small sandwich, bag of crisps and a small kit kat, Ray would produce a flask of soup, a big barm cake, a Galloways pie, a Muller rice, a banana and two cakes! And he always finished before me! But here's the strange thing. Unlike me, he always stayed slim.

If the weather was too bad for walking, we'd go to Liverpool and Manchester to visit the docks and museums. As we returned to the car one wet and windy Tuesday, a gust of wind blew Ray's cap into a crevice beside the Manchester Ship Canal. He was devastated. He'd grown so fond of his upmarket flat cap, a Christmas present, that he hardly took it off, even in the house. Secretly, everyone was relieved that at last we'd be able to see his head again, but, lo and behold, the following week he bought another.

I've mentioned Ray's love of rugby, gardening, National Trust properties and walking but without a doubt his greatest love was his family and friends. His wife June, his son Stuart, his grandaughter Jessica, Stuart's partner Katrina and her children David and Courtney. Ray adored Jessica. He cherished the moments he took her to feed the ducks at Pennington Flash and Orrell Water Park. He said many times that these moments of him and Jessica alone together were worth a million pounds. And he'd discussed plans with June to take Jessica on a caravan holiday.

To me, Ray was more than a brother-in-law. He was a true friend. He will be greatly missed by everyone who had the privilege of knowing him. In the words of Tina Turner, he was Simply the Best.

26.6 ELAINE AND KEITH'S WEDDING

It came as no surprise when, a few years after Ray and June's wedding, Vera's youngest sister, Elaine, also elected to get married at St David's. Elaine met her future husband Keith at Aspull Rugby Club where Keith played for the first team. They dated, the relationship flourished and the rest, as they say, is history.

One fine summer's day on Saturday 28 August 1982 Elaine Santus walked down the same aisle as her two elder sisters had before her to marry Keith Johnson. The reception was held at the nearby Haigh Hall where they posed for photographs and, as is evident from Image 251, they made a fine couple. At the last minute, George decided that he didn't want to make a Father-of-the-Bride speech and asked me to do it instead. I did but not, I think, very well.

As pageboys, both Andrew and Michael looked very smart in their outfits, as did Vera, June and Jane (Image 252). The wedding was wonderful but, unfortunately, it signalled the end of the weddings of our close relatives. It would be a long wait before the next one. However, as will become apparent later, the wait was worthwhile.

Elaine and Keith on their Wedding Day.

L to R: Jane (Elaine and Keith's friend),
June, Andrew, Vera and Michael.

437

At school, girls were never Andrew's priority. He preferred the company of boys and became good friends with several, especially Derren Castle and Andrew Stafford. As far as I am aware, his time at university was also romance free, but things would change.

On returning from his sojourn at university (Chapter 19), Andrew decided it was time to leave the family home. To leave the nest he had shared with his family for twenty-three years and become more independent. He moved into a rented, detached house in Sale, a house he shared with one other boy and two girls, and it was here that he met his future bride. But Helen wasn't one of the girls in the house or even someone local. She was from Bradford.

Andrew met Helen via the Internet. Despite having completely different backgrounds (Andrew is a scientist and Helen a musician and singer), it was a perfect match. They 'hit it off' together brilliantly and began dating on a regular basis. When I asked him what she was like, his response was a single word. Curvy.

Apart from Andrew, it was Michael and myself who had the privilege of being the first people from our family to meet Helen. It was a Friday evening and the Wigan Warriors were playing the Bradford Bulls in an important Super League game at the new JJB stadium in Wigan. It was a nervous and anxious few minutes as we waited in the car at the pre-arranged meeting point in Wigan for Andrew and Helen to arrive. Would it be a good evening or would things be awkward? These thoughts were whirling around my head when Andrew and Helen strolled into view. Big beaming smiles lit up their faces and, with their arms entwined around each other, they appeared to be a single entity. The evening went extremely well and, although Helen was disappointed that Bradford lost, she had a really good time.

To be near to Andrew Helen moved from her house in Bradford into rented accommodation in Sale. However, after several months, they decided to buy their own house in Westhoughton. At that time there were no new housing developments in Westhoughton, no 'New Build' homes, so they had to scour the area looking for houses 'for sale'. In 2002, even these were few and far between. One house in particular took their fancy. It was a three-bedroomed detached house on the Wayfaring estate but, at £87,500, it seemed just out of reach. The vendor wouldn't lower his price so, somewhat reluctantly, Andrew and Helen decided to settle for a much smaller semi-detached house on a nearby estate. We could see it wasn't what they wanted and offered them help with the deposit to purchase the house they really wanted. They accepted our offer and, having bought when prices were low, don't regret it one bit. As mentioned in Chapter

23, in 2015 they moved to a large 1930s semi-detached house in Standish, letting out their house in Westhoughton.*

Things didn't go smoothly. The mortgage provider's solicitors were based in Newcastle, a fact which almost caused the sale to collapse. The vendor's solicitors, based in Westhoughton, were pushing for a quick sale and Andrew's solicitors were dragging their feet. Dealing with his solicitors over the phone was extremely difficult and, in the end, we had to drive to Newcastle to collect the necessary paperwork to ensure the transaction was completed on time. (But we did get a discount because of the inconvenience.)

Helen is a lovely attractive girl with an outgoing personality who gets on well with everyone. She quickly became part of our family and it came as no surprise when, a couple of years after moving into their house, they announced their engagement. Like me, Andrew is a devout atheist and therefore wanted a civil ceremony for their wedding. Helen agreed and the search began for a suitable venue. Both Andrew and Helen love the Lake District, a place they visited often to indulge their photographic hobby, and eventually they chose the 'Inn on the Lake' at Glenridding for their wedding venue.

Everything was going fine then, out of the blue, Andrew informed us that the wedding was off. He and Helen had had a major 'bust-up' and cancelled it. We were devastated. They had seemed so happy together. What made it even worse was that, the following day, we had arranged to go with them on a tour of the Black Sheep brewery at Masham in the Yorkshire Dales. We asked them to go ahead, hoping there would be a reconciliation and, somewhat reluctantly, they agreed.

It was a difficult day. On the outward journey Andrew and Helen sat in stony silence on the back seat, making it a very uncomfortable experience. At the brewery, Andrew went outside to answer calls on his mobile phone, leaving Helen in tears thinking that he was speaking to another girl. Eventually, and I don't remember how, they began the making up process and ended a difficult day holding hands and talking to each other. The reconciliation continued apace and, a few months later, the wedding was re-arranged for the following year, this time at Armathwaite Hall, the sister hotel of the Inn on the Lake.

Helen held her hen night in London. One of her school friends, Liz Garner, had moved to Balham and helped enormously with the arrangements, including organising the hotel and an evening meal at an Italian restaurant. Vera, who is ultra conservative when it comes to food, enthused about her lamb shank for months, so it must have been good. However, the highlight of the weekend was a visit to the *Rocky Horror Show*. Dressed as vamps, they not only enjoyed the show but had a great time in a nearby pub, where Helen and her friends danced on the tables.

---

*   18 months later, they moved into a new detached house in the same area (Chapter 28)

Andrew went Dutch and held his stag night in Amsterdam. Dressed in his stag clothes (Image 253), he attracted lots of glances from bemused Dutch folk as he paraded the streets of Amsterdam. The centrepiece of the trip, organised by his best man, Keith McKnight, was a Saturday evening cruise around the bay on a boat. A boat equipped with a live singer and jazz band, plus free wine, beer and cheese (Image 254). Andrew's stag party were sat at the front and, during a short break, I informed the singer that it was Andrew's stag night. "Okay," she said, "I'll do something special for him." And she did. She sang a romantic love song in a very sexy way. But she sang it to the wrong person! Until informed of the error of her ways, she sang it to his best man, Keith. It was most amusing.

Andrew going Dutch in his 'Stag Outfit,'
Amsterdam, Spring 2006.

Andrew with the Jazz Band and
Female Singer on the boat.

No trip to Amsterdam is complete without a visit to the infamous Red Light District. I won't say too much but we did frequent a live sex show and visit several 'Brown Cafes'. Whilst drinking beer in one of the 'Brown Cafes', an almost naked lady in her glass fronted boudoir across the street continually beckoned Stuart, who was sat nearest the window, to join her. It was funny watching his dilemma of should I stay or should I go. (He stayed.)

Keith claimed he had lost an amount of money which, surprise, surprise, coincided with what the 'classier' ladies, who were located towards the centre of the Red Light District, charged for their services. (To be fair, he did lose the money whilst shopping earlier in the day, but it makes a good story.) And, during one of their late night (or, more accurately, early morning) forays, Michael and Stuart found out that the less classy ladies away from the centre offered a 'Buy One Get One Free' service for just 20 Euros, although they were vehement that they didn't take up the offer.

Most of the wedding guests stayed at the Castle Inn Hotel. Situated a mere 400 yards from Armathwaite Hall at the north end of Bassenthwaite Lake,[*] it was an ideal location. The only downside was that the extensive refurbishment started at the beginning of the year wasn't, as had been promised, completed. This meant that while some bedrooms were refurbished, others weren't but, more importantly, the main bar was out of commission and we had to make do with an improvised one.

None of these minor inconveniences detracted from the enjoyment. On the Friday evening we all enjoyed delicious bar meals followed by much drinking and merrymaking. And, before breakfast the following morning, many of us took a refreshing dip in the lovely pool.

The magnificent view from the
rear of Armathwaite Hall.

---

[*]   Bassenthwaite is the only lake in the Lake District. The rest are either 'meres' or 'waters'.

Andrew and Helen on their
Wedding Day, 15 July 2006.

The wedding itself matched the beautiful weather. It was an unforgettable occasion. Everything went as planned. The magnificent view over Bassenthwaite Lake (Image 255) provided a fitting backdrop to a lovely ceremony. Helen looked stunning, as did her bridesmaids, and she and Andrew made a most handsome couple (Image 256). Mum and dad didn't look too bad either (Image 257), and Michael and Kathryn completed a happy family photograph (Image 258).

Everyone thoroughly enjoyed the sumptuous three-course Wedding Breakfast, during which a helicopter landed on the lawn outside (Image 259). The occupants had, quite literally, 'dropped in' for lunch.

Vera and Me.

As is customary, Bill, Helen's dad, who was a chemistry teacher at a private school in Bradford, began the after dinner speeches. It was everything a Father-of-the-Bride's speech should be: witty, informative and just the right length. One bit I remember vividly. "Dad," said Helen. "Andrew's family are lovely, except…"

"Except what," demanded Bill. "They're not child molesters or drug addicts are they?"

L to R: Kathryn, Michael, Helen, Andrew, Vera and Me

The helicopter that 'dropped in.'

"No, it's worse than that. They're Wigan Warriors supporters." It brought the house down. (Helen's family were Bradford Bulls supporters.)

"A beautiful sandy beach on a far away Caribbean island. Waves lapping gently on the silver sand. The setting sun turning the sky a resplendent rustic red. And Helen and me strolling blissfully along, arms entwined and muttering sweet nothings in each other's ears. Then, at the right moment, I would get down on one knee and ask Helen to marry me. It would be so romantic. This was how I intended to propose to Helen. In the event, I asked Helen to marry me one rainy Saturday afternoon on the B and Q car park in Bolton." This is my abiding memory from Andrew's speech.

443

Keith McKnight, Andrew's best man, rounded off the speeches. It was much longer than the previous two, so much so that certain guests ran a book on how long it would be! It was, I think, about 25 minutes. After the meal, the bridesmaids plastered Michael's face with paper hearts (Image 260). He didn't mind one bit, knowing that his and Kathryn's big day wasn't too far away.

A happy Michael with his 'Love Hearts'.

Interspersed between the meal and the evening disco and buffet was a falconry display (Image 261). It went down a treat. At one point the instructor was saying how fearless one of the birds of prey was when, from around a corner a good hundred yards away, a small dog barked. Without hesitation, the bird flapped its huge wings and soared away to the safety of a tall tree and, much to the embarrassment of the instructor, didn't come down for over an hour. Everyone burst into laughter. It was hilarious. Finally, the evening disco and buffet brought the curtain down on a splendid day.

The instructor at the Falconry Display
with one of the Birds of Prey.

Andrew and Helen honeymooned in Italy, spending four days in Rome and seven in Florence. It certainly made an impression because the following year they asked Vera and myself to go back with them to Italy for a holiday. We did and had a most agreeable time, both in Rome and in Sermione, Lake Garda (Chapter 27). However, a few months later, I was struck with a bombshell. One of my best friends, Roy, died suddenly.

26.8 ROY

As was the case with Christine, I had known Roy for many years (Chapter 13). We had similar personalities and shared similar interests, including a love of rugby league. As mentioned above, Roy attended the meals at the *Three Arrows* pub. Furthermore, he always ensured that I was invited to my former Group's Christmas Party, a meal in Manchester followed by a pub crawl around the city. After we'd had our fill of pub crawling, Vera would come and collect us at the entrance to the Victoria Station car park and drive us to Roy's house in St Helens, where Roy would make us a brew before we departed for home.

This idyllic scenario continued for several years. Indeed, Roy and Lynne spent a weekend with us in our caravan in the autumn of 2004, less than two years before Andrew's wedding. It was a great weekend. It was, said Roy, one of the best they'd ever had. We took them to Holker Hall, where Lynne surprised us with her knowledge of the lineage of the Royal Family, to the Inn on the Lake at Ullswater, where Andrew and Helen were thinking of having their wedding, and to the heart of the Lake District, namely Windermere, Ambleside and Grasmere. They weren't walkers but said they fancied a short stroll somewhere pretty but not too strenuous. So we drove to White Moss Common, parked the car and did the short walk along the river to the edge of Grasmere Lake. It was a relatively flat, easy walk, little more than a mile in total, yet Lynne, but particularly Roy, found it hard going. I was surprised. However, I thought no more of it as we returned to

Allithwaite to enjoy our evening meal at the *Guide-Over-Sands* public house. A couple of years later, everything changed.

It was late evening and I was working in the study on my computer when the phone rang. It was after eleven-o-clock. No one rang that late. Vera brought the phone upstairs. "It's Lynne's mother," she said. "She wants to speak to you."

I took the phone and said hello. "Peter. I'm very sorry to bother you at this time but we have some bad news. Roy is dead. He collapsed and died of a massive heart attack in the front garden this evening. I'm really sorry to have to tell you over the phone but we don't know what to do about informing people at work. We don't know who to tell and thought you might know."

It was a bombshell. I was only speaking to him the previous day at work when he introduced me to a Japanese colleague who was also visiting. He seemed right as rain, just as he had at Andrew and Helen's wedding a few weeks earlier (Image 262) and at Lynne's surprise birthday party. These thoughts flashed through my mind like wildfire. I was speechless. "Are you still there?" Lynne's mother's voice seemed faint and far away.

Roy and Lynne at Andrew and
Helen's Wedding, 15 July 2006.

"Yes. I'm still here," I said. "It's just that I can't believe it."

"Neither can we," she said, "but I'm afraid it's true."

The following morning I phoned work to deliver the terrible news. They were as shocked as everyone else.

A few days later Vera and I drove to Roy's house to offer our condolences to Lynne and his family. It was a harrowing time but there was still a sense of humour. Apparently, when the vicar had asked Lynne if there was anything that Roy did particularly well, his youngest daughter, Vicki, had chirped, "Yes. He's brilliant at trumping."

Before we departed, Lynne's mother asked something which I was half expecting. "Peter. Roy talked a lot about you and thought of you as one of his best friends. Would you mind giving the eulogy at his funeral? It's what Roy would have wanted and it's what we want. But," she added quickly, "you don't have to if you don't want."

Delivering that eulogy in front of a packed church for the sudden loss of my best friend was, along with Ray's Tribute, one of the most difficult things I have ever done. I managed to get through most of it without faltering but, near the end, my voice betrayed the emotions I was going through.

26.9 ROY'S EULOGY

Stunned. Shocked. Complete and utter disbelief. These are some of the emotions that we all felt on hearing the terrible news about Roy, a man in the prime of his life.

Roy was unique. He was a kind, caring, softly spoken person with a wry sense of humour who was extremely well liked by everyone. In the 23 years that I have known Roy, I have never heard anyone, and I mean anyone, say a bad thing about him. Roy started work at ICI Runcorn in the 1970s as a Scientific Assistant working with Richard Hann. In 1980 ICI Electronics Group was formed and one of the key projects was electronic photography. At Blackley, our role was to invent new dyes but we were short of effort to meet the demanding targets of our Japanese collaborators. Richard said, "I have a good young lad called Roy Bradbury who you can borrow for six months." Well, we did "borrow" him, not for six months but 23 years! Roy took to dye chemistry like a duck to water and went on to become one of our leading dye chemists, reaching the lofty position of Senior Research Chemist.

Roy and his team successfully developed yellow, magenta and cyan dyes which helped the technology grow into a multi-million pound business.

Roy then moved into ink jet, one of our most successful businesses. Here, he was known as Mr Black and Mr Canon because he led the research into new black dyes (and invented several that are in modern ink jet printers), and was our technical contact with Canon in Japan, one of our major customers. The ink jet business, to which Roy made a major contribution, was recently purchased by Fuji for 150 million pounds.

Roy enjoyed his trips to Japan and it was on one of these that I found out that he could charm the ladies. The flight takes about 12 hours and I must have dozed off as we were approaching Tokyo. When I awoke, Roy's seat was empty. I thought he had gone to the toilet but when he hadn't returned after 5 or 10 minutes I had a look around the cabin. There was still no sign of him. I was getting a little concerned since by this time we had been told to sit in our seats with the seat belts fastened ready for landing. Then, the cockpit door opened and out strolled Roy having fulfilled a lifelong ambition. His charm had worked. He had sweet-talked the stewardess into persuading the captain to let him into the cockpit of the jumbo jet as it landed.

Roy was much more adventurous with food that me and on the trips to Japan, Bradburysan as he was known in Japan, would help to look after me. At dinner with Canon everyone would get their plate of sushi whilst mine would arrive with steak and chips.

Roy also spoke at and attended conferences around the world. Like most other things, he took this in his stride. In the evening, people would relax with a few drinks, a chat and some jokes. I remember Roy telling a joke which ended with him having to drink some beer with his mouth full of feathers, and to swallow the beer and spit out the feathers. An American colleague was so impressed that he asked Roy to teach him the joke so that he could tell it later, which he did. All went well until the end when, to everyone's amusement, he spit out the beer and swallowed the feathers!

Recently, many people have moved on to new companies or retired and Roy has endeavoured to keep in touch wherever possible, especially with those he had worked most closely with. Indeed, several people attending the church service today are evidence of this.

Roy was held in the highest esteem by all his friends and colleagues, both here and abroad. And he has a wonderful family at home. To me, Roy was much more than a friend and colleague. He was my best friend. He will be greatly missed by everyone who had the privilege of knowing him.

Roy, who had a mischievous sense of humour, had the last laugh. As we drove from the church to the crematorium, a violent thunderstorm erupted. The heavens opened as we dashed from the car and everyone got drenched. Looking up, I could almost see Roy's face in the clouds, smiling down at his little joke.

The sudden and unexpected deaths of two colleagues I had known and been close to for many years in the space of a few months affected me badly. Two people both cut down in their fiftieth year. Two people I was very fond of. Two people who were core members of the re-union meals at the *Three Arrows*. I know it's illogical, but ever since Roy and Christine's deaths, no further meals have been arranged. I don't want to tempt fate.

26.10 MICHAEL AND KATHRYN'S WEDDING

Michael and Kathryn met at a local pub, the *Three Pigeons*, when they were both in their early twenties. As Kathryn recalled later, Cupid shot his arrow and that was it. They were hooked. But the hook was loose. Although they began dating steadily, when Kathryn moved down south to train as an air stewardess, they drifted apart.

448

It wasn't a good start but Cupid had done his work. A couple of years later, when Kathryn moved back to her home in nearby Over Hulton, they met again whilst 'clubbing' in Bolton. One of Michael's friends, Phil, spotted Kathryn and urged him to speak to her. He did and the rest, as they say, is history.

After courting steadily for a few years, Michael and Kathryn, like Andrew and Helen before them, decided to buy a house of their own. Both wanted to live in Bolton, their preferred location being a development by Barrett on the site of the former Metal Box factory in Chew Moor. It was an ideal location, close to both Westhoughton, Bolton and the M61 motorway. They had registered their interest with Barrett but, on the day the houses were released, both Michael and Kathryn were unable to attend because of work commitments. Instead, they asked me and Vera to go and try to secure the house they wanted, a lovely, semi-detached house called the 'Maidstone'. We rushed to the site office and managed to secure the last remaining 'Maidstone' by putting down a small retainer of £100. (There was only a handful of Maidstone's on the mixed development.) All they had to do now was obtain a mortgage, which they did, and wait 12 months while the house was built.

During their courtship Michael and Kathryn enjoyed some fabulous holidays. First, it was Goa, partly, I suspect, to enable Michael to indulge his love of elephants. Then, it was South Africa. Although she is a British citizen, Kathryn was actually born in Johannesburg. Coupled with Michael's lifelong love of animals (Chapter 17) and his desire to go on safari, it was no surprise when they elected to have a two-centre holiday in South Africa. Capetown, they said, was absolutely beautiful, as was the five day safari near the Kruger National Park. Here, on the savannahs of South Africa, they saw lions, rhinos, elephants, leopards and buffalo. It was a dream come true.

One evening, as they prepared for dinner in the African bush, a dead antelope was discovered in the middle of the camp. It had been killed by a leopard. Taking no chances, an armed ranger escorted each couple from their hut to the dining area in case the leopard returned to claim its kill. It was pitch black and the ranger continually scanned the surrounding bush with his flashlight to ensure the leopard wasn't lurking around. Demurely, Kathryn asked him if he would direct the torch on to the ground in front of where they were walking. "Why do you want me to do that?" the surprised ranger asked. "I'm keeping a lookout for the leopard."

"Because," said Kathryn, who has a morbid dread of frogs, "I don't want to tread on any frogs!"

They enjoyed South Africa so much that, a couple of years later, the lure of Capetown proved irresistible. This time, however, they returned home with a surprise. It was a beautiful Sunday morning when the phone rang. It was Michael. "Would you and mum like to come round to our house for evening dinner?"

"Certainly," I replied. "We'd love to."

"That's great. But first, can we go and watch Wigan play at Huddersfield in the afternoon?" He had obviously missed his rugby.

Surprisingly, Wigan lost, but the biggest surprise still awaited. The dinner was served later than expected because the chicken took longer to roast than Kathryn had anticipated, but it was an excellent meal washed down with equally excellent (South African) wine. We chatted and drank and looked at their holiday photos until late into the night and, thinking they would be tired, made our excuses to leave. "No, no," said Kathryn. "You've not had dessert yet."

We had dessert followed by more wine and then slowly it dawned on us that there was going to be an announcement. And there was. With a beaming smile on her face, Kathryn proudly extended her left hand to reveal the most beautiful diamond engagement ring. Apparently, she had worn the ring on the flight back to avoid paying duty at customs, but removed it before meeting us at the airport. They had bought it and got engaged in Capetown, in the country where she was born. We were so happy for them.

In true romantic fashion, Michael had proposed to Kathryn on the previous Christmas morning by writing the message WILL YOU MARRY ME in rose petals on the lounge carpet. Kathryn looked at it, went back to bed, came down and said YES.

Unlike Andrew and Helen, Kathryn wanted a church wedding. After scouring the North West a suitable church and reception venue were found. The wedding would take place on Saturday, 8 August 2009 at All Hallows Medieval Church, Mitton, with the reception at the nearby Mitton Hall.

Perched atop a hill, All Hallows Medieval Church has sweeping views across the Ribble valley. Although relatively small, it is a beautiful old church, a truly fitting place in which to 'tie the knot'. And, at the bottom of the hill, the tastefully refurbished Mitton Hall provided an equally splendid venue for the reception (see later).

Kathryn held two hen parties. The first, for herself and her five bridesmaids, was a weekend in Edinburgh. The second was a 'Ladies Evening' at the JJB stadium in Wigan for her family and friends. Eagle eyed Michael had spotted this event whilst watching Wigan Warriors. It seemed excellent value at £20 a head for a four course dinner and live entertainment. I told Vera that 'Ladies Evening' was a euphemism for naked male strippers. "Don't be daft," she said. But it turned out to be true. Kathryn was mortified that her mother and Vera should be exposed to such things, but she needn't have worried. Everyone had a great time (and got some 'naughty' photographs).

It was the Bavarian city of Munich that beckoned Michael and his friends for his stag weekend (Image 263). Like Andrew before him, he also had to dress for the occasion (Image 264).

Michael and his friends in Munich on his Stag Weekend. L to R:
Mark Hinks, Keith Johnson, Phil Hinks, Richard Massey, Michael,
Andrew, Chris Lawson, John Hinks, Rob Thornley, Paul Hinks
and Paddy Barnes. Taken by Me.

After a brief familiarisation tour of the city centre pubs, the group made its
way through the English Gardens to hear the 'Oompah Band' and down a few
more glasses of excellent German beer. On the way through the nudist section, the
setting sun glanced off the pride and joy of a sunbathing naked man. "Bloody Hell!"
exclaimed a startled John. "I think he's polished it with Brasso."

The Saturday afternoon was spent alternating between eating and drinking, with
the latter predominating. It's strange but true that however much beer one consumes
in Munich, it never leaves you with a hangover. The reason, apparently, is because
the beer is fresh and pure and devoid of the chemical preservatives that are added to
mass produced beer.

Michael in his 'Stag Dress.' (Purchased
for four Euros at a local market).

451

In the evening, some of us went on a beer tour, ending up at the Hoffbrau House, famous as the place where Hitler gave his first speech. Then, after a delicious meal of steak and fries in a nearby restaurant, it was off to the outskirts of town for entertainment of the female kind. It was a classy joint with classy ladies. A place recommended by numerous taxi drivers. There were scantily clad ladies, lap dances, stage shows and a good bar. All I will say is that everyone had a thoroughly good time.

The wedding not only took an awful lot of planning, it also created an awful lot of stress. In addition to the usual problems of who to invite and where they would sit, there were the transport arrangements to sort out: a 'Poirot' car for Michael and an eight-seater coach for the bridesmaids (Images 265). But, without any shadow of doubt, the star of the show was the Hansom Cab. It was pulled by the most beautiful horse (Image 266). It's colour and demeanour reminded Vera and me so much of our beloved yellow Labrador (Chapter 17) that we named the horse 'Big Sam'. And, last but by no means least, there was the entertainment. A jazz band, a caricaturist, a harpist, a magician and the DJ and disco.

Michael's 'Poirot' car with David.

The Bridesmaid's eight-seater coach.

The Hansom cab.

On the Friday evening we arranged a meal at the Aspinall Arms for our family and friends. It was a meal that served a dual purpose. As mentioned in Chapter 23, not only was it was a meal for the wedding guests, it was also a meal to celebrate our Ruby Wedding Anniversary.

The wedding service was lovely. It went without a hitch. The female vicar, who I must admit reminded me of *The Vicar of Dibley*, put everyone at ease and conducted it extremely well. The choice of the hymns (Love Divine, Make Me the Channel of Your Peace and King of Kings) added to the occasion, as did the prank his two best men played on Michael. Unbeknown to him, they had stuck HELP ME on the soles of his shoes, a message which became visible to everyone in the congregation the moment he and Kathryn knelt down at the altar.

Kathryn looked gorgeous and Michael wasn't too bad either. Together, they made a most attractive couple (Image 267). Before leaving the church for Mitton Hall, they released two beautiful white doves as a symbol of peace and love (Image 268).

Michael and Kathryn on their wedding day.

Their arrival at Mitton Hall (Image 269) to the strains of *Ain't She Sweet* from the jazz band (Image 270) was stunning. Canapes and champagne taken on the front lawn in the beautiful summer sunshine kept the conversation flowing, but the real show stopper was the caricaturist (Image 271). He was in such demand that we had to extend his stay, causing the meal to be delayed by 45 minutes!

Releasing the doves outside the church.

The arrival of the bride and
groom in a Hansom Cab.

The jazz band.

The Wedding Breakfast of leek and potato soup, a roast beef dinner and a brandy snap basket, washed down with copious amounts of Merlot and Sauvignon Blanc, was delicious. The soothing sounds from the harpist added to the enjoyment. Then, it was time for the speeches.

A very nervous Father-of-the-Bride, Eric, spoke of Kathryn's birth in Johannesburg, and how, as a teenager, her long legs enabled her to become Bolton schoolgirls champion at hurdling for five consecutive years. Michael, and his two best men, John and Phil (Image 263, page 634), all delivered very witty speeches. "Kathryn. You look more beautiful today than I ever thought possible," is the quip I remember most from Michael's speech, a remark that caused the whole room to erupt in laughter (and Kathryn to look slightly bewildered).

John followed Michael and gave a very entertaining rendition of what a best man's speech should be. "Earlier, I asked Kathryn what she expected from today. To spend the rest of my life with the man I love, she said. When I posed the same question to Michael, he said, A new toaster!" Well done John.

"Michael, You're so lucky. Today, you'll leave here having gained a wife who's kind, loving and caring, a wife who radiates beauty wherever she goes. And Kathryn, you're so lucky too. You'll leave here with a lovely wedding dress and a beautiful bouquet of flowers," was just one of many witty phrases from Phil.

The caricaturist's images of Me* and Vera.

After the 'cutting of the cake' ceremony, a magician enthralled the guests with some truly wonderful tricks. The DJ was excellent too, playing just the right music to get everyone dancing, even Andrew and Helen and Katrina and Stuart! The buffet of bacon rolls, sausage rolls and chips was a hit too and, all too soon, a truly splendid evening came to a close.

Michael and Kathryn honeymooned in Thailand. It's a place they wanted to see and it gave them another opportunity to indulge their love of elephants. On their invitation cards, they had asked their guests to give them travel vouchers towards the cost of their honeymoon instead of traditional wedding presents as there was nothing they wanted for their home. Cheeky maybe, but it was done in a delightful way.

We haven't got a wedding list
The reasons we'll explain
Is to save you all the hassle
As shopping is a pain

We would appreciate help though
To send us on our way
And allow us to have our honeymoon
In a land quite far away

And now you know the reason
Behind this cheeky accord
Please help to give us memories
Of a dream honeymoon abroad

---

* This is the caricature on the front cover

'Our' children 1988. L to R: Natalie,
Michael, Michelle, Andrew and Stuart.

Weddings are also a time for reflection. A milestone on the path of life. A time to take stock. A time to risk a backward glance and see how your progeny have developed. A time to see if you have been good parents. We can feel proud. Not only Andrew and Michael, but all five of the children in our extended family have progressed from happy contented children to equally happy adults (Images 272 and 273). For me, the smiling, happy faces of the 'famous five' summed up the emotionally charged days of both our sons weddings.

The 'famous five' at Michael and Kathryn's wedding 2009.
L to R: Natalie, Stuart, Andrew, Michelle and Michael.

27

HOLIDAY TIME

The happy holidays with our children have been described in chapters 12, 13 and 18. This chapter describes some of the holidays Vera and I enjoyed after our offspring had flown the nest.

27.1 ROME AND LAKE GARDA

As mentioned in the previous chapter Andrew and Helen enjoyed their honeymoon in Rome and Florence so much they invited Vera and myself to go back with them the following year. Ray and June had just returned from a lovely holiday at Lake Garda, a place both Vera and I were keen to visit, so we agreed to a two-centre Italian holiday – one week in Rome followed by a week at Lake Garda. Andrew did a brilliant job booking the flights, transfers and hotels and, before departing for Manchester airport, we all ate a hearty lunch at our local garden centre.

It was evening when we arrived at our hotel in Rome. Located just a stone's throw away from the *Trevi Fountain*, it was an excellent location. Tired, hungry and thirsty after a days travelling we desperately needed some sustenance to combat the the hunger and the heat. Aware of our culinary traits, Andrew and Helen guided us through the narrow streets to a McDonalds they'd found on their honeymoon. The Big Mac and fries washed down with a cold diet coke tasted so good in the hot and sultry evening air.

Having been there the previous year Andrew and Helen worked out the week's itinerary. Not surprisingly, we saw the nearby *Trevi Fountain* many times, and the *Spanish Steps*, where Helen got accosted by a local selling trinkets. (She'd vowed she wouldn't get caught this time.) They took us along the River Tiber to the Vatican City, where we queued to see the famous ceiling in the *Sistine Chapel*, and to the nearby *Castel Sant' Angelo*. And, of course, we visited the *Coliseum* and *The Forum*.

Following a tip from Ian Taylor, we avoided the long queues at the *Coliseum* by purchasing a double ticket (for the *Coliseum* and *The Forum*) at the quiet and secluded Forum ticket office. Indeed, *The Forum* was one of our favourite sights. After exploring these ancient wonders, we toddled off for lunch at a restaurant near the *Coliseum*. Helen, who was the most gifted Italian speaker amongst us, did the honours and ordered our meals. Unfortunately, my cheese and tomato toastie was identical to Vera's cheese and tomato sandwich!

We tried different street restaurants for our evening meals but developed a fondness for one with a charming Italian waiter. He always greeted us with Mama, Papa, Big Boy (Andrew) and Princess (Helen). He was charming and friendly and, more importantly, efficient, and the food was good too. Although flattered, we knew it was a con because, on passing the restaurant one evening, we overheard him offering the same greeting to another family of four. However, what surprised us most was his name. He was so Italian yet he said his name was Eric!

The hot weather meant we always ate *al fresco*. Because of my love of soup, and to the annoyance of my companions, we had to search for restaurants serving soup. One evening, this backfired. I was the only one to order soup with my main meal (I don't know why I had hot soup when the weather was so hot) and was most surprised when my soup was served with the main courses of Vera, Andrew and Helen. I ended up eating my main course on my own.

At the next table an immaculately dressed woman wearing dark sunglasses and dripping in expensive jewellery sipped a coffee. She looked vaguely familiar, like a film star or singer, and was obviously important by the way the waiters deferred to her every whim. It was apparent she was waiting for someone since all she'd ordered in over an hour was a single espresso. And she was. Cradling her tiny white pooch in her arms, she stood up as a tall, handsome man approached. What happened next was so funny. This macho man had a large macho dog, a fierce looking German Shepherd. However, when the little pooch started yapping, this fierce looking brute cowered behind its master with its tail between its legs. Because the woman was holding the pooch in her arms, the dog must have thought the yapping pooch was a six foot monster!

Most days were ended by having a relaxing drink in one of the many street bars. One evening, whilst enjoying a cool beer and some nibbles in the *Campo dei Fioro* piazza (square of flowers), the very same square that Giordano Bruno was burned alive at the stake by the Roman inquisition for daring to suggest that the stars were just distant suns surrounded by planets that might harbour life like ours, Vera had a funny turn. The heat and humidity had taken their toll and she was on the verge of fainting. We had to give her lots of cold water and let her rest before escorting her back to the hotel.

Whilst in Rome we had time for just one excursion. Andrew and Helen insisted we had to visit Florence, regarded by many as the most beautiful city in the world. We duly booked our seats on the train (in Italy you're not allowed to board a train unless you have a pre-booked seat) and enjoyed our journey through the beautiful Tuscany countryside in an immaculately clean and comfortable train.

As we approached the *Duomo,* I remember Andrew's words well. "Prepare to be amazed," he said. And I was. The *Duomo,* the Italian word for cathedral, was a magnificent sight, as was the statue of David in the city square. Helen said his penis was made deliberately small to make the men feel good. The Ponte *Vecchio,* the old bridge full of (expensive) jeweller's shops over the River Arno, was equally impressive. Even Hitler loved it, ordering his bombers to leave it untouched during World War II. In the afternoon we walked up a lovely little hill beside the river to a cafe, where we enjoyed a relaxing drink whilst admiring the magnificent views over the city.

After a wonderful week my overriding impressions of Rome, apart from the famous sights, were the heat, the busy traffic (crossing the road could be a nightmare), and the delight of seeing something different around every corner.

For our holiday at Lake Garda we'd planned to stay in Garda itself but, after listening to Ray and June, we stayed at Sirmione. After a train journey from Rome to Verona, followed by a longish taxi ride, we arrived at our hotel. The Eden Hotel is in an excellent location. Not only is it beside the lake, it is also near the centre of the charming old town of Sirmione. Although the decor was dated, both ourselves and Andrew and Helen had large rooms overlooking Lake Garda. The staff were welcoming and friendly and the breakfasts delicious. There were spacious outdoor areas in which to relax, including a wooden jetty with steps down to the lake for those who wished to swim. We were all pleased, both with Sirmione and the Eden Hotel, and looked forward to having a relaxing week to recover from our exertions in Rome.

The first few days were spent exploring Sirmione itself. Its narrow, winding streets, squares, beaches, bars, cafes and shops were a delight. We visited Scaligera Castle, where Vera and Andrew stayed firmly rooted to the ground (they don't like heights) whilst Helen and I explored the ramparts, and the holiday home of Maria Callas, the famous Italian opera singer. We also lit some candles in a quirky little church. Whilst Vera and Helen rummaged in the shops, Andrew and I sampled the local beers. Later, we all strolled along the promontory past the bus station to a small park, where we played a game of crazy golf.

Helen and I paddled in the lake, walking on huge slabs of rock just beneath the surface. It was like we were walking on water. But we had to be careful. The rocks were very slippery and on more than one occasion we had the odd accident, slipping and falling into the warm waters of the lake.

We caught the small train to the *Grotto of Catullus,* some ancient ruins on a hill, which afforded excellent views to the impressive mountains surrounding Riva del Garda at the northern tip of the lake. On the hill we refreshed ourselves at a little cafe, where the birds were so tame they ate out of our hands.

The lovely Piccolo Castello restaurant.

In the evenings we sampled several restaurants but our favourite was the *Piccolo Castello* beside the castle. Andrew and Helen discovered this lovely little restaurant when they had their anniversary meal there (Vera and I ate at a different restaurant that evening) and enjoyed it so much that we all ate there the following two nights. We pre-booked tables on the first floor balcony overlooking the illuminated castle in order to get the best views (Image 275, page 463). Watching the swans gliding gracefully on the castle moat in the evening twilight as we wined and dined was so romantic.

We always ended the day in one of the many bars. Our favourite was the bar on the beach beside the castle. Watching the lizards dashing up and down the illuminated pink and green castle walls as we sipped our preferred tipples was a good way to end the day. The view over the lake wasn't bad either.

Ray and June had gone on about the boats on Lake Garda and we presumed that's how they'd done their excursions. Therefore, we used the boats for our trips, especially the fast boats. We used them for trips to Garda, Malcesine and Gardone, but they were expensive. (It transpired that Ray and June hadn't used the boats at all; they'd used the bus because the boats were so expensive!)

We all liked Garda. The waterfront restaurants along the sweeping expanse of the bay and the narrow roads and alleyways populated with quaint little shops made it a Mecca for cafe lovers and shoppers alike. Andrew and myself bought leather belts and wallets whilst Helen and Vera bought leather handbags. Our retail therapy sated, we walked along the lovely shoreline to Bardolino in sweltering temperatures, having an ice cream or two to cool us down. And yes, we did sample some Bardolino wine before catching the boat back to Sirmione. On our visit to Gardone, the heat was so overpowering that we had to seek sanctuary in the cool interior of the local church.

Romeo, Romeo, wherefore art thou? No trip to Italy is complete without visiting Verona, the city where Romeo and Juliet expressed their love for each other on the

461

now famous balcony. For this journey, we travelled by bus. On arriving in Verona we joined the throng of tourists from around the world in the small square as they jostled to have their pictures taken underneath the balcony. We also visited the office where several ladies were employed full-time writing handwritten replies to letters addressed to Romeo and Juliet. (Touching but how can people be so naive?) Not only did we see the famous balcony, we also saw the Coliseum. Perhaps not quite as impressive as its counterpart in Rome, it is famous for hosting a number of high profile music festivals.

All too soon it was time to return home. We flew back from the tiny airport of Brescia, a former Italian air force base, where Jackie Smith, Labour's Home Secretary at that time, was a fellow passenger.

27.2 SIRMIONE AND VENICE

In 2013, Vera and I returned to Italy for another two-centre holiday, ten days in Sirmione and five in Venice. Why? Mainly it was because we like Italy but also to do the things we hadn't had time to do before, like a round-the-lake tour, the Dolomites and Venice. We booked the holiday with Thomsons, electing to stay at the same resort and same hotel as before but, to our dismay, we didn't get a lake view room. However, on the plus side, the hotel had been completely refurbished.

The tour around the lake took a full day. Most of the tour was by coach, although part of the mountainous northern section near the remote town of Riva del Garda had to be done by boat. We stopped at some lovely little towns, such as Limone and Salo but, apart from Sirmione and Garda, Malcesine was one of our favourites. Sandwiched between the imposing Mount Baldo and the lake, we thought it a lovely place.

Perhaps our favourite excursion was the trip to the Dolomites, the imposing mountain range on the Italian – Swiss border. Our guide for this tour was Silke, a lovely German lady. She gave a most interesting commentary as the coach wove its way along the beautiful valley towards the Dolomites, pointing out the charming little hamlets nestled in the hillside, one of which we stopped at on our return journey. We passed the ski slope where the Italian skiers train for the Olympics and, a little further on, a cable car lift which was the scene of a terrible tragedy a few years earlier. A low flying American fighter jet crashed into the the cable, causing the cars to plummet to the valley below, killing all on board. Then, with impeccable timing, she asked how many people wanted to take the cable car to the summit of the Dolomites! At least twenty were required to obtain the massive group discount but, because of her tale about the crash, I feared she wouldn't get them. To my relief (I don't know about Vera), she did, just.

The view from the top of the Dolomites was amazing. The grey mountain peaks were so beautiful (Image 274). It felt like we were on top of the Himalayas. Even though it was a hot, sunny day in the height of summer, there was still plenty of snow about and it didn't appear to be melting. After a drink and a cake in the cafe, we boarded the cable car in readiness for the descent. It had glass sides and a glass floor so passengers could take full advantage of the magnificent views, but it was a long way down to the coach park and I think Vera closed her eyes as the cable car commenced its rapid descent.

Vera on top of the Dolomites in the snow.

Every morning at our hotel we heard the sound of Desenzano, Garda, Bardolino… as the boats arrived at the nearby jetty, so we felt we had to visit Desenzano. Located at the southern tip of the lake, it was only a short hop on the boat from Sirmione. Desenzano is a more modern, busier town than most other towns around Lake Garda, but pretty nonetheless, and we spent a most enjoyable day there.

In the evenings, we sampled the delights of several restaurants but went to the *Piccolo Castello* (Image 275) so often the proprietor presented us with a bottle of wine on our final night (Image 276).

Venice is something else. Its network of canals and narrow winding streets make it unique. The travel agent at Thomsons chose our hotel. Situated near the Rialto Bridge, the location of the Malibran Hotel was very good but the supposedly five star hotel was anything but. It was old and dated and had dirty mattresses stacked in the corridors. In our bedroom, a wardrobe door was hanging off and one of the drawers was broken. The bathroom wasn't brilliant either. Although it wasn't dirty, the rusty streaks on the old steel bath made it appear so. We should have complained, but didn't. Surprisingly, the American guests loved it. Its one redeeming feature was the evening meals. They were good and reasonably priced.

In Venice, we did the usual touristy things. We admired St Marks square (Image 277) but avoided paying 20 Euros for a coffee, had a gondola ride from the Bridge of Sighs (Image 278), and used the water taxis to get around. I thought it would be a good idea to take a water taxi tour of Venice by night, but Vera had reservations. And she was right. Except for the tourist attractions, most of the city was in complete darkness, so we saw very little. Even worse, it was so dark it was difficult to discern the names of the stopping points and we almost missed our stop for the hotel. However, we enjoyed our trips to Murano, the island where the famous glass is made, and Burano, the island famous for lacemaking. The latter in particular was very pretty (Image 279). We also bumped into Silke, the German guide for our trip to the Dolomites, who was hosting a trip to Venice.

Vera, the proprietor (on the right) and her
waitress at the Piccolo Castello restaurant.

Vera in St Marks Square.

On more than one occasion we almost got lost in the labyrinth of narrow streets, but discovered some beautiful secluded squares in the process. Whilst enjoying a coffee at one such square, a gondola stopped on the adjacent canal and the gondolier serenaded not only his passengers, but also the patrons of the cafe.

Me* and Vera on Gondola.

In the evenings we strolled along the canals searching for a quiet bar to end the day. One evening whilst strolling along the Grand Canal, I was shocked at the price of a beer. Fifteen Euros seemed pretty extortionate. Mean I am not but I hate being ripped off. We continued on towards a small wooden hut which seemed popular with teenagers. I quickly saw why. A frail old Japanese lady was selling bottles of wine for just 12 Euros. Not only that, she also opened the bottle and provided free plastic cups too. This was much better value so, armed with our opened bottle of red wine and two plastic cups, Vera and I became recycled teenagers sitting on the bank of the Grand Canal drinking our wine. It was like being young lovers all over again. The sitting down bit wasn't a problem, but getting up without falling into the Grand Canal after consuming a full bottle of wine was another matter entirely, but we managed it and made our way safely back to the hotel.

Market Square on the island of Burano.

27.3 CRUISE TO ICELAND AND NORWAY

We'd always fancied an ocean cruise so when Andrew and Helen asked us to join them on one we readily accepted their offer.

---

* This is the image I use for the 'About the Author' section at the end of my books

The company we chose, Celebrity, had just launched a brand new cruise ship, the Celebrity Eclipse, and it was this ship on which we booked our cruise (Image 280). Andrew said it was worth paying a little more to travel Concierge class because you got better facilities: larger outside staterooms with a private balcony, fast track boarding and a whopping $800 per cabin on-board spend, as well as other extras.

We hired a Ford Galaxy for the journey to Southampton, arriving at the Grand Harbour Hotel one late August afternoon in 2012. After dropping off the hire car, we freshened ourselves up in our rooms before enjoying evening dinner in the hotel dining room. As we stepped outside the hotel for a leisurely stroll along the quayside, we met a couple who'd just returned from a cruise. They enthused about the Eclipse, saying it was the best cruise ship they'd been on, and they'd been on many. After our stroll, we retired to the bar where Andrew and me had a few too many whiskies.

The Celebrity Eclipse cruise ship.

The following morning a mini-bus transported us and our luggage the short distance to the ship. After going through the check-in procedure (it was a breeze for Concierge class passengers), we were welcomed on board with a complimentary glass of champagne and directed to the main restaurant to enjoy a complimentary meal and further complimentary drinks whilst our staterooms were prepared.

The staterooms were lovely. Our stateroom was adjacent to Andrew and Helen's and the staff kindly agreed to remove the glass partition separating the two balconies, allowing the four of us to relax and enjoy our evening tipples together (Image 281). As the ship left port, we sat on the balcony as it sailed down the Solent and around the Isle of Wight before continuing its two day journey past the coast of Ireland to Iceland, our first destination. The two sea days were relaxing and allowed us time to explore the ship and get our bearings.

Andrew and Helen on balcony
enjoying an evening tipple.

The on-board facilities were first class. There were about 15 restaurants and cafes, a dozen bars, a casino, two theatres, a cinema, a swimming pool, a gymnasium and a shopping mall. Our favourite bars were the Wine Cellar, Michael's Club and the Ice Bar. The wine cellar was an oasis of tranquility. It was traditionally furnished with wooden panelling and sumptuous leather seats. By pre-paying we could dispense our chosen wines from the myriad of dispensers anytime we wanted.

The wine cellar was a quiet relaxing place to enjoy a glass of wine but if we fancied somewhere a bit more lively we patronised the Ice Bar, so named because the bar surface was made of ice. We got so friendly with the waiter that, as the cruise progressed, our whiskies grew exponentially!

Michael's Club was more akin to a Gentleman's Club with oak panelled walls, plush carpets and a resident pianist. It was the place we frequented for pre-dinner drinks.

At evening dinner we had a dedicated table for four in a secluded corner of the restaurant served by a head waiter, a wine waiter, a beer waiter and a soft drinks waiter (Image 282). The four course evening dinners were delicious and the service superb. The menu changed daily but there was always a default option of steak, chicken and fish. The only downside was that with the rich evening dinners and all the other free food available it was very easy to over indulge and pile on weight (Image 292, page 473).

Me, Vera, Andrew and Helen at our dinner table
(left) and with three of our waiters (right).

Reykjavik, the capital of Iceland, was a disappointment. However, the Golden Circle tour around the Thingwellir National Park was anything but. The contrasting scenery was absolutely amazing. Expanses of jagged, sharp black rock, reminiscent of the dark side of the moon, gave way to the lush greenery of Parliament Plain (Image 283).* We marvelled at the canyon which marks the fault line between the European and American tectonic plates but the highlight of the tour was the geothermal park of Geysir, where we witnessed 'Strokkur' spout towers of hot boiling water in the air every 20 minutes. Not only were the geysers spectacular, the vast reserves of subterranean hot water was the source of all of Iceland's heating and power. (You can't get greener than that.)

Our final stop on the tour was the amazing golden waterfalls of Gullfoss, one of the iconic waterfalls of Iceland.

Me and Vera on Parliament Plain.

---

*   The Icelandic parliament was founded on this plain

Our second day in Reykjavik was spent at the famous Blue Lagoon. Vera and Helen were a little wary but Andrew and I loved it (Image 284). It was like having a warm bath and the water was purported to have healing powers.

The ship then made the short journey to Akureyri. In contrast to Reykjavik, Akureyri was a town more like those in England's green and pleasant land, with lush vegetation and colourful flowers. We explored the lovely park and downed some cool drinks before returning to our ship for our next destination. The Faroe Islands.

Me before my dip in the Blue Lagoon.

Our ship docked in the picturesque town of Klaksvik, the second largest town after Torshavn, the capital of the Faroe Islands. We boarded a coach for our pre-booked tour. First, we travelled under the sea in the 6.3 kilometre long Norooyatunnilin road tunnel and then saw the iconic Eidi Football Stadium nestled by the sea, regarded by many as the most beautiful football pitch in the world. Later, we paused for photographs at The Giant and the Hag (witch), two rugged rocky pillars that rose from the sea. I couldn't resist taking apicture of Andrew and Helen with the Hag as the backdrop (Image 285) since her full name is Helen Anne Gregory (HAG).

Picture of Andrew and Helen with the
Giant and the Hag in the background.

Gerainger, our first port of call in the Norwegian fjords, was absolutely stunning. The fjords are awesome. They are so huge that the Eclipse, a very large cruise ship, was but a mere speck in these enormous natural structures.

The following morning dense low cloud engulfed the fjord and I feared our trip along the Snow Road to Laerdal would be cancelled as it would be extremely hazardous to drive in such conditions. To both mine and Andrew's relief (I'm not sure about the ladies) the driver decided the trip would go ahead.[*] It was a spectacular sight as the coach emerged from the cloud cover to reveal a cotton wool blanket of white floating above the fjord (Image 286). As well as stopping at Laerdal, the coach also stopped on the snow road to allow the passengers to frolic in the snow and throw snowballs at each other (Image 287).

For our wedding anniversary Andrew and Helen had bought us a dinner reservation in one of the 'Speciality' restaurants, and we'd been advised by the crew to have our dinner in the magnificent Tuscan Grille restaurant as the ship set sail from Gerainger. Having pre-booked the meal many months ago we were given the best table in the house, right in the centre of the panoramic glass window at the rear of the ship (Image 288). There must have been at least seven courses to the meal but the thing that sticks in my mind was that Vera had her first taste of ravioli – and loved it.

Vera and Me pictured above the
cloud layer covering the fjord.

---

* I suppose the experienced drivers are used to such conditions

Vera on the Snow Road to Laerdal.

We stopped at Flam, with its famous mountain railway, followed by Olden, Andrew's favourite. Here, we boarded a coach to Lake Stryn.

View as we left Gerainger from our
table at the Tuscan Grille restaurant.

Lake Stryn is one of the most beautiful places I have ever seen (Image 289). It was so beautiful that one of our fellow passengers remarked that if God came to Earth he would live at Lake Stryn. Vera and I loved it (Image 290).

471

Lake Stryn. No picture can
do justice to its beauty.

Vera beside Lake Stryn.

Me beside Lake Stryn.

Bergen, Norway's second city, was beautiful also (Image 291). We had a lovely time exploring the wooden buildings along the harbour, buying presents, such as coffee mugs and bob caps, for both our relatives and ourselves.

I know it was August but the warm and sunny weather surprised and delighted us. Indeed, it was so warm that I sunbathed on the balcony as we crossed into the Arctic Circle (Image 292).

Some of the lovely buildings in Bergen.

On the Eclipse a news sheet was issued daily describing the main events back home. Surprisingly, it also gave the rugby league results. Wigan had played Warrington in an important Super League match and I studiously avoided seeing the score as I'd recorded the game. However, one morning at breakfast a man sat at the next table voiced his disappointment that Wigan had lost.

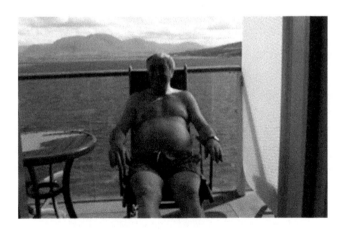

Me sunbathing on the balcony in the Arctic Circle.
The rich evening dinners and all the other free
food had taken their toll on my tummy.

On the journey back to Southampton Vera and I attended an evening show in the theatre whilst Andrew and Helen enjoyed a disco. The following afternoon Andrew and I went to a lecture on the workings of the ship (it used four tonnes of fuel per mile) while Vera won a T-shirt playing bingo. In the casino Andrew won a small amount at the roulette wheel and Helen won on a slot machine.

As is the custom we had our photographs taken at one of the formal dinners (Image 293). All too soon a wonderful cruise came to a close.

Me, Vera, Andrew and Helen in formal dinner attire.

27.4 NEW YORK

In the year of Vera's sixty-fifth birthday in 2012 not only did we have the cruise to Norway (Section 27.3) but Vera also overcame her fear of flying to go to New York, a city she'd always wanted to visit. We booked the one week holiday in June, so she would be in New York on the day of her birthday, 26 June. Displaying my stubborn streak, I insisted on flying British Airways from Heathrow to JFK, even though there were direct Virgin flights from Manchester, because that's the way I'd travelled on business trips. The shuttle to Heathrow wasn't a problem but getting through one of the world's busiest airports most certainly was. It was so hectic we almost missed our flight. The unfriendly staff didn't help matters either. Even though we'd booked with British Airways, the outward flight was with American Airlines, their partner airline. We had two standalone seats, a window seat and an aisle seat, the staff were obliging and friendly, and the food and service were first class.

At JFK the customs officer surprised us. "Are you going home the slow way?" he enquired. Seeing our puzzled looks he continued, "Well, you Brits, you normally arrive by plane and return on the QE2."

No, we assured him, we were returning the way we'd come, the fast way by plane.

The holiday didn't get off to a good start. As we travelled by taxi from JFK to Manhattan through Queens, the home of Flushing Meadows, the venue for the American Grand Slam tennis tournament, Vera was not impressed. She thought it a run down, scruffy area. As we neared our destination, the Crown Plaza Hotel* in Times Square, recommended by Ian and Sharon Taylor who'd stayed there earlier in the year, she was still unimpressed, especially when the taxi driver refused my 10 per cent tip and virtually demanded 18 per cent.

"Why on earth have you brought me here," were her exact words. "The noise, the traffic, the crowds, the concrete buildings. It's everything you hate." To a degree, she was right, but they seemed perfectly normal in New York. In fact, they epitomise the bustling city that never sleeps. To compound matters even more, in the evening we couldn't find the restaurant Ian and Sharon had recommended and ended up eating our evening meal in a McDonalds, where Vera got the wrong meal. (She always has plain hamburgers but occasionally they come full of relish, which she hates.) All in all, it wasn't a good first day. However, as for the rest of the holiday, she absolutely loved it.

As we do when visiting a city for the first time, we booked a two day ticket with a tour bus company. This allowed us to get our bearings, see the sights and to hop on and off the buses whenever we wanted. We went to the top of the Empire State Building (Image 294), originally dubbed the Empty State Building** by its rival, the owners of the Chrysler Building, because it was unoccupied for lengthy spells. The views from the top over Manhattan and the Hudson River were simply amazing. Vera also loved the Rockefeller Centre, especially the open air cafe on the ground floor where we ate lunch. Not surprisingly, she was enthralled by the shops on 5th Avenue, where we 'Built a Bear' for our niece, Layla, and the fabulous Grand Central Station, which is more like the foyer of a five star hotel than a train station. We took the bus over Brooklyn Bridge, where the tour guide pointed out the apartment owned by David Beckham, and the Italian restaurant on the other side where everyone has to queue, including the President of the United States.

---

*   We normally stay in Marriott Hotels but the Crown Plaza was a lovely hotel in a superb location in Times Square, although the restaurant facilities were somewhat limited

** The Empire State Building was built by the Ford Motor Company

Me and Vera at the top of the
Empire State Building.

The most moving part of our stay in New York was Ground Zero. It took ages to pass through the intensive security arrangements but, once inside, it was so beautiful. The atmosphere overwhelmed us. People spoke in hushed tones as they milled about the grounds, reading the thousands of names engraved in the slate walls surrounding the two enormous holes where the twin towers once stood. The sound of the water cascading down the sides, the floral tributes to those who had died, and the peace and solitude, was so poignant. Nearby, the new Freedom Tower soared majestically into the clear blue sky, emphasising that good will always prevail against evil. It was a most moving experience.

Before leaving Ground Zero, I asked an official for directions to Pier 42, which I'd visited on the 'Duty Case Trial' (Chapter 23), so we could enjoy some fish and chips for tea. After walking for some time there was no sign of Pier 42, so we turned back and headed to the other side of Manhattan. The pier was there but it wasn't Pier 42, it was Pier 17! We had our fish and chips, explored the quaint little shops on the wooden pier, then walked to Battery Park at the southern tip of Manhattan to catch the bus. A bus was just leaving but, rather than run to catch it, we decided to wait for the next one. It would be along in 15 minutes. Well, we waited and waited but no bus came. Getting rather worried, I checked the timetable given to us by the tour company. The last bus from Battery Park was 8-00 p.m., the one we'd just missed. Ignoring the underground and having only a few dollars on us, we decided to walk back to Times Square. It might not have seemed far viewed from the top of the Empire State Building, but the walk from Battery Park to Times Square was a good few miles. Along the way we asked a policeman if we were heading in the right direction. "You what! You're walking from Battery Park to Times Square," he gasped incredulously. "Take a taxi or the Metro." We didn't and, about an hour later, arrived at our hotel with feet that were so blistered and bleeding that we had to get some ointment and plasters to ease the pain.

From our hotel window we had a clear view of the port where the cruise ships docked and decided to book an evening cruise around the Statue of Liberty. The boat departed at 7-30 p.m. so we elected to eat in the hotel restaurant when it opened at 6-00 p.m. and catch a taxi to the port. I ordered soup and a well done steak and chips. It was a mistake. It took ages for the meal to be served and Vera became more and more agitated as the clocked ticked on (Image 295). (She'd ordered chicken.) At 7-15 we dashed out of the restaurant to the taxi rank and stated our destination. "Oh, I'm not authorised to take you there. I'm not allowed to cross the busy Boulevard," said the taxi driver.

"Okay, take us as near as possible," I replied, and jumped in. In the event, he did take us to the port and we caught the boat.

It was a fine evening so I chose seats on the outside deck. The views of the Manhattan skyline in the fading evening light were magnificent but Vera was disappointed with the Statue of Liberty. She thought it was dirty and needed a good clean. As the night closed in the temperature on board the boat plummeted and we began to shiver. "Let's go inside," I said, freezing in my shorts and T-shirt.

Vera with her angry face in the restaurant.

477

"No," replied Vera firmly, "we're staying here." She was getting her revenge for my earlier misdemeanours.

Without a doubt Vera's favourite part of New York was Central Park. Located just half-a-mile north of Times Square, it is absolutely huge. Enclosed by towering skyscrapers, it is an oasis of green in a vibrant, bustling city. We declined the offer of a horse drawn carriage ride, preferring instead to walk. It was wonderful watching the walkers, joggers, cyclists, carriages and the occasional car as we strolled through this vast expanse of parkland. The Turtle Pool, the lake, the bandstand made famous by the Friends programme, and the street artists were all fabulous, but Vera's favourite was the castle (Images 296), where couples got married and strolled barefoot through the park. She also liked the pond which people skate on in winter.

Overall, it was a marvellous holiday in an exciting city which I'm sure will lure us back.

Castle and lake in Central Park (left) and
Vera relaxing in Central Park (right).

27.5 VIKING RIVER CRUISE

It was Andrew and Helen who fancied a river cruise. Vera had occasionally talked about cruising down the Rhine so we agreed to join them. We chose a Viking river cruise from Amsterdam to Basel (Image 297) followed by an extra three days at Lake Lucerne and, in July 2015, boarded our flight to Amsterdam.

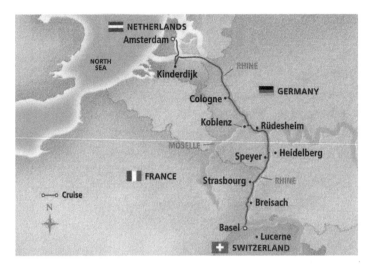

Cruise itinerary.

The holiday didn't start well. The plan was to spend the day in Amsterdam and board our ship in the evening. This didn't happen because the tall ships were in Amsterdam which meant we were bussed to Rotterdam to board our ship.

The ship was okay but tiny compared to the Celebrity Eclipse. After unpacking our luggage we enjoyed some relaxing drinks on the top deck. Andrew and Helen worked out that it would be cheaper to purchase the drinks package of 200 euros which covered all our drinks for the duration of the cruise.

The dining package included breakfast, lunch and evening dinner but the drawback, as far as we were concerned, was the open seating arrangement. Unlike on the Eclipse, we didn't have a dedicated table and had to sit with strangers on a large table at every meal, something which Vera hated. Not only that, the clientele were predominantly Americans, something we didn't expect on a European river cruise.

Our first stop was the UNESCO heritage site of Kinderdijk, an array of Dutch windmills nestled beside a network of canals. Our tour guide warned us to be extra careful as we explored the windmills as a number of people had been killed by the rotating arms.

Next up was the German city of Cologne. Our guide for the afternoon tour, Udo, was excellent. His funny and witty comments as he showed us the main sites made it a most interesting tour. As we entered the impressive cathedral he asked if we'd departed from Amsterdam or Basel. "Why?" someone asked.

"Because if you'd departed from Basel you'd have ABC syndrome."

"What's ABC syndrome?'

"Another Bloody Cathedral," he answered, laughing.

Udo was also our guide for the evening beer tour. He gathered our group of about a dozen outside a waterfront bar where a waiter stood outside. Then, in a loud voice he said, "Never, ever go into a bar where a waiter is stood outside. The better establishments don't do that. And never go in one which serves beer in large glasses," he continued, pointing to the steiners on the tables. I pitied the poor waiter. No wonder his bar was empty.

Udo led the group into some really interesting bars (Image 298) and explained the German etiquette of drinking. The fine beer was indeed served in small glasses and, as soon as your glass was empty, your attentive host immediately brought a fresh one. If, however, you wanted a break from drinking you placed a beer mat on top of your glass. Then, when you were ready to resume, the beer mat was removed and a fresh drink would arrive almost immediately. It was a system which worked really well.

At Koblenz, our next port of call, we visited Marksburg Castle. Perched on top of a hill the castle was quite impressive but our aged tour guide was anything but. However, the next phase of our journey more than atoned for that disappointment.

Me outside Peter's Beer House.

480

Andrew and Helen enjoying a beer.

The scenery along the Rhine, Germany's industrial river, was mostly unimpressive except, that is, for the Rhine Gorge. This beautiful stretch of waterway was absolutely spectacular. It was stunningly beautiful. The 132 metre high rock that jutted out into the river, with a 16 foot statue of Lorelei, the mermaid who lured ships on to the rocks, stood proudly on top, was simply breathtaking. To add to the wonderment, the Lorelei song was played as the ship sailed slowly through the gorge.

At Rudesheim, a picturesque little town, we had our evening meal in an Italian restaurant as a change from eating on the ship.

Heidelberg, Germany's university equivalent to Oxford and Cambridge, was absolutely lovely. With a river running along the valley and the castle sat atop the mountainside (Image 299), it was both spectacular and beautiful. On the castle tour we saw the biggest wine barrel in the world (Image 300) and, as our guide assembled his tour party in the castle square, he suddenly and unexpectedly burst into song, giving an excellent rendition of the German drinking song. He was so good he must have been a trained singer.

The enchanting city of Heidelberg
with the castle on top of the hill.

After Heidelberg we made a short stop at Speyer before enjoying a longer stop at Strasbourg, the home of the European Court of Human Rights. Strasbourg was captivating. It exuded character. A river flanked by beautiful old houses bedecked with flowers wound its gentle way through the city (Image 301). Criss-crossed with quaint bridges, it was most impressive. Cafes, shops and bars were everywhere. The hot, sunny day enhanced an already pleasing experience.

At our next stop, Breisach, we boarded a coach for an eagerly awaited tour around the famous Black Forest. The scenery didn't disappoint. We did a short walk along a wooded ravine before returning to the little village to sample some tea and, of course, Black Forest gateau. In the large craft shop I was amazed by the number and variety of cuckoo clocks. I never imagined there could be so many.

Wine barrel in Heidelberg Castle.

At Basel, the final stop on the cruise, we left the ship and boarded a coach to Lake Lucerne for the last three days of our holiday. As the coach approached Lucerne it stopped at the Lion statue. Sculpted in memory of the Swiss Guards killed at the Vatican, it is the most saddest looking, yet beautiful, lion I have ever seen (Image 302).

The Radisson Blue Hotel was modern, with large air-conditioned rooms, a spacious *en suite* and a king size bed. It was a welcoming abode in which to rest our tired bodies. We plonked on the bed and looked forward to a relaxing three days. Not only that, we'd be free of Americans.

The beautiful city of Strasbourg.

The lion of Lucerne.

After we'd rested awhile, we explored Lucerne looking for a restaurant to have our evening meal. All of us were impressed with Lucerne. Nestled between the lake and the mountains, it was a splendid place. A beautiful waterfront, quirky little back streets, a small harbour and numerous bars and cafes were just some of its delights (Image 303). The sunsets were spectacular too, as was the moonlight on the waters of the lake.

After selecting our restaurant on the waterfront we strolled back to our hotel to freshen up and change for dinner. As we approached the hotel a crowd was gathering outside the nearby Concert Hall for the evening performance. Curious, we looked who was performing. We couldn't believe our eyes. It was The Boston Philharmonic Orchestra and the gathering crowd was mainly Americans!

Me and Vera enjoying a beer (left) and
me and Helen enjoying a beer (right).

We took all our evening meals beside the water and all were delicious (and expensive). One sunny afternoon we sauntered down to a small beach. It was a hot, sunny day so I decided to have a paddle to cool my aching feet. I asked Helen to take a picture of me paddling, but she never arrived. However, she managed to take one as I was preparing to paddle (Image 304). Puzzled as to why she hadn't taken one of me paddling I returned to where they were sitting. She said that as soon as she got her camera out, a man appeared from nowhere and told her to put it away or he would call the police. Apparently, photography on beaches is forbidden in Switzerland.

We all really enjoyed Lake Lucerne and were sad when we had to leave for Zurich for our flight home. However, in just eleven days we had visited four countries: Holland, Germany, France and Switzerland. We couldn't have asked for more.

Me preparing to paddle.

27.6 SHORT BREAKS

Vera and I love short breaks in Britain. They are our best kind of holiday. There's no hassle with airports, taxis, passports, travel insurance or jet lag. You just jump into your car and off you go.

484

Our love of short breaks began with our children with walking holidays in the lakes and sightseeing trips to London and Richmond Hill (Chapter 12). As you will see later, it continued with both William and Jean and Brian and Valerie. Initially, we used Tesco vouchers (Vera shops at Tesco) to fund these breaks, enjoying stays at Glasgow and Bristol (Chapter 23). We also had short breaks in Cardiff, where the castle and Cardiff Bay were the highlights, Swansea, where we visited the beautiful Mumbles coastline, and the Thistle Hotels in London, the Westminster Thistle, which is no longer there, being our favourite. As time progressed the booking process with Tesco vouchers became a pain and the Marriott hotels were removed from their scheme, so now we either look for good offers on the internet with Amazon, Travel Zoo or Groupon, or book direct with our preferred hotels.

Over the years we've visited many areas of Britain – Stratford-upon-Avon, the birthplace of William Shakespeare, Northumbria, with its enchanting castles – Alnwick Castle is used in the Harry Potter films – and unspoilt coastline, East Anglia, where the jewel in the crown is the royal residence of Sandringham, and Oxford and Cambridge, two of our favourite cities. We've visited London many times, including Windsor and Greenwich, another two of our preferred places. One year, we treated our sons and their wives to a weekend break at the Guoman Hotel near Tower Bridge. Not only was the hotel expensive, so too were the taxis. A taxi is only allowed to carry five passengers so every time we went out we had to pay for two.

Some 40 years after our first attempt (Chapter 6), we finally managed a holiday in Oban. We booked a week's holiday with Highland Heritage but opted to travel by car and stay in a lodge. The lodge itself was somewhat dated but the food at the Alexandra Hotel was excellent. The homemade chocolates in the Oban Chocolate Shop were yummy but the highlight of the holiday was a day trip to the Isle of Mull on a Caledonian MacBrayne (Calmac) ferry. After arriving at the small port of Craignure, we travelled by coach to Fionnphort at the western tip of Mull, where we caught a small boat for the short trip to the tiny Isle of Iona, the final resting place of the respected Labour leader John Smith. His grave befits the surroundings, plain yet beautiful. We almost didn't make it back to Oban. A storm was approaching rapidly from the Atlantic and it was touch and go as to whether the ferry would risk sailing the treacherous Sound of Mull in bad weather. The alternative was to spend the night in the small port of Craignure. In the event, the captain decided to take the risk and managed to reach the relative safety of Oban before the full fury of the storm lashed the coast.

As well as Scotland, we also enjoyed a lovely holiday in Northern Ireland. On a Highland Heritage holiday in Scotland, Ray and June became friendly with Kathleen and Raymond, an Irish couple. They lived in a beautiful house on the shore of Lough Neagh but also had a holiday cottage in Port Stewart. As we had let them stay in our caravan in the Lakes, they reciprocated by letting us stay in their cottage for Ray's

60th birthday. Consequently, Ray and June, myself and Vera, and Keith and Elaine flew to Aldergrove airport for a week's stay in Port Stewart. We explored the awesome Giant's Causeway, crossed the daunting rope bridge at Carrick-a-Rede, some 100 feet over the Atlantic, to the tiny island of Carrickarede (Vera declined), and visited the Dough Famine Village in County Donegal, Ireland. The white sandy beaches and clear blue seas of the Donegal coastline were more in keeping with a tropical island than Ireland. They were pure paradise.

One day, we caught the train to Londonderry, where our guide for the bus tour, call me Gerry from Derry, was reputedly a former IRA terrorist. The massive murals on the buildings were a poignant reminder of the area's troubled past. Each one depicted an event of those troubled times. And the sectarian tensions were still evident. As we strolled along the city walls Loyalist drummers marched around the base of an enormous bonfire banging out Loyalist tunes. The looks on their faces warned everyone to stay away. They were guarding the bonfire before the main event – the burning of the Irish tricolour flag sat on top of the bonfire. We all quickened our pace and avoided eye contact to leave this intimidating scene.

Port Stewart itself is a charming, bustling little seaside resort. Not only are the people friendly, they are family friendly too. The many cafes stayed open until well into the night catering for extended families of parents, children and grandchildren. It was great watching them eat and drink until late into the night. The hot chocolate drinks were absolutely superb. Large mugs of steaming hot chocolate with masses of marshmallows, not only in the mug itself but also around its base, were a meal in themselves. And if you fancy fish and chips, just order one portion. We didn't and each person got two huge fish, loads of chips and a mountain of mushy peas. Overall, it was a holiday we all thoroughly enjoyed and Northern Ireland is a place I'd definitely revisit.

Our love of Llandudno stems, I think, from the many day trips we've enjoyed and the Masonic weekend that was held there (Chapter 11). However, the downside of day trips is the journey time: it can take up to two hours each way for the 180 mile round trip. As we got older, instead of day trips we preferred to spend three or four days at the Empire Hotel, usually as my birthday treat.[*]

It was William and Jean who introduced us to the Empire Hotel (Section 27.7). They'd stayed at this traditional family run hotel for a short break and recommended it to us. Owned and run by the Waddy and Maddocks families, it is a most welcoming hotel. It is in a good location, has a car park, which is rare for a hotel in Llandudno, and employs friendly, helpful, local staff, many of whom have worked there for a long time. The rooms are traditionally furnished and have a decanter of sherry, which is

---

[*]   Our stay at the Empire Hotel for my birthday treat has become an annual event

replenished daily. However, the main reason we love this hotel is the food. The breakfasts are cooked to order, and you can order whatever you want, but it is the four course evening dinners that are the highlight. The menu is extensive, the portions ample and the house speciality, roast Welsh lamb, is absolutely delicious. And all of this is served in the beautiful Watkins restaurant, where the tables are well spaced out providing privacy for the diners, something we like. After gorging ourselves, we retire to the spacious lounge to enjoy coffee and tea in the sumptuous leather seats whilst listening to the resident pianist playing songs of yesteryear. Then we (or should I say I), relax with a few beers and a glass or two of wine before retiring to our bedroom. There's absolutely no need to venture outside into the cold, chilly air of a March evening.

Llandudno itself is lovely. Its sweeping bay, flanked on either side by the Great Orme and the Little Orme, the wide, flat promenade, and the old fashioned pier, make it the archetypal Victorian seaside resort. The streets abound with shops and cafes, and it also boasts a modern retail park.

Normally we book either Monday to Friday or Thursday to Monday and set off around mid-morning, stopping at the Tweed Mill at St Asaph for brunch. For the final part of the journey, we take the coast road along Colwyn Bay and Rhos-on-Sea, arriving at our hotel at about two-o-clock. During our stay, we try and alternate our days between exploring Llandudno and having excursions. In Llandudno, we like to walk along the pier, stroll along the promenade, browse the shops (Listers, where both Andrew and ourselves have bought furniture, is our favourite) and patronise the cafes. However, without a shadow of doubt, our two favourite activities are walking around the top of the Great Orme and walking from the West Shore to Conway. Sometimes, we visit Harry and Maimi in Deganwy and spend a day with them. The year Ray died (Chapter 26), we took them for a day out. At Betws y Coed, Maimi was desperate for fish and chips but their preferred chippy was closed. However, we found one near the main car park. Maimi, who has a wicked sense of humour, remarked that the fish and chips were better than the first time she'd had sex! (She also said that the wrinkles in her heavily wrinkled face represented the number of times she'd had sex.) Suitably refreshed, we continued on over the stunning Llanberis Pass, then back along the coast road to Deganwy, where Harry and Maima made us most welcome in their bungalow.

All too soon it was time to bid farewell to the Empire Hotel and Llandudno for another year.

The Lakes is our other favoured destination. As mentioned in Chapter 12, we've stayed there many times with our children, enjoying some fabulous holidays. We usually stay at Keswick or Grasmere, two of the prettiest Lake District villages.

The Keswick Country Hotel was the venue for one of our stays. Its location near to Fitz Park, where we played a round of putting, was ideal for both the park and the town. We explored the town, where I purchased a new pair of Brasher walking boots, and strolled along the beautiful shore of Derwent water to Friar's Crag. Feeling more energetic, the following day we walked the entire 12 mile length of the lake, except for the final stretch where we caught the boat.

In Grasmere, we enjoyed a relaxing break at the Wordsworth Hotel. We took the free afternoon tea of homemade scones, jam and cream and a pot of tea in the pleasant hotel grounds, watching the rabbits as they gambolled around. The afternoon tea was simply scrumptious but the five course evening dinner was a little too rich (and posh) for our liking and we ended up eating one of our evening meals in the adjacent Bistro.

For my birthday in 2015 Andrew and Michael bought me a two night stay at the Daffodil Hotel, formerly the Prince of Wales Hotel, on the shores of Grasmere. It was a lovely birthday present but, although the hotel was really nice, it was very modern. On the second day we met up with Brian and Valerie, who were *en route* to a one night stay at the Borrowdale Hotel. The four of us climbed Easdale Tarn, marvelling at how warm it was for mid February. (Brian stripped down to his T-shirt and shorts!) On the descent, Vera offered to treat us all to coffee and cakes in the Miller Howe cafe. The cakes were delicious (and gigantic) and the drinks good, but not only did it cost her an arm and a leg (I think it was almost £30), it also dented our appetites for the evening meal. As Brian and Valerie departed for Borrowdale,* we departed for home, little knowing the tragedy to come in a few days time (Chapter 26).

27.7 SHORT BREAKS WITH WILLIAM AND JEAN

William and I had talked for a while about revisiting the Isle of Man, the island of our first holiday as children, partly for nostalgic reasons but also to play the golf course at Port St Mary again (Chapter 4). After searching the internet Jean discovered a lovely reasonably priced hotel in Douglas with excellent reviews. Kathryn, then an air stewardess with FlyBe, got us great discounts on the flights and so, in the August of 2010, we flew from Manchester to Ronaldsway, where we collected our pre-booked hire car. After piling our luggage into the small boot of the Ford Fiesta – it was a squeeze – we drove** the 12 or so miles to Douglas, saying Hello Fairies as we crossed the Fairy Bridge.

The hotel, situated just off the northern promenade, was really nice. It was unpretentious, clean and welcoming, and our two bedrooms were were both spacious

---

* In recent years we've joined Brian and Valerie for a February break at the Borrowdale Hotel and this has also become an annual event

** William and I shared the driving, driving on alternate days

and well furnished, with splendid views over Douglas Bay. The breakfasts were great too, as were the optional evening dinners.

After a wash and brush up followed by an evening dinner in the hotel we strolled along the promenade towards Summerhill Glen, the place were Vera and I got engaged many years earlier (Chapter 6). On the way back the weather began to change and rain threatened so we took refuge in a promenade pub, electing to sit in the outdoor patio area. Although protected from the rain, plus the fact the tables had heaters, it was still very chilly. No matter, we'd revive ourselves with a refreshing pint or two. As we were in the Isle of Man we ordered two pints of the local tipple, Okells bitter. It was a huge mistake. Both William and I agreed it was the worst pint we'd ever had. We had no more.

Later, in the hotel bar, we drank Peroni lager, more expensive but infinitely better (and stronger). It was reasonably priced too, especially for a hotel, except for the night when the barman brought the drinks to our table. For climbing just three steps, he charged an extra £3! After that, we always collected our own from the bar.

One morning we played putting at Onchan Head, where William and I delighted in shouting 'short' as Jean and Vera's putts invariably failed to reach the hole. We had a day out at Ramsey, visiting Mooragh Park, where we ate lunch in the little park cafe, then drove to the Point of Ayre at the northern tip of the island. After visiting the iconic lighthouse, we spent some time on the shingle beach looking for seals but, to our dismay, we didn't spot any.

One fine sunny day we drove to Laxey, first to visit Lady Isabella with its connections to Wigan, and then to the beach. For elevenses, we ordered some drinks from the small beach cafe; tea for me and Vera and coffee for William and Jean. Both William and Jean said it was the worst coffee they'd ever had. It was served in a polystyrene cup, was lukewarm, and so dilute (weak) that you could see the bottom of the cup. Not bad going that: in just two days we'd had our worst pint of bitter and our worst cup of coffee.

After a morning strolling around the historic streets of Castletown, the old capital of the island, where we visited the ancient castle and schoolhouse, we drove to the secluded cove of Port Soderick. Located just a few miles south of Douglas, this lovely spot could be reached either by land or sea. In the fifties and sixties the nightclub and entertainment complexes were the hub of Douglas's nightlife. The place throbbed with cabaret shows, talent contests and restaurants. Not any more. The deserted, boarded up, decaying buildings filled us with sadness.

That night, in Douglas, we ate fish and chips *al fresco* from a chip shop recommended to us by Kathryn, who often stayed in Douglas on her flights to the Isle of Man.

Peel, the home of Manx kippers, Niarbyl Bay and Tynwald, the home of the Manx Parliament, where I purchased a pair of navy blue Farah trousers at the nearby mill (I still have them), were also visited, but without doubt our best day was spent at the southern tip of the island. Our first port of call was Port St Mary, the place where William and I had our very first holiday (Chapter 4). Sadly, the guest house where we stayed, the Waters Edge, was now a private house and even the nearby Point Hotel, which was regarded as rather posh (and expensive) by the guests of the Waters Edge, had been converted into apartments. However, the cafe at the nine hole golf course was still there so me and William enjoyed a good round of golf (Chapter 4) whilst our wives enjoyed some refreshments and a gentle stroll around Port St Mary.

Afterwards, we drove to The Sound, the treacherous strip of sea separating the Isle of Man from its smaller cousin, the Calf of Man. Here, we did indeed see some seals as they sunbathed on the rocks and frolicked in the sea. A wonderful afternoon got even better with delicious tea and scones in Harry Kelly's Tea Rooms in Cregneash village. Before returning to Douglas, we stopped at nearby Port Erin to rekindle our memories of yesteryear.

Not only did the holiday provide lots of new memories, it also brought back lots of happy memories from years gone by.

Our second short break was in the Empire Hotel in Llandudno, one of ours, and William and Jean's, favourite hotels.

We set off on a beautiful Thursday morning and, as per normal, stopped at the Tweed Mill in St Asaph for brunch and a little shopping. Suitably refreshed, we arrived at the hotel in mid afternoon and, after checking in and having a quick wash and brush up in our rooms, had a leisurely stroll around the pier and nearby streets. Then it was back to our rooms to shower and change in readiness for the evening dinner.

The four course evening dinners in the lovely Watkins and Co restaurant are the highlight of the day. There's a choice of six starters (I usually have the Gaia Melon), followed by soup, then the main course, the dessert, and finally tea and coffee in the lounge. The house speciality is roast Welsh lamb and it is this dish that Vera and I normally have. It's so tender it literally melts in your mouth. William and Jean have similar culinary tastes and also like the roast lamb. We usually ordered two bottles of wine with our meal, taking any that was left into the lounge to consume later.

On the Friday we went to Betsy y Coed to do a little sightseeing and shopping. After a light lunch (you don't need much lunch after the Empire breakfast) we continued on to the Llanberis Pass. The scenery of the Snowdonia National Park is absolutely stunning but the pass itself, with its winding narrow road and steep descents, disconcerted both Jean and William.

The following day, on a recommendation from Brian, we drove to Red Wharfe Bay on the Isle of Anglesey. After driving along some tortuous narrow roads the place itself was a complete let down. It was just a restaurant and a pub in a small bay and both were heaving with people. The weather wasn't great either. It was cold and very windy. The only seats available at the pub were outside and that's were we had to drink our beers, shivering in the cold and windy conditions. The ramshackle toilets were also outside, so at least we didn't have far to walk.[*]

Whilst having our drinks we saw some very big women. And I mean big. Their breasts were huge. On pointing this out to Jean, she said that some men love their women big so they can bury their face in their huge breasts.

Brian and Valerie came down to visit on the Sunday. Before enjoying the traditional Sunday roast dinner in the hotel, we all had a stroll around the mountainside to the West Shore to work up an appetite. After the sumptuous meal, we caught the tram to the summit of the Great Orme. Before Brian and Valerie returned home, we all played a game of crazy golf. We took so long that the proprietor told us to hurry up – he wanted to close and go home. The weather didn't help – it was freezing cold and very windy.

After our evening meals, we retired to the comfortable lounge for after dinner drinks. Vera and Jean had just one then retired to bed, leaving William and me to consume more pints of Boddingtons and another bottle of wine whilst enjoying a good old fashioned singalong with the pianist.

27.8 SHORT BREAKS WITH BRIAN AND VALERIE

The first break we had with Brian and Valerie was Glencoe. We stayed in a Bed and Breakfast (B and B) in Ballachulish that Brian and Valerie had stayed in previously, but with different owners. On arrival, we asked the new owner if it was okay to take some beer into our rooms. He said it was fine but was amazed when he saw Brian and me carrying two large crates of the stuff.

The B and B was a very large detached house near the shore and we had the two best rooms overlooking the beautiful coastline. The breakfasts were good too but Brian remarked that the new owners weren't as friendly and had more rules than the previous owners, although Vera and I thought they were fine.

The first night we ate at a local hotel, the Loch Leven Hotel. It was a hot, sultry evening and we had a west facing window table. The additional heat from the setting sun proved too much for Vera and, like in Rome, she had another funny turn. However, she recovered and we all enjoyed a delicious meal. During our stay we ate at a number of restaurants and all of them were very good.

On the second day we drove a short way up Glencoe to a car park opposite Jimmy Saville's white cottage, where we were regaled by a Scotsman playing the bagpipes. After listening awhile to his melodious music, we embarked on

---

[*]   When we told Brian about our experience, he said it was over 30 years ago when he went

the strenuous ascent to the Hidden Valley. Located between the peaks of two mountains, it is a most serene spot. Part of the ascent involved negotiating a very narrow ledge on a rock face! Neither Vera nor I like heights but we managed. Apparently, in 1692 the Campbells took themselves and their cattle to the Hidden Valley to escape the MacDonald clan, but I'm sure they must have taken a different route as no cows could have crossed that ledge.

It was worth the effort. The Hidden Valley was beautiful, an oasis of peace and tranquility flanked by snow capped peaks. Brian even managed to scramble to the top of a large, slippery rock, a task that I chickened out of half way up. After eating our packed lunch (Image 305) we made the equally arduous descent, watching both the white speck of Jimmy Saville's cottage grow in size and the bagpipe music grow louder as we descended.

When Brian and Valerie told their daughter Catherine that we'd climbed the Hidden Valley, she was dumbfounded. "You can't have," she remarked, "it's far too difficult for you." But we had.

One evening we drove to nearby Cuil Bay to watch the sunset. It was spectacular (Image 306) but it came at a price. We were nearly eaten alive by the midges.

Brian, Vera and Valerie enjoying a
packed lunch in the Hidden Valley.

A spectacular Scottish sunset.

492

We also visited the secluded Singing Sands. After a scenic drive and a ferry crossing we parked the car near a small bay and walked a couple of miles through a dense pine forest to the Singing Sands. The beach was lovely (Image 307) and the clear blue sea enticed us to have a paddle, but we had to be extremely careful: the sea was full of stinging jellyfish. And yes, the sand did indeed 'sing' as you brushed your feet on it.

The nearby Silver Sands, a lovely stretch of beach sprinkled with rock pools and overlooked by a magnificent golf course, was also visited.

The following year we holidayed in Scotland again, this time on the Isle of Skye. Glencoe was far enough but the Isle of Skye was much farther, so we broke the journey by staying at a Premier Inn in Cumbernauld, just north of Glasgow. As we arrived in Glasgow I was bursting for a wee and stopped on a car park near a busy roundabout where, from my many visits to Strathclyde University, I knew there were toilets. They were still there but closed for refurbishment. Disaster. I had to relieve myself so, much to the disgust of Vera and Valerie, I did so in the middle of the shrub covered roundabout, with Brian doing his best to distract the passing motorists by waving his hankie in the air. Suitably relieved, we spent the afternoon in Glasgow showing Brian and Valerie some of the sights. Unfortunately, Scotland were playing an international match at Hampden Park and the city centre was full of Scottish supporters decked out in the dark blue of their team. Undeterred, we window shopped in Buchanan Street and Sauchiehall Street, enjoyed afternoon tea in the Willow Tea Rooms, and strolled beside the River Clyde. I showed them the entrance to Strathclyde University on 'Induction Hill', used as the location of Strathclyde Police Station in the TV series Taggart, before leaving to enjoy our meal at the Premier Inn.

Me and Vera on Singing Sands beach

On the way to the Isle of Skye we stopped at the Commando Memorial, marvelling at the bravery and courage of our soldiers, and sad that so many had given their lives for their country at such a young age.

Crossing from mainland Scotland to the Isle of Skye at the Kyle of Lochalsh, we proceeded to Portree, passing the imposing Cuillin Hills and the Talisker Distillery on the way. The landlady of our bungalow Bed and Breakfast (Image 308) was a Lancashire lass from Blackpool. Both she and her husband had been in the Royal Navy and 'retired' to the Isle of Skye, using their bungalow as a B and B to supplement their income. They were a lovely couple who made us very welcome.

Our B and B bungalow in Portree. Our
bedroom window is on the far right.

We visited several places and did several walks but the one that sticks in my mind was that at the 'end of the Earth'. Well, that's what it seemed like. We drove along tiny, narrow roads for ages before arriving at a completely remote campsite near Glenbrittle. After changing into our walking gear we set off along the base of the Cuillin Hills. The weather was fine but a black, thunderous storm cloud loomed in the distance. Still, there was nothing to worry about as it was heading away from us. Suddenly, and without any warning, the wind changed direction and blew the storm straight at us. Totally isolated and vulnerable, we turned back, but it was too late. The heavens opened and deluged us with water, not from above but from the side, driven by the fierce wind. It was horizontal rain at its most ferocious. It was akin to being hit with liquid machine gun pellets. Like most of the other walkers, we hurried back to the car to get changed. Within minutes, the car park was full of steamed up cars displaying fleeting glimpses of bare flesh as people struggled to remove their sodden attire and don dry, warm clothes.

The following day we went to the Beach of Shells near Dunvagan, a beach, as the name implies, made entirely of shells. Sod's Law struck again and I was caught short on this exposed stretch of coastline. Why is it that the urge to go always seems to happen in the most inconvenient of places! I couldn't wait so I had to 'do the business' in the only sheltered spot, a low stone wall near the sea. Unfortunately, a few minutes later a young couple visited the very same spot. Heaven knows what they thought.

Other places were visited too but those two incidents, together with the cosy restaurants and good food, were my abiding memories of Skye.

Our next two breaks were in Devon and Cornwall, two of mine and Vera's favourite places. As usual,* Brian found a charming B and B in Dartmouth, a place Vera and I had never been to before. In the afternoon we explored Dartmouth itself, searching out likely restaurants and pubs. On the first night we ate at the Station Cafe on the seafront, and on subsequent nights at the quaint Cherub pub and the Rockfish, a renowned seafood restaurant. All were good.

The weather on our second day wasn't great so we decided to visit the nearby National Trust House at Coleton Fishacre, a lovely old house with gardens that swept down to the sea some several hundred metres below. A sign warns the unwary that, to paraphrase Isaac Newton, what goes down has to come back up (Image 309).

In contrast to most of our breaks, on this one we did more sightseeing than walking. We had days out at Slapton Sands, the site of a terrible tragedy of World war II, where hundreds of lives were lost in a mock landing of D-Day. Because of a botch up, the allied warships fired their guns an hour before they should have, shelling the troops as they landed. A WWII tank on the car park serves as a poignant reminder of the tragedy.

Sign warning walkers that those who descend
the steep path have to climb back up.

---

* It was always Brian who searched the internet looking for really good Bed and Breakfast places, and he never disappointed

A little further on at Blackpool Sands Brian and I donned our swimming trunks and braved the freezing cold sea. We'd said all along that we'd take a dip in the sea and Vera and Valerie ensured that we kept our word. Not only was the sea absolutely freezing, an icy cold wind added to our misery.

Fowey is lovely. Although not big, it is a charming seaside retreat with narrow streets housing a host of shops and cafes. Sitting on the seafront licking a cold ice cream watching the world go by was a lovely way to relax.

Salcombe too was lovely but boy is it hilly. After parking our car at the top of the hill we trudged down to Salcombe several hundred metres below. Going down wasn't too bad but the return trek up the steep hill was an ordeal, especially on a hot summer's day. Half way up we took a breather at the church, admiring the stunning views.

We returned to Cornwall in 2017, the year of the snap General Election called by Theresa May, this time to Porthleven on the lizard peninsula. We visited the Lizard lighthouse and Kynance Cove, and did some exhilarating walks around Mullion Cove and Cadgwith, one of the prettiest seaside villages.

West Looe in Cornwall was lovely too. Vera and I had visited Looe on our forays into Cornwall with our children (Chapter 12), but never stayed there. After checking into our B and B I was intrigued by a statement in the holiday pamphlet. You must see the statue of Nelson in the harbour, but beware, it's not what you think. As we strolled the half mile or so into Looe for our evening meal, we saw the statue. It wasn't Admiral Nelson but a seal, a memorial to a friendly seal which had inhabited the harbour for many years.

One of the highlights of this holiday was the clifftop walk from our B and B in Looe to Polperro, about five miles away. It was a gorgeous summer's day and the views along the clifftop were stunning. At about the half-way point we stopped at a beachside cafe to enjoy some refreshing drinks and cakes. Because it was hot and we were tired we decided to catch the boat back to Looe but had to wait for the incoming tide to fill the harbour (Image 310). Still, it gave us time to explore the quaint little hamlet of Polperro, rummaging in the unique little shops for unusual trinkets. On the trip the captain of the small boat pointed out various places of interest, including the house where Charles and Camilla held their secret trysts.

Me, Brian, Vera and Valerie on Polperro beach waiting for the tide to come in.

Northumbria. A quiet, unspoilt gem of England and a place that Brian and Valerie had never been. On this break it was Vera and I who planned the itinerary.

Brian had found a charming B and B in a remote cluster of buildings just off the A1. It was run by a friendly lady and her husband from Yorkshire who'd fallen in love with Northumbria and couldn't resist buying this property. As we normally do on our first day away we asked our hosts for the best places to eat and later, in the darkening gloom of a Northumbrian evening, set off along pitch black, narrow country lanes to one of their recommended restaurants. It was worth it. The meal was delicious. However, I had to take extra care for the return journey after drinking two pints of beer with my meal.

The following day Bamborough and the iconic Bamborough Castle were our first destinations. Brian and Valerie were amazed, not only with the castle but also its position on top of a hill overlooking the fabulous beach. The panoramic vista was a joy to behold. From Bamborough we strolled along the wide sandy beach to Seahouses, a bustling commercial mini Blackpool and a complete contrast to to the quiet, sedate Bamborough. Nonetheless, we enjoyed exploring its winding streets and picturesque harbour. As it was early evening we decided to eat in Seahouses and sat ourselves down in a busy cafe. However, before the waitress came, Valerie decided she didn't like the fatty smell of the cafe so we all got up and went to a nearby chippy for fish and chips. We ate them *al fresco* on seats overlooking the little harbour but had to be very wary of the circling seagulls.

Rather than walk back to Bamborough (it was getting late), we opted to catch the bus. As one came in I stepped on board followed by Vera, Valerie and Brian. It's a good job Brian asked the driver if it was going to Bamborough otherwise we'd have ended up in Newcastle!

The next day we drove to Holy Island. It was scorching hot so we found a nice pub with cold beer to sate our thirst. After visiting the Abbey we walked to the castle before returning to the car to beat the incoming tide. After crossing the causeway we stopped for tea and scones at the lovely Barn Tearooms, recommended to us by the landlady of the B and B.

Craster, a quiet seaside resort famous for its kippers, was our next day out. We did the scenic coastal walk to Dunstanborough Castle that Vera and I had done on a previous holiday, and got talking to a German couple on our way back. They were retired and touring Britain in a camper van. It was their first visit to Britain and, because of the war, were apprehensive about the reception they'd receive. "We can't believe how friendly and helpful the people have been," said the lady. "They let us park outside their houses and even bring us fresh water." The conversation continued and somehow broached the topic of travellers. They asked if we had many travellers or Romany people in Britain. "Do you mean gypsies?" I said. "Yes," replied the German lady in a hushed voice, "but we're not allowed to call them that." It's a funny old world.

From watching the Robson Green TV series about Northumbria we paid a visit to Howick Hall, the birthplace of Earl Grey tea. Apparently, the flavouring was added to mask the taste of the local water and the rest, as they say, is history. For us, the reality of Howick Hall, both the Hall itself and the gardens, didn't live up to our expectations. However, we did enjoy a cup of the real stuff in the tea rooms before departing for the Ship Inn at Newton-by-the-Sea, where Robson Green sang in a group. This also was disappointing. Not the location of the pub. Nestled beside the village green and overlooking the bay, it was in a splendid spot, but the pub itself was a let down. Their best bitter was revolting, rivalling Okell's for the worst pint I've ever had (Section 27.7), and the solitary sit down cubicle in the men's toilet had a sign on the door proclaiming, 'Out of Order. Plumber will be here soon. Please be patient.' Charming, especially when you're desperate.

To complete a disappointing day, as we turned off the A1 on to the narrow, unlit road to our B and B, a truck appeared out of the night time gloom with two men standing in the back with rifles slung over their shoulders. Thoughts of the IRA sprang to mind but they were probably farmers (or poachers) on an evening shoot. Nonetheless, it was scary.

On our way home we stopped at Alnwick. Once voted the best place to live in Britain, it is a beautiful old town. Having only a limited amount of time, we visited Alnwick Castle, famous for its role in the Harry Potter films. We explored the magnificent gardens, including the Poison Garden, and the Tree House, reputedly the most expensive tree house in the world. Designed by Lady Jane Percy, Duchess of Northumberland, it cost over £15 million to build. After grabbing a bite to eat in Alnwick, we made the long journey home.

In 2015 it was back to Devon. Brian and Valerie had enjoyed a holiday in Lynton and Lynmouth in a previous year so that's where we headed. Brian decided we should break our journey at Burnham-on-Sea, a popular seaside resort where one of his friends holidayed every year, and he was curious to see what it was like. Popular it may be but impressive it is not. The promenade was flat and uninspiring and the resort bland and commercial, the same as countless other seaside resorts. We made a brief stop at Watchet, which was better, but I hoped Lynton would be better than both.

It was. Much better. Lynton, where we were staying, was situated on top of the cliff whilst Lynmouth, its sister resort, lay at the bottom. As ever, our B and B was lovely. Brian had chosen well yet again.

Our first walk was to Watersmeet, a National Trust place in a remote valley some four miles away. We set off from our B and B on a bright sunny day, climbing steeply out of Lynton to the wooded cliffs beyond. The walk continued for several miles along the ridge of the wooded valley into Exmoor Forest before we spied a deep cleft ahead – the valley housing Watersmeet. Relieved that a refreshing cream tea wasn't far away, we began the long descent. To our dismay, there was no Watersmeet at the bottom, just a sign directing us up the other steep, wooded side. We climbed back to the top and, to our relief, saw a sign saying Watersmeet 800 metres. We picked up the pace and carried on. After what must have been at least 800 metres, and more likely double that, another sign was encountered proclaiming, Watersmeet 400 metres. We duly carried on and asked a couple coming from the opposite direction how far it was to Watersmeet. About half-a-mile came the reply. Another 800 metres! These must be the longest metres in the entire world, I thought to myself as we carried on. Eventually, the trees cleared and, way below in the valley, we saw our destination. It had been a long arduous walk in hot conditions but the end result was worth it. Watersmeet was absolutely beautiful and we certainly deserved our cream tea (Plate 311).

When we told our hosts at the B and B where we'd been they were astounded. "What, you've walked from here to Watersmeet and back in weather like this!" they blurted out. "We did that walk a few weeks ago and it was very difficult. You've done very well." Like the Hidden Valley in Scotland, we had indeed done very well for a group of oldies.

We ate our evening meal at the The Nook restaurant, one Brian had found during his researches on Lynton. It was small and cosy having only six tables with wooden benches as seats, although they did have cushions on them. The young, local waitress was friendly and efficient and the ambience was good too. However, we became a little concerned when people started getting up and leaving the restaurant before their meals arrived. Had they been waiting for ages, got fed up and decided to leave? We needn't have worried. A few minutes later they all returned with pints of beer from the pub next door! Apparently, The Nook didn't serve alcoholic drinks but patrons could bring their own bottle of wine or nip next door if they fancied a beer. The service and the food were both excellent, so we ate there again. It was voted the best restaurant in Lynton, an accolade that we fully endorsed.

Watersmeet

Cream tea at Watersmeet

After a stroll around Lynton we popped into the pub, both out of curiosity and for a nightcap. It was nothing special and they didn't even have any plain crisps so I started a trend: I had a Mars bar with my pint of bitter!

The following day we drove to Ilfracombe. Much bigger, busier and more commercial than Lynton, it was a still a very pleasant seaside resort. After climbing to the top of the hill to admire the wonderful views, we strolled to the harbour where we were met by Verity. We could hardly have missed her. This 20 metre tall stainless steel and bronze statue of a pregnant woman created by Damien Hirst stands on the pier at the entrance to the harbour, towering over the inquisitive tourists. Some like the unusual statue but I was in the opposite camp. I found it weird.

Brian had found a pub/restaurant on the outskirts of Ilfracombe which had an excellent reputation for good food, and said we should eat our evening meal there. I think Valerie would have preferred to eat at one of the excellent restaurants in Lynton, but we parked at the pub anyway. The outside wasn't exactly inviting and the inside even less so. Valerie wasn't for staying* but in deference to Brian did so. It got even worse. The menu was restricted and unappealing. Apart from fish and chips there wasn't much else that took our fancy. And it wasn't cheap. The fish and chips cost £12.95 each so, with two rounds of drinks plus side orders, a fish and chip meal for four cost about £75.00. Watching Valerie sit there in stony silence reminded me of Vera in New York (Section 27.4).

Another walk we did was from Lynton to Woody Bay, passing a Christian retreat along the way. It was a magnificent building in a beautiful location. Like royalty, the Christians and monks certainly knew where to build their retreats and monasteries. A little further on we stopped for a cream tea. It was good but not as good as the one at Watersmeet. Suitably refreshed, we continued on to a secluded little cove, where I fell asleep on the rocks. Then, all to soon, it was time to return home.

In 2019 we holidayed in Bude, a place where our children spent many happy hours on the beach (Chapter 12). Bude itself wasn't that thrilling but Port Isaac, aka Port Wenn in the Doc Martin TV series, certainly was. We spent a most enjoyable day there, visiting all the major locations and enjoying a lovely snack in the 'School'. (It is a cafe in real life.) Also, we were lucky enough to see the filming of the scene where Ken Hollister (Clive Russell) died in the presence of his friend Bert Large (Ian McNiece), and to see the actors emerging from the shoot, with Ian McNiece making a beeline for the pie shop!

This year (2020) we had a holiday in the Isle of Wight, a place that neither Brian nor I had visited for many years (Chapter 29). However, it was our holiday in Pitlochry in 2016 that was to prove more eventful than most.

Neither Brian, Valerie, Vera or I had been to Pitlochry but on the return journey from Skye (see earlier) we'd been impressed with the scenery around Blair Castle, just a few miles from Pitlochry.

The week before we set off Neville and Phyllis had come down to our house to look at the extension and the new kitchen (Chapter 28). On hearing we were going to Pitlochry they insisted we call at their house in Arnside. It only involved a slight detour and so, on the Sunday morning, the four of us stopped at Neville's for coffee and biscuits, a chat, and a tour around their large, lovely garden.

We stopped at Gretna Green for lunch and then headed onwards and upwards towards Motherwell, our destination for the night. All was going to plan until we hit some major roadworks on the M74. There was stationary traffic for miles ahead. Rather than risk being stuck for hours, I took an exit on to a minor road and followed Brian's directions along winding country lanes and strange little towns. Eventually, we arrived at the Premier Inn. By now, the weather had turned nasty with heavy

---

*   Brian is keen on olde world pubs, Valerie less so

rain and dark, threatening clouds, so we booked a meal deal and, after freshening ourselves up, went to the adjacent Brewers Fayre for our evening meal. After some post meal relaxing drinks, we retired to our rooms to grab some much needed sleep.

Refreshed after a hearty breakfast, the following morning we headed towards Perth to visit Scone* Palace, the site where Scottish kings were crowned on Moot Hill. It was a beautiful sunny day and both the extensive grounds and the palace itself reflected this sunshine mood. Unlike some stately buildings, Scone Palace had spacious, bright, well furnished rooms that exuded character. The staff were friendly and obliging, including the doorman, who said he supported Hamiltonian Academicals and Warrington Wolves!

From Scone Palace we drove through beautiful countryside to the little village of Dunkeld. After mooching around the shops and buying some Tomintoul whisky for Keith, we treated ourselves to coffee and cakes at a quaint little cafe near the village church. Then, it was back to the car for the final leg of our journey.

Situated near the top of Bonnethill Road, Dunmurray Lodge had a well tended front garden** and splendid views. The effusive landlady, Lorraine, greeted us warmly, showed us our rooms (which were lovely) and explained the breakfast arrangements. She also told us the best places to eat and even booked reservations for us at Victoria's. Not only that, she gave us a card entitling us to a free round of drinks!

Both the ambience and the food at Victoria's were so good that we ate there on a second night. We ate our other two evening meals at the The Old Mill Inn, a restaurant owned by Victoria's husband.

As a starter for my breakfast I decided to try a bowl of porridge – well, we were in Scotland. Porridge is not a dish I normally eat but I was blown away by Lorraine's porridge. In contrast to some porridges, which can be thick and stodgy, this one had more fluidity and tasted absolutely delicious. The icing on the cake was that it came with three little jugs, one containing cream, one containing honey and one containing whisky. I enjoyed the first two but gave the whisky to Brian, since there is a zero tolerance policy to alcohol in Scotland and I was the driver. A plate of bacon, sausage, eggs, tomato, baked beans, black pudding and mushrooms (I passed on the haggis), followed by lashings of tea and toast, set me up nicely for the day.

Our first walk took us over the bridge on the River Tummel to the salmon ladder. We saw a few leap up the ladder but the most impressive feature was the viewing station where the salmon could be viewed up close and personal through a glass window. And boy, there were some big ones, big enough to fill hundreds of tins of John West.

After crossing the dam we walked along the loch shore, passing the imposing Green Park Hotel on the waterfront before stopping for lunch at the Pitlochry

---

*   Pronounced Scoon

**   Well tended gardens were a feature of Pitlochry. Some of them were magnificent.

Boating Station cafe. Foolishly, I bought a bag of duck food and regretted it almost immediately as I was besieged by a horde of hungry, noisy, quacking ducks, some of which pecked my legs for attention.

We continued on to the next small loch, pausing at a viewpoint to admire the stunning views. A sudden downpour sent us scurrying for shelter under some nearby trees, where we were joined by an elderly Scottish gentleman. We struck up a conversation and it transpired that he had also been an avid walker. Now in his eighties, he could only manage gentle walks but had used his passion for walking to write a book with his companion. "Give me the details and I'll buy one," I said, feeling somewhat sorry for this lonely old man.

"Oh, I just happen to have a copy with me," he replied, pulling a bread wrapper from his coat pocket. Carefully, and proudly, he extricated his book from the bread wrapper and handed it to me (Image 312).

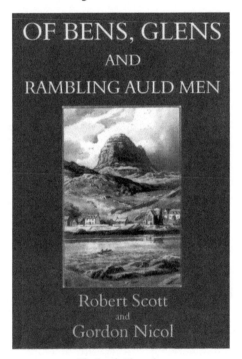

The book I bought.

"Good title," I said, "but which one are you?'

"I'm Bob Scott," he replied, and took back the book to show me a picture of the two authors.

"How much is it Bob?" I asked.

"£10.00."

"Fine, I'll take it," I replied and handed him a ten pound note.

"I'll sign it for you," he said enthusiastically. "What are your names, and the names of your wives? You never know, it might be worth a fortune in years to come." I am now the proud owner of a signed copy of the above book.

When the shower ceased, we bade farewell to Bob and continued on towards the next loch. However, after about a quarter-of-a-mile it began to drizzle again so we turned around and headed back.

A lonesome figure stood on the footbridge over the river. It was Bob. As we approached, he started another conversation, this time about the Green Park Hotel on the far shore. "It's absolutely superb isn't it?" I remarked.

"Yes, it is," he replied.

"I wouldn't mind staying there," I said.

"Oh, you can't stay there," he replied. "You have to be over 80 to stay in that hotel."

Blair Castle was a disappointment. Its location was fine but the Castle itself was dull and dingy, not at all like Scone Palace. After taking lunch in the cafe, we walked around Hercules Garden then drove to our next destination, the House of Bruar.

The House of Bruar is lovely. It is a beautifully laid out collection of shops and cafes offering an extensive range of goods. I bought some honey for my throat, which was still tender from the radiotherapy treatment (Chapter 29), and some real ales for Andrew and Michael. Before departing to visit Queens View, we enjoyed some refreshments in the new Victorian Conservatory.

When Queen Victoria visited in 1866, she assumed that the sweeping view westwards over Loch Tummel towards Rannoch Moor was named after her, but she was wrong. It is named after Isabella, the first wife of Robert the Bruce. The view is indeed befitting of a queen, especially in early evening as the sun is setting. Queens View must rank amongst one of the best views in Britain.

On the morning of Thursday 23 June, the day of the EU (European Union) referendum, Brian knocked on our door with the morning paper. "I just passed the Polling Station and there was a young girl with a 'Vote Leave' placard sat outside," he said.

"Good for her," I replied, "but I don't think it'll do much good up here."

At breakfast, Brian told Lorraine what he'd just told me. I said that we'd all done a Duncan Bannatyne. She seemed puzzled. "You know, Duncan Bannatyne's famous phrase on Dragon's Den, 'I'm out.' " She seemed a little surprised and said that she'd voted to stay in, mainly because places like Pitlochry relied on immigrant labour in the hotels and shops.

"I think Boris helped the Leave campaign enormously," she said. "I like him."

"Never mind," I replied. "You've got the two fishes." She stared at me blankly. "The two fishes, Salmond and Sturgeon." Well, she burst into a fit of laughter and couldn't stop.

"I've never heard them called that before," she replied eventually, "but it's very apt. Every time I see that Salmond I want to slap his face and Sturgeon is Miss Tippitoes." This time it was my turn to look blank. "Haven't you noticed, when she walks it's like she's walking on tiptoe." Obviously, she didn't like either of them.

On this historic day we walked to Edradour Distillery, the smallest distillery in Scotland. *En route*, we made a slight detour to the impressive Black Spout waterfall, where a sign warned us to be wary of ticks. After walking for a couple of miles through pleasant woodland and grassy meadows, we emerged on to a tarmac road. Turning left, we continued on for another mile or so but there was no sign of the distillery. Becoming a little concerned, we asked a dog walker where it was. "It's about a mile back that way," he said, pointing in the direction we'd just come. Thanking him, we turned around and headed back. If we'd turned right instead of left, the distillery was a mere 400 yards down the road nestled in a small valley.

By this time we were parched and ready for a drink. "Do you have a cafe?" I asked the man dressed in full Scottish regalia stood at the entrance.

He looked at me quizzically then said, "This is a distillery, sir. The cafes are in Pitlochry."

Disappointed, we signed up for the distillery tour and, lo and behold, our first port of call was a cafe!* After sating our thirst with tea and coffee (we got to keep the mugs), our guide, a pleasant young girl, escorted us to a room to watch a video and ply us with drinks. The men got two whiskies and the ladies a whisky and the Edradour equivalent of a Baileys. Watching Vera's and Valerie's faces as they tentatively sipped the 10 year old whisky was worth the entrance money. They hated the stuff. Vera didn't like the 'Baileys' either, although Valerie drunk hers. In the event, Brian and I had three whiskies each. The 10 year old Edradour was really nice (we had two of these) but neither of us liked the peaty one, although we drunk them. I was glad I didn't have to drive. Like in the cafe, we got to keep the glasses.

The tour was really interesting and enjoyable, enhanced by our lovely guide. The strong smell of bananas from the fermenting flasks, and the quarter-of-a-million pound wooden barrel stored near the exit door (in case of fire), were my abiding memories.

In the shop after the tour I complimented our guide on a wonderful tour. "Excuse me for asking, but are you Canadian?" I enquired. I was convinced she was.

"No," she replied with a smile. "I'm Scottish. I live just down the road in Pitlochry."

Someone was shaking my shoulder and saying wake up, wake up, you've got to see this. It was Vera. Always an early riser, she had switched on the TV and seen the

---

* Obviously, you had to sign up for the tour in order to use the cafe

505

referendum result. "We've voted to leave," she said excitedly. "I didn't think that would happen."

Neither did I. "That's great," I replied, and got up to watch the unfolding drama. We'd both used our postal votes and voted 'Leave' but I thought the 'Remain' camp would triumph. Just. I was shocked but happy that at last we'd got control of our own country again, free from the meddling bureaucrats of Brussels.

As we entered the dining room for breakfast on that historic morning, a German couple literally glowered at us. We didn't understand why but later, when they'd left, Lorraine told us they were devastated that the UK had voted to leave the EU. (And, judging from their reaction, I also think she'd told them how we had voted.) She said that Scotland had voted remain and that Nicola Sturgeon was once again advocating another referendum on Scottish independence. "Even if she gets one, she won't win," she continued, "because most Scots want to remain part of the UK."

On our journey home we visited Lanark Village, founded by the pioneer Robert Owen, the Scottish equivalent of England's Lord Lever. He provided decent homes, fair wages, free health care, education and the world's first workplace nursery for his textile workers. We took a ride back in time on the Annie McLeod experience, explored the Robert Owen school and the millworker's house, and visited the textile mill and the rooftop garden. Then, after purchasing ice creams from the village store, we strolled to Robert Owen's house. As we reached the front garden, we paused to watch a wedding. Vera and Valerie insisted we waited until the bride and bridesmaids arrived. (For some unknown reason, women always like to see the dresses of the bridesmaids and especially the bride's wedding dress.) After we'd seen his house, and the bride and bridesmaids' dresses, we set off on the long journey home.

On the final leg of our journey we stopped at Tebay, one of the best motorway services, for tea. Then it was back home to enjoy our new extension and receive a shock announcement from Andrew (Chapter 28).

28

MOVES AND EXTENSIONS

28.1 MICHAEL'S NEW HOUSE

After the birth of Joshua on 15 April 2013 Michael and Kathryn decided they needed a bigger house. They wanted to stay in Westhoughton and searched the property market for a large four-bedroomed house in that area. Eventually, they found one which was ideal. The four-bedroom detached property, which had just been extended, had a spacious hall, a good sized lounge and dining room, a large modern Wren kitchen boasting a central island unit, a utility room and a downstairs toilet. The master bedroom also had an *en suite* but the clincher was the extra, spacious reception room, a room ideal as Joshua's playroom. They put in an offer slightly below the asking price, which was accepted, then it was all systems go.

They'd already sold their own house to the first people who came to view, a young couple who'd been let down by Barrett. The price they got was a little less than what they'd paid for it* so the balance was substantial. Kathryn had given up her well paid job as an air stewardess with FlyBe, presumably to be a full time mum to Joshua in his early years, so it meant the mortgage would be based on Michael's salary alone. It wasn't easy, but, with a little help from us, they managed to secure one. Not only that, the couple buying their house were desperate to move in and pushed for a moving date in May, just six weeks away. In contrast, the vendors of Michael's new house wouldn't move until they'd found a place to live, which meant that Michael, Kathryn and Joshua would be homeless. "We're looking for a flat to rent for a couple of weeks," said Michael, "until our new house is ready." I didn't think it right they should have to live in a rented flat, especially with a young baby, and said they could stay at our house for a few weeks. It was the right gesture but a few weeks turned into

---

*   The property market was still recovering from the crash in 2008

five months! Eventually, in September 2014, Michael, Kathryn and Joshua moved into their new house at 55 Wharfedale (Image 313).

Joshua in front of Michael and Kathryn's new house (left)
and rear of Michael and Kathryn's new house (2018).
They had the garden landscaped (right).

28.2 ANDREW'S NEW HOUSE

Andrew has always had a fondness for older properties and so he and Helen decided to employ an interior decorator to transform the interior of their modern three-bedroomed detached house in Westhoughton to resemble that of an older house. Every room underwent a complete makeover: new decor, new furnishings, new fittings and even an old, authentic cast iron fireplace in the lounge. The finished result was stunning but they still longed for a real old house and began looking for one in Standish. After casting the net far and wide, it came down to just two properties. They viewed both then invited me and Vera to accompany them for a second viewing.

We didn't like the first one in Wigan Lane. It was on a narrow street with restricted parking and wasn't in a good state of repair. Doors wouldn't close, handles were loose and light fittings were hanging off the walls and ceilings. The current owners had had the kitchen extended, but on the cheap. Rather than move the sink, they'd left it in the middle of the room. It just didn't feel right. Even worse, part of a Wigan Hospital building jutted into the small back garden. Both Vera and I hoped they wouldn't choose this one.

The second house on Chorley Road, Standish, was better. It was a 1930s semi-detached house set well back from the main road with a good sized front garden, a large back garden and a long driveway. Both the interior and exterior exuded character but what clinched it for them was the basement floor. The basement had been converted into a large lounge/dining area, with a separate toilet room and a

508

separate utility room, and offered an extra floor of space. French doors looked out over the large back garden and the Douglas Valley beyond.

After the viewings we all went to the newly opened Central Station bar in Wigan to have a bite to eat and a drink to discuss the two houses. Obviously we let Andrew and Helen decide and, to our immense relief, they chose the one in Standish. They asked if we agreed with their choice and we said that we did. Their final offer for the house was accepted and Andrew and Helen moved into their 'new' abode in May 2015. They kept their detached house in Westhoughton, which they owned outright, and let it out to a school teacher and her two young daughters.[*]

When the extension to our house was complete (Section 28.3), we let Andrew and Helen have our summerhouse. After repainting it in pastel colours, it made a striking feature in their back garden.

About once a month Vera and I went to Standish to enjoy an evening drink with Andrew and Helen, either in The Albion pub or The Hoot wine bar. As we sat down in The Albion to enjoy our first drink Andrew undid his man bag and pulled out a sheaf of papers. Vera and I were intrigued. What was he doing? "We've been looking at some new properties," he said, "and we've put a deposit down on this one. What do you think?" he continued, handing me a photo of the Baybridge. To say we were shocked was an understatement. We were gobsmacked they were moving again so soon. However, the house was absolutely lovely (Image 314). By sheer coincidence, the plot number was 129, the number of our own house. Rightly or wrongly, I considered this to be a good omen. Also, the plot itself was a very good one, one of the best on the estate. Andrew said the builders had offered a good part exchange price for their house and so they'd agreed to go ahead.

"When are you thinking of moving?" I asked.

"Well, the builders want us in by Christmas."

"Christmas! That's less than six weeks away," I blurted out. "There's no way you'll be in by then."

The next few weeks were both frantic and fraught but, a few days before Christmas, they moved into their new home.

There were, I think, three reasons for this change of heart. The first was that Andrew had never lived in a semi-detached house before and wasn't used to the noise that could emanate from your neighbour. The loud playing of music at unsociable hours from Tony really irritated him, to the extent that he had their bedroom soundproofed, but even that didn't work. The second reason was that they'd underestimated the amount of work that had to be done to an old house to make it fit their requirements. The third reason, and the one that was the clincher, was that

---

[*]   They sold it a few years later after becoming disillusioned with the hassles of being landlords

Countryside, the builders of the new homes, had pushed leaflets through all the existing properties in the vicinity (the new development was only half-a-mile away) showing the styles of houses being built and offering a part exchange scheme whereby they would buy their current house.

The Baybridge, Andrew and Helen's new abode

Their old house was sold in the first week but, because of the tight timescale, they hadn't had time to arrange for the removal of the summerhouse. That's not a problem the new owners said, you can remove it later. A few weeks later I arranged with the builder who'd moved it from our house to Andrew's to move it once again. "I thought I'd seen the last of that," joked David Dobb, "but I'll be there at nine tomorrow morning."

A few hours later an angry Andrew rang and said the new owners were now reneging on their agreement to let him have the summerhouse. They were keeping it as 'compensation' for a couple of minor faults with the house. (A leaking tap and the fact that the water in the shower took a minute to warm up.) He wasn't happy and neither was I since I'd spent ages repainting it. However, both Andrew, Helen and their two cats have settled in really well and they all love their new home.

28.3 OUR EXTENSION

We'd considered extending our house for a number of years but the arrival of Joshua followed by both Michael and Kathryn's and then Andrew and Helen's house moves kept delaying it. One side of our house was wasted space – we never used it – and it was this space we used to enlarge our kitchen and add a new utility room. The wall separating the existing utility room from the downstairs toilet was also demolished and the larger room converted into a downstairs shower room. Vera and I spent ages evaluating different options, both for the new extension and the shower room, before coming to something we felt was close to what we wanted. Only then did we contact a builder.

Our neighbours across the street, Eileen and Michael, had recently extended their bungalow and the builder had done a very good job. Not only was the finished extension built to a high standard, the way he worked was also very good (some builders are totally disorganised) and so we asked them for his contact details.

David Dobb came when he said he would, listened to our ideas, and gave us the name of the architect he used to draw up some draft plans so he could provide us with a quotation for the work. We told him a main drain would have to be moved as it was in the way of the extension. "That's not a problem," he replied. "I do that all the time."

Mr John Holland, a knowledgeable, friendly, retired architect came and discussed our ideas with us, offering some major improvements to our design, especially the vaulted roof. We wanted a vaulted roof to give a feeling of spaciousness and to have three skylights to make the new kitchen light and airy (Image 315, page 723). After doing some quick, back-of-the-envelope calculations, he said it could be a problem because the window space would be too high in relation to the floor area. However, he said he'd circumvent the problem by adding an extra window to the existing kitchen before he submitted the plans.

The next few weeks were spent refining and modifying the plans until we were all satisfied with them. Then, he submitted copies to both the planning department and building regulations department of Bolton Council, to the builder and to ourselves. A few days later we received the quote from David for the extension, told him it was fine and said that he could begin whenever he was ready. In the meantime, Vera and I had to look for a new kitchen, a new utility room, and a new shower room.

We visited various kitchen showrooms, some we'd looked at a few years ago plus some new ones. It's amazing how your tastes change. A kitchen we'd really liked a year earlier we now hated and others we'd also liked fell out of favour. It made us realise you should never rush into things, especially major ones, but take your time. In the end it came down to two showrooms.

The Kitchen Emporium in Pemberton offered a reasonable selection of good quality kitchens and there was one in particular that took our eye, although we weren't fully sure. However, it was the Wren kitchens in Warrington that blew us away. The showroom was fantastic, the choice excellent and the kitchens superb. We were hooked. We quickly decided which units we wanted (gloss white with curved corners) with contrasting cashmere coloured units for the fridge/freezer, double oven and larder unit. Vera was so smitten with a striking wood effect worktop that she wouldn't compromise on it, as was I with a stunning white glass sink unit. Over the next few weeks we spent countless hours with the young kitchen designer, working off the plans for the extension. Putting our ideas into practice he designed and re-designed lots of kitchens on his computer until he arrived at one with which we were satisfied and then, and only then, did he present us with the price. It was substantially more than we'd anticipated. He could see we were shocked and said it did include fitting for both the kitchen and utility room.

"How much of that is for the fitting?" I asked, recovering from the shock.

"About four thousand pounds," he replied. "It's a big job."

Even after deducting the £4,000, it was still almost £2,000 over our budget.

"What if we have our own fitters?" I asked. "How much can you do it for then?"

"I'll see what I can do," he said, and went off to see his manager.

The figure he came back with was closer to our budgeted figure. "We can't go any lower," he said. "Remember, the price includes all the top quality appliances as well. The built-in Bosch 70:30 fridge/freezer, the built-in Neff double oven, the large Neff induction hob, the built-in CDA dishwasher and the CDA extraction hood. It also includes standard under cabinet lights. It's a good deal because it's a very big kitchen as well as a utility room."

He was right. It was a good deal for the amount and quality of the units and appliances we were getting, but I asked him to give us a few minutes to think about it. When he'd left I voiced the same views to Vera but said we should haggle a bit more. A further £500 discount, taking the price down to what we'd budgeted for, and better under cabinet lights, would be nice. The standard under cabinet lights were a bit on the clumsy side so I said we should push to have the swish, modern, under cabinet lighting system, which lit the inside of the unit as well as the worktop, but which was considerably more expensive, included as part of the deal. I wasn't sure he'd agree but there was no harm in trying, especially as we both knew this was the kitchen we wanted.

"Have you decided?" asked the young kitchen designer on his return.

"Well," I replied, "we like the kitchen very much and we'll sign now if you'll knock another £500 off the price and include the new under cabinet lighting system as part of the deal."

He was visibly taken aback. "I'm not sure we can do that," he said, "but if you'll definitely sign today and leave a deposit I'll tell my manager what you've said. He'll have to speak to Head Office. I'll be back in a few minutes."

"We've spoken to Head Office and they've agreed to reduce the price by a further £500 and include the new lighting system if you'll sign now."

"That's great," I replied, and duly signed the forms and paid the deposit.

With the builder sorted and the kitchen and utility room chosen, it was time to think of the logistics. Should we have the shower room and kitchen extension done together, or separately, and who should we get to fit the kitchen units and do the shower room?

The previous year we'd had a new bathroom. On the recommendation of our friends Ian and Sharon Taylor we'd employed Ian's nephew, Andy Hodges, a tiler, and Carl Liddell, a plumber, and they'd done a good job. They also fitted kitchens. Indeed, they'd just installed a new one for Ian and Sharon, and made a good job of it too, so we thought the best option was to have them do both the shower room and the kitchen, and to do them at the same time. It would be a horrendous two months without a downstairs toilet and especially a kitchen, but there was no other way. Furthermore, they'd fit in with the builder, as would the electrician they used, Sean Ratcliffe.

Work commenced in April 2015. David Dobb and Barry, his block paver and labourer, moved the main drain and then, to Joshua's delight, Barry dug out the footings with a mechanical digger, a digger he could sit on in Gaga's garden. He was thrilled to bits. However, the excavations unearthed a problem. The main gas pipe ran down the side of the house where the extension was being built and the building inspector insisted it had to be re-routed. You can't have a main gas pipe underneath the floor of a house. David duly dug the trench and laid new gas piping around the perimeter of the extension but he wasn't allowed to sever the old gas pipe and re-connect the new one. That had to be done by a Transco fitter. Even Shaun Lomax, a registered Corgi gas fitter who was removing our old gas boiler from the utility room and installing a new Combi boiler in the airing cupboard, wasn't allowed to do it, but he found someone who was, a retired Transco fitter. Transco wanted £1,250 just to re-connect the old gas pipe to the new one our builder had laid, an amount I found extortionate. Call me Jimmy Gas did it for £360. In conjunction with Shaun, he also relocated our gas meter to a white plastic box on the outside of the house.

There were no more hiccups and, after a further six weeks, the extension was built. I'd always wanted quoins (I think they add a touch of class to a house) and Tony, the bricklayer, incorporated them into both the extension and the front of the house (Images 315 and 316).

It was now time for the messy part – breaking through from the existing kitchen into the extension and removing the old kitchen. Knocking down the kitchen wall and installing the steel lintel was messy in the extreme. The dust and debris got everywhere. No matter how hard we tried, it found its way into every room in the house, even the upstairs ones. It was horrendous.

Rear of house showing new utility room with quoins and one of the three skylights (2018). One is obscured by the vaulted roof and the third one is on the front.

Front of house showing new garden room extension and front quoins, and the new windows, including the bow window (2020). The new doors are not visible.

Our old kitchen was completely gutted. Not only were all the units ripped out, so was the existing ceiling, and all the walls were stripped back to bare brick. Sean Ratcliffe, the electrician, did the same with the electrics. He ripped them all out.

Whilst David, Barry and Tony were focusing on the extension and kitchen, Andy and Carl were doing the same with the utility room. They too knocked down a dividing wall, installed a steel lintel, ripped out the ceiling and removed all the old wall plaster. Again, everything was reduced to bare bricks.

With the demolition phase over and the steel lintels in place, the construction phase commenced. Sean installed the new wiring, Carl installed the pipework for the plumbing and new ceilings were put up. Ken Roberts, the owner of Windowplas, who lived just four houses away from us, installed the new windows and doors.

Everything was going fine until Vera and I decided we wanted the fridge/freezer, double oven and larder units to become even more of a feature and protrude out like the hob (Images 317 and 318), which meant adding an extra two curved pieces. This increased the length of the kitchen by six inches and reduced the length of the utility room by the same amount. David measured and re-measured where the position of the wall dividing the kitchen from the utility room should be, and said it was going to be extremely tight to accommodate the units we wanted in the kitchen with those we wanted in the utility room. To compound matters even further, we were going away for a week's holiday to Lynton with Brian and Valerie (Chapter 27), a holiday we'd booked the previous year.

David actually built the wall and had the plastering done whilst we were on holiday. In the end, it worked out with just an inch to spare in the kitchen (Image 317). However, we had to buy a new slimline fridge/freezer for the utility room as our existing Bosch one was now too big* (Image 319).

Those six weeks from when the internal walls were knocked down to when the kitchen was complete were an absolute nightmare. We had to 'live' in the dining room with just a kettle and a microwave. Ready made meals were the order of the day, as were fish and chips from the local chippy. But we managed. We had to. I lost count of the number of brews I made for the workmen. At times, there were up to nine of them in the house!

Vera and I designed the layout of the shower room. As was the case with the kitchen, we spent lots of time until we felt we'd got it right. We chose the tiles from Tile Mart on Chorley Old Road in Bolton, as we had for the kitchen, and were extremely pleased with the end result (Image 320).

---

*   We gave this to Neil, William's son

Our new kitchen viewed from near the back door,
showing how the hob (see also Image 318), and the
fridge/freezer, double oven and larder units, stand proud.

Kitchen viewed from the far end, showing the radiator where Joshua dropped his tablet
(Section 29.2), and the wall plaques, one of which also fell behind the radiator (Chapter 29.)

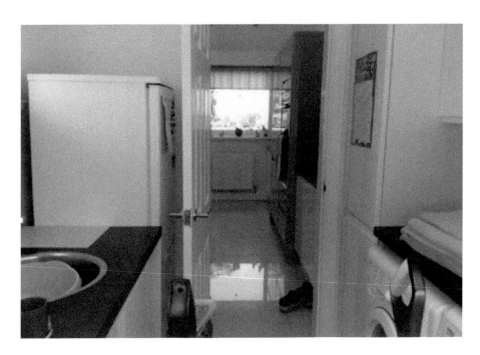

Utility Room with new slimline fridge/freezer.

Part of the shower room
(taken from window).

Hall and porch, with tiled floors and
new doors. The feature tile is also visible.

In 2016, we turned our attention to the hall and porch. We'd only planned to have the porch floor tiled but, when we saw how striking it was, plus the fact that a feature tile was left over, we decided to have the hall tiled too. New glass doors, new light fittings, a new radiator cover and redecorating completed the makeover (Image 321).

Landscaped back garden and new utility room.

The big job in 2017 was having the back garden landscaped. After drawing a draft plan and refining it countless times I asked David Dobb to do the work. It took David and Barry, with the occasional help of David's son, six and a half weeks to complete, removing 35 tonnes of rubble in the process. It was messy work, especially as the weather wasn't great, but the end result was definitely worth it (Images 322 and 323).

In 2018, we completed the last of our big jobs. Our original intention was to replace the polycarbonate roof on our 23 year old conservatory with a new solid roof. However, after discussions with the representative from Clearview,* the company we chose to do the work, we decided to replace the old frame as well and have a completely new building, a garden room. It wasn't straightforward. The conservatory is joined to the shower room (Image 207, page 363, and 323) and the box gutter meant that we had to have a bespoke garden room made (at additional cost). The end result certainly justified the additional expense (Image 323). Not only Vera and I, but also Joshua, love our new garden room. In fact, he loves it so much he regards it as his new playroom.

Rear of house showing new shower room, new
garden room with skylights, and new patio.

---

* We chose Clearview following a recommendation from Brian and Valerie. They built both their conservatory and that of a relative and did a very good job in both cases.

Part of interior of the garden room.

Getting the house and garden the way we want them has cost a lot of money. However, we'll reap the benefits as we grow older because we know it's where we'll spend a lot more time, not only by ourselves but with our grandson, Joshua.

29

A WELCOME ADDITION
AND
A SCARE

29.1 OUR FIRST GRANDCHILD

One autumn evening in 2012 Michael and Kathryn came round to our house to look at some holiday photographs from our cruise with Andrew and Helen (Chapter 27). They said they'd also had a short holiday while we were away and were bringing the presents they'd bought for us. When I asked them where they'd been, they looked at each other furtively and hurriedly blurted out something like York, or Chester, I can't remember which. This set the alarm bells ringing, but in a nice way. After handing us our presents, they sat back while we opened them.

Vera was the first to open her present. It was a mug. A puzzled look flashed across her face, then a smile. Mine was also a mug. Both had inscriptions. CONGRATULATIONS GRANDMA TO BE met my eyes whilst Vera's said CONGRATULATIONS GRANDAD TO BE. They'd got them mixed up but it didn't matter, we were about to have our first grandchild. I jumped up, hugged and kissed Kathryn and hugged Michael. I was so happy and so was Vera.

On the 15 April 2013 Kathryn presented us with our first grandchild, a beautiful baby boy. Everyone was thrilled to bits.

The first time we saw our new grandson at the Royal Bolton Hospital he seemed so tiny and fragile, like a little doll. We'd forgotten how tiny a new born baby was. Kathryn had experienced a difficult birth and was tired so we didn't stay long, but long enough to hold our new addition to the family.

As we were leaving I said to the nurse how beautiful he was. "All my babies are beautiful," she replied with a smile. It was obvious she took immense pride in helping bring new life into the world.

After a few days we asked Michael and Kathryn what they were going to call him. We've not decided yet, they said, but we'll let you know when we have. I thought this unusual since most parents decide their baby's name beforehand. A week passed, then two, then three and it was still baby no name. Then, one evening, the phone rang. "Dad, it's me. We've decided on a name. We're going to call him Brutus."

To say I was stunned was an understatement. I was speechless. Brutus, what a horrible name. Then it dawned on me that he was joking. "I had you going there," said Michael laughing. "We've decided to call him Joshua. Joshua Adam Gregory."

"That's nice," I replied. "I like those names." After informing Vera I rang Andrew and Helen. Quick as a flash, Andrew remarked that with a name like that he'd better be fast.* At first I wondered what he was on about then the penny dropped. Joshua Adam Gregory. JAG. The initials spelled the name of a renowned fast car. Maybe one day he would emulate Josh Charnley and play on the wing for Wigan!

When Joshua was just a few weeks old our two sons and their wives came round to our house for tea. Myself, Vera, Andrew and Helen ate first and retired to the lounge to change Joshua's nappy, leaving Michael and Kathryn to have their meal in peace. On hearing loud shouts from the lounge, Michael and Kathryn dashed from the dining room to see what all the commotion was about. As Joshua lay naked on the changing mat he'd unleashed an exocet missile of diarrhoea which shot halfway across the lounge before landing with a splat on the carpet. It was the first time that anything had been spilled on the carpet, but it most certainly wouldn't be the last, not with Joshua around.

Whilst he was young Kathryn introduced him to a number of activities, including Musicality and Water Babies. He enjoyed most of them but, like the rest of our family, he didn't enjoy the water, but that would change. He was a beautiful baby (Image 324).

Joshua at three months old.

---

* He was. In 2018 he won Bolton's 'Iron Kids' race.

We saw him a lot. He loved coming to his Nana's and Gaga's (Image 325) and slept at our house on a fairly regular basis. We read to him a lot and stimulated him with toys and he enjoyed it so much he quickly learned where we kept both the books and the toys (Image 326).

I love my grandad. Joshua aged about six months.

Joshua, aged about twelve months, playing
with Lego in the spare bedroom.

Like most children nowadays, Joshua went to nursery. Unlike most children, he started when he was just nine months old.

Vera and I were apprehensive on the first day that we took him to Rose Cottage Nursery at Chequerbent, worrying he might have a tantrum and refuse to stay.

After all, he'd spent his entire short life with either his mummy and daddy or his grandparents. Going to nursery was a big change for him.

Our fears were unfounded. Catherine, the young girl who looked after the newcomers, was lovely and quickly established a rapport with Joshua, allaying any fears he may have had. He did cry a little when we left him on that first day, but the crying only lasted for the first few days. After that, he was fine and really looked forward to going to nursery. Indeed, he went from age nine months until he was ready to start primary school in September 2017, aged four and a half, making many little friends and attending lots of birthday parties along the way.

In his final week he 'graduated' in his cap and gown, clutching his certificate (Image 327).

Joshua on his 'graduation' from nursery.

As he got older Joshua loved watching programmes on CBeebies. Initially, it was *In the Night Garden*, where his favourite character was Makka Pakka. In the January of 2014, when Joshua was nine months old, we took him to watch *In the Night Garden* at the Trafford Centre, where he had more fun tickling the head of the man sat in front of him than watching the show.

After *In the Night Garden* he moved on to *Dinopaws*, but his favourite was *Thomas the Tank Engine*. He knows the name, and number, of every engine and adores watching the feature length movies, especially his three favourites, *Blue Mountain Mystery, Tale of the Brave* and *The Great Race*. In *Blue Mountain Mystery* a yellow engine is knocked into the sea. Because of this he loves going to Southport to ride on the yellow road train to the end of the pier. "It's the yellow engine, Gaga. It's not fell into the sea," he says joyfully.

In the penny arcades he delights in rolling old pennies down the ramp to try and dislodge the ones at the bottom, and every time he replenishes his dwindling pile of pennies by inserting a pound coin in the change machine he thinks he's won the jackpot as the pennies come tumbling out.

Playing on the beach making sand castles and finding and throwing shells into puddles are other activities near the top of his enjoyment list, but at the very top is jumping into puddles. Most of the time he does this successfully, but not always. One day on Southport beach he misjudged his jump and fell headlong into a big puddle. Did he cry? He thought it was hilarious and burst into a fit of giggles, but Vera didn't. She had to change all of his sopping wet clothes.

Every time we ask him what he enjoyed most at the seaside his answer is invariably the same; the yellow engine.

But it's not just Thomas and the yellow engine he likes. He's simply mad about trains and tracks. We must have over fifty trains at our house and enough wooden track to go round the lounge ten times! He's a genius at laying tracks. His tracks have tunnels, bridges, junctions, turntables, level crossings, stations and even Gordon's Hill, and he plays with them for hours. In *Tale of the Brave* he's fascinated when a landslide deposits tons of rocks on the tracks and replicates this in our lounge by emptying a large bag of squirrel nuts over his tracks.

"Gaga, Thomas is broken. You need to mend him with batteries and a screwdriver." Joshua has got both the green Thomas and the blue Thomas and each needs two AAA batteries. He plays with them so much (and forgets to turn them off when he's finished) that we must have gone through more than 100 batteries. Because a screwdriver and batteries 'mend' Thomas, Joshua thinks they mend everything. The day I hurt my hand he said, "Don't worry Gaga. I'll get the screwdriver and batteries and mend it." He's so cute.

At the beginning of the Thomas DVDs they always advertise *Thomasland* at Drayton Manor so, in December 2015, myself, Michael and Vera took him to *Thomasland*. He was entranced. He rode on Thomas to the Dinosaur Park (he likes dinosaurs too), rode on several of the attractions, met the Fat Controller and enjoyed the (artificial) snow. However, his visit to meet Father Christmas was the highlight of his day. A fabulous day was ended watching the firework display around the lake.

He's also fond of diggers. Not only does he play with them, every time we took him out in the car we'd have to pass some diggers, otherwise he had a paddy. Fortunately for us, there were lots of roadworks and building works nearby. As mentioned in Chapter 28, he was overjoyed when he could sit on a real digger in our garden.

Although he was quick to talk (11 months) he was slow to walk (17 months).* Indeed, we were becoming a little concerned that he was taking so long to walk, but

---

* There are two reasons he was slow to walk. One, he was brilliant at crawling and two, boys are lazy.

we needn't have worried. When he was 17 months old he took his first, faltering steps in our lounge. Michael had brought him round to show us his new skill: standing upright on his own when, without any warning, he not only stood upright but also started to walk.

"Come on Gaga. It's playtime." It was Joshua shaking my arm to awaken me from my slumber at 7-00 a.m., an unearthly hour for me. "COME ON GAGA. IT'S PLAYTIME," he repeated, this time more loudly, whilst tugging my arm. It's great having a grandson but I miss my lie-ins when he has a sleepover. However, I just love it when he holds my hand and sits on my knee. There's nothing better.

Joshua loves the outdoors. From an early age we've taken him outside. In the garden he delights in digging up my plants, playing in his sand pit making sand castles with his bucket and spade, but his favourite activity is throwing things in the waterfall – everything is fair game. He then retrieves them, or tries to, with his fishing net. He also likes Mesnes Park, Wigan, climbing the steps to the cafe and playing on the playground. At Haigh Hall, he adores walks through the forest, finding a tree with a hole in its trunk and then filling it with twigs. And he makes it his mission to jump into every puddle along the way, making as big a splash as possible. (*Splish, Splash, Splosh* is another of his favourite Thomas movies.) He plays on the playground, walks through the tunnels and then walks on the train tracks in the forest to the miniature railway station. He's a creature of habit.

Rivington is another of his favourite places. He adores walking through the forest to Liverpool Castle where he gleefully jumps off every boulder and explores every nook and cranny of the castle ruins. He delights in jumping into all the puddles, creating as big a splash as possible. After he's exhausted the castle, it's off down to the reservoir. Here, Joshua delights in throwing countless stones into the water, especially the larger ones as they make the biggest splash.

He's also fascinated by wizards so we've built a den in the corner of our back garden for the wizard which he diligently inspects every time he comes to our house to see if the wizard has visited. He does the same near the reservoir at Rivington where there are several signs on the iron railings asking people not to pollute their drinking water. They all show a large cup of tea. "I think the wizard lives here," I say as we walk back to the car park, "and that's his garden behind the railings."

"Can we see him, Gaga?" he always asks excitedly.

"Well, I don't think he's in today," I reply, "because he's left a note saying that he's gone for a cup of tea," pointing to the sign on the railings, "but he might see us next time."

"Okay," replies Joshua, adding, "see you next time Mr Wizard."

For some reason Joshua has always been fascinated with caravans so, in 2016 Vera and I took him on a caravan holiday at Talacre Beach. As well as a bucket and spade we took his trains and track so he could play with them on the lounge floor. It was a wise move. He adored the caravan, running from one end to the other and building an enormous track on the lounge floor. He was enthralled with the children's TV programmes – they were in Welsh – and the fact that every room had a TV. "I think they've fallen into the sea and speak a different language, just like the yellow engine," I said. He thought that was hilarious.

We took him to the Welsh Mountain Zoo at Colwyn Bay, where he delighted in the antics of the penguins, but his favourite activity was riding on the yellow road train to the West Shore at Llandudno and playing on the lovely beach, collecting shells, throwing pebbles into the rock pools and racing his Gaga.

For the past two years myself, Michael and our friends Ian and Sharon have stayed at the Sunderland Marriott at Seaburn for the annual rugby league Magic Weekend in Newcastle (Chapter 16). Because Joshua enjoyed the caravan holiday at Talacre Beach so much, in 2017 Vera, Elaine and June took him, Layla and Jessica in a caravan at Cresswell Towers caravan site just north of Newcastle. Although it was hard work for the adults, the children absolutely loved it, despite the changeable weather. Indeed, even though it was pouring down, Joshua, to the amusement of the other people on the beach, sang, *Oh I do like to be beside the seaside*, at the top of his voice. However, I hope he didn't perform one of his more recent activities of weeing outdoors, an activity I hope he will outgrow.

August 2020. Joshua was now seven years old, old enough, we deemed, to have his first short break holiday in a hotel* with his Nana and Gaga. And so, on Tuesday 25 August we set off for the Empire Hotel in Llandudno.

It wasn't a good start. Storm Frances had just hit Britain meaning we had a difficult drive to our hotel through heavy rain on busy, windswept motorways. Over two hours later, I parked the car in front of the hotel, helped the porter take our luggage to our room, then drove to the Empire Hotel's garage. Its automatic door fascinated Joshua. He watched in anticipation as Vera swiped the card to open it and was amazed at how quickly it shot up, and then just as quickly down. We gathered the rest of our stuff from the car and then pressed the green button to exit the garage. We told Joshua he had just ten seconds to get out before the door came crashing down. He was outside in two!

It was still raining steadily as we walked the short distance to the hotel, where we climbed the staircase, a staircase with a blue carpet and 'gold' handrail, to Room 17 on the first floor. It was a superior room – the only room available when we booked – with two beds, a sofa bed, and a large *en suite* bathroom. Joshua was so impressed

---

* In 2018, we took him for a one night stay in the Hilton Hotel at Warwick to watch a dragon show at Warwick Castle he said it was better than the Ritz! Immediately, he chose his bed, the one in the middle, and mine, the one next to his, meaning Vera had to make do with the sofa bed (Image 328). The room also had several pictures of naked ladies on the walls so Joshua decided he'd follow suit and be naked too, but just in the room of course. (For some reason he likes being naked.)

A naked Joshua in Room 17 at the Empire
Hotel. His clothes are on his bed.

Because of the bad weather, we spent the next hour or so exploring the hotel. Joshua loved the lounges with their sumptuous sofas, the bar area and the large dining room, but his favourite was undoubtedly the indoor swimming pool. It blew him away. Even better, the entrance was just down the corridor from our room. He wanted to go in straight away, but it was too close to dinner and anyway, it was very busy. We told him we'd go in after dinner when it should be quieter. On returning to our room, Joshua played with his trains whilst Vera and I had a drink of tea and a biscuit before getting washed and changed ready for dinner.

Because of Covid 19, the hotel had decided to extend both the dinner times and the breakfast times and we thought it prudent to eat early, not only because there would be fewer diners but also to give us time to go to the pool. At 5-45 p.m., Elyse Waddy, the Empire Hotel's owner, escorted us to a large booth, which Joshua loved. It was a private space in which he could watch his tablet whilst eating his meal, yet another plus. When I told Elyse what he'd said about her hotel, she replied he had good taste.

Joshua had a large bowl of pasta and a bowl of fries, just like McDonalds, he said, and three or four bottles of Schweppes fresh orange juice. (They never charged for any of his orange juices and he had a lot.)

On the way back to our room at around seven-o-clock, we checked the pool. It was empty. Great. After changing into our trunks and putting on our robes, we made our way to the pool. Because of my ileostomy (Section 29.3), I also wore a

528

T-shirt to ensure that my pouch was fully covered. (Joshua doesn't know about my pouch.) I was a little apprehensive about entering a swimming pool having a pouch, but I needn't have worried. It was fine. We spent an enjoyable hour in the pool all by ourselves before towelling down and returning to our room, where Joshua played on his tablet then had his late night snack of orange juice and a Twirl. Lied in his bed next to his Gaga we had our customary chat before he fell asleep holding my hand.

After breakfast in our booth, where Joshua enjoyed his toast and orange juice, we made our way to the bus stop at the bottom of the street. In contrast to the previous day, Wednesday was a lovely, warm, sunny day. We'd just missed the 10-45 a.m. bus to Conway and waited for the next one which, according to the timetable, should arrive at 11-16 a.m. We waited and waited but no bus came. Whilst we were waiting, Joshua said a strange thing. He'd been asking Vera about Jessica's grandad. When she said that Jessica's grandad, Ray, had died (Chapter 26), he thought about this for a moment and then said, 'You and Gaga are legends and legends never die.' It's weird what thoughts go through young children's minds, especially with the Covid crisis and the lockdown.

After we'd waited over 45 minutes, a local elderly lady said the bus services had been severely curtailed because of Covid 19 and the next one could be another two hours. There was no way we were waiting that long and we hotfooted it to the pier and boarded one of the sightseeing buses, a red open top double decker. It was more expensive but they ran every 20 minutes, provided a commentary, an hop-on hop-off service, and the tickets were valid for 24 hours. Joshua elected to sit in the covered downstairs section and we enjoyed a pleasant 30 minute journey to Conway.

We had hoped to visit the castle but it was fully booked, so we did the next best thing and took Joshua to the Knights shop opposite. He absolutely loved it. The real swords, shields, axes, daggers, helmets and armour captivated him. And they had real muskets too. But he couldn't have any of those. Instead, he bought realistic replicas of a sword, a three birds shield, an axe, and a helmet, plus a bag of toy warriors. He left the shop a happy little boy, clutching his new sword and shield. After visiting Yesteryears toy shop, where he bought some wooden trains, we had lunch in the Illy cafe before strolling around the harbour and then catching the bus to Llandudno's West Shore. Much to Joshua's dismay – he wanted to sit downstairs again – I said we should sit upstairs on the open top double decker to get better views. It was a mistake. As the bus drove off, the sun disappeared behind a cloud and the wind increased. We all shivered on the cold and windy journey to the West Shore. To warm up, we had battles on the beach with his new swords and shield, and then with his warriors on the concrete steps. We were still cold so caught the bus back to the pier, this time in the downstairs section. After a short walk back to the hotel, we did the same as the previous evening: we got washed and changed, had dinner in a booth, and then went to the pool. This time, at Joshua's behest, I didn't wear a T-shirt. Once again, it was empty and we had a great time frolicking about (Image 329). We had races, sat in the Jacuzzi and I gave Joshua piggy back rides to the deep end.

Me and Joshua in the pool.

Thursday was a cloudy day, a day we'd hoped to go to the zoo but, like the castle, it too was fully booked. Instead, we decided to board the old charabanc for the scenic drive over the Orme. The driver gave an entertaining commentary and made several stops, allowing the passengers to admire both the stunning scenery and the wildlife. We saw seals on the beach and mountain goats and sheep on the mountain. One sheep looked a bit like Ralph, Joshua's favourite chubby sheep at AppleCast, near Parbold, a place that Joshua adores. He said that Ralph must have lived on this mountain before moving to AppleCast.

The driver's story about the haunted Lighthouse Hotel, where ghosts of shipwrecked sailors are said to roam the rooms, enthralled him, as did the fact that a phosphor bronze propeller of a sunken ship had never been found, and that divers still searched for this treasure, which is worth a cool £1 million. However, when he said that there were no wifi or mobile phone signals at the hotel, Joshua's interest waned. He loves playing on his tablet.

On returning from the coach ride, we spent some time on the busy pier, where Joshua tried his hand at a shooting game and bought two little Lego figures. As it began to drizzle, we returned to the hotel for lunchtime drinks in the lounge. Afterwards, as the rain had stopped, we strolled along the main shopping street then on to the beach, where Joshua and I built a large 'castle' from the many rocks and pebbles, and then watched to see if the incoming tide would demolish it. It didn't, so we had to demolish it ourselves by throwing rocks at it. To everyone's delight, two seals frolicked close to the shore. Joshua said they were the ones we'd seen on our scenic tour earlier in the day.

The evening was spent like the previous two with dinner, the pool, the 'secret' lounge and playing in our room. After breakfast on the Friday, we made the long journey home, our first holiday in a hotel with our grandson at an end. It was one we all enjoyed.

At just seven years of age, Joshua is already an inveterate traveller. His mum and dad have taken him to Tenerife (twice) to Disneyland Paris (also twice), where he met Father Christmas (Image 330), and Lapland, as well as many places in the UK. He's a lucky little lad.

Father Christmas with Joshua
at Disneyland Paris 2016.

Joshua is a lovely, well mannered, adorable little boy (Image 331) who, like his dad (Chapter 12, Images 121, 125 and 127), has a mischievous smile (Image 332) and some mischievous ways.

He is also very protective of his Nana and Gaga. If anyone calls us grandma and grandad, he shouts, "NO! IT'S NOT GRANDMA AND GRANDAD. IT'S NANA AND GAGA."

Joshua aged about 18 months.

Joshua, Layla and Jessica on the annual
Easter Egg Hunt at our house in 2016.

As mentioned in the Epilogue (which was written before the birth of our grandson), Joshua is the final piece in the jigsaw of my life.

29.2 A SCARE

It all started with a sore throat and a hoarse voice at the beginning of December 2015. As mentioned in Chapter 10 my throat is my Achilles Heel so I wasn't too concerned. In the past they cleared up of their own accord after a week or two, but this one didn't. As it was near Christmas I made the decision to make a rare visit to the doctors, but only after the Christmas and New Year festivities were over.

After giving me a thorough examination not only did the doctor prescribe a course of antibiotics, he also arranged for me to have a chest X-ray to rule out any underlying causes. He told me to come back and see him in two weeks time if the sore throat and hoarseness hadn't gone.

Two weeks later I was back at the doctors. The sore throat had gone but the hoarse voice hadn't. The doctor said that my chest X-ray was clear so there were no underlying causes connected to my chest for the hoarseness, and that it was most likely a problem with my vocal chords. In that case, he said, there's no point prescribing more antibiotics. Instead, he made an appointment for me at the Ear, Nose and Throat (ENT) Department at the Royal Bolton Hospital for 1 March.

On the morning of the 1 March 2016 Vera and I made our way to the waiting area of the ENT Department of the Royal Bolton Hospital. It was very busy and we anticipated a long wait. We weren't wrong. A nurse kept altering the waiting times. A 30 minute delay became 45 minutes, then 60 minutes and finally 80 minutes. Eventually, they called my name and Vera and I entered the room of a young female

Greek doctor. After asking a string of questions she examined first my ears and then my nose. Both were fine. "I'll take a look at your vocal chords now," she said, "using a camera. Have you had an nasendoscopy before?"

"No," I replied, "I haven't."

"It's okay, there's nothing to worry about," she continued. "It will just feel a little strange." She then handed me some tissues. "But you'll need these because it'll make your eyes water."

Everything was as she said. It did feel strange having a camera inserted up my nostril and down the back of my throat, and yes, it did make my eyes water. She wiggled the camera around my vocal chords for a few minutes, removed it – which also produced a strange sensation – before pronouncing that there was a 'lesion' on my left vocal chord which needed investigating. "I'll make you an appointment as a day patient for Mr Hargreaves to have a look at it and remove it by surgery if appropriate. Is Thursday 10 March convenient for you?' she asked.

"Yes, that's fine," I replied, thinking they weren't wasting much time.

"Okay, we'll see you on the 10 March," she said.

As we made our way back to the car, Vera obviously harboured the same thoughts. "That's quick," she said. "Do you think it's because it's something serious?'

"No," I replied. "They probably have to meet certain targets." She wasn't convinced and, in truth, neither was I.

On the 10 March we arrived at the ENT reception area at 1-00 p.m. After registering my details I bade farewell to Vera as a nurse escorted me to a small six bedroom ward. She took down further details and told me to remain dressed and sit on the solitary chair beside the bed until Mr Hargreaves came to see me. I did as instructed, reading the newspaper and doing the puzzles until I heard the unmistakable voice of Mr Hargreaves doing his rounds.

A nurse pulled the curtain around the bed and Mr Hargreaves breezed in. "Good afternoon. It's Peter isn't it?" he enquired.

"Yes, it is," I replied.

"Nice to meet you, Peter," he continued, shaking my hand. "Do you know what you're here for?"

"To have my vocal chords examined and a lesion removed," I responded.

"Very good," he said. 'That's right. I'm going to have a good root around using a camera with a microscope and excise the lesion if appropriate. Obviously, it will have to be done under a general anaesthetic. Are you allergic to anaesthetics?'

"Not as far as I'm aware," I said.

"Good. The anaesthetist will come to see you shortly. Before I go, I've got a few questions to ask."

He asked about any allergies, the medicines I was taking, my past medical history, if I had any dentures or loose teeth (your mouth is clamped open during the operation) and some other things. Then, he asked me to sign the consent form before moving on to his next patient.

As he departed a nurse drew back the curtain and said the anaesthetist would be along shortly.

The anaesthetist, a slim, pleasant lady in her mid-thirties, asked me virtually all the same questions as Mr Hargreaves had. She said it wouldn't be long before they took me to the anaesthetist's room in readiness for my operation.

About ten minutes later a nurse came and drew the curtains around me for a second time. She gave me a surgical gown and told me to get undressed and put it on. I did but it was one that fastened at the back and I couldn't do it. This presented me with a dilemma. I wanted to visit the loo before the operation but it was in the corridor outside the ward and I didn't fancy walking through the ward and along the corridor with a bare backside. Instead, I waited until the nurse came to collect me and let her fasten me up. I duly made my visit to the loo and then the nurse escorted me to the anaesthetist's room.

The anaesthetist greeted me warmly, loosened my surgical gown – she said it was too tight – gave me a pillow and lay me on my back on the gurney with my head resting on the clean, fresh pillow. She then found a vein in my right arm and connected the saline drip. After delivering the pre-op injection, she got the mask with anaesthetic and oxygen ready to place over my nose and mouth. "Aren't I having an injection?" I enquired. "It works much faster than gas and air."

"No," she replied, "I'm giving you gas and air," and placed the mask over my nose and mouth. "Breathe normally," she continued, "and try to relax. How are you feeling," she said softly.

"Drowsy," was my reply, and that was it. The next thing I remember was drifting in and out of consciousness in the Recovery Room. I glanced at the clock. It was 4-55 p.m. "How do you feel?" asked the male nurse sat by my gurney.

"Sleepy," I replied.

"That's okay," he said. "We'll keep you here for another 30 minutes until you've recovered, then take you back to the ward. I had a blood pressure monitor strapped to my left arm, a drip in my right arm, an oxygen mask over my face and a heart monitor. I closed my eyes and tried to rest.

"Are you famous?" a voice asked, "only a few of the nurses have remarked that you look like someone on the television."

"No, I'm not famous nor on the television," I replied sleepily.

At 5-30 p.m. the nurse disconnected all the apparatus and then he and another nurse began my journey on the gurney. They wheeled me out of the Recovery Room and through a maze of corridors to a large elevator. It stopped at the next floor and after yet more corridors we arrived back at the ward. "Shuffle across on to the bed," said the nurse after he'd positioned the gurney next to it. I did but it wasn't easy when you're still feeling groggy and woozy. He then adjusted the bed so I was in a sitting position and said a nurse would be along shortly with some food and drink. I thanked him and he left, leaving me to wonder what kind of food and drink I'd get. With my throat feeling rough and dry like sandpaper, I was really looking forward to a cold glass of milk and some fruit and ice cream. To my complete amazement, and disappointment, I got none of those. The nurse brought me a cup of tea, a glass of water and two slices of crusty toast. In the words of Victor Meldrew, I couldn't believe it. Still, it was late and it was better than nothing. I'd had nothing to eat for 24 hours and nothing to drink since 11-00 a.m. The only way I could eat the crusty toast was to take small bites and moisten them in my mouth with a sip of tea, and when that ran out, with water, before swallowing. By doing this, I managed to consume one slice, but it took me a long time.

I looked at the clock. It was 6-40 p.m. Had they rung Vera to ask her to pick me up? I was about to call the nurse and ask her when I heard footsteps approaching. It was Mr Hargreaves. He came and sat on the chair beside the bed. I waited for him to speak.

I remember his first words exactly. "I'm a little bit concerned," he began. Well, that set the alarm bells ringing and initiated a whole train of emotions stretching from one extreme to the other. "... that there are some cancer cells and cancerous tissue on your vocal chords." He must have seen the shock and disbelief on my face because he placed a reassuring hand on my knee before continuing. "But let's wait for the biopsy results in 7-10 days time. The hospital will contact you to arrange a date for you to see me to discuss the results. Is there anything you want to ask me?" Still feeling woozy from the general anaesthetic and in shock from the bombshell he'd just delivered, I shook my head slowly. "Okay," he continued, "I'll see you in about ten days time." Before getting up to depart, he once again placed his hand on my knee. Although it was meant to be a reassuring gesture it made me feel worse, as though it was someone saying a final farewell.

As Mr Hargreaves departed the nurse returned. It was 6-50 p.m. "Your wife will be here in ten minutes to take you home," she said. "Can you get dressed and pack up all your things. I'll come back for you when she arrives." I nodded meekly, my mind still in a whirl from the devastating news from a few minutes earlier.

Ten minutes later the nurse returned and escorted me to the reception area where Vera was waiting to collect me. "How did it go?" she asked. "Are you alright?"

I nodded my head. In the few minutes I'd had before meeting Vera I'd decided to tell her everything except the bit about cancer. It was a difficult decision. I didn't want to lie to her but I knew how she worried about things. In the words of our legal system, I'd tell her the truth but not the whole truth. I clung to the faint hope that the biopsy would prove fine and that there wouldn't be any cancer cells.

"How are you feeling?" she continued. "Are you alright to walk to the car?" Again I nodded my head. Realising I couldn't speak and that I was still a bit groggy from the anaesthetic, she said she wouldn't ask any more questions until we got home, when I could respond by writing down the answers.

When we got home she asked lots of questions and I wrote down lots of answers, but I never mentioned the C-word. Seeing I was tired, she said I should lie down on the couch and watch Widnes versus Hull on the television. I did but I didn't enjoy it. Not because of what Mr Hargreaves had said – I'd pushed that to the back of my mind – but because I wanted desperately to wee, but couldn't. I was bursting but every time I tried, all that came out were a few dribs and drabs. During the match I was up and down like a yoyo, but hardly anything came out.

The same thing continued when I went to bed. I was very tired but my brain wouldn't let me sleep. Instead, it kept telling me to go to the toilet because I needed a wee. I was toing and froing to the toilet without any success until the early hours of the morning before I finally managed to grab a few hours much needed sleep. In the morning, I did manage to wee a little and over the course of the day my waterworks returned to normal. I can only presume the problem was caused by the residual anaesthetic in my body.

The following few days were very harrowing. Vera kept asking more and more questions and I could tell she knew there was something I wasn't telling her. Finally, on the Sunday, I came clean and told her what Mr Hargreaves had said. She was dumbstruck. "It can't be," she said, "you only went in with a sore throat and a hoarse voice." That was true and I'm so glad I did because hopefully it meant they'd caught the cancer very early. I told her on our way to Housing Units to collect some light fittings we'd ordered for the hall, but it thoroughly spoiled the day.

"I knew there was something wrong the moment I saw you after the operation," said Vera later. "You're normally smiling and happy but you seemed, well, wild and not with it." I should have realised her perception would find me out.

Over the following few days Vera did two things. She asked me over and over again to remember everything that Mr Hargreaves had said. Everything. Exactly. Word for word. As accurately and precisely as possible in the hope of finding a ray of light. The second thing she did was to spend loads of time on the internet looking at cancer of the vocal chords. I wasn't convinced this was the right thing to do but in the event I was glad she did. One night, she showed me the fruits of her research. Cancer of the vocal chords is very rare – there are only about 2,500 cases per year in the entire UK – and is usually treated with radiotherapy. The success rate is high, 96 per cent for stage 2 cancer. (Stage 1 is the earliest form of the disease and stage 4 the most advanced.) This cheered me up a little, but not much.

Those ten days from being told the news on Thursday 10 March to the appointment with Mr Hargreaves on Monday 21 March were the worst of our entire lives. Every possible scenario flashed through my mind, from the worst to the best and every one in-between. In the worst case scenario, which I tried not to think about, I might only have a few months to live. If that was the case, and I hoped with all my heart that it wasn't, then I wouldn't see my beautiful grandson grow up, I wouldn't get much more time with Vera, my two sons, Andrew and Michael, and the rest of my family and friends. On a more practical note, I wouldn't get to enjoy our lovely new extension, kitchen, utility room and shower room, on which I'd just spent an absolute fortune (Chapter 28). However, on the optimistic side, if it hadn't progressed beyond stage 2 and spread, I had an excellent chance of a complete cure. It was this latter scenario that I kept at the forefront of my mind.

During those terrible ten days we decided not to tell anyone about the cancer, not even our two sons, Andrew and Michael, but to wait until we got the results of the biopsy, and to carry on as normal. That was hard enough but the situation was made even more difficult because the 23 March was my seventieth birthday, a special milestone which Vera and I always celebrate by having a few days holiday at the Empire Hotel in Llandudno, and then a meal for our family and friends. Given the circumstances, we decided to leave the meal until we knew the outcome of the biopsy, but we'd already booked our holiday at the Empire Hotel some months earlier for the 7-10 April and we wondered if we'd be able to take it.

Eventually the dreaded day arrived. Vera and I set off for the Royal Bolton Hospital on the morning of Monday 21 March to get the results of the biopsy. I can't describe my feelings, except to say they were all over the place, but I think I remained optimistic.

Only two people were in the waiting area of the Ear, Nose and Throat Department and I felt that this time our appointment would be on time. It wasn't to be. Lots of people came flooding in and began to be seen by the two doctors working under Mr Hargreaves, the young Greek doctor I'd seen and another female doctor. They were obviously new patients and it became apparent that those waiting for biopsy results had to be seen by Mr Hargreaves himself.

Whilst we were waiting a man and his wife, who were also there when we were on the 10 March, came and sat down beside us. His wife was very agitated, getting up and down and prowling around the waiting area picking up lots of leaflets. Living with Cancer, Surviving Cancer, MacMillan Nurses for Cancer Patients… As Vera and I glanced at the titles it did nothing to lift our spirits.

Suddenly, a female doctor in a white coat walked across the waiting area and stopped outside Mr Hargreaves door. She had a laptop displaying a coloured image of someone's throat. The door opened, a patient came out and she entered. A few minutes later the door opened again and a nurse called out the name of a woman in her sixties who was by herself. I knew I was next because she was the ten-o-clock patient and I was the ten-fifteen one.

By now both Vera and I were getting a little uptight, a little apprehensive, but what happened next was awful. Mr Hargreaves' door opened and the woman emerged in floods of tears supported by a nurse. It was obvious to everyone what she'd been told, and to make matters worse, she had to walk through the crowded waiting area to a private room. At that instant, my heart sank and my legs turned to jelly. The only thought flooding through my head was that Mr Hargreaves was getting all the bad news over with in one go and that I was the next one in!

"Peter Gregory," the nurse at Mr Hargreaves door called. It was only 30 feet or so to his door but on wobbly legs and a spinning head I don't think I'd have made it without Vera's support.

"Come in, come in," said Mr Hargreaves, "and take a pew." Trying to regain some sense of normality, I asked if it was okay for me to take off my scarf and coat. "Yes, that's fine," he said, and waited until I'd sat down. He then picked up my case file and seemed to study it for ages before uttering a word. I glanced over my shoulder to Vera, who was sat in a corner next to two nurses. Why did they need two nurses? Was it to support me after delivering the bad news? And why was he taking so long? Was he waiting for the right time to deliver the bad news? Vera must have felt the same and I thought she was on the verge of breaking down when Mr Hargreaves shattered the silence. Like before, I remember his first words precisely. "Well, it's not disastrous news," he said. What his next words were I can't recall with any certainty because of the overwhelming sense of relief that swept through my body, but it turned out that I had an *in situ carcinoma*, a localised pre-cancer which is classed as stage 0, the earliest possible form of the disease. It hadn't passed the epithelial layer and was localised in the vocal chords. Mr Hargreaves said he'd taken a large (10mm) biopsy sample and was pretty confident of his diagnosis. With my eyes I implored him to continue. "There are two types of treatment," he continued, "radiotherapy and laser surgery. Radiotherapy will consist of three to four weeks of continuous treatment at The Christie whereas laser surgery is done in a day at Manchester Royal. You'll need to have a CAT scan in the next few days and then a Multi Disciplinary Team of experts will decide which treatment is best for you. I can't guarantee 100 per cent that it will be a complete cure, but I'm 99.99 per cent certain that it will."

Having endured a crescendo of emotions, Vera and I could now relax for the very first time. We asked questions and even made some jokes. I told Mr Hargreaves that I could never have imagined that I'd be so elated to be told that I had cancer. He laughed and said they hardly ever caught a cancer at such an early stage. Continuing, he said that if I needed radiotherapy, I'd have to have a mask made at The Christie. "A bit like *Phantom of the Opera*," I said, feeling mightily relieved. We were assigned our own personal nurse, Korenza, who took us to another room to explain what would happen and hand out some leaflets. Vera told Korenza she'd looked on the internet about cancer of the vocal chords since that was her way of coping with it. Korenza said that was fine: people deal with it in ways that are best for them. Some bury their heads in the sand and pretend it's not happening whilst others, like you, want as much information as possible.

Two days later, March 23, was my seventieth birthday and both Andrew and Michael were coming to our house with their presents. We wanted both of them to hear the news at the same time and, even though my birthday was hardly the ideal time to tell them, it offered the best opportunity to do so.

Joshua presented me with his presents, a gigantic birthday card and a voucher for a massage at the Ribby Hall Hotel near Blackpool. Only two years old, he already knew what his Gaga liked. After handing me the usual chocolates and wine, my two sons surprised and delighted me with a voucher for a two night stay at the Swinton Park Hotel in Masham, the residence of Lord and Lady Masham, for me and Vera, plus three massages. It must have cost them an arm and a leg. I was deeply touched. Then came the horrible bit. As I told them what had happened and what the outcome would be, they just sat there in stony silence, as shocked as I was when Mr Hargreaves delivered his bombshell to me. I felt really bad having to tell them on my birthday, especially after receiving such lovely presents, but I emphasised that everything would be fine. Nonetheless, it put a dampener on the evening. Later that week, we informed our other relatives and friends.

A few days later I duly had my CAT scan at the Royal Bolton Hospital and received a letter from The Christie for my first appointment. Not knowing where The Christie was, on the day before my first appointment William kindly agreed to take us there. From our house it involved driving along the M61 to the M60 at Worsley, then along the stretch of the M60 being upgraded to a 'Smart Motorway', eight miles of motorway with a 50 mph speed limit. After leaving at junction 5, the Manchester Airport exit, we turned left on to Palatine Road to Northenden. Four miles later, The Christie was reached.

That stretch of the M60 past the Trafford Centre is notoriously bad for traffic congestion at the best of times, but with the road works it was horrendous, especially at rush hour. A journey which should take no more than 35 minutes could take up to two hours. Secretly, I hoped they'd opt for laser surgery, which would be over and done with in one day.

It wasn't to be. On Thursday 31 March Vera and I made our way to the Main Outpatients Department at The Christie. After a short wait we were directed to a private room where, some minutes later, the oncologist and his entourage, including Korenza, breezed in. He examined my larynx with the camera and pronounced that Mr Hargreaves' diagnosis was spot on. He said the Multi Disciplinary Team had studied my CAT scan and the biopsy sample taken by Mr Hargreaves and decided that radiotherapy was the best treatment for me. Laser surgery would necessitate removing a large part of the vocal chords which could impair my speech (see later).

"Have you anything you want to ask me?" he said.

"Do you know what's caused it?" I asked. "Could it be related to the polyp I had removed about 40 years ago," (Chapter 10).

"No," he replied, "that's most unlikely. Ninety-five per cent of vocal chord cancers are caused by smoking and the other five per cent by heavy drinking."

"But I've never smoked and I'm not a heavy drinker," I replied.

"Then you've been very unlucky," he said.

We were then taken to a different room where another oncologist explained what would happen next, including the side effects of the radiotherapy, and gave us some leaflets.

A few days later I received another letter from The Christie with the days for my treatment, as well as an appointment to have a blood test, a CAT scan and to have a mask made. The radiotherapy would begin on Wednesday 20 April for 16 consecutive days, excluding weekends but including Bank Holidays. This wasn't too bad since normally the treatment took 40 days, another reason to be glad they'd caught it early. As we'd requested, the appointment to have the mask made was 5 April, leaving our holiday dates free.

Vera's middle sister June accompanied us to The Christie on Tuesday 5 April. After having a blood test I was seen by my oncologist, Dr Garcez. She explained what would happen, especially the side effects. For the first eight sessions, she said, there wouldn't be any side effects other than reddening of the skin on my neck where the radiation would be directed. However, during the final eight sessions and for several weeks after, my throat would be extremely sore and I would have difficulty swallowing, eating and drinking. She prescribed a mouthwash, Difflam, and painkillers, a special formulation of liquid paracetamol and oral morphine. It was obviously going to be painful. She also said I'd get very tired and would need plenty of rest.

In the Mould Room I had to strip to my waist and lie down on a flat steel bed with my neck on a support. The white thermoplastic mask, which would cover my entire face, neck, shoulders and upper chest, was placed in a sink full of hot water to render it pliable. "Don't worry," said one of the three nurses, "it'll just feel like a warm facial."

"I'll let you know after," I replied, secretly dreading what was about to happen. As I lay on the bed with my arms by my side the nurses placed the warm plastic mask over my face and began the process of moulding it to the shape of my face and torso by massaging it with their hands. A small hole was cut into the mask for my nose to poke through, allowing me to breathe. Then, the mask was clamped to the bed, holding my face and upper torso in a vice like grip as they applied the finishing touches to the moulding process. Finally, they placed cold towels on the mask to cool it down. The whole process took about twenty minutes but it seemed much longer. If that was a warm facial, I thought to myself, I wouldn't be returning for an encore. But worse was to follow.

After waiting outside for a while I was taken for a CAT scan whilst wearing the mask. By now, the mask had cooled (and shrunk) and felt much tighter and more uncomfortable as it was clamped over my face and torso. I was glad when it was removed and wasn't exactly looking forward to sixteen sessions of radiotherapy in this helpless position, but I had no choice if I wanted to be cured.

We took our four day break from Thursday 7 April to Sunday 10 April at the Empire Hotel but didn't enjoy it as much as usual. There were, I think, two reasons for this. One, because of what we had just gone through plus what was to come, and two, the fact that the hotel was full to the rafters with with families still on their Easter holidays. (Easter had been very early.) Normally, the hotel wasn't full and there had never been any children on any of our previous visits. It was a break but we didn't feel as relaxed and refreshed at the end of it as we should have done, although I did enjoy a relaxing massage.

On the Saturday Vera received a call from Michael on her mobile phone. Andrew, Michael and Joshua had been round to our house to set up a surprise birthday present* for me and as they were about to leave Joshua dropped his tablet behind our new kitchen radiator. In their unsuccessful attempts at trying to retrieve it, they dislodged a glass plaque on the wall and it too fell behind the radiator (Image 317, page 516). They ordered a new one thinking it would have broken but when Carl, our plumber, removed the radiator on our return, both the tablet and the glass plaque were undamaged.

As me and Vera sat in the waiting area of Suite 2 in the Radiotherapy Department on Wednesday 20 April a sweet young girl called Rosie, dressed in the burgundy coloured uniform of a radiographer, called my name then escorted us to a small private room. Here, she took my details, explained what would happen and returned us to the waiting area.

When it was my turn Rosie called my name and beckoned me into Suite 2. She was lovely and I told her I could write a children's book about her, *Rosie the Radiant Radiographer*. I think she was blushing as she introduced me to the other radiographers, Neil, Lindsay and Holly. All of them were friendly and helped reassure and relax a nervous patient. Neil asked me my address and date of birth, a ritual performed each time I attended a session, and asked me to strip to my waist. Then, as instructed, I climbed on to the flat bed and lay on my back with my neck on the support. "Shuffle a little further up the bed," they said. "That's fine. Now move slightly to your left. Oops, that's too far. Move back a little." When I was positioned perfectly (determined by a laser line down my body), they always asked if I was ready for my mask. I never was but said yes anyway. The mask was then placed over my

---

* The surprise present was a Samsung tablet with loads of the latest films and box sets for me to enjoy whilst I rested

face and upper torso and clamped into position. It was so tight I couldn't move a muscle and hoped I wouldn't develop a tickle in my throat to make me want to cough because that would have been impossible.

It took a further few minutes to get the bed into the exact right position. I could hear them calling out numbers. Ninety-four point seven, ninety-five point one, fifteen point two... Then, when it was exactly right, they left the room whilst the intense X-ray radiation was delivered. It was the same every time. A burst of approximately 45 seconds, a short pause and then a shorter burst of about ten seconds. All I heard was a buzzing sound. I felt nothing on my neck or throat. The bed was re-positioned and two more identical bursts of radiation delivered. Then, to my intense relief, the radiographers returned to the room and removed the mask. (I tried not to think about what would happen if they didn't return.)

For the first three sessions I had a CAT scan as well as the radiation so these sessions took a little longer. I also had CAT scans very Friday, just to ensure the radiation was being delivered to the right place.

On Thursdays, in addition to having the radiotherapy, I also saw Dr Garcez, my oncologist. She was pleased with the progress. I hadn't lost any weight and the skin on my neck was standing up well to the radiation partly, I presume, because I applied E45 cream every morning and evening.

On Thursday 5 May, my twelfth session, Dr Garcez said that I wouldn't need to attend The Christie for a full six weeks after my final session. By that time, she said, all the side effects should have disappeared.

I asked her what happened to the dead cancer cells on my vocal chords.

"They just shrivel up, die and wither away," she responded, "and are excreted by the body. The radiation kills the cancer cells but it also damages, and kills, healthy cells as it passes through your neck and it's these damaged healthy cells which give the side effects. However, unlike cancer cells, the damaged healthy cells recover, usually within six weeks. But," Dr Garcez continued, "the side effects will be at their worst at the end of the treatment and for one or two weeks afterwards, so keep taking the paracetamol and morphine."

"I will," I replied, "and thank you for the explanation."

She wasn't wrong. My throat was sore in the extreme and swallowing, eating and drinking were extremely painful, even with the painkillers, but I managed to eat normal food for most of the time.

It was Sod's Law. Early in my treatment regime both Michael and Kathryn had busy work commitments, which meant that Vera and I had two-year-old Joshua quite a lot, including several sleepovers. We couldn't have managed if William and Brian hadn't shared some of the driving, taking me to The Christie whilst Vera looked after Joshua. We were so grateful for their help. Even so, it was Vera who did the bulk of driving me to The Christie for my 16 sessions of radiotherapy.

We'd heard a bell ring several times whilst sat in the waiting area of The Christie followed by loud clapping and wondered what it was for. "A patient rings the bell when their treatment is finished," said a lady sat next to us. "It's a new tradition started about a year ago by parents of young children. It gives them something to look forward to at the end of their treatment." They were right. It does give you something to focus on to mark the end of your radiotherapy treatment. And so, after my final session on Wednesday 11 May, I too rang the bell, thankful that my life saving treatment was over.

Everything was going fine. My three monthly checks at the Royal Bolton Hospital were clear. The cancer had gone. Then, after about two years, things changed. The young Greek doctor noticed a white spot on my vocal chords where the cancer had been. Concerned, she called for Mr Umapathy, the consultant, to have a look. With the camera down my throat, he asked me to cough. 'It's okay,' he said, 'it's just a spot of mucus. There's nothing to worry about.' I was mightily relieved.

At my next three monthly appointment, Mr Umapathy had moved on and the new consultant, Mr Malik, did the examination. The white spot, he said, wasn't mucus and needed to be removed, and arranged a date for the operation, which I duly had. To my horror, the biopsy revealed the excised tissue was cancerous. Either the radiotherapy hadn't killed all the cancer cells or the cancer had returned. Mr Malik said it was most likely the former since some cancer cells are resistant to radiation.

Bot Vera and I, as well as all our family and friends, were shocked. We all thought the cancer had gone.

Mr Malik explained the next steps. You can't have radiotherapy twice in the same area so if there were any more cancerous cells in my vocal chords they would have to be removed using laser surgery. Accordingly, he made an appointment for me to see Prof. Homer at the Manchester Royal Infirmary.

A few weeks later, Vera and I arrived at the Peter Mount Building at the Manchester Royal Infirmary for my appointment with Prof. Homer. After examining my vocal chords with a camera he concluded the best option was to take some tissue samples from my vocal chords, two from each side, and perform biopsies to see if there was any cancer present and, if there was, its location. A date was set for the operation and Vera and I returned home.

The Manchester Royal Infirmary is not an easy place to reach by car – Vera and I had used the train – but Michael agreed to drive us there on the day of my operation. It was scheduled for early morning which meant we had to leave home at an unearthly hour. As well as Vera, June also came along to provide support for Vera.

Watching the television in the waiting room we were shocked to see the tragic and unexpected death of the popular news presenter Diane Oxberry from cancer. It was a timely reminder what a killer disease cancer is.

The nurse informed Vera, June and Michael that I should be ready to go home by 1-00 p.m. so they stayed local, having a walk in the nearby park and patronising several cafes whilst I had my operation.

It was later than one-o-clock when I was discharged. The operation had gone smoothly but at a cost. I couldn't speak a word. I was, quite literally, speechless. The doctor said this was normal after having four chunks of my vocal chords removed but it should only be temporary. After they were satisfied I was okay, I rejoined my family and Michael drove us home.

About ten days later, Elaine and June accompanied me and Vera to the Peter Mount Building to get the results of the biopsies. We travelled by train to the Oxford Road station, ate some breakfast in a Costa cafe, then strolled the 1.5 miles down Oxford Road to the hospital, passing Manchester University, where both Andrew and Michael had their graduation ceremonies (Chapter 19). We entered the Peter Mount Building, sat in the waiting room and waited to be called. None of us spoke very much, each having their own thoughts about what was to come. Mine were optimistic. I hoped the cancer had gone. I don't know what Vera, Elaine and June thoughts were.

After a short wait, my name was called and me and Vera went to see Prof. Homer. The news was excellent. All four biopsies were clear. There wasn't any cancer. We were delighted and couldn't wait to convey the good news to Elaine and June and then to the rest of our family and friends. But there was a downside. Removing four chunks of my vocal chords meant my voice was a husky, hoarse whisper. Prof. Homer said it should improve over time and made an appointment to see me again in six months. Nonetheless, elated with the news that I was cancer free, the four of us went first to Primark to do a little shopping and then for lunch at the Metro cafe.

Over the next six months my voice did improve a little, but not much. After examining my vocal chords, Prof. Homer said that taking the samples for the biopsies had left a lot of scar tissue and this was inhibiting their vibration and causing the hoarseness. He said he would remove the scar tissue using laser surgery and arranged another appointment for November.

When we saw him in November I'd been diagnosed with bowel cancer (see later), something he was totally unaware of. This surprised us since we thought all my medical information would be at his disposal. He remarked that was the aim but the system wasn't yet fully functional. Therefore, because of my imminent operation to have my bowel removed, he said it was best to leave the vocal chord operation until my bowel treatment had been sorted out, and made another appointment for April 2020. Because of the Covid 19 pandemic, that was postponed and I'm still waiting, with my hoarse voice, for another date to remove the scar tissue and return my voice to some sort of normality.

29.3 AN EVEN BIGGER SCARE

After the successful treatment of my vocal chord cancer, I thought I was cancer free and could look forward to a happy and joyous 2019. After all, 12 July 2019 would be our Golden Wedding anniversary, a chance to celebrate 50 years of marriage. How wrong I was.

I'd been doing the bowel cancer screening test since I was 60 and the last one arrived in March. As per usual, I completed the rather unpleasant task and duly sent it off. A few days later, the result arrived. It was unclear. Strange, all the previous tests had been clear. After completing the test kit that accompanied the result, I posted that off too. To my utmost relief, it came back clear. But there was a caveat. Although the second test was clear, a further test kit had been supplied. They wanted 'the best of three'. To my horror, this one came back 'abnormal' and set in motion a chain of events that lasted for nearly a year.

Because of the abnormal result I was strongly advised to have a colonoscopy at the Royal Bolton Hospital. Reluctantly, I agreed. I also agreed to participate in the pioneering ERAS (Enhanced Recovery After Surgery) project, of which more will be mentioned later. In the week prior to the colonoscopy I had to follow a low residue diet, drink two litres of water a day, take two Senekot tablets per day, and, on the eve of the colonoscopy, empty my bowels by drinking two litres of MOVIEPREP, which tasted like lemon flavoured sea water. But it did the trick. Every time I went to the toilet it was like Niagra Falls.

On Monday 10 June, the day of my colonoscopy, I was injected with a relaxant and told to lie on my side with my legs tucked up towards my tummy. Before starting the procedure, the doctor asked what music I liked. 'ABBA,' I replied.

'Oh good,' said one of the nurses, 'some proper music at last.'

'Are you ready?' asked the doctor, as ABBA blasted out Dancing Queen.

'Yes,' I replied, although I wasn't really.

The feeling when someone blows cold air up your bottom in order to inflate your large colon is weird in the extreme. Even more weird is the feeling when the camera is inserted. I fervently hoped that I wouldn't fart to release the build-up of pressure in my bowel. It would have reverberated around the small room like a thunderclap and been most embarrassing.

On completion of the examination, the doctor remarked that mine was the cleanest bowel he'd ever seen! Most people, he said, can't drink all the MOVIEPREP but you obviously did.

After spending 30 minutes in the Recovery Room, I was told to get dressed and then escorted to a private room where Vera was waiting with a nurse. Shortly afterwards, the doctor breezed in with the results. His opening remarks, presumably to lighten the mood, were that his view of me now was much better than the one he'd had when doing the colonoscopy. He then showed us a diagram of the bowel. After a brief pause, he said they'd found a rectal cancer right next to my bottom, and an embryonic cancer on the right side of the bowel.

To say that Vera and I were shocked is a complete understatement. I was convinced the results would be clear. This was a bombshell. Even worse, the rectal cancer was quite advanced, probably stage two or three. Vera was very annoyed. She said that I'd done the test diligently for 12 years so why wasn't it picked up earlier. The doctor replied that the test only works if the cancer bleeds. He said it isn't ideal and that they were trying to develop a better test.

Continuing, he said the cancer was too close to my bottom to slice it out and reconnect the colon because doing that would affect the sphincter muscle and make me incontinent, something I certainly didn't want. The best, indeed the only option, was to remove the entire large colon (bowel) and have a bag. Furthermore, there was already another cancer and, if the bowel wasn't removed, it was extremely likely that other cancers would keep recurring.

It wasn't what Vera or I wanted to hear but removing the large colon was the only realistic option. I asked what the survival rate was after this procedure, since it is a major operation to endure. About 95 per cent, he replied, but we'll know better after the surgery and performed the histology on the tumour.

The doctor then explained that I'd need five weeks of radiotherapy and chemotherapy at The Christie to shrink the cancer prior to surgery. Clinging to straws, I asked if this might completely cure the cancer so that I wouldn't need any surgery.

"It's possible,' he replied, 'but extremely unlikely.'

I thought I hadn't had any symptoms of colon/rectal cancer but, on reflection, I had experienced problems in the last year or so with sudden urges to go to the toilet, both on our Thursday walks and on days out with Vera, including one or two 'accidents'. With hindsight, these were probably caused, at least in part, by the rectal cancer.

Vera and I decided not to tell anyone about what was happening until after the summer holidays. We didn't want to spoil peoples' holidays, including our own with Brian and Valerie in Bude. But we had to tell them before the commencement of the five weeks of treatment at The Christie. We had no choice since we'd have to make arrangements with Michael about Joshua. He stayed regularly at our house for sleepovers and Vera often took him to school and picked him up. Also, we'd need some help with the driving. It was too much to expect Vera to drive me to The Christie for five continuous weeks.

Telling our relatives and friends was very difficult, especially Andrew and Michael. They were all as shocked as we were, but everyone was supportive.

My diagnosis was bad enough but worse was to follow. Jean, William's wife, had been ill for some time with colon cancer but she became really ill in early summer. She was taken first to Bolton Royal Hospital and later to Bolton Hospice.

Because of bad weather, one Thursday myself, William and Brian, instead of walking in the rain, went to Oswaldtwistle Mill. We mooched around and enjoyed a light lunch in one of the many cafes. Suddenly, William's phone rang. It was his daughter, Helen. Jean was really ill and she wanted William present at her bedside. We asked William if he wanted to go straight to the hospice but, as a creature of habit, he said we should stop at The Tavern on the Hill in Bolton first and have a quick drink. We'd just ordered our drinks when his phone rang again. It was a desperate Helen. 'Dad, you'd better get here quick. Mum is going downhill fast. She hasn't got much time left.' We left our untouched drinks and raced to the hospice. We arrived too late. Jean had just died. Propped up in bed, in death she looked so ashen and frail, nothing like the 'real' Jean.

We were all shocked. We knew Jean wouldn't get better but no one expected the end to come so quickly. But it had. I don't know if William regretted his decision not to go straight to the hospice, but I know that Brian and I did.

Jean's humanist funeral was held at the lovely Charnock Richard Crematorium on a beautiful summer's day, followed by a wake at William's bungalow. Because of this tragic event, plus all the times he'd had to take Jean to The Christie, we never asked William to assist with the driving.

To celebrate our Golden Wedding anniversary on 12 July 2019, we'd booked a five night stay at Portpatrick in Dumfries and Galloway. Both Brian and Valerie and Elaine and Keith had enjoyed holidays there and recommended it. Unfortunately, the dates we'd booked fell slap bang in the middle of the scheduled five week course of radiotherapy and chemotherapy at The Christie. However, our oncologist, Dr Noreen Alam, said since it was such an important occasion, we should go ahead with the holiday. An extra few weeks delay wouldn't make any difference.

Although the Portpatrick Hotel was in a lovely location on a cliff overlooking the charming seaside resort, it was a Shearing's hotel which meant it was full of coach parties, something we are not fond of. The weather was warm and sunny too but we didn't enjoy the holiday as much as we should have because of what was to come. We did several walks and had days out at the Logan Botanic Gardens and the Mull of Galloway. Although Portpatrick is a pleasant resort, it is too isolated for our liking.

Five consecutive weeks of radiotherapy and chemotherapy at The Christie (25 consecutive days excluding weekends) is a tall order. Not just because of the treatment, but also because of the travelling. Travelling on the M60 past the Trafford Centre is difficult at the best of times, but with the upgrading to a smart motorway, it was horrendous. Vera was absolutely terrified of breaking down, or of me needing the loo urgently.[*] On more than one occasion we had to turn back or make an emergency stop.

---

[*]   One of the side effects of the treatment was sudden urges to go to the toilet

To her credit, Vera did most of the driving but was helped by Michael and Brian. As mentioned earlier, we didn't ask William. A journey that should have taken 35-40 minutes sometimes took almost two hours. And it wasn't just the travelling that took its toll, finding a parking spot at The Christie, especially at busy times, was nigh on impossible. However, as we did with the vocal chord cancer treatment, we got through it. Indeed, Dr Alam, who we saw on a weekly basis, remarked that we'd done extremely well and that I'd sailed through the treatment.

At the end of the treatment on 31 August, I had to wait 12 weeks for the inflammation to subside before the CAT and MRI scans could be done.

The results of both scans were very encouraging. Indeed, reading between the lines, both Vera and I thought the cancer had almost gone. During the treatment and afterwards, I took a daily dose of Manuka honey, which is claimed to be effective against colon cancer,[1] and whether this helped I don't know.

A few weeks later, after the Multi Disciplinary Team had met to discuss the results of the scans, we saw Mr Harris. He confirmed the treatment had really shrunk the tumour but reiterated that the best course of action was to take out the entire large colon, all five feet of it. He watched our reaction carefully as he delivered this news. Apparently, some patients take the news very badly, but Vera and I had already accepted that this was the best option. Relieved that we had taken the news so well, he booked the operation for 2 January 2020, saying it was best to avoid the Christmas period as it was chaotic. Neither Vera nor myself wanted me to be in hospital over Christmas anyway.

Unsurprisingly, our Christmas and New Year celebrations were somewhat muted, although Michael and Kathryn cooked a delicious Christmas dinner.

The next step was the pre-op. Elaine and June accompanied myself and Vera to Bolton One. We arrived a little late partly because of the traffic but mainly because I took short just as we were about to leave home.

A procedure that normally took about an hour took three hours! The nurses completed their tasks within an hour but Daniel, who went through every step both before, during and after the operation, took a whopping two hours. It was information overload in the extreme. He gave me a bag of goodies; 21 'Ensure Plus Juce' drinks to take, three per day in the week before the operation to build up my body's reserves; a breathing tube contraption to do breathing exercise five times per day; two DIY enemas, one to be administered on the evening before and one on the morning of the operation; plus a vast amount of literature. Both Vera and I left the meeting dazed by the amount of information he'd thrown at us.

A few days after the meeting I received a call from Carly, the ERAS coordinator. The aim of the ERAS programme was to get patients fitter, both before and after surgery, by doing some gym work in order to speed up their recovery. Now I have never been a gym person but I had three sessions at the Horwich Leisure Centre gym on the three weeks prior to my operation, two with Carly and one with my son, Andrew. To my surprise, I quite liked it, although once the programme has ended, I think I'll revert back to getting my exercise from walking and gardening.

The night before my operation, Elaine and June stayed at our house to support Vera. She hates hospitals, and their kindly support was most welcome.

My appointment time was 7-30 a.m. which necessitated an early start, especially as I had to administer the second enema at 6–00 a.m. The instructions said it would work in three minutes and they weren't wrong. I literally had to dash the short distance from the bedroom to the bathroom.

After I'd reported to reception, Vera and her two sisters departed for home, leaving me in the waiting area. A nurse escorted me to a ward where I got undressed, donned the surgical gown and saw first Mr Harris, the surgeon, and then the anaesthetist, who explained what was going to happen. Next it was the turn of the stoma nurse, Sue Poulson. She examined my abdomen to find the best place to position the stoma, and then marked the spot with black ink. I told her something that I'd forgotten to tell the surgeon, that I had an abdominal hernia. She said Mr Harris would probably fix that during the operation. With all the checks, and paperwork, done, a nurse then walked me to the anaesthetist's room.

After inserting several cannula's into my arms and fixing electrodes to my body, I was told to sit on the edge of the bed whilst they rooted around my spine finding the best spot to inject a powerful epidural. As soon as this was done, I had to lie down on the bed very quickly before it took effect. And when it did, the effect was scary. Very scary. I was completely paralysed from the waist down. No matter how hard I tried, I couldn't move a muscle, not even my toes. It was a frightening feeling.

Before the anaesthetic was injected, I glanced at the clock on the wall. It was 9-30 a.m. The next thing I remember was waking up in the Recovery room at 6-15 p.m., nearly nine hours later. After 30 minutes, a nurse transferred me, on a gurney, to the High Dependency Unit (HDU). I had loads of tubes and a catheter, as well as inflatable covers on my legs to prevent blood clots. I must have been a frightening sight for Vera and Michael when they visited in the evening. Prior to their visit Clare, the ward sister, said I should try to eat and drink something since I'd gone a long time without food or drink, not good for a diabetic person. I managed a small amount of minestrone soup followed by some custard (I couldn't face the main course), washed down with some orange juice. It was a mistake. About one hour later, in the presence of Vera and Michael, I got an unstoppable urge to vomit. Despite my best efforts to keep it down, I bowed to the inevitable and did a projectile vomit into a cardboard bowl. Clare said it was normal since the small intestine was still 'asleep' from the effects of the surgery, and the food had built up in my stomach. My body had to get rid of it and that's why I'd vomited.

I spent 48 hours in the HDU. The friendly and professional staff made my stay a pleasant one. They attended to my needs, emptying my bag, administering my medication, and even giving me full body washes, which were very welcome. The downside was the plethora of tubes meant I had to sleep on my back, something I never do, so I got very little sleep.

On day two I was being transferred to Ward E4 just as Andrew and Helen were arriving for the evening visit. Seeing all the tubes protruding from my body unnerved them a little but, apart from that, they said I looked very well.

Over the next day or so, the tubes were removed; the one for insulin; the one for morphine; and the one for the electrolyte; and the inflatable leg covers were replaced with stockings. The last tube to be removed was the catheter. 'Will it hurt?' I asked the nurse.

'No,' she replied. 'All you'll feel is a quick, sharp pain.' And then she yanked it out. It did hurt, but the sharp pain was only fleeting.

At last, free of all the tubes, I could get out of bed and walk around. I walked to the toilet/shower room and later, the full length of the hospital's main corridor, about 400 yards each way. I did this walk during Elaine and Keith's visit and I think it scared them a little. They thought it was too much for me so soon after major surgery, but it wasn't.

In addition to visits from Andrew and Helen and Elaine and Keith, I also got visits from Vera (nearly every day), Brian and Valerie, June and Stuart, Michael, and Ian and Sharon. Ian said he'd spoken to the nurse and she'd told him everything was fine except for one thing. They were running short of custard!

Once the doctors and nurses were satisfied that everything was fine and that I was confident changing my stoma bag, I was discharged on Thursday 9 January, exactly a week after my admission.

When Vera picked me up, I remarked that I'd really missed my roast beef dinners,* so she kindly made one for me that evening. It was delicious.

At home, the hardest thing was getting used to changing the stoma bags. In the first week I had one or two 'accidents' with leaking bags, which was very distressing, but I soon got the hang of it and, touch wood, I haven't had many since.

The stoma nurse, Fiona, made just one home visit, said I was coping extremely well, and that she didn't need to make any more visits.

On the day before we were due to see Mr Harris to get the histology results from my bowel, Sue Poulson, the head stoma nurse, rang to see how I was coping.**

'Fine,' I replied, surprised that Fiona hadn't communicated this to her.

Both Mr Harris and Sue greeted Vera and me in the consulting room to deliver the histology results. They were very good. The operation had been a complete success, so

---

* On hearing my request, the nurse said, jokingly I presume, that a take-away would do

** As a member of the Multi Disciplinary Team, she also told me what Mr Harris would say the following day

much so that I didn't need any further treatment whatsoever. No more radiotherapy or chemotherapy. Nothing. It was a huge relief. Neither Vera nor I wanted me to endure any more treatment. All that I needed was a blood test in six months and a CAT scan in 12 months, with the same the following year. After that, they would keep an eye on me for the next three years and then I would be discharged.

My weight before the operation was 14 stones. After the operation, it was 13 stone 2 pounds, a loss of 12 pounds. Most of this was attributable to the weight of the large colon, although some was also due to the small intestine taking time to fully recover and not absorbing all the nutrients. The upshot is that I now have a flat tummy, something I haven't had for a very long time, and I feel much better at my new slimline weight.

I sincerely hope this is the last scare. Surviving three cancer scares in the last four years is enough for anyone.

29.4 ANOTHER BOMBSHELL

One Monday morning in November the phone rang. I was in the shower and the Caller ID said it was William. Funny, he'd never rang me in the early morning before. I picked up the receiver and dialled his number. The voice that answered wasn't William's, but that of his daughter, Helen. 'I'm sorry to ring you so early in the morning,' she said, 'but I've got some terrible news. My dad passed away last night.'

I was gobsmacked. I was so shocked that I couldn't speak. 'Are you still there?' she asked.

'Yes, I'm still here,' I replied weakly.

'It happened last night as he was leaving the Hilltops club,' Helen continued. 'He collapsed on the car park. The ambulance crew think it was a massive heart attack.'

A few weeks earlier William had suffered a fall in his back garden, a fall which left him badly bruised and prevented him from having his usual Thursday walks with me and Brian. He didn't really know how it had happened, but it shook him up. With hindsight, he should have gone to the doctors, because it could have been a minor heart attack, a harbinger of what was to come.

On the morning that Helen rang with the terrible news I'd planned to see William at lunchtime to make arrangements for a short break at Glencoe with Brian and myself. Scotland was a place he'd studiously avoided but Brian and I had finally persuaded him to go. Unfortunately, it never happened.

Although William was officially my cousin, he was more like my brother. We'd been brought up together (Chapter 1) and shared many holidays together (Chapter 2). He was my walking companion and golfing companion but, most of all, he was a true friend. I miss him terribly.

William's death so soon after that of his wife, Jean, mirrors that of his dad, Evan (Chapter 24). He too died just a few weeks after his wife.

However, it wasn't all bad news in 2019. It was the year my first novel was published.

29.5 IN PRINT

Front cover of The Dark Freeze.

As well as this autobiography, I've been writing novels since my retirement in 2002, but never got around to having them published. *The Dark Freeze* (Image 333), a science fiction novel, was published in October. Not only did it receive good reviews, the local Wigan Post also ran an article on it[2] (Image 334). This year (2020), my second novel, *DARIT*, another science fiction story, was published (Image 335). Next year, 2021, The V-Girls, a crime thriller, and the book you are reading now, *Professor Custard: One boy's quest to fulfil his dreams,* my autobiography, will also be published.

Article in the Wigan Post.[2]

Front cover of DARIT.

29.6 A FEW LITTLE TREATS

After what Vera and I have been through in the past year, we decided to reward ourselves with a few little treats. In March I collected my brand new Mazda CX-5 Sport Nav+. I've had Jaguar saloons for over 20 years but as we've got older both me and Vera struggled to get in and out of them so we decided to get an SUV. We didn't like the Range Rovers and Land Rovers, nor the Jaguar F-Pace, although the E-Pace wasn't too bad, but the one we really liked was the Mazda CX-5. Ian and Sharon, our friends, have had Mazda's for many years and extolled the virtues of these Japanese cars. They were right. The Mazda CX-5, especially in the signature Soul Red Crystal colour, is a stunning car. I'm really pleased with it.

The second treat was our annual break at the Empire Hotel in Llandudno. We'd planned to go on the day of my birthday, Monday 23 March, for four days but, because of the Covid 19 lockdown, have had to postpone it until next year. However, we did manage a holiday at the Empire Hotel with our grandson in late August (Section 29.1).

Our third treat was a week's holiday in the Isle of Wight with Brian and Valerie. We'd booked to go in June but again, because of Covid, the holiday was delayed until early August. We had a good time driving down in my new car to Portsmouth, where Derek and Anne, Brian and Valerie's friends, treated us to a lovely meal. After an overnight stay in a Premier Inn, we spent a delightful morning in Portsmouth before catching the ferry to Fishbourne and then driving to the Foxholes Hotel in Shanklin. Sampling the island's delights was good, although a call from home midway through the holiday altered the mood somewhat. Brian's elderly mother had fell and had to be taken to hospital.

29.7 THE FINAL CURTAIN

Here, I think, is an appropriate point to end my story. A point in my life where both my sons are happily married and settled in their own houses. A point where I have a lovely grandson. A point where I have completed a satisfying career. And a point where I am enjoying retirement with my wife, a wife I have shared most of my life with. A wife I wouldn't swap for anyone. I trust that you too have enjoyed sharing the life of Professor Custard.

It is fitting, I think, to end the story of my life with some pictures of our grandson, Joshua (Images 336 to 338). He is now (August 2020) an inquisitive seven-year-old boy whose favourite word is why. He is the apple of our eyes.

Joshua at Christmas 2017.

Finally, I posed the question to you, dear reader, whether I had fulfilled my two dreams, the two burning desires that beat in the chest of a young boy and only became clear as he travelled along the path of life. The twin desires of becoming a respected and successful research chemist in colour chemistry, and helping to bring up our children as part of a happy and loving family. I hope your answer concurs with mine.

Joshua, age six, and his daddy.

Joshua with Father Christmas at
Knowsley Safari Park 2019.

REFERENCES

1. Life Extension Daily News at https://mycart.lifeextension.com
2. Wigan Post, Monday, 4 November 2019

EPILOGUE

And so, this almost completes my story. My journey along the meandering path of life. A path with many twists and turns. A path with many forks and branches. Many points where alternative routes could, and in some cases should, have been taken. But, in the end, I did my best. I did what I thought was right at the time. Of course, with hindsight, I would have done some things differently. Who wouldn't. But the bulk of my life; my chosen career, my friends and colleagues and, most especially of all, my wife and my children, I would change not one iota.

I said this ALMOST completes my story. Almost, because I am not dead yet and I hope to live for a good while longer. And almost, because however much you desire them, some things, like grandchildren, are completely outside your control. If I was granted one wish, it would be the fulfilment of that desire before I die.*

---

* The Epilogue was written before the birth of our grandson, Joshua (Chapter 29)

Appendix I

PUBLICATIONS, LECTURES AND PATENTS

PUBLICATIONS

(i) Books

1. P. Gregory (ed), 'Chemistry and Technology of Printing and Imaging Systems', Blackie, Glasgow, 1996.
2. P. Gregory, 'High Technology Applications of Organic Colorants', Plenum, New York, 1991.
3. P. F. Gordon and P. Gregory, 'Organic Chemistry in Colour', Springer-Verlag, Heidelberg, 1983.

(ii) Chapters

1. P. Gregory, 'Toxicology of Textile Dyes' in: Environmental Aspects of Textile Dyeing. R. M. Christie (ed.), Woodhead Publishing Limited, Cambridge 2007.
2. P. Gregory, 'Metal Complexes as Speciality Dyes and Pigments' in: Comprehensive Coordination Chemistry II: From Biology to Nanotechnology. J.A.McCleverty and T. J. Meyer (editors-in-chief), Elsevier, London 2004, pp. 549-579.
3. P. Gregory, 'Ink Jet Printing on Textiles' in: Textile Ink Jet Printing: A Review of Ink Jet Printing of Textiles, including ITMA 2003, TL Dawson and B Glover (eds), The Society of Dyers and Colourists Technical Monograph, 2004, pp. 69-97.
4. P. Gregory, 'Functional Dyes' in: Industrial Dyes: Chemistry, Properties, Applications. K. Hunger (ed.), Wiley-VCH, 2003, pp. 543-584.
5. P. Gregory, 'Important Chemical Chromophores of Dye Classes' in: Industrial Dyes: Chemistry, Properties, Applications, K. Hunger (ed.), Wiley-VCH, 2003, pp. 13-112.

6. P. Gregory, 'Dyes and Dye Intermediates' in: Kirk-Othmer Encyclopedia of Chemical Technology – 4th edition, Volume 8, Wiley, New York, 1993, pp. 542-602.

7. P. Gregory, 'Dyestuffs' in: The Chemical Industry, 2nd edition, A.R. Heaton (ed), Blackie, Glasgow, 1993.

8. P. Gregory, 'Colourants for Electronic Printers' in: Chemical Technology in Printing and Imaging Systems, J. A. G. Drake (ed), Royal Society of Chemistry, Cambridge, 1993.

9. P. Gregory, 'Colourants for High Technology' in: Colour Chemistry – The Design and Synthesis of Organic Dyes and Pigments, A. T. Peters and H. S. Freeman (eds), Elsevier, London, 1991.

10. P. Gregory, 'Classification of Dyes by Chemical Structure' in: The Chemistry and Application of Dyes, D. R. Waring and G. Hallas (eds), Plenum, New York, 1990.

11. P. Gregory, 'Dyes for Polyacrylonitrile' in: The Chemistry and Application of Dyes, D.R. Waring and G. Hallas (eds), Plenum, New York, 1990.

12. P. Gregory and P. F. Gordon, 'Non-textile Uses of Dyes' in: Developments in the Chemistry and Technology of Organic Dyestuffs, J. Griffiths (ed), CRAC 7, Blackwell, 1984.

(iii) Literature Papers

1. P. Gregory and C. Foster, 'Towards Enhanced Lightfastness of Azo Dyes by Selective Methylation.' In Press.

2. P. Gregory, 'Steamrollers, Sports Cars and Security: Phthalocyanine's Progress Through the Ages,' J.Porphyrins and Phthalocyanines 3 468-476, 1999.

3. M. G. Hutchings, P. Gregory, J. S. Campbell, A. Strong, J-P. Zamy, A. Lepre and A. Mills, 'The Comparative Solvatochromism of Arylazo and Heteroarylazo Compounds Based on N,N-Diethyl-m-acetylamino-aniline and N,N-Diethyl-m-toluidine.' Chem. Eur. J. 3 (10) 1719, 1997.

4. P. Gregory, 'Ink Jet Colorant Developments – Past, Present, Future', Toner Research Services Ink Jet Technology Monthly (J.Cooper, ed). Vol. 2, No. 1, 1995.

5. P. Gregory, 'Modern Reprographics', Review of Progress in Colouration, 24 1 1994.

6. P. Gregory, M. Paton, B. Tury, ,J. Chem. Res. 'X-Ray Crystallographic Structures of "2-Nitro-phenylthiocyanate and 1-Nitro-8-thiocyanato-naphthalene."' In Press. Peter Gregory, 'A Profile.' Chemistry Review, May 1992, p 36.

7. P. Gregory, 'The Role of Organic Molecules in Colour Hard Copy', Dyes and Pigments, 13 251, 1990.

8. P. Gregory, 'Colorants: Use in High Technology', Chemistry and Industry, 1989, 679.

9. P. Gregory, 'Electronic Photography – The Future', Chemistry in Britain, 1989, 47.

10. K. L. Birkett, P. Gregory, 'Metal complex dyes as charge control agents', Dyes and Pigments 1 341, 1986.

11. P. Gregory, 'Azo Dyes: Structure-Carcinogenicity Relationships', Dyes and Pigments 1 45, 1986.

12. A. J. Barnes, M. A. Majid, M. A. Stuckey, P. Gregory and C. V. Stead, 'The Resonance Raman Spectra of Orange II and Para Red: Molecular Structure and Vibrational Assignment', Spectrochimica Acta 41A, 629, 1985.

13. M. Ellwood, P. Gregory, J. Griffiths, 'First Examples of Phase Transfer Catalysis in Electrophilic Reactions. Acceleration of the Azo Coupling Reaction', J. C. S. Chem. Commun. 1980, 181.

14. D. Brierley, P. Gregory, B. Parton, 'Cationic Azo Triazolium Dyes: Elucidation of the Structure of the two Isomeric Components of CI Basic Red 22', J. Chem. Res. (S) 1980, 174.

15. P. Gregory, D. Thorp, 'The electronic absorption spectra of 2-substituted-4-NN-di-ethylamino-4"nitroazobenzene dyes and their mono acid cations: The applicability of Dewar's rule to these and related dyestuffs', J. Chem. Soc., Perkin I, 1979, 1990.

16. Gregory and C. V. Stead, 'The degradation of water soluble azo compounds by dilute sodium hypochlorite solution', J. Soc. Dyers and Colourists, 1979, 402.

LECTURES

1. *P. Gregory, 'A Waterfast Polymeric Black Dye for Ink Jet Printers', Diamond Research Conference, Las Vegas, 11-13 September 2001.

2. *P. Gregory, 'Colorants for Non-Impact Printing: An Overview', Advances in Ink and Paint Technology, Salford, 12-13 Sept. 2000.

3. *P. Gregory, 'The Future for Dyes in Ink Jet Inks and Toners', IMI's 3rd Annual Imaging Chemicals Conference, Orlando, 2-4 February 2000.

4. *P. Gregory and P. Wight, 'Colour Chemistry Course,' Strathclyde University, 17-19 January 2000.

5. *P. Gregory, 'From Obscurity to Stardom: The Story of Ink Jet Printing and Colourants', RSC Industrial Affairs Lecture, Edinburgh University, 16 November 1999.

6. *P. Gregory, 'Advances in Colorant Chemistry', Diamond Research Conference, Santa Barbara, 3-5 October 1999.

7. *P. Gregory, 'Steamrollers, Sports Cars and Security: Phthalocyanin's Progress Through the Ages', Phthalocyanines: 70 Years of Scientific Progress, RSC, Edinburgh, 21-23 September 1998.

8. *P. Gregory, 'Enhanced Lightfastness from Photofading Studies', International Congress on Imaging Science (ICPS '98), Antwerp, 7-11 September 1998.

9. *P. Gregory, 'Ink Jet Colorants: Current and Future Trends', 3rd International Conference on Imaging Science and Hardcopy (ICISH '98), Chongqing, China, 26-28 May 1998.

10. *P. Gregory, 'Steamrollers, Sports Cars and Security', Leeds University, 20 April 1998.

11. *P. Gregory, 'Ink Jet Colourants: Current and Future Trends', Colour Science '98, Harrogate, 30 March -1 April 1998.

12 *P. Gregory, Ink Jet Colourants: Current and Future Trends', Japan Hardcopy 1997, Tokyo, 9-11 July 1997.

13. *P. Gregory, 'Phthalocyanines: An Old Dog with New Tricks', Chemichromics '97, Manchester, 16-17 June 1997.

14. *P. Gregory, 'From Obscurity to Stardom: The Story of Ink Jet Printers and Colorants', Andersonian Chemical Society Lecture, Strathclyde University, 6 March 1997.

15. *P. Gregory, 'Tutorial: Colour Chemistry', IS&T's NIP 12, San Antonio, 27 October- 1 November 1996.

16. *P. Gregory, 'Trends in Ink Jet Inks,' IMI's Fifth Annual Ink Jet Printing Workshop, Cambridge, Mass. USA, 29 March 1996.

17. *P. Gregory, 'Trends in Ink Jet Inks', CAP-Ventures Communication Conference, Orlando, 15 February 1996.

18. *P. Gregory, 'Colorant Chemistry, an Advanced Tutorial', IS&T's Eleventh International Congress on NIP, Hilton Head, 2 November 1995.

19. *P. Gregory, 'Dyes vs Pigment Inks', BIS Strategic Decisions Ink Jet Printing Conference, Berlin, 17 March 1995.

20. *P. Gregory, 'Ink Perspective – Dyes and Their Capability', BIS Strategic Decisions Ink Jet Printing Conference, Monterey, 12 October 1994.

21. P. Gregory and J. D. Schofield, 'Research: Past, Present and Future, Specialist Colours Conference', Knutsford, 6 October 1994.

22. *P. Gregory, 'Leading the Jet Set', Parliamentary Links Day, Houses of Parliament, Westminster, 30 June 1994.

23. *P. Gregory, 'Choosing Colorants for Ink Jet Printers: Dyes vs Pigments: The Truth', IMI's Third Annual Ink Jet Printing Workshop, Cambridge Mass., USA, 6 April 1994.

24. *P. Gregory, 'Dyes vs Pigments – The Truth', Ninth International Congress on Advances in Non-impact Printing Technologies/Japan Hardcopy '93, Yokohama, 4-8 October 1993.

25. *P. Gregory, 'Phthalocyanines: Colorants with an Invisible Future', Fourteenth International Congress of Heterocyclic Chemistry, Antwerp, 1-6 August 1993.

26. *P. Gregory, 'Metal Phthalocyanines in High Technology', Royal Society of Chemistry 1993 Autumn Meeting, Warwick, 21-23 September 1993.

27. *P. Gregory, 'High Technology Applications of Functional Dye Materials', Second International Symposium on Chemistry of Functional Dyes, Kobe, Japan, 23-28 August 1992.

28. *P. Gregory, 'Colorants for Electronic Printers', Royal Society of Chemistry: Chemical Technology in Printing and Imaging Systems, York, 6-7 October 1992.

29. J. S. Campbell, P. Gregory and P. M. Mistry, 'Novel Waterfast Black Dyes for Ink Jet Printing', IS&T's Seventh International Congress on Advances in Non-Impact Printing Technologies, Portland, Oregon, 6-11 October 1991.

30. Gregory, R. W. Kenyon and P. M. Mistry, 'The Discovery of a Novel Alcohol Soluble Black Dye for Industrial Ink Jet Printing', SPSE's Sixth International Congress on Advances in Non-Impact Printing Technologies, Orlando, Florida, 21-26 October 1990.

31. P. Gregory, 'The Use of Colorants in Important Hi-Tech Areas', SCI Colour Chemistry Symposium, London, 11 May 1989.

32. P. Gregory, J. S. Campbell and A. Quayle, 'Novel Infrared Absorbers for Non-Impact Printing Applications', SPSE's Fifth International Congress on Advances in Non-Impact Printing Technologies, San Diego, 12-17 November 1989.

33. P. Gregory, 'Novel Phthalocyanines for Positive Charging OPC's', SPSE's Fourth International Congress on Advances in Non-Impact Printing Technologies, New Orleans, 20-25 March 1988.

34. P. Gregory, 'Dye Diffusion Thermal Transfer Dyes', SPSE's Fourth International Congress on Advances in Non-Impact Printing Technologies, New Orleans, 20-25 March 1988.

35. P. Gregory, 'The Role of Organic Molecules In Colour Hardcopy', Institute for Graphic Communication (IGC) International Conference, Amsterdam, October 1987.

36. Gregory and K. L. Birkett, 'Metal Complex Dyes as Charge Control Agents', Thirtieth International Congress of Pure and Applied Chemistry (IUPAC), Manchester, September 1985.

*   Denotes an invited lecture

PATENTS

(Number of patents in each discipline)

Textile Dyes

Reactive Dyes	6
Cationic Dyes	19
Phase Transfer Catalysis	1
Biocides	2
Ink Jet	55
Electrophotography:	
Organic Photoconductors	5
Charge Control Agents	4
Infrared Absorbers	6
Thermal Printing	15
New Opportunities	2
TOTAL	115

CHAIRPERSON

1. Innovations in Modern Colour Chemistry, SCI, Manchester, 2 May 1996. Colour Chemistry Sessions of the Fourteenth International Congress of Heterocyclic Chemistry, Antwerp, 1-6 August 1993.

2. Ink Jet Printing Session of Imaging Science and Technologies Eighth International Congress on Advances in Non-Impact Printing Technologies, Williamsburg, Virginia, 25-30 October 1992.

3. Society of Chemistry and Industry Colour Chemistry Symposium, London, 9 May 1991.

4. Photoreceptor Session of SPSE's Sixth International Congress on Advances in Non-Impact Printing Technologies, Orlando, Florida, 21-26 October 1990.

5. Photoreceptor Session of SPSE's Fifth International Congress on Advances in Non-Impact Printing Technologies, San Diego, 12-17 November 1989.

6. Society of Chemistry and Industry Colour Chemistry Symposium, London, 11 May 1989.

Appendix II

THE FLAG EXPERIMENT

I've included the full details of the Flag Experiment to preserve it for posterity so that future generations can enjoy this wonderful experiment.

The flyer used to attract people to the event is shown below. It never failed to attract a large audience, either schoolchildren or adults.

COLOUR CHEMISTRY MAGIC

Are you wearing clothes? Are they coloured? Do you ever wonder how this was achieved?

This magical demonstration shows how the colorant, a dye, imparts colour to a garment, the textile fabric. And it shows why over 5,000 colorants are needed to colour the vast array of everyday materials.

Come along and be amazed.

INSTRUCTIONS AND DYES

- Place 1,500 ml of water from a boiled kettle in a 2 litre glass beaker with a thermometer and a glass rod. The water should be around 85 – 90⁰C.

- Add the dyes:-

i. The yellow dye (2g) DISPERSOL YELLOW B-6G (WAXOLINE YELLOW G-FW)
    This dye should be present as a dispersion in water.

ii. The red dye (1g) ACID RED 249

iii. The blue dye (0.25g) DIRECT BLUE 80

- Add the cloth. This is three equal pieces of viscose, silk and acetate rayon either sown or stapled together. The size of each piece should be approximately 8 inches by 6 inches.

- Add:-

i. Sodium sulphate (10g)
ii. Acetic acid 1M (20ml)

- Stir occasionally at 85 – 90°C with a glass rod for, ideally, 10 – 15 minutes, although a good result is obtained after 5 minutes.

- Remove the cloth with the glass rod and dunk into 1,500 ml of cold water in a 2 litre beaker. This is both to cool the hot cloth and remove any residual dye. Then pull out the brightly coloured yellow, red and blue tricolour flag.

NOTE: It is best to have all the ingredients pre-weighed in glass bottles before commencing the experiment

BANTER TO USE DURING THE FLAG EXPERIMENT

Good afternoon (or evening) ladies and gentlemen (or children). Welcome to …

I'm glad (and relieved) to see that you are all wearing clothes. And even more glad that most of them are coloured.

In the next 10 minutes or so I'm going to show you some Colour Chemistry Magic, a magical demonstration before your very eyes. So take your places to get a good view.

Before I begin, have you ever wondered how your clothes, and most other things, acquire their colour? Well, textile fibres are coloured by a process known as 'dyeing'. In this process, a coloured material, a dye, becomes attached, or bound, to the fabric.

The dyeing process is very simple. The fabric is placed in hot water containing the dye and, after a few minutes, the dye becomes attached to the fibre.

This beaker contains hot water from a boiled kettle at about 85°C.

First, we add a yellow dye. As you can see, this is a water insoluble dye called a disperse dye because it forms a very fine dispersion of dye particles in the water.

Next, we add a red dye. What colour do you think the mixture will go when we add the red dye to the yellow dye? As you can see, it goes a scarlet – orange colour, just like mixing yellow and red paints. Unlike the yellow dye, the red dye actually dissolves in the water.

And then, we add a blue dye. This produces a murky brown colour. If other yellow, red and blue dyes are chosen, it is possible to produce a black. This technique is used in the printing industry to produce 'composite' blacks, for example, in ink jet printer inks.

Now, we add the fabric.

Finally, we add the salt and vinegar. Just like salt and vinegar make your fish and chips taste better, they also make the dyeing process better. The salt helps the blue to dye the fabric whilst the vinegar (acetic acid) helps the red dye.

To get the best result you normally leave it for 10 – 15 minutes but we won't wait that long. We'll just leave it for a few minutes.

WHILST WAITING

Virtually every textile fabric is dyed in this way, just by placing it in hot water with the dye. There's nothing fancy about the dyeing process.

I see that some of you are wearing patterned garments. These patterns are produced in two main ways.

i. By weaving together differently coloured yarns.
ii. By a printing process.

The printing process is slightly different from the dyeing process but still embodies the same basic principle of applying a dye to a fabric using heat.

As a matter of interest, how many commercial colorants do you think there are at any one time? The answer is approximately 5,000. Why are there so many?

There are so many because of the vast array of different substrates to be coloured. Apart from textiles, such as cotton, polyester, nylon, silk, viscose, acetate rayon… there are also:-

Paper
Plastics
Leather
Wood
Metal
Glass, and many more.

Not only does each one require its own type of colorant, each type has to have a spectrum of colours, ranging from yellows, through oranges, scarlets, reds, purples, blues and greens to the tertiary shades such as greys and blacks. Furthermore, many companies market their own brands of colorants. This is why there are so many.

Does anyone know how many colours are possible theoretically? No? The answer will astound you. There are 16.7 million possible colours. Even more surprising, the average human eye can detect about 10 million of them. Amazing.
As well as colouring textiles and other materials, colorants are also used to colour humans. To colour us! For example, we use dyes to colour our hair, lipstick to colour our lips, and tattoos to colour our skin. Indeed, the first recorded use of any colorant by mankind was by the Neanderthals over 18,000 years ago when they used ochre (rust or iron oxide) from dried river beds to daub on to their dead prior to burial.

Now, it's had long enough so I'll take it out and give it a quick rinse. And Hey Presto, we have a beautiful tricoloured flag.

That's because the yellow dye just dyed the acetate rayon, the red dye the silk and the blue dye the viscose rayon.

Thank you for your attention.

INDEX

Acknowledgements

I would like to thank my eldest son, Andrew (Image 298, page 674), for his invaluable help in showing me how to convert my Apple Pages manuscript into a Microsoft Word document, and especially for showing me how to convert all the images into the correct size and format for the book. I wouldn't have had a clue.

I also wish to thank my youngest son, Michael (Image 337, page 780), for transferring the files from my computer to a memory stick to send to the publishers. The files were far too big to send by email.

Finally, special thanks go to my nephew, Stuart Gent, a graphic designer, for designing the front and back covers of Professor Custard. I think they are brilliant.

Thank you to all of you.

ABOUT THE AUTHOR

Professor Peter Gregory spent his entire career in chemical research, first with ICI, then AstraZeneca and lastly Avecia. His hi-tech colours group were the world leaders in inventing and supplying ink jet dyes and inks to the major ink jet printer manufacturers such as HP, Canon, and Seiko Epson. During his time at work Peter was in constant demand as a speaker at prestigious international scientific conferences, published numerous literature papers and has over 100 patents to his name. He co-authored a best selling text book *Organic Chemistry in Colour* and is the author of *High Technology Applications of Organic Colorants*. He retired in 2002.

Whilst at work, Peter always had a dessert with custard at lunchtimes. During his 37 years, he calculated that he had consumed 3.5 tonnes of the stuff, and that's without the jam roly polys, spotted dicks, etc.

In his retirement Peter has used his scientific background to write two sci-fi novels, *The Dark Freeze* and *DARIT*, both published by Troubador, and a crime thriller, *The V-Girls*, yet to be published. His autobiography entitled, unsurprisingly, *Professor Custard,* is what you have just read.

In addition to writing, Peter is an avid fan of Wigan Warriors Rugby League Football Club, a keen gardener, and a walker, his favourite area being the Lake District. He lives in West Bolton with his wife Vera. They celebrated their Golden Wedding in 2019 and have two grown-up married sons, Andrew and Michael, and a grandson Joshua.